Sectarian Violence in India

Readings on the Economy, Polity and Society

This series of readers is meant to introduce university students and research scholars to important research that has been published in the *Economic and Political Weekly* in specific areas. The readers draw on the large number of research articles that has been published in *EPW* over the decades. Each set of readings is compiled by a senior academic who has also written an introductory essay for the volume. *EPW* is grateful to the authors of the articles included here for permission to reproduce them. This series with two titles published every year between 2016 and 2019 has been produced with the help of a grant from the Tata Trusts. *EPW* is grateful to the Tata Trusts for supporting this venture.

Published

Economic Reforms and Growth in India, ed. **Pulapre Balakrishnan** (E-book)

Environment, Technology and Development: Critical and Subversive Essays, ed. **Rohan D'Souza**

Village Society, ed. **Surinder S. Jodhka**

The Adivasi Question: Issues of Land, Forest and Livelihood, ed. **Indra Munshi**

Women and Work, ed. **Padmini Swaminathan**

Decentralisation and Local Governments: The Indian Experience, ed. **T. R. Raghunandan**

Higher Education in India: In Search of Equality, Quality and Quantity, ed. **Jandhyala B. G. Tilak**

The Problem of Caste, ed. **Satish Deshpande**

Social Policy, ed. **Jean Drèze**

Water: Growing Understanding, Emerging Perspectives, eds **Mihir Shah and P. S. Vijayshankar**

A Handbook of Rural India, ed. **Surinder S. Jodhka**

Sectarian Violence in India

Hindu–Muslim Conflict, 1966–2015

Edited by

SANJAY PALSHIKAR

and

SATISH DESHPANDE

TATA TRUSTS

Orient BlackSwan

SECTARIAN VIOLENCE IN INDIA: HINDU–MUSLIM CONFLICT, 1966–2015

ORIENT BLACKSWAN PRIVATE LIMITED

Registered Office
3-6-752 Himayatnagar, Hyderabad 500 029, Telangana, India
e-mail: centraloffice@orientblackswan.com

Other Offices
Bengaluru, Bhopal, Chennai, Guwahati, Hyderabad, Jaipur, Kolkata, Lucknow, Mumbai, New Delhi, Noida, Patna, Visakhapatnam

© Orient Blackswan Pvt. Ltd. and *Economic and Political Weekly* 2019
First published by Orient Blackswan Pvt. Ltd. 2019

ISBN 978-93-5287-585-6

029289

Typeset by
Le Studio Graphique, Gurgaon
in Adobe Garamond Pro 10.5/12.5

Printed in India at
BB Press, Noida

Published by
Orient Blackswan Private Limited
3-6-752, Himayatnagar, Hyderabad 500 029, Telangana, India
e-mail: info@orientblackswan.com

Contents

SECTION II

Theoretical and Conceptual Issues

SECTION III

Communal Politics

SECTION IV

Accounts and Analyses of Specific Riots

Tables and Figure

Tables

Figure

Acknowledgements

This volume has been in the making for a long time. Along the way, we have received generous and conscientious help from several persons and it is our pleasure to thank them all. The project began when Ram Reddy, then Editor of the *Economic and Political Weekly*, invited us to put together a collection of essays on communal violence published in the *EPW* between 1966 and 2015. Madhav Kumar and Pankti Dalal, interns at the *EPW*, combed through the entire set of almost 50 years' issues of the journal and identified over 400 contributions on the subject including Special Articles, Correspondents' Reports and Editorials. Out of these, we selected around 40 pieces for the volume.

Editing the essays in order to keep the length of the volume manageable was our next task. Tejaswi Chatwal and Azim Ahmed, research scholars at the Department of Sociology, Delhi University, helped with the arduous job of converting the original file formats so that we could edit them. While we were working on the essays, we thought of including a map showing the places where riots had taken place. Aparna Vincent, a research scholar at the University of Hyderabad, helped in preparing a riots table on the basis of the annual surveys of riots by Asghar Ali Engineer. Arvind Susarla, University of Hyderabad, put us in touch with a young geographer, Aquib Jamal, who is currently at the IIIT, Hyderabad. Soon, the first version of the map was ready. With some helpful suggestions from Arvind Susarla, the map was finalised.

We also benefited from our discussions with P. Salah (who generously shared his unpublished work with us) and Jyotirmaya Sharma, both of the University of Hyderabad. Through this unreasonably long period when the volume was getting ready, Lubna Duggal of the *EPW* readily responded to all our queries and sent us much needed reminders. We appreciate her patient and diligent help. At Orient BlackSwan, we thank Nilanjana Majumdar and especially Parvati Mohan, who handled all the copy-editing and the numerous delays and interruptions—with exemplary diligence, courtesy and cheerfulness.

We are grateful to all the authors who gave us the permission to republish their essays and also graciously allowed us to abridge their original articles. Ram Reddy and Paranjoy Guha, both former editors at the *EPW*, and Gopal Guru, the current editor, persisted with us and continued to believe in the importance of the project. We sincerely appreciate their support and thank them all.

6 April 2018

Sanjay Palshikar (Hyderabad)
Satish Deshpande (Delhi)

Abbreviations

BJP	Bharatiya Janata Party
BSF	Border Security Force
BSP	Bahujan Samaj Party
CBCID	Crime Branch-Criminal Investigation Department
Congress (I)	Congress (Indira)
CrPC	Criminal Procedure Code
CRPF	Central Reserve Police Force
DC	District Collector
DMK	Dravida Munnetra Kazhagam
ENPV	effective number of parties
IB	Intelligence Bureau
INC	Indian National Congress
IRS	institutionalised systems of riot production
LDF	Left Democratic Front
NCM	National Commission for Minorities
NTRO	National Technical Research Organisation
OBC	other backward classes
PAC	Provincial Armed Constabulary
PMA	Pottery Manufacturers Association
PUCL	People's Union for Civil Liberties
PUDR	People's Union for Democratic Rights
RAW	Research and Analysis Wing
RSS	Rashtriya Swayamsevak Sangh
SC	scheduled caste
SDM	Sub-divisional Magistrate
SP	Samajwadi Party
ST	scheduled tribe
UDF	United Democratic Front
VHP	Vishva Hindu Parishad

A Tribute to Asghar Ali Engineer (1939–2013)

This volume featuring the *Economic and Political Weekly*'s coverage of the incidents of communal violence will not be complete without a special mention of the contributions by Asghar Ali Engineer over a period of nearly 25 years. He wrote indefatigably on communal conflicts between the Hindus and the Muslims in India, the history of their relations, the underlying reasons of disharmony and the circumstances leading to the worsening of this disharmony in hostility and violence.

In an early piece in the *EPW* (17 June 1978), entitled 'What Have the Muslim Leaders Done?', Engineer said that while the leaders of the community have paid attention, sometimes disproportionately, to the religious and cultural issues, they have done hardly anything to solve the economic problems of ordinary Muslims, most of whom are poor. Muslims are a large minority. Electorally, Engineer says, they are crucial for any political party. Aware of this, the Muslim leaders have made opportunistic use of the numerical strength of their community, and struck deals instead of doing something for the community. Unless a new leadership, committed to the economic improvement of the poor Muslims, and open to working with other progressive forces emerged, there was no hope for the Indian Muslims. He closed that article by saying, 'To me it appears certain that the poor and exploited Muslims will have to take part in the class struggle which will get sharpened in the coming days rather than rely on the traditional Muslim leadership which is corrupt and dishonest.'

Engineer's first signed piece covering a communal riot appeared in the issue of 15 August 1981. For some time, he reported on incidents of communal violence in the 'From Our Correspondents' column. From 1995 to 2005, every year, he wrote on incidents of communal violence that had taken place during that year (or in the previous year). Apart from these annual reviews, he also wrote on the long-term themes which he thought were relevant to the inter-community relations. In these, he took up questions like do Muslims vote as a block (March 1977), is Islam an intrinsically intolerant religion (13 February 1999), and is it correct to project backwards our current notions of conflict between the Hindus and the Muslims on the history of pre-modern India (13 February 1999).

Engineer's understanding of the problem of communalism in India was based on some simple, clearly articulated premises which he often reiterated: religion cannot be blamed for its practitioners' actions; Islam is theologically tolerant, Muslims are not always so; common people are more religious than communal; their leaders, and the elite generally, are more communal than religious; communal conflict takes place because of political competition among leaders and because of economic conflict among the poor; the root cause of conflict is not religious disputes but material interests, though it takes 'religious' form; there are very few spontaneous riots; most riots are pre-planned; if police is asked not to allow any communal violence, and if there is no interference from politicians, any riot can be quickly brought under control; for almost all riots politicians and their 'power-politics' are responsible; all communalism is bad, it is wrong to separate and defend 'minority communalism' from 'majority communalism', because they intensify each other.

These were Engineer's basic convictions. Some of them can be selectively and mischievously used. Others can be criticised for being too simple. But together, they gave his writings clarity, consistency and force. If he was forthright in holding the Hindutva organisations responsible for communal tensions in many cases, he was blunt in saying that Muslim organisations like SIMI were responsible for spreading 'communal poison among unemployed Muslim youth' (12 January 2002: 102). In spite of the depressing communal scene (which he surveyed for decades!), he remained optimistic about riots being eliminated by 'people-oriented politics' (ibid.: 104), and whenever he came across instances of ordinary Hindus and Muslims helping each other, saving each other during riots, he pointedly mentioned those instances in his coverage.

As Hilal Ahmed points out in his tribute (June 2013), Engineer distinguished between 'communalism' and 'communal violence' (1 February 1992) as 'two distinct stages'. In a general communal atmosphere, an incident or two may trigger violent outburst. In reconstructing the circumstances that led to a riot, Engineer looked for what he called, 'provocative factors'. Engineer's annual surveys in the *EPW* identify such provocative factors in riot after riot. Comprehensive in their coverage, these surveys can be used to compile a list of the immediate causes of riots. But such incidents by themselves are not capable of always triggering group violence. They do so because they are the culmination of a series of interconnected happenings at a particular place. Engineer's other writings in the *EPW*, where an entire piece is devoted to one major riot, build a narrative. Typically, following standard journalistic practice, he starts with a paragraph or two about where and when the riot took place, human and monetary losses, and how long it took for normalcy to return. Then the demographic profile of the town, major occupations of different communities, and a brief history of the place would follow.

On this factual background, Engineer places the sequence of events, building of tensions, opportunism of leaders and the inaction or the excesses of the police. He remained careful with details and remembered to qualify his factual claims where necessary. It is through countless such stories that Engineer tried to make sense of the senseless and inhuman phenomena of communal riots. It must have been a far from easy exercise. It must have been not only physically demanding but psychologically exhausting to go from one riot affected town to another and be confronted by the same political machinations and wilful administrative paralysis resulting in a great suffering by the poor and the receding prospect of 'peaceful coexistence of different communities'. However, without getting dispirited by the depressing sequence of events repeating themselves at different places, Engineer kept reporting on communalism and communal riots. Referring to Iqbal in one of the pieces, he says, what we have lost is the sense of a loss. It is this sense of a loss that Engineer must have hoped to awaken through his writings.

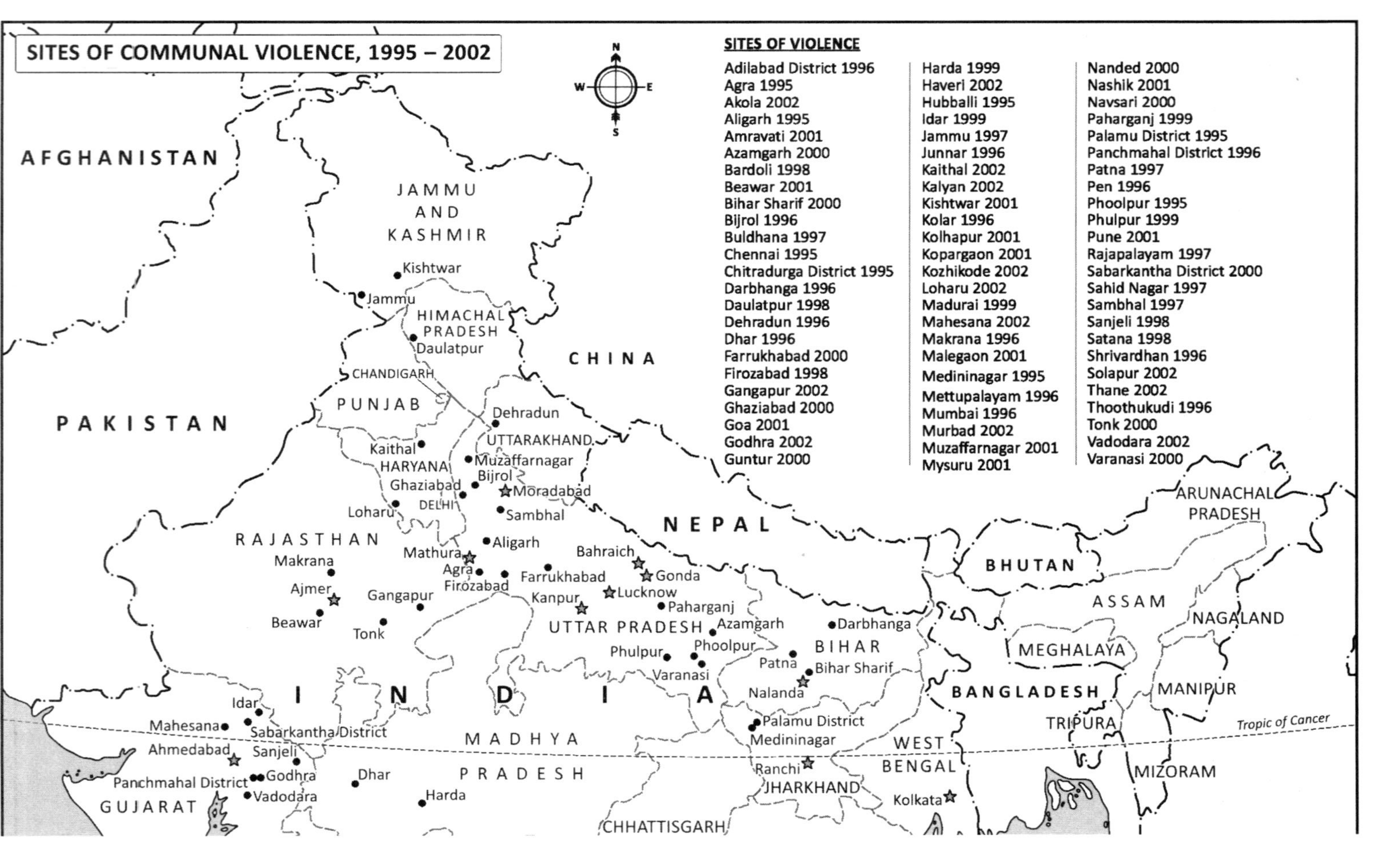
SITES OF COMMUNAL VIOLENCE, 1995 – 2002
SITES OF VIOLENCE
Adilabad District 1996
Agra 1995
Akola 2002
Aligarh 1995
Amravati 2001
Azamgarh 2000
Bardoli 1998
Beawar 2001
Bihar Sharif 2000
Bijrol 1996
Buldhana 1997
Chennai 1995
Chitradurga District 1995
Darbhanga 1996
Daulatpur 1998
Dehradun 1996
Dhar 1996
Farrukhabad 2000
Firozabad 1998
Gangapur 2002
Ghaziabad 2000
Goa 2001
Godhra 2002
Guntur 2000
Harda 1999
Haveri 2002
Hubballi 1995
Idar 1999
Jammu 1997
Junnar 1996
Kaithal 2002
Kalyan 2002
Kishtwar 2001
Kolar 1996
Kolhapur 2001
Kopargaon 2001
Kozhikode 2002
Loharu 2002
Madurai 1999
Mahesana 2002
Makrana 1996
Malegaon 2001
Medininagar 1995
Mettupalayam 1996
Mumbai 1996
Murbad 2002
Muzaffarnagar 2001
Mysuru 2001
Nanded 2000
Nashik 2001
Navsari 2000
Paharganj 1999
Palamu District 1995
Panchmahal District 1996
Patna 1997
Pen 1996
Phoolpur 1995
Phulpur 1999
Pune 2001
Rajapalayam 1997
Sabarkantha District 2000
Sahid Nagar 1997
Sambhal 1997
Sanjeli 1998
Satana 1998
Shrivardhan 1996
Solapur 2002
Thane 2002
Thoothukudi 1996
Tonk 2000
Vadodara 2002
Varanasi 2000
N
W
E
S
AFGHANISTAN
PAKISTAN
JAMMU AND KASHMIR
CHINA
NEPAL
BHUTAN
BANGLADESH
INDIA
HIMACHAL PRADESH
CHANDIGARH
PUNJAB
HARYANA
DELHI
UTTARAKHAND
RAJASTHAN
UTTAR PRADESH
BIHAR
MADHYA PRADESH
GUJARAT
JHARKHAND
WEST BENGAL
CHHATTISGARH
ARUNACHAL PRADESH
ASSAM
NAGALAND
MEGHALAYA
MANIPUR
TRIPURA
MIZORAM
Tropic of Cancer
Kishtwar
Jammu
Daulatpur
Dehradun
Kaithal
Muzaffarnagar
Bijrol
Ghaziabad
Moradabad
Loharu
Sambhal
Aligarh
Mathura
Agra
Firozabad
Farrukhabad
Bahraich
Gonda
Lucknow
Kanpur
Paharganj
Azamgarh
Darbhanga
Makrana
Ajmer
Gangapur
Beawar
Tonk
Phulpur
Phoolpur
Varanasi
Patna
Bihar Sharif
Nalanda
Palamu District
Medininagar
Ranchi
Kolkata
Idar
Mahesana
Sabarkantha District
Ahmedabad
Sanjeli
Godhra
Panchmahal District
Vadodara
Dhar
Harda

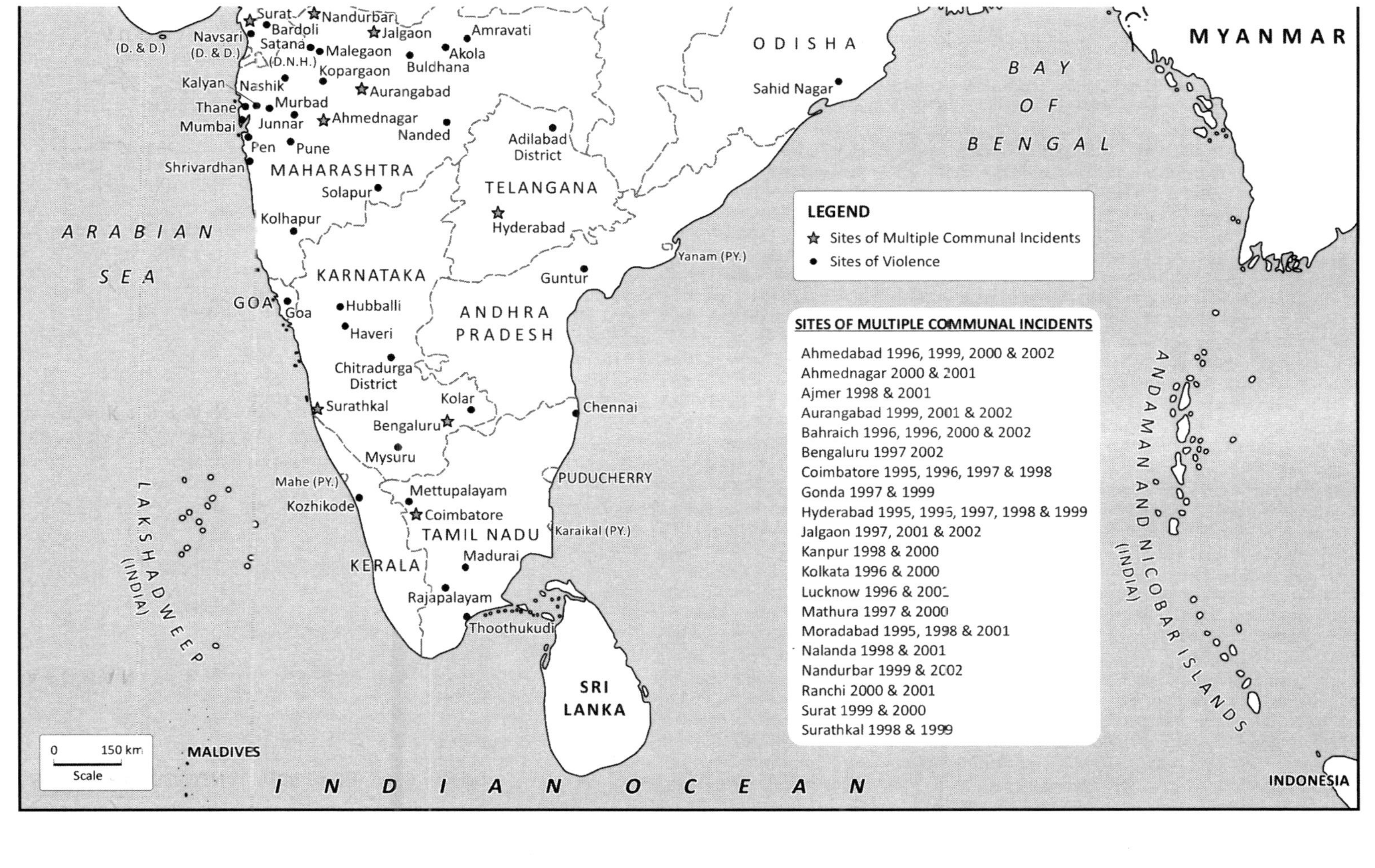

MYANMAR
ODISHA
BAY OF BENGAL
Sahid Nagar
Surat
Nandurbar
Bardoli
Jalgaon
Amravati
Navsari
(D. & D.)
(D. & D.)
Satana
Malegaon
Akola
(D.N.H.)
Kopargaon
Buldhana
Kalyan
Nashik
Aurangabad
Thane
Murbad
Mumbai
Junnar
Ahmednagar
Nanded
Pen
Pune
Adilabad District
Shrivardhan
MAHARASHTRA
Solapur
TELANGANA
Kolhapur
Hyderabad
ARABIAN SEA
KARNATAKA
Guntur
Yanam (PY.)
GOA
Goa
Hubballi
Haveri
ANDHRA PRADESH
Chitradurga District
Kolar
Surathkal
Chennai
Bengaluru
Mysuru
PUDUCHERRY
Mahe (PY.)
Mettupalayam
Kozhikode
Coimbatore
TAMIL NADU
Karaikal (PY.)
KERALA
Madurai
Rajapalayam
Thoothukudi
LAKSHADWEEP (INDIA)
SRI LANKA
ANDAMAN AND NICOBAR ISLANDS (INDIA)
MALDIVES
INDIAN OCEAN
INDONESIA
0 150 km
Scale
LEGEND
Sites of Multiple Communal Incidents
Sites of Violence
SITES OF MULTIPLE COMMUNAL INCIDENTS
Ahmedabad 1996, 1999, 2000 & 2002
Ahmednagar 2000 & 2001
Ajmer 1998 & 2001
Aurangabad 1999, 2001 & 2002
Bahraich 1996, 1996, 2000 & 2002
Bengaluru 1997 2002
Coimbatore 1995, 1996, 1997 & 1998
Gonda 1997 & 1999
Hyderabad 1995, 1995, 1997, 1998 & 1999
Jalgaon 1997, 2001 & 2002
Kanpur 1998 & 2000
Kolkata 1996 & 2000
Lucknow 1996 & 2001
Mathura 1997 & 2000
Moradabad 1995, 1998 & 2001
Nalanda 1998 & 2001
Nandurbar 1999 & 2002
Ranchi 2000 & 2001
Surat 1999 & 2000
Surathkal 1998 & 1999

A Note on the Map

A visual representation of the spatial distribution of riots is too obvious a need to require explicit justification. The map given here is an attempt to meet this need. It was prepared by Aquib Jamal, a geographer based at the IIIT, Hyderabad. The map is based on Asghar Ali Engineer's annual surveys of communal incidents across the country from 1995 to 2002, and is intended to supplement earlier attempts at such an exercise.

We are aware of at least two earlier attempts to prepare a comprehensive dataset on communal violence in India, one by Violette Graff, published in the French journal *Herodote* and available on the Sciences Po website, which covers the period from 1978 to 1993.[1] The other attempt is by Ashutosh Varshney and Steven Wilkinson, who have compiled data for the period 1950 to 1995. Though there is a continuity and overlap of periods covered in these three exercises, identifying trends across the three datasets is not easy because the sources used by the respective scholars are not identical. Newspapers, particularly a newspaper of record like *The Times of India*, are common to the three but beyond that there is variation.

For the map presented here, cities, towns and, in some cases, districts mentioned in Engineer's annual surveys were noted down and then located on the map. Though this gives us a general picture of the spread of communal incidents during the period beyond that covered by Varshney and Wilkinson, and therefore may have some use, the two are not comparable. Since the places where riots took place were identified entirely on the basis of Engineer's write-ups and not cross-checked independently, there is some inexactitude with locations. In some cases, for example, only the district was mentioned and not the village or town and therefore, the precise place could not be shown on the map. In the Varshney-Wilkinson data, incidents of Hindu or Muslim groups clashing not with each other but with the police were categorised separately. If there was a lull in the rioting, it was entered as two separate cases. Wherever caste or some other mobilisation seemed to have taken place along with the communal, those incidents were categorised differently. As for the precipitating causes, accidents, eve-teasing, inter-religious marriages, a construction or an attack on a building led to 'group clashes', again those incidents were entered in the dataset separately. Since the map presented here and the dataset on which it is based did not follow these protocols in coding the events, it must be regarded as a very preliminary exercise.

The list of places called 'The Frequent Riot Spots' simply follows the frequency of riots. But that does not necessarily make the place 'riot prone' in the strict sense. From the state-wise data on riots presented by Wilkinson (see figures 1.2, 1.3 and 1.4 in Wilkinson 2004), it is clear that the frequency and the intensity (measured by the number of deaths) do not always go together. By combining the two for the period 1950–95, Varshney has come up with a list of 'riot prone' cities which include, in descending order, Bombay, Ahmedabad, Hyderabad, Meerut, Aligarh, Baroda, Delhi and Calcutta (Varshney 2002: 7).

One can see why Varshney has taken the number of deaths to be one of the indicators. Apart from being countable, 'deaths' provides the investigator with an unambiguous criterion whereas injuries are a matter of degrees of seriousness not easy to classify. But dimensions like how many were injured seriously, how many were displaced, how much of personal property was lost, etc., do matter in gauging the seriousness of a riot. The riot proneness of a place can manifest itself in very different ways. A place may be prone to frequent low intensity incidents resulting in what Sudha Pai and Sajjan Kumar (2018) call 'everyday communalism'. Another place may witness communal violence far less frequently, but these are 'deadly riots', 'pogroms', preceded and followed by a different politics. So, depending on the definition of a 'riot', different cities will emerge as trouble spots in different datasets.

The reason why different cities emerge as trouble spots in different analyses is also likely to be because of the different sources of the data and different definitions of a 'riot'. According to the Indian Penal Code (in 1992), a 'riot' was defined as taking place 'when an assembly of five persons or more uses force or violence in pursuit of a common aim'.[2] Wilkinson himself defines a 'deadly ethnic riot', mostly following Donald Horowitz, as 'an intense, sudden, though not necessarily wholly unplanned...attack by civilian members of one ethnic group on civilian members of another ethnic group, the victims chosen because of their group membership'.[3]

Despite all these caveats, a simple map of the sort presented here is nevertheless an invaluable aid to visualising the location and extent of recurrent communal violence in contemporary India. We are grateful to Aquib Jamal for enabling us to present it here.

Notes

1. Available at https://www.sciencespo.fr/mass-violence-war-massacre-resistance/en/document/hindu-muslim-communal-riots-india-i-1947-1986 (accessed 27 July 2018). The map is titled: 'Map 2. Locations of Main Riots between Hindus and Muslims (1978–1993)'. The orignal source for this map is cited in this article as: Graff, Violette. 1993. 'Le désarroi des musulmansindiens.' *Hérodote* 71, October–December, 129.

2. This is cited by Wilkinson (2004) in footnote 4 on p. 244.

3. Footnote 25, p.10 in Wilkinson 2004. Further details of the problems regarding sources and definitions are found at Appendix A and B in Wilkinson 2004, the latter also being available in Varshney 2002 as Appendix B. In addition, see chapter 4 in Varshney 2002 and pp. 9–16 in Wilkinson 2004 to get an idea of the stupendous problems facing the researcher—and the ingenious solutions found by these two scholars—in compiling reliable statistics on riots in post-Independence India. Problems become more daunting for the pre-Independence period as Wilkinson shows. However, Varshney and Wilkinson have sharply divergent theses on communal conflict in India. An exchange between the two which appeared in the EPW is reproduced in this volume in an abridged form.

References

Pai, Sudha, and Sajjan Kumar. 2018. *Everyday Communalism and Riots in Uttar Pradesh*. New Delhi: Oxford University Press.

Varshney, Ashutosh. 2002. *Ethnic Conflict and Civic Life: Hindus and Muslims in India*. New Delhi: Oxford University Press.

Wilkinson, Steven I. 2004. *Votes and Violence: Electoral Competition and Communal Riots in India*. Cambridge: Cambridge University Press.

Note to the Reader

As you begin to read this rich and varied collection of articles and commentaries written over the past half century, please do keep in mind the following points:

1. We have edited many of the pieces here in order to shorten them and accommodate the largest possible selection. Places where text has been cut are marked with ellipses (...). Where the ellipses occur within square brackets on a line of their own, they indicate that a paragraph or more of the original text has been omitted. However, in the altered contexts of today, it is important to note that in general, we have made only the absolutely minimum changes while abridging the essays. This has sometimes meant that we have retained words or phrases that we would not use today because they no longer carry the connotations they once did, or because they have acquired new shades of meaning. In fact, we explicitly requested our copy editor to *not* subject these texts to the usual modes of copy-editing in order to stay as close to the original as possible. The intention of this volume, and the series of which it is a part, is to make available to the contemporary reader a handy compendium of social science research and commentary published over several decades in the *Economic and Political Weekly*. Readers are, therefore, urged to revisit the original articles—easily accessible on the online archives of the *EPW*—whenever they wish to pursue a particular argument or description.
2. Please note that temporal references have not been changed. For example, phrases like 'last year', 'the current decade', etc. have been left as in the original. The date of original publication is shown at the bottom of the title page of each chapter, along with volume and issue details, for ease of reference, and to help the reader to locate each piece in its original context.
3. We have made a sincere effort to correct obvious errors and to fill gaps wherever possible, especially with regard to incomplete or missing references. However, we have been unable to do this in some cases: for instance, the place of publication is sometimes missing due to the citation style used in some of the earlier essays; references to unpublished work, or work in ephemeral magazines or newspapers; and out-of-print or otherwise untraceable sources.
4. Tables and charts not mentioned in the excerpted portions have been omitted. Also, all the tables that are included have been reformatted.

INTRODUCTION

The Social Sciences and the Economic and Political Weekly *on Hindu–Muslim Conflict*

SANJAY PALSHIKAR AND SATISH DESHPANDE

Communal clashes between Hindu and Muslim groups have been endemic to India's public life. Academics and commentators have therefore been understandably concerned with communalism and its violent manifestations. Writing in the *EPW* in 1987, Gyanendra Pandey began by saying that, '[O]ne needs to make no apology for yet another article on "communalism"...given the current political situation in India.' He was no doubt alluding to the spate of clashes at several places in the north following the (1 February 1986) order of the District and Sessions Judge of Faizabad to unlock the Ramjanmabhoomi temple. A little earlier, Chris Bayly (1985) began his now famous essay on the 'pre-history' of communal conflicts in modern India by referring to some other equally disturbing events that served to renew interest in the 'well-worn topic of conflict between members of India's major religions'. More than three decades since those fateful days, we are yet to witness any tapering of either the scale or the frequency of communal riots. Violent incidents still rock the public life of the nation, and academics trying to understand these phenomena continue to struggle to keep pace with them.

This volume bears witness to that ongoing struggle. It is a cumulative account, albeit a selective and abridged one, of what social scientists have had to say—in the journal that arguably represents them the best—on the crucially important subject of communal violence from the late 1960s until about 2015. In sum, this volume offers a broadly representative overview of what the social sciences have had to say on Hindu–Muslim conflict in independent India.

THE RATIONALE OF THIS BOOK

In speaking of the organising principles of this collection, the obvious starting point is its single source, namely the *Economic and Political Weekly* (*EPW*). This is clearly a limitation since significant social science research on communal violence in India has of course been published elsewhere as well. However, the uniqueness of the *EPW* offers ample justification. The breadth of its content, spanning not only academic articles ranging across the humanities and social sciences but also journalistic commentary, and its weekly cycle of publication make it an unmatched—and hence an indispensable—repository. This is particularly true for the subject matter of this volume: it is fair to say that no other academic journal has devoted as much space and sustained attention to communal violence. Indeed, the *EPW* would almost certainly be the single largest source for any volume on this subject.

Despite the single source, there were as many as 430 articles, reports or other columns (not counting editorials or letters to the editor) on communal violence and riots published between 1966 and 2015 to choose from. In choosing just 38 from among these—a selection rate of about one in 11—we have been guided by considerations that are inevitably more or less subjective. Some of these have taken the form of relatively precise demarcations, while others are more fuzzy.

For example, the decision to restrict the volume to the post-Independence era yielded a well-defined selection criterion. The *EPW* has many excellent articles on communalism and sectarian violence in the colonial period, and a case can be made for the lingering salience of colonial policies and discourses. But the modalities of contemporary communalism have been so decisively shaped by Partition (or the creation of Pakistan) and postcolonial phenomena like electoral politics, that it constitutes a distinctive period with its own trajectories. In terms of the types of writings chosen, we have generally preferred the longer pieces that are called 'special articles' in the *EPW* to the shorter reports and commentaries. This is because we felt that the better researched pieces with longer gestation lags tend to stand the test of time much better than the valuable, but more ephemeral shorter journalistic or fact-finding pieces. However, the short reports have been discussed in detail later in this Introduction.

Collectively, the contents of this volume are intended to answer the question: what can the social sciences tell us about communal violence? This is admittedly an imprecise criterion, but it comes closest to capturing the way we went about making our selection. Within this broad remit, we have tried to choose writing that may be said to be 'representative' in one or more senses. For instance, we have tried to incorporate a variety of disciplinary perspectives including political science, political economy, history, sociology and other social sciences and humanities. This is perhaps the place to point out that a representative collection is not necessarily a collection of the *EPW*'s 'top 10'—or in this case, the top 38—essays on the subject found in the *EPW*.

We have also tried to ensure an adequate regional spread, but this has proved more difficult because we were constrained by what was available. Also, the significant sites of communal violence have tended to be concentrated in northern India. The south has not been as active, and is therefore largely absent, though in recent times Karnataka, Tamil Nadu and even Kerala have reported recurrent clashes that are finding their way into the *EPW*.

Conceptual boundaries have been the most difficult to draw. 'Communalism' is itself a broad category that has seen some definitional variation. The term 'riot' is also a fuzzy term, beyond its core entailment of violent deaths and localised destruction of property and terrorisation of neighbourhoods by mobs. Moreover, to understand the 'communal riot' as a recurrent, widespread, and far-from-accidental phenomenon, it is necessary to step back from the actual sites and forms of violence to background factors. This has led to the inclusion of more general articles that analyse the growth and nurturing of sectarian animosities in specific contexts, and the theoretical issues involved in studying them. Political science and history are especially important in this regard, and the *EPW* has hosted debates on the methodology and theory that ought to inform research on communal violence. (See, among others, the contributions of Wilkinson, Varshney, Kumar and Pandey in this volume.) Overall, we have generally tried to stay close to communal violence, and we have restricted this to Hindu–Muslim antagonisms because the anti-Sikh and anti-Christian instances are too specific and localised compared to the spread and longevity of the former.

We move on next to a quick survey of the field that is represented by the pieces in this collection.

Hindu–Muslim Conflict in Independent India

In the history of India as an independent nation-state, the decade of the 1950s was perhaps the only period when no major communal conflicts took place. It was possible to entertain the hope then that the Partition-related violence in 1947, unprecedented and horrific though it was, was the climactic end to the series of Hindu–Muslim clashes that had been going on since at least 1893. The 1961 Jabalpur riots dashed that sombre hope. It is not clear what started the riot. As always in these cases, facts are disputed. But it seems that a Hindu businessman's daughter eloped with the son of his Muslim rival. According to the other version, a girl raped by two Muslim youths committed suicide and that triggered inter-community violence. The Jabalpur riot was followed by one each in Calcutta, Jamshedpur and Rourkela in 1964 and one in Ranchi in 1967. The decade closed with the 1969 Ahmedabad riot in which over 600 people are said to have died, and the 1970 Bhiwandi riot. After that there has been no respite. Asghar Ali Engineer, who wrote extensively on communal conflict and also contributed to the *EPW* over a decade (see the tribute to him that follows this Introduction), says:

> In the sixties major riots used to take place one at a time and at comparatively long intervals. In the seventies ...the intervals became shorter....In the early eighties the interval became so short that I had hardly finished investigation of one major riot before I had to rush to investigate another major one. In 1983, I returned from Meerut and hardly unpacked my luggage when I had to dash off to Baroda for investigating another riot (Engineer 1986: 994).

In the late 1980s and in the following decade, the situation got worse. The frequency and the scale of incidents of communal violence have led commentators and scholars to search for the period in the South Asian history when these incidents began. There is no consensus over the genesis of communal violence. The difficulty is partly empirical. We know that groups of Hindus and Muslims clashed at various places on several occasions in pre-modern India. The number of such incidents is of course not comparable to that in the nineteenth and twentieth centuries. But the silence of historical sources is by itself no guarantee that communal violence did *not* take place. It is difficult to arrive at any reliable statistics for the pre-modern period. But more challenging are the conceptual issues. When we apply modern terms to describe pre-modern events, we invite the charge of anachronism.

'Communalism', as we know it, has had the context of mass politics, the supposedly neutral state, and pan-Indian identities. To call religion-linked collective violence in pre-modern India (of which there is evidence) 'communalism' in the absence of these conditions would be incorrect. The dominant view among Indian historians is that the Hindu–Muslim animosity is the legacy of the British rule (see Upadhyay and Robinson 2012, included in this volume). The three interrelated things that were decisive were: separate electorates from the Morley-Minto reforms onwards which recognised and legitimised religious identities, encouraged the formation of organisations around these identities, and incited political rivalry between them; Census, or the exercise of counting and the use of religious categories for that purpose; and the colonial historians' view of the medieval period in Indian history as a period of Muslim rule marked by religious persecution of the Hindus. Underlying these three factors was the assumption that the pan-Indian religious identities of the people in the subcontinent as Hindus and Muslims had already crystallised before the British came. Indian historians across the ideological spectrum have argued, with different nuances, that much of the communal trouble in the post-Independence India has been because of the British policies. This view, and an occasional counter, finds an echo in some of the contributions to the *EPW*, though most of the debate around this question has taken place elsewhere in history journals.

Chris Bayly countered the dominant view and argued that 'the widespread Hindu-Muslim symbiosis of the pre-colonial period did not totally exclude the possibility of riot and disturbance along communal lines' (1985: 181). Marshalling evidence from a wide variety of sources, Bayly showed that Hindu–Muslim riots did take place at several places in the north during the eighteenth and early nineteenth century. What is more, in many cases the triggering incidents—religious processions, killing of a cow, music in front of a mosque—had an uncanny resemblance to the riots in the modern and post-Independence period. But this article, and much of the later debate on whether Hinduism is a colonial/modern construct, appeared elsewhere. For example, Gyanendra Pandey (1990: 15) reacted sharply to Bayly's revisionist intervention in his now quite famous work, *The Construction of Communalism in Colonial India*, by saying that there is in Bayly's argument 'no sense of context', 'not a hint that human beings and their actions...derive their meaning' from the overall context. If, what appears in the twentieth century is the same as what took place in the eighteenth century, then nothing has changed in the history of South Asia in spite of the colonial intervention. 'The context disappears' (Pandey 1990: 16). Little later, the revisionist side in the debate was joined by Sanjay Subrahmanyam (1996:

44–80), who was convinced that the 'medieval and late pre-colonial Indian society was violent', and that 'the texts and ideological statements produced in the epoch were often suffused with this violence, which was seen as legitimating for a number of reasons'. However, he clarifies, 'there was relatively little harnessing of devices of collective memory or the recollection of "historical grievances" to orchestrate mass violence' (57–58).

Adam Bowles et al. (2012) came close to this position in their ambitious survey of the state–religion relationship in India from the earliest times to the present. They said that they 'searched hard for pre-modern riots and did not find very many'. Of course, this relative lack of evidence did not necessarily mean that 'Indian society in pre-modern times was completely harmonious' (2012: 257). In an important chapter called 'Cohesion and Conflict', they present some case studies from pre-modern India and conclude that 'pre-modern India was not free from religiously linked collective social violence', that they were not cases of purely religious violence, nor was the violence always between the Hindus and the Muslims, and that the rulers, though at times brutal, were often 'even-handed' in their intervention (2012: 130–32). It would appear then that 'there were more clashes over religion than most historians and anti-secularist warriors such as Ashis Nandy would allow, but still far fewer than in colonial times...' (2012: 259). This debate, and the closely related debate on the alleged 'invention' (or 'construction') of Hinduism in modern times was not prominent in the *EPW*'s discussion of communalism.

On its part, the *EPW* has focussed on the events of the post-Independence period and its contributors too have mostly confined themselves to finding the genesis of the riots in the economic and political processes of the post-1947 period and not traced it further back. This meant that perspectives taking the discourse analysis approach have not found significant representation in the *EPW*. By way of an example, one could refer briefly to the work by Gyanendra Pandey (1990: 1–14) again. In the introductory chapter of that book, Pandey, who prefers to speak of 'sectarian strife', says that '"Communalism" ... is a form of colonialist knowledge. The concept stands for the puerile and the primitive....' Communalism, in this perception, is a 'pathological condition', the Other of secularism, liberalism and nationalism; it is 'nationalism gone awry'. It is supposedly a feature of the South Asian region, a region that cannot produce genuine nationalism, or cannot be genuinely liberal and secular. The primordial religious loyalties and their mutual hostility in this society are a given. Calling this an essentialist view of Indian society and history, Pandey argues that traces of this view persist even in ostensibly nationalist or leftist analyses.

Another example of discourse analysis of 'riots' (to use official or governmental terminology) is the Special Issue (No. 3) of the journal *Domains*. As the editors Deepak Mehta and Roma Chatterjee (2007: 8) explain, for the papers in this issue 'the communal riot is both a practice and a discursive condition, anchored in documentary, pictorial, ethnographic, narrative and judicial accounts'. Deepak Mehta's own paper in the issue is partly about how the Srikrishna Commission Report on the 1992–93 Bombay riots follows, in its official account of the riots, documentary procedures established by the colonial enquiry commissions. Mehta then goes on to 'juxtapose' to the Report the testimony of a riot survivor and problematises the relationship between the two. Work of this kind, which over the years has found its niche in certain journals, has been almost absent in the *EPW* with its search for objective facts in the midst of contested claims.

SOME FEATURES OF THE CORRESPONDENTS' REPORTS ON RIOTS

For many years, the *EPW* covered communal riots in its issues through the 'From our Correspondents' column. This was unique to the *EPW* because among the academic periodicals, no other publication reported communal disturbances so regularly. Moreover, these were not merely factual reports of where the riots took place, how many died and whether the situation was now under control or not. The *EPW* reports presented more than just the details of the incidents. They helped readers see those incidents in the context of the socio-economic history of the place and were complementary to the longer pieces published as 'Special Articles'.

The correspondents' reports were based on field visits. The 'correspondents' made use of a variety of sources including newspapers, the local police, NGOs working among minorities or working for better inter-community relations, residents of the areas affected by the riots, reports of fact-finding teams, reports of organisations like the Peoples Union for Democratic Rights (PUDR) and the People's Union for Civil Liberties (PUCL), interviews with the local notables, etc. Piecing together bits of information from all these sources, they constructed an account of what happened, what led to the riot, its intensity, and the human and material losses it resulted in.

Though the reports were written by different authors, some common features are noticeable. Most of them pay attention to the details of the locality of the city where the riots were most intense. The numerical proportions of different communities, their occupations, the main economic activities in the town, competition over resources and opportunities, the role of communal organisations, and electoral competition are the factors which in their interrelationship are presented in most of the reports.

The *EPW*'s correspondents are unsparing towards the police and the local administration, explicit about the organisations they think are responsible for the trouble, and clearly state which community suffered the most. Against the background of the standard practice of the big newspapers using allusions like 'one community' and 'the other community', this is bold and has sometimes invited the charge of being partisan. But if the communal violence that has taken place in the last five decades or more is a gruesome aspect of relations of domination and resistance—resistance that at times takes equally ugly form—then stance of neutrality may be artificial and, at best, misplaced. That does not mean that the correspondents pre-judge the specific events that have taken place in the riot-affected area. On the contrary, one can see them attempting a balanced picture, putting together facts collected from as many different sources as possible. Riots begin with rumours and leave behind more rumours. Usually, journalists or members of a fact-finding team visit the affected area a few days or weeks after the riot. The intervening period may facilitate clarity as to what exactly happened or the hardened animosity may make things more opaque.

It is not easy to sift through allegations, hearsay and very understandable exaggerations. Commenting on the Gian Prakash Committee report on the Meerut riots, Ashghar Ali Engineer is critical of the committee's reluctance to fix responsibility for the riot but at the same time, he is candid in admitting that it is never easy to find out the truth. He says,

> ...after marshalling all this evidence, the committee could not reach any firm conclusion as to how the riot began....No doubt the situation was confusing in the city on that fateful night. Even for this writer it was very difficult to obtain an authentic version as to who exactly started the trouble and how. Various stories were circulating. In fact there were as many versions as the number of individuals one met. The community to which one belonged also mattered very much.

But, he asserts that 'to say this does not mean that truth could not have been ascertained. It certainly could have been' (Engineer 1988, 31). It is this sober optimism that seems to have motivated the correspondents to go to the field, collect various accounts, recognise them to be partial, but use them carefully to tell the *EPW* readers a more complete story.

As part of their reports, the correspondents often state whether the town or the city where the riot took place has had a history of communal tensions. If yes, then that becomes an implicit, albeit unargued explanation of the current trouble. This is slightly problematic since a longer perspective shows that barring cities like Ahmedabad, most other 'trouble spots' have been 'riot prone' only during specific periods. Hyderabad was one such city in the 1980s, but in the later period, the frequency of riots has come down remarkably. On the other hand, when the correspondents express surprise over a riot having broken out where there had been no history of communal disturbances, one has the sneaking suspicion that behind this factual statement there is a postulate of a peaceful past. This stage of communal harmony also doubles up as a methodological beginning, a starting point of an enquiry into gradual communalisation culminating in riots. Thus, in *Communal Violence in Indore* (2008), Jaya Mehta and Vineet Tiwari write of the 'glorious past of communal harmony' during the Holkar period and of the non-communal working class culture in the city. Following Indore's industrial decline, the authors tell us, the working class culture also faded and it was replaced by business, real estate, unaccounted money, unemployment and poverty—the last two more pronounced among the Muslims. Communal propaganda found it easier to strike roots in these conditions and then, when on the day of a bandh called by the BJP–VHP, some Muslim shopkeepers refused to shut their shops, trouble broke.

A related but methodologically different feature of the reports is the way the economic factors are connected by some of the correspondents to communal tensions and to the eventual riots. In the report, *Ferozabad: Anatomy of a Riot* (Chopra and Singh 1972), the attack on the Union office is explained thus: '...the Glass Workers' Union office was attacked for no obvious reason than that the union president was a Muslim. The other reason, and probably a more genuine one, was that the workers were proposing to go on strike for higher wages' (1,713). Another correspondent, reporting the 1973 Poona riot, suggests that the Maharashtra government may have engineered the riot with the help of Shiv Sena to divert people's attention from price rise and food shortage: 'The successive food riots in Nagpur, Nasik and other parts of the state', the various bandhs, and its own intelligence reports, seem to have convinced the government that there is widespread discontent over the economic situation. 'In this situation, what could be better than communal riots to divert people's attention from their economic plight and frustrations' (*EPW* Correspondent 1973: 887).

We mention these write-ups only as illustrations and do not mean to single them out. What is common to all three reports is that communal violence is understood as an interruption of or departure from politics around material interests or an abnormal way of continuing that politics. There is more than a suggestion here that class solidarity is normal, anti-price rise agitation is reasonable, communal riots are neither. That the governing class or the ruling class stands to gain in some situations from communal riots (as suggested by the *EPW* editorial of 9 May 1981, on the Biharsharif riots) is not at all implausible. But unless the relation between the two forms of subaltern collective action is spelt out more systematically, the analysis can attract the kind of criticism Gyanendra Pandey (15 October 1983) makes of the liberal and left writings on communalism. They share the European Enlightenment belief in the superiority of the national and the economic over the religious or the communal. These latter are seen as subordinate factors making or unmaking the nation, or class struggle, or development. When the *EPW* correspondents speak of riots as engineered to divert people's attention from other (real) issues, they do unwittingly treat 'the people' as objects of forces beyond them and not actors with their own consciousness. This does pose a problem and is shared to a greater or lesser extent by many reports in the *EPW*.

There is another issue involved here, namely the way material interests and the communal consciousness are believed to be related to each other. The *EPW* correspondents seem to share an unarticulated ontological faith in causality as the motor force that keeps the social world going. And there is the belief in the 'communal' being the (distorted) expression of the economic. With these two underlying assumptions, many of the narrations of riots mention the political, economic, demographic happenings and their culmination in riots. The account that emerges is not at all implausible, but the linkages are assumed or merely gestured at. When this happens, the report hovers between a journalistic story and a social scientific exercise. It is the special articles which make up for this shortcoming.

The question of how to define communalism is obviously related to the issues we are discussing here but does not seem to have been prominent in the *EPW*. John Oommen (1995) quotes the definitions by Bipan Chandra and Louis Dumont but that is not the focus of his article. For Bipan Chandra, communalism is the belief that 'because a group of people follow a particular religion, they have as a result, common social, political and economic interests'. And Louis Dumont sees a parallel between communalism and nationalism: nation replaced by community. In a 2002

EPW article, Gyanendra Pandey says (though one is not sure if he subscribes to this view) that 'communal conflict...has to do with worldly issues between people belonging to different religious denominations whom political leaders of different stripes have sought to mobilise on the basis of political, economic, social and cultural demands that they supposedly share in common'.

It can be argued that just as communal conflict cannot be understood without communalism, communalism too cannot be understood without secularism from which it is conceptually inseparable. And yet, except for the piece by Sasheej Hegde, we have not included essays on secularism in this volume. In the political polemic in India, 'communal', hardly a term of commendation, is often traded against 'pseudo-secular', a description meant to be equally insulting. Taking these terms with their intended illocutionary force and not literally, the 'pseudo-secular' are those hypocrites who, at best, perversely refuse to see Hindutva as legitimate expression of cultural nationalism, and who, at worst, indulge in minority appeasement out of political opportunism. On the other hand, the project of cultural nationalism is seen by its opponents as 'communal' in the sense of a project of the Hindu majority's dominance of the minorities in all the spheres. Here it should be pointed out that such dominance has been already accomplished at the middle and top levels in various fields. The politics of Hindutva is about making this dominance permanent and official. Apart from resisting cultural expressions of this dominance, minorities, especially the Muslims, are also locked in a grim battle over resources and opportunities at the level of the lower classes. Their resistance gives Hindutva its *raison d'être* and provides it with a mass base.

But the urban and the semi-urban lower classes are mobilised for many different kinds of politics and taking up their issues is not what makes a party or an organisation communal. Consciousness of being part of a community, too, is not sufficient to make it communal. What is crucial is the nature of the 'community' one identifies with and the manner of identification. Apart from being enumerated and kept jealously distinct, the community that a communalised person belongs to is typically imagined to be facing threats from an antagonistic community. Once these threats, constructed by political imagination, are presented to the consciousness of its putative members, they work like a self-fulfilling prophecy and serve as a standing justification of aggressive politics on behalf of the 'beleaguered community'. Communal consciousness, and hence the communal mode of identification, is thus distinct in that the adversarial orientation towards the 'other community' within the nation space is basic to it (Zavos 1999). This identification is essential and not accidental, temporary or issue-specific and therefore, it is supposed to be the orientation of all the members of the community.

Perhaps we should not be talking of 'consciousness' alone because it is the 'doing' of a certain kind that is important here. Communal riots are not communal because or only because they express already prevalent communal feelings, but because they successfully call into existence mutually hostile religious groups by invoking them (Brubaker 2002). The modality specific to the existence of groups threatening each other is not natural in the sense of surviving and flourishing by itself once it has originated for some reason. It has to be enacted from time to time and riots are an enactment of that modality.

It is, therefore, not a good idea to ask what the necessary and sufficient conditions of a riot are or to attempt an INUS model[1] (Mackie 1965) of the causality of riots. Because both the ostensible provocation and the violent response that it elicits time and again in such a predictable manner, are perhaps better understood as ways of 'performing' communal relations. Keeping this in mind, let us look at the various acts—or rumours of such acts—that usually succeed in triggering a communal conflict.

CAUSES OF RIOTS

So what causes a riot? One can prepare a long list on the basis of the *EPW*'s reports. But a simple answer would be that anything can start a riot. Looking at some of the reports, it is amazing how little it takes to trigger communal violence. A quarrel between two groups of children, a minor road accident, eve-teasing, elopement, India losing a cricket match, a fight breaking over kite flying, throwing colour on a person of another community during the Holi celebrations... anything will do. There are also incidents which may not have anything to do with the other community but, because of the low level of mutual trust, are readily attributed to the adversaries: a mosque catches fire due to short-circuit, a boy being treated in a private clinic dies, dead bodies of four Muslim girls surface. The third category would be of incidents which by now anyone who knows anything about the Hindu–Muslim conflict would be familiar with: a piece of meat thrown in a mosque by 'miscreants', music played outside a mosque, aggressive slogan shouting in a procession which takes a route for which it has no permission, throwing stones on a Ganesh (or Durga or Shivaji) procession, burning of a copy of the Koran, etc. Fourth set of incidents or the so-called causes are disputes over the use of public spaces and pieces of land with unclear ownership status: one group wants to use it for hoisting the national flag, the other insists that it has been used for Id prayers for years; a mosque is being built on a piece of land, the other group comes and claims it for a Hanuman temple; Muslims want to build a wall around their cemetery, Hindus object to a tree being included inside the compound. Fifth type is incidents of Muslims clashing with the police, or attacking a police station, or having an argument with the police over the alleged arbitrariness or excesses of the police. It is clear that the police or the local administration is not trusted by the Muslims. So when the local authorities demolish a part of a mosque complex on the ground that it is an unauthorised construction, Muslims react belligerently and attack offices and police stations. Now, there is no reason why such events should lead to a general *Hindu–Muslim* conflagration, but they do, confirming the Muslim suspicion of collusion.

The last category consists of reactions to something that has taken place elsewhere in the world. After the US invasion of Iraq, parts of India saw protest marches and bandhs called by some Muslim bodies. Some Hindu shopkeepers refused to down their shutters and that led to tensions. A soldier, who happened to be a Hindu, died in a bomb blast in Kashmir. When his body was brought to his native town, Shiv Sena gave a call for a bandh and there was stone throwing when some Muslim shopkeepers refused to join. In the late 1960s, there was a sudden rash of riots in the eastern part of India as a result of the stories of persecution carried by the Hindu refugees fleeing from East Pakistan.

It is a useful preliminary exercise to classify 'causes' into such categories. But perhaps more important are the trends across categories. First, throwing a piece of meat in a mosque or playing music outside a mosque while there are prayers going on inside, are deliberate acts calculated to incite. Those who do it know why they are doing it and those who are targeted know that these are meant to provoke them. These are attacks on the community's symbols, on its ideas of the sacred and the sacrilegious. They are meant to be so and the targeted community almost never fails to take offence. There is something routine about these incidents of mischief and the responses and counter responses they generate. Communal riots do not happen out of accidents, random events or out of misunderstanding. In article after article, Asghar Ali Engineer keeps arguing that most riots are pre-planned, not spontaneous, and Paul Brass, in an article included in this volume, argues that 'the production of...riots involves calculated and deliberate actions by key individuals, the conveying of messages, recruitment of participants', and provocative actions 'that are part of a performative repertoire'. He calls it the 'institutionalised riot production system', put in place in the northern parts of the country sometime in the 1960s and perfected over the following decades in the context of electoral competition. If Brass and Engineer are right, then neither an exhaustive list of the 'precipitates' of riots nor an analysis of the necessary and sufficient conditions of riots will be adequate as long as riots are not seen as command performances.

What helps riot production is the community consciousness of a kind which it feeds off and heightens in turn. This heightened community consciousness produces uniform and predictable responses to incidents which are otherwise quite different from each other. An elopement is at best a matter between two families, eve-teasing is a gender issue, and a dispute over a piece of land is a property issue. But they are all seen as community issues because they are all about the community's assets—women, children, land, buildings—and assets of the community need to be protected from the other community. Similarly, the idea of a religious community, extending beyond the nation-state, demands that any suffering that one's co-religionists go through elsewhere must be not only protested against here, in India, but, by the same logic, members of the other community must be made to pay for the atrocities perpetrated by their co-religionists elsewhere. Systematic riot production is helped by this 'community at war' perception that a sizeable number of people come to have.

Role of the Police

If communal conflict is a result of such systematic riot production, then the role of the police—either way—becomes crucial. Most of the *EPW* reports of individual riots are critical of the police. The criticisms range from indifference and inaction to active participation in a riot. (See the Editorial, 'Dhule's Uniformed Riots', in the 16 February 2013 issue of the *EPW*). Instances where the 'correspondent' acknowledges the police impartiality and firmness or concedes that they were badly outnumbered by the rioters are very few. Far more often, we read of complaints by those affected in the riot that in spite of repeated calls, the police did not come. Or that in spite of palpable tension in parts of the city, police took no preventive measures. Or that even as a mob went around forcing shopkeepers to close down and threatening the reluctant ones, the police merely looked on. Going by a textbook understanding of rule of law, this is already quite serious. But inaction, it seems, is the most benign form of police lapses (except, of course, when your house is surrounded by a large and hostile mob and your frantic calls to the local police go unanswered). If the complaints and allegations of the riot victims (corroborated in many cases by fact-finding teams and judicial inquiries) are true, then the police are capable of much worse. If we were to attempt listing dubious police actions in an ascending order of gravity, the list would be as follows:

- Incompetence
- Inaction
- Participation in looting
- Indiscriminate action
- Excess
- Partisan action
- Inciting violence
- Partisan brutality

As an example of the last item in the list—partisan brutality—read this account of an incident during the 2008 Indore riots: a Muslim boy was going for work. 'According to his 14-year old younger brother, a policeman caught him, dragged him down to the ground, put the gun on his face, pulled the trigger, and walked away' (26 July 2008, 12). It is important to mention here that there was already tension in the town and a group of Muslims had earlier attacked a police station. This background makes the alleged act of the policeman look like an act of retaliation. But it was more than that. The boy had not participated in the attack on the police station. His killing by the policeman, in its general, misdirected nature, was an expression of a communalised mindset.

If we disregard this as an aberrant behaviour of an individual policeman, there is the infamous case of the Provincial Armed Constabulary (PAC) of Uttar Pradesh, which is hard to explain away. Iqbal Ansari, in a piece included in this volume, says:

> On May 22, 1987, during curfew in Meerut in UP, the PAC picked up several hundred innocent Muslims mostly youth from their homes and took them away in trucks, while there was no rioting in that area of the city. A few days later about 40 dead bodies of some of the arrested were found floating in the Upper Ganga Canal... (30 December 2000). (There are also other versions of the incident.)

These are a couple of the most glaring instances. But apart from murder in cold blood, the police have been accused of many other misdeeds. Use of brute force, deployed in a blatantly partisan manner, is obviously serious. But perhaps more exasperating than serious are the instances of police participation in looting during riots. In a letter to the *EPW* editor, 'A Reader' claims that during the 1984 Hyderabad riots, he saw shops, mostly belonging to Muslims, being looted and burnt and whenever a shop was broken into, he saw people, including policemen, rushing in and taking away whatever they could from the shop (6 October 1984).

In a hard-hitting editorial in the 6 June 1987 issue, the *EPW* says: 'The Indian police, it seems, is adept at missing the culprit and killing the innocent....The recent communal flare-up in Old Delhi provided the police with yet another opportunity to prove their dexterity in letting off the guilty and killing the innocent'. It quotes a damning observation from the Sixth National Police Commission Report: in many instances 'police officers and men appear to have shown unmistakable bias against a particular community while dealing with communal situations'. The Report recommends recruitment of the members of the minority community and other weaker sections, a suggestion which has kept coming from many quarters. As long as the police and paramilitary forces do not have men and women from the minority communities in sufficient numbers, it will be perceived with distrust. A number of *EPW* articles on riots narrate instances where Muslim groups have clashed with the police. These clashes arise out of the Muslim hostility towards the police. But the fact that in some cases such clashes have metamorphosed into a general Hindu–Muslim conflagration (for example, in Hyderabad in 1981) shows that their perception of the police as an organised coercive force acting on behalf of the majority community needs to be taken seriously.

Judicial Inquiries

Every time incidents of communal violence take place, there is a clamour for a probe and the government in office sometimes institutes a judicial enquiry. Ideally, this should be a welcome exercise. It can prepare the ground for the eventual prosecution of the guilty, point out administrative lapses, help us understand the dynamics of riot-like phenomena, and suggest ways of improving inter-community relations. In practice, however, enquiry commissions rarely succeed in doing any of these things despite their voluminous reports. *EPW* has, on many occasions, editorially commented on this, its contributors have pointed out problems with such exercise, and the piece included in this volume (by Rajeshwari) shows with specific examples why in spite of many judicial commissions from 1961 onwards, very little has changed on the ground.

To understand why inquiry commissions are often an exercise in futility, we need to remember that the power to order an inquiry lies with the government—state and the central. It is the same government which has failed to anticipate or control a riot. It cannot be too keen to have its machinery exposed to a neutral scrutiny. It can subvert the inquiry it has instituted. The composition of the commission, its chairperson, whether the inquiry is going to be an administrative or judicial, its terms of reference, the staff made available to it, the time within which it is asked to submit its report, extensions granted or not granted, are all crucial matters on which the government has the power to decide. Those threatened by the inquiry can approach the High Court, and then the Supreme Court, causing delays. Witnesses are not always willing to come forward and depose. The interpretation of the terms of reference and laying down the procedure are the commission's prerogatives and so is the interpretation of evidence it collects. And after all this, if it does manage to submit a unanimous report, it is after a long time, during which the political situation may have changed, and the government of the day may not take any action on it.

Not all commission reports are made public; commissions themselves take a long time, and their findings are merely 'noted for future guidance' by the government (*EPW* Editorial, 19 September 1981; see also an earlier editorial, *Aligarh Riots*, 18 November 1978). Governments do not always table Action Taken Reports, witnesses die, and evidence is lost. No wonder few are prosecuted and even fewer are convicted. Of course, the limitations of the commission alone are not responsible for this. In 'Recalling Bhagalpur' (4 May 1996), John Zavos clarifies that a commission is not a substitute for normal investigations under the criminal justice system. The two are separate and can function simultaneously. But the very visible act of appointing a Commission of Inquiry considerably reduces the pressure on the government to take action after a riot when in fact the government should be filing cases on the suspects on the basis of the information it has and pursue them vigorously. This is rarely done.

Commission reports themselves sometimes suffer from serious shortcomings including systematic biases. The Nanavati Commission appointed after the Gujarat 2002 riots became controversial for a number of reasons. Justice Nanavati was criticised for clearing the police and the administration of any charges of lapses in handling the riots even before the inquiry was complete. There were also doubts raised about his impartiality after the contents of a sting operation became public (See Part 2.2.1 of Jaffrelot 2012). Earlier, in case of the 1984 Hyderabad riots, the Justice Krishnarao Commission Report was criticised for not taking into account the large number of affidavits submitted to it and also for its uncalled for advise to the Muslim community to adopt family planning and accept the Common Civil Code (See Rao 1986). So, in addition to the deliberate subversion of the process by the state machinery, the outlook of the judge presiding over the enquiry also obviously makes a difference.

The Working Group of the National Integration Council submitted in 2007 a study of 29 reports of commissions of inquiry from 1961 to 2003. Chapters III and IV of the Working Group's report give a summary of the findings of all the previous enquiry commission reports and a list of causes of riots (See Ministry of Home Affairs 2007).

AFTER THE RIOT

Riots are often talked about in terms of the number of persons killed, property destroyed, curfew imposed, whether army had to be called in or the State Reserve

Police (SRP) controlled the situation, and so on. While these are the standard indicators of the intensity of a riot, the aftermath is no less important. Every major riot produces multiple consequences which continue to be felt long after the so-called return to normalcy. Even as the curfew is lifted, shops open, streets get crowded again and the city wears its normal busy look, those whose houses have been burnt down and family members attacked and killed, start their lives far away from their homes in relief camps.

Relief colonies usually come up on the outskirts of the city. The site is far from ideal. The houses are poorly built; there is no ventilation, no potable water and no drainage. There may even be a huge garbage dump nearby. When it rains, there is water logging, seepage, and in such conditions diseases spread quickly (Mander 2006). Despite all this, life must go on. Adults have to go to work and children have to go to school. It may not be possible any longer to simply walk down to the school or cycle to the workplace from the new place. There may be no city transport available. Girls' education is the first casualty. In the long run, it may even reflect in the lowering of the age of marriage of the girls (Sheth and Haeems 2006). Among working adults, those whose carts or shops have been destroyed must look for ways of raising money to recover and rebuild. Women earlier working as domestic labour in middle-class houses closer to their homes must now look for alternative sources of income. Providing for a large number of uprooted people and families is not easy and government's efforts and resources often do not match the scale of the tragedy. There are charges of incompetence, bias and discrimination. Voluntary organisations of various sorts step in to provide what the government cannot or may not give. Some of these organisations use the situation to entrench themselves among the displaced and try to draw them into identity politics. While the riot affected need help and appreciate it wherever it comes from, not many of them want to be part of such politics.

This is when some of them decide to go away to some other town or city. The use of the word 'migration' to describe this relocation is controversial (Badigar 2012). 'Forced migration' is better. To call such people 'internally displaced' would be more accurate. The UN definition of the 'internally' (that is, within the national boundaries,) 'displaced persons' speaks of persons having been 'forced or obliged to flee or to leave their homes or habitual residence'. The reasons include 'situations of generalised violence' and 'violations of human rights'. The riot affected are displaced in this sense. In fact, they are doubly displaced—first, from their homes and then, from the relief colony. The new place they settle at sometimes brings them into conflict over resources with groups already living there. This means fresh trouble, perhaps another displacement, and new groups being communally mobilised. (See the report on the Jamshedpur riots in the *EPW* issue of 19 May 1979 for an example of this.) Thus, one major riot prepares the ground for many small and big riots in future.

Among those who stay back in the city where their lives were devastated by the riot, there are some who seek legal redressal. This is a 'mistake', but it takes them a long time to realise it. The way our criminal justice system works, it is not easy for the victims of communal riots to get justice. Either their complaints are not registered accurately or the investigation is shoddy. So their case is already weakened and the chances of the acquittal of the accused are high. But before that, there is the agonising wait for the case to come up for hearing. The defence lawyers are adept at securing endless adjournments resulting in the dragging of the case. The complainants also find criminal cases slapped against them. Pursuing their complaint already takes a toll on their time, energy and earnings. Now they have the additional burden of defending themselves against false charges. As this goes on for months and years, they get tired. In the meantime, feelers are sent to them to 'compromise'. If the offer of 'compensation' does not induce them, there are threats of various kinds. They resist for some time, but then give in to the pressures. In an extra-legal negotiation forbidden by the law but encouraged by the way the system works, they settle for a compromise. They know that the violent death of their kin cannot be compensated, nor is the paltry amount offered enough to repair the material damages. But their lives have been already disrupted, the case is going nowhere, and regardless of the court's verdict, it is the same neighbourhood, or the same job that they have to return to. All this breaks their resolve and, in spite of the support of activists, they settle for a 'compromise' (Mander 2012).

The case then meanders without lawyers from either side vigorously pursuing it and at some point, long after we have forgotten about the case, we read in the newspapers that the accused have been acquitted for want of sufficient evidence. This is a settlement, not a closure that comes after justice is done and is believed to have been done. There is a resolution but no reconciliation. Reconciliation between the attackers and the attacked is perhaps a very distant goal. But reconciliation in the sense of the victims' sense of the fairness of the system being reaffirmed also proves to be elusive. Embittered and feeling defeated, if some of them participate in a future violent confrontation of a communal nature, it should not surprise us.

There is yet another way in which a major riot leaves many reminders behind. Changes in the human geography of the city are among the most permanent and manifold of them. Already in cities like Hyderabad, Delhi and Ahmedabad, the old, 'walled' part is very different from the new part of the city and the difference has not come about naturally or spontaneously. The new part looks clean, spacious, planned and relatively prosperous. The old part is congested, crowded, and 'trouble' prone. Economic activities are also spatially distributed in such a way that they reflect and reinforce social divisions. You do not find malls and flyovers and corporate offices in the old city. With riots, the division between 'two geographically distinct and socially disconnected parts' is accentuated (Chaudhury 2007). Muslims have often complained of not being able to rent a house or a shop in the cosmopolitan areas of our cities. The less resourceful among them go to the old city. There is some comfort and a sense of security in huddling together, but ghettoisation can work both as a target in a future riot and also as an encouragement to aggressive 'retaliation'.

Everything that follows a riot then acts as an incitement to another riot. The so-called period of peace in between the two is taken up by electioneering. The connection riots have with electoral fortunes is now so well-known that it can be called a social science common sense. There are articles in this volume (Wilkinson, Varshney) which discuss this correlation but here we would like to refer to a relatively old *EPW* article by Jaya Kamlakar (1988). The author says that while cities are ethnically heterogeneous, electoral constituencies have homogeneous pockets. Speaking of municipal elections and the politics around them, the author says that 'Municipal election constituencies are... much smaller' compared to the assembly constituencies and therefore 'it is the municipal constituencies which tend to circumscribe entire pockets of ethnic groups. These constituencies are, therefore, easily mobilised into vote banks.' As the population increases, constituencies are delimited and with that, the trend of homogeneity gets accentuated. The electoral success of the Shiv Sena in Bombay and the AIMIM in Hyderabad is, it is argued, largely in homogeneous constituencies. From municipal to assembly and parliamentary constituencies, the size and the composition change, caste becomes an important factor, and more complex electoral strategies are required. But the belief that communal riots are started by politicians with an eye on the elections remains strong among commentators, academics and others. In article after article, we find the *EPW* contributors holding politicians (and the 'anti-social elements'!) responsible for riots.

It should be clear by now that the absence of a communal riot does not necessarily mean communal peace and that the period between two riots must be understood differently. The images and stereotypes circulating in the media during 'peace time', the portrayal of historical figures and events in the text books which are being read by children, are obviously relevant and the *EPW* has published some essays highlighting these.

Towards a Sustainable Communalism?

One issue that we have been very conscious of, which readers may have noticed as well, is the striking difference between the times in which these chapters were written and our own location in what is already being termed the 'Modi era'. Today, the concerted attempt to *normalise* communal politics is well under way, and the Indian society and polity are feeling the effects of this drive. By contrast, most of the chapters in this volume were written in more confident times, when the abnormality of communal violence was taken for granted, and 'secularism'—whatever the meaning attached to it—was merely a contested but not an embattled term. The ascendance of right wing politics espousing Hindutva has shaken up the hitherto taken-for-granted status of older national and social values even as it produces paradoxical effects.

Relevant here is the apparent paradox of the decline in the older type of riot—understood as a major if relatively short-lived conflagration that engulfed a town, city or region for some days, weeks, or occasionally, months. As the model of 'sustainable communalism' that began (arguably) with Gujarat 2002 is exported to other parts of the country, including Uttar Pradesh, Rajasthan, Madhya Pradesh, Maharashtra and Karnataka, a change in the pattern of communal violence is visible. Major riots are few and far between; instead, we have a constant stream of almost daily provocations and incidents, usually without any fatalities, but with considerable loss of property, severe physical assaults, often accompanied by the forcible eviction of Muslim populations from the village or urban neighbourhood.

These concerns are echoed by Badri Narayan in his article on 'Communal Riots in Uttar Pradesh' (published in the *EPW* in September 2014, chapter 28 in this volume). Speaking of the phenomenon of 'small riots', Narayan points to their contribution towards the 'constant reproduction of communal consciousness'. Major riots require a lot of hard work (on the part of its instigators) and carry high risks, whereas small riots involve less work and less risk, but are equally successful in polarising voters on communal lines and ensuring the electoral victory of the sponsoring elements. Narayan quotes a practitioner of this form of politics who asks: why should we take big risks when it is possible to get the same results with less investment, less work and less risk? Narayan also reminds us of a survey report in the *Indian Express* that had found evidence in police records of more than 600 incidents of 'small' violence in Uttar Pradesh in the months following the 2014 elections.

In its issue dated 27 June 2015, the *EPW* carried an editorial titled 'Resisting "Sustainable" Communalism'. Noting that the BJP's victory in the 2014 general election had, for the first time, placed the Indian nation 'on the uncharted terrain of an uninhibited majoritarian communalism backed by state power', it goes on to speak of the 'acceleration of the insidious process by which majoritarian communalism is being normalised'. The editorial further argues that such a normalisation 'enables and requires the transition from spectacular, wholesale acts of violence to the retail violence of everyday humiliations'. It is significant that this editorial provokes C. M. Naim (a well-known scholar of Urdu language and literature, and professor emeritus at the University of Chicago) to write a letter to the editor (25 July 2015) pointing out that 'there is another similarly corrosive "sustainable" communalism, and that is of a large portion of the Muslim community', that is expressed through 'sectarian' bias and antagonism.

Judging by these symptoms, it is very likely that the most urgent task in this era of 'the new normal' will be to name, rigorously describe, and challenge this routinised form of communalism.

GAPS AND SILENCES

Brief mention must be made of some notable absences in the material on Hindu–Muslim conflict made available by the *EPW*. The first and most obvious feature here is that while most authors deal with Hindu communalism, there are really very few who analyse Muslim communalism. To be sure, we cannot expect any easy symmetry here given the vast differences between the two communities, and therefore of their respective communalisms. Nevertheless, it is a matter of some concern that we do not have very many scholarly descriptions of Muslim communalist organisations or their modes of operation.

There are several essays on the Muslim community in India (for example, those by Asghar Ali Engineer, Imtiaz Ahmed or Balraj Puri), and some of these also speak of communal forces within it. But there is nothing to compare with the kind of engagement visible in, for example, Tanika Sarkar's essay on the Rashtra Sevika Samiti or the interviews with Hindu communal leaders in the study of the Nizamuddin riots (Pradip Datta et al.). There may be many objective reasons why it is more difficult to research Muslim communal organisations than Hindu ones, but these reasons cannot be treated as justifications. Particularly from the point of view of the community of scholars, it is urgently necessary to overcome these barriers at least in a few instances.

At a very different but perhaps equally significant level, it is astonishing that one of the largest massacres in independent India—that in Nellie, Assam in 1983—did not get adequate attention in the *EPW*. This is all the more surprising when the other major massacres on a similar scale—Delhi 1984 and Gujarat 2002—have understandably provoked a slew of articles and commentaries. This is all the more regrettable because the incredible social and ethnic complexity of the north east provides rich material for the social sciences.

Perhaps this is also the place to indicate our own biases and preferences that have influenced the editing and abridgement of most of the pieces included here. (This is different from the question of the criteria by which these pieces themselves were selected.) Since most of these articles and essays have been written soon after the events they describe, they are understandably full of contextual references that may not always make sense when read in a different time and setting. On the whole, we have tried to exclude the more graphic descriptions of violence as part of our overall inclination to privilege analysis over description, in so far as the two can be distinguished. We have also usually left out references to specific individuals and organisations and their alleged acts, since these were reported at second or third hand, and could invite unnecessary controversy that would detract from the main objective of this volume.

Quite apart from the question of sensitive material, there is the factor of abridgement. In order to accommodate as wide a selection of material as possible, we have shortened the longer articles to an approximate average of 5,000–6,000 words. Roughly one-third of the entries here did not need to be abridged; seven of the articles were longer than 15,000 words, with five of them being above 20,000 words. While exceptions have been made for some general surveys, we have carefully abridged the rest. While we have tried our best to ensure that the authors' narrative retains its coherence and that its most distinctive aspects are highlighted, the fact remains that two-thirds of the articles here are only partial versions of the original. Readers are therefore reminded that all these essays are available in their original and complete form in the archives of the *EPW*, and should be consulted wherever it is necessary to get a fuller sense of the authors' intent or the specifics of the events being described.

This volume has been put together in the hope that bringing together a representative sample of the social scientific work on communal violence over the past five decades will help us to gain a historical perspective on the challenges that face us in the present. Such a perspective has become an urgent necessity in a time when the effort to normalise and justify sectarian violence is gaining ground.

THE STRUCTURE OF THIS BOOK

The 38 articles that form this volume have been divided into four sections or parts. Section I is concerned with 'General Surveys' that look at riots over a long period or as a recurring phenomenon. Section II takes up 'Conceptual Issues' raised by the subject of sectarian violence. Section III deals with the broad field of 'Communal Politics', the causal context out of which communal violence emerges. Finally, Section IV consists of the self-explanatory category of 'Accounts of Specific Riots'. As might be expected, this is a rough classification of convenience, and several chapters may arguably be included in sections other than the one in which they are currently located. But by and large, this loose framework helps to impose a minimal structure while being hospitable to the many overlaps and continuities across sections. In terms of numbers, Section I is the smallest with only four entries, while Sections II and IV have 10 essays each, and Section III has as many as 15 articles. Brief prefatory notes are placed at the head of the four sections of this volume to introduce the specific set of articles in each section.

NOTE

1. Proposed by J. L. Mackie, this refers to a model of causality. The acronym INUS stands for the Insufficient but Necessary (or Non-redundant) part of a causal condition which is Unnecessary but Sufficient to produce the outcome. When we identify a short circuit as the cause of a fire in a house (an example given by Mackie), we do not mean that short circuit always causes fire, nor do we mean that all fires are caused by short circuits. For a short circuit to cause a fire, several other factors—like some inflammable material lying around, absence of a fire extinguisher—must also be present. Together with the short circuit, the whole causal condition can be said to have produced the fire. But this causal condition is not necessary for causing a fire since other causal conditions producing the same effect are conceivable. Replacing short circuit by some event which acts as a trigger for a communal riot, we can assess the causal condition that led to the riot in a non-necessary way. How illuminating such analysis can be is, however, debatable (Mackie 1965).

REFERENCES

Ahmed, Hilal. 2013. 'Asghar Ali Engineer (1939-2013): Emancipatory Intellectual Politics'. *Economic and Political Weekly* XLVIII (22), 20–22.

Ansari, Iqbal. 2000. 'Hashimpura Riots: Is there any Hope of Justice?'. *Economic and Political Weekly* 35 (52–53), 30 December, 4601–02.

Avchat, Anil. 1973. 'Poona Riots: Can Government Complain?' *Economic and Political Weekly* 8 (20), 886–87.

Badigar, Sanjeevini. 2012. 'A "Normal" Anomaly: Displacement due to Communal Violence in Gujarat'. *Economic and Political Weekly* XLVII (3), 42–47.

Basu, Kaushik, and Sanjay Subrahmanyam, eds. 1996. *Unravelling the Nation: Sectarian Conflict and India's Secular Identity*. Gurgaon: Penguin.

Bayly, C. A. 1985. 'The Pre-History of "Communalism"? Religious Conflict in India, 1700–1860'. *Modern Asian Studies* 19 (2), 177–203.

Bowles, Adam, Ian Copland, Ian Mabbett, Asim Roy, and Kate Brittlebank. 2012. *A History of State and Religion in India*. Oxfordshire: Routledge.

Brass, Paul. 2004. 'Development of an Institutionalised Riot System in Meerut City, 1961 to 1982'. *Economic and Political Weekly* 39 (44), 30 October, 4839–48.

Brubaker, Rogers. 2002. 'Ethnicity without Groups'. *Arch. europ. social.* XLIII (2), 163–89.

Chaudhury, Anasua Basu Ray. 2007. 'Sabarmati: Creating a New Divide?'. *Economic and Political Weekly* 42 (08), 24 February, 697–703.

Chopra, Suneet, and N. K. Singh. 1972. 'Ferozabad: Anatomy of a Riot'. *Economic and Political Weekly* 7 (34), 19 August, 1711–13.

Editorial. 1978. 'Aligarh Riots'. *Economic and Political Weekly* 13 (46), 1869–70.

———. 1981a. 'Biharsharif'. *Economic and Political Weekly* 16 (19), 833–34.

———. 1981b. 'The Guilty of Jamshedpur'. *Economic and Political Weekly* 16 (38), 1513–14.

———. 2013. 'Dhule's Uniformed Riots'. *Economic and Political Weekly* XLVIII (7), 9.

Editorial Note. 1987. 'Communal Riots: The Role of the Police'. *Economic and Political Weekly* 22 (23), 6 June, 864.

Engineer, Asghar Ali. 1978. 'What Have the Muslim Leaders Done?'. *Economic and Political Weekly* 13 (24), 17 June, 985–86.

———. 1981. 'Trouble at Aligarh Muslim University: A Report'. *Economic and Political Weekly* 16 (33), 15 August, 1340–42.

———. 1986. 'Maharashtra: Engulfed in Communal Fire'. *Economic and Political Weekly* 21 (23), 7 June, 994–97.

———. 1988. 'Gian Prakash Committee Report on Meerut Riots'. *Economic and Political Weekly* 23 (1–2), 2–9 January, 30–33.

———. 1999. 'Resolving Hindu-Muslim Problem: An Approach'. *Economic and Political Weekly* 34 (7), 13 February, 396–400.

———. 2002. 'Communal Riots: Review of 2001'. *Economic and Political Weekly* 37 (2), 12 January, 100–04.

EPW Correspondent. 1973. 'Some Notes on the Poona Riots'. *Economic and Political Weekly* 8 (26), 30 June, 1138–42.

Jaffrelot, Christoff. 2012. 'Gujarat 2002: What Justice for the Victims? The Supreme Court, the SIT, the Police and the State Judiciary'. *Economic and Political Weekly* XLVII (8), 77–89.

Kamalakar, Jaya. 1988. 'Ethnic Politics in Municipal Corporations'. *Economic and Political Weekly* 23 (19), 7 May, 945–46.

Mackie, J. L. 1965. 'Causes and Conditions'. *American Philosophical Quarterly* 2 (4), 245–64.

———. 1980. *The Cement of the Universe: A Study of Causation*. Oxford: Oxford University Press.

Mander, Harsh. 2006. 'Inside Gujarat's Relief Colonies: Surviving State Hostilities and Denial'. *Economic and Political Weekly* 41 (51), 23 December, 5235–39.

———. 2012. 'Broken Lives and Compromise: Shadow Play in Gujarat'. *Economic and Political Weekly* XLVII (8), 90–97.

Mehta, Deepak, and Roma Chatterji. 2007. 'Introduction: Riot Discourses'. *Domains* 3, 8–13.

Mehta, Jaya, and Vineet Tiwari. 2008. 'Communal Violence in Indore'. *Economic and Political Weekly* 43 (30), 26 July, 10–13.

Ministry of Home Affairs. 2007. 'Report of Working Group of National Integration Council to Study Reports of the Commissions of Inquiry on Communal Riots', Government of India. Available at https://mha.gov.in/sites/default/files/NIC-W-Group.pdf (accessed 2 January 2019).

Oommen, John. 1995. 'Politics of Communalism in Kerala'. *Economic and Political Weekly* 30 (11), 18 March, 544–47.

Pandey, Gyanendra. 1983. 'Liberalism and the Study of Indian History: A Review of Writings on "Communalism"'. *Economic and Political Weekly* 18 (42), 15 October, 1783–91.

———. 1987. 'Questions of Nationalism and Communalism'. *Economic and Political Weekly* 22 (25), 983–84.

———. 1990. *The Construction of Communalism in Colonial India*. New Delhi: Oxford University Press.

———. 2002. 'India and Pakistan, 1947–2002'. *Economic and Political Weekly* 37 (11), 16 March, 1027–33.

Rajeshwari. 2013. 'Judicial Inquiries into Communal Violence: Relevance of Vishnu Sahai Commission'. *Economic and Political Weekly* XLVIII (40), 13–15.

Reader. 1984. 'Hyderabad Riots'. *Economic and Political Weekly* 19 (40), 6 October, 1721–22.

Sheth, Suchitra, and Nina Haeems. 2006. '"Sisters under the Skin": Events of 2002 and Girls' Education in Ahmedabad'. *Economic and Political Weekly* 41 (17), 29 April, 1708–12.

Subba Rao, C. V. 1986. 'Story of a Judicial Enquiry'. *Economic and Political Weekly* 21 (7), 15 February, 284–86.

Subrahmanyam, Sanjay. 1996. 'Before the Leviathan: Sectarian Violence and the State in Pre-Colonial India', in *Unravelling the Nation: Sectarian Conflict and India's Secular Identity*, eds Kaushik Basu and Sanjay Subrahmanyam. Gurgaon: Penguin, 44–80.

Upadhyay, Surya Prakash, and Rowena Robinson. 2012. 'Revisiting Communalism and Fundamentalism in India'. *Economic and Political Weekly* XLVII (36), 35–57.

Varshney, Ashutosh. 2002. *Ethnic Conflict and Civic Life: Hindus and Muslims in India*. New Delhi: Oxford University Press.

Wilkinson, Steven I. 2004. *Votes and Violence: Electoral Competition and Communal Riots in India*. Cambridge: Cambridge University Press.

Zavos, John. 1996. 'Recalling Bhagalpur: Aftermath of 1989 Riots'. *Economic and Political Weekly* 31 (18), 4 May, 1055–59.

———. 1999. 'Searching for Hindu Nationalism in Modern History: Analysis of Early Ideological Developments'. *Economic and Political Weekly* 34 (32), 7 August, 2269–76.

SECTION I

General Surveys of Sectarian Violence

Introduction to Section I

This section consists of contributions which have a broad sweep. These are either historical surveys of the Hindu–Muslim relations, with an emphasis on the vicissitudes of the Muslim community, or surveys of the literature on communalism. Asghar Ali Engineer's essay is of the first kind. In an overview of the Hindu–Muslim relations, he takes us through the series of events through which a community, demoralised and terrorised after the Partition, first got disillusioned with the Congress and then got restive and assertive in its defence of the community's interests, and how this, seen as new aggressiveness by the then Jan Sangh, set in motion (yet another, we should add), political consolidation of the Hindu identity. One of the main arguments he makes is that there is competitive communalism from (some of the) leaders of both the communities and, though the minority community's communalism can be said to be mainly defensive in nature, it legitimises the majority community's communalism and then both keep reinforcing each other.

Some observers may feel uneasy about equating the communalism of two very unequal communities, but most will appreciate how difficult it must have been for Engineer to take this position and stick to it. More discomfort is likely to arise out of his return to the point in history when bitterness was created (at least in north India) because of the power struggle between the Hindu rulers and the Muslim invaders, a struggle which the Hindu rulers lost. In the south, the Muslims came as traders and got assimilated into the local population since they constituted no immediate challenge to the power relations there. Engineer seems to be suggesting that the Hindu rulers losing power to the Muslims was one of the first in a chain of events that led to the permanent bitterness between the two communities. There may be a conflation of temporal sequence and causal sequence here. Moreover, historical memories, far from being a natural phenomenon, are at least partly a result of active and selective remembering and forgetting.

However, Engineer's essay and the one by Imtiaz Ahmed in this section have the distinction of drawing our attention to the importance of historical development for a better understanding of the communal problem. Imtiaz Ahmed's essay from 1969 ('Secularism and Communalism') is one of the early overviews of the Hindu–Muslim 'problem' that resists popular, 'politically correct' constructions, which often romanticise and exaggerate the role of 'syncretic culture'. Ahmed insists that there have been strong and persistent cultural differences between the two communities, but he also argues that these differences cannot be said to have made the Partition inevitable. It is the political strategies of both Hindu and Muslim elites that had a much more consequential role.

The essay by Surya Prakash Upadhyay and Rowena Robinson is a survey of the literature on communalism. It is a remarkable survey both for the long period it covers (the entire post-Independence period), and also for the range of works it looks at: academic, journalistic, literary and artistic (mainly films). Its main aim is to classify the literature on communalism but along the way, it also presents discussions on how to define 'community' and 'communalism'. It then proceeds to classify the literature into four categories (essentialist and constructivist, instrumentalist and institutionalist) depending on the theoretical perspective from which a given work has understood communalism. The difference in perspective has sometime produced sharp exchanges among scholars (say, between the instrumentalists and the institutionalists), but it is worth noting that some aspects of their theories are mutually compatible and even mutually strengthening. Instrumentalist and institutionalist views of communalism stress on different things: cynical mobilisation and use of identities for political gain in one case and discrimination and inequalities in the other. But unless there are grievances, partly based in real injustices and inequities, using them for polarising politics will not be easy.

Sometimes, debates produce diametrically opposite positions. This is true of essentialism versus constructivism. The essentialist view believes that Hindus and Muslims were already two distinct, homogenous, self-conscious, territorially anchored communities when they first met and they were so utterly different from each other that there was bound to be enmity between them. A lot of liberal and 'left secularist' scholarship has strenuously, and often convincingly, argued against this by giving examples of the porous boundaries between the two communities and their mutual influences. Countering the left secularists, it is said that Islam was so different from the Indic religions that several centuries of living under the Muslim rulers must have produced an awareness of a distinct religious identity among the Hindus. But as the inscriptional evidence presented by Brajdulal Chattopadhyay (1998) shows, the 'Muslim invaders' and the Muslim rulers were often identified by the Hindus by their ethnicity and rarely by their religion. The essentialistic view of communities does look weak. But its opposite, the constructivist view, when applied to the history of Hinduism on the subcontinent, is also in need of more refinement. Afterall, as David Lorenzen (1999) asks rhetorically, Hinduism may have been a construct but what was it constructed out of? Clearly, the future development of these theses depends on further historical investigations into the middle period of the Indian history.

To return from this brief historiographical digression, there is one more essay in this section, a 1985 article by Gopal Krishna. Compared to the theoretical nature of the issues covered by Upadhyay and Robinson's survey, Gopal Krishna's essay is about more concrete things. Taking the riots of the 10-year period from 1961 to 1970 as its focus, it presents a lot of data about the states in which these riots took place, names of places, whether urban or rural, the causes, the main organisations which participated in the riots, towns where riots happened frequently, and so on. The exercise here of generating a dataset on riots is similar to the one Varshney (2002) and Wilkinson (2004) did later for a longer period. This overall survey forms the first of a two-part article by Gopal Krishna; the second part (on the Delhi riots of May 1974) is included in Section IV of this volume.

References

Chattopadhyay, Brajdulal. 1998. *Representing the Other? Sanskrit Sources and the Muslims (Eighth to Fourteenth Century)*. New Delhi: Manohar.

Lorenzen, David. 1999. 'Who Invented Hinduism?' *Comparative Studies in Society and History* 41 (4), 630–59.

Varshney, Ashutosh. 2002. *Ethnic Conflict and Civic Life: Hindus and Muslims in India.* New Delhi: Oxford University Press.

Wilkinson, Steven. 2004. *Votes and Violence: Electoral Competition and Communal Riots in India.* Cambridge: Cambridge University Press.

1

COMMUNAL CONFLICT AFTER 1950*

A Perspective

ASGHAR ALI ENGINEER

There are different views about Hindu–Muslim relations in India. No view, the matter being extremely complex, can be above controversy. Also, the Hindus or Muslims cannot be treated as entirely homogeneous communities. Different traditions in the two communities play their own role in determining this relationship. There are orthodox and liberal traditions and theocratic traditions on one hand, and 'sufi' and 'bhakti' traditions, on the other. There are, besides religious conflicts, conflicts of interests too. On occasions, conflicts of interests sharpen religious conflict. Not only this, religion is often used to provide legitimation for conflicts of interests and thus, what appears to be religious conflict may in fact be a cover-up for a conflict of interest. This is, of course, not to suggest that there has been no religious conflict between the two communities.

The fact that Muslim dynasties ruled over India for about eight centuries also colours this relationship. Liberal scholars have tried to show how Muslim influence had a benign effect on Indian culture and how the impact of Islam generated a composite culture. At least in north India, the centre of Muslim rule, no sphere of public life could escape the Muslim influence.

Interestingly, Hindu–Muslim conflicts are also of much greater intensity in the north. The reasons are not far to seek. Muslim invaders came from northern mountain passes and conquered northern parts of India. Thus, the struggle for power between Hindu rulers and Muslim invaders took place in this region, leaving their bitter memories behind. No such power struggle took place in the south, as Muslims came there mostly as traders. Again, it was in this region [northern India] that the battle for the division of the country in pre-1947 days was fought. This division was accompanied by considerable bloodshed.

The Partition riots ranged up to 1948 with some skirmishes occurring up to 1950. The period from 1950 to 1960 proved to be quiet, with few riots being reported. There are several reasons for this. After the formation of Pakistan,

---

* *Economic and Political Weekly* 27 (34): 1782–85 (22 August 1992).

Muslims were reduced to a much smaller minority. Apart from this, a large number of Muslims were killed in Partition riots on the Indian side (a large number of Hindus were killed on the Pakistan side) and they were in a state of terror. Muslims could hardly then assert themselves or compete with the Hindus politically or economically. The Muslims were too subdued in this period to provoke the Hindu ire. The other important reason was that the Muslim elite, both power elite and economic elite, had migrated to Pakistan and those left behind could hardly offer any serious economic competition, at least in the 'cow belt'.

JABALPUR, 1961

The first major communal bombshell in the post-Partition period exploded in Jabalpur in Madhya Pradesh in 1961 (see Engineer 1984). One of the reasons for this riot was acute economic competition between two *bidi* manufacturers in the town—one Hindu and one Muslim. The Hindi press played an inflammatory role. It all started with the daughter of the Hindu bidi manufacturer falling in love with the son of the Muslim bidi manufacturer. The Hindi press, at the instance of the daughter's father, described it as a Muslim boy attempting to rape a Hindu girl. Muslims were killed in this riot and they were terrorised by the armed police. The Urdu press carried many stories of police atrocities. A team of senior journalists from Bombay investigated the Jabalpur riot and mainly blamed the Hindi press for provocation. S. B. Kolpe, a senior journalist from Bombay who visited Jabalpur wrote,

> Most of the newspaper reports were identical, obviously emanating from the same source. On reaching Jabalpur... I found that two or three stringers working jointly for several national dailies were responsible for these reports which had a damaging effect on the political life of a nation as a whole. Only one of the three knew enough English to write readable reports. The others copied these with minor changes.

Kolpe further informs us,

> The facts reported were 'collected' from the local police who were not free from communal bias, and no reporter ever bothered to verify the facts doled out to him. Since I was known to most senior journalists in Jabalpur as an activist of the working journalists' trade union movement, I had no difficulty in mixing with the local fraternity.

The Jabalpur riot was so severe that Jawaharlal Nehru took the initiative of setting up the National Integration Council to promote emotional integration in the country. Nehru thought a body like this would succeed in bringing about some measure of accommodation between Hindus and Muslims.

The Muslim leadership was greatly perturbed by this fresh outburst of communal violence in post-Partition India. They were far from aggressive in this phase. So far, they had looked to Nehru for protection and security. However, with the emerging forces in the political scene, Nehru also appeared to be a helpless spectator. Some Muslim leaders like Faridi, a former socialist, and Syed Mahmood, who was very close to Nehru and was minister of state in the foreign ministry, felt disillusioned with the Nehruvian policy and formed the Majlis-e-Mushawarat, a consultative body of various Muslim groups and political parties. The Mushawarat was not a political party of Muslims. It was the first attempt, in post-Independence India, to bring together Muslims to pool their energies and intellectual powers not only to find solution to their problems, but also to exert pressure on the political system for realising their demands. The Urdu press, by and large, welcomed the move and published articles and editorials to this effect. But it also sent alarm signals to Hindu communalists and right-wingers. Though the Muslim masses had taken no initiative in the formation of Pakistan, all Muslims in India were seen as guilty of the creation of Pakistan by communal Hindus and any attempt on the part of Muslims to form any organisation with political implications was seen as an attempt to create another Pakistan.

The formation of the Majlis-e-Mushawarat was also seen in this light by the national press, especially the Hindi press, despite assertions to the contrary by the Mushawarat leaders. The Mushawarat started a debate about the plight of Muslims in post-Independence India, but could hardly succeed in achieving anything. There was, of course, no question of its success in stopping communal riots. Even leaders like Zakir Husain who subsequently became President of India could not achieve much. After the death of Maulana Abul Kalam Azad, a towering Muslim leader who had fought against idea of Pakistan and had seen its harmful effects for Indian Muslims, Zakir Husain was the senior-most Muslim leader of high credentials. He was close to Nehru and also enjoyed respect from Muslims, though a small section of angry Muslims saw him and similar other Muslims holding power in the Congress ministry as mere show-boys.

After Jabalpur, a chain of riots broke out in Ranchi, Jamshedpur, Aligarh and other towns. The immediate cause was the stream of Hindu refugees coming from the erstwhile East Pakistan. In Jamshedpur and Bhilai steel factories, some Muslim workers were thrown into steel furnaces and burnt alive. These riots continued up to 1965, when war with Pakistan broke out. Nehru, in his last meeting with senior IAS officers, described communalism as the greatest internal enemy of India, but was helpless in preventing these riots. All the states where riots broke out were Congress-ruled and yet, he could not persuade his own party chief ministers to curb communal violence. The Majlis-e-Mushawarat could, at best, submit memoranda and issue statements. Zakir Husain's personal intervention could bring no relief either. At the most, Muslim leaders could threaten to vote against the Congress, But there too, Muslims had hardly any alternative. There was no strong secular opposition party which could replace the Congress in the states or at the centre.

It was only in 1967, when some opposition parties combined to provide a united front, that such an opportunity arose. The Congress was voted out of power in some states including Uttar Pradesh, the most populous state of the cow-belt, where the Muslim population is around 15 per cent. Muslims voted against the party in protest, against the Congress apathy towards their plight. But then Jan Sangh, a Hindu communal party, was part of this SVD (United Front) government.

However, in 1968, the Congress was rejuvenated by Indira Gandhi. She nationalised major banks with a stroke of the pen and won laurels from Indian people. Her slogan, 'garibi hatao', electrified the atmosphere and she became an unquestioned leader of the Indian masses. In order to woo Muslim masses, she laid great emphasis on secularism. For her electoral arithmetic, Muslim and Harijan (now called 'dalit') votes were of importance. Both Muslims and dalits were totally opposed to the Jan Sangh. Thus, Muslims and dalits readily rallied around Gandhi.

The Jan Sangh was extremely worried by the left-wing policies of Gandhi and more so because of her popularity among Muslims and dalits. They could counter Gandhi only by engineering serious communal trouble in the country, which they did in Gujarat. The Gujarat riots exploded on the Indian political horizon with such tremendous force that the whole atmosphere changed in the country. Law and order being a state subject, Gandhi was totally helpless. Moreover, Gujarat was ruled by the opposition. Congress and any intervention by the centre would have been easily construed as politically motivated and Gandhi, at that stage, could not afford any adventurist action. Our investigations show that more than a thousand people perished in Ahmedabad alone.

[...]

A resolution was passed in ... the Jan Sangh's [eds] conference in Ranchi, demanding Indianisation of Indian Muslims, thereby implying that the Muslims in India were alien, had not adopted Indian culture and did not respect Hindu deities. Surprisingly, some national dailies wrote editorials in support of this demand and compared it with the demand for Indianisation of services during the British period, quite a false comparison. Also, the Hindus strongly resented the fact that Muslims were not prepared to accept change in their personal law. In response to a demand for a uniform civil code, Muslims formed the Muslim personal law board in the late 60s to protect their shari'ah law, according to which Muslim men could marry up to four wives and could seek unilateral divorce. The government had to assure Muslims that it had no intention of interfering with Muslim personal law. This was construed by the Hindus as 'appeasement' of Muslims.

To this day, this remains a sore point and the Bharatiya Janata Party (BJP) has begun to describe Nehruvian secularism as 'pseudo secularism' and describes its own version of secularism as 'positive secularism'.

Emergency and After

Several major riots took place around this time, the worst being the Bhivandi-Jalgaon riots of 1970 in which not less than 400 people died. However, the period until 1977 was comparatively quieter. Gandhi declared emergency in 1975, which continued up to 1977, when general elections were declared. During the emergency, both Hindu and Muslim communal parties were banned and there were hardly any major riots. However, in the 1977 elections, the Congress was voted out of power and the Janata Party, which again included the Jan Sangh and other centrist parties, came to power. The Muslims had also greatly suffered during emergency due to excesses in enforcing family planning measures, and enthusiastically voted for the Janata Party. The Jan Sangh leaders, before merging with the Janata Party, took an oath at Mahatma Gandhi's 'samadhi' (memorial) that they would renounce communalism and adopt the Gandhian programme. The Muslims, tired of the Congress rule, accepted the professions of the Jan Sangh leaders and voted massively for the Janata Party, at least in the north, where they had suffered most. The prayer-leader of the Jama Masjid, Delhi, popularly known as the Shahi Imam, emerged as a strong Muslim leader who lent his support to the Janata Party.

The emergence of the Shahi Imam was an unfortunate development for the Indian Muslims. He had neither participated in the freedom struggle, nor had any worthwhile knowledge of the intricacies of the Muslim problems, much less any experience of evolving proper strategies. He adopted aggressive postures towards the Janata government and was soon alienated from its leaders. The Janata government did not last long as there was neither any ideological cohesion nor any unity of purpose among its constituents. The communal problem surfaced once again and major riots broke out in the north in Jamshedpur, Aligarh and Benaras. Muslims were once again at the receiving end.

When the Janata government at last fell under its own weight, the Shahi Imam too showed political opportunism in the ensuing elections in 1980 and supported the Congress. Muslims too, once again, supported the Congress and Indira Gandhi was voted to power. However, she remained unsure of Muslim support and tried to woo the emerging Hindu middle castes.

There were a series of major riots, particularly in Moradabad in 1980, and in Biharsharif in 1981. Another Muslim leader, Syed Shahabuddin, began to emerge on the political scene. He was brought into politics by the Jan Sangh leader Atal Bihari Vajpayee, who was foreign minister during the Janata regime. Shahabuddin resigned from the foreign service and joined the Janata Party. Though well informed, dynamic and shrewd, he was inexperienced in politics and was ambitious to emerge as the sole Muslim leader. He achieved prominence in the early 1980s and issued aggressive statements on the Biharsharif riots and also on the issue of conversion of a few hundred dalits to Islam in Tamil Nadu, popularly known as the 'Meenakshipuram conversions'. This was fully exploited by the communal Hindus...to communalise the Hindu mind. The aggressive stance assumed by the new Muslim leadership had a very adverse effect on the Hindu psyche.

A minority—it may be ethnic or religious—has to adopt proper strategies for its own safety and security. If it adopts an aggressive stance, even for its legitimate demands, it ends up by further antagonising the majority community. Even the legitimate demands must be couched in a well-thought out manner. This is something which the new Muslim leadership could not properly appreciate. A proper strategy for minority demands becomes all the more necessary if the majority community, for historical reasons, is already hostile towards it. In case of Muslims, there was one more factor: they were seen as being responsible for the division of the country in 1947.

The new Muslim leadership did not realise these intricacies and began to press its demands more and more aggressively. Moreover, new factors were emerging on the political and economic scene. By the early 1980s, the population of Muslims had doubled (now they were 80 million as per the 1981 Census) and hence, had gained political significance. No party aspiring to come to power could ignore this vote-bank and hence, the centrist parties sought to woo them and conceded their religious demands like preserving Muslim personal law. Muslims were thought to be voting *en bloc* and any party securing their votes was certain to come to power.

For the BJP, this was highly frustrating. Also, by the 1980s, a small section of Muslims in the north, especially those areas which were traditional centres of Muslim artisans like Meerut, Aligarh, Moradabad, Benaras and Azamgarh, became prosperous by developing entrepreneurship on a small scale and this section of Muslims began to adopt a high-profile style of politics, and was led by the newly emergent leadership. It was this leadership which led two major movements, that is, the Shah Bano movement and the Babri Masjid movement in an aggressive manner, which made the average Hindu hostile towards Muslims.

Shah Bano Controversy

Shah Bano was a Muslim woman who had filed a case under section 125 of the Criminal Procedure Code (CrPC) for maintenance, against her husband, from whom she had separated. She was awarded maintenance under this law by the Madhya Pradesh High Court. Her husband filed an appeal against this judgment in the Supreme Court claiming that the high court judgment was in violation of the provisions of Muslim Personal Law according to which a divorcee was entitled to maintenance only for a period of three months, called the 'iddah' period, whereas under the CrPC, section 125, maintenance to a divorcee is to be paid by the husband for life or until she remarries. The Supreme Court, however, upheld the lower court judgment arguing that it was given under a common secular law and that as argued by Shah Bano's advocate, it is in keeping with the Quranic verse 2:241. The Supreme Court did not accept the plea by the advocate of the Muslim Personal Law Board that it was violative of Muslim Personal Law. Muslim leaders protested against the Supreme Court judgment saying that it was interference in the Muslim Personal Law and that the Supreme Court had no right to interpret the holy Quran. The liberal and progressive Muslims supported the judgment, arguing that it was a question of Muslim women's rights and that the judgment, delivered under the common criminal law of the country must be respected. However, liberal Muslims were a small minority. The protest movement against the Supreme Court judgment soon gathered momentum and acquired aggressive proportions. Large numbers of Muslims came out on the streets to protest and to demand that either the Supreme Court judgment be declared invalid or the law be changed, exempting Muslims from the provisions of CrPC, section 125.

This aggressive protest against a common criminal law of the country was strongly resented by the Hindus. They also made it an issue of women's rights. The left parties also made it a question of strengthening secular forces in the country and opposed the Muslim orthodox or view that a Muslim woman could not, on being divorced, claim maintenance beyond the iddah period. But the Muslim leadership stood its ground and put tremendous pressure on the Rajiv Gandhi government to change the law. The government accepted the Muslim demand and enacted the Muslim Women (Protection on Divorce) Law which exempted Muslims from application of CrPC, section 125.

Much before the ink of the new law was dry, a new controversy arose. Under pressure from Hindu fundamentalists, the doors of the Babri Masjid, closed for more than four decades, were thrown open to the Hindus to worship Lord Rama, whose idol was installed inside the mosque during Partition riots in 1948. Some knowledgeable sources even maintain that the Rajiv Gandhi government did a trade-off and acceded to Muslim fundamentalists' demand to enact the Muslim Women's Bill and conceded Hindu fundamentalists' demand to throw open the doors of the Babri Masjid. Whatever be the case, the fact remains that another Pandora's Box was opened.

Hindu communalists had acquired a legitimacy of sorts, thanks to the Shah Bano movement. They now sought to further consolidate their position through the Ram Janmabhoomi movement, which claimed that the Hindu deity Lord Rama was born at the spot where the Babri Masjid stands today and that in fourth century CE, a Hindu ruler Vikramaditya had constructed a temple commemorating Rama's birth. This temple was demolished by Babar, the Mughal ruler, when he conquered the province of Awadh and at his command, a mosque was constructed there and was known after the emperor as Babri Masjid.

Senior historians in India have effectively challenged this point of view and have tried to show that there is no proof that Rama was born at that spot nor that any temple existed at the spot where Babri Masjid stands today. However, the question was no longer a historical one. It had acquired serious political proportions. The BJP reaped its political harvest in the 1989 election by increasing its strength in the Lok Sabha to 80 seats.

In this controversy too, the Muslim leadership played no less an aggressive role. They organised many meetings, rallies and conferences. Syed Shahabuddin even gave a call for boycotting the Republic Day celebrations on 26 January 1987. It again had a very adverse impact on the Hindu mind. It was construed as a declaration of disloyalty towards the Indian Republic. Of course, Shahabuddin had to withdraw his boycott call under pressure from liberal and progressive Muslims, but the damage was done. During this period, many communal riots took place in Uttar Pradesh, Bihar, Madhya Pradesh, Rajasthan, Gujarat, etc. Now the arena of communalisation was so wide that even the south was deeply affected and riots broke out in some states like Karnataka, Tamil Nadu and even Kerala, normally the leftist stronghold. In places like Bhagalpur in Bihar, the casualties were very high; 800–1,000 people died in communal violence in October–November 1989, most of whom were Muslims.

The 10th Lok Sabha elections in May 1991 were mainly fought on the issue of Ram Janmabhoomi-Babri Masjid and all important and basic issues facing the people were pushed to the background. The BJP felt that it had a chance to come to power by playing up the Ram Janmabhoomi controversy and, if one goes by the statements of the BJP leaders, they perhaps felt this controversy would see them into power both at the centre and in some of the northern states. Though they captured power in Uttar Pradesh, they could not make it to the centre.

Thus, we see that competitive communalism proves most dangerous for the country and for the minority community. Even if minority communalism is defensive (though it is not always so, as shown by the Shah Bano controversy), it provides legitimacy for majority communalism which, in turn, strengthens minority communalism, thus creating a vicious circle which is difficult to break. It is unfortunate that though the Indian state is secular, religion has come to acquire a premier place in Indian politics.

Nothing could be a greater disaster for this multi-religious and multi-ethnic society.

Reference

Engineer, Asghar Ali. 1984. *Communal Riots in Post-Independence India*. Hyderabad: Sangam Books.

2

Secularism and Communalism*

Imtiaz Ahmad

'Communalism', wrote Thompson and Garratt, 'is an old Indian problem that time does little to solve'.[1] Anyone who has carefully observed recent political developments will easily appreciate the truth of this statement. Official statistics indicate that there are, on an average, more than 100 communal clashes every year.[2] These repeated outbreaks of communal frenzy destroy more than just a few lives and property. The claim of the Hindus that India is a secular state, the hope of the Indian Muslims that they can live in peace and communal amity, and the conviction of the progressive and liberal-minded intellectuals in the possibility of the emergence of a secular social order in India in the future, all suffer a serious blow.

Yet, a great deal of this loss is still not recognised. The typical response of the Indian Government and the national political leaders towards communal riots is to condemn the commercial political parties for making increased use of religion for political mobilisation, to pass resolutions calling for national unity and occasionally to set up a commission to inquire into the factors which led to a particular flare-up. According to the official view, repeated outbursts of communal violence are regarded as a vitiation of Indian social and cultural life. It is suggested that historically, there is no basis for estrangement between Hindus and Muslims: Hinduism and Islam have interacted closely for centuries and this interaction has produced a composite national culture in which Hindus and Muslims are equal participants.[3] Sometimes, this view is reinforced by adding that Hinduism is fundamentally a tolerant religion and this rules out the possibility of any actual or potential religious conflict between Hindus and Muslims. The argument is similar to one advanced during the latter phase of the freedom movement. In those days, the villains were the British and the Muslim League and the cause of vitiation was supposed to be foreign domination, the conscious policy of the British to divide and rule. Since Partition, the role of the villain has been transferred to Hindu and Muslim communal organisations.

* *Economic and Political Weekly* 4 (28–30): 1137–58 (July 1969).

Glorified Past

To argue that the problem of communalism today is a creation of the communal parties alone amounts to granting them a kind of semi-divine role, or, at any rate, to making politics an autonomous power. If the communal parties are able to arouse communal feelings and tensions successfully, it is because the prevailing social climate is favourable for such a development. Even the so-called secular political parties and organisations, including the Congress, are at present pursuing many policies and using electoral strategies which can be shown to have directly contributed to the intensification of communal tensions. It might be argued that this development is a kind of adventitious growth which has been dictated by considerations of political expediency and it does not affect the genuine secular character of these parties. Still, the close link between such a development and the Indian social situation is part of the political reality.[4] It is, therefore, necessary that an effort should be made to explore the causes for the persistence of communalism, to examine the depth and seriousness of our commitment to secularism, and to pinpoint the barriers to our realisation of the ideal of building a secular social order.

One of the principal difficulties in this connection arises from the view that Indians take of Indian society, and the place of communalism in it. In India, intellectuals and laymen alike tend to take a somewhat exaggerated view of the Indian past, and try to trace almost all aspects of human civilisation back to their ancient and rich cultural heritage. This tendency was strongest during the freedom movement. In those days, Indian past was glorified and elements which seemed to give the Europeans a sense of superiority—and consequently enabled them to justify their right to rule—were seen as existing in the Indian past. For instance, it was asserted that democracy was characteristic of the Indian way of life, and democratic institutions could be traced back to ancient Indian political traditions.[5] Few Indians realised that social inequality was religiously sanctioned in ancient India, and the close congruence between religious sanctions and social practice which must have existed within a social system which was otherwise closed militated against democratic principles. In recent years, secularism too has been traced back to Indian traditions. Sardar Panikkar writes, 'But the composite character of Indian political structure is not derived from European traditions. Even in the days when the kings professed orthodox Hinduism, they welcomed and gave not only protection but special rights and privileges to religious minorities'.[6]

One can easily understand the tendency among scholars to glorify the past during the freedom struggle.[7] The nationalist historians were writing at a time when the national movement was demanding political rights and representation in the government, and political life and institutions of the past were probably the most sensitive areas of disagreement with British historians. It was, therefore, natural that matters relating to political institutions and values current in European thought were accepted and their equivalents sought in the Indian past. However, persistence of this tendency with respect to secularism, especially, has had somewhat unfortunate consequences. It has encouraged the belief among a large number of Indian intellectuals and public men that there already exists a sufficiently strong basis for the secular state, and there is no special need to promote secular values in society. In fact, the view to which I referred earlier, namely, that riots and communal disturbances are occasional episodes which will settle themselves in course of time, stems mainly from such a belief.

SECULARISM IS A RADICAL BREAK

The evidence of history does not support the view that secularism, as embodied in the Indian Constitution, is derived from ancient Indian traditions, or that there is a pre-existing place for secularism in the Indian system of values. The Indian Constitution postulates that political institutions must be based on the social and economic interests of the entire community, without reference to race, religion or sect; that all citizens must enjoy equal rights, but no privileges; prescriptive rights or special claims should not be allowed to any group on the basis of religion.

It is no doubt true that the state in ancient India was often tolerant of all religions, but the promotion of dharma was regarded as the foremost responsibility of the state. In promoting dharma, the king built temples, granted them large endowments, and exercised strict control over their affairs. Moreover, the system of justice in ancient India was founded on the principle of inequality. Special treatment meted out to religious minorities was dictated by considerations of commercial interests and political expediency, not a conscious acceptance of the principle that adherents of all religions were equal in the eyes of the state. In fact, religious minorities were protected and granted special rights, but the rights enjoyed by them were not on a par with the majority of the population. During the medieval period, too, the religious policies of the Muslim rulers were characterised by bigotry and fanaticism. Akbar no doubt gave official encouragement to the spirit of religious tolerance, but the institutional separation of religion and state was probably as foreign to his political theory as it was to those of the ancient Hindu kings.[8] In essence, therefore, the ideal of secularism as embodied in the Indian Constitution is derived from European political traditions, and its acceptance after Partition constitutes a radical break with India's past traditions.

I emphasise the uniqueness and radical nature of the decision by Indian leaders to make India a secular state for two main reasons. First, it serves to highlight the fact that there was no basis for secularism in ancient and medieval India. Second, it suggests that the promotion of secularism called for unusual energy and efforts. It was required that certain tendencies which had dominated social and political life for centuries and had become particularly pronounced in the second half of the nineteenth century should be consciously and systematically curtailed and discouraged. In the course of our discussion, I shall try to pinpoint some of these tendencies in somewhat greater detail.

In the historic past, Indians had not been seized with that spirit of nationalism which so radically changed the face of Europe in the nineteenth century. The principal reason for this was that the concept of nationalism itself was lacking in Indian thought. 'In our language', declared the Bengali poet Harish Chandra, 'we have no such words as "nationality" and "patriotism"'.[9] Bipin Chandra Pal echoed the same feeling after a lifetime spent in politics, 'Our language has, in fact, no word corresponding to the English word "nation" . . . And the reason is that our social synthesis stopped with the race idea. We never had, therefore, this nationalist sentiment before'.[10] Indeed, differences of race, language, religion and caste had conspired to keep the various sections of the population divided.

Concept of Nationalism Lacking

This traditional absence of patriotism or national feeling had important consequences for future political developments. When the nationalist sentiments began to germinate in the minds of Indian leaders in the latter half of the nineteenth century, these were driven to develop the nationalist doctrine from scratch, so to speak, since Indian history could not provide any adequate framework upon which a theory of nationalism could be erected. Moreover, there was no tangible basis upon which such a theory could be made to rest. Utindra Nath Tagore had once stated that patriotism was a plant which could not thrive except in the soil watered by the hand of faith.[11] The concept of nationalism was improvised with the assimilation of certain deities from the Hindu pantheon. Symbolised by the figures of Hindu goddesses Durga, Vani and Lakshmi, India was deified as the Mother to whom her children owed the highest loyalty.

In Bengal, Bankim Chandra Chatterjee was the first to popularise a religious conception of nationalism through his well known novel, *Ananda Math*, and his poem, *Bande Mataram*. As the theme of his novel was built around the struggle of Hindus to free themselves from Muslim misrule in Bengal at a certain period in the eighteenth century, ... the 'children' were intended to personify Hindus pledged to redeem the 'Motherland' from its contemporary misery. And the lesson which the author intended to teach was that only when all Hindus acknowledge their nationality, that is, recognised the 'Mother', would the 'Motherland' be regenerated.

Bankim's patriotism was intensely provincial, but Hindus all over India soon adopted the symbol of the 'Motherland'. It provided a frequent theme for nationalist poetry and continued usage broadened its connotation. The Motherland of *Ananda Math* was extended to include the whole subcontinent. 'India stands to us in the relation of Mother', proclaimed Narendra Nath Sen, 'and we are her children. Mother India has been too much neglected by us—her unworthy, degenerate and unfaithful sons; and it should be the endeavour of every Indian ... to serve her as a sacred duty'.[12]

Missing Homogeneity

Hindu patriotism fostered the notion, as Lingam Lakshmanji and others had said, that India was after all the land of the Hindus and that Aryavartha had been the seat of the most venerable and magnificent civilisation the world had ever known. The plains and valleys of northern India were redolent with memories which carried the mind back to the heroic age of Indian history. There was no mistake about the localities either; the details had been transmitted from generation to generation, and every step over the area carried the mind back to the days when the Hindu was strong, noble and illustrious.

Such a view of nationalism could hardly be expected to appeal to the Muslim mind. The Muslims were adherents to a different religio-centric manner of life and they did not share the Hindu veneration of the country as mother. It is true that the Muslim community in India was formed gradually through absorption from Hinduism over the centuries, yet the two communities remained distinct with an emphasis on their separateness. It is often argued that the social and cultural differences between Hindus and Muslims were never as sharp and clear as they have been made out to appear. The vast majority of Indian Muslims being descendants of indigenous converts, the distinction between the two communities could not have been socially clear. The convert group, so the argument runs, embraced a new religion but its customs, rituals and the style of life generally remained patterned on the Hindu model. 'I have never heard', declared Gandhi once, 'of a body of converts constituting a separate nation from the parent stock'.[13] M. Mujeeb has recently tried to show that Hindu customs, values and forms of worship were pronounced among Muslims all over India until recently, and as late as 1959, 'a Hindu temple near Suratgarh in Rajasthan has Muslim priests who perform the worship of the idol and receive offerings from devotees'.[14]

There is no doubt that Hindus and Muslims shared, and still share, many common cultural values and practices, and that they were often bound together in close social and economic relationships. Cultural habits die hard. Having converted from Hinduism, it was natural for Muslim groups to continue to practise many customs and rituals which had no place in strict Islamic theology. But it is not necessary that these common social practices should have made for a lasting homogeneity between the two communities. As Louis Dumont has rightly suggested, the significance of the difference between Hindus and Muslims is generally missed because religion is not taken as constitutive of society.[15] Moreover, a clear distinction is also not drawn between the various levels at which the religious conflict between Hindus and Muslims found its expression.

For a proper understanding of the differences between Hindus and Muslims, it is necessary to draw a distinction between the ideological and interactional levels and to consider the religion of the masses separately from that of the educated Hindus and Muslims. Ideologically, Hinduism and Islam are quite antithetical to each other. It is true that Islam in India adopted many elements which were quite foreign to it. On the one hand, the Muslims tolerated the infidels alive and as part of the socio-political system which they established in India, abolishing, from Akbar to Aurangzeb, the capitation (*jizya*) tax on them. On the other hand, the Hindus accepted as rulers people who could not be transformed into kshatriyas, as they denied the supremacy of the brahmins and, theoretically at least, the validity of caste distinctions. But this co-existence produced no general ideological synthesis. Islam refused to be completely fused into Hinduism, although it adopted several elements from it. Hinduism ossified itself in self-defence; the Hindu social system put itself on the defensive after the Muslim conquest and tightened itself more than ever before. Although there were movements and individual efforts at harmony, synthesis and even composite development, the two religions remained widely separated.

Varying Strength of Links

At the interactional plane, the common links between the two religions were indeed numerous, though the strength of these links varied according to the social and cultural level of the adherents. Perhaps the links were strongest at the base of the social system, and the two communities touched one another in positive ways. Edward C. Dimock, Jr[16] has recently shown, using literary evidence from the Muslim Vaishnava poets of Bengal, that Hindus and Muslims shared pastoral and other festivals, and that the similarities of devotional *sufi* doctrines to those of Hindu *bhakti* made it but a short step from one religion to another. On the other hand, the educated or otherwise culturally sophisticated members of the two communities recognised differences between themselves and operated in different social orbits. For instance, the middle-class Hindu, especially of the twice-born status, was never quite comfortable with his Muslim neighbours whom he regarded as rude in their manners and unclean in their customs. The Muslim, on his side, did not forget that he had conquered India, and he was apt to assert an importance which only irritated and annoyed the Hindus. He was also unable to conceal his contempt for the Hindu as an idolater.[17] There were, of course, cases of close affection between individual Hindus and Muslims, but the normal attitude was not one of cordiality. In fact, despite the relatively high-level syncretistic attempts as those of Akbar and Dara Shikoh on the one hand and Kabir and Nanak on the other, 'neither educated Hindus nor educated Muslims accepted cultural co-existence as a natural prelude to cultural assimilation. Cultural apartheid was the dominant ideal in mediaeval Muslim India, in default of cultural victory'.[18]

It needs to be emphasised here that the distinction between those who accepted the absolute requirements of the faith and those whose behaviour was guided by the custom of the village rather than by the precise prescriptions of Islamic law was not absolute. The different categories were characterised by considerable fluidity and there was constant circulation of personnel from the bottom upwards. An individual whose religious belief was compounded of elements of animism, magic, mysticism and the teaching of the Prophet could be, and frequently was, transformed into a relatively orthodox Muslim. It is essential to appreciate this dynamic character of the categories, since because of it, people who merely shared common cultural elements were unable to develop any special sense of identity. It tended to encourage the development of a consciousness of community, although the conflict of interests among the social strata within the community was often acute and occasionally came to the surface. Whenever conflict arose between the communities, it tended to be posed in terms other than those of cultural similarity and to run along the cleavage which was most sharply defined in the social structure, namely, religion.

Certain cultural processes tended to sharpen the differences between the two communities and to contribute to the development of community feeling among them. For want of better words, I use the terms 'Sanskritisation' and 'Islamisation' to refer to the processes operating among Hindus and Muslims respectively. Sanskritisation refers to a process by which the customs, rituals, beliefs, ideology and the pantheon of orthodox Hinduism spread to low Hindu castes and outlying groups. It had both positive and negative aspects. On the positive side, a Sanskritising group adopted the customs and rituals of the higher castes and claimed that its lifestyle fitted the more extreme Hindu image. On the negative side, it discarded those customs and practices which were associated with magic, animism and mysticism, and proclaimed its distance from groups whose culture was influenced by village ways. Srinivas[19] has recently noted that Sanskritisation arose from, among other things, a higher group consciousness resulting from a group's contact with a source of the Great Tradition of Hinduism, such as a pilgrimage centre or monastery or proselytising sect, and that it has been largely responsible for the spread of a uniform Hinduised culture throughout the country. Sanskritisation was a slow process until the forces set in motion by the establishment of British rule accelerated its pace, but it served to increase the distance between those members of the two communities who rubbed shoulders together daily and shared common customs and beliefs.

PARALLEL PROCESS OF ISLAMISATION

The parallel process among the Muslims was Islamisation. It involved the spread of the customs, ideology and practices of the orthodox Muslims belonging to the upper strata of the Muslim society. When a Hindu group was converted to Islam, it was immediately pushed out by the Hindu social system. It no doubt continued to perform certain socio-economic functions for the Hindu castes, but the degree of its contact was restricted, especially so far as commensality was concerned. Moreover, the convert group realised that its status within the Muslim community depended upon its distance from Hindu castes. As a result, it soon discarded the un-Islamic practices which formed part of its general lifestyle, adopted a new name designed to connote a better social status, and advanced a claim to have descended from one of the noble-born (*ashraf*) families of Arabic or Persian origin. All this naturally had the effect of blurring its Hindu ancestry and widening the distance between it and the Hindus in the local area. Like Sanskritisation, Islamisation helped in the spread of a relatively uniform Muslim culture throughout the country, and it was aided by the presence of certain orthodox movements, such as *tabligh* and *tanzim*.

It may be objected that I am advocating what is commonly known in the historical literature as the 'two-nation theory'. There is no doubt that lasting heterogeneity between Hindus and Muslims was emphasised as one of the cardinal points of that theory. Its proponent, the Muslim League, used this lasting heterogeneity between the two communities as a justification for its claim to be the sole representative of the Muslims and to support its demand for a separate homeland for Muslims. This theory was constantly repeated by the Muslim League during the freedom struggle, although the League leadership was unable to provide any factual support to it. In recent years, historians in Pakistan have directed their scholarly energies toward providing a historical basis for the two-nation theory. Most historical studies in Pakistan insist that the creation of Pakistan was a logical development of Indian history, since Muslims remained a separate nation despite the efforts toward cultural synthesis between Islam and Hinduism.[20]

Historical Separateness

This trend in Pakistani historical writings has its counterpart in India. The principal concern of many Indian historians seems to be to counteract the Muslim League's two-nation theory and to provide a historical basis for modern India's choice of secularism as a goal of national policy. Many historians who have recently written on the national movement have sought to prove that India is characterised by a fundamental cultural unity and that the national culture of India is a happy blending of the elements drawn from different cultures and religions, particularly Hinduism and Islam.[21] One consequence of this tendency among Indian historians has been that the viewpoint holding that Indian culture is composite in character has come to be regarded as the only truly nationalist point of view. Anyone who stresses the lasting heterogeneity between Hindus and Muslims is usually branded as a communalist and a supporter of the Muslim League's two-nation theory.

The standpoint taken here is that the case for arguing that Hindus and Muslims remained separate despite mutual interaction is historically sound. It is undoubtedly true that Indian culture has imbibed a number of different cultural streams over the centuries. From times immemorial, India has attracted peoples of different cultures, religions and races and the interaction among them, whether military or peaceful, helped to create a culture which would have to be regarded as syncretic. However, the dominant strain of this culture was always Hinduism, and, to the extent that Indian civilisation remained an amorphous entity, other cultural streams were only partially integrated into the national culture. In my opinion, therefore, the Indian civilisation was more like a wall on which the elements of the different cultures and peoples were loosely hung against the background of Hinduism. Even a slight tilt of the wall shook the loosely hanging canvases of the other cultures and made them come out of their hooks and fall apart.

As I shall show soon, the idea of a composite national culture in India was propounded by the secular leadership in the Congress during the 1920s to counteract the development of two parallel nationalisms in India and to deny the claim of the Muslim League to be the sole representative of the Indian Muslims. It was repeated again and again and came to be identified as the truly nationalist point of view. Nowadays, it is accepted as an a priori fact and no attempt is made to examine its historical validity. Where, in my opinion, both the Pakistani and Indian historians are wrong is the importance they attach to the heterogeneity between Hindus and Muslims. Pakistani historians assume that the cultural differences between Hindus and Muslims were in themselves an adequate reason for the creation of Pakistan.

Indian historians, on the other hand, assume that this must be true and, therefore, immediately hasten to deny the very fact of difference between the two communities. Partition is a complex problem and any attempt to explain it in terms of a single factor is bound to be misleading. It should be recognised that religious differences between Hindus and Muslims did not make Pakistan inevitable. On the contrary, it was the subsequent development of Indian politics which made the idea of Pakistan emotionally appealing to the Muslims.

The Muslims were slow[22] to respond to Western education and there was far less intellectual ferment among them. When they did take to Western education nearly 50 years later, they found that the whole idea of nationalism was deeply embedded in orthodox Hinduism. Naresh Chandra Sengupta, Bankim's translator, had warned that the anti-Muslim spirit of Bankim's novel and his use of Hindu religious symbolism would hinder the growth of a true Indian nationhood by preventing the participation of Muslims and other religious communities.[23] Indeed, as Louis Dumont has rightly remarked: 'There [could] be no place for Muslims in a patriotism whose images [were] the Hindu gods and goddesses'.[24] As with the Hindus, their nationalism took the form of Muslim nationalism, looking back to Islamic traditions and culture, and fearful of losing those because of the reassertion of orthodox Hinduism.

Some secular-minded leaders in the Congress were disturbed by the development of two parallel nationalisms in India and they tried to broaden the concept of Indian nationalism to include both Hindus and Muslims. For this purpose, it was necessary that the religious undertones of nationalism should be seriously and systematically curtailed, and a set of ideas should be postulated to provide an adequate framework for a secular Indian nationalism. In a series of writings beginning with the *Glimpses of World History*, Jawaharlal Nehru tried to show that the Hindu–Muslim schism in Indian life was a superficial phenomenon, since there could be no real conflict between them just because they had different religious views. India, he postulated, was a unity in which people of different races, cultures and religious outlooks had intermingled to constitute a composite national culture. Nehru was not a historian in the technical sense of the term. He was chiefly concerned with counteracting the development of parallel nationalisms in India, and the idea of composite culture came in useful for that purpose. In order to further reinforce the secular character of the national struggle, he tried to place the growth of Indian nationalism in the world context and added a socio-economic side to it. He showed that Indian nationalism represented the urge of the people all over the world to be free from colonial domination and this urge arose from the desire of these peoples to bring about their social and economic development. As Michael Brecher has noted, 'Nehru was not alone in this view, but his influence gave it special weight in the party'.[25]

SECULAR IMPACT AT INTELLECTUAL LEVEL ONLY

The impact of the secular leadership of the Congress was confined to the intellectual level. However, on the popular level, the leadership of the Congress after the death of Tilak to the time of Partition remained in the hands of Gandhi. Gandhi's religious background was the popular Vaishnava tradition which provided him with an intimate knowledge of the legends and symbolisms of the religious folk heroes of India. Vaishnavism was a creed of personal devotion and less esoteric and abstract than the monoistic Shavaism which had provided the substance of the traditionalism of earlier nationalists. Until his advent on the political scene, the national movement as represented by the Congress was restricted to the Western-educated elite who generally came from one of the dominant minority castes of Bengal or Maharashtra, such as the *bhadralok* and *chitpavan* Brahmins. It had no mass base. Gandhi was quick to realise that a political movement could not succeed without mass support, and he directed his energies to carrying the political movement to the masses.

It is difficult to say whether Gandhi wanted to appeal to the masses of all religious persuasions or, first and foremost, to the Hindu peasantry and, only secondarily, to the non-Hindu communities. It can be shown, however, that Gandhi took the Indian masses into groups and tried to enlist their support for the national movement separately, making an appeal to each group on an issue which was likely to have some emotional appeal for it, and at a time which appeared suitable for his purpose. This can be seen clearly in his political strategy. He made a directly emotional and religious appeal to the Hindu masses from the beginning, and, when the occasion presented itself, tried to enlist the support of the Muslims on the khilafat issue. In any case, to carry the political movement to the countryside, Gandhi expressed himself in a Hindu idiom. As Srinivas states:

> India was thought of as 'mother India', Bharat Mata, and patriotism was love for one's mother, freeing her from the thraldom of an alien ruler . . . During the Civil Disobedience Movement, for instance, the resisters (satyagrahis) were garlanded, their faces marked with titak, and arati, a solution of turmeric and lime powder kept in a tray, was waved before them. Mahatma Gandhi . . . saw God Narayana in the poor (daridranarayana), the millennium which he wanted for India was conceived of as Rama Rajya, and he shared the Hindu veneration for the cow. Two of his central ideas, satyagraha or civil resistance, and ahimsa or non-violence, had their roots in Hindu and Jain customs and thought.[26]

Gandhi cast his political personality into a saintly mould and the prevailing public attitude towards him is one of reverence. This mitigates against a critical assessment of his political strategy and the place of religion in his political philosophy. Louis Dumont has suggested that Gandhi's objective was two-fold: to attain independence and to consolidate Hinduism. In order to attain both ends, it was necessary to show the beginning of reform, but reform was subordinated to independence. Dumont writes:

> Gandhi did not only want to show to the British, but also to persuade himself, that India was in the process of reforming herself: he must have had some doubts on this score, and his doubt became overwhelming when circumstances showed him the country as unregenerated. A revealing instance of Gandhi's conception of reform as having to take place within Hinduism occurred when, in Poona in 1931, he fasted to exact from Ambedkar his renunciation of a separate electorate for the Untouchables.

> This showed that the right to dispose of oneself could be opposed to England, not to Hinduism.[27]

Gandhi's approach to politics brought him in direct conflict with the secular leaders in the Congress. These leaders were vexed by the increasing part played by religion in organised politics. In the mid-1920s, Nehru wrote to a friend: 'The communal frenzy is too awful to contemplate. We seem to have been caught in a whirlpool of hatred and we go round and round and down and down this abyss'.[28] About religion itself, he said: 'No country or people who are slaves to dogma . . . can progress, and unhappily our country and people have become extraordinarily dogmatic and little-minded'.[29] On the other hand, Gandhi asserted that 'those who say that religion has nothing to do with politics do not know what religion means'.[30] In fact, men like Nehru and Bose found Gandhi's political tactics somewhat ideologically frustrating,[31] though they were unable to make a clear break with him for reasons of political expediency (Bose, of course, parted company with Gandhi subsequently).

CONGRESS DUALITY

This created a duality of character in the Congress organisation. On the level of principles, it claimed to be a truly secular organisation, refusing to take into consideration the religious differences found in Indian society and presenting itself as a representative of the nation. On the level of fact, on the other hand, it tended, or at least appeared to the Muslims, to be a predominantly Hindu organisation, identifying in the first place the Indian nation with the high-caste Hindus. Indeed, Dumont's characterisation of the organisation seems to fit the facts aptly: 'One is led to speak of "Hindu nationalism", an expression which, were it not self-contradictory, would well describe the common ground between tendencies as different as those of Tilak and Gandhi'.[32] It may be mentioned here that the secular nationalism of Nehru and other liberal-minded leaders had much in common with the nationalism of the founding fathers of the Indian National Congress, but these were by now mere shadows in the national pantheon and hardly anyone cared to remember them.

It is not my intention to suggest here that Gandhi was a communalist. In fact, his religious faith was different from that of the earlier extremists like Tilak, and, while his approach to politics was basically traditionalistic, he broadened the nationalism of the Congress to include the Muslims. The fear which spread throughout the Muslim world after the Armistice, namely that the Christian powers were going to destroy Turkey and thereby the last remaining bulwark of Islam, gave Gandhi, as he himself stated, 'such an opportunity of uniting Hindus and Muslims as would not arise in a hundred years'.[33] It is nevertheless evident that Gandhi's efforts to bring about Hindu–Muslim unity made little sense to the majority of the Muslims. His use of the religious terminology of Hinduism alienated the majority of Muslims. They felt that his primary sympathies lay with the dominant majority community and were unwilling to accept his leadership. They continued to rally under the banner of the Muslim League. It should, however, be emphasised that the Muslim image of Gandhi underwent a radical change in the mid-1940s when the

Mahatma travelled across the country protecting Muslims against communal frenzy. But this change in the Muslim image was far too late: the seed of communal discord had already grown into a large and shady tree and was bearing its bitter fruits.[34]

It is often difficult for politicians to control the forces which they themselves set in motion. Gandhi had taken the Indian masses in groups and tried to incorporate them into the national movement in their own right, hoping that they would be able to share power together. On the other hand, the leadership of the Muslim League, not to speak of other communal parties, failed to see how the inherently Hindu character of the Congress organisation could make for a peaceful and fair political co-existence. They exploited the Muslim alienation which Gandhi's political tactics had accentuated, and used the combined Muslim support for political bargaining. All this had already sharpened the Hindu–Muslim friction. The partition of the Indian subcontinent and the large-scale movement of population across the borders gave an impetus to the social animosities between the two communities. There was mass killing on both sides and communal tensions mounted to a point which is rare, though not unknown, in human history.

Two Nations in Perversity

The creation of Pakistan brought the Indian Muslims face to face with a difficult problem. Throughout the freedom struggle, the Muslim support for the idea of Pakistan was derived from the community's fear of submergence in the face of reassertion of orthodox Hinduism. When Pakistan came into existence, some of the areas where the movement for a 'separate homeland for Muslims' was most popular remained in India. The Muslims living in those areas naturally had to make a choice between staying on in India or migrating to the country they had fought to establish. The choice was relatively simple and easy for those Muslims who were on the side of the Congress during the freedom movement. It was, however, not so easy for those Muslims who had been involved with the idea of Pakistan. There were many practical difficulties which stood in the way of a clear-cut choice. Many of the Indian Muslims were in Government or private jobs and leaving for Pakistan could involve loss of the advantages of seniority, provident fund and pension. The main source of income for the upper and upper-middle-class Muslim in north India had been jagirdari and zamindari; if these Muslims left for Pakistan, they were liable to lose their title to the land. In this situation, the choice of a large number of Muslims was made on the basis of pragmatic considerations. W. C. Smith has argued that Partition shocked the Muslim community because the struggle for Pakistan was based on the grounds that the community was a unity, and the success of the League policy led to the fact of their becoming two nations.[35] In fact, the sense of shock arose more from the choice which faced Indian Muslims rather than the objective realisation that they were divided into two separate nations.

In India, the Muslims were not faced with the same kind of threat to personal security and material assets as were the Hindus and Sikhs in the Punjab, or at least, not to the same extent. In West Punjab, as Parash Tandon's autobiography[36] shows, the Hindus and Sikhs wanted to stay on, but it was the political situation which forced them to flee. In India, on the other hand, the presence of a secular leadership, more significantly Nehru, gave the Muslims assurance that their lives and personal property will be protected. The Muslims living in areas which were not directly affected by communal riots largely stayed on even though many of them were involved with the idea of Pakistan. It may be mentioned that the decision of a large number of Muslims to continue to stay in India after Partition was reinforced by a vague idea which many of them entertained at the time, namely that India and Pakistan shall not remain separate states for a long time; they will rather form a confederation in which the interest of the community shall be safeguarded, but there will be free movement of individuals from one part of the country to another.

SOURCE OF IRRITATION TO HINDUS

The continued presence of the Muslims in India was, however, a source of irritation for the majority of Hindus. They now asked how the followers of the two-nation theory, who had argued on the assumption that Hindus and Muslims could not co-exist together as their principles of life were opposed to each other, could become faithful citizens of India. They found it hard to believe that the Muslims who remained in India were not emotionally committed to the idea of Pakistan. In fact, they looked upon the Indian Muslims with suspicion and hatred for the division of the country, this hatred sometimes leading to violent attacks on Muslim lives and property.

Hindu antagonism and hatred toward the Muslims were so strong within the first few months of Partition that one would not have been surprised if India had emerged as a Hindu state. It is well known that certain elements within the Congress were favourable to the idea of India becoming a theocracy. However, there were other factors which were not quite favourable to such a development. For one thing, the leadership of the Congress and the country had passed, by this time, into the hands of leaders who were intellectually and emotionally committed to the idea of secularism. Second, India's declaration of becoming a theocracy would have seriously damaged the image of the Congress. The Congress had presented itself as a secular political organisation and rested its claim to speak for the whole country on that ground. If India became a theocracy after Partition, this would have meant that its earlier claim was false. Third, the assassination of Gandhi created a favourable climate for the acceptance of the concept of a secular state. Following the assassination, Hindu opinion was deeply smitten by a sense of remorse at its own fanaticism and considered itself responsible for the death of the Mahatma. It accepted secularism as an act of penitence at the assassination. Finally, the attainment of Independence infused the Hindus with a novel sense of power and, in the wave of liberalism which often comes with the acquisition of such power, they committed themselves to the idea of a secular state as a concession to the Muslims. Many orthodox Hindus entertained the belief after Independence that in accepting secularism, they were making a gesture of goodwill towards Muslims for, as masters of India's destiny, they could as well make it a theocratic state.[37] All these factors were not equally significant, but they all contributed to the emergence of India as a secular state.

Jawaharlal Nehru was the most outstanding advocate of the secular state in India. For him, secularism was an important element in his total social philosophy, not simply an empty political slogan. At the risk of oversimplification, it can be stated that Nehru saw the prevalence of the rational and scientific attitude as the essence of secularism. He said in 1936:

> Our politics must either be those of magic or of science. The former of course requires no argument or logic; the latter in theory at least is based on clarity of thought and reasoning, and has no room for vague, idealistic or religious or sentimental processes which confuse and befog the mind.[38]

In India, he thought, the mode of thinking was dominated by religion because it had missed the Industrial Revolution and its people had been unable to imbibe the scientific spirit. It was for this reason that Indian leaders sought communal and sectarian solutions to political problems. The first necessary step towards the goal of the secular state in India, according to Nehru, was the creation of a rational and scientific outlook and world-view among the people.

The rational outlook could not, however, be imposed from above. It was closely related to the economic and social structure of society and there was little hope for secular values to become accepted so long as these aspects of Indian society remained stagnant. It was, therefore, necessary that rapid social and economic changes must be initiated in society so that traditional cleavages may give rise to new ones based on economic criteria. It was Nehru's contention that communalism, a dismal aspect of Indian political life on the whole, was mainly a reflection of its backward economic organisation and stagnant social structure. 'I am afraid I cannot get excited over the communal issue, important as it is temporarily', he wrote.[39] Elsewhere, he noted:

> I do not think that Hindu-Muslim unity or any other kind of unity will come merely by reciting it like a mantra. That it will come, I have no doubt, but it will come from below, not above . . . Social and economic forces will bring other cleavages to the front, but the communal cleavage will go.[40]

Soon after Independence, Nehru initiated large-scale programmes of economic development and social change, and launched the country on the road to modernisation.

Conflict with Strong Orthodoxy

However, Nehru's forward-looking programmes were essentially the programmes of a small minority. A second class of opinion, with its roots spreading through all the main interest groups in the country, was the body of orthodox and traditionalist Hindu opinion. Its extreme expression was in the Hindu Mahasabha, the Rashtriya Swayamsevak Sangh (RSS) and the Jan Sangh, but it had the sympathy of a large majority of Congressmen. This class of opinion was opposed to most of the programmes and policies advocated by Nehru. It disliked the efforts to raise the Untouchables, to treat the Muslims as equal citizens in a predominantly Hindu India, and to extend the rights relating to inheritance and divorce to women. In short, it disliked the whole concept of a secular state. If Nehru insisted that there should be complete religious tolerance—and more than this, complete elimination of religion from public life—the orthodox Hindu opinion wanted that Hinduism should become the guiding principle of state policy. It sought to recreate in India a social order which, though it had hardly ever existed in the past, was supposed to symbolise the glory of Hinduism.

The traditionalist opinion as represented by orthodox Hindu organisations, such as the Hindu Mahasabha and the RSS, fell in disrepute for some time after Independence on account of Gandhi's murder at the hand of a fanatical Hindu who had past associations with both the Hindu Mahasabha and the RSS, and who was known to have been a trusted lieutenant of V. D. Savarkar. The Mahasabha was obliged to suspend its political activities, the RSS was banned, and Guru Golwalkar was arrested along with several other prominent members of his organisation. During this time, the principal opposition to Nehru's liberal programmes came from within the Congress organisation. It is well known that one of Nehru's most outstanding opponents in the Congress was Sardar Patel who, as Percival Spear has remarked, 'represented militant . . . Hindu feelings of solidarity, rather than secular nationalism'.[41] Sardar Patel pressed for some recognition of Hinduism in Indian national life.

Incidentally, one of the arguments urged in Hindu Mahasabha circles against resumption of political activity in 1949 was that it was not necessary, since Sardar Patel was pursuing a strong Hindu policy.[42] After the Sardar's death, Purshotam Das Tandon, Pandit Thakur Das Bhargava, Seth Govind Das and several other prominent Congressmen continued the ideological tendency represented by him. In fact, the duality which had characterised the Indian National Congress during the freedom movement became much more clear-cut: it claimed to be the voice of the nation at the all-India level, proclaiming its commitment to secularism, socialism and democracy, but kept within its fold a strong body of orthodox and conservative opinion.

Revivalist Demands

Soon after Independence, the traditionalist opinion called for formal recognition of Hinduism in the Indian Constitution and social directives of state policy. Sardar Patel vowed that he would not rest until the Somnath temple, partially destroyed during the Muslim invasion in the eleventh century, was reconstructed and restored to its old glory. For him, as for many others, this project symbolised the repudiation of over a thousand years of Muslim domination in India, and the restoration of Hindu supremacy. As the Constituent Assembly began its task of drafting the Constitution of free India, Ramakrishna Dalmia launched a nation-wide campaign for the inclusion of a clause forbidding cow slaughter. K. M. Panikkar called for the revival of Sanskrit on the ground that, 'It is to the classics of that language that our traditions are to be traced. Without the continued cultivation of Sanskrit by the intelligentsia of the country, the cultural unity of India will suffer.'[43] Sampurnanand, the Chief Minister of Uttar Pradesh, insisted that India should break free from the leading strings of the West, ignore the accusations of revivalism, and devote itself to the re-moulding of the whole educational system in independent India on the basis of dharma.[44] He saw a bright future for India if it could surmount the obstacles of a 'false emphasis on secularism' and 'spurious intellectualism'. There were many others who expressed similar views and sentiments.[45]

Of course, these revivalist demands were a natural outcome of the manner in which Indian nationalism had developed and the ideology which had provided substance to it. We have shown that Indian nationalism was nurtured by memories of a glorious past of the ancient Indian civilisation which flourished at a time when the rest of the world was still struggling in the stone age. Cultural decline in India, the early nationalists had asserted (needless to say that the idea was implicit in Gandhi's conception of Rama Rajya), was associated with political subjugation, and the imposition of alien cultures, first Islamic and subsequently Western. With the attainment of Independence, it was only natural that the demand should have been made that the state get rid of the cultural vestige of alien rule and set about restoring the past greatness of traditional Indian culture.

Michael Brecher wrote in *Nehru—A Political Biography*, 'With each passing year of Nehru's tenure as Prime Minister the forces of communalism are weakened'.[46] Although recent political developments show that the conservative communal elements have consolidated themselves in Indian political life, this statement nevertheless serves to highlight the crucial role played by Nehru's towering position in restraining the active campaigns of the traditionalists at the beginning of the post-Independence period. To begin with, Nehru stood at the helm of national affairs and had a powerful charisma around him. He used his personal influence to promote his programmes. Thus, we find that the constitutional debates were on the whole a tremendous success, a reaffirmation of liberal and forward-looking views. Secularism, socialism and democracy with universal suffrage extending to over 175 million people were all accepted without any serious opposition. Even the social disavowal of caste and untouchability were accepted without demur. This is not to suggest that there was no opposition. There were many sectional interests which disliked these measures, but they acquiesced even if they did not approve.

Parochial Strength

However, Nehru's success was not altogether a loyal course. He had to make important compromises with and concessions to orthodox opinion. For instance, Nehru hoped to pass the Hindu Code Bill in a single session of the Constituent Assembly. It took him nearly six years to pass the two important measures giving Hindu women equal rights with men in inheritance, succession and holding of property, establishing monogamy and providing for divorce. Moreover, the measures were processed piecemeal rather than as a single comprehensive enactment. As Percival Spear has remarked, 'Nehru regarded these reforms as an essential part of his liberal secular state and his sincerity is shown by the persistence of his struggle. That he had to struggle at all shows the strength of the covert opposition based on traditional feeling.'[47]

There was a second limitation too. The Indian political leaders were divided into two major groups. The first contained the all-India politicians who had been mainly interested in the theoretical side of nationalism before Independence. After Independence, it was mainly the leaders of this group who spearheaded the processes of secularism, socialism and economic development. The other group consisted of provincial leaders amongst whom commitment to the ideals of secularism and socialism was considerably diffused, varying in its form, character and intensity. Moreover, these provincial leaders retained their political influence through an articulation of various regional and local interests. Sometimes these interests ran counter to the ideals accepted at the all-India level. Thus, we find that, whether on the question of equal treatment of Muslims and other religious minorities, removal of untouchability or elimination of religious symbolisms from the state, the provincial leaders often went their own way. Although Nehru and many other central leaders explicitly rejected the demand for legislation banning cow slaughter and considered the passing of such legislation 'a wrong step', the chief ministers of many states disregarded the centre's directive and passed laws against cow slaughter.

REINFORCEMENT OF TRADITIONAL VALUES

Elsewhere,[48] I have said that there was no strong movement for secularism in the country and the processes of social change in independent India were characterised by a reinforcement of traditional values. There is now ample evidence in support of such a view. It can be seen in the changing fortunes of the traditionalist and conservative political organisations. To begin with, thanks to the strong campaign carried out by Nehru against the traditionalist forces, the Hindu...parties generally fared poorly in electoral contests. In 1951–52, the Hindu Mahasabha won only four seats in the Lok Sabha, and the Jan Sangh and the Ram Rajya Parishad captured three seats each. Their representation in the state legislatures, although somewhat better, was far from impressive. However, since 1957, the Jan Sangh has achieved notable successes in the elections at practically all levels. It has been most successful in the municipal elections and it now controls more than half of the corporations of the *kaval*[49] towns in north India, including the Delhi Corporation.

Within the Congress, the trend towards the consolidation of traditionalist forces is reflected in the changing character of the leadership. The leaders who earlier advocated secularism, socialism and economic development have been either gradually pushed out of the Congress (or put in the background) or have voluntarily left the organisation. Their place has been taken by the so-called political bosses who control the party machinery, organise factional politics and engineer the elections through their links with the cadre at the grassroots level. These leaders do not share the conviction of the earlier leaders nor are they afraid to lose anything if the programmes of secularisation, modernisation and economic development are abandoned. In fact, they have a vested interest in maintaining the status quo, for the success of the programmes of economic development and social change may bring about significant changes in people's attitudes and values and thereby undermine the real bases of their power and influence.

Weakened Commitment to Secularism

On the whole, therefore, the national commitment to secularism has weakened and the efforts for the promotion of secularisation and modernisation of the state and society have slackened. Even the presence of Indira Gandhi as the Prime Minister does not provide an adequate assurance that the commitment to secularism will be upheld in the future. While there is no doubt that she shares the convictions of her father, she does not owe her power to the same charisma which enabled Nehru to override the opposition to his programmes. She owes her power to articulation of various sectional interests and she can scarcely press for programmes which run counter to the prejudices of large sections of society.

The consolidation of orthodox forces has been accompanied by an increase in the spread and revival of traditional values and a growing communal consciousness. In the words of Srinivas:

> School text-books contain incidents from the Hindu epics and Puranas, the lives of regional saints, the extracts from old poets whose themes are almost always religious or moral. Journals and books contain religious matter, and the popular children's story magazine Chandamama exploits the inexhaustible mine of the epics, Bhagavata, the Puranas and others, for children's stories. All-India Radio broadcasts devotional music every morning and, occasionally, harikathas. It also marks the big festivals by special programmes which again draw on the traditional culture of the Hindus. The themes of many films are drawn from the epics, although 'social themes' and romantic stores are not unimportant.[50]

Srinivas rightly insists that the spread of traditional values, whether through films or All-India Radio or in popular books, brings about radical changes in the content of traditional culture. Indeed, from an academic point of view, it is possible to see the revival and revitalisation of traditional symbols and values in contemporary India as an aspect of modernisation.[51] However, for a variety of reasons, we can still characterise the spread of traditional values as a reassertion of orthodox Hinduism. For one thing, the content of Sanskritic values, symbols and mythologies retains its religious and moral character and does not undergo secularisation in the course of their spread through mass media or school textbooks. For instance, the Ramayana and Mahabharata were seen as sources of the Hindu religion, not as literary classics, and there is no attempt to undeify their heroes, Rama and Krishna. In fact, any attempt to undeify the characters of the epics is considered 'futile and positively mischievous'.[52] Second, these values are frequently characterised as a part of the cultural heritage of all Indians, not only of the adherents of Hinduism. For instance, the Basic Hindi Reader for the fifth class, edited by the Director of Education, Uttar Pradesh, contains the following description of the river Ganges:

> Indians regard the river Ganges as sacred. It is said that, emerging from the feet of Lord Vishnu, the Ganges came to the thick hair of Lord Shiva and from there to the Himalayas . . . The Ganges is believed to wash away all sins (literally, to be the destroyer of sins).[53]

Clearly, the belief in the sacredness of the river or its power to wash away sin is shared only by the Hindus. Religious minorities are not to blame if they have seen in this an attempt to impose Sanskritic values on all Indians. Finally, and this is a significant consideration, the revival of traditional culture is viewed by the majority of Hindus as a symbol of Hindu resurgence and dominance.

Greater Communal Consciousness

Sanskritisation served as an effective source of cohesion in Hindu society in the past. It bound together Hindus belonging to different castes, sectarian and regional or linguistic groups and lacking an overarching formal structure like the Roman Catholic Church or a trained body of missionaries devoted to the task of strengthening the practice of a uniform religion.[54] The increase in the pace of Sanskritisation in recent years has heightened the communal consciousness among the Hindus. This is not to suggest that the internal cleavages within the Hindu community have become obsolete or that they have lost their social significance. Paradoxically, while on the one hand the democratisation of the Indian social system has revived the role of the traditional groupings based on caste, sectarian and regional or linguistic identity, increased Sanskritisation has brought about the consolidation of the Hindus as a religious community on the other. Some people are often inclined to believe that the two types of communal consciousness (those of the traditional grouping and the religious community) are similar in character and tend to neutralise one another. What is generally forgotten by the proponents of this view is that they are situationally determined and operate at different levels of segmentation. Broadly speaking, the identity of the traditional grouping based on caste or sect is effective only so long as the conflict or competition is confined within the religious community. When, on the other hand, competition involves two or more religious communities, the internal cleavages within each community usually merge together to form the wider religious community and consequently, it is the religious identity that assumes greater prominence.[55]

The two wars in which India became involved during the last decade contributed a great deal to the intensification of communal consciousness and the consolidation of the traditionalist forces in the country. On both occasions, the upsurge of nationalism had strong undertones of Hinduism. Particularly during the Indo-Pakistan war, the whole concept of patriotism was deeply embedded within Hinduism. The Muslims were a priori suspect in the eyes of the majority of the people and their houses were closely watched against possible sabotage. Even a dim ray of light emanating from a Muslim house during blackouts was considered a signal for the invading Pakistani planes. Organised rumours circulated throughout the country against the character and political integrity of some of the most prominent Muslim leaders in the country. Innocent Muslims were apprehended in the streets on suspicion of being Pakistani paratroopers and were subjected to all kinds of harassment. It speaks a great deal about the nature of Indian society that during the final phase of the war, the entire propaganda machinery of the Government of India had to be directed towards projecting an image of Indian Muslims as loyal Indian citizens and rescuing them from a possible onslaught of Hindu communal violence.

Srinivas recently pointed out that the pace of Sanskritisation had increased in India since Independence. He did not indicate the implications of this development for the realisation of the goal of secularism which the country has been trying to pursue probably because his major concern was Hinduism, not Indian society.[56] However, any such development is bound to produce a deep impact upon the religious minorities in the country. Let us therefore consider in some detail how the Muslims have been affected by it.

In order to gain an understanding of the implications of increased Sanskritisation for Indian Muslims, it may be useful to briefly review the situation of the community immediately after Partition. Percival Spear has recently summarised the picture of the Indian Muslims fairly objectively and we may reproduce his summary here. He writes:

> At Partition the official class largely, though not entirely, disappeared. The cultivators of the East Punjab and some in West Bengal migrated to their respective wings of Pakistan. But there were still left agricultural pockets all over North and Western India and in Hyderabad ... In general the urban artisan class east and south of Delhi remained, though reduced in Delhi itself by riot and migration. But even where they were still numerous as in Agra, they were overawed by the knowledge that authority was now in Hindu hands. The professional and commercial classes remained in large measure, though there was considerable 'skimming off' from both classes, especially from Uttar Pradesh and Bihar. Many families were divided, one branch migrating and the other electing to stay on. Indian Islam was now left a bleeding trunk of cultivators, bereft of its professional and intellectual head. The head had been scarred, not severed. Politics, for Muslims as Muslims, was virtually dead, for there was clearly no room in India for a Muslim League advocating Pakistan.[57]

In this situation, the Indian Muslim community had to reorient itself and readjust to the changed circumstances. The Indian Muslim had to learn to regard his brothers-in-faith in Karachi or Lahore, whom he had supported in the demand for Pakistan, as foreigners. He had to learn to view his Hindu neighbours with whom he has never had much social intercourse as a fellow-citizen. And, he had to reconcile himself to the fact that political power now lay in Hindu hands and he occupied only a secondary position in the power structure. These were difficult emotional adjustments in themselves. The difficulty was accentuated by the hostile attitude of the majority community. The vast majority of the Hindus blamed the Indian Muslims for the division of the subcontinent and doubted their political loyalty to the country.

SUBDUED ISOLATION

The process of adjustment to the post-Partition situation produced two different political tendencies among Indian Muslims. Some Muslims isolated themselves from the mainstream of national political life and turned to the world of religious preoccupations. They were encouraged in this by certain Muslim religious or semi-political organisations, such as the All-India Tablighi Jamat and the All-India Jamat-e-lslami, which had come into existence shortly before Partition and whose members had offered their support for the creation of Pakistan. The Tablighi Jamat put its emphasis on strengthening the observance of religion among the Muslims as it believed that the decline of the Muslim community in India was a result of its having lost touch with the cardinal principles of the faith. It sent out deputations of missionaries from place to place to sustain and strengthen the believers in the practice of their religion. The Jamat-e-Islami, on the other hand, believed that a true Muslim society could exist only in a country where the government was in the hands of the Muslims and it was carried out according to Islamic principles. It advised the Muslims that India was a *dar-ul-harb* ('place-of-war', but used more generally to refer to states or countries ruled by non-Islamic laws) and the Muslims should refrain from taking part in its political structure until political power was restored to the Muslims.

For obvious reasons, the movement represented by the Jamat-e-Islami could not be very popular. Its theory that it was possible in India to have a Muslim majority and to establish an Islamic state was quite fantastic, in India, where the Muslims constituted hardly more than 10 per cent of the total population, there was obviously no scope for the development of an Islamic state. Even though some ardent supporters of the movement deceived themselves into believing that the number of Muslims could be increased through missionary activity, the masses were not much attracted by it. But its political and social separatism, with its roots extending to the movement for religious puritanism which had been influencing Muslim thought since Shaikh Walliullah, attracted many people.[58]

However, the tendency towards isolation from participation in political life was restricted to only a small section of the Indian Muslim society. The majority of Indian Muslims were quick to see that too effective a participation in the political process would arouse the hostility of the Hindus and withdrawal from it would reinforce their charge that the Muslims were keeping themselves aloof from the mainstream of national life. So, led by Muslim leaders in the Congress and the All-India Jamiat-ul Ulema-e-Hind which alone among the Muslim organisations had some influence in the community after Partition, the Indian Muslims extended their political support to the Congress Party. Between 1952 and 1962, the Muslims usually stood behind the Congress, supporting the candidates put up by the Congress and electing Muslim candidates largely on Congress Party tickets. Among the Muslims elected to the Lok Sabha and the state legislatures, those belonging to the Congress constituted the vast majority in the first three elections.[59]

Congress as Political Umbrella

It would be a mistake to assume that the Muslim support for the Congress was based on a conscious realisation that political integration was the most desirable course open to the community from the viewpoint of the future development of Indian polity. It was based on pragmatic consideration: the community saw in the Congress a political umbrella which could offer it protection against Hindu communal forces and safeguard its political interests. It may seem somewhat paradoxical that the Muslim community should have viewed the Congress as a political umbrella when only a few years ago, it had rallied against it under the banner of the Muslim League. It is necessary to realise, however, that the Congress was the only party which had advocated secularism during the nationalist struggle and which had remained committed to that ideology after Partition. Although the Indian Muslims would have preferred to have an organisation of their own, the basis of sectarian politics was gone with the creation of Pakistan and there was no place for an organisation which represented barely 10 per cent of the population diffused in different parts of the country. In the situation, therefore, the only feasible alternative for the community was to support the party which could best protect its interests.

The support for the Congress brought some enlargement for the Muslims in public life. Those Muslims who had been loyal Congressmen as Muslim nationalists were cherished and often promoted by a government anxious to prove that it was secular and non-communal. Sometimes, even those Muslims who had earlier supported the Muslim League, such as Chowdhary Khaliquzzaman, were also promoted as a gesture of goodwill and faith. In the elections, Muslim candidates were often granted nominations to run for elective offices. It is true that such nominations were generally motivated by considerations of electoral strategy; they nevertheless increased Muslim representation in elected bodies. Indeed, the number of Muslims elected to the Lok Sabha during the first two elections was in excess of their proportion in the total population in the country. However, this enlargement of political representation produced little change in the mood of the community. The Indian Muslims, at least the majority of them, continued to feel frustrated and disillusioned, believing that their real grievances had failed to attract the attention of the national leaders.

The sense of frustration arose from two main reasons. First, the great majority of Muslims believed themselves to be discriminated against, especially from an economic point of view. The All-India Muslim Convention, held at Aligarh in 1953, expressed grave concern at and dissatisfaction with the central government's policies toward their community. It called upon the government to fix a certain percentage of seats for Muslims in the government services. In 1955, Mohammed Ismail, president of the All-India Muslim League, declared that the number of Muslims being recruited to the various services was dwindling in a fearful manner. Speeches made at the All-India Muslim Convention held at Delhi in 1963 emphasised similar facts, although no demand was made for reservation of seats. More recently, Ansar Harvani complained that, 'After two decades of Independence, the Muslims hardly find any place in the economic structure of the Indian society. They have almost no place cither in the corporate or public sector, and feel that they are being reduced to be the hewers of wood and drawers of water.'[60]

DEGREE OF DISCRIMINATION

It is difficult to ascertain with any degree of certainty whether there is, in fact, any discrimination against Muslims in the matter of jobs, or it is merely a fiction of their mind, a reflection of their fear of persecution in a predominantly Hindu India, that they are subject to continuous economic discrimination. For one thing, the basic statistics required to prove or disprove the fact of discrimination are not available. Second, discrimination is something that is as difficult to prove objectively as it is easy to feel subjectively; there can be no way of showing whether a candidate for a particular position has been rejected on the basis of an objective assessment of his qualifications or the communal biases of the selectors. Nevertheless, in a society where communal consciousness is sharply developed and the outlook of the people is clouded by a communal world-view, it would be wrong to assume that communal biases do not enter in recruitment at least at certain levels of government and private jobs. It is well known that the leading commercial firms in the country are reluctant to employ Muslims in top managerial positions as a matter of policy. Again, there is some evidence that at lower-level government jobs, Hindu administrators sometimes manage to misplace applications bearing Muslim names, and the system of recruitment is such that it allows the communal biases of the selectors to influence the recruitment procedure.[61] But, of course, the important thing is not that there is discrimination against Muslims in the economic structure. What is important is that Muslims have felt so insecure as to believe themselves to be the target of continuous economic discrimination. The fact of their belief has been crucial in their social adjustment in the country.

The second reason which contributed to the sense of insecurity and apprehension in the minds of the Indian Muslims was a belief that the Hindu majority was trying to break down their cultural identity and to deprive them of their religious and cultural symbols. I have discussed the reasons underlying this belief at some length elsewhere.[62] It is sufficient here to state that the spread of Sanskritic cultural values and symbols through school textbooks and mass media, the attempt to project these values as the values of all Indians, the repeated utterances of some traditionalist leaders suggesting that Muslims must accept Hindu values and discard Arabic and Persian names in order to become acceptable in the Indian state of the future, the diffusion of non-Islamic elements in some of the Muslim institutions, such as the Aligarh Muslim University, which they regard as symbols of their cultural heritage in India (especially since diffusion of non-Hindu elements in Hindu institutions has been seriously resisted), the threat of reform of Muslim Personal Law and the decline of their language are some of the factors which have contributed to their sense of insecurity and to their belief that their cultural heritage is threatened by the resurgence of Hindu culture. All these factors are not equally relevant. Nor are the Muslims justified in feeling threatened by all of them. Clearly, changes in Muslim

Personal Law are immediately called for in the context of the emerging secular values, especially since similar changes have been undertaken in the laws of the Hindus. Muslim fear on that score would be based on a conscious distortion of the intentions of the government.[63]

But the fear of submergence arising from the treatment meted out to Urdu or the spread of Sanskritic symbols would not be altogether imaginary. Despite the constitutional guarantee that, 'Any section of the citizens residing in the territory of India or any part thereof having a distinct language, script or culture of its own shall have the right to conserve the same',[64] Urdu has been eliminated from schools throughout long areas of northern and central India. Moreover, the efforts of Muslim leaders to urge the government to provide facilities for the teaching of Urdu to Muslim children have been nipped in the bud and dismissed as communalism. In the situation, the question posed by Eugene Smith in his book assumes some relevance, 'Precisely how could the Indian Muslims conserve their culture if their mother-tongue was banished from the primary school attended by their children?'[65] Indeed, as W. C. Smith wrote in 1953, the conclusion is inescapable that, 'The [Indian Muslim] community is in danger of being deprived of its language, than which only religious faith is a deeper possession. Nine years of gradual adjustment in other fields have brought no improvement in this, and little prospect of improvement.'[66]

Clinging to Faltering Traditions

It is a matter of common knowledge that when a religious minority feels seriously threatened, the machinery of its faith begins to wear out and its traditions begin to falter against those of the majority, it turns worriedly in upon itself and its members cling even more intensely to the faltering traditions. That something like this has happened in the case of the Indian Muslim seems quite certain. Studies of religious change in some parts of the country where Muslims are found in substantial numbers show that the social and political developments in the country have precipitated a renewal of interest in religion among the Muslims and given rise to revival movements. I shall here like to refer the reader to the study of the Meos of Rajasthan carried out by P. C. Aggarwal.[67] My own research on the process of social change in some of the Muslim-dominated rural areas of eastern Uttar Pradesh confirms the observations offered by Aggarwal in his paper.

These changes are not confined to the rural areas. My research among Muslims in Uttar Pradesh shows that similar changes are taking place in the urban areas also. In all large towns and cities in the state, the number of traditional Muslim schools has increased over the last two decades (even though the population of Muslims was somewhat reduced after Partition) and there is a tendency among the Muslims to send their children to these schools. Moreover, Muslim festivals and ceremonies are now celebrated with greater pomp and show. The Id-e-Milad or the birthday of Muhammad is celebrated on an elaborate scale in all towns and cities which have a sizeable Muslim population and their importance is often enhanced by the presence of Muslim dignitaries. In the month of fasting (Ramadan), Muslims gather in large numbers for the evening prayers (*taruvi*) in the mosques and the conclusion of the recitation of the Quran undertaken on the occasion is marked by a great deal of religious zeal. This revival of interest in religion is not merely an expression of an amorphous 'primordial identity', but also a pragmatic adaptation to a social setting where religious barriers are still strong and the secular melting-pot has not yet begun to boil.[68]

Meanwhile, the death of Nehru, whom the Muslims considered a shield and protector, the erosion of the image of the Congress umbrella as the protector of the religious minorities, the change in the character of the Congress leadership, and the consolidation of the conservative communal forces in the country as a whole alienated the Muslims from the Congress and encouraged a tendency towards political consolidation among them. The most direct evidence of this tendency is to be found in the emergence of the All-India Muslim Majlis-e-Mushawarat as a fairly influential political force in north India. At the last general election, the Majlis-e-Mushawarat did not enter the election as a political party; it rather entered into alliances with individual candidates or opposition parties on the basis of a nine-point mandate earlier formulated by it and offered its support to them.[69] More recently, however, the Majlis has assumed the character of a political party. In the mid-term election in Uttar Pradesh, the Majlis played a direct role by entering electoral contests as a political party. According to a news item in *The Times of India*, there is a possibility that the seven candidates elected on Majlis support will help the Congress form a coalition government in Uttar Pradesh, provided the demands laid down in the Mushawarat's mandate are accepted. This shows that Muslims are trying to consolidate themselves in Indian political life so as to be able to influence the political process directly.

Whether consolidation on the basis of religious identity is likely to prove detrimental to the secularisation of Indian society is a debatable question and cannot be discussed here. Beteille has recently argued that,

> The growth of 'communal consciousness' need not be viewed as necessarily an unhealthy or disruptive force. It may, on the contrary, be a precondition for the integration of *a minority group* into the wider body politic. For the measure of integration lies not so much in a passive acceptance of the *status quo* as in the adoption of a body of common political rules through which divergent interests are organised and articulated.
>
> Thus what has been viewed by some as an increase in communal consciousness may be only a step forward in the politicisation of Indian society (first italics mine).[70]

UNFAVOURABLE FRAMEWORK

However, the revival of traditional Islamic culture and the political consolidation of the Indian Muslim community has been seen by many as an expression of Muslim separatism and militancy. For instance, *Enlite* news magazine suggested in an editorial article in 1968 that the communal disturbances in Mysore State last summer were directly traceable to 'the rising Muslim militancy in the South'.[71] After tracing the past associations of the Muslim leaders of the state to the Muslim

League, the article concluded, 'Even today the Muslims of the State have not joined the mainstream of national life'.[72] Again, referring to the proceedings of the Muslim League Conference held at Calicut, it commented:

> One of the resolutions passed unanimously demanded the creation of a separate Muslim majority district. It was evident that it all meant the revival of the old cry of Moplastan. The Pakistan originally visualised by the Jinnah group was a state with an eastern and a western wing, with a centre in Hyderabad, with its crona in Kashmir and footholds in Goa and Malabar, thus facing to the west—to Mecca—religiously. The League was resuscitated in Kerala first on account of the Congress and now due to the Left Communists, in Madras by the blessings of Rajaji and Swatantra party and in Mysore and Hyderabad with the aid of the Muslim Leaguers of Kerala and Madras. *In all these four States largescale smuggling activities are going on unchecked and Muslims have grown rich in these years by leaps and bounds* (emphasis added).[73]

Perhaps, this *Enlite* comment represents a rather extreme communalist position, but the sentiment expressed by it is widely shared by a great majority of the Hindus.

Separatist or militant politics requires a special legal framework for its operation. It generally operates in a political framework wherein two or more parties can vie with one another for political favours from a superior arbiter. Until Independence, the presence of the British created a political system in which both Hindus and Muslims sought to appropriate as many advantages for themselves as they could bargain for. Thus, if the communal riots of the pre-Independence period are carefully analysed, it becomes quite clear that communal violence was equally instigated by Hindus and Muslims in those days, because each group was interested in asserting its distinct cultural identity and its political claims. Indeed, Muslims insisted on slaying the cow and the Hindus claimed the right to play music in front of mosques, because these activities had come to symbolise a means of cultural self-assertion, and the presence of the British as arbiters created a political situation in which such cultural self-assertion was politically meaningful and significant.

However, since Independence, the political balance of power has undergone a significant change, and the politico-legal system does not provide an operative framework for separatist or militant politics: there is no superior arbiter and the Muslims in the country have had to reconcile themselves to the fact that they could no longer assert themselves without the risk of arousing the hostility of the majority community. Thus, they are no longer in a position to instigate communal riots, especially since they are likely to be the principal sufferers of such events on account of the indifferent attitude of the police and the administration of which there is overwhelming evidence in the report of Ray and Chakravarty on the Meerut riots.[74] This is not to suggest that Muslims are free from blame for the heightened communal feelings and tensions in India today. It is necessary to realise, nevertheless, that Muslim communalism does not any longer enjoy a favourable legal framework for its operation and has consequently been rendered ineffective, although it has not died out any more than Hindu communalism.

Moreover, Muslims are not the only group which has consolidated itself in order to influence the political process. Even a casual look at the political developments which have been taking place over the last two decades will show that political consolidation has taken place at almost all levels of Indian society, and social groups based on different kinds of communal loyalties have tried to use their combined strength to influence the political process. Political scientists have commented on the democratic reincarnation of caste for a long time. In addition, regional and linguistic groups all over India have been consolidating themselves during the last decade to count for more in political life. Thus, political consolidation among the Indian Muslims would seem to be a development which is in keeping with the general trend of Indian politics. Indeed, the demand of the Muslims of Malabar to have a separate Muslim majority district is similar to the demands of the peoples of Haryana, Himachal Pradesh, Vidharbha and the Punjab to have separate states. Yet, the demands made by Muslims are often seen by the people as an expression of communalism and are characterised as separatist or militant. This shows that the majority of Hindus have not taken Muslims to be a part of the wider Indian polity and subject to the same political influences as every other group.

REVERSAL OF TREND

In a way, the process of cultural and political consolidation among the Indian Muslims is a reversal of an earlier trend towards the integration of the community into the national body politic. On the basis of election statistics, Gopal Krishna argued that while there was no evidence to prove or disprove that the Muslims had held aloof from national political life, there was evidence of increased political secularisation of the community during the last two decades. He concluded that,

> Competitive electoral polices has probably begun to break down the isolation of the Muslim electorate from the political process. Communal solidarity is clearly being subjected to pressure by electoral competition; more than one Muslim candidate contesting from the same constituency indicates that the community does not operate as a monolithic entity in politics. That those seeking election have to depend on the support of communities other than their own has the effect of broadening their horizons, extending their area of concern and in the process promoting the slow integration of their community into the emerging secular society. The increasing tendency for Muslim candidates (who presumably represent the politically active element in the community) to assume national party identifications shows that the integrative process is at work.[75]

That the reversal of the process towards integration has been influenced by the consolidation of the traditionalist and communal forces within the Hindu community is almost certain. In any multi-ethnic society, the burden of promoting the secularisation of the political system rests largely, though not exclusively, with the dominant majority community, because it alone is in a position to take a comprehensive view of the social and political process and to create a favourable atmosphere for the promotion of secular values. Indeed, the actions and attitudes of the Hindus are of crucial importance at present, because Muslim attitudes are still reactions to the pattern of Hindu politics, rather than independent initiatives.

In the face of the spread of traditional Hindu culture and the consolidation of the traditionalist Hindu forces, the Muslims have reacted by recreating their communal solidarity. On the other hand, the consolidation within the Muslim community has brought back in the minds of a large majority of the Hindus the association of the Muslim League and Partition. In the situation, social tensions have been high and communal violence has broken out on the slightest provocation. For provocation, unfortunately, the issues are many, and certain economic and political factors have served to accentuate the communal hostilities.

Secular State, Communal Society

It is beyond the scope of this chapter to make suggestions towards the reduction of social tensions or the solution to the communal problem in contemporary India. Our aim here has been to survey the development of Indian politics over the last 50 years or so and to examine the part played by the ideologies of secularism and communalism in it. Our analysis has shown that the problem of communalism has deep social roots in Indian society which go back to the origins of the national movement, in fact even before, and the choice of secularism as a principle of state policy constituted a radical breach from India's past historical traditions. In conclusion, I should like to make a distinction between the secular state and secular society and to show that such a distinction is especially meaningful in the case of India because a series of interactions has coloured the attitudes of the great majority of the people in the country.

In India, the state is committed to the ideology of secularism. The Indian Constitution guarantees equality of opportunity to everyone without the distinctions of race, religion and creed. Moreover, religious or other kinds of minorities have been provided with special safeguards to protect their interests. It is now increasingly becoming obvious, however, that these constitutional guarantees and protective measures have not worked well in practice because those responsible for controlling the machinery of the state have often allowed their attitudes and values to influence the administrative and political processes. In their report on the Meerut riots, Ray and Chakravarty have provided impressive evidence to show that the very agencies charged with the task of safeguarding the interests of the minority community were callous and indifferent, and allowed the Hindu communal forces to have free play. They point out that during the riots, the telephones of all the local Muslim leaders were placed out of order, and a complaint by a prominent Muslim to the Deputy Commissioner did not bring about restoration of the service. The police was partisan and the local District Magistrate admitted that the administration was infiltrated by orthodox and communal elements.

It is obvious that a distinction can be meaningfully drawn between secular society and secular state. Society is wider than the state in its operation. In a society where the outlook of the people is dominated by communalism, the state usually cannot function for a long time on secular lines because the prevailing social tendencies, sooner or later, find their expression in the policies of the state. On the other hand, when a society is organised on secular principles or respect for secularism as a social ideology is diffused throughout the society, the state is generally likely to function on secular lines. In India, the state has remained committed to secularism but the widely diffused communalism and the highly strung atmosphere of the country has made it impossible for the secular values and ideals to be realised. The champions of the ideology of secularism were conscious that the constitutional declaration of India as a secular state was not likely to be particularly meaningful unless the basic orientations of society were radically altered. Hence, Nehru and his trusted lieutenants initiated movements from the top and from the bottom to create a society in which religion was to play no role in political cleavages, in which all religious groups were to have the same economic and political opportunities, the jockeying for power caste by caste and community by community was to be replaced by functional groupings in which people would choose representatives standing for real economic and political positions.

For Nehru, the problem of communalism was a problem in which overemphasis had been given to religion or social diversities. The primary task consisted in insisting resolutely on mutual respect and developing just and positive projects of secular education and industrialisation to give support to the movement for secularism led from the top. In recent years, unfortunately, the programmes which could help create a secular society have been gradually discarded or slowed down. It has been commonly assumed that so long as the constitutional provisions are not altered, there is no cause for worry. In my opinion, the only guarantee for the constitutional provisions to be translated in practice is that a consolidated and continuous effort should be undertaken to create a society in which mutual respect and freedom of opportunity can be given actual shape. And, it is to the task of creating such a society that the political leadership in the country should address itself in the future.

NOTES AND REFERENCES

1. Thompson, E., and G. T. Garratt. 1934. *Rise and Fulfilment of British Rule in India*. London: Macmillan, 623.

2. Based on a statement by the Home Minister, Y. B. Chavan, in the Lok Sabha. See *The Hindustan Times*, 12 June 1968.

3. Recently, this view was reiterated by the Deputy Prime Minister, Morarji Desai, at the concluding session of the National Integration Council Meeting at Srinagar.

4. Studies by sociologists and political scientists show that the chances of the success of a candidate in the elections depend on his ability to manipulate the traditional groupings in his favour. Indeed, in a tradition-bound society, traditional groupings are bound to be an important resource of power.

5. I refer here to the statement made by Surendranath Banerjee while speaking to a group of students at the University of Cambridge.

6. Panikkar, K. M. 1963. *The Foundations of New India*. London: George Allan and Unwin, 169. Of course, Panikkar was not consistent on this point. Elsewhere he wrote, 'Clearly, our new democratic, egalitarian, and secular state is not built upon the foundations of ancient India, or of Hindu thought.' (See Panikkar, K. M. 1956. *The State and the Citizen*. Bombay: Asia Publishing House, 28).

7. See Thapar, Romila. 'Ancient Indian Historiography'. Paper presented at the South Asia Seminar in the University of Chicago, Spring 1968.

8. See Smith, D. E. 1963. *India As a Secular State*. New Jersey: Princeton University Press, 62–65.

9. Appendix to the report of the Education Commission. Report by the North Western Provinces and Oudh Provincial Committee, 202.

10. Pal, B. C. 1916. *Nationality and Empire*. Calcutta: Thacker, Spink & Co., 78.

11. Tagore, U. N. 1865. *Bengalis as They Are and as They Ought to Be*. Calcutta, 35.

12. *Indian Mirror*, 6 November 1883, 'Letter to the Editor: "Indian Emigrants"', signed Purno Chander Mukerjee; *Indian Mirror*, 17 April 1884, 'Letter to the Editor: "New India"', signed S. Govinda Rao.

13. Quoted in Khan, S. H. 1959. *The Muslim League Movement: Second Phase*. Lahore, 14.

14. Mujeeb, M. 1967. *The Indian Muslims*. Montreal: McGill University Press, 19.

15. See Dumont, L. 1964. 'Nationalism and Communalism', in *Contributions to Indian Sociology* 7, 53–56.

16. Dimock, Jr, Edward C. 1967. 'Muslim Vaishnava Poets of Bengal', in *Languages and Areas: Studies Presented to George V Bobrinskoy*. Chicago: University of Chicago Press, 28–36.

17. The animosity between the communities permeated the vocabulary of the people. Hindus and Muslims referred to one another as *malechas* and *kafirs*. Indeed, there were also differences in dress, household utensils, house types, especially the construction of the house, and the words used for different kinds of activity.

18. Hardy, P., in W. T. de Bary et al. 1958. *Sources of Indian Tradition*. New York: Columbia University Press, 369–70.

19. See Srinivas, M. N. 1967. 'The Cohesive Role of Sanskritisation', in *India and Ceylon: Unity and Diversity*, ed. P. Mason. London: Oxford University Press, 77–81. For a detailed discussion of Sanskritisation, see his paper 'Sanskritisation and Westernisation' in the collection of his essays (1962) titled *Caste in Modern India and Other Essays*. Bombay: Asia Publishing House.

20. See, for instance, Qureshi, I. H. 1962. *The Muslim Community of the Indo-Pakistan Subcontinent*. The Hague: Mouton & Co.; Ministry of Information and Broadcasting, Government of Pakistan. 1957. *The History of Freedom Movement in Pakistan*. Karachi: Ministry of Information and Broadcasting, Government of Pakistan; Qureshi, I. H. 1965. *The Struggle for Pakistan*. Karachi: University of Karachi; Khaliquzzaman, C. 1961. *Pathway to Pakistan*. Lahore: Longmans; Ali, C. M. 1967. *The Emergence of Pakistan*. New York: Columbia University Press.

21. See, for instance, Chand, Tara. 1959. *History of the Freedom Movement in India*. New Delhi: Publication Division, Ministry of Information and Broadcasting, Government of India; Mujeeb. *The Indian Muslims*; Gopal, Ram. 1959. *Indian Muslims*. Bombay: Asia Publishing House; Husain, S. Abid. 1964. *The Destiny of Indian Muslims*. Bombay: Asia Publishing House. I should like to stress here that the fundamental unity of Indian civilisation has more often been assumed than empirically demonstrated. Dumont and Pocock recently laid down the postulate, India is one, as a necessary precondition to a sound development of the sociology of India. The tone of their argument is revealing, '[W]e learn in the first place never to forget that India is one. The very existence, and influence of the traditional higher, Sanskritic civilisation demonstrates without question the unity of India . . . Indeed, the unity of India is sort of commonplace ...' (Dumont, L., and D. F. Pocock, eds. 1957. *Contributions to Indian Sociology* 1, 9). Indeed, as Bailey has rightly observed,

> [there is] no doubt that, as an exercise, the editors [Dumont and Pocock] could find some common ground between Hinduism, Buddhism, Islam, Christianity, Utilitarianism, Marxism, Socialism, and all the other ideas and values which are relevant to social behaviour in India ... But the editors are in fact concerned with only one system of values—Hinduism ... At the outset the editors have taken a seven-league step towards proving the unity of India, for they have excluded from their definition of India all ideas and values which are not going to fit even into the Procrustean bed which the editors have constructed ... (Bailey, F. G. 1959. 'For a Sociology of India?', *Contributions to Indian Sociology* 3, 91–92).

22. I use the word 'slow' in a relative sense here. Western education was first introduced in the presidencies of Bengal and Bombay. Muslims in these areas were slow to respond to Western learning. Muslims in Uttar Pradesh were quick to see the advantage of education from the beginning and they took to the learning of English with equal readiness.

23. Quoted in Chatterjee, Bankim Chandra. *The Abbey of Bliss*, tr. Nares Chandra Sen-Gupta. Kolkata: Padmini Mohan Neogi, viii–x.

24. Ibid., 60.

25. Brecher, Michael. 1959. *Nehru—A Political Biography*. London: Oxford University Press, 617.

26. Ibid., 80–81.

27. Ibid., 63–64.

28. Quoted in Ibid., 99.

29. Ibid., 99.

30. See *Complete Works of Mahatma Gandhi*, Volume 3, 217.

31. For the differences of viewpoint between Gandhi and Nehru, see Brecher. *Nehru—A Political Biography*, 122–29, 247, 268–83.

32. Brecher. *Nehru—A Political Biography*, 60.

33. Quoted in Garratt, G. T. 1938. *The Legacy of India*. Oxford: Oxford University Press, 138.

34. It is necessary to remind ourselves at this point that there was an important economic side to this problem too. Strong vested interests had developed by this time for the maintenance of the communal cleavage and they were unlikely to give up the advantage of reservation of seats in the administration, representation in public bodies, etc.

35. Smith, W. C. 1957. *Islam in Modern History*. Princeton: Princeton University Press, 257.

36. Tandon, P. 1961. *Punjabi Century*. London: Chatto and Windus.

37. Numerous statements expressing this viewpoint were made in the Constituent Assembly when the sections relating to fundamental rights were under debate. It was most strongly expressed by M. Misra.

38. See Brown, Dorothy, ed. 1965. *Nehru: The First Sixty Years*. New York: John Day & Co., 302.

39. Ibid., 198.

40. Ibid., 328.

41. Spear, Percival. 1967. 'Nehru'. *Modern Asian Studies* 1 (1), January, 16.

42. See Smith. *India As a Secular State*, 480.

43. Panikkar. *The Foundations of New India*, 90.

44. See Sampurnanand's (1956) essay in *The Future of Education in India*. New Delhi: Publications Division, Government of India, 73–75.

45. Such sentiments were not very modern nor were they widely expressed in the English language. They were nevertheless widely and deeply felt.

46. Brecher. *Nehru—A Political Biography*, 626.

47. Spear. 'Nehru', p. 27.

48. See Ahmad, I. 1967. 'Muslims and Social Change', *The Hindustan Times*, 9 November.

49. The term 'kaval' (rarely used now) refers to the cities of Kanpur, Agra, Varanasi, Allahabad, and Lucknow (KAVAL). [eds]

50. Srinivas, M. N. 1966. *Social Change in Modern India*. Berkeley: University of California Press, 132.

51. See Rudolph, L. I., and S. H. Rudolph. 1967. *The Modernity of Tradition*. Chicago: University of Chicago Press, 1–14.

52. See C. Rajagopalachari (1954) quoted in *The Guardian*, Volume 32, 223.

53. Quoted in Smith. *India As a Secular State*, 389.

54. See Srinivas. 'The Cohesive Role of Sanskritisation', 68–69.

55. For a detailed discussion of this process, see my essay 'Political Process in Rural Uttar Pradesh' to be published in the collection of studies of the Fourth General Election under the editorship of M. N. Srinivas and A. M. Shah.

56. See Srinivas. 'The Cohesive Role of Sanskritisation', 67–82.

57. Spear, Percival. 1967. 'The Position of Muslims, Before and After Partition', in *India and Ceylon: Unity and Diversity*, ed. P Mason, 45.

58. For an elaborate discussion of this point, see Husain, S. Abid. 1964. 'The Destiny of Indian Muslims'. Bombay: Asia Publishing House, 142–44.

59. See Krishna, Gopal. 1968. 'Framework of Politics'. *Seminar*, No. 106, 34.

60. Harvani, Ansar. 1968. 'Whither Indian Muslims?'. *Link*, Republic Day Special, 17.

61. Smith. *India As a Secular State*, 416–18.

62. See Ahmad, I. 'Modernisation and the Indian Muslims', to be published in *Modernisation of the Indian Society*, A. K. Singh (ed).

63. See Ahmad, I. 'Muslims and Social Change' for a discussion of the Muslim attitude to changes in Muslim Personal Law.

64. Constitution of the Republic of India, Article 29(1).

65. Smith. *India As a Secular State*, 426.

66. Smith. *Islam in Modern History*, 266–67

67. Aggarwal, P. C. 1968. 'Islamic Revival in Modern India: The Meos'. Paper presented at the Annual Convention of the Association of Asian Studies held at Philadelphia, March 1968; and Aggarwal, P. C. 1969. 'Changing Religious Practices: Their Relationship to Secular Power in a Rajasthan Village'. *Economic and Political Weekly* IV (12), 22 March, 547–51.

68. Ibid.; also see Shils, Edward. 1963. 'On the Comparative Study of the New States', in *Old Societies and New States*, ed. Clifford Goertz. London: Free Press, 1–26.

69. For a discussion, see Ahmad, I. 1967. 'Indian Muslims and Electoral Politics'. *Economic and Political Weekly* 2 (10), 11 March, 521–23.

70. Beteille, A. 'Future of the Backward Classes', in *India and Ceylon: Unity and Diversity*, ed., P. Mason, 115.

71. 'Hindus Take a Rap'. *Enlite* (Baroda), 18 May 1968.

72. Ibid.

73. Ibid.

74. See Ray, A. K., and S. Chakravarty. 1968. 'Meerut Riots X-Rayed'. *Link*, 25 February, 18–20.

75. Krishna, Gopal. 1967. 'Electoral Participation and Political Integration'. *Economic and Political Weekly* Annual Number, February, 187.

3

COMMUNAL VIOLENCE IN INDIA*

GOPAL KRISHNA

[...]

THE EXTENT

Although communal violence had become an endemic feature of Indian life before Independence, it declined markedly after 1947. There are no adequate data on communal incidents between 1947 and 1954, but there is good ground for believing that there were not many of them. Such information, as is available, shows that for India, except Bihar and Uttar Pradesh, there were only 20 incidents in 1950 (11 of them in West Bengal), seven in 1951, 12 in 1952 and four in 1953. Their numbers were not large for the subsequent decade. The great divide in the history of communal riots in India is 1964. This is borne out by the statistical compilation put together by the Government of India, Ministry of Home Affairs. Whereas the total number of reported communal incidents over the period 1950–63 was 1,141, giving an average of 81.5 per year, in 1964, it had risen to 2,115. Admittedly, 1964 was a particularly bad year for communal violence, but there is no mistaking the fact that it represented a major change in the communal climate in the country. For the seven years between 1964 and 1970, the average number of incidents per year was 1,025, as against 81.5 for the preceding 14 years.

Not only had the number of incidents increased, but the area affected by communal violence had steadily expanded. In 1961, there were 61 districts in the country which had experienced communal troubles in that year; by the end of the decade, their number had gone up to 216, representing about 70 per cent of the basic administrative units. Again viewed as an administrative task, whereas in 1961, 61 district authorities had to contend with communal violence, by the end of the decade, their number had risen to 116. The number of districts affected in the various states over the years is given in Table 3.1.

It is evident that progressively, communal conflict has emerged as one of the major problems in most of the states and increasing administrative and political

* *Economic and Political Weekly* 20 (2): 61–74 (12 January 1985).

Table 3.1: Number of Districts Affected by Communal Violence, 1961–1970

State	*1961*	*1962*	*1963*	*1964*	*1965*	*1966*	*1967*	*1968*	*1969*	*1970*	*Total No. of Districts*	*Total No. of District Affected*
Andhra Pradesh	–	2	2	–	3	2	3	6	3	4	20	11
Assam	4	2	4	5	6	3	3	4	2	8	11	9
Bihar	11	4	9	12	9	11	14	15	16	14	17	13
Gujarat	2	3	4	7	5	3	1	2	14	5	17	16
Haryana	–	–	1	–	1	–	–	–	–	–	7	1
Jammu and Kashmir	–	–	–	–	–	–	–	–	–	1	9	1
Karnataka	2	1	2	2	4	2	2	4	4	6	19	14
Kerala	2	2	–	1	3	2	2	4	5	4	9	8
Madhya Pradesh	8	4	1	7	5	2	6	6	9	13	43	29
Maharashtra	4	5	3	10	13	11	7	9	12	17	26	25
Orissa	1	–	1	5	3	3	2	2	4	5	13	10
Punjab	–	–	–	–	–	–	–	–	–	1	11	1
Rajasthan	–	1	–	1	2	3	3	3	2	7	26	11
Tamil Nadu	2	1	1	5	2	2	2	2	3	4	11	11
Uttar Pradesh	13	11	6	9	12	9	10	14	9	16	54	31
West Bengal	10	9	5	11	8	5	7	5	10	8	16	15
Delhi	1	1	1	–	1	–	–	1	1	1	1*	1
Manipur	–	–	–	–	–	–	1	–	–	–	1*	1
Arunachal Pradesh	–	–	–	–	–	–	–	1	–	–	1*	1
Tripura	1	1	–	1	–	–	–	1	–	1	1*	1
India	61	47	40	71	77	58	63	79	94	116	316	216

Source: Author.

resources have to be applied to its containment. There are three states with very low incidents of communal violence, namely Haryana, Jammu and Kashmir, and Punjab. The primary factor accounting for it is the population composition of these states. In Haryana and Punjab, the Muslim population is small and consequently, the potential for Hindu–Muslim conflict is much less. In Kashmir, the situation is reversed, that is, the Hindu population there is small and consequently, there is less potential for Hindu–Muslim conflict. The situation in Jammu is rather different. Here, the Hindus enjoy preponderance in the population. The communal situation in Jammu has deteriorated over the past 14 years.

From the territorial spread of communal violence, we move to examine the actual incident of it in different states over the 1961–70 decade, subjecting the available data to detailed scrutiny with a view to determining the rural–urban distribution of incidents, the areas of repeated violence, the intensity of violence and identification of the riot-prone towns and districts. Table 3.2 gives state-wise distribution of communal incidents for this period.

Communal violence occurs in areas of mixed population. There are fewer incidents in districts with small proportion of Muslim population; they also appear to correlate with the size of the Muslim population as a proportion of the urban population in several districts. While a precise relationship between communal incidents and the proportion of Muslim population in rural/urban areas cannot be established, available data do suggest a broad pattern; more riots occur in districts with Muslim population varying between 10 and 30 per cent and above. Table 3.3 supplies the details for all the states.

In the following pages, a detailed state-wise analysis of these data are presented, first for urban areas and then for rural areas.

Andhra Pradesh

(1) Towns with persistent violence: Hyderabad experienced riots in eight out of 10 years. The 1968 riots were serious, lasting for as long as 36 days, 1967 for nine days, 1970 for 11 days, and Nizamabad town experienced riots successively for three years—1965, 1966 and 1967, lasting for four, four and six days respectively. The number of incidents was unusually large in 1967; 510 spread over six days. Of the total 100 days of communal violence in the state spread over 10 years, Hyderabad accounted for 65 and Nizamabad for 14, and the rest 21 days by the remaining 11 towns, giving the average duration of riots less than two days per town over a 10-year period.

(2) The number of incidents may be similarly analysed. Of the total 737 incidents reported, Hyderabad accounted for 115 and Nizamabad 587, leaving 35 incidents to the remaining 11 towns, averaging 3.2 incidents per town over a 10-year period.

(3) The rural–urban distribution of incidents: 737 urban, 22 rural.

(4) Hyderabad emerges as the single major centre of communal trouble in Andhra Pradesh. Hyderabad has been a centre of communal politics. It has a large Muslim population, a part of which has experienced reverse social mobility.

Table 3.2: Communal Violence, 1961–1970 Rural/Urban Distribution

State	1961		1962		1963		1964		1965		1966		1967		1968		1969		1970		Total	
	R	U	R	U	R	U	R	U	R	U	R	U	R	U	R	U	R	U	R	U	R	U
Andhra Pradesh	–	–	1	4	1	6	–	–	15	34	–	54	–	528	4	77	–	13	2	23	22	737
Assam	9	1	4	3	31	11	15	4	8	6	9	1	9	6	27	3	8	2	37	20	157	59
Bihar	24	10	5	2	12	8	97	331	25	7	22	5	337	315	55	20	48	21	66	120	691	839
Gujarat	–	2	1	4	2	17	5	37	4	26	1	2	1	–	–	4	94	578	6	15	114	685
Haryana	–	–	–	–	3	–	–	–	–	1	–	–	–	–	–	–	–	–	–	–	3	1
Jammu and Kashmir	–	–	–	–	–	–	–	–	–	–	–	–	–	–	–	–	–	–	3	1	3	1
Karnataka	1	7	1	1	–	4	2	1	22	17	–	4	5	–	4	20	1	26	3	17	39	97
Kerala	3	–	6	–	–	–	3	–	4	–	4	–	1	1	6	–	8	1	4	4	39	6
Madhya Pradesh	53	180	5	6	–	1	9	12	3	4	2	15	1	19	–	14	7	148	11	38	91	437
Maharashtra	10	7	5	27	1	14	10	67	16	210	8	238	2	163	6	29	5	35	153	194	216	984
Orissa	–	2	–	–	–	2	252	440	1	6	6	4	–	2	2	4	6	2	2	7	269	569
Punjab	–	–	–	–	–	–	–	–	–	–	–	–	–	–	–	–	–	–	2	–	2	–
Rajasthan	–	–	–	2	–	–	–	1	–	5	–	42	–	4	–	6	–	8	5	9	5	77
Tamil Nadu	2	–	1	–	3	–	3	4	8	–	2	–	2	1	2	–	2	2	9	3	34	10
Uttar Pradesh	15	76	14	17	7	5	14	7	12	27	8	121	21	26	10	147	11	18	15	38	127	482
West Bengal	35	–	66	34	9	1	456	339	23	1	13	12	15	11	5	26	63	17	78	32	763	473
Delhi	–	1	–	1	–	1	–	–	–	4	–	–	–	–	–	1	–	2	–	5	–	15
Manipur	–	–	–	–	–	–	–	–	–	–	–	–	1	–	–	–	–	–	2	–	3	–
Arunachal Pradesh	–	–	–	–	–	–	–	–	–	–	–	–	–	–	4	–	–	–	–	–	1	–
Tripura	4	–	1	–	–	–	6	–	–	–	–	–	–	–	–	2	–	–	6	–	14	2
India	153	286	110	101	68	70	872	1,243	141	146	75	498	395	1,076	122	353	253	873	403	526	2,592	5,372

Source: Author.

TABLE 3.3: Muslim Proportions in the Rural/Urban Population of Districts (1961) and the Number of Communal Incidents, 1961–1970

(*In Per Cent*)

State	*5*		*5.01 to 10.00*		*10.01 to 15.00*		*15.01 to 20.00*		*20.01 to 30.00*		*30.01 and Above*		*Total No. of Incidents*		*Total*
	R	*U*	*R*	*U*	*R*	*U*	*R*	*U*	*R*	*U*	*R*	*U*	*R*	*U*	
Andhra Pradesh	1	–	21	–	–	4	–	3	–	607	–	123	22	737	757
Assam	7	2	7	3	–	36	5	2	–	14	138	–	157	57	214
Bihar	178	–	95	–	354	429	12	365	–	45	15	–	691	839	1530
Gujarat	38	1	70	–	6	99	–	472	–	108	–	–	114	685	799
Haryana	–	1	–	–	–	–	–	–	3	–	–	–	3	1	4
Jammu and Kashmir	–	–	–	–	–	–	–	–	–	–	3	1	3	1	4
Karnataka	20	–	12	–	7	67	–	9	–	7	–	14	39	97	136
Kerala	–	–	3	–	8	4	–	1	12	1	16	–	59	6	45
Madhya Pradesh	71	–	20	126	–	213	–	2	–	66	–	29	91	437	528
Maharashtra	124	–	79	223	3	187	–	116	–	409	–	39	206	994	1200
Orissa	269	26	–	441	–	–	–	–	–	2	–	–	269	569	838
Punjab	2	–	–	–	–	–	–	–	–	–	–	–	2	–	2
Rajasthan	1	–	4	3	–	3	–	65	–	1	–	5	5	77	82
Tamil Nadu	34	–	–	5	–	5	–	–	–	–	–	–	34	10	44
Uttar Pradesh	–	–	58	–	16	–	21	15	17	260	10	207	127	482	609
West Bengal	1	18	27	15	17	397	23	–	589	43	106	–	763	475	1236
Delhi	–	–	–	15	–	–	–	–	–	–	–	–	–	15	15
Arunachal Pradesh	1	–	–	–	–	–	–	–	–	–	–	–	1	–	1
Tripura	–	–	–	–	–	–	–	–	14	–	–	–	14	–	14
India	746	48	396	833	411	1,444	61	1,055	635	1,562	288	438	2,592	5,372	7,964
	794		1,229		1,855		1,336		2,197		726		7,964		

Source: Author.

There was considerable Arya Samaj activity in the city over a long period. In recent years, the growth of communal organisations has contributed to the accentuation of communal tension in the city.

Assam

(1) The district capital Silchar shows incidents more persistently: in five out of 10 years, Silchar, Dhubri and Karimganj, all class III towns, recorded 12, 11 and nine incidents over the decade, leaving 25 incidents distributed over the remaining 15 towns. The class I towns, namely Gauhati and Shillong, recorded only one incident each throughout the decade—Gauhati in 1965 and Shillong in 1970. In both cases, the trouble lasted for only one day.
(2) Of the 42 days of communal riots in the state, Silchar, Karimganj and Dhubri accounted for 21 days, leaving 21 days of rioting in the remaining 15 centres. Of these, another class III town, Tinsukia, experienced two riots of two days each.
(3) The main towns of communal trouble seem to be three, possibly four (all of them class III): Silchar, Karimganj, Dhubri and Tinsukia.
(4) In Assam, the incidence of communal violence is much greater in rural than in urban areas: 157 against 57 incidents.

Bihar

(1) Of the 839 incidents, 84 per cent are accounted for by two industrial centres—Ranchi and Jamshedpur, and its adjacent areas Chaibasa and Chakradharpur.
(2) Ranchi and Bihar Sharif have had recurring riots: in seven out of 10 years in Ranchi and six out of 10 years in Bihar Sharif, the Jamshedpur–Chaibasa area had riots in five out of 10 years.
(3) Of the 171 days of rioting, Ranchi accounted for 33, Bihar Sharif 10, and Jamshedpur 28; Chaibasa and Chakradharpur accounted for eight and 18 days respectively. Thus, the three centres of riots accounted for 97 out of 171 days, that is, about 57 per cent. Bhagalpur appears to be another centre of rioting: it experienced riots in three out of 10 years, and in 1967 had nine days of rioting. The worst years for riots were 1964, 1967 and 1970, which accounted for 766 of the 839 incidents, and 117 of the 171 days of rioting. In Bihar, class I towns are the worst affected.
(4) There was a large number of incidents in rural areas in this state—691 over the 1961–70 decade.

Gujarat

(1) Most of the riots in Gujarat took place in 1969. Of the total 685 incidents over the 10-year period, 578 took place in that single year. Only two towns, namely Ahmedabad and Godhra, show a recurring pattern. During the decade, Ahmedabad had riots in six years, and Godhra in five years.

(2) Of the 152 days of riots, 98 were during 1969, and Ahmedabad, Baroda and Godhra accounted for 59 of the total number of days (that is, about 40 per cent of the total). The remaining 42 towns experienced communal violence of varying duration, totalling 93 days over the decade. Even in Ahmedabad, the duration of riots was not more than two or three days before 1969.
(3) Communal disturbances in Gujarat have been mainly in urban areas. The state capital Ahmedabad has had an old legacy of communal trouble, going back to 1714. In the decade under review, the urban areas accounted for 685 incidents, while the rural areas accounted for 114 incidents.

Haryana

The state experienced a communal riot only once, during 1965, at Nuh (VI class) in Gurgaon district.

This incident lasted only for one day. The place affected was a class VI town.

Jammu and Kashmir

Jammu and Kashmir experienced a one-day communal riot in 1970. The affected town Kistwar (in Doder district) is a class VI town.

Karnataka

(1) There were no places except one, Bidar, which experienced repeated rioting in Karnataka. Bidar had riots in four out of 10 years under review.
(2) The number of days of rioting for the decade was 33, and the worst year of rioting was 1970, when six towns had riots; in 1968, there were five.
(3) The number of incidents in the rural areas was 39 for the decade.

Kerala

(1) Throughout the decade, Kerala experienced communal rioting only in four places, and each had only one riot. Of the six incidents, three occurred in Trivandrum, and of the five days of rioting, Trivandrum accounted for two.
(2) There were many more rural incidents than urban: 39 as against six in the towns.

Madhya Pradesh

(1) 328 of the 437 incidents took place in two years—1961 (180) and 1970 (148).
(2) Indore had riots in four out of 10 years, one every year beginning 1967. Jabalpur had riots in three out of 10 years, and so did Bhopal and Satna. Vidisha had riots in four out of 10 years.
(3) Of the 119 days of riots, Indore accounted for 25, Jabalpur 14, Bhopal six and Vidisha five, leaving 69 days to 37 towns.
(4) Indore is the prime centre of communal violence in Madhya Pradesh. For it, 1969 was the worst year, with 114 incidents spread over 11 days.

Maharashtra

(1) The worst year for communal violence in Maharashtra was 1970, when the state experienced 85 days of rioting, out of the total of 193 days for the decade. Twenty-two towns had communal riots in 1970, as against 12 in 1968, and 16 in 1966, the previous peak year.

(2) The towns experiencing repeated rioting were Greater Bombay, Poona, Sholapur, Malkapur, Aurangabad, Ahmednagar, Akola, Bhiwandi and Malegaon. The first four of these had communal riots in five out of the 10 years, while the remaining ones had them for four years out of 10.

(3) Bhiwandi, Poona, Aurangabad, Thana and Greater Bombay experienced intense forms of rioting in 1970. Bhiwandi had 20 days of rioting in that year, Poona had 10 days, Thana 13 days, Aurangabad eight days and Greater Bombay six days—together, 57 days out of the total of 85 days of rioting during that year. Washim in Akola district and Malegaon in Nasik district are two other towns which experienced communal rioting of the same scale in 1966 and 1967 respectively. Poona had its worst riots in 1965, when 201 incidents occurred over 6 days.

(4) There was substantial communal violence in the rural areas of Maharashtra, accounting for a little over one-sixth of all the incidents over the decade.

Orissa

(1) In Orissa, the main incidents of communal violence occurred in 1964. In that year, riots took place in 11 of the 15 towns in which riots have occurred during the 1969–70 decade.

(2) There is only one town—Cuttack—with a recurring cycle of communal violence. Here, riots have taken place in six out of 10 years.

(3) Of the 62 days of rioting, Rourkela accounted for 17 (15 in 1964, two in 1970), and Cuttack 13, leaving 32 days for 13 other towns, averaging two-and-a-half days of rioting over a 10-year period.

(4) There was a large number of communal incidents in rural areas during the decade—264 were reported. They were mostly part of the 1964 outbreak.

Rajasthan

(1) The main centres of communal violence in Rajasthan were the cities of Jaipur, Jodhpur and Udaipur. They all experienced rioting in four out of 10 years. Udaipur had its worst riot in 1966, when 40 incidents took place in two days of rioting.

(2) The three cities accounted for 19 days of rioting, leaving 12 days of it to the remaining eight towns, thus averaging for them one-and-a-half day's rioting for each over the decade.

(3) The incidents of communal violence in the rural areas of the state were negligible.

Tamil Nadu

(1) The decade recorded very few communal incidents in the state. No town, except Madras, had more than one riot over the period; and even Madras had only two of them, in 1964 and in 1969.
(2) No riot lasted beyond one day.
(3) There were 34 rural incidents, 3.4 times more than the urban ones.

Uttar Pradesh

(1) 14 class I towns account for 311 incidents out of the total of 482 for the decade. Of these 310, Allahabad, Meerut and Aligarh account for 208, that is, over 67 per cent.
(2) Aligarh and Meerut have had riots in seven out of the 10 years under review. Moradabad has had riots for eight out of 10 years. Agra and Bareilly had them for six out of 10 years, and Allahabad and Varanasi had them for five years.
(3) Of the 179 riot days, Allahabad accounted for 32, Meerut 25, Aligarh 20, Moradabad 19, and 11 each in Agra, Bareilly and Varanasi—together 129, representing just over 75 per cent of the total, leaving 50 days to 32 towns for the whole decade.
(4) The number of rural incidents was relatively few—127 out of the total of 609.

West Bengal

(1) The major outbreak of communal violence in West Bengal was in 1964: 339 of the 473 incidents occurred in that one year in 32 towns, most of which have had no riot afterwards in the decade under review.
(2) Calcutta city has suffered communal violence on a modest scale every year since 1964.
(3) Of the 150 days of rioting, 86 were in 1964, and Calcutta accounted for 30 more in the subsequent years of the decade.
(4) The rural incidents of communal violence were substantial, accounting for over 60 per cent of all the incidents.

Delhi

Delhi experienced communal incidents every year during the decade except in 1964, 1966 and 1967.

The total number of incidents was 15, resulting in 15 days of communal violence for the decade.

Tripura

Tripura reported two incidents in 1968, resulting in two days of violence.

From the analysis of the data on communal violence available to us, it would appear that the following urban centres are prone to periodic rioting:

1. Andhra Pradesh: Hyderabad, Nizamabad

2. Assam: Silchar, Dhubri, Karimganj, Tinsukhia
3. Bihar: Bhagalpur, Bihar Sharif, Jamshedpur (with Chaibasa)
4. Gujarat: Ahmedabad, Godhra, Baroda
5. Madhya Pradesh: Indore, Jabalpur, Bhopal, Vidisha
6. Maharashtra: Bombay, Poona, Sholapur, Malkapur, Aurangabad, Ahmednaga, Akola, Bhiwandi, Malegaon
7. Rajasthan: Jaipur, Jodhpur, Udaipur
8. Uttar Pradesh: Agra, Allahabad, Meerut, Aligarh, Varanasi, Bareilly, Moradabad
9. West Bengal: Calcutta
10. Delhi: Delhi

Table 3.4 presents in a summary form the data on all the 335 towns which together recorded 5,766 communal incidents over the 1961–70 decade.

While the average number of incidents per town affected is a little over 17 for the decade, it is 33 for class I towns, 25.4 for class II towns, 9.80 for class III towns, 4.82 for class IV towns, 1.94 for class V towns and 1.5 for class VI towns.

Taking the 1971 town classification, we find that 10.77 per cent of all the towns in the country had experienced communal violence. The percentage figures for different classes of towns were: 15 per cent in class I; 25.45 per cent in class II; 15.33 per cent in class III; 7.71 per cent in class IV; 5.13 per cent in class V; and 3.37 per cent in class VI towns.

The pattern of violence in rural areas is as follows:

(1) *Andhra Pradesh:* Of the 22 rural incidents reported, 14 occurred in Nizamabad district in 1965.
    Medak reported 3 rural incidents in 1968.
(2) *Assam:* Of the 157 rural incidents, 88 were reported from Cachar, 31 from Goalpara and 11 from Kamrup. 1963, 1968 and 1970 accounted for 95 of the 157 incidents.
(3) *Bihar:* Of the 691 incidents, Muzaffarpur accounted for 245, Ranchi 107, and Singhbhum 62, a total of 414, about 60 per cent. Of these, 304 took place in Muzaffarpur and Ranchi in 1967, and 60 in Singhbhum in 1964.
(4) *Gujarat:* Of the 114 rural incidents reported, 94 took place in 1969: 45 in Kaira, 16 in Mehsana, nine in Baroda.
(5) *Karnataka:* Of the 39 reported incidents, 16 took place in Mandya in 1965. The rest were spread over the remaining 13 districts over the decade.
(6) *Kerala:* Of the 39 reported incidents, 11 took place in Kozhikode, which experienced communal rioting in six out of 10 years of the 1961–70 decade; the rest were scattered over the remaining seven districts.
(7) *Madhya Pradesh:* Of the 91 reported incidents, Sagar accounted for 25 and Jabalpur for 20. They took place in 1961.
(8) *Maharashtra:* Of the 216 incidents, 104 took place in Thana, and of these, 101 occurred in 1970; 38 in Kolaba (34 in 1970); 10 in Greater Bombay (all in 1970); a total of 152 (of which 145 in one year, 1970), representing 70 per cent of the cases.

Table 3.4: Communal Violence 1961–1970 Class of Towns and Number of Incidents*

State	I		II		III		IV		V		VI		Total	
	1	*2*	*1*	*2*	*1*	*2*	*1*	*2*	*1*	*2*	*1*	*2*	*Towns*	*Incidents*
Andhra Pradesh	3	119	1	587	6	23	2	3	1	5	–	–	13	737
Assam	2	2	1	4	5	37	2	3	4	4	4	7	18	57
Bihar	9	609	4	17	10	184	8	20	3	8	1	1	35	839
Gujarat	3	420	10	139	13	77	14	40	5	9	–	–	45	685
Karnataka	4	12	3	9	5	25	4	45	3	5	1	1	20	97
Kerala	2	4	–	–	1	1	1	1	–	–	–	–	3	6
Madhya Pradesh	11	281	4	29	13	72	5	38	8	17	–	–	41	437
Maharashtra	14	484	7	87	11	320	12	83	5	10	–	–	49	984
Orissa	1	14	2	388	3	20	7	41	2	6	–	–	15	469
Rajasthan	4	66	1	1	3	4	3	4	–	–	–	–	11	75
Tamil Nadu	1	4	1	2	3	3	1	1	–	–	–	–	6	10
Uttar Pradesh	14	311	8	12	10	115	5	40	2	4	–	–	39	482
West Bengal	9	235	15	174	13	60	3	4	–	–	–	–	40	473
Delhi	1	15	–	–	–	–	–	–	–	–	–	–	1	15
	78	2,576	57	1,449	96	941	67	323	35	68	6	9	336	5,766

Notes: 1. No. of towns. 2. No. of Incidents
*Haryana, Jammu and Kashmir and Tripura are excluded from the table. They reported four incidents between them over the decade, spread over four towns (2 class V and 2 class VI).

Source: Author.

(9) *Orissa:* Of the 269 incidents, 223 took place in Sundargarh and 21 in Sambalpur in 1964, which represents over 83 per cent of the cases.
(10) *Tamil Nadu:* Of the 34 incidents, nine were reported from Tiruchirapalli, which experienced communal riots in four out of 10 years of the 1961–70 decade.
(11) *Uttar Pradesh:* Of the 127 incidents reported, 20 were from Gorakhpur, 17 from Allahabad, 10 from Bareilly, and nine from Meerut. Allahabad reported riots in rural areas in six years of the 1961–70 decade, Gorakhpur four, and Meerut five.
(12) *West Bengal*: Of the 763 reported rural incidents, 395 were from 24 Parganas, 138 from Nadia, 63 from Murshidabad, 53 from Cooch Behar, 23 from Malda, 20 from West Dirajpur. Of the 763 incidents, 456 took place in 1964, and 424 of them in two districts, 24 parganas and Nadia.

There are 30 districts in the country which can be identified as being prone to communal violence in rural areas:

- Andhra Pradhesh: Nizamabad, Medak
- Assam: Cachar, Goalpara, Kamrup
- Bihar: Muzaffarpur, Ranchi, Singhbhum
- Gujarat: Kaira, Mehsana, Baroda
- Karnataka: Mandya
- Madhya Pradesh: Sagar, Jabalpur
- Maharashtra: Thana, Kolaba, Greater Bombay
- Orissa: Sundargarh, Sambalpur
- Tamil Nadu: Tiruchirapalli
- Uttar Pradesh: Gorakhpur, Allahabad, Bareilly, Meerut
- West Bengal: 24 Parganas, Nadia, Malda, West Dirajpur, Murshidabad, Cooch Behar

Causes of Communal Violence

It is a general finding of nearly all the enquiries into communal riots that their immediate causes tend to be almost always trivial. The remarkable feature of communal incidents is, however, not that they begin with trivial friction, but that once begin, they acquire a collective aspect. The riots in Delhi in 1973 and 1974 started over petty personal quarrels, but soon developed into group conflict, leading to much loss of life and property, and increased communal hostility. The major riots of the 1960s had insignificant beginnings. Of the 841 incidents over the 1961–70 period whose causes have been identified by the Ministry of Home Affairs, the details are given in Table 3.5.

A little over half of the total number of disputes relate to private causes (52.66 per cent), while the rest relate to religious/public causes. The largest category of incidents, 6,815 out of 7,964, representing 81.80 per cent of the total, are identified by the Ministry of Home Affairs as 'chain incidents', that is, have no independent cause(s), but result from some major outbreak and are in the nature of a spillover. Almost three quarters of these 'spillover' incidents occurred in four

TABLE 3.5: Causes of Communal Violence

	No. of Incidents	*Percentage*
Festivity/celebrations	225	26.75
Private property disputes	162	19.26
Quarrels over women	142	16.89
Personal transactions, enmities, etc.	139	16.53
Cow slaughter	121	14.39
Desecration of religious places	34	4.04
Disputes over graveyards	18	2.14
Total	841	100.00

Source: Author.

TABLE 3.6: Causes of Communal Violence, 1961–1970

State	*Cow Slaughter*	*Desecration of Religious Places*	*Festivity/ Celebrations*	*Graveyards*	*Total*	*Chain Incidents*
Andhra Pradesh	–	1	21	1	23	680
Assam	7	1	11	–	19	106
Bihar	56	4	64	8	132	1,199
Gujarat	6	2	6	–	14	724
Haryana	–	–	–	–	–	2
Karnataka	1	1	8	2	12	100
Kerala	–	1	4	1	6	9
Madhya Pradesh	6	–	11	–	17	429
Maharashtra	8	18	35	2	63	1,022
Orissa	5	–	9	–	14	699
Punjab	–	–	–	–	–	1
Rajasthan	–	–	4	–	4	51
Tamil Nadu	–	1	5	1	7	17
Uttar Pradesh	17	4	27	3	51	425
West Bengal	15	1	17	–	53	1,040
Delhi	–	–	2	–	2	–
Arunachal Pradesh	–	–	1	–	1	–
Tripura	–	–	–	–	–	11

Source: Author.

years—1964, 1967, 1969 and 1970, and were related to the wave of violence that swept eastern India in 1964, Bihar in 1967, and Gujarat and Maharashtra in 1969 and 1970 respectively. These together accounted for 54 per cent of the 'chain incidents' of the decade. The state-wise distribution of incidents by identified public causes is given in Table 3.6.

(1) Bihar leads in having the higher number of public causes for communal violence, and is followed by Maharashtra, Uttar Pradesh and West Bengal. Between them, these four states account for over 70 per cent of the cases.
(2) The cow slaughter question is important in Bihar, Uttar Pradesh and West Bengal.
(3) The incidents of desecration of religious places are most important in Maharashtra, and to a small extent in Bihar and Uttar Pradesh.
(4) The graveyards issue is of importance in Bihar, and to a lesser extent in Uttar Pradesh.
(5) The festivity/celebration occasions have occasioned communal violence in all the states save Punjab, Haryana and Tripura (also in Jammu and Kashmir, and Manipur).
(6) Here too, Bihar takes the lead, followed by Maharashtra, Uttar Pradesh, Andhra Pradesh and West Bengal. Between them, these five states account for 72.88 per cent of the cases of communal violence on this score. The rural–urban distribution of these incidents shows that 55 per cent of them occurred in rural areas. The rural/urban and state-wise distribution is provided in Tables 3.7 and 3.8.
(7) As is to be expected in predominantly rural Bihar, there are more incidents on every count in the rural areas there as compared with the urban areas. This is especially so with regard to cow slaughter. This issue is also important in rural Uttar Pradesh and rural West Bengal. In Maharashtra, on the other hand, it has been an entirely urban problem.
(8) Festivities/celebrations give rise to communal incidents in rural areas in every state except Andhra Pradesh and Delhi, and in urban areas in all states except Kerala. In rural incidents of violence on account of festivity, Bihar takes the lead, followed by West Bengal and Uttar Pradesh, while in urban disturbances on this count, Maharashtra takes the lead, followed by Andhra Pradesh, Uttar Pradesh and Bihar.
(9) The largest number of incidents of desecration of religious places was reported from Maharashtra, where they were recorded in seven out of 10 years under review. Here, they were predominantly in urban areas.
(10) Incidents related to graveyards occurred mainly in rural Bihar.

TABLE 3.7: Rural/Urban Distribution of Causes of Communal Incidents

	Rural	*Urban*
Cow slaughter	88	33
Festivity/celebrations	104	121
Desecration of religious places	16	18
Graveyards	11	7
Total	219	179

Source: Author.

TABLE 3.8: State-wise Distribution of Causes of Communal Incidents

State	*Cow Slaughter*		*Festivity*		*Religious Places*		*Graveyards*		*Total*
	R	*U*	*R*	*U*	*R*	*U*	*R*	*U*	
Andhra Pradesh	1	4	–	21	–	1	–	1	28
Assam	4	3	4	7	1	–	–	–	19
Bihar	44	12	48	16	3	1	6	2	132
Gujarat	3	3	5	1	2	–	–	–	14
Karnataka	1	–	3	5	1	–	1	1	12
Kerala	–	–	4	–	1	–	1	–	6
Madhya Pradesh	3	3	2	9	–	–	–	–	17
Maharashtra	–	8	7	28	4	14	1	1	63
Orissa	4	1	2	7	–	–	–	–	14
Rajasthan	–	–	1	3	–	–	–	–	4
Tamil Nadu	–	–	4	1	1	–	1	–	7
Uttar Pradesh	14	3	11	16	2	2	1	2	51
West Bengal	15	–	13	4	1	–	–	–	33
Delhi	–	–	–	2	–	–	–	–	2
India	88	33	104	121	16	18	11	7	398

Source: Author.

The identified private causes of communal violence related to women, private property and personal transactions, feuds, etc. Over the 1961–70 decade, these together numbered 443. Their distribution for rural and urban areas is given in Table 3.9. It should cause no surprise that more communal incidents occur in rural areas than in urban areas, given that almost four-fifth of the Indian population still lived in rural areas in 1961.

TABLE 3.9: Rural/Urban Distribution of Private Causes of Communal Violence

Issues	*Rural*	*Urban*
Women	65	77
Private property	134	28
Personal transactions, etc.	55	84
Total	254 (57.33) per cent	189 (42.67) per cent

Source: Author.

The proportions between rural and urban incidents alter dramatically when we come to the 'chain incidents'. Here, the rural areas account for only 28.77 per cent of the total number of such incidents reported for the 1961–70 decade. Riots in rural areas are sporadic and generally do not spread.

Our understanding of the 'causes' of communal violence can now be deepened somewhat with the help of the findings of the various Commissions of Enquiry that have reported on some of the major riots. There are six reports of the Raghubar Dayal Commission reporting on six riots that took place between August and October 1967, the Reddy Commission's report on the Gujarat riots in 1969, the D. P. Madon Commission's report on the Maharashtra (Bhiwandi, Jalgaon and Mahad) riots of 1970, the Tandon and Prasad reports on riots in Delhi in 1973 and 1974, and the Jitendra Narain Commission's report on the Jamshedpur disturbances of April 1979. I have not been able to consult the report on the Tellicherry (Kerala) riots of 1970.

Among the general causes of riots these commissions mention are a history of communal conflict, which creates a recurring cycle of confrontation between communities. These confrontations result in violence on some provocation or the other. The immediate factor in such a case is not the 'cause' of communal violence but only an occasion. The true, deeper, cause is elsewhere. Among these deeper causes identified are: (1) the Partition of India and resulting hostility of Hindus towards Muslims; (2) the activities of communal organisations and political parties; (3) religious disputes arising from cow slaughter, music before mosques, desecration of religious places (temples, mosques, graves), possession of graveyards; (4) affront to women; and (5) conversion activity.

In their report on the Ranchi-Hatia riot of 22–29 August 1967, the Raghubar Dayal Commission reported that the riot was preceded by several incidents causing communal animosity; the overall political situation in the state (Bihar) had become unstable in the aftermath of the general election of that year; the communal organisations...had been active in the area and had, by their activities poisoned, inter-community relations; and, the Muslim demand for the recognition of Urdu as the second official language of the state was greatly resented by the Hindus.

This last was the immediate cause of a protest procession which sparked off the communal riot.

The disturbances in Jainpur and Suchetpur in Gorakhpur district of Uttar Pradesh on 24–25 September 1967 centred around the question of ownership of a piece of land claimed by Muslims to be their graveyard and by Hindus as their cremation ground.

In Sursand (district Muzaffarpur, Bihar), the disturbances of 13–15 October 1967 were sparked off by the controversy over the route of the Durga procession. The village had received full impact of communal tension over several years and had entered even into the cultural programmes organised during the Vijayadashami festival.

Disturbances in Sholapur (Maharashtra) on 17 September 1967 started during the passage of the Ganapathi procession. Sholapur has a long history of communal conflict, going back at least to 1925. Sectarian religious organisations and communal political parties have been active in the town for several years.

The Ahmednagar (Maharashtra) riot of 18 September 1967 was occasioned by the disfigurement of idols in a local temple. Ahmednagar too has a long history of communal conflict. The Pakistan factor has also operated in the local inter-community relations. Communal organisations have been active.

Malegaon (Maharashtra) also has a long history of communal conflict. The riot on 24 September 1967 was focused on a case of cow slaughter. Molestation of women, music before mosques and cow slaughter have agitated the town population at least since 1922. Communal organisations have been active.

The Ahmedabad riot of 18 September 1969, which spread to several other areas in Gujarat, took place over the alleged attack on the sadhus of a local temple by a group of Muslims. Although there have been communal riots in Ahmedabad before, the city had no entrenched tradition of communal conflict. The tension was building up over the preceding three or four years, especially in the aftermath of the 1965 India–Pakistan war. Communal organisations were active in the city.

In Bhiwandi (Maharashtra), the May 1970 disturbances occurred on the occasion of the Shiva Jayanti celebrations. The town had become a victim of communal politics since 1963, largely as a result of the activities of communal political organisations.

The riots in Delhi in 1973 and in 1974 had entirely private origins, but the area in which the disturbances occurred has had a history of communal conflict going back to 1924. Communal organisations have been active in the area for several years.

The Jamshedpur disturbances of April 1979 arose over the Ram Navami procession route. The city has experienced communal conflict since 1964. Communal organisations have been active, especially with the *akhadas*.

In recent years, two further causes of communal conflict have emerged, namely conversion and economic competition. Conversions have been an explosive issue in India since the mid-1920s. For several decades, it had Iain dormant because there was no large-scale conversion activity. Its re-emergence is owed to the reported mass conversions of Harijans to Islam in Tamil Nadu in 1981.

Economic competition as an underlying cause of communal conflict is being frequently mentioned in some recent writing on the subject, and the cases cited are those of riots in Aligarh, Moradabad, Bihar Sharif and Udaipur. Of these, only the last case had been carefully researched by Zerah Banu and her data demonstrate that the riots of 1965–66 have had a devastating impact on the Bohra businesses in the city.[1]

All the inquiry commissions have rejected pre-planning as a cause in any of the riots they investigated.

THE PARTICIPANTS

It is difficult to determine who participates in the disturbances. Communal disturbances entail both group activity and individual acts. Group activity is demonstrative, while individual acts pertain to arson, stabbing or use of fire arms against the adversaries. The various inquiry commissions, to whose reports reference has been made above, speak of riotous crowds of 100 to 10,000 or more. The figures of those arrested by the state authorities in the course of controlling riot situations, either before, during or immediately after a riot, provide a poor guide to the scale of participation and no guide at all to the social background of the participants. The inquiry commissions' reports are also of little help here. But it is obvious that in Ranchi and Jamshedpur, Ahmedabad, Bhiwandi, Malegaon and Sholapur, the participants were mainly industrial workers; there was some student participation in the Ranchi and Ahmedabad riots. In Sursand (Muzaffarpur district, Bihar) and in Jainpur and Suchetpur (Gorakhpur district, Uttar Pradesh), the participants were agriculturists. In Delhi, they were factory workers, petty traders and local gundas. In all urban riots, the gunda element is strongly represented.

The available data on arrests (see Table 3.10), though of only limited value, throw some light on the scale of comparative participation in riots in different states by different communities (in this case, Hindus and Muslims). Unfortunately the 'not-known' category is too large (71.30 per cent of the total).

TABLE 3.10: Communal Violence—Arrests, 1961–1970

State	*Hindus*	*Muslims*	*Not-known*	*Total*
Andhra Pradesh	256	166	315	727
Assam	331	398	899	1628
Bihar	2,005	1,560	2,076	5,641
Gujarat	122	241	6713	7076
Haryana	–	4	–	4
Jammu and Kashmir	9	7	–	16
Karnataka	11	29	580	620
Kerala	47	9	31	87
Madhya Pradesh	3,266	1,292	1,216	5,774
Maharashtra	334	356	9,591	10,281
Orissa	26	39	1,013	1,078
Rajasthan	24	71	266	361
Tamil Nadu	58	75	15	148
Uttar Pradesh	1,375	1,797	2,801	5,973
West Bengal	2,756	618	17,567	20,941
Delhi	31	34	16	81
Arunachal Pradesh	–	–	4	4
Tripura	17		42	59
India	10,668	6,696	43,145	60,509

Source: Author.

Among the participants, we ought to include those communal organisations and political parties which have been active on behalf of communal causes, for their activity certainly contributes to the development of a climate of conflict, and in the course of actual disturbances, their workers and sympathisers must be presumed not to be passive spectators of events.

For the Hindus, the various inquiry commissions have identified the Rashtriya Swayamsevak Sangh (RSS), the erstwhile Jan Sangh, and the Bombay-based Shiv Sena as of prime importance. There are also local organisations—such as the Rashtriya Utsav Mandal in Bhiwandi, an organisation dominated by the RSS and Jan Sangh elements—which played a critical role in the communal disturbances of May 1970. For the Muslims, these organisations include Majlis Ikmir-e-Millat, Muslim Majlis, Majlis-e-Mushawarat, the Indian Union Muslim League and the Jamat-e-Islami. There are also local Muslim organisations which surface during riots.

It is now conceded on all sides that non-communal political parties also make their contribution to the aggravation of communal climate in the country. They do this by paying close attention to the communal factor in their electoral calculations and by submitting to communal pressures in order to secure group support in elections.

The communal parties are engaged in continuous activity that promotes tension. Religious celebrations provide frequent occasions for expression of communal hostility, and in this, on available evidence, Hindu communal elements seem to be more active than the Muslim communal elements.

A section of the intelligentsia makes its own contribution through production of communal literature. It has not been possible to estimate the number of newspapers, especially weeklies in local languages, and other publications which promoted communal hostilities, but their influence must be substantial.

This will require a careful investigation.

THE COST

The human, material and spiritual costs of communal violence are very high. Its cost to the nation in terms of negative impact on national integration is even greater. The data available to us enable us to consider the human cost in terms of casualties and, somewhat less adequately, the damage of property. For the decade 1961–70, communal riot caused 3,195 deaths and injuries to 12,155 persons. The details for the different states are given in Table 3.11. 5,022 of the 7,964 incidents involved damage of property. Among the places attacked were religious shrines, markets, factories and private dwellings. There are no estimates of losses suffered in these attacks for the country as a whole, but the inquiry commissions provide details for the cases they investigated, and these must suffice as illustrations for our purpose.

[...]

One of the distressing aspects of casualties in communal violence is the marked preponderance of Muslims killed and injured. Among those identified by religion, numbering 2,679 killed and 9,272 injured, 2,397 among the killed and 5,138 among the injured were Muslims. A scrutiny of the data shows that in all states save Haryana, Karnataka, Punjab and Tamil Nadu, more Muslims were killed than Hindus; among the injured Muslims preponderated in all states except Andhra Pradesh, Assam, Jammu and Kashmir, Madhya Pradesh, Maharashtra, Karnataka and Delhi. To a student of communal violence, communal proportions among the

Table 3.11: Casualties 1961–1970 (Killed and Insured)

State	1961		1962		1963		1964		1965		1966		1967		1968		1969		1970		Total	
	K	*I*	*K*	*I*	*K*	*I*	*K*	*I*	*K*	*I*	*K*	*I*	*K*	*I*	*K*	*I*	*K*	*I*	*K*	*I*	*K*	*I*
Andhra Pradesh	–	–	–	3	–	44	–	–	–	66	–	63	13	160	3	211	–	19	3	28	19	594
Assam	2	24	–	6	14	128	2	18	1	67	1	8	–	43	10	98	2	14	7	91	39	497
Bihar	6	86	1	24	1	96	339	417	5	92	–	48	197	346	15	295	12	170	34	196	610	1,670
Gujarat	–	5	–	14	1	63	1	187	8	101	–	15	–	16	4	58	469	1,083	1	46	484	1,588
Haryana	–	–	–	–	2	–	–	–	–	25	–	–	–	–	–	–	–	–	–	–	2	25
Jammu and Kashmir	–	–	–	–	–	–	–	–	–	–	–	–	–	–	–	–	–	–	–	7	–	7
Karnataka	–	23	–	–	1	24	1	16	1	11	–	8	–	16	4	107	3	75	–	46	10	326
Kerala	–	31	3	53	–	–	–	15	–	16	–	15	2	21	1	22	–	28	–	13	6	214
Madhya Pradesh	85	205	2	38	–	1	20	38	–	24	5	22	–	51	–	22	15	368	8	155	135	924
Maharashtra	1	65	5	61	6	122	–	111	3	216	29	213	9	188	3	185	2	168	220	783	278	2,122
Orissa	–	3	–	–	–	4	985	257	–	17	–	20	–	1	–	4	4	14	–	9	989	329
Punjab	–	–	–	–	–	–	–	–	–	–	–	–	–	–	–	–	–	–	–	2	–	2
Rajasthan	–	–	–	19	–	–	–	–	1	32	1	26	–	13	–	6	1	10	1	9	4	115
Tamil Nadu	–	28	–	–	–	–	–	26	1	28	–	10	1	42	1	18	–	25	1	69	4	251
Uttar Pradesh	40	185	10	56	2	31	6	60	8	94	3	62	23	247	42	380	14	309	8	69	156	1,493
West Bengal	5	90	21	114	3	53	349	958	2	29	3	78	8	158	4	69	49	213	12	153	456	1,915
Delhi	–	1	–	7	–	3	–	–	–	21	–	–	–	–	–	–	–	11	–	2	–	45
Manipur	–	–	–	–	–	–	–	–	–	–	–	–	–	6	–	–	–	–	–	–	–	6
Arunachal Pradesh	–	–	–	–	–	–	–	–	–	–	–	–	–	–	–	2	–	–	–	–	–	2
Tripura	–	9	–	–	–	–	–	2	–	–	–	–	–	–	–	–	–	–	–	–	–	11
India	139	755	42	395	30	569	1,703	2,110	30	870	42	588	253	1,308	87	1,377	572	2,507	297	1,676	3,195	12,155

Source: Author.

killed and the injured can hold no intrinsic interest, but the disparity between the two communities in this horrible count exerts profound negative influence on the community which suffers a comparatively larger loss of life and hence, this aspect of the data needs to be seriously noted.

The available data disclose a similar tale regarding damage of property. Of the 3,167 incidents identified as involving damage to property, 2,609 resulted in damage to the properties of Muslims, 558 resulted in damage to the properties of Hindus, and 14 to the properties of both.

[...]

It is a very puzzling and deeply disturbing feature of many of the communal incidents that they were started or aggravated by a section of the Hindus. This is the evidence of most of the inquiry commissions' reports. The data on communal incidents compiled by the Ministry of Home Affairs for the period 1961–70 show that of the 5,189 incidents for which 'first resort to violence' by Hindus or Muslims could be identified, Hindus accounted for 3,888, that is, about 75 per cent of the cases. While the 'first resort' data carry no explanatory value for making sense of communal riots, they nevertheless betray a profound feeling of hostility among the Hindus towards Muslims.

Detailed data are not available for the period since 1970, but overall figures are available for the decade 1971–80. From them, it is evident that during that decade, the number of communal incidents was fewer than for the preceding decade. There were, between 1971 and 1980, 2,572 communal incidents against 7,964 for the 1961–70 period. This could be a misleading statistic in that the definition of 'incident' employed for the 1971–80 decade might be different from the one employed for the preceding decade. There were no 'major' riots during the 1971–80 period, and consequently the number of persons killed in riots is much smaller: 1,185 against 3,195 during 1961–70. Table 3.12 gives comparative data for the two decades.

TABLE 3.12: Communal Incidents and Casualties (Killed and Injured) 1961–70 and 1971–80

Decade	*No. of Incidents*	*Casualties Total*	*Killed*				*Injured*			
			Hindus	*Muslims*	*Not Known*	*Police*	*Hindus*	*Muslims*	*Not Known*	*Police*
1961–70	7,964	K 3,195 I 12,155	282	2,397	515	1	4,134	5,138	1,888	995
1970–80	2,572	K 1,185	373	766	33	13	6,674	5,683	1,072	1,772

Source: Author.

The figures reflect greater violence in the 1970s than in the 1960s despite the fact that the 1960s were characterised by at least six major riots namely, Rourkela, Jamshedpur and Calcutta in 1964, Ranchi in 1967, Ahmedabad-Baroda in 1969, and Bhiwandi-Jalgaon-Mahad in 1970. The death toll per incident in the 1961–70 decade was 0.40; in the next decade, it was 0.46. The difference on account of injuries is much greater: the number of injured per incident was 1.52 in the 1961–70 period; it was 5.94 for the next decade. The number of policemen killed had risen from 1 in 1961–70 to 13 in the 1971–80 period and the number of policemen injured had gone up by 78 per cent for almost a quarter of the incidents.

The scale of communal violence has increased over the years. The states which were once free of it have now been affected. The issues continue to be those which agitated the rival communities in the past, that is, music before mosques, cow slaughter and affront to women. To these has been added the new source of economic competition. Communal confrontations, when they take place, result in loss of life and property and damage to sacred places. Nearly all social groups, except the top elite, seem to participate in one way or another in these communal conflicts. They bear the characteristics of a semi-permanent group warfare which erupts without prior warning, the eruption often sparked off by some trivial incident, and at the end of it leaves everyone injured, impoverished, embittered and confirmed in their hostilities.

Note

1. Banu, Zerah. 1982. 'Emerging Class Relations among Caste Hindus' in *Inter-Religious Perceptions of Hindus and Muslims*, ed. K. S. Durany. New Delhi: Indian Institute of Islamic Studies.

4

Revisiting Communalism and Fundamentalism in India*

Surya Prakash Upadhyay and Rowena Robinson

Introduction

Communalism has been commonly understood in the literature as conflicts over secular issues between religious communities, particularly between Hindus and Muslims.[1] Deliberations around communalism have, to a large extent, linked it with the colonial period in India and with particular religious communities, such that the concept has acquired a definite and definitive association. It is true that there were struggles in the pre-colonial period, but they cannot be said to have taken the form of full-blown communalism.

Communalism may be said to be rooted in power relations between communities, histories of togetherness and a disposition to dominate others. Communalism's political, economic, social and other associations are linked to assertions for community identity that trigger communities to seek or to resist domination. Communalism may be seen as a process of the competitive aspirations of communities to dominate and/or resist domination of others over perceived and real threats, grievances, insecurities and distrust. This aspiration to dominate others took a concrete form during the colonial period, but it has been spreading, bringing new issues and new groups into its ambit. Communities have been drawing contentious boundaries differentiating others, adding sources of 'marginalisation', selectively constructing histories, recalling 'humiliations' and 'defeats', remembering 'violent times' and unleashing all kinds of violence. The origins and causes of communalism have been explored at several levels in the literature, which the rest of this chapter surveys.

We have reviewed journal articles, books, dissertations, seminar and conference reports, films, documentaries, novels and editorials in major dailies published in post-Independence India. From the literature on communalism, we would like to point out certain important aspects that are worth noting. First, arbitrary definitions

* *Economic and Political Weekly* 47 (36): 35–57 (8 September 2012).

and explanations, often due to the development of opposing schools of thought, have created vagueness around the phenomenon of communalism and its associations with the concept of community.[2] Second, most of the writings on communalism are not on communalism per se. They are on Hindu communalism, Muslim communalism and Hindu fundamentalism and, as said already, the connection between communalism and communities is not addressed properly. Third, features of religious communalism—a presumed homogeneous community identity and community consciousness—are also exhibited by sects, cults, castes and linguistic and regional communities. Such communities and their politics are not seen as part of the restricted idea of communalism. This is why the use of the idea of the 'ethnic' is considered more appropriate, for it can bring under its consideration the full range of such expressions. Fourth, occurrences of communal violence in southern Indian states, its spread to rural and hill areas where tribals and dalits are either involved or attacked, and a range of new subjects for contestation in contemporary times show that communalism is not a peculiar north Indian and urban phenomenon.

Community and Communalism

To begin a discussion on communalism, it is necessary to see how it has been defined and explained, and how it has been associated with the term 'community'. In a crude way, a group of people with some common bonds or notion of common identity can be treated as a community. Apparently, the association of communalism with community looks simplistic. An analysis of the characteristic features of communalism shows that the complex relationship between communalism and community has largely been overlooked. Jones defines 'communalism as consciously-shared religious heritage which becomes the dominant form of identity for a given segment of society' (1968: 39).[3]

Community, or *Gemeinschaft*, denotes a group of people organised along some common social markers with a certain degree of identity transferred into a sense of 'we-feeling'. In this sense, social groupings along various social ascriptions and affiliations, such as caste groups, linguistic groups, sects and cults are also communities. Writings on communalism, even while highly analytical, consider community in terms of religion. This narrowing of communalism to apply only to religious communities has been uncritically inherited from colonial understandings of communities in India. 'Under colonialism, the religious definition of community has become so predominant that in common discourse communalism has become more or less synonymous with communalism of the religious variety' (Kooiman 1995: 2,123). Pandey clarifies that 'specification of communal with religious communities is not derived from the community but from the tension between religious communities' (1990: 9). However, the same applies to other communitarian groupings as well. Whenever a community forms, tension forms along with it. Though scholars have debated this issue, it has not been given adequate attention in the literature.

There are fragmented debates on communalism's association with the term community. Pandey (1990) recognises significant flexibility in the term communalism and argues that it could be applied to any form of community that displays an antagonistic stance towards another community based on the same kind of signifier. For a few scholars, antagonism is not important. For example, Mukhia argues that 'community should constitute a continuum as an operative category rather than being diametrically opposed to another community' (quoted in Srimanjari 1990: 59).

Scholars have also argued over the inclusion of other types of communities under communalism and the usefulness of communalism as a conceptual and analytical category. For example, Vanaik (1997) argues for the consideration of only religious communities under communalism. For him, incorporating other communities under communalism would lead to a loss of focus and then, communalism as a conceptual category becomes too broad to be useful. On the other hand, Zavos says that 'this flexibility strips the concept down to the level of a framework, narrowing rather than broadening its possibilities' (1999: 2,270). Jones (1968) refers to a few other ways of defining communalism. For instance, he uses the term 'social communalism' for the non-brahminical movement in Tamil Nadu. He asserts that by incorporating other identities under its purview, 'communalism then would become a broader concept applicable to a wider variety of social and historical processes' (Jones 1968: 39). While scholars have argued for incorporating other varieties of communities under the concept of communalism, it is essentially the Hindu–Muslim relationship that forms the core of the debate on communalism in the literature. It is not essential to the concept of religious communalism or ethnocentricity in other parts of the world; for example, the ethnic cleansing in the Balkans was a conflict between Christians and Muslims.

Communalism has been defined and explained from a variety of theoretical perspectives—essentialism, instrumentalism, constructivism and institutionalism.[4] Essentialism or primordialism is the perspective that believes Hindus and Muslims have formed monolithic communities since the time Muslims arrived in India, and the two communities have always been at odds with each other. Such a position is generally taken by Hindu communalists. Scholars such as Dumont also believe in 'primordial conflict' between the Hindus and the Muslims. This perspective ignores the symbiosis between communities and highlights only animosities. It tries to draw up a picture of monolithic communities, particularly that of the Hindu community as something that has remained unchanged since antiquity.

For constructivists, on the other hand, communalism is not merely a reflection of a pre-existing community, but the will to create a bounded community in which groups play down internal divisions to create the broadest possible unity against the group defined as the 'other' (Pandey 1990; Thapar 1989). This theoretical strand mainly focuses on colonial policies that resulted in the hardening of religious identity and the formation of community consciousness.

With the British taking over India, new elements entered into the administrative system. During the colonial period, new areas—in political and economic institutions—opened that were previously available to only a very limited section of society. The domain of conflict extended from the religious to the secular sphere. For

Hasan (1979) and Chandra (1984), communalism is not a religious phenomenon, but a secular one. Similarly, for Engineer, communalism is 'an attempt to achieve secular goals through religious means' (1997: 703). In the colonial period, the old contentions were strengthened by new elements. Communalism was 'modified during the 19th century by the dual influences of modernisation and Westernisation' (Jones 1968: 39). It has been argued that communalism is a modern phenomenon (Chandra 1984; Mukhia 1972). The roles of ideology and ideologues have also been given importance. Bipan Chandra (1990) understands communalism as an ideology. For him, communalism is a belief system through which society, economy and polity are viewed; a way of looking at society and politics. Similarly, P. R. Ram says, 'One needs to understand different levels, layers and mechanisms through which an ideology gets actualised through the actions of an individual' (1996: 2,266).

For institutionalists, communal conflict/violence is structured in economic and political institutions. They locate economic hardships, slow economic development and paucity of resources as the reasons for communalism. 'Increasing social tensions are not only a function of ideology, they are no less a function of hard economic realities on the ground' (*Economic and Political Weekly* 1998: 686). Communalism has also been described as an aberration that retards the economic growth of the country. 'If religion today in India acts predominantly...much is to be attributed to the character of economic development and the social relations that it has generated' (Bharadwaj 1990: 67).

For instrumentalists, communal conflict/violence is seen as a consequence of the vested interests of political leaders, elites and the middle class. Communalism has been seen as 'perversion of religion from a moral order to temporal arrangement of contemporary convenience, from a faith into a constituency, from a strategy of living into tactics of politics, from an end into a means' (Khan 1989: 138). Scholars such as Engineer (1984) and Gupta (1991) have argued that communal tensions are the creation of vested political interests. Similarly, Mukhia says, 'The ruling class itself is seldom communal in its own economic or even political behaviour, but it spreads the ideology of communalism in the classes which are its adversaries' (1972: 53). Political parties and extra-political organisations create propaganda of the injustices apparently experienced by their community. However, a few scholars argue that communalism is 'group solidarity' (Bhaskar quoted in Oommen 1995: 544). Thus, we can see that communalism has been understood from various perspectives, which indicates that communal tensions are not located within any particular institution. The vastness and spread of communalism makes it difficult to arrive at a coherent understanding of it.

In India, communities form along a variety of affiliations and social ascriptions such as caste, class, region, language and religion. Often, an individual affiliates himself or herself to many groups. 'Having more than one set of identities, an individual can belong to several communities at the same time and may be mobilised along different, mutually exclusive lines of communal identity' (Alavi and Harris 1989: 223; Shah 1994: 1,133 quoted in Kooiman 1995: 2,123). Mahmood asserts, 'While scholars working in other parts of the world argue over whether particular movements are linguistic, ethnic, religious, regional or any other wide variety of adjectives, Indians have solved the problem nicely by thinking in terms of "communities" whose identity may be defined in diverse ways' (1993: 722).

Perhaps Mahmood overstates the situation. Scholars in India have designated specific concepts for community formations and conflicts between caste, region and language as casteism, regionalism and lingualism, respectively. In fact, a few scholars have designated very specific terms even for caste movements—for example, 'social communalism' (Jones 1968) and 'social revolution' (Omvedt 1972). However, if the literature makes a distinction between communalism on the one hand, and lingualism, regionalism and casteism on the other, it would be interesting if future researchers could expound on how community formation at a religious level is different from caste, region or language. What set of questions differentiate religious communalism from clashes of other social ascriptions?

[...]

HINDU AND MUSLIM GROUPS

The communal atmosphere changed after the Sangh parivar launched the Ram Janmabhoomi/Babri Masjid movement. This movement had all kinds of support and was not located only in the political realm. Hindus were emotionally charged and wanted to replace the mosque with a Ram temple (Raychaudhuri 2000). Raychaudhuri writes, 'The Babri Masjid Ram Janmabhoomi controversy is not a symptom of religious revivalism or any spontaneous resurgence of Hindu concern for the honour of their ancient faith' (2000: 260). It was in effect the successful end result of a sustained organisational and propaganda campaign launched by the Sangh parivar (Raychaudhuri 2000: 260). For the Bharatiya Janata Party (BJP), electoral success is envisaged as the end product of the social acceptance of its cultural and ideological hegemony (Pannikar 1993: 24). Riots in India are often 'incited through religious discourses' (Lobo 1995). Or, to quote Nandy (1995), in using religious symbols, politicians, land developers and bootleggers make 'dispassionate use of passions' (quoted in Bock 1997: 18). 'The danger of Hindu communalism is far broader than the influence of the RSS, which no doubt is the arch villain of the piece' (Desai 1984: 1,196).

The liberalisation of the Indian market, the growth of opportunities and the subsequent growth in the size of the middle class have aggravated the communal situation in contemporary India. The Ram Janmabhoomi movement resulted in a series of communal riots in various parts of India, including Bombay, Surat, Ahmedabad, Kanpur and Delhi. Rajagopal has argued that 'Hindu communalism could and did serve... as an ideology reinforcing economic liberalisation and its accompanying consumerist ethos' (1996: 341). He holds that there was an overlap between the narratives of communal and consumer identity formation.

It is not only the Sangh parivar that exploits religious sentiments for political gain and the establishment of cultural hegemony. If the parivar has made its slogan *garv se kaho hum Hindu hain* (say with pride we are Hindu), Islamic groups have asserted their cultural purity and have appealed to people to go 'Back to Islam', the original Islam followed by the Prophet, and in Mecca. Religious sentiments are exploited and the appeal to follow Muslim Personal Law is always made. *Madrasas* are seen as sources of growing Islamisation. There may be formal schooling in religious texts, and often the *maulana* and *mulla* socialise students into Islamic traditions. Islamisation and political communalism are engineered by the religious groups and exploited by the political elites.

Within the Muslim community, various orthodox groups such as the Jama'at-e-Islami and Tablighi Jama'at and terrorist outfits such as the Lashkar-e-Taiba and Hizbul Mujahideen invoke different religious interpretations that may or may not have direct political aims. Similarly, for groups such as the Students Islamic Movement of India (SIMI), Islam is a complete world view and ideology that governs every aspect of a Muslim's personal and collective life. For it, it is not the Constitution of India, but Islam that lays down a complete code of conduct. Unfortunately, its activities stereotype the entire Muslim population in India. As scholars point out, they have also established close links with various Islamist groups in several other countries (Mayaram 2004; Sikand 2001). For them, democracy and secularism are un-Islamic. 'In SIMI discourse, Hinduism is painted in the most lurid colours, and as an inveterate foe of Islam and its followers. The only way to salvation, then, is by converting to Islam' (Sikand 2001: 3,804).

Communal controversies emerged from the mid-1980s around the issues of Shah Bano, Roop Kunwar, the opening of the lock at Babri Mosque and later its demolition. These controversial decisions of the government did have political ramifications but they were politicised largely on the issues of minority consciousness and pseudo-secularism. A minority consciousness does not emanate only from low numerical strength of a community or the ethnic history of a community.

Gupta (1985), drawing from the case of Sikhs during the 1980s, says the new phenomenon of minority consciousness should be read jointly with the alienation of minorities from the contemporary Indian political system and the judiciary. Much of the strength for communalism comes from the idea of minority consciousness. Let us take the case of the Hindus, particularly the upper caste and middle class, and how they are sometimes able to construct themselves as a minority. The development of a minority consciousness within the majority has been a characteristic of several South Asian countries, not only India, in recent times (Pfaff-Czarnecka et al. 1999). The reversal of the Supreme Court's decision in the case of Shah Bano increased the minority consciousness among Hindus because there were already problems with a certain percentage of reservation in government jobs for Muslims in Gujarat. This was followed by the Mandal Commission recommendations.

Class and Communal Consciousness

Generally, studies on communal consciousness have focused on the elites to point to the source, as it were, of communal consciousness. At the same time, it is generally accepted in the literature that the actual violence is committed by others—the working classes, the slum-dwellers, the lumpen proletariat. This view was to be sharply disturbed when in Gujarat in 2002, there was documented evidence of the middle classes, including women, participating in looting and violence. This will be discussed later. Returning to the point under discussion, we find that the section of the population largely seen to participate in the violence during the colonial period is the working class. The phenomenon of migration and the presence of migrants in riot-prone cities have also been included in analyses of communalism and communal conflict in modern times. Communal consciousness among peasants and agricultural workers has also been explored. This has generally been discussed in relation to land politics.

Instances of Hindu–Muslim communalism in north India in the colonial period go back to the early nineteenth century (Pandey 1983: PE20). The Julaha of Banaras were called 'bigots' by Robinson (1974) because many of them were involved in communal clashes that took place in the nineteenth century in several north Indian towns. Severe dislocations in the social and economic spheres during the colonial period contributed to widespread communal tensions. The subaltern school of scholars began exploring the field of community consciousness and the impact of communal politics on peasants and on workers. These studies are focused, for instance, on millworkers in colonial India who migrated to urban areas for work. Chakrabarty (1981) explains important aspects of politics among peasants and millworkers in Calcutta. Instead of 'class consciousness of labour', the worker in the mills exhibited community consciousness and participated in communal clashes.

Upadhyay (1989), looking at the Bombay workers, asserts that though workers participated in communal riots, communal consciousness did not develop. For him, participation in communal riots by workers was more about personal rivalries and the desire to settle scores. Ghosh (1990) argues that colonialism was the biggest determinant and the workers in the jute mills displayed two selves—the self of the peasant and the self of the worker—as many migrated from rural Bihar and had close associations with the middlemen who recruited them—the 'jobbers'. Banu (1994) talks about the migration of entrepreneurs and asserts that the decision-making power of migrant entrepreneurs and competition with members of the receiving society can develop into communal animosity. More elaborately, migrant labour participates in communal rioting to settle scores with the local community. Presenting the case of communal violence in Surat, Breman (1993) says it is immigrant labour that is largely responsible for creating violence among Hindus and Muslims. It is observable from the above discussion on communalism and its various trajectories that it emerges from the competition to maximise resources to dominate the other community. Apart from direct sources, there are various indirect sources that communities may take as reasons to claim their own marginalisation, and thereby seek greater assertion or promote conflict.

As the literature demonstrates, communalism serves the interests of the dominant classes in various ways. In the colonial period, communalism helped the feudal class and the middle class because it strengthened their position both in the administration and in the polity (Bal 1988). Several scholars have written on how the elite and the middle classes were a contributing factor in communalism in independent India as well. Desai notes, 'Hindu communalism and Muslim communalism, with all their never-ending feuds, meet in pro-imperialism, anti-communism and anti-Sovietism. Further, both of them are defenders of landlordism and free "enterprise" in India' (1984: 1,196). Chhachhi et al. (1993) say that communal violence in India seems to hold in its grip the middle-class Hindu psyche as the Hindus view themselves as the victims of the state, a state which by its policies of 'pseudosecularism' and 'appeasement of minorities' has frustrated their genuine aspirations and diminished their position.

Similarly, Kothari (2002) writes on the role of the middle classes during the Gujarat riot in 2002 (also see Parthasarathy 2002). In independent India, as mentioned earlier, slow economic growth, scarce opportunities and rising unemployment heightened competition among segments of the petty bourgeoisie. 'The urban petty bourgeois—shopkeepers, clerks, lower level professionals and the like—are highly politicised by now and they share the multiple aspirations of their more fortunate fellow citizens' (Raychaudhuri 2000: 271). Economic stagnation and rising unemployment heighten competition among segments of the petty bourgeoisie for scarce opportunities and political parties benefit by claiming to represent these interests.

The majority community homogenises the socio-economic conditions of the Muslims. For the majority community, the reference point for comparison with their own position is the affluent Muslims who have collected political and economic clout and can compete with Hindus. In such a situation, any attempt by the state to make special provisions for Muslims is seen as Muslim appeasement, pandering to the Muslim vote bank and pseudo-secularism. For Hindus, Muslims are in a better-off condition because there are Muslim entrepreneurs who engage in business with the Gulf countries. Muslim migration to the Gulf countries and remittances make the Hindus more insecure and competitive. For Hindus, what they perceive as the inflow of 'Arab money' is one of the reasons for increased mosque construction and the financing of terrorism in India (Ahmad 1984). The flow of Arab money formed a core issue for Hindus and, accordingly, it was construed that the Muslim Jamaats were well-funded through Arab money (Thapar 1980). Bakshi notes that by the 1970s, 'a sizeable section of the poor Muslims and Hindus were reaping the benefits of Gulf money. The new wealth brought with it a greater self-confidence and a wish to translate it into other spheres as well such as reaffirmation of their religion through building of mosques and elaborate ceremonies' (1984: 2,152).

As a result of growing economic muscle, the political assertiveness of Muslims increased, which translated into cultural and social visibility and a triumph of their community. The economic changes and thereby political, social and cultural visibility aroused a number of latent fears among Hindus, which were frequently voiced at the time of the Moradabad riots (Ahmad 1984). Hasan (1982: 33) discusses the case of the Muslim businessmen of Moradabad, which was the cause of much antagonism in the city.

[...]

The leads and lags of communities in the Indian economic system have been seen as part of the reasons for the rise in communalism (Dutta 1972). 'The theory of Muslim backwardness...regards communalism as the result of tensions between poor Muslim cultivators and Hindu landlords, or of competition for government posts between ill-educated Muslims and better-educated Hindus' (Heehs 1997:101). Similarly, Shakir asserts, 'The Muslim elite in India has been indulging in the practice of articulating its grievances, for communicating with the Muslim masses, for framing its political strategies and for maintaining a separate political status for the community' (1979: 469). Shakir's observations of political leaders could be correct, but the socio-economic condition of Muslims in India is generally poor. The Sachar Committee (2005) makes some important observations on the socioeconomic situation of Muslims in contemporary India. Its examination of the social, economic and political place of Muslims in modern India shows that the community is largely backward and deprived in terms of access to education, financial services and resources, and employment. Similar observations were made earlier as well, though without the support of the wealth of data the Sachar report provides.

For instance, during a convention in 1986 referred to as 'The Call', it was emphasised that 'there was no inherent resistance to modern education among the Muslims but that severe economic, cultural and social discrimination had crippled the community' (Raman 1987: 175).

NATIONALISMS, COMMUNALISMS AND SECULARISMS

Is India a secular nation? Can secularism survive in India? Can India grow with secular ideals in the midst of communal and partisan politics? These questions are not new but come to the fore after any communal event. Views abound on the nature, form and credentials of India as a multicultural, secular nation state. However, this debate regarding secularism, nationalism and communalism has, to a large extent, to do with community formations in the colonial period. 'Colonialism was the major force in producing religion-inflected nationalism as a form of anti-colonial resistance in colonies' (Needham and Rajan 2007: 7). As has been shown in this chapter, one of the principal causes of communalism lay in colonial policies. However, one also has to look at cultural formations in pre-colonial and colonial India and their evolution in independent India, and the changes in the dynamics of community relations, to find answers for the problem of communalism and its relationship with nationalism and secularism. There are good reasons to argue why communities may have resorted to communalism, how they imagined the nation, why communities believed in the superiority of their form of nationalism, how communal practices effected secular nationalism, and how conflicts between the Hindu Mahasabha, the Muslim League and the Congress resulted in the Partition.

In the pre-Independence era, debates on nationalism projected an opposition between the secular nationalism of the Indian National Congress (INC), and the communal practices of the Muslim League and the Hindu Mahasabha. Political groups used 'communal' as a negative attribute to malign the practices of other parties. In the process, Hindus, Muslims and Sikhs formed their own communal spaces and contended for self-determination. The Hindu Mahasabha and the Muslim League mixed their nationalism with communalism. In independent India, this debate has expanded and now revolves not only around communal practices but also, critically, the Indian Constitution and practices of secularism. Secular nationalism during the pre-Independence period involved attempts to take up the interests of all communities, while versions of Muslim nationalism or Hindu nationalism were specifically looking out for the interests of their respective communities. Mukhia argues, 'The Muslim League and the Hindu Mahasabha of the pre-Independence India are the king examples of such communal organisations' (1972: 46). The Muslim League and the Hindu Mahasabha both threatened and hindered the growth of a national movement. 'The propaganda of the Muslim League and the Hindu Mahasabha...produced communal feeling and a tendency among the middle class to criticise the Congress for not supporting the Hindu cause as against the Muslim League' (Pandey 1987: 984).

These groups were involved not only in creating schisms in secular nationalism but also in creating cultural nationalisms. The Hindu Mahasabha blamed the Congress for its mild attitude to Muslim aggression and for Muslim appeasement. Singh (1990) argues that nationalism and communalism need not always be considered antithetical; they come together in religious nationalism. For example, the Hindu Mahasabha insisted on the idea of the Hindu Rashtra. Savarkar termed India as 'Bharat' and used the concept of *Punyabhumi* for the Indian land. Savarkar's and the Sangh parivar's idea of the nation is defined by religion. In the case of Hindu and Muslim, communalism and nationalism are same. 'Both communalisms started parallel to each other. Both communalisms did begin together, in response to secular nationalism and both hated "secular nationalism" (Gandhi-Nehru), both boosted each other, both were aloof from the freedom struggle and both created "fear" of the other, within their own constituency' (Ram 1996: 2,266).

Three Versions of Nationalism and Secularism

This resulted in the emergence of at least three versions of nationalism and secularism. The INC pushed for a secular form of statehood where citizenship would be based on equal representation of all, irrespective of social ascriptions. The Hindu Mahasabha visualised a Hindu Rashtra, while the Muslim League advocated the formation of Pakistan (Mahajan 2000). Scholars have argued that these three visions on the nature of the post-Independence state were 'primarily reactions to the process of colonisation and desire to be free from alien rule' (Das 2010). But it is necessary to perceive that these visions originated keeping in view the others and to understand what these visions have produced in independent India. Zavos argues that the 'development of Hindu nationalism as an ideology needs to be identified autonomous of Hindu communalism which emerged in the 1920s as a historical condition channelling ideological forces of Hindu nationalism towards particular objectives' (1999: 2,269). However, Zavos misses the ideological links of Hindu nationalism to propaganda and movements that began much before the RSS and the Hindu Mahasabha were established. 'One can very well supplement a big list of Hindu communal actions even before the formation of RSS' (Ram 1996: 2,266).

The contemporary ideas of Hindu nationalism are not different from the founding ideas of nationalism of the Hindu Mahasabha. In fact, these are supplemented with more additions of a similar kind. Along with this, many other elements have developed. The colonialist construction of history produced Muslims as alien on Indian soil. This vision of the Hindu Mahasabha and the RSS was boosted by the Muslim League's demand for a separate state for Muslims and thereby the Partition. The demand for partition and separate statehood made Muslims an enemy of united India or *Akhanda Bharat*. The separatist image of the Muslims has been reproduced in almost all the propaganda of the Sangh parivar in the post-Independence period. A separate Muslim identity, the apparent 'growth' of the Muslim population, and the alleged affiliation of Muslims to West Asia and Pakistan have all become part of the commonsense of Hindu nationalist ideology.

Secular nationalism that largely rests on equal rights, citizenship and the separation of the state from religion has been questioned both by academics and political actors in independent India. Communities question the constitutional ideal of secularism. Concessions to minority communities are considered as curbs on the freedoms and rights of the majority community. Partisan politics that began in the late 1960s have produced communal politics. Parties align with particular communities to achieve political power; for example, the Hindu card played by Indira Gandhi and the Hindutva card of the BJP. 'Parliamentary parties have talked of equal respect to all religions, but in practice have fostered communal vote banks of different religions, deepening and expanding communal tension' (Wantoo et al. 2002). At the same time, scholars argue that secular nationalism and the idea of democracy have also found acceptance in India (for instance, see Khilnani 1997). As Archer points out, 'The antisecularists are right when they say that India has a political culture which is deeply influenced by religious traditions. But they are wrong when they say that India does not have a secular political culture' (1999: 891).

Communal violence should be understood within the larger context of the struggle and debate over secularism in the postcolonial Indian state (for perspectives on secularism in India, see Bhargava 1998). The Constitution promises that the state shall have no religion of its own. However, in practice, many of the elements of national culture are highly brahminical. Ahmad (1969) asserts that the national culture has a heavy content of Hinduism. 'Brahmanical features of Hinduism were deliberately selected, promoted and projected at the national level in a manner that, for all practical purposes, blurs the distinction between Hindu nationalism and Nehruvian secular composite nationalism' (Alam quoted in Singh 2005: 916). One can find that most of the time, the nomenclature of tanks and missiles in India has been derived from Hindu gods and symbols—agni, nag, trishul, and so on. This has been in vogue for a very long time in Indian defence policy. Hence, it does not appeal to Muslims. For Ahmad (1969), 'the choice of secularism as a principle of a state policy constituted a radical breach from India's past historical traditions'. Dixit questions Ahmad's approach to secularism and calls Muslim non-adherence to secular norms as 'Communal Secularism' or 'Compartmentalised Secularism' (1969: 1,752).

When the state accedes to the pressure of minority demands, the majority group feels threatened. At the same time, the idea of secularism in India involves recognising the religious minorities and allowing them to act according to secular principles in politics and society without giving up their distinct religio-cultural identities. However, the 'assimilative', 'tolerant' nature of Hinduism creates dilemmas for other communities. Saraswati *vandana*, lighting of the lamp, classical music, and festivals and celebrations with Hindu elements marginalise the cultural elements of other religious groups.

> An emphasis on the adoption of symbols such as Dharma Chakra, popularisation of festivals as Ramlila, broadcasting of Bhajans and devotional songs in the early morning programme of All India Radio, extension of the governmental patronage to the Sadhu Samaj, etc, betray a strong Hindu bias in the approach of the new rulers (Shakir 1979: 471).

Singh (2005) discusses Hindi-Hindu biases in the Indian Constitution. He demonstrates flawed aspects of the Constitution such as the insertion of the term Bharat in Article 1, which reflects the power of the Hindutva-minded sections (also see Shakir 1979). Similarly, Article 25 (2) (b) fundamentally undermines the secular character of the state in favour of Hindus.[5] Article 48 of the Constitution, part of the Directive Principles of State Policy, enjoins upon the state that it 'shall endeavour to organise agriculture and animal husbandry on modern and scientific lines and shall, in particular, take steps for preserving and improving the breeds, and prohibiting the slaughter, of cows and calves and other milch and draught cattle'. Singh (2005) considers this an unmistakable reflection of the religious preferences and powers of the dominant upper-caste Hindus among the Constitution makers.

Articles 343 and 351 urge the state to promote Hindi (of a Sanskritised kind) as the 'all-India' language and to strengthen the Hindi language and Devanagari script, which again reflects a Hindi-Hindu bias in the Constitution. Several scholars have discussed how the privileging of Hindi has led to the marginalisation and inhibition of other languages (Brass 1974; Rai 2000; Singh 2005). On these fronts, minorities feel that the Hindus have been recognised by the state, which empowers them and allows them to hegemonise other groups. While on the practical level, when minorities are recognised and empowered through amendments and verdicts, the majority community looks at it as minority appeasement.

Notes

1. On the other hand, scholars such as Robinson (2005) and Varshney (2002) now employ the more neutral and established sociological concept of the 'ethnic'. It could also be looked at as an ethnocentrism based on an exclusive community identity, which is totalising

and eventually finds expression is many kinds of antagonisms. See Pandey (1990) for how 'communalism' was constructed by colonial authors to describe what in other parts of the world was seen as ethnic discontent. However, since a lot of the literature continues to employ the term communalism, we follow the practice in this article.

2. Heehs (1997) draws attention to the issue and calls for an interdisciplinary approach to reflect on communalism in India.

3. In most of the works, as has been remarked on above, communalism has been associated with religious communities. One influential author is Louis Dumont (1970).

4. Varshney (2002) uses these four theoretical strands for understanding the debates around ethnic conflict.

5. Article 25 Freedom of conscience and free profession, practice and propagation of religion

(1) Subject to public order, morality and health and to the other provisions of this Part, all persons are equally entitled to freedom of conscience and the right freely to profess, practise and propagate religion.

(2) Nothing in this article shall affect the operation of any existing law or prevent the State from making any law-

(a) regulating or restricting any economic, financial, political or other secular activity which may be associated with religious practice;

(b) providing for social welfare and reform or the throwing open of Hindu religious institutions of a public character to all classes and sections of Hindus.

Explanation I: The wearing and carrying of kirpans shall be deemed to be included in the profession of the Sikh religion.

Explanation II: in sub clause (b) of clause reference to Hindus shall be construed as including a reference to persons professing the Sikh, Jaina or Buddhist religion, and the reference to Hindu religious institutions shall be construed accordingly.

REFERENCES

Ahmad, Imtiaz. 1969. 'Secularism and Communalism'. *Economic & Political Weekly* 4 (28–30), 1137, 1139–45, 1147–52, 1155–58.

———. 1984. 'Political Economy of Communalism in Contemporary India'. *Economic & Political Weekly* 19 (22–23), 903–06.

Alavi, Haniza, and John Harris, ed. 1989. *Sociology of Developing Societies: South Asia.* Houndmills: Macmillan.

Archer, Robin. 1999. 'American Communalism and Indian Secularism'. *Economic & Political Weekly* 34 (15), 887–92.

Bakshi, Rajni. 1984. 'Changing Dimensions of Communalism'. *Economic & Political Weekly* 19 (51–52), 2152–53.

Bal, S. S. 1988. *Political Parties and Growth of Communalism in Punjab, 1920-47.* Chandigarh: CRRID Publication.

Banu, Zainab. 1994. 'Immigrant Groups as a Factor in Communal Riots'. *Economic & Political Weekly* 29 (37), 2408–11.

Bharadwaj, Krishna. 1990. 'Economic Development and Communalism: A Note'. *Social Scientist* 18 (8–9), 66–70.

Bhargava, Rajeev. 1998. *Secularism and Its Critics.* New Delhi: Oxford University Press.

Bock, Joseph G. 1997. 'Communal Conflict, NGOs, and the Power of Religious Symbols 1'. *Development in Practice* 7 (1), 17–25.

Brass, P. 1974. *Language, Religion and Politics in North India*. London: Cambridge University Press.

Breman, Jan. 1993. 'Anti-Muslim Pogrom in Surat'. *Economic & Political Weekly* 28 (16), 737–41.

Chakrabarty, D. 1981. 'Communal Riots and Labour: Bengal's Jute Mill-Hands in the 1890s'. *Past and Present* 91, 140–49.

Chandra, Bipan. 1984. *Communalism in Modern India*. New Delhi: Vikas.

——. 1990. 'Communalism and the State: Some Issues in India'. *Social Scientist* 18 (8–9), 38–47.

Chhachhi, Amrita, Khalid Hameed, Ali Khaqan Mirza, C. Parthmanoharan, Narendr Singh and Others. 1993. 'Concern on Communalism'. *Economic & Political Weekly* 28 (17), 778.

Das, Runa. 2010. 'Colonial Legacies, Post-Colonial (In)Securities, and Gender(ed) Representations in South Asia's Nuclear Policies'. *Social Identities* 16 (6), 717–40.

Desai, A. R. 1984. 'Congress (I), Communist Parties and Communalism'. *Economic & Political Weekly* 19 (30), 1196–97.

Dixit, Prabha. 1969. 'Secularism and Communalism: A Comment'. *Economic & Political Weekly* 4 (44), 1751–54.

——. 1974. *Communalism: A Struggle for Power*. Hyderabad: Orient BlackSwan.

Dumont, Louis. 1970. *Religion, Politics and History of India*. Paris: Mouton Publishers.

Dutta, Ratna. 1972. 'Social and Economic Compulsions behind Communalism'. *Economic & Political Weekly* 7 (5/7), 255–57 + 259–61 + 263–64.

Economic and Political Weekly. 1998. 'Not So Hung After All!'. *Economic & Political Weekly* 33 (13), 686.

Engineer, Asghar Ali, ed. 1984. *Communal Riots in Post-Independent India*. New Delhi: Sangam Publications.

——. 1997. 'Religious Fanaticism and Communalism'. *Economic & Political Weekly* 32 (14), 701–04.

Ghosh, Parimal. 1990. 'Communalism and Colonial Labour: Experience of Calcutta Jute Mill Workers, 1880–1930'. *Economic & Political Weekly* 25 (30), PE61–72.

Gupta, D. 1985. 'The Communalising of Punjab, 1980–1985'. *Economic & Political Weekly* 20 (28), 1185–90.

——. 1991. 'Communalism and Fundamentalism: Some Notes on the Nature of Ethnic Politics in India'. *Economic & Political Weekly* 26 (11–12), 573–83.

Hasan, Mashirul. 1979. *Nationalism and Communal Politics in India*. New Delhi: Manohar.

Hasan, Zoya. 1982. 'Communalism and Communal Violence in India'. *Social Scientist* 10 (2), 25–39.

Heehs, Peter. 1997. 'Indian Communalism: A Survey of Historical and Social Scientific Approaches'. *Journal of South Asian Studies* 20 (1), 99–113.

Jones, Kenneth W. 1968. 'Communalism in the Punjab: The Arya Samaj Contribution'. *The Journal of Asian Studies* 28 (1), 39–54.

Khan, Rasheeduddin. 1989. 'Secularisation Process in India: Problems and Prospects' in *Development, Politics and Social Theory*, ed. Iqbal Narain. New Delhi: Sterling Publishers.

Khilnani, Sunil. 1997. *The Idea of India*. New Delhi: Penguin.

Kothari, Rajni. 2002. 'Culture of Communalism in Gujarat'. *Economic & Political Weekly* 37 (48), 4823–25.

Kooiman, Dick. 1995. 'Communalism and Indian Princely States: A Comparison with British India'. *Economic & Political Weekly* 30 (34), 2123–33.

Lobo, Lancy. 1995. 'Communalism and Christian Response in India'. *Journal of Theological Reflection* 59, 365–74.

Mahajan, S. 2000. *Independence and Partition: The Erosion of Colonial Power in India*. New Delhi: Sage.

Mahmood, Cynthia Keppley. 1993. 'Rethinking Indian Communalism: Culture and CounterCulture'. *Asian Survey* 33 (7), 722–37.

____. 2004. 'Hindu and Islamic Transnational Religious Movements'. *Economic & Political Weekly* 39 (1), 80–88.

Mayaram, Shail. 2004. 'Hindu and Islamic Transnational Religious Movements'. *Economic & Political Weekly* 39 (1), 80–88.

Mukhia, Harbans. 1972. 'Communalism: A Study in its Socio-Historical Perspective'. *Social Scientist* 1 (1), 45–57.

Nandy, Ashis. 1995. 'An Anti-Secularist Manifesto'. *India International Centre Quarterly* 22 (1), Spring, 35–64.

Needam, Anuradha Dingwaney, and Rajeshwari Sunder Rajan, eds. 2007. *The Crisis of Secularism in India*. Durham: Duke University Press.

Omvedt, Gail. 1972. 'Jotirao Phule and the Ideology of Social Revolution in India'. *Economic & Political Weekly* 6 (37), 1969–79.

Oommen, John. 1995. 'Politics of Communalism in Kerala'. *Economic & Political Weekly* 30 (11), 544–47.

Pandey, Gyanendra. 1983. 'The Bigoted Julaha'. *Economic & Political Weekly* 18 (5), PE 19–28.

____. 1987. 'Questions of Nationalism and Communalism'. *Economic & Political Weekly* 22 (25), 983–84.

____. 1990. *The Construction of Communalism in Colonial North India*. New Delhi: Oxford University Press.

Pannikar, K. N. 1993. 'Culture and Communalism'. *Social Scientist* 21 (3/4), 24–31.

Parthasarathy, D. 2002. 'Women, Communal Violence and Right Rhetoric'. *Manushi* 129. Available at http://www.indiatogether.org/manushi/issue129/rights.htm (accessed 11 May 2012).

Pfaff-Czarnecka, Joanna, Darini Rajasingham Senanayake, Ashis Nandy, and Edmund Terence Gomez. 1999. *Ethnic Futures: The State and Identity Politics in Asia*. New Delhi: Sage.

Rai, Alok. 2000. *Hindi Nationalism*. Hyderabad: Orient BlackSwan.

Rajagopal, A. 1996. 'Communalism and the Consuming Subject'. *Economic & Political Weekly* 31 (6), 341–48.

Ram, P. R. 1996. 'In Praise of RSS'. *Economic & Political Weekly* 31 (34), 2266.

Raman, Vasanthi. 1987. 'Communalism and the Threat to Diversity: A Report'. *Economic & Political Weekly* 22 (5), 174–76.

Raychaudhuri, Tapan. 2000. 'Shadows of the Swastika: Historical Perspectives on the Politics of Hindu Communalism'. *Modern Asian Studies* 34 (2), 259–79.

Robinson, Francis. 1974. *Separatism among Indian Muslims, The Politics of the United Provinces Muslim, 1860-1923*. Cambridge: Cambridge University Press.

Robinson, Rowena. 2005. *Tremors of Violence: Muslim Survivors of Ethnic Strife in Western India*. New Delhi: Sage.

Sachar Committee. 2005. 'Sachar Committee Report', available at http://www.prsindia.org/administrator/uploads/general/1242304423--Summary%20of%20Sachar%20Committee%20Report.pdf (accessed 30 April 2012).

Shah, Ghanshyam. 1994. 'Identity, Communal Consciousness and Politics'. *Economic & Political Weekly* 29 (19), 1133–40.

Shakir, Moin. 1979. 'Religion and Politics: Role of Islam in Modern India'. *Economic & Political Weekly* 14 (7/8), 469–71 + 473–74.

Sikand, Y. 2001. 'Countering Fundamentalism: Beyond the Ban on SIMI'. *Economic & Political Weekly* 36 (40), 3803–04.

Singh, Pritam. 2005. 'Hindu Bias in India's "Secular" Constitution: Probing Flaws in the Instruments of Governance'. *Third World Quarterly* 26 (6), 909–26.

Singh, Randhir. 1990. 'Communalism and the Struggle against Communalism: A Marxist View'. *Social Scientist* 18 (8/9), 4–21.

Srimanjari. 1990. 'Seminar on "Communalism in India": A Report'. *Social Scientist* 18 (6/7), 49–72.

Thapar, Romesh. 1980. 'Muslim Communalism'. *Economic & Political Weekly* 15 (35), 1463.

Thapar, Romila. 1989. 'Imagined Religious Communities? Ancient History and the Modern Search for a Hindu Identity'. *Modern Asian Studies* 23 (2), 209–31.

Upadhyay, Shashi Bhushan. 1989. 'Communalism and Working Class: Riot of 1893 in Bombay City'. *Economic & Political Weekly* 24 (30), PE69–75.

Vanaik, Achin. 1997. *The Furies of Indian Communalism: Religion, Modernity and Secularization*. London: Verso.

Varshney, Ashutosh. 2002. *Ethnic Conflict and Civic Life: Hindus and Muslims in India*. New Haven: Yale University Press.

Wantoo, Pran et al. 2002. 'Separate Religion from Politics'. *Economic & Political Weekly* 37 (20), 1854 + 1949.

Zavos, John. 1999. 'Searching for Hindu Nationalism in Modern Indian History: Analysis of Some Early Ideological Developments'. *Economic & Political Weekly* 34 (32), 2269–76.

SECTION II

Theoretical and Conceptual Issues

Introduction to Section II

Communal strife in modern India is approached from different theoretical positions and has been explained in many different ways. This diversity in the general literature on the subject is reflected to some extent in the *EPW* essays as well. But if there are a few things that are common to these diverse analyses, then rejecting the spontaneity thesis is one of them. Most riots are planned, as Asghar Ali Engineer never tired of reminding us. This planning is well characterised by Paul Brass as the Institutionalised Riot System: a system of riot production which is activated from time to time. Who puts in place this system and for what reason?

If we take the second question first and see what the answer is, it will be easy to guess who the actors are. The purpose of the routinised periodic riot production, according to Brass, is to influence electoral outcomes. Obviously then, the members of the political class or the political elite are the actors in this game (though, the less visible involvement of those outside the political class need not be ruled out). This connection between elections and riots, in its more elaborate and formal form, can be found in Wilkinson's work. We have given in this section a sample of it in the form of his debate with Ashutosh Varshney, hoping that the exchange will bring out more sharply the details of his analysis. Riots, Wilkinson says, are caused by politicians who also have the power to prevent them. Whether they will do the first or the second depends on their electoral interests, which, in turn, are determined by how effective the competition between parties is and how close the elections are. But whoever plans the riots and benefits from them, the actual participants in the violent incidents on the streets are not all mercenaries or criminals. Several commentators and analysts have pointed to the involvement, at once sad, sobering and perplexing, of the subalterns. Perplexing not because it contradicts our assumption of the essential goodness of the poor, but because it is difficult to see why they should be doing something which brings disproportionately greater loss and suffering to them, especially when their interests are not identical with those of the political elite.

One possible answer, found in Berenschot's essay in this section, is that the poor are bound to the elite in a patronage network. The elite use their control of the bureaucracy to give the poor access to basic civic amenities, jobs, etc., something which in theory the state ought to be ensuring not as a favour but as part of its functions. In exchange, the poor not only vote for the relevant faction of the elite but also become part of its polarising politics. This still does not explain the scale and intensity of communal violence and one needs to go to the longer version of

Berenschot's work for a better understanding. This is true of others mentioned here as well. Otherwise, their analyses will appear to be far more vulnerable to easy criticism than they are. It should also be kept in mind that the evolution of the scholarship on this subject has not taken place in the sequence in which it is presented here for expository purposes.

While introducing the essays of the previous section, we had observed that the future development of the contending theses in the debate on Hinduism and the Hindu–Muslim relations in pre-colonial India depends on further historical investigations into the middle period of Indian history. The difficulty is with the limited and fragmentary nature of evidence. In her essay in this section, Dharma Kumar points out that much of what we know of medieval India and the inter-community relations in that society is about the court culture and events. We know comparatively very little about the general life and how the ordinary Hindus and Muslims related to each other. She makes this point while criticising the 'left-secular model' of Indian history.

But suppose there is lot of evidence about some period, and some part of the subcontinent. A historian will then be able to present a picture of what that society was like. Armed with this historical knowledge, should s/he take active part in the fight against communalism (which often uses communal interpretations of the past)? There are several things that can be said about this issue but two points are especially relevant here. The historian's history is but one of the ways in which the past is apprehended. There are myths and memories and their political efficacy has for long been recognised and harnessed by political parties as Badri Narayan's essay in Section III ('Memories, Saffronising Statues and Constructing Communal Politics') shows. Left secularist history is surely needed to combat right-wing writing, especially when it has historiographical pretensions. But when confronted by (politically modified) popular memories, folklore and legends, it is either an encounter of the incommensurable or the historian has to claim scientificity for her/his enterprise. The presumption of superiority implicit in this move is not without its problems. Gyanendra Pandey's essay ('In Defence of a Fragment') departs from scientific history writing to raise the question of how to write about violence, particularly sectarian violence. The problem is partly how to represent pain and suffering, how to ask the victims of terror to give us—the investigators from outside—the details of that very terror. But it is also about the highly compromised nature of the state 'archives'. Sectarian violence 'produces the necessity of evidence-gathering', but also 'wipes out evidence'.

Essays in this section thus deal with 'communalism' at different levels: adequacy and reliability of data, rival theoretical explanations, methodological issues, difficulties in identifying the very object of enquiry namely, 'communalism', theory dependence of definitions, talking at cross purposes that it produces, location of categories like 'secularism' and the conventions governing their use, and exploring analytical alternatives to perspectives which unquestioningly use humanist conceptions of 'actors' and 'subjects'. This entire discussion of communal violence is animated by the hope that with more data and better theories, we will be able to make sense of what appears to be abrupt, sudden and inexplicably inhuman.

Whether that hope will be fulfilled remains to be seen. In the meantime, scholars continue to grapple not only with data, sources, definitions and methodologies, but also with the larger entanglement of communal strife with certain dimensions of modernity like democracy, rule of law and demands for equality of opportunity and equality of treatment. Here, particularly in the context of the demands for—and expectations of—equality, the salience of the 'institutional racism' framework, developed in the UK, for understanding communalism in India can be seen. Institutional racism is embedded racism built into institutions like the police, bureaucracy, educational system, etc. It is a bias built into the normal functioning of institutions and results in systematic discrimination against certain groups. Pritam Singh's essay suggests that we understand the problem of communalism in India as institutional discrimination against the minorities. The importance of Pritam Singh's essay is that it takes the discussion of communalism beyond elections, political parties and 'communal' organisations to the shared, collective orientations of the organs of the state. In so doing, it quietly explodes the myth of the neutrality of the modern state.

5

An Electoral Theory of Communal Riots?*

Ashutosh Varshney#

[...]

The Argument

Why do communal riots take place? Wilkinson's central argument is that 'democratic states protect minorities when it is in their government's electoral interest to do so' (p. 6). But when, one might ask, is it in the government's interest to protect minorities?

Wilkinson points to two principal possibilities: (i) 'when minorities are an important part of their party's current support base, or the support base of one of their coalition partners in a coalition government' (p. 6); or (ii) 'when the overall electoral system in a state is so competitive ...that there is therefore a high probability that the governing party will have to negotiate or form a coalition with minority supported parties in the future, despite its own preferences' (p. 7).

Of the two parts of the argument, thus, the first concentrates on the support base of the governing party or coalition; and the second focuses on the level of electoral competition. The higher the competition between political parties, says Wilkinson, the lower will be the incidence of riots. 'Politicians in government will restrict the supply of security to minorities if...overall levels of party competition in a state are so low that the likelihood of having to seek the support of minority-supported parties in the future is very low' (p. 7). In short, in highly competitive electoral contexts, Muslims would be protected by ruling parties, even when targeted by mobs in riots, because small groups could be critical in swinging closely contested elections.

* *Economic and Political Weekly* 40 (39): 4219–24 (24 September 2005).

This is a review essay on Steven Wilkinson's *Votes and Violence: Electoral Competition and Communal Riots in India* (New York: Cambridge University Press, 2004; first South Asian edition, 2005). The reply by Wilkinson is the next chapter.

How is the level of electoral competition to be measured? In terms of the effective number of parties (ENPV), says Wilkinson. The virtue of ENPV, a commonly used measure to determine the level of party competition, is that it does not count the total number of parties contesting an election and weigh them equally, for that can only demonstrate the formal, not real, level of competition. ENPV gives greater weightage to parties with a larger vote share than to parties with a smaller vote share, thus showing what the degree of effective, not formal, competition is. [1] The state of Madhya Pradesh may have as many political parties participating in the elections of late as Uttar Pradesh, but Madhya Pradesh normally has a straight contest between the Congress and the Bharatiya Janata Party (BJP), whereas in Uttar Pradesh, the electoral field has for over a decade been four-cornered, split between the Samajwadi Party (SP), Bahujan Samaj Party (BSP), the BJP and the Congress. The effective number of parties, and therefore the level of party competition, in Uttar Pradesh is higher than in Madhya Pradesh, even if the total number of political parties contesting in the two states is about the same.

In my critical appraisal below, I will first deal with the second argument. The reason is quite simple. The argument linking electoral competition and riots is quite novel. Moreover, claims about electoral competition—what it is, how to measure it, and how it is connected to riots—dominate the book and also provide its title. I turn subsequently to the argument about the role of the state, which has been standard fare in the literature for a long time.

Party Competition and Riots

Does higher competition for votes between political parties lead to lower communal rioting and lower party competition to higher rioting, as Wilkinson claims, or is it the other way round? Consider Figure 5.1, derived from the 46-year database (1950–95) that Wilkinson and I jointly created. It presents data (i) on the number of deaths; and (ii) on the number of riots for each year between 1950 and 1995.

Figure 5.1: Hindu–Muslim Riots 1950–95

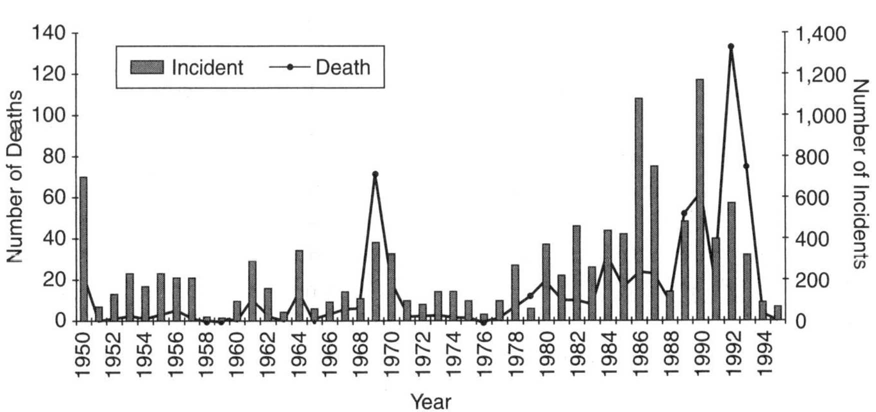

Source: Varshney 2004a, p. 95.

Note that between 1950 and roughly 1975–76, the figures reveal no upward or downward trend. The ups and downs in riots appear to be a random walk. Starting with the late 1970s, however, there is a clear upward trend—ups and downs in riots each year are around a rising trend. Compared to 1950–76, more riots took place in India in 1977–95 and more people died in them.

Wilkinson's central argument says: the higher the competition, the fewer the riots. Was party competition between 1977 and 1995, a period of rising riot frequency, less vigorous than during 1950–76, when riots were fewer?

The answer is an unambiguous no. Roughly till 1967, the Congress had a nearly hegemonic hold over power and no other parties came close. The Congress began to lose power in 1967 at the state level and by 1977, the Congress was voted out at the centre as well. Since then, the party competition, if anything, has been more vigorous. Indeed, at least since the late 1970s, incumbency has not been an advantage in Indian politics. Roughly three out of four incumbents have been thrown out of office in elections.

How do these considerations tie up with ENPV? ENPV is, by definition, higher for a period when many more parties become effective contestants for power than for a period when the domination of one party was rarely challenged. In short, India has had more riots in a period of greater party competition, not less. Wilkinson's theory proposes the opposite:

> The effect of the decline of the dominant Congress Party and the resulting party competition in recent years has not, as some have argued, been to increase the level of communal violence. On the contrary, the increasing party competition for minority voters has led to a reduction in Hindu-Muslim violence, as politicians are forced by electoral incentives to take firm action to prevent Hindu-Muslim riots (pp. 169–70).

Here, then, is a direct clash between theory and evidence. But Wilkinson does have a way out. He can say that his argument applies to the state level, not to the national level. Logically speaking, it is possible for the country as a whole to have more riots and higher party competition at the same time, because (i) a few states may have low party competition and a lot of riots, even when (ii) most states have higher party competition and fewer riots. In theory, an increase in (i) cannot only fully cancel out the decrease in (ii), but also produce an overall national increase in riots if the jump in (i) is big and the decline in (ii) low.

It would have been instructive to discover whether states with small effective number of parties in the post-1977 period—let us say, Gujarat, Rajasthan, Madhya Pradesh, Andhra Pradesh, Himachal Pradesh—have indeed more than spoiled the overall downward effect that the states with higher number of effective parties—Uttar Pradesh, Bihar, Haryana, Maharashtra, Tamil Nadu—have, according to Wilkinson, brought about. No such exercise is undertaken. Instead, Wilkinson calculates the ENPV for various states in 2002 (p. 143) and then presents his regression results for the period 1961–95 (p. 151), leading to his major conclusion that 'the number of Hindu-Muslim riots goes down as the effective number of parties goes up' (p. 150). If this argument does not work for India as a whole, does it for the state level?

SURPRISING EXCLUSIONS

Wilkinson's book is silent on two major issues, raising serious doubts about the validity of the argument even at the state level. First and foremost, one of Wilkinson's key causal variables—low or high party competition, or closeness of the election race—is at the level of electoral constituencies, but his riot data are town-based. It is well known in India's election studies that administrative units like towns and electoral units like constituencies do not normally coincide. Most towns of India are part of a larger or smaller electoral constituency, both for the national parliament and state assemblies, or alternatively, they are so large that they have split into several constituencies.

Potentially, this creates insurmountable problems for Wilkinson's argument. Let me give an example. The town of Aligarh is split into two state assembly constituencies, Aligarh and Koil. Aligarh constituency incorporates a large part of the town, but Koil is both urban and rural, made up of some parts of Aligarh town and some contiguous rural areas. Wilkinson can measure electoral competitiveness at the level of Koil or Aligarh constituency, but the riot data we jointly collected are not for constituencies. [2] Incidents that are coded as riots in Aligarh town (including when the riot took place, how many people died, where the riot took place), may have taken place either in Aligarh constituency or in Koil constituency.

There is no way of knowing this, unless one meticulously disaggregates riot locations below the town level—down to the *mohalla* or neighbourhood level—and then begins to map neighbourhoods with the constituencies in which they fall. Our database, as it currently exists, does not allow this. Wilkinson simply cannot be sure that riots at the town level are connected to the competitiveness of elections at the constituency level.

If this is true for Aligarh, a medium-size town, consider the enormous measurement problems that this incorrect equation raises for riots that took place in the bigger riot-prone cities—Ahmedabad, Vadodara, Hyderabad, Mumbai and Delhi. These five cities accounted for a very large proportion (nearly 38 per cent) of all deaths in Hindu–Muslim riots during 1950–95 (Varshney 2002a, 104–05). Moreover, each of these cities has many more than two state assembly constituencies that Aligarh is split into. The city of Delhi, for example, has seven national parliamentary and, currently, 70 state assembly constituencies. Our dataset simply does not allow us to determine which Delhi riots fell in which of Delhi's many constituencies. No analyst can derive conclusions about towns from electoral constituencies unless we incorrectly assume that the town and constituency tend to coincide.[3]

Another big silence, perhaps inadvertent, calls attention. Why have the regressions been run only for a truncated period, that is, 1961–95 (p. 151)?[4] Why not for the entire period of 1950–95 included in our database? This matter is important, for the period left out of regressions, 1950–60, saw a much smaller number of riots than the later period, and also had a low level of party competition. Is the negative relationship between party competition and riots by any chance an artefact of the truncation, or does it hold up even when the entire period is covered? Wilkinson provides no assistance in the matter.

INCONSISTENT INCLUSIONS

Wilkinson's argument becomes even more troubling when the reported regression results are carefully examined. Instead of a clearly demonstrable and robust inverse relationship between the degree of party competition and occurrence of riots, we get radical indeterminacy and a lot of what statisticians call 'noise'.

Wilkinson has presented his regression results at two levels—for Uttar Pradesh, 1970–95 (pp. 43 and 45) and for 15 major states of India, 1961–95 (p. 151).[5] When the latter is analysed, 'there is a negative relationship between the degree of electoral competition in a state and its level of communal riots' (p. 150). But in Uttar Pradesh, the relationship is positive (Table 2.1 of the book, p. 43). 'The closeness of the previous Vidhan Sabha election ... seems to be positively related to the likelihood of a riot taking place before the next election' (pp. 42–43). Are close races likely to reduce, or increase, the odds of riots?

When one looks at the relationship between electoral competition and the number of deaths, not number of riots, the plot thickens even further. Closeness in previous national election is negatively correlated with the number of deaths, but positively correlated with the closeness in the previous state election (p. 45). In short, the relationship between electoral competition and riots is not uniformly negative. Rather, it is both positive and negative, depending on (i) whether we are looking at India as a whole, or at Uttar Pradesh, and (ii) whether we are looking at national or state elections. Closely contested national elections appear to produce a tendency towards fewer, smaller or no riots, but closely contested state assembly elections generate the opposite result.[6]

More confusion is added by the variable 'proximity to elections'. In Uttar Pradesh, the odds of riots go up if national or state level elections are within six months (p. 43), but at the all-India level, riots are positively correlated with 'state elections within six months' and negatively correlated with 'national elections in six months' (p. 151).[7] Statistically, then, we have no uniquely acceptable and generalisable pointers to whether elections and riots are clearly related.

The indeterminacy, one should emphasise, is not confined to statistical results only. The text also says quite contradictory things. In the opening chapter, as quoted above, the relationship between electoral competitiveness and riots is called negative (pp. 6–7), an assertion repeated in several other places (pp. 137, 144, 147, 150 and 152). Elsewhere, however, Wilkinson equally clearly states: 'towns with a close electoral race are considerably more likely to have a Hindu-Muslim riot' (p. 16); 'increases in electoral competition are associated with a rise in the likelihood of communal riots' (p. 47); 'violence...was most likely to break out in those places where political competition was most intense' (p. 205).

What might account for these contradictions? Let us give the argument the benefit of doubt and point to two theoretical possibilities. First, it may be that the relationship between electoral competition and riots is neither uniformly positive, nor uniformly negative, but curvilinear. That is, it is positive (or negative) up to a threshold of competitiveness and turns negative (positive) once party competition crosses that threshold. There is, in other words, a 'tipping point' somewhere, which transforms a negative or positive linear relationship into its opposite. If so, Wilkinson should have tested for it, just as he has for the percentage of Muslims in a town's population, which he finds curvilinearly related to riots (p. 41).

Second, it may be that Wilkinson has measured electoral competitiveness for his India-level analysis in one way and measured it for the state of Uttar Pradesh quite differently. As we look carefully, that does turn out to be the case. For Wilkinson's national-level analysis, the indicator of electoral competitiveness is ENPV, and for the analysis of Uttar Pradesh, the indicator is 'how close the last election race was'.

These are, of course, two different things, for it is possible for races to be quite close even if the contest is bipolar, not multi-cornered. Of late, election races between the Congress and the BJP have been roughly as close in Madhya Pradesh and Rajasthan as in the multi-party contests of Uttar Pradesh. Wilkinson should have specified what matters most for his theory: closeness of races, or number of effective parties. They are conceptually separable. Wilkinson should also have used an identical measure for India and Uttar Pradesh, and at the very least, might want to re-run the regressions.

To conclude, if the exclusions generate doubts about Wilkinson's central argument, the inconsistencies and contradictions of what has been included seem to undermine it. This does not, of course, mean that there is no link between elections and riots. All it suggests is that Wilkinson has not been able to establish it.

State and/or Civil Society?

Let me now turn to the first part of Wilkinson's argument. It concerns the relationship between the state and riots. 'The response of the state', says Wilkinson, 'is the prime factor in determining whether ethnic violence breaks out' (p. 6). Further, 'in virtually all the empirical cases I have examined, whether violence is bloody or ends quickly depends not on the local factors that caused violence to break out but primarily on the will and capacity of the government that controls the forces of law and order' (p. 5).

A great deal has been written about the role of the state in communal riots.[8] But before I analyse Wilkinson's version of it, let us first note that Wilkinson's views have dramatically changed over the last 10 years. In his first publication on the subject, jointly authored with me (Varshney and Wilkinson 1996), Wilkinson had drawn a distinction between the normative and empirical sides of a state-based explanation, suggesting that if the state repeatedly does not stop riots, even though it is constitutionally supposed to, scholars should stop asking what the state should do and start investigating why the state in fact does not perform its constitutionally assigned functions:

> Justice Raghubar Dayal's commission summarised almost all of the main measures to reduce violence as long ago as 1968: that state governments should not undermine or interfere with local law enforcement; that speedy and firm action should be taken at the first sign of trouble; that prosecutions of offenders should not be withdrawn for political reasons; that officers in service should not be transferred for reasons other than the requirements of service; that the press should be stopped from making false and deliberately inflammatory statements; and that textbooks should be cleansed of deliberately communal interpretations of history (Varshney and Wilkinson 1996, p. 38).

After outlining this list, Wilkinson, along with me, concluded that 'another riot commission which tells us what ought to be done is not as helpful as finding out why previous recommendations have not been followed and then deciding which policies can be carried out' (Varshney and Wilkinson 1996, p. 46).

Moreover, Wilkinson at that time firmly veered towards an explanation based on civil society: 'Local inter-group ties...seem to provide the best defence against the spread of communal violence' (Varshney and Wilkinson 1996, p. 39). Many examples of integrated ties preventing riots were cited. One such example stood out:

> Disha is a women's NGO working in Saharanpur district of Uttar Pradesh. Disha's workers (sakhis and sahyoginis) are drawn from both religious communities... As part of the Mahila Samakhya (MS) initiative in the state, Disha worked to improve women's education and awareness about a wide range of social issues...In Bateda village, before MS started, the women from the Muslim mohalla did not speak to the women from the Hindu basti....Gradually, a relationship of trust was built. ...(T)he sakhis and sahyoginis did not find it difficult to mobilise the two communities on a common basis like ration cards. Once the barrier was broken there was no going back. ....They were even supported by the men in their efforts. Such contacts helped to stop communal violence in the autumn of 1990. Women mobilised by the NGO were active in stopping the controversy over the Ram janmabhoomi from destroying local communal harmony. Hindu women who had met Muslims through Disha's social work persuaded local Hindus to reassure Muslim families—who were about to flee their homes—that they would be in no danger if they stayed (Varshney and Wilkinson 1996, pp. 43–44).

This previous writing is not referenced at all in this book. If considerably greater research since 1996 has led to a change in Wilkinson's views, it should of course be accepted as something to do with professional evolution. But does the new argument stand up to scrutiny?

[...]

Politics and the Muslim Vote

To support his theory, Wilkinson has marshalled qualitative empirical materials primarily from five states: Gujarat, Kerala, Tamil Nadu, Bihar and Uttar Pradesh. When the 2002 riots broke out in Gujarat, the riots on the whole did not spread beyond the state,[9] though it should be noted that despite the enormity of violence, several towns within Gujarat, including Surat, remained quiet, or had small incidents only.[10] Wilkinson argues that the clearest support for his theory comes from how Indian states other than Gujarat handled the 2002 riots. In 2002, Gujarat was among the states having the lowest number of effective parties, the BJP was in power in the state all by itself (not in a coalition) and it had no need for Muslim votes. The states of Madhya Pradesh and Rajasthan—adjacent to Gujarat and like Gujarat, having only two main parties, the BJP and the Congress—had no riots because the political party in power, the Congress, needed Muslim votes to compete with the BJP. In short, for riots not to take place, a state does not have to have a high ENPV, though it would be better if it did. All that is required is that a ruling party should have a need for the Muslim vote.

Wilkinson's interpretive account of qualitative political materials, which he needs to establish causality, is remarkably selective. First of all, it is worth asking if the Gujarat riots in 2002 had something to do with the fact that the central government in Delhi, in which the BJP was a primary partner, did not suspend the BJP government in the state, using Article 356 of India's Constitution. Second, more critically, one can think of not one or two, but many instances when the ruling party was not the anti-Muslim BJP, or its analytic equivalent, the Shiv Sena, but deadly Hindu–Muslim riots nonetheless took place.

If Gujarat in 2002 was ruled by the BJP, the Congress Party ruled Gujarat on the following occasions when riots broke out: January 1982; March 1984; March–July 1985; January, March and July 1986; January, February and November 1987; April, October, November and December 1990; January, March and April 1991; and January and July 1992.[11] The BJP came to power in Gujarat state only in 1995. Moreover, in the early to mid-1980s, the Congress in Gujarat also unveiled the so called KHAM (Kshatriya, Harijan, Adivasi and Muslim) strategy, aimed at putting together an alliance of these groups as a basis for power. The Congress aggressively courted the Muslim vote; it was in power, yet Hindu–Muslim riots were endemic.

Consider now the period of the Ayodhya agitation, 1990–92. During 1989–90,Uttar Pradesh was ruled by Mulayam Singh Yadav, whose commitment to Muslims and cultivation of the Muslim vote is well known. In 1990, he did order the police under his command to shoot on the masses mobilised by Hindu nationalists, earning the famous epithet 'Maulana Mulayam'. Yet, awful riots took place in Uttar Pradesh in 1989–90. In supporting his theory, Wilkinson notes how Mulayam Singh Yadav in 1994–95 succeeded in preventing riots (p. 93), but surprisingly omits his failure to do so in 1989–90.

To make sure that these illustrations are not simply viewed as a few exceptions, to only proving the rule, let me give some more critical examples. During the infamous Mumbai riots in January 1993, the Congress ruled the state of Maharashtra. During the 1980s, riots in the Moradabad, Aligarh and Meerut towns of Uttar Pradesh, the Congress ran the state governments there. Between 1978 and 1983, riots repeatedly rocked the city of Hyderabad, even as the state of Andhra Pradesh had Congress governments. And most remarkably of all, the riots of 1961, the worst year for riots in the first decade and a half of independent India, occurred when Nehru was India's prime minister, with an unquestionable commitment to India's Muslims, and almost all states then were Congress-ruled. Counterexamples undermining Wilkinson's theory are simply too many to be brushed aside as occasional deviations from the rule.

Why should the Congress, even under Nehru and Indira Gandhi, have failed to prevent riots? Why was Mulayam Singh Yadav successful in 1994–95 but failed in 1989–90? Why did the Gujarat government fail to prevent riots in the early to mid-1980s? Can we prove that the Congress governments (and Mulayam Singh Yadav in 1989–90) were not cultivating, or did not need the Muslim vote? Not having used the many counterexamples above, Wilkinson does not formulate the question this way.

Fundamentally, Wilkinson's understanding of the state is at issue here, especially the relationship between the ruling party on the one hand and the permanent bureaucracy and police in a parliamentary system on the other. The theory that riots would not take place if only the government could order the police or armed forces 'to use deadly force to stop them' (p. 20) betrays a monolithic and omnipotent view of the state. The state is not a monolith, nor is it omnipotent or omniscient. Ruling politicians are indeed the bosses of bureaucrats and police officials, but that does not mean that ruling parties will always get what they want.

Consider Indira Gandhi, who had a remarkable hold over state chief ministers after 1971. Can we really show that the many riots during her years, especially during 1981–84, took place because she allowed her chief ministers to order the police not to protect Muslims during riots—in the cities of Aligarh, Moradabad, Meerut, Hyderabad, Bhiwandi and Ahmedabad? In all of the states where these cities fell, the Congress ran governments during 1981–84.

Quite often, if not always, the relationship between ruling parties and the bureaucratic–police establishment is one consisting of serious principal–agent problems. If peasants can subvert the landlords through 'weapons of the weak' without frontally defying them (Scott 1985), police officers and bureaucrats, with much greater power than the peasants, can also subvert the ruling parties through subterfuge, dissimulation and feigned compliance, even when one can demonstrate that the ruling party would not benefit from having riots and would like to prevent or control them.

If riots took place under Nehru and Indira Gandhi's Congress rule, despite their pro-Muslim political ideologies, why might that be so? Because some police officers and bureaucrats had very different ideological persuasions; or because officers at the top levels shared the ideological proclivities of the rulers but officers at the district level did not; or because police officers were heavily compromised in that the criminals who led the mobs in riots had developed an extensive network of relationships with them and with important local politicians; or because the police officers and bureaucrats, despite political orders and their desire to control riots, were simply unable to do so, either due to the fact that information flows on the ground were defective, or the ruling politicians were divided on what to do, or opposition politicians, especially the Hindu nationalists, were strong enough to ignite riots and had enough links in local society to incite mobs. Other than ruling parties, opposition parties in a democracy also matter, and even while not ruling, can wield a lot of power. The argument that the state can stop riots at will can only be premised upon an assumption that there are either no principal–agent problems at the level of state institutions and/or the state is all-powerful and opposition parties of no consequence. Both assumptions are flawed.

This view of the state, of course, does not mean that the state is never interested in riots. It may be, but that, as the examples above show, is not always the case. That being so, one cannot build a general theory of state involvement in riots. State involvement of the kind Wilkinson talks about is linked conceptually to pogroms, not riots. Gujarat comes closest to Wilkinson's theory because it was one of the few pogroms in independent India. Riots have often taken place in India; but there have been very few pogroms.[12]

This view of the state also does not mean that one should stop critiquing the state for failing to protect the lives of its citizens. In terms of action, citizens should of course exercise pressure on the state to behave better. But in terms of analysis, one needs to draw a distinction between empirical and normative theories of the state. The state quite often does not, or is unable to, do what it should. Political scientists have long known that.

[...]

Notes

1. The formula is ENPV = $1/S\ v_i^2$, where v_i is the vote share of the ith party.

2. For each district, our riot data is split into two parts: urban and rural. For our template, see Wilkinson 2004, p. 256; and Varshney 2002a, p. 309. No further disaggregation of urban and rural is available in the template.

3. One can theoretically connect riots in towns and the degree of electoral competition, if in each of the many constituencies of the city, the election race is equally close or has an equal number of effective parties. This assumption, if true, can allow Wilkinson to equate a lot of towns and constituencies, but still not all of them, for some will continue to be in constituencies that have significant rural citizens as well. One should, however, note that election studies in India have often shown that constituencies in the same city—whether Bombay, Delhi or Hyderabad—often seriously differ in how close the election races are.

4. This period is covered by Wilkinson for the country as a whole, but for Uttar Pradesh, regressions cover a still shorter period, 1970–95 (pp. 43, 45).

5. I am only concentrating on those results reported to be statistically significant by Wilkinson—at 105, 5 per cent or 1 per cent. For one of the clearest statements on how to interpret statistical significance by one of the best practitioners of the craft, see Christopher Achen 1982, pp. 46–51.

6. At the very least, this is a paradox that calls for an explanation in a book that presents an electoral theory of riots. Sadly, Wilkinson does not provide an explanation, deductive or empirical.

7. It is not obvious what this variable really means. In presidential systems, the election dates are typically cast in stone, and politicians know for sure how far the elections are. In parliamentary systems like India's, the legislature can be dissolved by the existing governments and elections must typically be held within 10-12 weeks of dissolution, unless the Election

Commission overrules the incumbents. To have riots within six months of elections seems to add a fixity to legislative elections that has not existed in India since 1962.

8. See Brass 2003; Varshney 2002a, chapter 12; and Varshney 2004a, Preface.

9. There were small riots in Andhra Pradesh and Maharashtra.

10. See Varshney 2004b. See also Wilkinson 2002.

11. See Varshney 2002a, chapter 10.

12. See Varshney 2002b.

REFERENCES

Achen, Christopher. 1982. *Interpreting and Using Regression*. Newbury Park: Sage.

Brass, Paul. 2003. *The Production of Communal Violence in Contemporary India*. New Delhi: University of Washington Press, Seattle and Oxford University Press.

King, Gary, Robert Keohane, and Sidney Verba. 1994. *Designing Social Inquiry*. Princeton: Princeton University Press.

Ragin, Charles. 2004. 'Turning the Tables: How Case-Oriented Research Challenges Variable Oriented Research' in *Rethinking Social Inquiry*, eds Henry Brady, and David Collier. Lanham, MD: Rowman and Littlefield.

Scott, James. 1985. *Weapons of the Weak*. New Haven: Yale University Press.

Varshney, Ashutosh. 2002a. *Ethnic Conflict and Civic Life: Hindus and Muslims in India*. New Haven: Yale University Press; and New Delhi: Oxford University Press.

———. 2002b. 'Understanding Gujarat Violence', in *Items and Issues*. New York: Social Science Research Council, Fall 2002.

———. 2004a. 'Preface', *Ethnic Conflict and Civic Life*. New Delhi: Oxford University Press, paperback edition.

———. 2004b. 'States or Cities? Communal Violence in India', in *Regional Reflections: State-Level Factors in Indian Politics*, ed. Rob Jenkins. New York: Oxford University Press.

Varshney, Ashutosh, and Steven Wilkinson. 1996. 'Hindu-Muslim Riots 1960–93: New Findings, Possible Remedies', RGICS Project No 12, Rajiv Gandhi Institute for Contemporary Studies, New Delhi.

Wilkinson, Steven. 2002. 'Putting Gujarat in Perspective'. *Economic and Political Weekly* 37 (17), 27 April, 1579–83.

6

Communal Riots in India*

Steven I. Wilkinson

What causes communal riots in contemporary India? In my book *Votes and Violence* (2005), I argue that politicians both cause them and, more importantly, have the power to prevent them, through their control of the state governments responsible for law and order.[1] Riots in India, I argue, are the product of incentives at the local level and the state level. At the local level, I argue that the most important cause of riots is the intensity of electoral competition. Where political competition is most intense, 'parties that represent elites within ethnic groups' use anti-minority protests, demonstrations and physical attacks that precipitate riots in order to 'encourage members of their wider ethnic category to identify with their party and the "majority" identity rather than a party that is identified with economic redistribution or some ideological agenda' (p. 4).

However, the real issue in explaining riots, I argue, is not which local political or sociological factors increase the likelihood of violence, but whether the level of government responsible for law and order (the 28 states, in India's federal system) chooses to prevent violence or intervene quickly to stop it when it does break out. Rioters are not heroes and the state police and paramilitary forces—even in states like Bihar where the general quality of administration is far from high—have.shown themselves capable of preventing communal riots when given the right direction by their ministers.[2]

What then determines the reaction of state governments? I argue that state governments protect minorities when it is in their electoral interest to do so:

> [P]oliticians in government will increase the supply of protection to minorities when... minorities are an important part of their party's current support base, or the support base of one of their partners in a coalition government; or when the overall electoral system in a state is so competitive—in terms of the effective number of parties—that there is therefore a high probability that the governing party will have to negotiate or form coalitions with minority supported parties in the future... (pp. 6–7).

The growing competitiveness of state politics in India, in other words, much of it the result of backward caste mobilisation, is a positive thing for communal relations.[3]

* *Economic and Political Weekly* 40 (44–45): 4768–70 (29 October 2005).

An increase in the number of parties competing for Muslim votes increases the incentives for state governments to prevent anti-minority violence.

Many Indians, and scholars of Indian politics, will not be surprised by these arguments, and my work is in a rich tradition of studies on the connection between electoral competition and riots. But my book, I hope, makes a contribution in two ways: first, by explicitly theorising about the precise conditions under which electoral competition matters for riots at several levels, and second, by using a great deal of new data (a joint 1950–95 dataset on Hindu–Muslim riots Ashutosh Varshney and I collected, and a great deal of other riot, election, census and socio-economic data that I collected independently) to test my hypotheses against other leading explanations for communal riots. The book uses some statistical analysis, but it also contains a great deal of qualitative evidence based on archival research, fieldwork and extensive reading in primary and secondary sources.

ALTERNATIVE APPROACHES

My focus on the importance of politics at the state level presents an alternative, however, to some recent scholarly work that identifies town-level factors as key to explaining the prevalence of communal riots. Paul Brass (2003), for instance has focused on the importance of 'institutional riot systems' in producing large-scale riots in towns in which they are endemic. And Ashutosh Varshney (2002: 11) argues in his book that state and national-level politics are less important than town-level civic organisations and networks: where a town's civic organisations are inter-ethnic and associational, '...polarising politicians either don't succeed or eventually stop trying to divide communities by provoking and fomenting violence'.

The fact that several political science research projects have been looking at the issue of communal violence at the same time has been very productive in terms of helping each of us sharpen our arguments and explanations, and hopefully in terms of building wider cumulative knowledge about what causes riots. Brass's work for instance, because it acknowledges the importance of electoral incentives at different levels and the role of the state, is largely compatible with my own. But of course differences in approach and emphasis remain. In a recent review of my work, (Varshney 2005; chapter 5 of this volume) Varshney draws attention to some of these differences, and I would like to turn now to a specific discussion of the criticisms he makes of my electoral arguments.

ELECTORAL INCENTIVES

The most important substantive question that Varshney raises about my book is how local and state-level incentives interact to lead to violence (p. 4221). Why, he asks, should intense competition at the local level often lead to anti-minority polarisation while an increase in party competition at the state level leads to states acting more aggressively to prevent violence? The answer, clearly stated in the book, is that party competition is bipolar at the local level (p. 23) but multipolar at the state level in most Indian states, meaning that different groups of voters are pivotal at each level (pp. 138–46). Misunderstanding the fundamental nature of this argument, unfortunately, leads to further misunderstandings about the theoretical and analytical choices made in the book.

At the constituency level, as the work of Pradeep Chhibber and others has shown, electoral competition in India tends to follow the bipolar pattern that Maurice Duverger long ago predicted would obtain under a first-past-the-post electoral system. Given that upper-caste Hindus and Muslims are disproportionately urban communities throughout much of the country (West Bengal is one notable exception), we often therefore have a situation in towns in which a party from the majority community confronts a Muslim-supported party, with the winner of the two-party race being decided by who can win over the remaining Hindu voters, something that I show in the book is frequently achieved through communal polarisation and riots.[4]

At the state level, however, because India is highly diverse, its state electoral constituencies relatively small, and the different social groups that support different parties are mobilised and distributed unequally across each state, the number of parties in most states now aggregates to considerably more than two.[5] In 2002, for instance, my data show that the average number of effective parties in the 15 major states was 4.4, with only three of these 15 states (Andhra Pradesh, Himachal Pradesh and Gujarat) having fewer than three effective parties (p. 143). I suggest that this multipolar competition among parties, many of which have strong caste or redistributional ideologies, is a good thing for communal relations because Muslims thus become an important swing vote for parties from the majority community. The advantages of multiparty competition for ethnic moderation have of course been raised by others, such as Donald Horowitz, but my book is, as far as I am aware, the first to show, using data on every Indian major state election from 1961–95 (not just data from 2002, as Varshney implies), that a greater number of parties at the state level leads to fewer communal riots, even when we control for socio-economic factors and a state's previous level of violence.

The fact that I hypothesise different theoretical mechanisms at different levels explains why different measures of electoral competition are appropriate. At the town level, where competition is bipolar, I predict that violence will take place in seats with the tightest electoral races (measured by the margin at the previous election), the party representing the elite within an ethnic category that can potentially unite a majority of voters will have a greater incentive to foment polarising events and riots in order to solidify its vote. But at the state level, it is not the previous electoral margin that is important, but whether the government in power at the time of the riot might (i) break apart due to inter-party differences over the threat of communal violence and (ii) whether the overall competitive environment in a state is so intense that a substantial riot-induced shift in Muslim votes to other parties might cause the incumbent party or parties to lose ground to competitors. The appropriate measures at the state level, therefore, are the number of parties that are competing for office and the Muslim support for the major parties.

THEORIES AND NON-EXCEPTIONS

Varshney cites a number of riots that he thinks are 'exceptions' to my general electoral arguments, and he argues that these exceptions are so frequent that they undermine the argument as a whole. Without getting into the interesting methodological issue of how many exceptions it might take to invalidate any particular thesis, let me simply make two points. First, there are not so many exceptions as to invalidate the significance of the main explanatory variables in my multivariate statistical analysis. Second, many of the 'exceptions' that Varshney claims undermine my argument are not exceptions at all but are entirely consistent with my theory.

To reiterate, my book makes a general argument about the conditions under which democratic governments prevent riots. In the Indian context, the theory does not associate riots with government by any particular party—rather it predicts that democratic governments led by any party will prevent riots when they depend for votes directly or indirectly upon the minority groups. But Varshney says my theory is undermined because 'one can think of not one or two, but many instances when the ruling party was not the anti-Muslim BJP [Bharatiya Janata Party], or its analytic equivalent, the Shiv Sena, but deadly Hindu-Muslim riots nonetheless took place'. Having framed my argument in this way, he then points to riots that happened during Congress rule (for example, in Ahmedabad, Moradabad, Meerut, Hyderabad and elsewhere) as damning exceptions to my theory.

This portrayal unfortunately rests on a misunderstanding of my argument, which offers a general theory of the way in which party competition can affect governments' response to riots, not the anti-BJP thesis that Varshney describes. In the book, I highlight examples of Congress and Muslim League politicians' complicity in Partition-era riots in Bihar, Uttar Pradesh, and in Calcutta (pp. 5, 74). I also point out that in the post-Independence era Congress has, at times, benefited electorally from Hindu–Muslim violence (p. 50) and I find that we can identify no robust statistical relationship between Congress rule and the level of riots, a result I attribute to the widely varying communal character of the party and its leadership across time and place (p. 153). Lest anyone be in doubt about my position, I say on p. 153 that

> [A]t one time or another, Congress politicians have both fomented and prevented communal violence for political advantage. Congress governments have failed, for example, to prevent some of India's worst riots (e g, the Ahmedabad riots of 1969, the Moradabad riots of 1980, and the Meerut riots of 1987) and in some cases Congress ministers have reportedly instigated riots...and have blocked riot enforcement.

So, of course, I wholeheartedly accept Varshney's point that riots can occur under governments of many political stripes, because that is my point as well.

FUTURE RESEARCH POSSIBILITIES

The obvious direction for the future study of communal riots—at least from the perspective of my own discipline of political science—is to try to build explanations that work across many different levels (*mohalla*, town, state and national) and then test these explanations against plausible alternatives using good qualitative and quantitative data from at least several decades. This is a challenge, because the real world does not always provide us with the data we would wish to test our theories. I speak from experience, because even after spending many years working on my own book, I was not able to gather material to test all the explanations I wished using the whole 45 years of data on which I had data on riots.[6] Such testing is even more of a challenge for those scholars who focus on the role of inter-ethnic economic competition, town-level riot networks or social capital, where our most systematic data tends to be cross-sectional rather than time-series.[7]

One point that Varshney makes about the data I use is the question of whether it is legitimate to match constituency-level electoral data and town-level riot data, because some towns have more than one constituency. 'Wilkinson simply cannot be sure', he says, 'that riots at the town level are connected to the competitiveness of elections at the constituency level'. The first response to this criticism is to say that the multiple constituency-single town issue applies to only a small minority of the towns in my sample. The average constituency in Uttar Pradesh now has around 4,00,000 inhabitants and this population total is exceeded in only a dozen or so of the 167 towns in my sample; moreover, we know that the Election Commission tries to draw boundaries to avoid crossing administrative boundaries wherever possible.[8] Second, the procedure I use for the dozen remaining towns in the sample (seeing whether they contain constituencies that are highly competitive) is appropriate because we have good theoretical reasons to believe—on the basis of Brass's study of Aligarh, for instance—that competitive races in individual constituencies often lead to violence that ultimately affects the town as a whole.

Would my town level findings (reported in Table 2.1 of the book) about the importance of electoral competition in predicting riots at the local level go away if I were to drop the largest towns with multiple constituencies from my statistical analysis? I reran the statistical analysis to find out, and they would not.[9] I do not, of course, disagree with Varshney that it would be better and more conclusive if we had data on riots that always perfectly matched the boundaries of our electoral units. In fact, after my book was sent to the publishers, I was able to create such a dataset (for Gujarat, using electoral and census data I collected and constituency-level riot data obtained by Yogendra Yadav), and I have recently used it to analyse the pattern of electoral competition and riots in Gujarat before and after the 2002 riots to see, among other things, if the closeness of electoral competition there predicted violence. The findings—that competition at the constituency level predicts the location of riots—are entirely consistent with those in my book.

Ultimately, the best long-term test of any explanation is whether it seems to work with new data, or be successful at predicting what will happen in new situations. Do other scholars looking at communal riots identify the same factors as important and does my explanation seem to make more sense than the alternatives in explaining patterns of violence? I am optimistic, because other scholars using their own data have found very similar patterns to the ones that I identify in my own work. Yogendra Yadav (2003), for instance, examined the patterns of violence and the electoral swings in Gujarat in 2002 and found that 'the BJP managed to recover its eroding social base with carefully crafted and subtly executed politics of hatred.... Anti-Muslim violence played a crucial role in this process of recovery, damage control and acquisition'. I hope that my work, and the work of the many scholars who wrote in the pages of the *Economic and Political Weekly* and other Indian journals after the 2002 riots, will help to contribute to an emerging consensus on the crucial role of electoral competition and the actions of state in explaining patterns of peace and violence.

NOTES

1. See Wilkinson 2005. I am grateful to several colleagues who provided valuable comments on this piece.

2. *Indian Express* (New Delhi), 26 March 2002, p. 1. Wilkinson 2005a (pp. 63–96) explores in-depth the issue of state effectiveness.

3. I point out (pp. 8–9) that in systems where responsibility for law and order is shared across several levels of government such as national and local, the model can be extended 'to incorporate electoral incentives and power asymmetries across these different levels'. Although in India, states are by far the most important level to look at (national governments have in the past been loath to impose president's rule on states in which they or their allies are in office), I have recently argued that the 'changing dynamics between the central and state governments should also have a beneficial effect in reducing anti-Muslim violence' and in this and other papers I describe the ideological and pragmatic reasons why the current national Congress government is more likely to intervene against state governments that allow riots to break out. See Wilkinson 2005b.

4. Wilkinson 2005a, pp. 21–26, Muslims are 18 per cent of the total population and 32 per cent of the urban population in Uttar Pradesh, 6 per cent and 15 per cent in Madhya Pradesh, 8 per cent and 18 per cent in Rajasthan, 11 per cent and 25 per cent in Maharashtra, and 9 per cent and 14 per cent in Gujarat according to the 2001 Census.

5. For the general link between ethnic heterogeneity, constituency size and the number of parties in a plurality system, see Cox 1997, pp. 205–21.

6. Varshney states that there is a 'big silence' in my book on the issue of why my regressions were 'run only for the truncated period 1961–1995...' and that 'Wilkinson provides no assistance in the matter'. In fact, I would have liked to include data from 1950–60, and I explain clearly on p. 147 why I was not able to do so: 'I select 1961 as a starting date because state reorganisation was largely complete for major states by this date, and because the key demographic data for these new states is only easily available for 1961 onward'.

7. Achen (1982: 54–55) points out the very real problems with using cross-sectional data to sort out causality.

8. Varshney also raises the issue of cases with towns whose population is smaller than the total population of a constituency, but he provides no reason to convince us why it does not make sense to assume, as I do, that political life in a constituency of 4,00,000 probably revolves around the 2,00,000 population city that lies at its centre.

9. The statistical output from the replication and study referred to below is online at http://www.duke.edu/~swilkins/research.html.

References

Achen, Christopher H. 1982. *Interpreting and Using Regression*. Newbury Park, London and New Delhi: Sage Publications.

Brass, Paul R. 2003. *The Production of Hindu-Muslim Violence in Contemporary India*. New Delhi: Oxford University Press.

Cox, Gary. 1997. *Making Votes Count: Strategic Coordination in the World's Electoral Systems*. Cambridge: Cambridge University Press.

Varshney, Ashutosh. 2002. *Ethnic Conflict and Civic Life: Hindus and Muslims in India*. New Haven: Yale University Press.

———. 2005. 'An Electoral Theory of Communal Riots'. *Economic and Political Weekly* 40 (39), 24 September, 4219–24.

Wilkinson, Steven I. 2005a. *Votes and Violence: Electoral Competition and Communal Riots in India*. New Delhi: Cambridge University Press.

———. 2005b. 'Elections in India: Behind the Congress Comeback'. *Journal of Democracy* 16 (1), January, 153–67.

Yadav, Yogendra. 2003. 'Gujarat: The Patterns and Lessons'. *Frontline*, 21 December 2002–3 January 2003.

7

Development of an Institutionalised Riot System in Meerut City, 1961 to 1982*

Paul R. Brass

In many parts of India where Hindu–Muslim riots are endemic, especially in the northern and western states, institutionalised systems of riot production (IRS) have been created in the years since Independence, which are activated during periods of political mobilisation or at the time of elections. Far from being spontaneous occurrences, the production of such riots involves calculated and deliberate actions by key individuals, the conveying of messages, recruitment of participants, and other specific types of activities, especially provocative ones, that are part of a performative repertoire. Moreover, all these actions may require frequent rehearsals until the time is ripe, the context is felicitous, and there are no serious obstructions in carrying out the performance.

That Meerut has been in the past a site of endemic Hindu–Muslim riots is clear enough from the list of such events shown in Table 7.1. Serious riots, that is to say riots with deaths, have occurred in Meerut city since before Independence—in 1939 and 1946—and after Independence in 1961, 1968, 1973, 1982, 1986, 1987, 1989, 1990 and 1991.[1] Although no major riots have occurred in Meerut city since 1990, I have confirmed in recent visits to the city (January 2004) that an IRS continues to function and could be activated in the future. However, this chapter will focus on the riots of 1961 and 1982, leaving the other riots and an explanation for the current dormancy of the IRS for analysis in later publications.

While my last book,[2] which focuses on the history of riot production in the town of Aligarh, has been, for the most part, favourably received so far, legitimate issues have been raised concerning whether or not one can infer from the mere frequency of riots at a particular site the presence of an IRS and, secondly, whether the frequency of such riots in the past is a predictor of future riots.[3] A third issue has arisen as a consequence of the argument presented in the work of Ashutosh

* *Economic and Political Weekly* 39 (44): 4839–48 (30 October 2004).

TABLE 7.1: Riots and Riot Deaths in Meerut City, 1939–90

Date	*Official Death Toll*[a]	*Unofficial Estimates*
1939 (2 October)	8	
1946 (7–11 November)	29	
Pre-Independence total	37	
1961 (5–8 October)	14	17[b]
1968 (28–30 January)	13	17[c]
1973 (11 December)	7	
1982 (7–11 September; 29–30 September–1 October)	42[d]	85[e]
1986 (1 March)	3	
1987 (April–July)	136[f]	163[g]/329[h]
1989 (11 August)	1	
1990 (22 September)	1	
1990 (2–3 November)	12	16[i]
1990 (12–13 December)	1	4[j]
1991 (20 May)	32	
1991 (12 June)	1	
Post-Independence total	263	
Grand total	300	

Notes: [a] Figures are from the Varshney-Wilkinson dataset derived from *The Times of India*, kindly provided to me by Steven Wilkinson.
[b] Interview with Tanzim Ali Shah, in Meerut, 18 August 1983.
[c] Of which 16 were Muslims, one Hindu 'killed due to mistaken identity', according to Ray, Aswini K., and Subhash Chakravarti. 1968. Meerut Riots: A Case Study. New Delhi: Sampradayikta Virodhi Committee, 11.
[d] Wilkinson's dataset divides this long period of violence in Meerut into two separate riots, for which he gives the figure of 11 dead in the first, 31 in the second.
[e] S. A. A. Sabzwari. 1983. 'Meerut in Law Court', Meerut.
[f] Wilkinson's dataset gives death tolls in 1987 on seven different dates; I have combined them all into one figure.
[g] 'Muslim India 73', January 1989, 18, citing Kuldip Nayar in *Sunday Observer, 27 November 1988.*
[h] Muslim Advocate's Council. 1989. *'An Objective Study of 1987 Meerut Riots to Assess, How Deep is the Injury? and What Loss the Country Suffered?'*. Meerut, A-1–A-23.
[i] *ToI*, 3–4 November.
[j] 'Muslim India 98', February 1991, 78.

Source: Author.

Varshney concerning the critical importance of what he calls 'civic engagement' in riot prevention and the absence thereof as equally important in explaining the occurrence of riots.[4]

With regard to the first two issues, I have first to clarify my position as follows. The mere frequency of riots at a particular site does, to my mind, warrant the inference that a system of riot production exists, but does not prove its existence. The latter must be demonstrated. Quantitative, statistical analyses cannot demonstrate the existence of a dynamic process. The latter can be revealed fully only by ethnographic research. Press reports and other documentary sources may also be useful in providing evidence for or against the existence of an IRS. The primary scientific value of the discovery of the importance of the IRS as an explanatory factor in the production of riots is that it directs attention away from spurious explanations of riot occurrences, particularly those that argue that they are spontaneous occurrences arising out of historical animosities between peoples. But, the discovery also has policy implications since it demands that attention be paid to the actual instigators and perpetrators of acts of collective violence that everywhere have for far too long and far too often gone unrecognised and unpunished.

With regard to the second question, Wilkinson's data have identified previous frequency of riots as a significant explanatory variable in riot production.[5] But it certainly does not have universal power. One important reason that it does not have higher explanatory power is that local conditions that have provided the context for the creation of an IRS may change over time, placing the activation of the riot system in dormancy or, rather, to use my own metaphorical terminology, reducing it to the rehearsal phase, but not eliminating it from the site, thereby ensuring its availability if and when the political context changes.

With regard to the issue of the critical importance of civic engagement, that is, the existence or absence of inter-religious associations and interpersonal relations, I have found this argument of little value. It has neither statistical nor persuasive ethnographic support.[6] Most important, my research demonstrates that, even where elements of civic engagement do exist in civil society in India, they cannot withstand the power of political movements and forces that seek to create inter-communal violence. I believe that what is true for India is true elsewhere as well. Therefore, from a policy point of view, it is a pure diversion to invest resources in promoting civic engagement, when attention and resources should be directed towards uncovering the system and process of riot production and the producers thereof.

In the remainder of this article, I will provide ethnographic evidence to support my arguments on these three issues primarily from my own original research in Meerut between the years 1983 and 2004.[7] This article discusses only two of these riots, those of 1961 and 1982. I use the 1961 riots as a kind of benchmark to contrast with the later riots, to illustrate the changes that took place in the intervening period in their intensity and deadliness, and to explain how and why those changes have taken place.

RIOTS OF OCTOBER 1961

The Meerut riots of October 1961, which were enacted on 5–8 October, followed two days after the Aligarh riots of 1–3 October in which 15 people were reported to have been killed. The Meerut riots were almost equally deadly. Thirteen people were reported killed during these days and one other person was killed on 11 October during curfew relaxation, bringing the reported death toll to 14. Riots also occurred during this month in 13 other cities and towns in western Uttar Pradesh, but did not extend further to other parts of the state. These western Uttar Pradesh riots occurred four months before the third general elections. The Congress was the ruling party at the centre and in the state as well as the dominant party in Aligarh city and Meerut city. The communal composition of the populations of Aligarh and Meerut cities were roughly similar. Hindus and others constituted a majority in both towns, comprising 55 per cent and 58 per cent of the total respectively, compared to Muslims with 35 per cent and 37 per cent.

The home minister of the state government, responsible for law and order, was Chaudhuri Charan Singh, who took a hard stand against the communal riots in Meerut and elsewhere; he instructed the district magistrates to take firm action and sent police reinforcements to Meerut. On 8 October, additional forces were also sent to Meerut from both the Provincial Armed Constabulary (PAC) and the army, as they had been previously sent to Aligarh as well.[8]

[...]

Political Context of Riot Production

Let us now look more closely at the political context in which these riots were produced. The Congress was in power in Uttar Pradesh. Further, ... the entire period between 1952 and 1962 in Meerut city was one of Congress dominance: in municipal, legislative assembly, and Lok Sabha elections, all of which were won by the party in this period. Moreover, in the first two post-Independence legislative assembly elections, the Jan Sangh candidates polled poorly, losing their security deposits in both elections, and the party's candidate in 1957 polled fourth, with only 4.43 per cent of the vote.

As the rioting spread in Aligarh and Meerut, the chief minister and the home minister of Uttar Pradesh declared that these riots had been organised by political parties and unnamed 'communal organisations'[9] with the specific purpose of taking advantage of the situation for their own political benefit. Prem Bhatia, a columnist for *The Times of India*, was certain that the riots would cause 'considerable political damage' to the Congress in the forthcoming general elections and that 'the Hindu and Muslim communal parties' would gain from them. He argued that it would greatly increase both 'the Hindu and Muslim vote against the Congress', naming the Jan Sangh as the likely chief beneficiary.[10] The Home Minister, Charan Singh, made precisely the same assessment of the situation after a five-day tour of the riot-struck towns, saying that there was definitely a political conspiracy behind the riots, which displayed 'a common pattern' in the affected towns and that the purpose was 'to discredit the Congress among the Hindu and Muslim masses with a view to capturing political power'.[11]

The results of the February 1962 legislative assembly elections, held only four months after the September riots, confirmed Congress fears, though they do not prove the charges. The Congress vote declined precipitously, by approximately 20 per cent, while the Jan Sangh vote increased by approximately the same amount (Table 7.2). Moreover, the combined vote of the two militant Hindu candidates, from the Jan Sangh and the Hindu Mahasabha, was 31.40 per cent, a mere 175 votes short of the Congress total. Further points to note are, first, that both leading

TABLE 7.2: Election Results for Meerut City Legislative Assembly and Parliamentary Segment, 1952 to 1962

Year	*Turnout (Valid Votes Only)*		*Candidates*	*Caste/Community*	*Party*	*Votes Polled*	*Percentage of Total Valid Votes*
	No.	*Per Cent*					
1952[a]	43,988	53.39	Kailash Prakash	Bania	INC	26,542	60.33
			Ram Sarup Sharma	Brahman	IND	6,943	15.80
			Raja Ram		Jan Sangh	4,957	11.27
			Madan Mohan		Socialist	4,626	10.52
			Madho Prasad		IND	490	1.11
			Kashi Ram		IND	430	0.97
1957[b]	52,915	67.56	Kailash Prakash	Bania	INC	27,059	51.14
			Aizaz Hussain	Muslim	CPI	18,604	35.16
			V. S. Vinod	Vaish	IND	3,130	5.92
			Pershadi Lal		JS	2,344	4.43
			Bishan Sarup		RRP	1,115	2.11
			Ghamandi Lal		IND	663	1.25
1962[c]	56,849	62.31	Jagdish Saran Rastogi	Bania	INC	18,026	31.71
			Mohan Lal Kapoor	Khatri	JS	14,683	25.83
			A. Majeed [Abdul Majid]	Muslim (Ansari)	PSP	12,072	21.24
			Hakim Ullah	Muslim (Lohar)	CPI	4,499	7.91
			V. S. Vinod	Vaish	HMS	3,168	5.57
			Shiva Nand	NA	IND	2,049	3.60
			Others (5)			2,352	4.14
1962 Lok Sabha, Meerut segment	58,793	64.44	Shah Nawaz Khan	Muslim	INC	32,450	55.19
			Maharaj Singh Bharati	Jat	Socialist	21,340	36.30
			Shiv Datt Singh	Jatav	JS	4,361	7.42
			Ratish Mohan Agarwal	Bania	IND	642	1.09

Note: a. 3–25 January 1952; b. 9 March 1957; c. 23 February 1962.
Source: Author.

candidates in 1962 were Hindus, whereas the runner-up in 1957 was a Muslim member of the Communist Party of India. Second, the combined vote for the two Muslim candidates in 1962 was less than that of the sole Muslim candidate in 1957. So, the riots were followed by a diminution of the electoral strength of the Congress and an increase in that of the Jan Sangh, and probably was a direct political consequence of the riots. Further, the circumstantial evidence suggests that the riots were produced with the political complicity of the Jan Sangh and other militant Hindu elements,[12] with the hope that it would enhance their vote in the upcoming elections.

Riots of 1982

I want to fast forward now 20 years to the riots of 1982, by which time the Meerut IRS was fully developed, and the political context had changed significantly. The riots of 1982 were ultimately overshadowed, and have since been almost forgotten, in the aftermath of the even more horrendous massacres of 1987 in Meerut and nearby localities of Maliana and Hashimpur. These massacres were so horrific and went so far beyond anything that had happened before, either in Meerut or in other parts of the country since Partition, that they received quite considerable national and some international attention. Moreover, efforts continue to this day to bring to book through the Indian courts the principal culprits in those great massacres. 1987 was, in effect, the culmination of a quarter century of development of the Meerut IRS, but the way was paved by the great trial run of 1982. It is important, therefore, for many reasons, not to forget 1982 if we are to understand how riots become endemic in a particular site and how their perpetrators are enabled to move from transgression to transgression with relative impunity. In contrast to the situation with regard to the 1961 riots just discussed, information on the 1982 riots from my own interviews and from the documentary record are ample.[13] This in itself constitutes an important difference, the significance of which will be discussed in the conclusions.

Changed Political Context

The political context had changed dramatically during the previous two decades. Jawaharlal Nehru was prime minister in 1961; he had never deviated from devotion to secular principles and had broad support among the Muslims in the country. However, over the years during Indira Gandhi's turbulent rule, she and the Congress had lost much of their former support among Muslims, especially in north India. This change occurred partly because of a general rise of Muslim political assertiveness on many issues, including the increasing frequency and scale of rioting during the preceding 20 years, and Muslim disillusionment in consequence of these riots. At the same time, Indira Gandhi had changed her political tactics and had begun to appeal more and more directly to Hindus, in Jammu and Kashmir and elsewhere in the country. The opposition to her had also changed. The former Jan Sangh had been transmuted into the Bharatiya Janata Party (BJP) and was projecting a moderate face, which made possible inter-party alliances between it and other non-Congress parties. However, many in the Rashtriya Swayamsevak Sangh (RSS), the organisational base of the BJP, distrusted the new face of the BJP, preferred Gandhi's new face, and, in my personal knowledge, did support Congress candidates in Uttar Pradesh in the ensuing elections of 1984 and 1985.

The political context in Meerut had also changed dramatically, twice over in fact, since the riots of 1961 and 1968. Between 1967 and 1974, the Jan Sangh had captured the Meerut city legislative assembly constituency. ... Its candidate, Mohan Lal Kapoor, had won the elections of 1967, 1969 and 1974. However, between 1974 and the Meerut riots of 1982, the political context had once again been transformed. The emergency had come and gone, the Jan Sangh had merged into the Janata Party, along with other parties, to defeat the Congress in the 1977 elections, and, after the disintegration of the Janata Party, the BJP had not been able to retain the Jan Sangh's hold on Meerut city, though its candidate remained Mohan Lal Kapoor. Instead, the Congress appealed directly to the Muslim voters in its efforts to regain both the Meerut city legislative assembly constituency and the Meerut Lok Sabha constituency by running Muslim candidates in both constituencies, who had been loyal to Indira Gandhi during the Emergency. The Congress, with Manzur Ahmad as its candidate, succeeded in wresting the Meerut city constituency in the June 1977 elections, and secured it again with the same candidate in 1980. It regained the Lok Sabha constituency in 1980, with Mohsina Kidwai as its candidate. But now, in the highly competitive political and electoral context that had emerged in the aftermath of the Emergency, Indira Gandhi had once again changed her tactics, as above noted, towards more conscious efforts to retain and expand the hold of the Congress among the Hindu majority population of the country.

Origin of the 1982 Riots

There is a virtually universal tendency to seek a precipitant or cause for the beginning of every large-scale riot, to give it a central focus, a date and an explanation. I have also noted elsewhere that this type of effort is misleading, distracts our attention from the activities, incidents and preparations that are involved by riot producers, who fasten upon local controversies when the time is ripe to let loose the violence. Further, there are always multiple narratives concerning the unfolding of events, including the singular event upon which the effort of explanation is focused.[14] That was the case in the 1982 Meerut riots, where the central focus was upon a site in the *mohalla* of Shaghasa variously described to me, and visited by me, in August 1983. That site was described alternatively as a temple or a 'mazār', or a drinking water well that was either in use or not in use, and even as a site adjacent to a latrine. The ownership of the site was also disputed. And the so-called real reasons for the dispute and its transformation into a great riot are also contested.

In my experience, this type of controversy, or description of a controversy, between Hindus and Muslims, is virtually universal in the cities and towns in north

India where Hindu and Muslim populations live in mixed neighbourhoods. These local disputes, some of them completely fabricated, as I believe was the case in Meerut in 1982, are mini-Ayodhyas, the source of the provocative and disingenuous militant Hindu claim that there are some 3,000 sites where Hindu temples were destroyed in the distant past to make way for Muslim mosques. These controversies can rise to the level of widespread rioting only if external political forces are brought to the scene to make use of them for their own purposes. In Meerut, as elsewhere in India at this time, the Vishva Hindu Parishad was active, in the early stages of the Ayodhya movement itself, and it and other elements in the Sangh parivar also became involved in this affair.

But it is my contention that this local dispute had even then a much broader political significance in Indian politics and society that continues up to the present day. The Meerut site is merely one location in a huge grid or lattice-work of such sites that are laced together especially, but not exclusively, in northern and western India. The grid is much denser in these parts, but it extends to many other parts of the country, including the deep south, where new sites of this type are currently being activated.[15] Further, the Meerut situation had multi-level political-electoral ramifications: it was used to mobilise Hindus and Muslims on opposite sides in municipal elections that were held in the midst of the controversy; the local politicians also had their sights set on its consequences for them in future legislative assembly elections; and it was a replica of the developing conflict in Ayodhya.

Another way of seeing the creation of these little sites of conflict, with only slightly different variations to fit each local context, is to consider them as an element or, as Tilly has put it, a 'routine' in a political repertoire of staged conflicts.[16] Far from springing directly out of the history of Hindu–Muslim relations, religious differences, and social animosities, or even out of long-simmering local disputes, these temple–mosque and mandir–mazār conflicts are recently learned forms of collective action,[17] with specific aims of producing the very animosities, controversies, and violence (when desired) from which they are alleged to have sprung. Moreover, their purpose is also clear: to produce electoral benefits and, in the Indian political scene of the past two decades, to produce a complete shift in the forms of political domination in the country. The routines are well known, widely spread and are probably not centrally directed. But they are often—if not generally—deliberately staged. They are staged in the same way as Gandhi's mass movements, which selected particular foci that would arouse the people of India against the British and British rule, but in a disciplined, peaceful, non violent manner. In Indian politics of the past two decades, however, the organisations in the militant Hindu family have deliberately chosen to focus on issues that will divide Hindus and Muslims, knowingly inciting crowds to turbulence and violent action. Muslim politicians, religious leaders and other Muslim organisations have also contributed to the process, but the main driving forces behind the spatial extension of these local conflicts, and the main beneficiaries, have been the militant Hindu family of organisations.

CONCLUSION

I want to conclude by summarising the similarities and differences between the riots of 1961 and 1982. First, the similarities. There is a clear connection in both cases between the timing of the riots and elections—legislative assembly elections in 1961–62 and municipal elections in 1982—and the involvement of local politicians in the events that led up to the riots. Inter-communal associations existed in Meerut at the time of both riots, but were overpowered by the momentum of events and the passions aroused by them at the time, leading to polarisation on both sides and consolidation of communal voting in subsequent elections. On both occasions, the police were partial to the Hindu side and acted in a hostile manner towards Muslims. The riots on both occasions, though they originated in local disputes, had multilevel political significance and involved politicians and other activists from the local level to the state to the national level.

Finally, with regard to the question of civic action to prevent, contain and control riots, it is evident that the political mobilisation of communal sentiment overpowered whatever civic engagement existed in Meerut and that civic action to contain and control rioting once started was ineffective. The ability to sustain inter-communal relations, sentiments and actions, and thus provide a barrier to communal violence, decreases the longer the authorities delay, procrastinate and thereby allow the momentum of the move towards a communal riot to accelerate. At some point, if no action or insufficient or incompetent measures are taken, the end result is total communal polarisation that overwhelms all existing inter-communal feelings of commercial, professional and interpersonal solidarity.

The differences between the origins, development and denouement of the two riots are profound. First, the 1961 riots arose out of student fracases into which others, especially local politicians, were drawn, and from which they sought political advantage. The 1982 riots, in contrast, were a staged performance in a new repertoire that was being enacted in other parts of the country and that continues to be enacted up to the very present. Second, there is the shadowy presence, if not the direct, active involvement, of a national militant Hindu organisation, the Vishva Hindu Parishad, and the issues raised by it during that time up to the present, that enables the incorporation of local issues into a national frame. Third, stable governments and a unified stance towards containment of the riots, however ineffective, existed in 1961, but were absent in 1982. Indeed, there were deep political divisions at all levels in 1982—local, state and national—that prevented uniform, prompt and decisive action.

The district administration of the time was incompetent, and some of its officers were partial to the Hindu side. The Congress was in power in the state government, whose Chief Minister Sripat Misra was one of the weakest in the state's history, whose government was unstable and divided by factional divisions concerning the distribution of portfolios. Moreover, in those days, no Congress chief minister could do anything of political importance without consulting the prime minister or her son, Rajiv Gandhi, or other close associates of the ruling family in New Delhi.

While the rioting was spreading in Meerut, the chief minister held on to the home portfolio, that is, the ministerial position whose occupant is responsible for law and order in the state, including control of the police forces. In the political conditions of the time, Sripat Misra, otherwise occupied, subject to control from Delhi, had neither the will nor the capacity to issue the necessary orders to bring the Meerut rioting to an end. Such orders should have begun with the transfer of the senior administrative and police officers of the district as soon as it was evident that they had failed in their duties, a practice that has since become the norm.

As for New Delhi itself, it has already been noted above that the prime minister was herself seeking to transform the Congress support base in the country, especially in the north, by courting militant Hindu support, including that of the RSS. So, the central government itself procrastinated. It need not have waited for the state government to request the deployment of central forces since the state government would bow to the merest wish of the prime minister in those days. In short, at no level of government whatsoever in India at that time was there any disposition to exercise effective force to bring the Meerut rioting to an end until the massacre at the Feroze Building[18] drew sufficient media and public attention to the consequences of this total failure of government responsibility in India.

Fourth, we witness in 1982 not merely police partiality, not merely a riot, but a vicious police (PAC) attack upon the Muslim population at the termination of the riots in a pattern that, again, has not only continued up to present times, but became even more extreme at this site (in 1987) and at other sites (Gujarat, 2002). All these differences add up to the demonstrable presence of a system and a set of practices that constitute what I have characterised as an institutionalised riot system, a system that can be activated when the time is ripe and that involves the utilisation of a coherent repertoire of routine actions.

The differences clearly outweigh the similarities in their implications for inter-communal relations in contemporary India, which can only be seen in negative terms. There is, however, a difference, with more hopeful implications, between the two situations, namely the extent of documentation that exists for 1982 and later riots compared to what existed in 1961. There exists now in India an institutionalised system of riot documentation (call it an ISRD) that comes into play after each riot, that embraces a range of civil liberties organisations, secular intellectuals, retired Supreme Court judges, English-language press journalists, and others who go to the sites of these riots, pogroms and massacres, record for all time the actions of IRS actors, including often the names of the leading perpetrators, and create a body of truths to counter the mendacities of the perpetrators and the blame-displacing claims of their apologists. Up till the present, the force of the institutionalised riot systems that continue to exist at numerous sites in India continues to outweigh the ISRD, but the latter provides a ground for hope that this form of extra-local civic action may acquire sufficient political force and backing to ultimately displace and contain the former.

NOTES

1. Although the data are unreliable, Meerut also ranks very high in the list of 'riot-prone towns' in India in the period from 1960 to 1993, in Varshney, Ashutosh, and Steven I. Wilkinson. 1996. *Hindu-Muslim Riots 1960–93: New Findings, Possible Remedies.* New Delhi: Rajiv Gandhi Institute for Contemporary Studies, 27; and also in the period from 1950 to 1995 in Varshney, Ashutosh. 2001. 'Ethnic Conflict and Civil Society: India and Beyond'. *World Politics* 53 (3), April, 372. In the latter, Meerut and Aligarh rank fourth and fifth respectively in the number of deaths in the period, just below the three metropolitan cities of Bombay, Ahmedabad and Hyderabad.

2. Brass, Paul R. 2004. *The Production of Hindu-Muslim Violence in Contemporary India.* Seattle: University of Washington Press; New Delhi: Oxford University Press.

3. Wilkinson, Steven I. 2004. *Votes and Violence: Electoral Competition and Ethnic Riots in India.* Cambridge: Cambridge University Press, 52–53.

4. Varshney, Ashutosh. 2002. *Ethnic Conflict and Civic Life: Hindus and Muslims in India.* New Haven: Yale University Press. I have outlined some of the numerous deficiencies in this work in Brass 2004, 418–19 fn.

5. Wilkinson 2004, 44.

6. See Wilkinson 2004, 53–57 on the absence of statistical data; and on the paucity of either quantitative or qualitative data, see Dipankar Gupta's review of Varshney's book, under the title, 'Fanaticising Religion' in *The Book Review,* September 2002.

7. My research in Meerut city and district actually began in 1962, but my focus was different at that time and did not touch upon the 1961 riots.

8. *The Times of India,* 9 October 1961.

9. *The Times of India,* 8 October 1961.

10. *The Times of India,* 10 October 1961.

11. *The Times of India,* 11 October 1961.

12. Among those reported to have been arrested for curfew violation on 7 October was the Rashtriya Swayamsevak Sangh organiser, Rameshwar Dayal; *The Times of India,* 8 October 1961.

13. There are also two other published reports, based on original research in Meerut undertaken shortly after these riots, by Asghar Ali Engineer. Engineer, Asghar Ali. 1984. 'An Analytical Study of the Meerut Riot' in *Communal Riots in Post-Independence India,* ed. Asghar Ali Engineer. Hyderabad: Sangam Books, 271–80 and Saxena, N. C. 1999. 'Inquiry Report on Meerut Riots, September–October, 1982' (abridged version), in *Communal Riots: The State and Law in India,* ed. Iqbal A. Ansari. New Delhi: Institute of Objective Studies, 356–66. See also a later report by Anamika Srivastava. Srivastava, Anamika. 1999. *Communal Violence and Administration.* New Delhi: Rawat, chapter 8.

14. I have demonstrated this especially in Brass, Paul R. 1997. *Theft of an Idol.* Princeton: Princeton University Press.

15. For example, the recent controversy fomented by the RSS in Chikmagalur in Karnataka concerning the Bababudangiri Sufi shrine, *Frontline* 20 (26), 20 December 2003–2 January 2004.

16. Tilly refers, for example, in his discussion of the development of mass politics in Great Britain, to 'repertoires of contention'. The word repertoire identifies a limited set of routines that are learned, shared and acted out through a relatively deliberate process of choice: 'People learn to break windows in protest, attack pilloried prisoners, tear down dishonored houses, stage public marches, petition, hold formal meetings, organise

special-interest associations. At any particular point in history, however, they learn only a rather small number of alternative ways to act collectively'; Tilly, Charles. 1993. 'Contentious Repertoires in Great Britain, 1758–1834'. *Social Science History* 17 (2), Summer, 264.

17. Or relearned, if one accepts the view of C. A. Bayly: Bayly, C. A. 1998. 'The Pre-history of "Communalism"? Religious Conflict in India, 1700–1860', in *Origins of Nationality in South Asia: Patriotism and Ethnical Government in the Making of Modern India*, C. A. Bayly. New Delhi: Oxford University Press, 225 ff.

18. This refers to a major incident in the 1982 riots: 'The most infamous and atrocious incident during the 1982 riots was the massacre of an estimated 29 people—men, women, and children, all Muslims—by the PAC at a site known as the Feroze Building.' Please see full original version for details. [eds]

8

Muzaffarnagar Riots

*Perils of Patronage Democracy**

Ward Berenschot

The recent upsurge of communal violence in Uttar Pradesh has allayed hopes that India's economic growth would gradually put an end to a long history of Hindu–Muslim strife. Since 7 September 2013, at least 52 people (15 Hindus and 37 Muslims) have died and 50,000 people were displaced around the town of Muzaffarnagar. Subsequently, about 30 children have frozen to death due to the appalling conditions in the refugee camps where thousands are still staying out of fear of returning to their ransacked homes.

The immediate trigger had been a dispute over, apparently, the stalking of a girl. This dispute led to the death of the alleged stalker, a Muslim, and two family members of the girl, Hindu Jat farmers. In this region, Muslims have been working the field of Jat farmers for generations, but this interdependence did not prevent politicians from both communities to react to the incident with incendiary speeches. As the Uttar Pradesh government wavered in its response and community mobilisation got underway, a gruesome spectacle of mass violence enfolded. The Muzaffarnagar riots have been the largest outburst since the 2002 violence in Gujarat, but it is by no means an isolated incident: after the Samajwadi Party (SP) under Akhilesh Yadav came to power in Uttar Pradesh in March 2012, the police has counted 39 outbursts of communal riots (Rai 2013).

To explain this upsurge, we need to go beyond the usual political incriminations and look at the nature of Uttar Pradesh's political arena instead. Sure enough, there are plenty of reasons to blame political strategising for the violence. Ahead of the 2014 general elections, the Bharatiya Janata Party (BJP) badly needs to recover lost ground in the state. ... Their militant defence of the Jat community seems a calculated attempt to solidify Hindu support.

Similarly, there are good reasons to suspect that the wavering response of Yadav's government have been guided by the need to maintain the support of Uttar Pradesh's Muslim community, so crucial for the SP's electoral victory in the 2012

* *Economic and Political Weekly* 49 (12): 15–18 (22 March 2014).

state elections. This might explain the perceived bias of the police against the Jat community, the release of Muslim suspects and the transferring of police officials who arrested these suspects. Because of these observations, it has been argued that the recent violence is the result of an implicit 'deal' between the BJP and the SP, intended to polarise society along communal line (see Centre for Policy Analysis 2013; Rao et al. 2013). Intense polarisation might serve to weaken the mobilisational capacity of competing political parties like the Bahujan Samaj Party (BSP) and the Congress.

Such political machinations are a recurring element of reporting on communal riots and they also figure prominently in academic explanations for India's Hindu–Muslim violence. They are, however, unsatisfying on two accounts: first, such a focus on the strategies of political elites leaves unexplained why common villagers—who do not share the same political interests—could be instigated to participate in the violence. And second, the observation that politicians can benefit from the resulting social polarisation begs the question: what is it about India's political arena that makes social polarisation such a profitable political strategy?

After a year-long period of fieldwork on the organisation behind Gujarat's 2002 violence, I feel that the answer to these questions lies in the dependence of particularly poorer citizens on patronage networks to gain access to state institutions. Such an analysis is not meant to refute political explanations for violence, nor does it exonerate individuals of their responsibility for stoking communal embers. But it might help to understand why they do so.

Patronage networks are exchange networks: through these channels, political elites mobilise (electoral) support—votes and campaign support, but also campaign budgets—while compensating their supporters by providing them with access to state resources such as jobs, public services or business contracts. The widespread dependence of citizens on such patronage networks is strengthened by a largely self-enforcing mechanism: as citizens reward politicians for providing them with access to state resources, political success is largely premised on developing control over the functioning of state bureaucracies, which in turn reinforces the dependence of voters on political mediation. It is because of this entrenched political meddling in the functioning of state bureaucracies that India has been called a 'patronage democracy'.

Infrastructure for Violence

So what does this dependence on patronage networks have to do with the violence that engulfs a community after a relatively small incident such as eve-teasing? A focus on the functioning of these patronage networks yield two important mechanisms of how and why a patronage democracy engenders—under certain conditions—communal violence. One mechanism is related to the actual organisation of violence, the other to the political exploitation of social identities.

First, the organisation of violence. A recurring element in studies on the 'groundwork' of Uttar Pradesh's politics are descriptions of how political parties are using their control over the distribution of state resources to attract and reward voters

(Chandra 2004). Such clientelistic strategies require effective networks: informal links between local (community) leaders, political workers and state officials are necessary to ensure that efforts to distribute state resources—jobs, public services, government contracts, etc.—will indeed be reciprocated by voters at the time of elections.

Furthermore, clientelistic strategies lead to the politicisation of state bureaucracies. The inability of police officials in Uttar Pradesh to arrest politically well-connected criminals—yielding perceptions of a 'goonda raj'—is just one visible effect of the control that politicians wield over the bureaucracy. As a result, for less privileged citizens, the access to, say, a secure land title, a government job or a loan is not based on one's individual rights as a citizen, but rather the result of the negotiations and exchanges of favours with political intermediaries (Jeffrey 2002).

In this way, clientelistic electoral strategies are generating widespread patronage networks that, at times of communal tensions, can serve as the infrastructure for the mobilisation of mobs and the organisation of violence. Not just party members or local strongmen but also criminal actors, state officials, businessmen and police officers derive at least a part of their livelihood from the (business) opportunities and state resources that can be obtained through political connections. Such benefits give these actors various incentives to nurture their contacts with politicians and influential bureaucrats. These incentives make the instigation of violence possible: the capacity of political actors to mobilise large mobs, distribute weapons and prevent police intervention is related to the rewards that individuals at lower levels in the clientelistic pyramid can reap by performing favours for their patrons.

POLICE, GOONDAS, LEADERS

Take, for example, the failure of police officials to stem the violence and the accusations that minister Azam Khan ordered the transfer of police officials and a district magistrate for arresting Muslims. For police officials, maintaining good relations with politicians serves to streamline a steady stream of bribes. By crossing politicians, by for example, attempting to prevent violence, police officials risk being transferred to 'punishment postings'. Given the considerable bribe they often had to pay to secure a good posting, such a transfer would imply a serious financial risk. As a result of this dependency on political patrons, the police force cannot function as a bulwark against the instigation of ethnic violence; the control of politicians over the postings of police officers undermines the capacity and willingness of individual officers to function as custodians of the law.

A similar argument can be made about another important type of contributors to communal violence: local criminals or goondas. Patronage channels need individuals known for their capacity for violence, not only for the (campaign) money that their illegal activities bring in, but also because of the need for 'muscle power' to establish local authority to provide protection in the absence of a fully sovereign police force. For their part, local goondas face strong incentives to attach themselves to political patrons, since their livelihoods—extortion, gambling, illegal trade, etc.—often depend on political contacts to ward off police intervention. As a result, political actors dispose of a lot of 'muscle power' that can be asked to take the lead during outbursts of violence.

A third group of contributors are community leaders. Local leaders come in various forms and sizes, but a recurring aspect of local leadership is that it is bound with a capacity to 'get things done', that is, to deal with state institutions on behalf of their community members (Krishna 2007). For ambitious individuals, the development of ties with influential power holders can thus hardly be avoided—which makes them and their community vulnerable to political manipulation. In a similar manner, one can analyse the local popularity of militant organisations like the Vishva Hindu Parishad (VHP) or the Rashtriya Swayamsevak Sangh (RSS). Their appeal is not just based on ideology or the invocation of a shared enemy. Their popularity is also related to the way these organisations are integrated into local patronage channels and, consequently, the capacity of these organisations to provide followers with a government job, a business opportunity or preferential treatment by the police.

In short: the networks involved in the instigation and perpetration of violence are not just 'institutionalised riot systems' (Brass 2003); they are patronage networks. Their capacity to instigate violence is related to their capacity to provide access to state resources.

Patronage and Identity Politics

A second important mechanism linking the daily machinations of a patronage democracy to outbursts of violence concerns identity politics. It is often commented that India's pervasive identity politics stems from the usefulness of social identities to mobilise electoral support. A focus on the intricacies of clientelistic exchanges can help understand why this is so.

When access to public services is shaped by political intercession rather than policy provisions, candidates do not need to convince voters of the effectiveness or reasonableness of policy proposals. They need to find ways to credibly convey the promise that after elections, they will be willing to devote time and energy to solve their problems. Social identities provide useful means to convey this promise. A shared social identity—whether in terms of caste, regional background or religion—provides a candidate with the (symbolic) arguments to convince voters that he will be 'their man' and empathises with their needs. The different identity dimensions among the electorate are instruments for politicians to make these promises more convincing. Through the use of different identity symbols, and through the invocation of antagonisms between voters, politicians can convey their most important message: after the elections, I will be more helpful to you than other candidates.

Furthermore, a clientelistic political arena generates important incentives for political leaders, their clients and brokers to structure their clientelistic exchanges along the lines of social divisions such as religion or caste. As both voters and politicians exchange political support for access to state resources, ethnicity provides them with a very useful tool to do so. A shared caste background of candidates gives voters some reassurance that an elected candidate will actually be of help after the elections to deal with state institutions. For politicians, the invocation of identity symbols provides them with a useful means to convey a credible promise to the electorate that they will be more helpful to the voter then the opposing political party.

And for brokers—the local leaders and 'fixers' who mediate the interaction between politician and voters—their leadership of a community can be used to reassure politicians of their capacity to deliver a large number of votes. As politicians need to use their limited resources efficiently, they prefer to deal with brokers who possess authority over a large number of voters. In the absence of strong civil society organisations (like trade unions, cooperatives, business organisations), brokers can invoke their membership of a community to reassure politicians of their capacity to deliver a large number of votes. After elections, this membership is again invoked to pressurise politicians into delivering the promised public resources.

COMMUNITY MOBILISATION

This imperative to organise election campaigns around us–them divisions stimulates politicians to engage in attempts to manipulate the importance that voters attach to different identity dimensions. While, for example, the BJP targets a religious divide, BSP, Congress and SP particularly target caste divisions. As political campaigns are thus organised around different identity dimensions—caste, religion, and class and region—electoral success depends to a certain extent on heightening the public awareness of one such dimension at the expense of other dimensions.

Campaign speeches of politicians can often be interpreted as attempts to manipulate this salience of 'their' identity dimension. Outbursts of communal violence serve this purpose very effectively: by polarising society along a religious divide, such violence hinders the mobilisation efforts of parties who target caste divisions. A patronage democracy thus stimulates a constant manipulation of the importance that people attach to different dimensions of their social identities.

The process of invoking social divisions to facilitate clientelistic exchanges has the important side effect of associating the membership of a community to the access to (state) resources. As the contacts and solidarity that these networks offered proved essential to secure education, healthcare or security, the impression is generated that the election of someone from another community to a key position would form a real threat to one's well-being and one's chances to succeed in life. When the networks that provide access to state resources become organised around social divisions, the potential power-shifts that elections bring about thus provide ample motivation for not only elites, but also their followers to mobilise.

In this way, one could interpret the remark of a Jat farmer from Muzaffarnagar that, 'There will be no peace until the balance of power is sorted out' (Jha 2013). This remark is not just about community honour. As Muslim votes have helped the SP come to power in Uttar Pradesh, their access to state institutions, particularly the police, has improved. This increased closeness to state authorities yields not only material benefits, but also symbolically shifts perceptions of power and superiority between communities. Take this quotation from a Meerut resident:

> This government has been trying to show itself as pro-Muslim. As a result, young and irresponsible groups among Muslims too race about on mobikes, violate traffic signals and, when stopped, stick their mobiles on the ears of the policeman and put a local leader on the line, frightening the cop (Chishti 2013).

Such community-based shifts in access to state institutions create tensions. In this way, the fragmented and versatile nature of local patronage channels can help explain the current upsurge in violence in Uttar Pradesh. The national elections in 2014 are creating tension in the state not only because Narendra Modi's candidacy is bringing Muslim–Hindu divisions to the fore, but also because these elections provide an occasion for local communities to rally against (or defend) uneven access to state institutions.

References

Brass, Paul. 2003. *The Production of Hindu-Muslim Violence in Contemporary India*. Seattle: University of Washington Press.

Centre for Policy Analysis. 2013. 'Muzaffarnagar 2013—Violence by Political Design', available at http://kafi la.org/2013/09/18/muzaffarnagar-2013-violence-by-political-design-centre-for-policyanalysis/ (accessed 11 October 2013).

Chandra, Kanchan. 2004. *Why Ethnic Parties Succeed: Patronage and Ethnic Head Counts in India*. Cambridge: Cambridge University Press.

Chishti, Seema. 'Western UP on Edge'. *The Indian Express*, 7 October 2013, available at http://www.indianexpress.com/news/western-up-on-the-edge/1179208/0 (accessed 11 October 2013).

Krishna, Anirudh. 2007. 'Politics in the Middle: Mediation Relationships between the Citizens and the State in Rural North India', in *Patrons, Clients and Policies: Patterns of Democratic Accountability and Political Competition*, eds H. Kitschelt and S, Wilkinson. Cambridge: Cambridge University Press, 141–58.

Jeffrey, Craig. 2002. 'Caste, Class and Clientelism: A Political Economy of Everyday Corruption in Rural North India'. *Economic Geography* 78 (1), 21–42.

Jha, Prashant. 'We Have Been Reduced to Strangers in Our Own Land'. *The Hindu*, 16 September 2013, available at http://www.thehindu.com/news/national/other-states/wehave-been-reduced-to-strangers-inour-own-land/article5133814.ece (accessed 8 October 2013).

Rai, Manmohon. 'Samajwadi Party Ruling: Over 3 Dozen Riots Reported in Less than Two Years'. *The Economic Times*, 9 September 2013, available at http://articles.economictimes.indiatimes.com/2013-09-09/news/41903441_1_akhilesh-yadavgovernment-muzaffarnagar-two-youths (accessed 9 October 2013).

Rao, Mohan, Ish Mishra, Pragya Singh, and Vikas Bajpai. 2013. 'Communalism and the Role of the State: An Investigation into the Communal Violence in Muzaffarnagar and Its Aftermath', available at http://www.epw.in/system/fi les/Muzaffarmagar%20Report%20-%20Final%20(1).pdf (accessed 11 October 2013).

9

Institutional Communalism in India*

Pritam Singh

[...]

Progressive discourse around the critique of communalism in India has focused primarily on instances of inter-religious violence and the activities of political and social organisations that are characterised as communal—that is to say 'engaged in articulating the demands or viewpoints of one or other religious community'. The fundamental weakness of this discourse is that it neglects the deeper and less visible political, socio-economic and cultural structures that give birth to sectarianism/communalism and to sectarian/communal organisations. Furthermore, such a discourse has an inbuilt bias in that it equates, what are normally referred to in the literature as, majority and minority communalisms. This chapter is an attempt to develop a critique of this discourse by delving deeper into the institutional structures of communalism in India. I have chosen to name this deeper structure of communalism as institutional communalism, drawing on the experiences of anti-racist activism and theories of institutional racism in the UK.

[...]

Defining Institutional Communalism

It may be useful for getting a sense of the term institutional communalism to mention here that the inspiration for using it came from the term 'institutional racism', used in Britain initially in the context of racism in the police force, but eventually extended to identify racism in many other institutions. William Macpherson, who headed the inquiry into the death of a black teenager Stephen Lawrence, used the term institutional racism to characterise the systematic racism prevalent in London's Metropolitan police force. Lawrence was an 18-year-old from London, a student, who was murdered in a racist attack while waiting for a bus on the evening of 22 April 1993. After the initial investigation, five suspects, all white, were arrested but not convicted. It emerged during the course of this investigation that the murder

* *Economic and Political Weekly* 50 (28): 48–56 (11 July 2015).

was racially motivated and that the handling of the case by the police and the Crown Prosecution Service was influenced by considerations of race.

The public outrage at the handling of this case by the police and the prosecution service, the media campaign on the case, and the public campaign led by Lawrence's parents forced the government to order a public enquiry in 1998 that was led by William Macpherson. The inquiry report, published in 1999, which came to be known as the Macpherson Report, concluded that the Metropolitan police force that had originally investigated the case was 'institutionally racist'. The systematic/ institutional racism was not about one or more individuals in the police force being racist; instead, it was about the entire gamut of functioning of the police force in its dealings with minority ethnic groups.

The general definition of institutional racism provided by Macpherson (1999) was: 'the collective failure of an organisation to provide an appropriate and professional service to people because of their colour, culture, or ethnic origin'.[1] Extending the scope of his recommendations beyond police reforms, Macpherson called for institutional reforms in the civil services, local governments, the National Health Service, schools and the judicial system to address issues of institutional racism. The term 'institutional racism' had been used before, most famously by Stokely Carmichael, the Black Panther, in the 1960s and the 1970s in the USA,[2] but the Macpherson Report triggered a resurgence of interest in this term and shifted public attention from the physically violent racist actions of individual racists to the racism inherent in the day-to-day practices of these state and other institutions. The focus on institutional racism triggered by the report helped extend the public debates on racism beyond the criticisms of political organisations that were considered racist, such as the British National Party, to the investigations into racism in the mode of functioning of a wide variety of institutions of British society and state.

Employing the concept of institutional communalism in India, in the manner in which institutional racism has been used in the UK, can offer us a new perspective on communalism/religious sectarianism that extends beyond the political activities of 'extremist' political, social and cultural organisations. One major weakness of the anti-communalism discourse in India has been the excessive focus on political activities of organisations that are considered communal, for example, the organisations associated with what is called the Sangh Parivar, the group of organisations that are considered advocates of Hindu majoritarian dominance in India. The same method is employed to examine political organisations that are considered advocates of any minority religious community, such as Muslims, Sikhs and, to a lesser extent, Christians.

[...]

Evidence of Institutional Communalism

In the same manner that institutional racism represents the dominant power status of the white ethnic group in Western societies, institutional communalism in India represents the dominant power status of India's majority religious community, that is, Hindus. The overwhelming numerical majority of Hindus in India[3] (80.5 per cent according to the 2001 Census) accords them a privileged location in the political, social, cultural and eventually economic networks, while disadvantaging the religious minorities (Muslims [13.4 per cent], Christians [2.3 per cent] and Sikhs [1.9 per cent]) in these networks (GoI n.d.).[4] Hierarchical relations constituted through class, race, gender, religion, ethnicity and nationality operate through diverse ways and have an impact upon the precise location of individuals and groups in society and economy. Bourdieu's social capital theory[5] can provide us with a framework, here, with which to encapsulate the privileged location of upper-caste Hindus in India. Bourdieu defines social capital as:

> ...the sum of the resources, actual or virtual, that accrue to an individual or a group by virtue of possessing a durable network of more or less institutionalised relationships of mutual acquaintance and recognition (Bourdieu 1986: 248; Bourdieu and Wacquant 1992: 119). ...which provides each of its members with the backing of the collectively-owned capital, a 'credential' which entitles them to credit, in the various senses of the word. These relationships may exist only in the practical state, in material and/or symbolic exchanges which help to maintain them (Bourdieu 1986: 248–49).

A majority has an inherent advantage by virtue of being a majority, unless these advantages are counteracted and contained by other social forces. In other words, to use Bourdieu's social capital theory, a majority has accumulated social and cultural capital, and hence economic and political capital, by the simple fact of being socially and culturally positioned as a majority. Institutional communalism is, therefore, the exercise of accumulated power—the power of its social/cultural/political/economic capital—by the majority.

[...]

In India, with 80.5 per cent share of the population being Hindu and most institutions of power being dominated by upper-caste Hindus, there is an inbuilt bias towards privileging of Hindus, but almost non-existent institutional mechanisms to counteract this inbuilt bias. Apart from affirmative action in the form of reservations for scheduled castes and scheduled tribes, that has been a positive force in neutralising upper-caste dominance, there is nothing in India on the lines of equal opportunity legislation, monitoring and accountability that track systematic bias and discrimination against religious minorities in India. The National Commission for Minorities constituted as late as 1993—more than 43 years after the formation of the Indian Republic in 1950—remains a mere paper tiger without the power and institutional infrastructure to track systematic inbuilt bias against religious minorities, leave aside neutralising this bias.

Institutional communalism in India, that is to say Hindu majoritarian bias, pervades the Indian Constitution, bureaucracy, security forces, parliamentary institutions, judiciary, prisons, academic institutions, health services, media, and the cultural and art organisations. The exact nature and extent of institutional communalism in these institutions is uneven, and deserves further detailed investigation. There is, however, a reasonable amount of evidence and research already in circulation, which indicates the pervasiveness of Hindu-communalist bias in a range of institutions in India. I outline these below.

Constitution

I have previously challenged the existing consensus, or near consensus, among Indian academics and opinion makers about the secularism of India's Constitution and, through a scrutiny of various clauses in the Constitution, have demonstrated the existence of strong Hindu bias in that claimed secularism (Singh 2005). My conclusion was that India's Constitution

> ...has several elements of Hindu bias in it. The symbolic insertion of 'Bharat' in the opening article naming the country; the provision for strong centralisation supportive of Hindu nationalism; the active intervention of the state to consolidate Hindu identity through reform of the Hindu religion; the definition of 'Hindu' supportive of a Hindu assimilative agenda towards Buddhists, Jains and Sikhs; cow protection; pre-eminent status for Hindi in the Devanagari script and special importance for Sanskrit are all features of the constitution which make its secularism seriously Hindu-tainted (Singh 2005: 921).

Rochna Bajpai (2002, 2009, 2011) points to the weakness of minority rights in the Indian Constitution, and James Chiriyankandath (2000) demonstrates the compromised nature of Indian secularism due to the impact of religion, particularly the Hindu religion, in the making of the Constitution.

Judiciary

Cossman and Kapur (2001) have examined several judgments and judicial interventions of India's Supreme Court in cases that required consideration of religious issues, and have demonstrated (especially in chapter 2 of the book, *The Supreme Court Hindutva Judgments*) the prevalence of Hindu bias in the working of this highest judicial institution of India. Similarly, Sen (2010) examines a range of cases that had a religious component in them, and demonstrates that the Supreme Court's responses to them have contributed to 'homogenisation of religion' and nation, which is favourable to the Hindu world view and insensitive to pluralism and religious minorities.

Vrinda Grover (2004, 2006) demonstrates systematic Hindu bias in the working of the police and judiciary in the way evidence regarding the massacre of Sikhs in 1984 in Delhi was collected (or not collected) and interpreted. The Congress, the ruling party at the time of the anti-Sikh carnage, is widely believed to have protected the guilty perpetrators of the massacre. The significance of Grover's work is that it highlights how the majoritarian Hindu bias in the institutions of the police, investigation agencies and judiciary is not limited to periods of Congress Party rule at the centre, but transcends a specific political party's control of state power at any point of time. It is due to this institutional communalism, embedded in the agencies of the state, that even during the non-Congress regimes at the centre, the victims of the Delhi massacre could not get justice (Kaur 2004; Mitta and Phoolka 2007). The resurgence of the recent Sikh resentment against the acquittal of Sajjan Kumar, a prime suspect in the organisation of anti-Sikh violence in Delhi in 1984, by a Delhi Court, has been primarily ignited by the fact that the judge in this case did not respect and accept the eyewitness accounts of women whose family members had been killed during the violence and who had testified in the court that they had seen Sajjan Kumar leading the mobs that killed their family members (Dogra 2013).[6]

[...]

Another example of institutionalised Hindu bias in India's judiciary was revealed by Justice S. S. Sodhi, a former Chief Justice of Allahabad High Court, in a public meeting in Chandigarh. Justice Sodhi revealed that 'no Sikh Judge was trusted to deal with Sikh terrorist cases' (*Tribune* 2008).

A more glaring case of majoritarian mindset and institutional communalism became evident in the Supreme Court decision to award the death sentence to Mohammed Afzal Guru, a Kashmiri militant who was secretly hanged on 9 February 2013. The bench deciding his case said that the death sentence was necessary in order to satisfy 'the national conscience', which is a surrender of the legal reasoning to a structure of biases (Peer 2013).

Security Services

Manisha Sethi (2013) demonstrates brilliantly the systematic bias in the working of intelligence agencies and police in their dealings with the minority Muslim population. Her quotes from two police officials are worth repeating here:

> In cases of terror attacks or communal riots, if the police goes after the perpetrators of the violence, and they happen to be mostly Muslim, you cannot, in the name of secularism, expect the police to act in proportion to their population (Prakash Singh, former DG, BSF).
>
> There is nothing like Saffron terrorism. It just doesn't exist in the Hindu pantheon (M. N. Singh, former Commissioner of Police, Mumbai).[7]

Since there is no evidence that there was any protest at these remarks or official contestation of them by anyone in the police force, these views can reasonably be taken as representing a wide consensus in the Indian police's perceptions regarding Muslims and Hindus.

It is very difficult to get hard data on the representation of different religious communities in the intelligence agencies of the Indian state. A human rights activist, who shared with me some confidential information he was able to gather, was of the view that there were many layers of secrecy associated with different intelligence agencies of the state and that it was an unwritten rule that the more secret an agency was, the less was the likelihood of non-Hindus being given a job or role in it. Other information that has come to light seems to confirm this view. Subhash Gatade (2008), writing on the emergence of Hindu terror groups, notes that one problem in investigating these groups is 'the near absence of Muslims or Sikhs in the different intelligence wings of the government'. Saikat Datta (2006), in an article titled 'Muslims and Sikhs Need Not Apply', pointed out that barring the Intelligence Bureau (IB), which has a handful of Muslim officers, none of the other wings of intelligence have a single Muslim officer in their ranks. According to him,

> From 1969 till today—RAW's [Research and Analysis Wing, perhaps the most secret agency] current staff strength is about 10,000—it has avoided recruiting any Muslim officer. Neither has the National Technical Research Organisation (NTRO), a crucial arm of external intelligence. The IB with 12,000 personnel has been a little more open. It has a handful of Muslim officers, the senior-most is a joint director.

In 2012, for the first time, a Muslim officer, Asif Ibrahim, was made the director of the IB.

Forced by a petition to the Supreme Court, the Army has admitted that bodyguards to India's President are recruited only from Hindus (*rajputs* and *jats*) and it seems, since a considerable part of India's jat population that is in Punjab is Sikh by faith, the jat category has been extended to include Sikh jats also (*Tribune* 2013).

Media

Analysing the media coverage of the Punjab crisis in the 1980s, I have documented extensively that Doordarshan (central government-owned TV channel), All India Radio (AIR) and the mainstream English language media displayed deeply embedded institutional communalism in systematically pandering to Hindu biases, prejudices, and sentiments in reporting and commenting on Indian army's Operation Blue Star action at the Golden Temple—the holiest Sikh shrine—in June 1984, and the massacre of Sikhs in November 1984 after the assassination of Indira Gandhi by Sikh bodyguards, the then Indian prime minister who had ordered the army action at the Golden Temple (Singh 1984, 1985a, 1985b). Patwant Singh (1985) also demonstrates how in the media reportage of Punjab, the inherent bias due to the majoritarian Hindu control of Indian media led to distorted reports and commentaries that perpetuated pre-existing prejudices against the Sikhs and led to distorted information being fed to the citizens of India.[8] In more recent years, since the massacre of Muslims in Gujarat in 2002, the Kargil war with Pakistan and the global rhetoric on 'war on terror', the majoritarian bias in media and popular culture, especially in Indian cinema, is particularly directed against the Muslim minority (Kumar 2013).

What I have outlined thus far is merely the tip of the iceberg, a few examples to initiate a debate on embedded Hindu bias and institutional communalism in India. A thorough and collective examination is required not only of state institutions (civil services, security forces, judiciary and prisons), but also of non-state institutions (corporate world and non-governmental organisations [NGOs]) and the ideological apparatus (universities, research institutes and media establishments). A critique of organisations and institutions beyond the organisations that are popularly perceived to be overtly 'communal' (such as the Sangh Parivar), which is to say, a critique of the deeper structures of communalism at work within the Indian state, would give us a much more complex understanding of institutional communalism.

EQUATING MAJORITY AND MINORITY COMMUNALISM

Theoretical and political work against institutional racism has highlighted one aspect that is crucial to further work on institutional communalism, that racism, if any, of minority ethnic individuals or groups against dominant white racism is of very little significance, and any energy devoted in the direction of exploring and critiquing minority racism (sometimes referred to by white racists as 'reverse racism') is a diversion from the central task of fighting racism. The central core of racism is not just about racially charged beliefs and attitudes, but also the power to put into practice those beliefs and attitudes in a way that has differential impact on the lives of members of different races. Many institutions in the Western world have been characterised as racist because of the 'culturally sanctioned beliefs which, regardless of the intentions involved, defend the advantages whites have because of the subordinated position of racial minorities' (Wellman 1993: xi). Therefore, there is no substance in what is claimed as minority racism or reverse racism. Even if some individuals or groups in minority ethnic groups harbour prejudices against the dominant white race, they would not be able to cause any substantial disadvantage to the dominant group because they do not possess the power to oppress the dominant group. This does not mean that marginal cases of harassment of individual members of the dominant white race by some members of any minority racial group cannot take place. However, what is crucial is that minority racial groups do not have institutionalised power to systematise their harassment of the members of the dominant racial group.

[...]

CONCLUSIONS

[...]

The lens of institutional communalism allows us to see beyond the surface-level communal activities of political and social organisations to the deeper roots of communalism embedded in the working of a diverse range of public, semi-public and private institutions in Indian society. In the same way, as the tool of institutional racism highlights the racism of the majority white community, because of the power the white mainstream community enjoys in Western societies, the tool of institutional communalism helps us highlight the communalism of the majority Hindu religious community, because of the power the Hindu religious community enjoys in India. The important implication that follows from this is that, as in the case of anti-racist theorising and practice, the focus is on critiquing majority racism. The focus on anti-communalism theorising and practice has to be the critique of majority Hindu communalism in India. Racism as a social phenomenon exists, in its current form, because of the supremacist thinking, behaviour and practices in the dominant white community in the West. Similarly, communalism in India exists, in its current form, because of the supremacist thinking, behaviour and practices in the dominant Hindu community in India.

The fight against institutional communalism in India alerts us to a challenge bigger than merely inflicting electoral defeats on Hindu communal parties and organisations. Causing electoral defeats of Hindu communal parties and organisations remains an important strategic task and needs to be seen as part of eradicating institutional communalisms. However, even if such parties are defeated electorally, institutional Hindu communalism remains pervasive in varying degrees in India's constitution, judiciary, civil services, electoral and parliamentary institutions, security forces, prisons, academia, media, corporate business, and even NGOs. It will continue as a social, cultural and politico-economic force to disadvantage the lives of minority communities in India. Thinking from the perspective of institutional communalism alerts the anti-communalism practitioners in India not only to the massive challenge they face, but also to the need for devising practical devices to monitor communalism in the everyday working practices of a vast range of institutions in India.

[...]

NOTES

1. A similar kind of institutional racism has been identified in the German police's investigations into neo-Nazi terror groups. For over a decade now, there has been a consistent pattern of bomb attacks and murders where a majority of the victims were of Turkish origin. '[I]n spite of the indications of a racial motive for the serial murders, the police and security services insisted at the time that their prime suspects were rival Turkish gangs or drug runners' (Peel 2013: 4). Thinking and activities based upon biases, prejudices and stereotypes are central to both institutional racism and institutional communalism.

2. I am thankful to Tanya Singh for very valuable information on the use of the term 'institutional racism' by black American theorists in the early twentieth century and by anti-racist/black activists in the UK.

3. It is a demonstration of the institutional power of upper-caste Hindus that despite consistent opposition by sections of dalit communities to their inclusion in the category of Hindu, they continue to be counted as Hindus. This exercise of institutional power by upper-caste Hindus to keep enumerating the dalits as Hindus is used by them to continuously reinforce their claims to be an overwhelming majority community in India.

4. See Harriss-White (2003) for a detailed empirical, ethnographic and theoretical investigation of the religious dimension in the working of Indian capitalist economy and the privileging of Hindu upper castes in India's capitalist economy. T. P. Wright Jr (1981; cited in Harriss-White 2003) and A. Ali (1992) have argued that the privileged location of upper-caste Hindus in India's state apparatus (especially after the 1947 Partition of India that led to migration of many Muslim entrepreneurs to Pakistan) has led to the Indian state helping upper-caste Hindu capitalists in their business ventures, and that this has contributed to the weakness in the growth of the Muslim capitalist class in India. See also Rehman 2012. Arvinder Singh (1999: 152–53) has cited data from the Centre for Monitoring Indian Economy that shows that out of the 10 largest corporate businesses in Punjab in 1994, only one was Sikh-controlled, while by population size the Sikhs were more than 60 per cent of the state's population (Singh 2008).

5. I am thankful to Shirley Velasquez and Oxford's Capitalism Study Group for very fruitful discussions on Bourdieu's work.

6. For a general mapping of embedded Hindu communalism in the working of the police, which also contributes to judicial disempowerment of minorities, see Vijapur and Haque 2006, and for more specific examination of police prejudice against Muslims, see Khan (2006).

7. See also Sethi 2014.

8. Patwant Singh was once a part of India's elite, especially in the world of architecture and art, but the Indian army's attack on the Golden Temple and the anti-Sikh carnage in Delhi turned him into a sharp critic of the Indian political, judicial and media establishments. For my tribute to him and his work, see my obituary of him and that of Ram Narayan Kumar, one of the finest human rights campaigners in India, who also reported extensively on the Hindu bias in police, bureaucracy, media and judiciary in dealing with human rights violations of India's Sikh minority (Singh 2009).

REFERENCES

Ali, A. 1992. 'The Quest for Cultural Identity and Material Advancement: Parallels and Contrasts in Muslim Minority Experience in Secular India and Buddhist Sri Lanka'. *Institute of Muslim Minority Affairs Journal* 13 (1), 33–58.

Anderson, Perry. 2012. *The Indian Ideology*. New Delhi: Three Essays Collective.

Bajpai, Rochna. 2002. 'The Conceptual Vocabularies of Secularism and Minority Rights in India'. *Journal of Political Ideologies* 7 (2), 179–98.

———. 2009. 'Constitution-making and Political Safeguards for Minorities: An Ideological Explanation'. *Journal of Contemporary Thought* 30, Winter, 57–87.

———. 2011. *Debating Difference: Group Rights and Liberal Democracy in India*. New Delhi: Oxford University Press.

Bourdieu, P. 1986. 'The Forms of Capital', in *Handbook of Theory and Research for the Sociology of Education,* ed. J. Richardson. Westport, CT: Greenwood Press, 241–58.

Bourdieu, P., and L. J. D. Wacquant. 1992. *An Invitation to Reflexive Sociology*. Cambridge: Polity Press.

Chandra, Bipin. 1984. *Communalism in Modern India*. New Delhi: Vikas.

Chiriyankandath, James. 2000. '"Creating a Secular State in a Religious Country": The Debate in the Indian Constituent Assembly'. *Commonwealth and Comparative Politics* 38 (2), 1–24.

Cossman, Brenda, and Ratna Kapur. 2001. *Secularism's Last Sigh? Hindutva and the (Mis)Rule of Law*. New Delhi: Oxford University Press.

Datta, Saikat. 'Muslims and Sikhs Need Not Apply'. *Outlook,* 13 November 2006.

Desai, Darshan, and V. Venkatesan. 'There is a Case for Commuting Bhullar Sentence: M B Shah'. *The Hindu*, 21 April 2013, available at http://www.thehindu.com/news/national/there-iscase-for-commuting-bhullar-sentencembshah/article4637577.ece (accessed 17 June 2015).

Dogra, Chander Suta. 'How the Centre and the Police have Shielded Sajjan Kumar since 1984'. *The Hindu*, 8 May 2013, available at http://www.thehindu.com/news/national/how-thecentre-and-police-have-shielded-sajjan-kumarsince-1984/article4693431.ece?homepage=true (accessed 17 June 2015).

Gatade, Subhash. 2008. 'Terrorism's New Signature: Enter Hindutva Terrorists'. *Mainstream* 46 (6).

GoI. n.d. 'Census of India: Religion'. Office of the Registrar General & Census Commissioner, Ministry of Home Affairs, Government of India, New Delhi, available at http://censusindia.gov.in/Census_And_You/religi on.aspx (accessed 17 June 2015).

Grover, Vrinda. 2004. 'Prejudice and Democracy: Law, Police and Anti-Sikh Massacre, 1984'. Paper presented at the Workshop on 1984 Anti-Sikh Pogroms, Coventry University, 30 October, unpublished.

——. 2006. 'Role of Police in 1984 Anti-Sikh Massacre, Delhi', in *Minorities and Police in India,* eds Asghar Ali Engineer, and Amarjit S. Narang. New Delhi: Manohar, 193–208.

Harriss-White, Barbara. 2003. *India Working: Essays on Society and Economy.* Cambridge: Cambridge University Press.

Juergensmeyer, Mark. 1991. *Radhasoami Reality: The Logic of a Modern Faith.* Princeton, NJ: Princeton University Press.

Kaur, J. 2004. *Twenty Years of Impunity: The November 1984 Pogroms of Sikhs in India.* A Report by ENSAAF, London: Nectar Publishing/Bookmarks.

Khan, Arshi. 2006. 'Police Prejudice against the Muslims' in *Minorities & Police in India,* eds Asghar Ali Engineer, and Amarjit S. Narang, New Delhi: Manohar, 141–62.

Kumar, Sanjiv H. M. 2013. 'Constructing the Nation's Enemy: Hindutva, Popular Culture and the Muslim "Other" in Bollywood Cinema'. *Third World Quarterly* 34 (3), 458–69.

Macpherson, W. 1999. *The Stephen Lawrence Inquiry: Report of an Inquiry by Sir William Macpherson of Cluny.* London: The Stationery Office.

Mitta, M., and H. S. Phoolka. 2007. *When a Tree Shook Delhi: The 1984 Carnage and Its Aftermath.* New Delhi: Roli Books.

Pearl, Martyn, and Pritam Singh, eds. 1999. *Equal Opportunities in the Curriculum.* Oxford: Oxford Brookes University.

Peel, Quentin. 'Germany on Edge over Trial of Neo-Nazis'. *Financial Times,* 6 May 2013.

Peer, Gazala. 'When the Indian Nation's "Conscience" was Satisfied'. *Kafila,* 15 February 2013, available at http://kafi la.org/2013/02/15/when-the-indian-nations-conscie ncewas-satisfi ed-gazala-peer/ (accessed 17 June 2015).

Portes, A., and J. Sensenbrenner. 1993. 'Embeddedness and Immigration: Notes on the Social Determination of Economic Action'. *American Journal of Sociology* 98 (6), 1320–50.

Rehman, Mujibur. 2012. 'Indian Capitalism and Future of Indian Muslims'. Paper presented at the annual conference of the British Association of South Asian Studies, School of Oriental and African Studies, London, 12–14 April, unpublished.

Sayeed, Khalid Bin. 1963. 'Religion and Nation Building in Pakistan'. *Middle East Journal* 17 (3), 279–91.

Sen, Ronojoy. 2010. *Articles of Faith: Religion, Secularism and the Indian Supreme Court.* New Delhi: Oxford University Press.

Sethi, Manisha. 'Sinful Liberals and the War against Jihadi Terror: Manisha Sethi Responds to Praveen Swami'. *Kafila,* 9 May 2013, available at http://kafi la.org/2013/05/09/sinfulliberals-and-the-war-against-jihadi-terrormanisha-sethi-responds-topraveen-swami/ (accessed 17 June 2015).

——. 2014. *Kafkaland: Prejudice, Law and Counterterrorism in India.* New Delhi: Three Essays Collective.

Singh, Arvinder. 1999. *Industrial Transition in an Agricultural Surplus Region: A Study of Punjab.* PhD thesis, Jawaharlal Nehru University, Delhi, and Centre for Development Studies, Trivandrum.

Singh, Patwant. 1985. 'The Distorting Mirror' in *Punjab: The Fatal Miscalculation,* eds Patwant Singh, and Harji Malik. New Delhi: Crescent, 9–32.

Singh, Pritam. 1984. 'AIR and Doordashan Coverage of Punjab after Army Action'. *Economic & Political Weekly* 19 (36), 1569–71.

———. 1985a. 'Government Media and Punjab'. *Economic & Political Weekly* 20 (2), 79–80.

———. 1985b. 'The Role of the Media' in *Punjab in Indian Politics*, ed. Amrik Singh. New Delhi: Ajanta Publishers, 155–84.

———. 2005. 'Hindu Bias in India's "Secular" Constitution: Probing Flaws in the Instruments of Governance'. *Third World Quarterly* 26 (6), 909–26.

———. 2008. *Federalism, Nationalism and Development: India and the Punjab Economy.* London/New York: Routledge.

———. 2009. 'In Remembrance: Ram Narayan Kumar and Patwant Singh'. *Journal of Punjab Studies* 16 (2), 295–301, available at http://www.global.ucsb.edu/punjab/journal/v16_2/articles/8-Obituaries16.2.pdf (accessed 17 June 2015).

———. 2010. *Economy, Culture and Human Rights: Turbulence in Punjab, India and Beyond.* New Delhi: Three Essays Collective.

Tribune. '1984 Riots a Blot on Nation'. 24 February 2008.

———. 'Prez Guard Job Only for Rajputs, Jats & Sikhs', 3 October 2013.

Vijapur, Abdulrahim, and Mohibul Haque. 2006. 'Endangered Minorities in India: Understanding the Role of Police', in *Minorities & Police in India,* eds Asghar Ali Engineer, and Amarjit S. Narang. New Delhi: Manohar, 111–121.

Wellman, David T. 1993. *Portraits of White Racism.* New York: Cambridge University Press.

10

Communalism and the Consuming Subject*

Arvind Rajagopal

[...]

Contemporary Communalism and Electronic Capitalism: Imagining Whose Community?

The growth of communalism is all too often firmly harnessed to one agency, notably the Bharatiya Janata Party (BJP) and its affiliates, spotlighted as a threat to be understood and fought. The danger of such a view is that an entire set of phenomena tends to get reduced to the success or failure of a particular party. The wide variety of environmental factors enabling the rise of the party, its support by various social groups, including many that were previously uncommitted, the communalisation of everyday life and practices, changes in the wider culture reflected in and resulting from its propaganda even in the absence of its decisive political victory (as yet): all of these factors tend to get ignored. The extent to which the ruling party colluded in the Ram temple movement is one of the more important of a series of relevant factors here. Such factors should force a rethinking of the 'usual suspects' approach to communalism, one that holds the Congress as the secular party of last resort. It is much more useful to think of the Hindu right as having not one, but two parties, the Congress and the BJP, operating gyroscopically to keep an upper-caste ruling alliance in power. That is to say, it is in the opposition of the two parties that space for the Rashtriya Swayamsevak Sangh (RSS)/Vishva Hindu Parishad (VHP) is won, an opposition bounded and contained within a larger unity. This was succinctly expressed by Govindacharya in conversation: BJP minus RSS equals Congress.[1] Extrapolating, RSS equals BJP minus Congress, Thus, the progress of the Ram temple movement could be accompanied by the appearance of political resistance at the centre, even if this resistance was often perceived as Congress inertia or incompetence.

---

* *Economic and Political Weekly* 31 (6): 341–48 (10 February 1996).

In attempting to situate and understand the recent phase of communalism, several writers have distinguished, very roughly, between the period of Nehruvian consensus, of a relatively secure Congress ideology of secular, autarkic developmentalism, and that which succeeded it: it is in the latter period that communalism has been on the ascendancy. In this phase, one which is yet to take full definition, there is a concerted attempt to reduce the redistributive functions of the state, and to render the market as the pre-eminent means of resource allocation. The increased reliance on the market and the concomitant dependence on foreign loans, reinforced by IMF–World Bank strictures, opens up domestic markets and 'globalises' the economy in unprecedented ways. Together with the declared failure of state-led development and of the old Congress ideology, these changes make earlier modes of conceiving of the nation non-viable (Deshpande 1993), and indeed, cast them in crisis. It is in this context that the increased concern with national identity and the political resort to Hindu or Hinduised definitions of national identity, such as the use of the 'Hindu card' in electoral campaigns or the decision to serialise epics on national television, can best be understood.

[...]

With the large-scale introduction of electronic communication, the staging of Indian politics undergoes a qualitative transformation; hereafter, any broad analysis of political culture would be incomplete without figuring the media into it. This is not a result of the 'impact of the media' in any simple sense. Rather, it has to be understood in terms of the relations of 'electronic capitalism' within which it is effective. Just as the commodity preserves a certain in-built openness to difference (Chakrabarty 1993), the commodified image as well accommodates and subsumes the variety of interpretive stances arising from uneven social development. In commodified image systems, production and consumption are alienated from each other, so that consumers have no direct input into the production process. Although consumption is private, it is an act duplicated numerously and simultaneously, thereby allowing a social character to be imputed to it and it is here that the crucial ideological force of television's 'representation' lies.

Television secures the social time of viewers via its 'free' images which are scrupulously gauged in regard to productivity and rate of return. Television creates a space for its own time, one that is shared by all its viewers collectively. Just as the 'freedom' of wage labour is its ideological underpinning and the source of its appeal, the freedom with which time is granted to television enables viewers to treat it as their own, and thus help secure television's power all the more effectively. The time spent on television is experienced as unthreatening and is thus freely given, because it accrues elsewhere, in a mediated fashion as it were. As television becomes a key locus of collective activity, albeit in a serialised and individuated fashion, it comes to 'stand for' society and serves as a crucial ruse of consent.

What we have is in fact the preservation of two distinct sets of time: the time of the image and the time of viewing, and not the reduction or the supercession of one to or by the other.[2] A tele-centric view would be one that regards the time of the image as the effective level, and the one that matters, for instance, as the stage of 'global capital' where value is delivered to its ultimate beneficiaries. The special quality of television rather is to harness diverse temporalities together, the time of viewers and that of the image, in one imperturbable 'flow', to re-deploy Raymond Williams's term.

[...]

The distinctness of the televisual medium is in the way it appears to implode a diversity of viewing contexts and a range of interpretive responses in the singularity of a broadcasting event. A plurality of readings and reading practices can thus be presented as co-located in the simultaneous reception of the telecast image. This plurality can then be re-inscribed in homogeneous terms such as 'ratings' or 'popularity'. But it is well to remember that no single 'class base' can stand for and explain an event occurring in the context of and mediated by electronic capitalism. At the same time, no single set of interpretations and no unitary subject position provides access to the meanings mobilising the event. We need to acknowledge, on the one hand, the plurality of social groups involved, and on the other hand, the multiple subject positions characterising any particular social group.[3]

Gramsci formulates the notion of 'contradictory consciousness', arising from the opposition between theoretical consciousness, which is inherited from the past, and the consciousness implicit in practical activity, which in a sense involves pre-critical, unrecognised 'stratified deposits' of history, in religion, common sense and folklore (1988: 325–34). Ideological analysis has then to address multiple levels of consciousness and epistemically diverse data. Not only the 'official' ideology of communal parties contained in its manifestoes and pronouncements, but as well the myths, common sense, faiths and folklore it draws on, join to comprise the contradictory consciousness of communal ideology.

The notion of contradictory consciousness points to the multiplicity of subject positions, and the inadequacy of positing a unitary subject adhering to a rational, internally coherent ideology, understood in the singular. Rather, there are articulations between diverse arguments, images and themes which have no necessary class-belonging (Laclau 1977), but constellate together in contingent formations spanning a diverse class base. These various class fractions and groupings may finally be delivered up to serve the interests of a far narrower section, but the heterogeneity of the ideological formation must be recognised. Misunderstood as a unitary entity, there develops the consequent error of re-describing real diversity and discrepancy in terms of a binary classification: either 'communal' or 'secular'. Thus, I hypothesise a partial overlap between communal and consumer identity formation as a way of addressing the specificity of this heterogeneity. The consequence of the overlap between communal and consumer identity is a shifting subject position not foreseeable in advance or mappable in terms of objective coordinates. This can be illustrated in the phenomenon of the *Ramayan* tele-epic.

A serial like the televised *Ramayan* was able to appeal across diverse social contexts, provoking a range of understandings of its significance but 'uniting' them in the event of the serial's transmission. The importance of the telecast is hard to estimate, but there is no doubt that it was crucial.[4] The VHP mobilisation played on the discrepancies and paradoxes contained in the tele-event. The *Ramayan* serial offered an opportunity to appeal to a shared symbolic background in more ways than one, portraying as it did images of an idealised golden age behind and above contemporary divisions. The serial offered a seemingly impossible idealisation of selfless and harmonious relationships that presented an implicit rebuke to modern individualist and instrumental relations. By relegating it to a presumed past, both its believability and its unbelievability could be accommodated together in a dynamic contradiction. What critics dismissed as naive credulity on the part of audiences, in this view becomes more plausible. Images of Ram Rajya stood as memory and myth, religion and history all at once, hard to dispel or refute, haunting people with the globally alternative possibilities they seemed to offer.

Thus, the serial provoked a collective 'remembering' of a society that everyone agreed had disappeared, and that some observed had never existed. The idealised past presented in the serial was Utopian, in the sense that it inverted dystopic perceptions of contemporary society. The desire for this 'past' was legitimated in various registers: as moral and social critique, as history, as religious epic, and as soap opera. A rationalist critique of the *Ramayan* would therefore hardly be adequate to the polyphonous character of its appeal.

The desire to transcend the present, which cut across all categories of viewers, presented a 'resolution' of the serial's contradictions (a state-sponsored, commercial-financed, soap operatic rendition of a religious epic broadcast on national television) or accommodated them as non-contradictory, or unimportant. The VHP drew on the *Ramayan*'s appeal and extended it, using symbols and themes with a broad reach at the same time as it deployed a stratified system of propaganda, combining a sophisticated set of communication strategies with intensive grassroots work. A succession of tasks, from the 'tala kholo andolan' and the 'shila puja' to the various kar seva[5] summons, served as the equivalent of a series of calls to arms, bringing the diverse strands of the movement together. It was primarily in performance that the movement as such came to be sustained.

A cloth trader and RSS member in Berasia, MP offered a summary view of the variety of mobilisational strategies deployed by the VHP-RSS combine, one that Hindutva supporters in the capital might have shared but were perhaps too wary to articulate before an inquiring academic: 'There are two kinds of people associated with the Ram Janmabhoomi movement. There are uneducated people, who are affected by religious feeling. And there are educated people, who are nationalist in their thinking. The intention of the Ram Janmabhoomi movement is a nationalist intention' (Interview in Berasia, 10 May 1994). The BJP's purpose was to bring the two together, so that those who were religious-minded could be made to serve a higher, national cause, he said.

If the distinction between 'educated' and 'uneducated' is too literal and crude a way of referring to a diverse class base, and the implication of separate spheres too sharply drawn, what this emphasises, at any rate, is the variety of discursive registers at which VHP publicity worked. Those making visits to Ayodhya when the movement was in progress received pamphlets not necessarily offered to visitors to the New Delhi VHP office, for instance. In these pamphlets, it was explained that Ram's birthplace was a site made more auspicious by the deaths of innumerable Hindus over centuries, martyred while fighting for it against Muslim rulers (Garg n.d.).

Paintings arranged 'chronologically', in a gallery behind the VHP office at Ayodhya, described these battles in graphic detail. Paragraph-long captions sequenced the 'history' accompanying the pictures, telling how devotees of Ram (or the Bajrang Dal of those days, one activist explained to me) would strike at night, attempting to rebuild the temple that the Mughal emperor Babar's forces would dismantle by day. This kind of vivid re-creation of detail created an immediate link between earlier events and the task of the moment, simulating the signs of historicity while in fact mythologising the past.

As against the above, there was literature that included more abstract arguments about the hurt to national sentiment, the importance of Ram as a national symbol, or the injustice of 'pseudo-secular' policies. Accompanied by copious references to colonial records and legislative acts, with citations of volume, section and page number, such literature projects an aura of erudition, and tends to gloss over more explicitly mytho-historic 'details'.[6] Clearly, the 'history-effects' attempted in Hindutva propaganda strike a variety of notes, indicating the awareness of diverse reading contexts ranging from the scholarly to the mytho-poetic. The Berasia trader referred to this diversity in a rudimentary and indeed ideological fashion, describing a division between leaders and followers and justifying it as such. Against the simplistic compartmentalisation between educated and uneducated, or nationalist and religious, we may note that readers may themselves place texts against different contexts and thereby accommodate appeals to the fabulous and to faith as well as to argument and to fact.[7] Here, we can distinguish between the discursive character of support for movements from the effects of such discourses, developed and shaped in the practice of politics, and manifesting as 'retail Hindutva' consumers, Hindu vote banks, kar seva volunteers, mosque demolition squads and anti-Muslim rioters. It is in performance that political lines are drawn, as people cast their lot with one side or another in electoral, ideological and, indeed, life-or-death battles.

Growing Aestheticisation of Politics

[...]

Walter Benjamin has observed that the logical result of fascism is the introduction of aesthetics into politics: the right of the masses to change property relations is replaced by the opportunity to express themselves (1969: 241). Contemporary communalism bears similarities with German and Italian fascism (Sarkar 1993), but has its own historical specificity. Electronic capitalism re-codes class differences to structure a shared fantasy space where class contradiction is transformed into consumer longing. The achievement of the aestheticisation of politics is to change the setting of desiring from the private to the public realm, or to extend it across the private and the public. Now, market liberalisation witnesses the mobilisation of national sentiment to create the consensus for the aggressive privatisation of the economy. The glorification of the nation, in this scenario, foregrounds individual initiative and private desires, while in fact masking the decline and suppression of existing public space. Communalism, in this sense, is symptomatic of global trends, inflected variously in Thatcher's Britain, and Reagan and Bush's USA, to cite two instances in the West. Hindu nationalist politics, or a soft saffron Hindutva, emerge, in the Indian context, as a contested means of articulating a new hegemonic consensus, feeding and supported by the permeation of everyday life by communalised culture.

The introduction of aesthetics into politics is no mere recrudescence. It represents a form of power that cannot simply be subsumed as part of the 're-feudalisation of the public sphere' (Habermas 1989). Aestheticised politics exhorts individualised expression. It encourages new forms of self-fashioning that can be tailored to one's particular needs, even while it enables the organisation of large masses of people in oppressive social relations. It dismantles older forms of social life and institutes new and different conditions in its place. It replaces relatively embedded contexts of expression related to work and community life, by more impersonal, mediated contexts within which those in diverse occupations, classes and regions may rejoice in the similitude of emotions and styles. The ability of electronic capitalism to yoke discrepant temporalities together indicates the parallel processing involved. There is both an unprecedented centralisation in the production of expression with mass media, and an unprecedented dispersal of effect, as messages reach audiences widely separated from each other. Yet this dispersal only adds to the power of the media, as wider arrays of viewing contexts are subsumed within the scope of the same images.

The aestheticisation of politics might be seen as complementary to and convergent with Foucault's concerns in his discussion of 'governmentality' (1991). He uses the term to refer to a new form of governance, one that emerged in early modern Europe, that combines two apparently contrasting modes of power, one totalising and centralising, the other individualising and normalising. The term allows us to conceptualise how power may be exercised while permitting free exchange and free expression, and indeed precisely as a consequence of such liberties. It is through the constitution of individuals as free, rational subjects that governmental power evolves, attending simultaneously to the particular characteristics of each person under its purview, and distributing and organising these elements within a larger system of control. The value of the term is in its acknowledgement of a bilateral character to power, top-down and bottom-up as well, as technologies of government intersect with technologies of the self. The normalisation of the self as a voluntary process undertaken through self-surveillance and self-discipline is complementary to a mode of governance that, although overarching in scope, remains sensitive to the extremities of its points of application.

Liberalisation and the devolution of the powers of the sovereign state to the economy involves as its complement a social devolution of power as well, from the community or the extended family to the nuclear family and to the individual. Now political power in India has long coexisted with a durable and decentralised form of cultural power, embodied in caste and community relations, even while those forms of cultural power were being extensively reworked under colonialism and independence. The notion of caste, for instance, has functioned as a substitute for 'civil society' in attempts to think Indian society (Dirks 1993). The colonial heritage of Indian society created a system of power alternate to traditional power, one that reshaped and finally supplanted it. In the process, as Chatterjee has noted, nationalists created a notion of an 'inner' Indian culture that was inviolate; social reform was undertaken by Indians themselves and British incursions into this realm were fiercely contested. With the coming of 'self-rule', the gap between cultural or spiritual power and more formal, state power was theoretically closed, in a sense. Narratives of community nevertheless played an important part in the political struggle for independence (Freitag 1991). While they no longer had the same official valency in postcolonial India, they were sustained in a variety of ways, as part of lived customs and traditions, and as a reliable mode of electioneering. The commitment to a certain notion of 'secularism' by an English language elite, and to a top-down state-led form of development (Kaviraj 1990) retained a disjuncture between these forms of power then. To some extent, communalism represents the repositioning of narratives of community, while retaining mechanisms of modern state power. There is thus a discrepancy in the subject-position of Indian governmentality; the dissonant and mutually contradictory narratives of capital and community are sought to be sutured together under the sign of the Indian consumer.

The cultivation of self-expression and self-fashioning are 'rights' afforded to consumers in lieu of political power. The existence of community points in one sense to the context of individual fulfilment and to its enabling basis, to the matrix within which decisions on and practices of consumption occur. The nucleation of the family unit represents an attempt to delimit this expression of community, as it doubles up as a unit of governmental administration and surveillance. The entry of aesthetics into politics is not itself in aid of administration and surveillance, however, although it is complementary to it. Rather, it evokes and channels the desire for self-expression, and works to orchestrate the collective expression of this desire. In communalism, self expression is oppositional in its lived meanings, seeking to harness the memories of alterity in community as means of resistance to oppression. Community represents a claim on resources and a source of authority that are on a narrative trajectory orthogonal to those of capitalist relations. The ceaseless emphasis on mobilisation and performance, whether in kar seva or in riots, is both a sign and an outcome of the contradictions coiled within communal politics, between individual expression and a coercive political regime, between the claims to community and the otherisation through which community is 'realised'.

With the near absence of legitimacy accorded to state institutions, however, coercion and the violence of communal assertion could not issue from centralised apparatuses of government in any direct or explicit manner. With the growing crisis of political institutions, resulting from both historical and structural causes, the state comes into enormous disrepute. In this context, the ideological charge of liberalisation and the boost given to private, market forces assist in the entrepreneuralisation of social function. The familiar notion of the edifices of the state at work, then, must now reckon with the informal character of centralisation, dispersed in the quieter, more inconspicuous and so less culpable forces of voluntary initiative. Thus, organised and systematic communal violence may be inflicted by scattered and nameless rioters, striking terror all the more effectively for their apparently spontaneous mob action.

State extortion of income and bureaucratic rent-seeking may themselves become shrouded in mystery as they reappear in the guise of a stock market collapse, with a long bullish trend successfully engineered to lure crores from hapless small investors (Dasgupta 1993). The seemingly chaotic character of the violence (financial and bodily), and the diffuse signs of its origins, testify to a form of governmental power that works in a distinct fashion. Rather than provoke a call to 'get the state off the people's backs', for instance, the sense of lawless violence generates a sentiment in favour of stern 'discipline', with authoritarian, honest, efficient leaders in charge. The phenomenal popularity of the Chief Election Commissioner T. N. Seshan, and of the former Bombay municipal corporator G. R. Khairnar, both bureaucrats famous for a swift and ready technocratic vigilantism, can be considered indicative of an influential diagnosis of the problem. Incorruptible disciplinarians, ready to cut through due process and exercise arbitrary personal authority for the greater good of the public, are seen as the answer, one that points towards a stronger, not a weaker state—indeed, there is the fantasy of a dictator present here.

I had noted, in my essay, the enablement of communal politics through consumer culture, through the purchase of 'retail Hindu' commodities including buttons, pamphlets, stickers, bricks for the Ram temple, bottled holy water, audio and video cassettes, and viewers' consumption of other media products including commercially sponsored tele-serials. The promotion of Hindutva through the circuits of commodities gave communal politics much greater visibility and, thereby, access to a far wider public. The solicitation of consumer desire to complement the Hindu right's currents of nationalist fervour helped reproduce communalism while advertising it at the same time. At the same time, it signalled an important shift in Hindu right strategy, embracing what Golwalkar had earlier condemned as today's method of more advertisement than actual work. From its inception, the RSS had aimed at conducting a far-reaching, long-term programme of building a universalist national 'brotherhood' insulated from the vagaries of the marketplace and the fickleness of electoral democracy. The move to retailing Hindu identity declared an intention to seek and build on far more partial forms of support, with the explicit aim of securing political power. The taste of power at the centre during the Janata government, an awareness that the BJP could benefit in comparison to the Congress's relatively spasmodic and timid use of the Hindu card, as well as a keen sense that in the current political conjuncture, there were few strong contenders to oppose its quest for power, were among the factors combining to instigate this important shift.

The harnessing of the circuits of commodity power, however, entailed a certain vulnerability to the rhythms of market cycles, and the need to bolster demand by keeping alive the political promises of Hindutva. Benjamin's discussion of the aestheticisation of politics does not include the submission of aesthetic judgment to market testing or voter preference. Writing in 1936, he was contemplating its deployment by well-ensconced fascist regimes. In a competitive context, the judgment is not only of aesthetics, but also of success. To quote L. K. Advani (1993), 'For the purpose of securing the non-committed vote, you must at least create an illusion that you are likely to come to power'. When the illusion is revealed as such, and the seemingly unstoppable momentum of its political purveyors is checked, the identification of the images and symbols of 'retail Hindutva' with its political proponents is loosened.

The cycle may turn again for the BJP, as recent events in Maharashtra and Uttar Pradesh suggest; the Hindu right may once again be within striking distance of power at the centre. ... Even in the absence of Hindutva's political triumph, then, we find the appropriation by the consuming subject of a kind of retail Hindu identity. The relevance of the latter, it appears, lies in notions of authenticity and strength, in its invulnerability to the corruption and violence of the public realm on the one hand, and its freedom from the entanglements of actual community relations on the other. Liberalisation proceeds with its reorganisation of public and private spaces in ways that are articulated to the Hindu right's political project, but not necessarily identical with it. Late capitalism's attempts to revitalise itself demonstrate an eruption of the contradictions of community onto the stage of capital, and an effort to harness these contradictions in furthering accumulation. ...

Notes

1. Personal interview with Govindacharya. Madras, 25 May 1992.

2. Richard Dienst in 'Still Life in Real Time', a recent work that attempts to theorise television in provocative ways, offers this useful distinction between the 'time of the image' and the 'time of viewing.' However, he glosses over the crucial disjuncture between these temporalities, staying at a level of abstraction that leads him to explain television's power as illustrative of 'capitalism', without reference to historical or social context. His integration of television as a mechanism in the circuits of capital turns into making television metonymic of capital itself. Thus, the implications of the dual temporality of television are steered towards understanding television's power in a way that I would call 'tele-centric' (Dienst 1994: 58–59).

3. It is important to note that the psychoanalytic subject of fantasy, privileged in cinema studies, and the spectator-subject (here, of television) are not synonymous entities or coeval theoretical constructs. The danger of merging the psychoanalytic subject of fantasy with spectatorship is that we might then substitute a limitlessly mobile subject for the specificity of a historically located subject; at the same time, we risk eliding the social and technological specificity of the medium (see de Lauretis 1994: 125, 140–41).

4. BJP member and RSS ideologue Jay Dubashi spoke of a BJP meeting in Ahmedahad that coincided with the telecast of an episode of the *Ramayan*. The meeting had to be deferred until the serial was over. Hundreds of people joined them in watching it. It was then that they realised, Dubashi disclosed, that this was no ordinary programme, nor any ordinary popularity. It was something different, he said. This was of course a retrospective judgment on Dubashi's part, but there was no mistaking his view that the popularity of the serial was a significant political event (personal interview, New Delhi, 18 May 1994).

5. These refer to the agitations of the latter half of the 1980s for, respectively, opening the locks of the temple claimed to be Ram's birth place, for laying the foundation for a new temple there, and finally the call for holy public service towards building the temple. [eds]

6. See VHP. 1991. *The Great Evidence of Shri Ram Jamabhoomi Mandir*. New Delhi: Vishva Hindu Parishad; and Nandan n.d.

7. It would not be possible, then, to neatly separate a 'legitimate' mode of history writing from that of the Sangh parivar with the latter understood to be 'fundamentally ahistorical' (Pandey 1994).

REFERENCES

Advani, L. K. 'Interview'. *The Economic Times*, 10 August 1993.

Benjamin, Walter. 1969. 'The Work of Art in the Age of Mechanical Reproduction', in *Illuminations: Essays and Reflections*, ed. Hannah Arendt, trans. Harry Zohn. New York: Schocken Books, 217–51.

Chakrabarty, Dipesh. 1993. 'Marx after Marxism; A Subaltern Historian's Perspective'. *Economic and Political Weekly* 28 (22), 29 May, 1094–96.

Chatterjee, Partha. 1993. *The Nation and its Fragments: Colonial and Postcolonial Histories*. New Delhi: Oxford University Press.

Dasgupta, Gurudas. 1993. *The Securities Scandal: A Report to the Nation*. New Delhi: People's Publishing House.

de Lauretis, Teresa. 1994. *The Practice of Love: Lesbian Sexuality and Perverse Desire*. Bloomington: Indiana University Press.

Deshpande Satish. 1993. 'Imagined Economies: Styles of Nation-Building in Twentieth Century India'. *Journal of Arts and Ideas* 25–26, December, 5–35.

Dienst, Richard. 1994. *Still Life in Real Time*. Durham, NC: Duke University Press.

Dirks, Nicholas. 1993. *The Hollow Crown: The Ethnohistory of a Little Kingdom*, second edition. Ann Arbor: University of Michigan Press.

Foucault, Michel. 1991. 'Governmentality', in *The Foucault Effect*, eds Colin Gordon et al. London: Harvester Wheatsheaf.

Freitag, Sandria. 1991. 'Enactments of Ram's Story and the Changing Nature of "the Public" in British India'. *South Asia* 14 (1), 65–90.

Garg, Balwant Rai. n.d. *Sri Ramjanmabhumi Mandir Ayodhya ki Rakt Ranjit Gaurav Poorn Gatha*. Ambala: Bharat Vidya Vihar.

Gramsci, Antonio. 1988. *An Antonio Gramsci Reader*, ed. David Forgacs. New York: Schocken.

Habermas, Jurgen. 1989. *The Structural Transformation of the Public Sphere*, trans. Thomas Burger. Cambridge, Massachusetts: MIT Press.

Kaviraj, Sudipta. 1990. 'Capitalism and the Cultural Process'. *Journal of Arts and Ideas* 19, May, 61–75.

Laclau, Ernesto. 1977. *Politics and Ideology in Marxist Theory: Capitalism-Fascism-Populism*. London: New Left Books.

Nandan, Deoki. n.d. *Shri Rama Janma Bhumi: Historical and Legal Perspective*. New Delhi: Vishva Hindu Parishad.

Pandey, Gyanendra. 1994. 'Modes of History Writing: New Hindu History Writing of Ayodhya'. *Economic and Political Weekly* 29 (25), 18 June, 1523–28.

Prasad, Madhava. 1995. 'Ideology as Contagion'. Economic and Political Weekly 30 (11), 18 March, 587–88.

Ross, Andrew. 1993. 'The Chicago Gangster Theory of Life'. *Social Text* 35, Summer, 93–112.

Sarkar, Sumit. 1993. 'The Fascism of the Sangh Parivar'. *Economic and Political Weekly* 28 (5), 30 January, 163–67.

11

Always Already Secular?*

Afterthoughts on the Secular–Communal Question

Sasheej Hegde

> We are not in the realm of causal explanations, and every such explanation sounds trivial for our purposes.
>
> —Wittgenstein (1974: 63)

One of the characteristic features of the many disagreements underwriting what can be termed 'the secular–communal question' is that the parties to them are simply opposing one strand of thought to another. The overall effect has been one of controversy no doubt, but without any apparent move towards a decisive outcome. ... In the pages that follow, ... I ... engage with the dominant line on the secular–communal question in India. This is the line that can be identified broadly as the cultural inadaptability thesis about secularism in India. The thesis, broadly stated, is that secularism cannot take root in India because of its peculiar cultural and religious conditions. It is further maintained that, since religion itself is a 'Western' category, versions of secularism that take for granted that what needs separation from politics is something called religion get their basics wrong.

[...]

A Thesis Revised/Revisited

Invariably, in much discussion about secularism in India, it has been emphasised that the latter is a 'Western' concept and indeed that, since the meanings that attach to the word in the Indian context are very different from their English counterpart, the Indian debate on the subject can and should proceed independent of the European or American discourse of the same. Facing up to precisely this point, Partha Chatterjee has noted:

> Unfortunately the matter cannot be settled that easily. The Indian meanings of 'secularism' did not emerge in ignorance of the European or American meanings of

* *Economic and Political Weekly* 40 (4): 322–34 (22 January 2005).

> the word ... To pretend that the 'Indian' meaning of secularism has marked out a conceptual world all of its own, untroubled by its differences with 'western' secularism, is to take an ideological position which refuses either to recognise or to justify its own grounds (1994: 1,769).

... Chatterjee further notes ... that while the Indian usage 'might open up conceptual or referential possibilities in Indian discourse which were unavailable to the concept of "secularism" in the west', the continued use of the concept, either in its native idiom or in its English usage, 'indicates that the more stable and well-defined reference for the concept lies in the western political discourse about the modern state' (Chatterjee 1994). ...

Chatterjee clearly is resting his case on considerations of an economy of argument emphasising, at once, a certain distrust ... of the modern state, and yet looking for (in his own words) 'political possibilities within the domain of the modern state institutions as they now exist in India' (1994: 1,776–77). All the necessary explaining is sought to be done in terms of a recognition ... that there is the 'very real theoretical possibility that secularisation and religious toleration may sometimes work at cross-purposes' (1994: 1,768). Accordingly, ... Chatterjee, even as he is concerned to affirm the positive question 'Is the defence of secularism an appropriate ground for meeting the challenge of the Hindu right?', also confronts the failure of the attempt (at least on the part of the modernising elite) 'to see the "original" meaning of the concept actualised in India', while going on to detail the anomalies in the 'career of the secular state in India' (Chatterjee 1994: 1,771–73). This is a perilous passage however, something that Akeel Bilgrami latches to, but is concerned to pick on and disintricate only the 'anti-statism' of Chatterjee's manoeuvre.

Bilgrami (1997) does not deny that the Indian state ever since Independence (and especially since Nehru's departure) has shown an inability to cope with communal conflict, but maintains that the phenomenon cannot be grasped as something wired into the very idea of the modern state and its forms of rule. He proposes an alteration in the way in which the modern liberal state is theoretically viewed, which should allow for possibilities 'which necessarily happen on intra-community sites (as in Chatterjee's picture of things) to ... happen on a statist site' (1997: 2,535). And then, in what seems to me a shift of gear, orients his analysis towards a diagnosis of the way that a self-proclaimed secular state has dealt with the question of religious communitarian substantive conceptions of the good, arguing that there is much to fault here. Bilgrami's argument here, we need to reiterate, is also part of the clarifications that he seeks to effect upon his idea of 'emergent' and 'negotiated' secularism, one which would issue from a 'descriptive acknowledgement of community by the state' but which would also disclose 'no normative commitment to community' (1997: 2,538). In terms of the theoretical space that he has been trying to clear, removed from both 'archimedean' secularism and 'communitarianism', Bilgrami is seeking to innovate conceptually from within liberal thought the axes for coping with the specific problems of governance in multi-communal societies. The 'faults' he records, therefore, are nothing intrinsic to the sites he deconstructs, so that in picking off one (say, the archimedean secularism of the Indian state before and after Independence), he is not concerned to foreclose possibilities for an alternative (what he has termed a 'negotiated' secularism) within the same site.

My problem ... concerns less the content of these conclusions themselves than the ideas being brought to mediate the record. The issue of course is not delimited to Chatterjee and Bilgrami, or even the contexts they speak off and against. ... Rather, it involves broader ranges of scholarship and commitment vis-à-vis the secular–communal question. Consider, for instance, a recent redrawing of the map of secularism ... [by] Neera Chandoke (1999). ... Chandoke seeks to avoid the sharp polarisations that have underscored the framing of questions. According to her, there is a need to shift the ground of the debate 'so that we produce some consensus both on the desirability of secularism, as well as on the need to buttress it' (1999: 3). Along this course, she pursues two questions—one, how do people belonging to diverse persuasions come to live together in a polity ... and, two, what is the status that the polity should grant its minorities—but clearly the burden of the argument is concerned to mediate a space 'beyond secularism'. For Chandoke, secularism 'in its present form ... has simply exhausted its potential' (1999: 96) and, what is more, places a constraint upon how the state ought to protect its minorities. Secularism, particularly, is marked out as failing to manage interreligious relationships, and therefore constraining the pursuit of substantive equality.

Gurpreet Mahajan is concerned to address this point in a recent review, observing that 'it is necessary to rescue secularism from readings that posit an antagonism between secularism and minority rights' (2002: 406). But crucially, in a larger tract, Mahajan (1998) encounters this ground from within specific intimations of failure (or, rather, incompleteness). As she maintains therein: 'The point that needs to be emphasised is that the mere separation of religion from state cannot guarantee the extirpation of community sentiments. Tolerance and secular politics are the end products of the process of secularisation; hence, it is this dimension of democratic life that needs to be strengthened' (1998: 23). Or, again, that the '[f]reedom and equality granted to the religious domain, rather than absence of an individualist ethic, shaped Indian democracy, creating a situation in which the logic of cultural pluralism has frequently obstructed the process of secularisation' (1998: 39). ... We have here a way of animating the secular-communal question ... in a specific modality ... of reversal, whose question apropos ... the secular-communal problematic, is never (or not quite) 'What is secularism?' or even 'What is communalism?' but rather, 'Secularism for whom? To do what? Who advocates communalism, when and where, how and how much?'. In effect, these two gestures point to different worlds for their answers.

[...]

Let me try to elaborate in context and in the process weave a consideration that would bear especially on any enunciation of a thesis of cultural inadaptability. ... Such a focus ... is meant to avoid reducing a problem (in our case, the secular-communal question) to a particular determination of it. ... This gesture of avoidance—of deferral, we can even say—is also capable of yielding an interpretation which opens out the space of the record from the inside. ... Consider Chatterjee: even as he poses directly the question of grounding a challenge to the Hindu right from within secularism, the analysis inscribing this focus also confronts the failure of this ground. Particularly, he is concerned to emphasise that the concept 'secularism' carries within itself the fate of a failure of a certain secular-modernising discourse to seize the world, as it were. Likewise, for Bilgrami, the concept, at least in India, seems to bear the brunt of a certain liberal archimedean stance which did not—and indeed does not?—have enough place for a politics of recognition. Both answers may have a suggestiveness in connection with the specific situations they address. What is being overlooked, however, is the possibility that the failure they pick on and thematise could yet be the mark of an excess that necessarily attaches to the secular-communal question, one which tends both to universalise the latter and to particularise it.

The failure is then the determination's inherent limit, but is also, on that count, bearing upon an excess which prevents it (the secular-communal question) from achieving an identity with itself; and thus keeps alive the possibility of its re-articulation across diverse socio-political fields. [...] to think it's 'fate', its inscription and its politics, the standard repertoire of a genealogical mode (a la Foucault or even Nietzsche). But where it seems to err is in positing that this is all that one needs to do in both opening up to an idea (or ideal) and instituting a modality. There remains, of course, the question of this reversal, of ... whether something—an idea, an ideal, a modality, any given cultural form—can be universalised or not, that is to say, grounded in itself, without reference to its contents, and applied across contexts? Or whether ... one can say what the necessity of a form (an idea, an ideal, a modality) is, by 'developing' this necessity? ...

Something of the order of this enumeration is implied by Javeed Alam's arguments grounding what he has termed (in a loaded phrase) the 'indispensability of secularism' (1998). It is very hard to give a critical justification for juxtaposing secularism and modernity, although it has been constantly resorted to in the historical study of cultural forms (and Alam is clearly not outside the sway of this frame). One cannot doubt a certain causal connection between them, of course. But what seems even more pertinent is how this causal relation is effected and being mediated by what kind of necessity? Summarily, for Alam, it is necessary to ground secularism in the historically emergent and the culturally encoded, without of course rendering the latter into an immutable principle (a rendering which he believes is the wont of 'foundationalism' conceived in Cartesian or Kantian terms). Interestingly, the entire argument is structured by the expectation that some form of causal activity—in his case, the processes internal to modernity—procured certain effects by means of some kind of force or immanent logic. Secularism is treated 'not as an innate feature inherent to the human situation but as a need at a specific moment in history in different societies' (1998: 9); and, what is more, goes on to claim that 'many concepts that originated in western modernity are not only living needs—to capture and nurture new expectations, aspirations and telos of life—but can also become rooted in many different cultural situations' (1998: 15).[1]

In grounding secularism thus, Alam is also interested to pose the question of the relation between religion and politics, to try and draw a scrupulous separation, as it were, between the two. Now, it is not that such consequentialist (one may even read them as 'functionalist') arguments are in principle unjustified or in practice useless; they could correspond to the way things (have) come to be and thus elicit something internal to a process of being (or becoming). But it is frivolous to keep pressing the inquiry in such terms when the answers do not always justify them; and it leads only to confusion and miscomprehension then to posit classes of phenomena which correspond not to the answers received but to the questions put. The philosophically minded historian Hans Blumenberg has called attention to the ease with which we confuse 'preconditions' (plainly, the histories of what led up to something) and 'effects' (the aggregate of the changes which that something causes or that unfold in respect to it).[2]

I suspect that such a conflation underwrites Alam—a necessary derivative of his consequentialist (and functionalist) mode of theorising and doing history—although it should be mentioned in his defence that in determining what conditions are necessary (vide the indispensability of secularism) one may actually be involved in determining what is sufficient (apropos the logic immanent to modernity) for those very conditions. It is nevertheless by no means clear, within the space of this argument, how the deliverances of secularism are to be either derived or secured. A most charged issue turns on the question whether secularism implies neutrality—and again, on what site, the state and/or its communities?—or even whether secularism as process can take shape only gradually and in definable stages (apropos the secularisation of civil society),[3] and Alam's terms clearly sidestep these questions. Nor is the position, it seems to me, clarified by affirming, against the consequentialist (or functionalist) preoccupation with 'results' and 'effects', that the concern can and ought to remain the securing of certain acts 'in themselves' (in the Kantian mode, say, of deontology). Indeed, there is no clear line between acts and consequences; and, one might add, consequentialists can be just as concerned about acts, regardless of their consequences, usually those which maximise wellbeing overall (see Bennett 1996).

This general methodological point is essential to understanding the limits of the epistemology of value underscoring Alam, as indeed any engagement with the secular-communal question per se. It is not so much that arguments both grounding and asserting the necessity of secularism are inevitably flawed; rather, that such reasoning may indeed very often be the source of our arriving at our values. What Alam fails to do, thus leaving himself open to objection, is to explain adequately how secular obligations (and therefore secularism) are related to the good life as a whole, let alone consider whether, and if so in what sense, such obligations lie at the heart of the good life, or whether without them life cannot be good. I am not, of course, concerned in this chapter to offer such an argument; rather, only just about clearing a space for it.[4] But, as I indicate later on, we may require a 'philosophy' in order to tell a story after all! It is towards a more precise determination of these contours that

I shall now turn. In doing so, however, let me set up a further consideration upon the variation wrought within the thesis of cultural inadaptability.

'RELIGION IS A WESTERN CATEGORY...'

Consider now the claim that 'religion' is a Western category—as indeed the deduction that comes to be placed thereupon, that versions of secularism which take for granted that what needs separation from politics is something called religion get their basics wrong. The question to be considered here is: what should we understand by the statement 'religion is a Western category'? As an illustration of the general point that all concepts are bounded by time and place, as the concepts of a particular society or tradition, this formulation (as indeed the wider axis of theoretical intervention that it provokes) could scarcely be altered. But if this is so, it can still be asked how far one is justified in detaching a concept from its social matrix and presenting it as having applicability outside the form of society in which it bears expression. This question is obviously relevant in any consideration of the claim—voiced most insistently by Ashis Nandy above all (and perhaps also T. N. Madan)—that we would do well to abandon secularism for some more proximate ideal or norm. However, for now, my interest attaches to the proposal 'religion is a Western category'.

To be sure, the claim is a precipitate one, condensing much that is both factual and normative. The burden of this testimony, taken as it stands, is the subject of a book by Balagangadhara (1994), who, speaking about the conviction that religion is a cultural universal, discerns here a claim that is ultimately 'theological', being itself part of a Christian religious framework. Is it, on this reading, a statement of fact, a judgment of reality? It is very hard, I realise, to give a critical justification for any clear contrast between fact and value; and, to be sure, no such contrast has been presupposed here. If, however, as the 'classical' sociological theorist Emile Durkheim has noted, '[a] value judgment expresses the relation of a thing to an ideal' (1974: 95), then, in this case, it might be affirmed that it is a certain official definition—an ideal type?—which determines the character of the claim in question. The considerations thus adduced could be added to endlessly of course, and indeed there is no end to the question of fact and value to which they respond.

It is important to be quite clear what is at issue here. There are, it seems to me, grave difficulties facing the idea of difference, of radically distinct communities, concepts and/or discursive agendas. For instance, where do we or us (or our) stop and they or others (or them) begin? Certainly, geography and time may help implicate separateness, even exclusivity, and therefore difference, but this does not, of itself, establish the difference as difference. What has to be shown—and this is important—is that there are points of separation—exclusivity—beyond these spatial and temporal ones, which constitute incommensurable differences. A line of reasoning familiar from Wittgenstein and Davidson suggests that this may not be possible.[5] Indeed, if one must respond to the secular-communal question by devolving upon that very mode (namely, secularism) which the question is meant to answer, then, perhaps, there must be something attaching to that very mode which can only be the object of normative appropriation, and cannot remain strictly or only a factual reordering. Our accounts, of ourselves, of the secular-communal question per se, to the extent that they can, and ought to, obtain as normative, require us to have an independent conceptual grasp of the relevant identifying norms. We might require a 'philosophy' in order to tell a story after all.

To generalise our terms somewhat: the point, note, is not that if there are no decisive reasons to live in one way rather than in another (among the more or less disparate forms of life that are known or that can be conjectured), then we may as well conduct ourselves as the people around us expect—whether or not they themselves have any good reasons for regarding their rules of life as right and proper. This would be to take for granted the relativist arguments that since forms of life differ, none of them are absolutely right. But this is logically mistaken. Numerous though forms of life may be, and however discrepant they may be from one another, it could still be the case that just one of them was (or is) absolutely right. It is not self-contradictory to assert as much, and plainly it is a logical possibility. The question, however, as to how we should discover the one right form of life is separate, and not a purely 'logical' matter. But the consideration that has to be borne in mind is that the relativist has given us no proof that it is not to be found.

One might confess to a certain perplexity about what is being entailed. Could not the claim 'religion is a Western category' be taken to signify, precisely, the axis of such a retrieval—that it could yet constitute the basis of a higher order conviction, an independent conceptual grasp of the relevant identifying norms vis-à-vis the secular-communal question? Perhaps, but I have the problem of reconciling this near-relativist construal with the fact of 'difference' being, while salient, not of itself crucial. What must preoccupy us is the question of the conclusions to be drawn from a proper recognition of this fact. Indeed, the question will only be seen in sharp relief when one weaves the position that our point of view has led us to with (yes) the work of Wittgenstein. Consider the following:

> But how can a rule show me what I have to do at this point? Whatever I do is, on some interpretation, in accord with a rule.—That is not what we ought to say, but rather: any interpretation still hangs in the air along with what it interprets, and cannot give it any support. Interpretations by themselves do not determine meaning (1968: 198).
>
> Can one say that at each step of a proof we need a new insight? Something of the following sort: If I am given a general (variable) rule, I must recognise each time afresh that this rule may be applied here too (that it holds for this case too). No act of foresight can absolve me from this act of insight. Since the form in which the rule is applied is in fact a new one at every step. But it is not a matter of an act of insight, but of an act of decision (1974: 301).

The challenge is what construction to put on these remarks? Wittgenstein's point would be missed by anyone who took him to be simply arraigning against the realist case (the thesis, broadly, that thoughts are either true or false, and are so antecedently to our knowing which; in short, that there is something in virtue of which they are true or false). Again, it seems to me that the characteristic concerns of these passages has nothing to do with the reality of rules, but are (as one might say) 'epistemological'. Read straight, they amount to a sort of idealist construal, in which the determinacy of reality comes from what we have decided or are prepared to count as determinate. But it is important to reiterate that the 'determinacy' in question is one of sense, not of truth: 'don't think, but look' (Wittgenstein 1968: 66). There is again no special problem, for this position, as to the relation between the sense and the reference it determines: it simply is in the nature of a sense to determine a referent. But ultimately the question would have to be faced, why this sense, and not another? Also, how is it that the existence of an activity or an idea could constitute grasping any particular sense?

Wittgenstein, in the remarks cited, is trading on the possibility of an oscillation between two orders of sense—between what one might term a descriptive pole (where, for a given order of entailment relations, it could be affirmed that they are necessary yet contingent, that is, they could be false and/or refuted by new experience) and a normative pole (where everything is what it is and not another, not just happening to be so but also, what is more, cannot be otherwise). And yet, it is important to note, not quite obliterating the difference between the two roles. When Wittgenstein states that 'interpretations by themselves do not determine meaning' and/or that there need not only be one correct way of being guided by a rule, he is supposing that the order of reasons can be separated from what those reasons are about, and hence what we are responding to when we raise validity claims. The latter too are responses, that is, they record the place of the pull of the world in claims of that kind. What all this would require is an order of appraisal which asks, of any given claim—be it of what can be known or what must be done, or even what should be hoped for—not only why it must be so, but also the relevant identifying norms that bear upon it.

In focus, then, is not some ultimate truth about the secular-communal question, but rather the cultivation of an attitude—an order of conviction, something not strictly moral in a reductive and utilitarian sense—proper to that question. The tendency to think that something is not quite right about a concept or an ideal, as indeed the thought that there can only be one correct way of applying the concept/ideal, leads us to think that the conventions proper to the latter could not possibly guide another concept or ideal, since (as is claimed) the situations specific to them are so different. Clearly, there is a need to dispel ourselves of this fixation. ...

[...]

NOTES

1. I have a long paper commenting on the contours of Alam's and parallel work on modernity in India and elsewhere (Hegde 2000), and am therefore abridging the terms somewhat.

2. Blumenberg (1987: 127) was, of course, alluding to the history of science.

3. The latter is more easily asserted than accomplished—for variations on this argument, see Thapar (1996) and Vanaik (1997)—but for a closely argued appraisal concerning the former, see Bilgrami (1997). Note, however, the turns in our text.

4. For an alternative take on this, see Bharucha (1998). But surely it is simply not enough to hold that secular constituencies have characteristic discourses or 'plots', or that the development and control of a given discourse may provide a key to social power, or even that an inquiry into the processes of dissemination of knowledge(s) ought to be high on the agenda for researchers today.

5. See Davidson (1985). He has argued that, as a consequence of the nature of interpretation, 'we could not be in a position to judge that others had concepts of beliefs radically different from our own' (143), that therefore, there could not be others with concepts or beliefs radically different from ours, and thus the idea of a dualism of 'scheme' and 'content' is incoherent. I shall return to Wittgenstein presently, and am therefore avoiding a reference here.

References

Alam, Javeed. 1998. 'Indispensability of Secularism'. *Social Scientist* 26 (7/8), 3–20.

Balagangadhara, S. N. 1994. *The Heathen in His Blindness...: Asia, The West and the Dynamic of Religion.* Leiden: E. J. Brill.

Bennett, Jonathan. 1996. *The Act Itself.* Oxford: Clarendon Press.

Bhargava, Rajeev. 1997. 'A Note on the Secular/Communal Question', circulated to Participants of Study Week on 'The Secular-Communal Question' at the Indian Institute of Advanced Study, Shimla, 8–14 May.

———. 1998. 'What is Secularism for?', in *Secularism and Its Critics*, ed. Rajeev Bhargava. New Delhi: Oxford University Press, 486–542.

Bharucha, Rustom. 1998. 'The Shifting Sites of Secularism: Cultural Politics and Activism in India Today'. *Economic and Political Weekly* 33 (4), 24 January 24, 167–80.

Bilgrami, Akeel. 1997. 'Secular Liberalism and Moral Psychology of Identity'. *Economic and Political Weekly* 32 (40), 4 October, 2527–40.

Blumenberg, Hans. 1987. *The Genesis of the Copernican World.* Cambridge: MIT Press.

Chandoke, Neera. 1999. *Beyond Secularism: The Rights of Religious Minorities.* New Delhi: Oxford University Press.

Chatterjee, Partha. 1994. 'Secularism and Toleration'. *Economic and Political Weekly* 29 (28), 1768–77.

Davidson, Donald. 1985. 'On the Very Idea of a Conceptual Scheme', in *Post-Analytic Philosophy*, eds John Rajchman, and Cornel West. New York: Columbia University Press, 129–44.

Durkheim, Emile. 1974. *Sociology and Philosophy.* New York: Free Press.

Hegde, Sasheej. 2000. 'Modernity's Edges: A Review Discussion'. *Social Scientist* 29 (9–10), 33–86.

Mahajan, Gurpreet. 1998. *Identities and Rights: Aspects of Liberal Democracy in India.* New Delhi: Oxford University Press.

———. 2002. 'Review of Neera Chandoke's Beyond Secularism'. *Contributions to Indian Sociology* 36 (1–2), 405–07.

Thapar, Romila. 1996. 'The Tyranny of Labels'. *Social Scientist* 24 (9–10), 3–23.

Vanaik, Achin. 1997. *Communalism Contested: Religion, Modernity and Secularisation.* New Delhi: Vistaar.

Wittgenstein, L. 1968. *Philosophical Investigations.* Oxford: Basil Blackwell.

———. 1974. *Philosophical Grammar.* Oxford: Basil Blackwell.

12

LEFT SECULARISTS AND COMMUNALISM*

DHARMA KUMAR

A group of Indian historians, whom I call the left secularists, have embarked on a collective project to combat communalism in India by their professional writing. While I share their aim of a secular India today,[1] I feel that this venture is misguided, both as regards current political strategy, and as questions of historical scholarship. Only the latter are considered in this paper. At the outset, I should make it clear that I have chosen to criticise only reputable historians, and that I respect many of them not only professionally but for the courage and integrity they have shown in their personal actions.

[...]

The activities of left secular historians have become more hectic in the last few years, but many of the core group have been writing in this vein for much longer. The core group is mainly Delhi-based, and drawn very largely from the Jawaharlal Nehru University, with the addition of Gyanendra Pandcy, Tanika and Sumit Sarkar, and R. S. Sharma from Delhi University, and Mushirul Hasan from Jamia Millia. This group is not confined to Delhi; there are important members from Aligarh, Calcutta and elsewhere. These historians have been very powerful in intellectual life in India. Many people assume that they are the sole voice of secularism in India as is obvious in the statements even of opponents of their views. In my experience, educated people are often afraid openly to voice different views from these historians, for fear of being thought reactionary or communal. Needing a name for this group, I chose 'secular leftists', a term they would probably accept. 'Politically correct' is defensible, but unnecessarily offensive.

LEFT SECULAR MODEL

Based on my reading of their work, I have constructed a basic model, setting out what seem to me to be the essential propositions of the group. Wherever possible, I have quoted from these writers themselves,[2] but readers should remember that this model is my construction, intended to show the logic of their credo, and individuals

---

* *Economic and Political Weekly* 29 (28): 1803–09 (9 July 1994).

may object to one or other of the propositions, though not to all of them. Members of this group, being intellectuals, often differ from one another, but there is a wide area of agreement. Differences between them (such as between Pandey and Bipan Chandra) do not seem to me to destroy the left secular (LS) model, so I have ignored them. Before going on to the propositions, one should note that nearly all LS historians use 'communalism' in its common north Indian sense of tension between religious communities; some may qualify the term to signify political action based on such discord. Pandey recognises that in south India, 'communal' refers to caste divisions; thus, the famous Communal Government Order of 1921 prescribes caste-wise reservations in government employment. But then, he too lapses into saying,

> In its common Indian usage the word 'communalism' refers to a condition of suspicion, fear and hostility between members of different religious communities. In academic investigations, more often than not, the term is applied to organised political movements based on the proclaimed interests of a religious community, usually in response to a real or imagined threat from another religious community (or communities). It denotes movements that make sectional demands on state policy for a given share in jobs, education and legislative positions, leading on in some instances to demands for the creation of new provinces and states.[3]

The essential propositions of the LS model, in chronological order, are as follows. The first proposition is that Hindus and Muslims by and large lived in harmony in medieval society, before British rule. To quote Hasan,

> [W]hile there were stray, localised and sporadic incidents of conflicts over religious symbols, the integrative and syncretic forces were at work amongst the elites as well as the common people. The dominant picture of the 17th and 18th centuries is not of the Hindus and the Muslims forming exclusive and antagonistic categories but of their co-operating in cultural life and social affairs.[4]

The reason for this, according to Hasan, was that 'religious solidarity was not the basis of collective socio-economic experience. The ideology of the state did not rest on the notion of a "unified" community, with identifiable interests, which forms the main pillar of modern day "communalism".'[5]

Second, the seeds of communalism in its modern form lie in the colonial period. Indeed, they were deliberately planted by the colonial rulers; in Pandey's phrase, communalism was a colonial 'construction'. The writing of history was a major element in this strategy.

> Both as an ideology and as a movement, communalism derives ideological sustenance from the view, which was popularised by Henry Elliot and other colonial writers, that Islam and Hinduism, as indeed their followers, co-existed uneasily in India and that religious conflicts rather than harmonious living was the hallmark of the medieval Indian ethos.[6]

The third proposition is that the colonial period marks a sea-change in Hindu–Muslim relations.

> For the first time, signs of Hindu-Muslim friction surfaced in some areas and amongst certain groups. Now, the terms of dispute were articulated differently. The language

> and vocabulary of discourse changed. Muted expressions were replaced with angry exchanges. Mild protests took the form of violent outbursts. The reasons for this were quite numerous, ranging from the introduction of western-style institutions to the emergence of religio-revivalist trends, stimulated by powerful socio-religious reform movements in Bengal, Punjab and Maharashtra.[7]

Fourth, the greatest danger facing India today is Hindu communalism.[8] In S. Gopal's words, 'the main attack on secular objectives in free India has come from the ranks of Hindu bigotry'.[9] This is because Hindus are the majority community. 'It is for the Hindus to be secular and thereby help the minorities to become secular. For it is the majority community alone that can provide the sense of security'.[10] Bipan Chandra argues that '[m]ajority communalism inevitably leads to fascism, while minority communalism leads to separatism or separatist sentiments'.[11]

Fifth, Hindu communalists have played on the false notions of history put forward by colonialists, and embellished by Hindu chauvinist writers. Sixth, this leads to the conclusion that this 'political abuse of history' necessitates intervention by 'the historian'. A manifesto prepared by 25 members of the Centre for Historical Studies of the Jawaharlal Nehru University declares:

> Each individual has a right to his or her belief and faith. But when beliefs claim the legitimacy of history, then the historian has to attempt a demarcation between the limits of belief and historical evidence. When communal forces make claims to 'historical evidence' for the purposes of communal politics, then the historian has to intervene.[12]

The different steps in the argument presented here and the links between them are not equally strong. One essential point is the change brought about in the colonial period in the way in which religious communities were organised and interacted with other communities and with government. This change is attributed in the most general terms to capitalism and colonialism. Although this is not logically necessary, many authors also stress the general harmony that prevailed between Muslims and Hindus in the medieval period, thus reinforcing the argument that colonialism created communalism. The next crucial stage is the transition to adult suffrage, mass politics and majority voting after 1947.

The view that communalism took its modern form during the colonial period is certainly tenable, but requires complex analysis bringing in the new political forms of the colonial period, many of which most of us would consider desirable—new ideas of equality, new ideas of the scope and possibilities of state action, the effects of economic growth, limited though it undoubtedly was, and the effects of political unification and peace.[13] And one change is that the British were neither Hindu nor Muslim—the fact that this is obvious does not make it irrelevant.

The LS model has been very influential and in my view has damaged historical research and writing in India. Many subjects are considered dangerous or irrelevant, especially those relating to religion, even though at least two major world religions originated in India, and others that originated elsewhere have spread throughout India over the centuries. To support my view, I have considered a range of topics, from the decline of Buddhism to the consequences of colonialism. None of these is dealt with in depth; my object has been to show the effects of the LS model on the writing of history, by considering the work of leading LS historians in significant areas.

[...]

Treatment of Hinduism

The LS treatment of Hinduism bears several marks of politically motivated scholarship. In fact, the problems begin with the very term 'Hinduism'. There has been a sad expenditure of intellectual energy by scholars on the definition of Hinduism, and indeed on whether the term can be used for any religious community. This may be connected with the belief instilled in Indian students that no discussion can begin without definitions. Those wanting to use the term 'Hinduism' must jump over two hurdles. The first is the absence of boundaries of the kind found in the so-called Semitic religions, and the second is that the term 'Hindu' itself occurs relatively late. But neither of these hurdles makes the use of the term 'Hinduism' inadmissible today.

The question of when the term 'Hindu' was first used is an interesting philological question, but the argument that it was first used only in Arab texts does not make the application of the term Hinduism to earlier periods invalid, any more than that scientists cannot use the term 'elephants' because the animals in question do not use it.[14] There is no reason whatsoever why the modern scholar should not apply the term to a set of beliefs held by people in the distant past, regardless of their own usage. He can then consider the set of beliefs held by people in a different period, and decide whether there is enough in common with the earlier set to warrant the use of the term 'Hinduism' for the later set also. He may decide that while there are similarities, there are also significant differences, so he may add a qualifier. Thus, Halbfass describes the writings of Radhakrishnan and others as neo-Hinduism,[15] and his distinction between Hinduism—a term he does not hesitate to use for works written well before the Christian era—and neo-Hinduism is not only clear but very informative.

Having queried the existence of Hinduism, LS historians distinguish between 'brahminical Hinduism' and popular Hinduism. Brahminical Hinduism is bascially bad Hinduism as distinct from the good Hinduism of the people[16] or 'true Hinduism'.[17] The term 'brahminical Hinduism' abounds in current LS literature, and evokes knee-jerk hatred from modern radicals.

The term 'brahminical Hinduism' is inaccurate to describe modern urban religiosity, or even the political Hinduism of the Bharatiya Janata Party (BJP) or the Rashtriya Swayamsevak Sangh (RSS). The RSS itself realises that caste is divisive and so weakens the Hindu community.[18] In fact, 'brahminical Hinduism' tells us what it is that the users of the term hate most—brahminical Hinduism has been described as racist, inegalitarian, and now it is said to have a gender bias. It is, in short, politically incorrect, in American terms; in post-modern idiom, it is the Other to 'progressives'.[19]

This emphasis on the caste-ridden nature of brahminical Hinduism is not merely inaccurate; it obscures a fascinating development taking place before our very eyes. Hinduism, whose elastic and flexible nature so many commentators stress, is assuming a yet new shape (or shapes) of a completely unprecedented kind. Genuinely devout Hindus, including Vivekananda and Mahatma Gandhi, have long attacked untouchability on moral grounds. Political Hindus have decided that all caste distinctions are an encumbrance; in a mirror image the left has apparently decided that caste divisions are useful politically. Priests in south Indian Adi Saivite temples have declared that they are not brahmins, while once they would have insisted that they were brahmins. In Pune, Hindu women are being trained to be priests. What does all this leave of brahminical Hinduism?

In short, there have been two different, sometimes inter-related, developments in modern India. The first is that a large number of Indians feel Hindu in a religious sense, as shown by the proliferation of gurus, bhajana samajas and so on. Whether this is a growing tendency is a moot point. Second, politicians have found it useful to get votes on the plank of 'Hinduism'.[20]

In my view, faith in the necessity or the inevitability of caste boundaries has declined considerably in both groups. Many other changes have taken place, giving rise to sneers about 'syndicate Hinduism' or appeals to 'true Hinduism', as defined by Marxists. Is not denying the possibility of change amongst Hindus an act of 'reification' the intellectuals among 'orientalists' are accused of?

HINDUS AS MAJORITY COMMUNITY

A common ploy is to refer to Hindus merely as 'the majority community', thus reducing communalism to the conflict between the majority and minority communities, a simple question of numbers. LS historians also seem to have the need to reduce the size of the Hindu 'majority' as far as possible; thus Buddhism and Jainism are included amongst the 'minority' religions. Thapar writes, 'Religions such as Buddhism, Jainism, Islam and Christianity see themselves as part of the historical process of the unfolding and interpreting of the single religion and sects are based on variant interpretations of the original teaching'.[21] It is undoubtedly correct that Hinduism is and was organised very differently from Islam or Christianity, but the point at issue is the classification of Buddhism and Jainism. There is of course no reason why one should not classify religions as one likes, having first expounded and justified the principles of classification. But this particular division is at variance with general scholarly practice, and requires greater justification than what Thapar provides. Moreover, many Hindu sects, such as the lingayats, could fit Thapar's definition of Buddhism and Jainism. One can certainly draw a line between Buddhism and Jainism on the one hand and designated Hindu sects on the other, but the line will vary in width and sharpness according to region and period, especially since Hinduism was deeply influenced by other faiths.[22] And surely, Buddhism and Jainism are much more like Hinduism than like Islam and Christianity?

Similarly, Hindu numbers are kept down by excluding tribals and lower castes. To quote Thapar again, 'In this sense Hindu in the Arabic texts included both the brahmanas and the lower castes, an inclusion which was contrary to the precepts of brahmanism'.[23] Presumably 'lower castes' is wider than 'untouchables', a term Thapar also uses in this essay. Perhaps Thapar refers to the fact that sudras were not one of the thrice-born varnas, but they were obviously part of the varna scheme conceptually. You cannot criticise 'brahminical Hinduism' for being hierarchical, and at the same time refuse to see that castes cannot be 'higher' without 'lower' castes. (The only point to be made here is that the best test of membership of Hinduism is to ask what the groups in question themselves believe.)

The trouble with this bland division into majority and minority communities is that it overlooks the huge differences between Islam and the Indic group, which must include 'brahminism' and folk Hinduism, and in which most scholars would include Buddhism as it was practised in India, and Jainism. Writing in 1962, Aziz Ahmad endorsed the statement made by an Englishman in 1892 that 'Islam is in most respects the very antithesis of Hinduism', adding that 'The Hindu has been a spiritual anarchist, his faith being intensely personal and individualistic'.[24] Moreover, it is anachronistic to call the religion of the Tughlaqs, Lodis and Mughals a 'minority religion'. Differences in psychology, theology and social philosophy between Islam and the Indic religions raise fascinating historical questions which have been overlooked by modern Indian historians. For instance, did the consciousness of sharing a religion with rulers play a part in the identity formation of Muslims in the past and today? How do other communities remember their pasts? Again, the history of the application of the term 'minority community' to Muslims in India is itself an interesting historical question.[25] Of course this is politically dangerous ground, but it would be sad if historical scholarship were deterred by current political fears. When historians take part in politics, they should not assume that history is their private property, to use old-fashioned language, or that they can 'appropriate history', to be modern. The trouble is that LS historians need the notion of putting right 'historical injustice' (for instance, to support affirmative action) but they have decided that the only historical victims are the lower castes, and hence the only oppressors upper-caste Hindus, especially brahmins. In view of India's long, complex and still little known history, this is dangerous self-deception.

Composite Culture

A very important component of the LS tradition is the belief that a 'composite culture' had evolved when Muslims and Hindus lived together in harmony before the British.[26] This evolution, it is believed, shows that Hindus and Muslims can live together in harmony today too, especially if, some might add, Hindus went back to 'true', that is, non-Vedic, non-brahminical, Hinduism. In some respects, this 'composite culture' is an aspect of the Golden Age myth, the myth that all was well before the British (or the Muslims), into which even careful scholars in other disciplines lapse. Thus to Susanne and Lloyd Rudolph, 'The question is not why old conflicts are flaring up anew, but rather why traditionally harmonious mosaics have been shattered'.[27]

There are, sadly, few accounts of life as it was lived under the various Muslim rulers; the references in LS writing are often only to court life and, moreover, only north Indian court life. Undoubtedly, a courtly culture in art, architecture, music and literature evolved under certain rulers, welding various strains—Hindu, Persian, Saracenic and so on. But this never spread all over India, nor one must forget that under some Muslim rulers, one pan-Indian element in north Indian urban high life was supplanted—many educated men who would once have learnt Sanskrit learnt Persian instead. Undoubtedly, this north Indian courtly culture can accurately be termed a composite culture, and in my view its achievements in architecture and music are glorious. But this was a very small part of north Indian life. The beauty of the Taj tells us nothing about the absence of conflict between Muslims and Hindus at the time it was built, nor about Muslim arrogance, nor the suppressed feelings of resentment on the part of the Hindus, or distrust between various communities. Distrust and fear of authority may have to be read between the lines, for instance from Hindu behaviour after the end of Muslim rule. Thus, a historian of the early colonial period remarks in passing: 'It is rarely acknowledged how much Hindu festivity came out into the open during the 19th century'.[28] Reading between the lines is undoubtedly difficult and risky, but the historian should at least be aware of the possibility of suppressed feelings. Many Indians even today seem afraid of open expression of their feelings.

Exactly, or even approximately, when and where did communal harmony reign, and what were the conditions under which it worked? (The implicit answer, 'When the British were absent'—is hardly satisfactory.) When detailed accounts of medieval life in town and country, court and camp, are available, one will have a better sense of the variations in inter-communal relations, and the extent and causes of conflicts of different types. Till then, the historian should refrain from appeals to the myth of communal harmony, especially since other scholars have come to other conclusions. For instance, Aziz Ahmad: 'The history of medieval and modern India is to a very considerable extent a history of Hindu-Muslim religio-cultural tensions, interspersed with movements or individual efforts at understanding, cultural harmony and even composite developments'.[29] Again, LS historians often argue that religious syncretism was the pre-British norm, and frequently refer to Akbar's Din llahi and the similarities and interaction between the Sufism and Bhakti movements. However, this is apparently not the view of all scholars. For instance, the radical partiality for Din llahi is ironic in view of Aziz Ahmad's opposition of Akbar's 'imperial and aristocratic' Din llahi to the 'popular and demotic' Kabirpanthis.[30]

[CONCLUSION]

[...]

On one point, I partly agree with LS history; the nature of communalism may well have undergone an alteration in the colonial period. But the reasons for this are more complex than in LS accounts. A central fact is that the British were, by and large, neutral between Hinduism and Islam. Other factors include urbanisation, industrialisation, and the worldwide rise in Islamic fundamentalism. Factors specific to India include the nationalist movement, and the rise of political parties and a relatively free press. Some of the changes which originated in the colonial period are working themselves out today, for instance, in the appeal of competitive democratic politicians to group vote banks, first discussed by M. N. Srinivas, and in government policies of affirmative action. Other recent developments cannot be attributed to the colonial period, or at least not directly. The most important may be the decay of political parties. To force these profound complex changes into the simple LS model greatly damages historical research and writing, and probably harms their short-term objectives as well.

[...]

One would expect LS historians to be insensitive to the vast differences between Islam and Hinduism,[31] differences obliterated by the stress on syncretism and composite culture. Modern unbelievers (such as myself) have to make a special effort to comprehend these differences, but overlooking these issues drains Indian history of much of its meaning. It is significant that LS historians take such a partial view of political power. Muslim emperors and kings ruled far longer than the British, and they did not subscribe to modern notions of neutrality in state policy, however much they recognised political exigencies. This simple fact has surely left a deep impact on the consciousness of both Muslims and Hindus. Historians will have to overcome this lack of accounts of how Hindus felt, and the paucity of descriptions of life as it was actually lived in the medieval period. This may reflect the Hindu tendencies to ignore experience and to shut out unpleasant facts, tendencies well in evidence today.

Finally, I myself believe passionately in secularism, but to achieve it we must reform our institutions and laws as they are now, not construct an unconvincing version of history.

Notes

1. The word 'secular' has many meanings. When I use the term here, I simply mean that I desire an India where people of different faiths can live together in peace, so a secular policy is one that furthers this ideal. The difficulties of achieving this ideal are often underestimated; perhaps one reason is that we do not reflect upon our experience and are not ready to admit our mistakes.

2. In addition to the works cited, see *Social Scientist* 21 (3–4), March–April 1993. Every time I go to a library, I see a new article or book on communalism (sometimes under the guise of ethnicity), I do not claim that I have made a comprehensive study of even the secondary literature, but I have tried to be fair to the authors I criticise.

3. Pandey, Gyanendra. 1992. *The Construction of Communalism in Colonial North India*. New Delhi: Oxford University Press, 6.

4. Hasan, Mushirul. 1991. 'Competing Symbols', in *Anatomy of a Confrontation: The Babri Masjid–Ramjanmabhumi Issue*, ed. S. Gopal. New Delhi: Viking, 103.

5. Ibid.

6. Ibid.

7. Ibid.

8. I am not asserting that each of these ideas originated with LS historians, but the derivation of their ideas, for example from Jawaharlal Nehru, is not my concern.

9. Gopal, S. 1991. 'Introduction', *Anatomy of a Confrontation*, 14. Similar views were put forward by Nehru, but he is not the subject of this chapter.

10. Ibid., 18.

11. Chandra, Bipan. 1993. *Essays on Contemporary India*. New Delhi: Haranand Publications, 189. 'Hindu fascism' is another much-used term.

12. 'The Political Abuse of History', *Seminar* 364, December 1989.

13. See Srinivas, M. N. 1966. *Social Change in Modern India*. California: University of California Press.

14. Those who think I am attacking a straw man should refer to Irfan Habib. 1993. 'Medieval Popular Monotheism and Its Humanism: The Historical Setting'. *Social Scientist* 21 (3–4), 79.

15. Halbfass, William. 1988. *India and Europe: An Essay in Understanding*. New York: Suny Press; also see Halbfass, William. 1991. 'The Idea of the Veda and the Identity of Hinduism' in *Tradition and Reflection*, ed. Wilhelm Halbfass. New York: State University of New York Press, especially 7–9, where Halbfass quotes (and later disputes) several versions of the view that 'Hinduism is a European invention'. Similarly, Gonda distinguishes between 'ancient' and 'more recent Hinduism', cited in H. von Stietencorn, 'Hinduism: On the Proper Use of a Deceptive Term', in *Hinduism Reconsidered*, eds Gunther D. Sontheimer, and Hermann Kulke. New Delhi: Manohar, p. 23.

16. I suspect that a careful reading of current writings would reveal that any Hinduism is mistrusted (a good subject for psychologists), but the inconvenient fact that large numbers of the 'oppressed' are clearly Hindus makes the distinction necessary.

17. After the destruction of the Babri masjid, there was a spate of articles by LS journalists about 'true' Hinduism, which is tolerant and belongs to the people, and some of them quoted the upanishads or even the Ram Charat Manas of Tulsidas. Bhaktism and Sufism are particularly good, prompting Ramachandra Guha to coin the phrase 'Bhakti Marxism'. Note also Smith's warning that

> it is only partially valid to term bhakti movements as popular, for their leadership often came from those born to higher castes, even if their appeal is largely to lower caste groups because of the emphasis upon egalitarian ideals and the promise that birth presents no barrier in access to the divine.

Smith, Bardwell. 1976. 'Introduction', in *Hinduism*, ed. Bardwell Smth. Leiden: E. J. Brill, 3.

18. Anderson, Walter K., and Shridhar D. Damle. 1987. *The Brotherhood in Saffron*. New York: Westview Press; New Delhi: Vistaar Publications, 95. This is supported by hearsay about the attitude to the Mandal Commission by RSS activists today, but a serious study of this issue is required. This is not to deny that sadhus and some Hindu politicians do assert that the laws of Manu should form the basis of the Indian Constitution, but the beliefs of the lunatic fringe are not our concern.

19. It is difficult to keep pace with this hydra-headed monster. One night, I joked to a friend that I was waiting to learn of the connection between brahminical Hinduism and multinational corporations. The next morning, the journalist Praful Bidwai linked BJP leaders to the 'hedonistic world of Indian big business' and RSS workers to employers of child labour and excise tax evaders. *The Times of India*, 10 September 1993.

20. For a good but brief discussion of the dynamics of mass politics and Hindutva see, Thomas Blom Hansen, 'RSS and the Popularisation of Hindutva', *EPW*, October 16,1993. pp. 2270–73.

21. Thapar, Romila. 1993. 'Imagined Religious Communities?', in *Interpreting Early India*, Romila Thapar. New Delhi: Oxford University Press, 69.

22. On south India, see Shulman, David. 1984. 'The Enemy Within: Idealism and Dissent in South Indian Hinduism', in *Orthodoxy, Heterodoxy and Dissent in India*, eds S. N. Eisenstadt, Reuben Kahanc, and David Shulman. Berlin: Mouton.

23. Thapar, Romila. *Interpreting Early India*, 77.

24. Ahmad, Aziz. 1964. *Studies in Islamic Culture in the Indian Environment.* Oxford: Clarendon Press.

25. T. N. Madan has pointed out to me that both Jinnah and Azad rejected this use.

26. Significantly, the term 'composite culture' is only applied to Hindu–Muslim interaction, although, as T. N. Madan reminds me, Indian history provides many other (and genuinely mutual) examples of composite culture, such as Hindu–Buddhist cultures.

27. Hoeber, Susanne, and Lloyd Rudolph. 'Modern Hate', *The New Republic*, 22 March 1993. The notion of traditional harmony is pervasive and both T. N. Madan and Ashish Nandy refer to it in their essays.

28. Prior, Katherine. 1993. 'Making History: The State's Intervention in Urban Religious Disputes in the North Western Provinces in the early 19th Century'. *Modern Asian Studies* 27 (1), February, 180.

29. Ahmad, Aziz. *Studies in Islamic Culture in the Indian Environment.* On a practical note, the concept of 'composite culture' does not solve current political problems, as the political history of Uttar Pradesh shows. Brass, Paul R. 1974. *Languages, Religion and Politics in North India.* Cambridge: Cambridge University Press, 220–23. T. N. Madan has denounced the habit of 'dogmatic language of a so-called composite culture'. T. N. Madan. 'Urdu in India', *The Times of India*, 16 October 1989.

30. Ahmad, Aziz. *Studies in Islamic Culture in the Indian Environment*, 179–80. Akbar is indeed a fascinating figure, but not as the author of a successful composite culture and religion.

31. Gopal betrays not only his 'rationalism', but also his unconscious Hinduism when he writes, 'To the person moved by the religious impulse, the ultimate truth is one, every religion shows some traces of it and it is a matter of indifference to which religion one adheres'. Gopal, S., ed. *Anatomy of a Confrontation*, 14.

13

In Defence of the Fragment*

Writing about Hindu–Muslim Riots in India Today

Gyanendra Pandey

I

This is ... a preliminary statement regarding some of the difficulties of writing the history of violence, more specifically in this instance, the history of sectarian violence in colonial and post-colonial India. The history of violence is written up in the historiography of modern India as aberration and as absence. *Aberration* in the sense that violence is treated as something removed from the general run of Indian history, its distorted form, its exceptional moment: not the 'real' history of India at all.[1] *Absence*—and here the point applies more emphatically to a field wider than Indian history—because historical discourse has experienced very great difficulty in capturing and representing the moment of violence. The 'history' of violence is, therefore, almost always about context—about everything that happens around violence.[2] The violence itself is taken as 'known'. Its contours and character are simply assumed: its forms need no investigation.

[...]

The present statement deals with the historiography of sectarian strife. This historiography functions, and has long functioned, in a political context where the rhetoric of nationalism is of central importance. In recent times, especially over the last two decades, this rhetoric has taken on a new tone and a different kind of stridency. The highly centralised state power that now goes by the name of the Indian nation-state has spoken more and more brazenly on behalf of a get-rich-quick, consumerist 'middle class' and its rural rich ('rich peasant') allies. In furthering the ambition of this sectional interest, the state has shown its willingness to mark out all opposition as 'anti-national'—whether this opposition has been located in the industrial working class, among the rural poor, or in other regional and local movements.

* *Economic and Political Weekly* 26 (11–12): 559–72 (23 March 1991).

The 'fragments' of Indian society—the smaller religious and caste communities, tribal sections, industrial workers, activist women's groups, all of which might be said to represent 'minority' cultures and practices—have been expected to fall in line with the 'mainstream' (brahminical Hindu, consumerist) national culture. This 'mainstream', which represents in fact a very small section of the society, has indeed been flaunted as *the* national culture. 'Unity in Diversity' is no longer the rallying cry of Indian nationalism. On the contrary, all that belongs to any minority other than the ruling class, all that is challenging, singular, local—not to say, all difference—appears threatening, intrusive, even 'foreign' to this nationalism.

Writings on Indian politics need to foreground this state-centred drive to homogenise and 'normalise', and to foreground also the deeply contested nature of the territory of nationalism. Part of the importance of the 'fragmentary' point of view lies in this, that it resists the drive for a shallow homogenisation and struggles for other, potentially richer definitions of the 'nation' and the future political community.

I do not suggest that resistance by the 'minority' always, or even usually, functions consciously in this way. But the historian, social scientist or political activist who stands back to analyse the conditions of Indian society will perhaps agree that this is an important part of what is happening. There is a historiographical contest involved here too. For the narrow and diminishing view of nationalism described above is bolstered not only by a reference to current world trends in the economic and political practice of states, nor only by those who speak of ancient India as the cradle of civilisation and the storehouse of all that is good and valuable in the contemporary world, but also by a 'modern' and avowedly secular nationalist historiography that has reinforced notions of a natural Indian unity and an Indian nationalist essence.

This historiography has elevated the nation-state—indeed, a contingent form of the nation-state as found in India today—to the status of the end of all history: so much so that 'History', throughout schools, colleges and universities in India, still ends for the most part in 1947. It has also crafted for us the neat binary categories with which we have all had to work: secular/communal/national/local (all too often read as 'anti-national'); progressive (= 'economic)/reactionary (= 'cultural'), categories that historians have only recently begun seriously to question.[3]

Even today, after decades of powerful and sophisticated history-writing by left-wing, nationalist and other liberal scholars, the view from the 'centre' remains the recognised vantage point for a meaningful reconstruction of 'Indian' history, and the 'official' archive (government records or, for an earlier period, court records) the primary source for its construction. This historiographical practice fails, it seems to me, to lay sufficient stress on the provisional and changeable character of the objects of our analysis: 'India' and 'Pakistan', 'Awadh' or 'Andhra Pradesh', the Hindu or the Muslim 'community', the 'nation', 'nationalism', 'communalism'.

By attributing a 'natural' quality to a particular unity, such as 'India', and adopting its 'official' archive as the primary source of historical knowledge pertaining to it, the historian adopts the view of the established state. This has surely happened in the historiography of modern India. The inordinate emphasis placed on the (given) unity of India and the unity of the struggle to realise 'her' independence has meant that the history of India since the early nineteenth century has tended to become the biography of the emerging nation-state. It has also become a history in which the story of Partition, and the accompanying Hindu–Muslim and Muslim–Sikh riots of 1946–47, is given short shrift.

The history of sectarian strife in general, and of what is called 'communalism' in India, is written up as a secondary story. 'Hindu' politics, 'Muslim' politics and Hindu–Muslim strife appear as a minor element in the main drama of India's struggle for independence from colonial rule; and they are associated usually with the machinations of the colonial ruling class. Histories of Partition too are generally written up as histories of 'communalism'. These are, as one might expect, anything but histories of noble endeavour. They are not even, in any substantial degree, histories of confused struggle and violence, sacrifice and toss, histories of the tentative forging of new identities and loyalties, or of the rise among uprooted and embittered people of new resolutions and new ambitions. They are, in the main, accounts of the 'origins' or 'causes' of the Partition, investigations of the chances, the political mistakes or the less amenable social and economic developments that allegedly brought about this tragic event. In this account, moreover, the tragedy appears as one that, for all its consequences, miraculously left the course of Indian history unaltered. In spite of the emergence of two, now three, independent nation-states as a result of this partition, 'India', this historiography would seem to say, stayed firmly—and 'naturally'—on its secular, democratic, non-violent and tolerant path.

[...]

The reasons for the kind of suppression described above are not far to seek. Difference and strife between Hindus and Muslims persists in India today, and in relating the history of such strife, there is the real danger of reopening old wounds. In addition, there is no consensus amongst us about the nature of the Partition. We have no means of representing such tragic loss, nor of pinning down—or rather, owning—responsibility for it. As a consequence, our nationalist historiography, journalism and filmmaking have tended to generate something like a collective amnesia. Consciously or otherwise, they have represented Partition and all that went with it as an aberration. 14 August 1947 (the day of the establishment of Pakistan) becomes an accident, a 'mistake'—and one for which not we, but 'others' were responsible.

I should like to suggest, further, that our analyses of politics and strife in post-Independence India have run pretty much along the same lines. I will seek to demonstrate this through an examination of the historiography of 'contemporary communalism'. There is another incidental benefit that may flow from such an examination. Recent events and the writings upon them reveal, by their immediacy and uncertainty, many of the hazards of evidence and of representation from which historians of earlier periods sometimes believe themselves to be immune.

Although the immediate context for the observations that follow is the experience of recent 'riots', especially one in Bhagalpur in 1989, I wish to stress that the difficulties of evidence-gathering and representation encountered here point to the folly of our using 'evidence' of, say, 50 or 100 years ago as if it were somehow 'transparent': biased accounts to be sure, but accounts that may be balanced by setting them off one against another, by appropriate additions and subtractions, to give us a more or less adequate reconstruction of 'history'.

II

It has become common in recent writings to describe one instance of strife after another as 'perhaps the worst since 1947'; such has been the magnitude and brutality of sectarian violence in the 1980s.[4] Bhagalpur 1989 was one of these devastating outbreaks. This round of violence in Bhagalpur began in the last week of October 1989. Arson, loot and murder spread from the city to the surrounding countryside and raged practically unchecked for several days. The situation was then brought under some sort of control by military and paramilitary forces; but an atmosphere of fear and terror remained for months afterwards.[5]

Given the scale of the 'riots', and the infamous role of the local administration in encouraging the attacks and suppressing evidence, it is impossible to establish the 'facts' of this occurrence—what traditional historians like to call the 'nuts and bolts' of the story. Possibly as many as 1,000 people were killed in the course of the violence, most of them Muslims: but estimates of the casualties still vary enormously.[6] During the first days of the 'riots', trains were stopped repeatedly at different places in Bhagalpur and its neighbouring districts, and from several of these, Muslim travellers were dragged out and lynched: but no one can say for certain how many were killed in this way—not even disturbed Hindu travellers who happened to be caught on one of these trains and saw people being pulled from their particular carriage. In the major attacks, in the rural areas and in the city, neither old people nor infants, neither women nor children were spared. There is widespread feeling that women were abducted and raped on a large scale, but none of the surviving victims will talk about rape: the five specific cases recorded by the PUDR team that conducted investigations in Bhagalpur in January 1990 were incidents which the Muslim women informants had themselves heard about.

What is beyond question is that the extent and ferocity of the attacks was quite unprecedented, even for a district which has seen much sectarian strife before, including 'riots' in 1946. At the worst stage of the violence in October–November 1989, some 40,000 people were forced to leave their homes and live in makeshift relief camps. Destruction and looting of property occurred on a massive scale for several weeks. The fears generated among the heavily outnumbered Muslims were such that a great many were unwilling to return to their homes even three months after the initial outbreak of violence: an estimated 10,000 were still in 'relief camps' towards the end of January 1990, apart from those who had moved in with relatives or friends in 'safer' places in or outside Bhagalpur district. At this time, many Muslims were pressing for the permanent retention of military or paramilitary forces in the vicinity of their villages or wards ('*mohallas*') as the only trustworthy means for their protection, and some were demanding that they be given arms by the government for the same purpose. The air was still thick with rumours, and isolated attacks and looting continued to occur: one such incident was reported as late as March 1990.

How do we write the history of such an event? In Bhagalpur, the state's 'archives', those official sources that generations of historians and social scientists have treated as core accounts, more 'reliable' or at least more 'comprehensive' than any other source, are largely missing. Like historians generally, various teams of independent investigators visiting Bhagalpur have been eager to obtain the official account in order to establish 'some overall picture' in the midst of an otherwise confusing investigation.[7] But the view from the centre has largely been destroyed in this instance, at any rate for the first few, absolutely critical days of the 'riots'. A *Sunday Mail* report of 11 February 1990, made after a fortnight-long investigation into the Bhagalpur carnage and its aftermath, sums up the situation in this regard:

> Crucial records of the period, especially those from the tables of [the] then district magistrate [DM]. . and superintendent of police [SP]. . are missing. Evidence strongly suggests that [the DM]... in all probability destroyed the log book of the central control room in which the many SOS received in the fateful week were recorded. The fresh log book that has been placed in the office strangely makes no mention of the incidents.
>
> ... [the SP at the time], who has since gained notoriety, too has left his successor... without a clue to work [with]. His records too show a single joint report on the Chanderi massacre (one of the worst incidents in the countryside), just because Patna High Court had issued a notice.
>
> Even the joint report of the DM and the SP on the first incident at Tatarpur Chowk [in Bhagalpur city] on October 24 that had lit the fuse is among the papers not traceable. The fact, incredible as it may sound, is that there is no statement of facts available in either the DM or the SP's office.

This kind of destruction or removal of records is, of course, not unprecedented: the British practised it on a large scale in India after 1937, and no doubt there have been many other instances since Independence. What is less frequently observed, however, is the destruction entailed in the systematic construction of evidence on all sides, official and unofficial, when an event of this kind occurs. Violence produces the necessity of evidence-gathering, of uncovering hidden processes and contradictions that we might normally prefer to ignore; but violence also wipes out 'evidence' and even, to a large extent, the possibility of collecting it in a manner and form that is deemed acceptable by today's social science. Let me illustrate this with reference to the PUDR team's work in Bhagalpur.

In spite of the size of this team[8] and the very long hours it put in during its eight-day visit to the district, we were bound by serious limitations. The majority of the people we spoke to in Bhagalpur were Muslims. They were the primary victims of the 'riots'; they were in the relief camps; they were the people who were willing to, perhaps had need to, talk. Hindus in many of the badly affected areas met us with studied silence, if not hostility.[9] The Hindus we could speak with easily were from a narrow stratum: middle-class intellectuals, political activists, professionals and officials with established opinions (or 'theories') about what had occurred.

In addition, we were confronted with the problem, when we met victims of the violence, or other eyewitnesses, of what questions to ask, and how. The form of a question suggests particular answers, and there were particular answers that we were more ready to hear than others. This is a point to which I shall return. But we faced a further difficulty at the outset: how does one ask the victims of such barbarism—the father and son, or the mother and four little children who survived because they were away or managed somehow to hide in the fields, from where they saw elders and young ones, women and men, everyone to be found in the Muslim quarter of their village being slaughtered—how does one ask such victims of terror for details of what thcy saw?

And yet 'investigators' are bound to ask. And sometimes the victims, survivors and others standing by begin to talk without even being asked—because they have been asked so many times already, or because there is need for a public narrative of their suffering. However, this narrative too assumes a set form. It appears as a ritualised account, a collective memory or record that has been generated on behalf of the entire community—'Muslims' or 'Yadavs' or 'Hindus', or whatever. The standard practice in the affected 'mohallas' and villages we visited was for us to be taken to a central spot where many people gathered, and the 'elders' or the 'educated' gave us what might be called the authorised account of local happenings.

Even in those places where women, youths or for that matter children spoke up separately, and differences of emphasis and priority surfaced in their different accounts, their reports still emerged as part of a collective statement. The broad outlines of what occurred appeared to be known to everyone in the same way, and the concerns were common: the suffering of the collectivity, the need for protection and compensation, the identification of those who had proved to be friends in need (mainly religious organisations and, in places, where the left had a presence, left-wing activists and associations).

The PUDR team went to Bhagalpur three months after the outbreak of this violence, and it is possible to suggest that the ritualised nature of these collective accounts was much more firmly set by then. Yet I have no doubt that a collective memory, in a set form, will have come into being very soon after the occurrence of the events it describes. This has to do with the living conditions of the local communities, the history of past strife and the difficult relations with the state. But it has to do with another factor as well, that the purpose of the public narrative is at least partly to impress a particular point of view on the state and its agents.

The situation produced by any large-scale outbreak of violence deepens the division that may at any time be seen to exist between privileged people and common folk in India. Such situations also work to level communities and make entire groups that are under suspicion a part of the 'common folk'. At these times, the informant—distant villager, illiterate artisan, faceless member of a makeshift relief camp, and even the elite of a community such as medical practitioners or university professors—tend to become part of a collective subject that approaches the investigator as 'a person of influence' and appeals to her/him for relief, justice, mercy.

Consequently, much of our conversation with local people in Bhagalpur had to do with minute details of property losses, injuries and deaths which we did not necessarily consider central to our investigation. We were asked repeatedly to come a little further, to this village or the next, to see for ourselves the destruction of this house, to make a note of these names too. We were asked also to record 'First Information Reports' and evidence where the police had allegedly failed or refused to record these, or at least to help in getting them recorded because, as a number of informants said, 'We live under constant threat and may well be killed before anyone bothers to take down our evidence'. We were met in other places with the bare response: 'We don't know anything. We were not here.'

Very often, the accounts we were given partook of the character of pre-emptive narratives. They were constructed, more or less consciously, in order to falsify particular 'theories' or explanations of the course of events. 'Hindus', who were accused of taking out an armed procession and adopting extremely aggressive tactics during its course through the city of Bhagalpur, thus sparking off the violence of 24 October, declared that the procession was an ordinary religious one, like any other on important festive occasions, and that it was accompanied by very large numbers of women and children singing devotional songs and playing on musical instruments as they went along. 'Muslims', who were accused by the local administration and by others of making preparations for a 'riot' from long before 24 October, declared all over the district and almost without exception that they had never had any quarrel with the Hindus and had no reason to fear a riot, that perfect amity had always existed between the Hindus and Muslims of the district, and that 'even in 1946–47', while the rest of northern India burned, there was no (or very little) trouble in Bhagalpur.

Even where the defence of the immediate group or collectivity was not an issue, as when we spoke to urban professionals and intellectuals, the defence of something larger and more intangible was sometimes at stake: the 'good name' of the city (or region), for example, or the very possibility of Hindus and Muslims living together in the future—as of course they must. It was this kind of thinking that led many people to stress the importance of letting bygones be bygones. Some similar reasoning perhaps lay behind the pronounced tendency to lay the blame for the strife on 'outsiders': political leaders in Patna and Delhi, 'criminal gangs', a corrupt and spineless administration. The theory of 'criminal' instigation and conduct of the riots has been especially popular. The argument is that 'criminal castes' from across the river Ganga (which flows west to east through the district just north of the city of Bhagalpur) came into the city and other strife-torn places in large numbers, that these castes (designated 'criminal' by the erstwhile colonial regime) are the cause of much of the lawlessness in Bhagalpur even at other—'normal'—times, and that criminal gangs making free use of these 'outside' elements were largely responsible for the violence of 1989.

The difficulties of evidence-gathering are, however, only a part of the problem of reconstructing the history of such events. The question of how to write about such experiences, already hinted at, is equally hazardous. For there is the obvious danger of sensationalising and over-dramatising, thus rendering such strife and its consequences as extraordinary—aberrational. Yet there is, on the other hand, at least an equal danger of surrendering to the demands of an academic discourse, of sanitising, 'naturalising' and thereby, making bland and rather more palatable what is intensely ugly and disorienting. Academic discourse too tends to push the moment of violence into the realm of the exceptional and aberrant, as I shall try to show in a moment.

Discussions of sectarian strife in India find it necessary to try and balance an account of 'Hindu' atrocities by some account of 'Muslim' (or 'Sikh') atrocities. So, a few weeks after our visit to Bhagalpur, the chief minister of Bihar spoke, in a public announcement on the steps being taken to restore normalcy, of the numbers of Hindu temples and shrines destroyed in the district along with large numbers of Muslim holy places; against all the evidence, for no investigating team had reported a single Hindu temple or shrine damaged or destroyed on this occasion. So too, a documentary film on the Bhagalpur violence, made by an independent and enterprising filmmaker, Nalini Singh, and shown on national television in March 1990, equated Jamalpur (the one Hindu village to be attacked in the course of the 'riots') with Logain (the site of one of the worst massacres of Muslims), implying that the attacks and casualties were of the same order; although the most reliable estimates suggest that seven people were killed and some 70 houses and huts partially burnt and looted in Jamalpur against 115 killed and the entire Muslim 'basti' looted, burnt and destroyed in Logain.[10]

This allegedly 'liberal' demand to document and present 'both sides of the case' is frequently accompanied by the social scientists' search for 'outside forces' and 'exceptional circumstances' which are, in this reckoning, very likely to be found at the back of such acts of extraordinary violence. For Bhagalpur, journalists and other investigators have pointed the finger at 'criminal' elements, at the local administration and at the vicious propaganda of the Vishva Hindu Parishad (VHP) and other militant Hindu organisations. As a newspaper report of 19 November 1989 has it,

> Is it possible that people who live together [have always lived together] and share each other's daily concerns—about food and drink, the marriage of daughters, and electoral politics should become enemies overnight? What have these people to do with the Babri Masjid and Ram Janmabhoomi controversy? But the criminal elements of both communities saw their opportunity and very quickly indeed they filled the minds of the people with a poisonous insanity.

That this task of poisoning the minds of the people could be accomplished so quickly does not seem to raise any problems for the writer: its significance is never discussed. Instead, we are told: 'The Bhagalpur riots are not so much the product of sectarian ['communal'] feelings as a calamity brought about by the criminals'.[11]

The moral of the story, which carries over from nationalist accounts of the pre-Independence period, is that 'the people' are essentially secular. The same newspaper report goes on to say:

> The criminals are armed with rifles, guns, bombs, axes, choppers, spears and the blessings of [powerful] political leaders. What can the people possibly do? *[Bechari janta kare to kya kare?].* The members of both [Hindu and Muslim] communities wished to live together in peace and friendship, but the criminals ultimately succeeded in spreading the poison among them.[12]

Explanations of violence in terms of 'larger historical processes' are not so far removed from this kind of analysis as might appear to be the case at first sight. Instead of the activities of VHP propagandists and criminal elements, or dereliction of duty on the part of local officials, these deal in the 'criminalisation' of politics; the 'communalisation' of Indian public life, not excluding the administration; longer-term economic changes—the rise of the 'backward castes', emergence of new trading groups, unionisation, labour trouble and the like. The PUDR's careful and detailed report on the 'Bhagalpur Riots', for instance, makes an elaborate—if somewhat confusing—statement regarding the complex of circumstances surrounding the outbreak of violence:

> A common simplification of the riots has consisted in placing the responsibility for them on criminals. We feel it may be more accurate to say that it was the sum of relations between criminals, the police, administration, politicians, the dominant elite and the economy which are responsible and, at any given time, one or all of these—along with some local people—were significant factors and agents in the riots.[13]

Too often, however, the statement of complex, long-term historical processes leaves little room for human agency and human responsibility, and becomes a statement about the essential and unchanging ('secular') character of the majority of the people concerned. The 'economic dimension' particularly tends to emerge as the master of all.

[...]

In its more extreme versions, this economists' viewpoint tends to reduce all history to a fight for land and profit. Here is a journalist's account of the 'Economy of Communalism' in Bhagalpur: 'It would be simplistic to dismiss the recent Bhagalpur communal riot as a manifestation of the ugly face of our civilisation. Attention must be focused on [the] ruined economy, dying industry and the decadent feudal agrarian structure of the area which provides food [fuel?] to such an event.'

Further, 'Religion is no consideration among the buyers and sellers [of firearms]. Profit is the overwhelming motive. They have a vested interest in keeping the communal tension going... Another factor that keeps it going is [the] profitability of relief camp operations [sic]'.[14]

Obviously, it is not my submission that economic interests and contradictions are unimportant. However, there is more than a narrowly conceived material interest to the history even of our times. Yet some of the most sophisticated writing in the social sciences continues to reduce the lives of men and women to the play of material interests, or at other times to large impersonal movements in economy and society over which human beings have no control. The thrust of this writing is to suggest that the 'real' battle lies not where it might appear—say, in matters of history or notions of honour, not in the centrality of religion or people's attachment to particular cultural and religious symbols—but in the question of immediate material interests. In the quarrels at this level, furthermore, it is above all the elite groups that count. Let me quote the PUDR report once more: 'The major material long-term benefit the (rural) elite groups are likely to get from the present riots is land'. Or again, regarding continuing tension between Hindus and Muslims in the villages: 'one of the major factors contributing to this state of affairs is property, especially land, of those who left their homes. Threats continue to be made by those who have now set their eyes on either grabbing or buying land cheap.'[15] (By them alone?).

Let me reiterate, at the risk of superfluity, that my point is not that land and property are of no importance in bringing about or perpetuating sectarian conflict. My point is that the emphasis placed upon these factors often leaves little room for the emotions of people, for feelings and perceptions—in a word, insufficient room for agency.

There is one particular aspect of this question of agency that may be spelt out further. The mass of 'the people' appear in a quite passive role in many of our analyses of 'riot' situations. It is economic interests, land struggles, the play of market forces and frequently, elite manipulation, that make the running. 'The people' find their place, once again, outside history. By that means, perhaps, their pristine qualities (their 'purity') are preserved. For the message of much of the writing on sectarian violence in India in recent times is the same as that found in the nationalist histories of the pre-Independence period. It is to suggest that events like Bhagalpur 1989 do not represent the real flow of Indian history: they are exceptional, the result of unusual conjunctures. It is to pretend that their occurrence on the scale and with the frequency that we have seen in the 1980s still makes no fundamental difference to the essential 'secularism' of the people[16] and to our cherished national traditions: 'secularism', 'nonviolence', 'peaceful co-existence'.

[...]

III

This is, to my mind, an unacceptable history. It is unacceptable not only because it tends to be reductionist and not only because it continues to ply a tired nationalist rhetoric. It is unacceptable also because, willy-nilly, it essentialises 'communalism' and the 'communal riot', making these out to be transparent and immutable entities, around which only the context changes.

A point that I have already made but should like to emphasise is that the grand narratives which we produce—and must continue to produce—as historians, political scientists, sociologists or whatever, tend to be about 'context' alone, or at least primarily: the 'larger forces' of history that assemble to produce violent conflicts of the kind discussed above. One advantage, or if you prefer consequence, of this is that we are able to escape the problem of representing pain. This is a sanitised history with which we are relatively comfortable. In it, violence, suffering and many of the scars left by their history are suppressed.

It seems to me imperative, however, that historians and social scientists pay closer attention to the moment of violence and try in some way to re-present it in their writings. There are at least two reasons for this. First, the moment of violence, and suffering, tells us a great deal about our condition[17] today. Second, the experience of violence is in crucial ways constitutive of our 'traditions', our sense of community, our communities and our history.

[...]

IV

Standard historiographical procedure since the nineteenth century appears to have required the taking of a prescribed centre (of a state-formation, nation-state) as one's vantage point and the 'official' archive as one's primary source for the construction of an adequate general 'history'. The power of this model can easily be seen in the writing of modern Indian history.

This is a procedure which is not easily discarded, both because states and nations are central organising principles of human society as we know it, and because the historian must necessarily deal with periods, territories, social groups and political formations constituted into unities or blocs. However, the fact of their constitution—by historical circumstance and by the historian—needs to be borne in mind. The provisional and contested character of all such unities (the objects of historical analysis) must be underlined.

I should like to suggest, in opposition to the established procedure, that, with all their apparent solidity and comprehensiveness, what the official sources give us is also but a fragment of history.[18] More, that what the historians call a 'fragment'—a weaver's diary, a collection of poems by an unknown poet (and to these we might add all those literatures of India that Macaulay condemned, creation myths and women's songs, family genealogies and local traditions of history)—is of central importance in challenging the state's construction of history, in thinking other histories and marking those contested spaces through which particular unities are sought to be constituted and others broken up.[19]

If the provisionality of our units of analysis needs stressing, so does the provisionality of our interpretations and of our theoretical conceits. The arrogation of 'total' and 'objective' knowledge is no longer anywhere near as common as it used to be in historical writing. Nevertheless, the temptations of totalising discourses are great. The yearning for the 'complete' statement, which leaves out nothing of importance, is still with us.

That urge will remain an important and necessary part of the historiographical endeavour. At the same time, however, it would be well to acknowledge the provisionality of the statements we make, their own historicity and location in a specific political context, and consequently their privileging of particular forms of knowledge, particular relationships and forces to the exclusion of others. None of this is to deny the importance or efficacy of certain subject positions in a certain historical context. At the present juncture in India, however, the totalising standpoint of a seamless nationalism that many of us appear to have accepted as social scientists and historians seems especially inappropriate.

The dominant nationalist historiography that insists on this standpoint needs to be challenged not only because of its interested use of the categories, 'national', 'secular' and so on. It needs to be challenged also because of its privileging of the so-called 'general' over the particular, the larger over the smaller, the 'mainstream' over the 'marginal—because of its view of India, and all of South Asia, from Delhi alone.

[...]

Notes

1. See the many reviews of *Subaltern Studies* and of Guha, Ranajit. 1983. *Elementary Aspects of Peasant Insurgency in Colonial India* (New Delhi: Oxford University Press), which make the criticism that these works have concentrated too greatly on the moment of open revolt and violence. The criticism fits in with a more general trend in 'peasant studies' and social history that has led to the recent emphasis on 'everyday forms' of people's existence and resistance. See Scott, J. C. 1985. *Weapons of the Weak: Everyday Forms of Peasant Resistance.* New Haven: Yale University Press.

2. Mani, Lata. 1989. 'The Female Subject, The Colonial Gaze: Eyewitness Accounts of *Sati*'. Paper presented at a workshop on 'Culture, Consciousness and the Colonial State', held at the Isle of Thorns, UK, 24–27 July, which makes a similar point about agency and the moment of suffering, among other propositions.

3. See, for example, Nandy, Ashis. 1985. 'An Anti-Secularist Manifesto'. *Seminar* 314, 14–24; Madan, T. N. 1987. 'Secularism in Its Place'. *Journal of Asian Studies* 46 (4); Chatterjee, Partha. 1984. *Bengal 1920-47: The Land Question*. Calcutta: K. P. Bagchi and Co., 'Preface'; Chakrabarty, Dipesh. 1985. 'Invitation to a Dialogue', in *Subaltern Studies, Volume IV*, ed. Ranajit Guha. New Delhi: Oxford University Press; G. Pandey. 1990. *The Construction of Communalism in Colonial North India*. New Delhi: Oxford University Press.

4. The strife in Delhi 1984, Meerut 1987, Bhagalpur 1989 has been reported in this way. For a still more recent example, sec Tavleen Singh's report regarding comments on the Gonda riots, *Indian Express*, 14 October 1990.

5. The details in the next two paragraphs are taken from the PUDR report, *Bhagalpur Riots* (New Delhi, April 1990), and the notes upon which it is based.

6. While many local people put the death toll at not less than 2,000, the official figure for the number of people killed was 414, as of April 1990. The most careful unofficial calculations suggested that perhaps 1,000 people lost their lives, over 90 per cent of these being Muslims; Ibid., 1.

7. I refer here to our own efforts as a team of investigators. Satish Saberwal and Mushirul Hasan also note the '[w]holly unjustified confidence' of the mass media in the official version of events in recent instances of strife; Saberwal, Satish, and Mushirul Hasan. 1984. 'Moradabad Riots, 1980: Causes and Meanings', in *Communal Riots in Post-Independence India*, ed. Asghar Ali Engineer. New Delhi: Sangam Publications, 208.

8. As the PUDR report notes, the support given to its 10-member team by local activists of the Communist Party of India (Marxist) 'effectively doubled our strength'; *Bhagalpur Riots,* 70.

9. It is worth noting, indeed, that we were repeatedly pressed to go and see those places also where Hindus had been the victims of attacks—notably, a village named Jamalpur and a few sections of Bhagalpur city. We had decided to visit these places in any case, even before our on-the-spot investigations began in Bhagalpur, precisely in order that we might see and hear 'both sides'.

10. PUDR, *Bhagalpur Riots,* 17.

11. Vajpayee, Ved Prakash. 1989. *Navbharat Times*, 19 November 1989 (translation mine).

12. Ibid. Here is an even cruder example of the same kind of argument: 'In India the basic material is very good, I mean, the people. They are honest, intelligent and generous. They are only waiting to be drawn into the national mainstream. What is absent is leadership of the right type.' Raman, A. S. 'Leaders to Blame for Communalism'. *Sunday Mail,* 14 October 1990.

13. *Bhagalpur Riots,* 6.

14. Jain, Sumitra Kumar. 'Economy of Communalism'. *The Times of India*; reproduced in *India Pakistan Times*, May 1990.

15. *Bhagalpur Riots*, 32 and 37.

16. I should add that 'secularism' and 'communalism' are perhaps not the most useful terms to be applied in our investigations of the social and political consciousness of different sections of the Indian people. This is a point that is made by several scholars and also by me in my book on *The Construction of Communalism* (Pandey, Gyanendra. 1990. *The Construction of Communalism in Colonial North India.* New Delhi: Oxford University Press).

17. A detailed newspaper report on the rape of two nuns teaching at a convent school in Gajraula, Uttar Pradesh, notes that the three rapists, wearing nothing but undergarments, addressed one another as 'ustad' and 'guru' while they held the nuns at gunpoint; *Hindustan Times,* 23 July 1990. This is the kind of brag commonly associated with young louts found teasing women and girls on Delhi buses and in Bombay films. It is worth pondering the question how large is the step from this kind of molestation of women to the kind of violent assault involved in rape.

18. 'Is it possible to write (conceive of) a history of Europe in the 19th century without an organic treatment of the French Revolution and the Napoleonic wars....One can say, therefore, that [Croce's] book on the *History of Europe* is nothing but a fragment of history'; Gramsci, Antonio. 1971. *Selections from the Prison Notebooks of Antonio Gramsci*, eds Q. Hoare, and G. N. Smith. London: Lawrence and Wishart, 118–19. It will be clear, of course, that I am not advocating the kind of 'objective', 'integral' history that Gramsci called for.

19. I might add that, given the very great difficulty, if not impossibility, of translating cultures and consciousness into alien languages, a new historiography also requires a more concerted effort to recover, what we continue in India to call the 'vernacular' (and also the dialect) in terms both of sources and of the medium of historical debate. Along with that, there is the need to recognise that the 'vernacular' may also be the 'national', in more ways than one.

Section III

Communal Politics

Introduction to Section III

The 15 pieces in this section cover the general field of 'communal politics'. On the one hand, this is the field that lies between the two sections of this book that precede and follow this section—Section II on conceptual issues relating to Hindu–Muslim communal violence, and Section IV containing accounts of specific riots and eruptions of violence. On the other hand, 'communal politics' is the immediate context from which communal violence emerges, and with which it has a strong and almost inevitable causal relationship. At the same time, communalism is also a broader topic which, especially with its counterpart, 'secularism', has been a matter of sustained debate in India. Given this, we have tried to keep this section as close to communal violence as possible, and hence we have excluded the larger question of secularism (which is the explicit focus of only one essay in this book). Though this was not planned, we find that most of the authors in this section are also those who have written on communal violence as well.

Since this book is intended to be a reference work, it is not meant to be read in a linear sequence like most other books. The essays in this section are arranged chronologically so that writings from the same or nearby times are placed together, and the changes over time are also visible. The range in this section is of about 40 years, with the earliest piece dating from 1972 and the most recent from 2014. There is a roughly uniform distribution across decades. There are two essays from the 1970s, four from the 1980s, three from the 1990s and three from the 2000s, within which two are from 2002 and the other from 2014 respectively.

Four of the essays in this section are specifically on the Indian Muslim community, including its own varieties of communal politics. Romesh Thapar's brief intervention (provoked by the Moradabad riots) forthrightly names Muslim communal acts and the complicity of the Congress in abetting violence. The other three essays, those by Moin Shakir, A. A. Engineer and Balraj Puri, discuss Muslim community politics more generally while placing it in a multi-religious socio-historical context that includes the massive trauma of Partition. They offer an overview of the Muslim community's history from the time when the possibility of Partition first appears. Divisions within the community come in for detailed discussion, especially the regional and class divides that played a decisive role.

Ratna Dutta (later Ratna Naidu) offers one of the first detailed, fieldwork-based accounts of the concrete histories that shape political economy and eventually facilitate the outbreak of communal violence. Her essay is important because her field site was one where Muslim dominance in economy, polity and society was a very recent experience kept alive in popular memory. Imtiaz Ahmed's second contribution ('Political Economy of Communalism') follows Ratna Dutta in detailing the economic reasons for rivalry. Ahmed is particularly interested in examining and explaining the correlation between the upward economic mobility of Muslims in small pockets of north India (such as Moradabad and its environs) and the tendency towards recurrent communal violence.

A. R. Desai's piece here is notable because it explicitly criticises the Marxist parties of India (CPI and CPM) for their tacit refusal to tackle communalism frontally. While criticism of the Congress Party is common to many essays in this section, Desai's is unique for targeting Marxists. Rajni Kothari's essay is an extended reflection on how the emerging cultural politics of caste, class and community has provided fertile ground for the growth of communal hatred. Bhavna Mehta and Trupti Shah report on a survey of women in Baroda following the 1991 riots there. While gender perspectives appear in several essays in this volume, this essay and the one by Tanika Sarkar on the Rashtra Sevika Samiti are the only ones that are based exclusively on research among women.

The contributions of Steven Wilkinson and Jan Breman are attempts to make sense of the Gujarat carnage of 2002. But the perspectives in each essay are very different. Wilkinson emphasises the role of political competition in shaping the response of state governments to communal violence, while Breman offers a strongly economic and specifically labour-centred view of why violence of the sort seen in 2002 did not (or was not allowed to) happen earlier.

The essay by Badri Narayan that concludes this section is also the most recent and flags an issue of growing concern in recent times, namely, the trend towards the routinisation of communal violence. Badri Narayan is concerned about the trend towards 'small riots' in Uttar Pradesh, which imply a creeping process of 'normalisation' of communal tension. This is a very significant development in communalism, especially after the Gujarat 2002 watershed, and is discussed in the main Introduction to this volume.

14

Social and Economic Compulsions behind Communalism*

A Case Study

Ratna Dutta

[...]

In this chapter, I will report merely the case study of a small town to illustrate how the leads and lags of Hindus and Muslims in entering the modern economic age have completely reversed the bargaining strength of one community vis-à-vis the other. Perhaps conflict between Hindus and Muslims on this subcontinent became non-negotiable because the Muslims felt a presentiment of the facts we describe in this case study.

The decision to do intensive fieldwork in a small town was made on the assumption that I could get a better understanding of the communal conflict by studying the problem in the context of the 'total system', albeit at a micro level. This town, which for purposes of this report may be labelled as X, happened to be an excellent choice for the purpose, as I hope will become apparent presently.

By the 'total system', I refer to the different facets of the urban community, that is, the civic, the political, the administrative, the economic, the educational, cultural, religious, and so on. ... In a small municipality like X (population: 43,156), it was possible to study the communal question in relation to all these various processes.

X is situated in the heart of the Deccan Plateau, far from the northern storm centres of communal tension of pre-Partition days. The interstate highway approaching X from the east takes a sudden turn to reveal a skyline studded with the beautiful domes of Islamic culture. X was under Mohammedan rule uninterruptedly for more than 500 years—indeed, until it was violently taken over by police action under the Government of India in 1950. It was part of the dominion of the Nizam of Hyderabad prior to police action. As a matter of fact, the history of Muslim rule in the area goes back to much before the first Nizam of Hyderabad.

* *Economic and Political Weekly* 7 (5–7): 255–64 (5 February 1972).

In this town and the surrounding district, as also in the state of Hyderabad, the ruling Muslim community was a tiny percentage of the total population. Only one out of every five persons in the Nizam's state was a Muslim; the rest were Hindus. In the district in which town X is located, 119,742 out of 663,172, that is, 18.1 per cent of the total population are Muslims (1961 Census).

Five hundred years of dominance by such a minority community has left its legacy on the demographic, political and economic divisions in the social structure. The Muslim community is found mainly in the urban centres of the district. ... In terms of percentages, the Muslims living in the rural areas in the district are only 14 per cent of the total population. The figure for the urban concentration of the Muslims is as high as 47.27 per cent of the total in the district. In X municipality, Muslims constitute 45 per cent of the total population. The figures for the community-wise distribution of the total population in the municipality are as in Table 14.1.

TABLE 14.1: Community-wise Distribution of Population in X

		Percentage of Total
Muslims	19,627	45.4
Hindus	18,806	43.5
Scheduled Castes	3,063	7.1
Christians	1,665	3.9
Sikhs	61	0.1
Total	43,222	100.0

Source: Census of India, 1961.

NOT SO DIFFERENT

This concentration of the minority community in urban centres is a pattern not so different from that in the rest of India—or, for that matter, anywhere else in the world. ... However, whereas in India this minority psychology may have accentuated the urban concentration of the Muslim population in recent years, the roots of the trend in the Nizam's dominion are to be traced back to the hundreds of years of rule by the Muslim community. The ruling Muslim community had for generations converged onto the centres of patronage and power. Obviously, since such magnetic centres attract all classes of the ruling cultural group, there was room both at the bottom and at the top of the civil, political and military hierarchy for the absorption of the group. Urdu was the language of the administration, of the courts, and of the educational system, but only the Muslims spoke Urdu. The mother tongues of the people of the district were Telugu, Marathi and Kannada. Interpreters had to be used even low down in the administration. Almost the entire Muslim community, therefore, was absorbed into the administration, police and military establishment. Except for the crafts, such as in silver or metal, which catered to the esoteric tastes of the ruling noblemen, Muslims were not to be found in the primary agricultural and industrial sectors of the economy. The Muslims with land-based wealth were mainly *jagirdars* and *inamdars*,[1] and there were hardly any industries in the district at the time. Trade and commerce are activities which are inimical to Islamic culture (among other reasons, because of the taboo against the acceptance of usury). However, upon deeper inquiry, one always finds the cultural deterrents to commercial activity to be spurious. ... Suffice it to say that, to the Muslims in X, trade and commerce held less attraction than did the lucrative and prestigious positions in the administration.

Nor did the Muslims in the district go into the educational line on any large scale—even though the medium of instruction favoured them. The Nizam's government had established a high school as early as in 1885; children from all communities went to the school, although the medium of instruction was Urdu only. There is no evidence that, even with this advantage on their side, the Muslims took to education on any large scale. ...

[...]

The entire Muslim community in the Nizam's days was sustained by the tertiary sector of the economy in the district, whereas the Hindu community, though lower in social status, was sustained by the primary and secondary sectors of the economy. The two major communities, therefore, were caught in different stages of preparedness when the excitement of industrialisation and modernisation took grip of the rest of the country and the expanding market and money economy began to penetrate into X.

Convertibility into Cash

X is surrounded by a number of tiny villages, and each of them had survived for centuries as self-sufficient economic units. But once the transport and the communications systems spread their antennae into these villages, the agricultural goods which the peasants produced began to be diverted to the town market. Those who had hard cash found a lucrative investment outlet in the commission agencies. The commission agents provided the marketing link between the district and the rest of the country. Twenty years ago, there were only one or two commission agents, but now there are about 60 agents in X. ... There is a large and growing cooperative sector—a modern sugar factory being one of the more recent ventures. Most of the stores, hotels, cinema houses and small-scale industries in the town are sustained by growing consumer demand generated by both the local people and the many professional and technical persons who man the new ventures sponsored by the central government.

The question which is of relevance for us is how is this expanding market being shared by the major communities in the town? Table 14.2 gives the community-wise distribution of all the establishments in the town which employ more than one labourer.

... Since most of the urban trade and industry is fed by land-based wealth, the Muslims have been left out of these expanding sectors. The jagirdars and inamdars

TABLE 14.2: Community-wise Distribution of All Establishments in X Employing more than One Person

Kinds of Establishment	*Hindu*	*Muslim*	*Sikh*	*Christian*	*Cooperatives*	*Total*
Commission agents	46	1	–	–	–	47
Cloth shops (including readymade clothes)	76	22	1	–	–	99
Dealers in metal goods	11	5	–	–	–	16
Dealers in mechanical, electrical and agricultural equipments	13	7	–	–	–	20
Mechanical workshops	2	12	–	–	–	14
Small-scale industries	3	4	–	–	–	7
Mills and factories—Oil	4	–	–	–	–	4
—Khandsari/sugar	4	–	–	–	–	4
—Dal	3	–	–	–	–	3
Washing soap	3	–	–	–	–	3
Biscuits	3	2	–	–	–	5
Mathh	–	–	–	–	1	1
Zardh	–	2	–	–	–	2
Medical stores	5	1	–	–	1	7
Kirana shops	87	32	–	–	–	119
General stores	8	6	–	–	4	18
Handicrafts	1	8	–	–	–	9
Petrol pumps	2	1	–	–	–	3
Fireworks	–	5	–	–	–	5
Hotels and restaurants	12	3	–	–	–	15
Printing Presses	3	2	–	–	1	6
Total	286	113	1	–	7	407

Source: Author's Fieldwork.

were abolished in 1950. The compensation money enabled a very few of the Muslims to invest in the trade in the town. But the large tenant farmers, into whose hands most of the land was retained, are the winners today. This landed class today consists almost entirely of Hindu *lingayats*. The community-wise distribution of those who live in the municipal area of the town but have land in the district are as in Table 14.3. Whereas 45 per cent of the total population in X are Muslims, only 16 per cent of the citizens of the town who own land are Muslims. Of the town's people who own land, 83 per cent are Hindus, although they consist only of 43 per cent of the total population.

As for the professions, out of the 81 lawyers in the district, only 10 are Muslims (except for one Christian, the rest are all Hindus). Of the 20 doctors in the town, not one is a Muslim. The Muslims in the district lag way behind the other communities

TABLE 14.3: Community-wise Distribution of Landowners in X

		Percentage of Total
Muslims	81	16.0
Hindus	425	83.8
Scheduled Castes	1	0.2
Christians	–	–
Sikhs	–	–
Total	507	100.0

Source: Author's Fieldwork.

in the competition for a share in the expanding economy of the development decades.

[...]

Thus it is that 20 years after Independence, the Muslim population in X is uprooted from the feudal economy, is ill equipped for the new, and carry in addition the burden of the sins of their forefathers who conquered and ruled this country.

In X, almost 99 per cent of the cycle *rikshaw* pullers (a mode of transport introduced only about a decade ago in the town) are Muslims. The petty vegetable and fruit sellers are Muslims. ... Workshops requiring relatively less capital and mechanical skills are being run by Muslims. Most of the handicraftsmen are Muslims. Participation of the Muslim masses in the educational institutions and the professions is dismal, and X is probably a fairly representative sample of India in this regard. My data show that Muslim children attending high school number less than half of the total number of Hindu children attending school in a town where 45 per cent of the total population are Muslims. ... The data show not only that Muslims constitute a very low percentage of the total student population in the college, but also that these percentage figures have been falling over the last 10 years. ... The relative strength of the Muslim students in the science classes is again ... very low.

Two Questions

There are two questions relevant to the data on the dismal educational and economic livelihood pattern of the Muslim community. (1) How far is this pattern different from that in the pre-Partition days? (2) Whether, and how far, the economic backwardness of the Muslims as a community is due to discriminatory practices of the majority community.

To answer the first question, one has to remember that educational or technical qualifications were not a very important criterion for employment in the earlier days. For one thing, the state of the economy was not such as to require a great deal of the skills which are acquired through formal education. The channel for upward mobility was the family tree.

In any case, just being a Muslim was an overwhelming advantage in the Nizam's dominions, just as today, a lingayat Hindu is undoubtedly in a better position to compete for jobs. Then again, whereas the Urdu medium administrative language favoured the Muslims, the Kannada medium no doubt favours the Hindus at least in this state today. If one were to set aside all these ascriptive attributes—most of which favoured the Muslims in earlier times, but favour the Hindus now—then it is higher educational qualifications which makes the difference in the ability to get jobs today.

In a way, there is a load of double disadvantage working against the Muslims, because they lag behind the Hindus in educational qualifications and the ascriptive attributes which had helped for centuries have overnight become irrelevant as criteria for jobs placement. Here again, I would like to point out that the situation for Muslims in X is perhaps not so different from what it is for them in Uttar Pradesh and Punjab, where Urdu used to be the court language. Our evidence from this district exhibits, in the ideal typical form, the pattern existing in the rest of the Mughal empire. The only difference is that the districts under the Nizams were sheltered from change for a longer time with the help of the British.

To turn to the second question we raised: whether and how far the economic backwardness of the Muslims as a community is due to discriminatory practices of the majority community. It is, of course, quite difficult to get statistical data on this question on any large scale. However, my observations in this town gave me the impression that a qualified and skilled Muslim would not remain unemployed because of the fact that he is a Muslim. Indeed, even at the level of unskilled labour, Muslims are looked upon favourably, by potential employers, the reason being that they have been found to give better service than their Hindu counterparts. ...

Thus, it seems to me that a hostile attitude towards a particular community need not necessarily manifest itself in the economic exchange relationships. However, if the economic venture happens to be in the nature, for instance, of a cooperative, then it is likely that the hostile attitude will have its impact. Also, in the case of employers for whom job distribution involves patronage distribution rather than any immediate economic return, attitudes towards the minority population will determine their chances of employment. Such is very often the case in educational institutions, where economic returns are neither immediate nor very specific.

Since the primary or high schools are separated by the medium of instruction, opportunities for teaching and admission to schools are also differentiated accordingly. The medium of instruction, of course, nearly equates with the different religious groupings.

However, since the situation is different in the college in X, where the medium of instruction is English, I had a look at the community-wise distribution of the members of the staff. The total staff strength consists of 38 members. Of this, only one person is a Muslim. His designation is that of a lecturer and he teaches Urdu and holds an MA degree. However, out of the 13 peons in the college, five are Muslims (which is a proportionate representation of the strength of the communities in the town). Among the lower level staff, out of 13 members only one is a Muslim and he is a laboratory assistant in physics holding an SSLC degree. Except for two Christians—a lecturer in Botany and the Physical Director—the rest of the staff of the degree college consists entirely of Hindus.

Difficult to Generalise

It is, of course, difficult to generalise from these figures either that qualified Muslim teachers are difficult to get or that they fall out of the system due to actual discrimination. I would suspect, however, that the Muslims who are slightly more qualified would want to move into more metropolitan pastures, such as Hyderabad, both for economic and psychological reasons.

Since there were some serious allegations that Muslims have been almost totally left out of the cooperative venture in the district, I tried to collect some data with regard to this ... and found that 35 per cent of the shareholders from X town of the leading industrial cooperative bank are Muslims, 21 per cent from the district are Muslims. However, if one looks at the composition of the office bearers, not only of the industrial cooperative but of most of the other important cooperatives in the district, they will be found to be entirely Hindus. ... The point to note is that Muslims have been left out of the political field in the district in recent years. Nor have they as yet organised themselves as a separate political entity in the district. Hence, they very rarely hold any important office in any of the cooperatives. Even when they are members, they possibly feel somewhat left out and may even feel more difficulty in getting a loan or some other facility from the cooperative than do the Hindus who have greater leverage with the office bearers. In any case, it is obvious that, whether or not discriminatory practices operate on grounds of religion and caste, there is always psychological predisposition to give credence to these factors.

Vociferous Allegations

The Muslim population is vociferous in their allegations that they suffer discrimination in employment opportunities and in sharing the benefits of the expanding market and of government development plans. ...

At least two prominent Muslim leaders told me at some length about the difficulties which a Muslim faces if he requests for a permit, licence or loan from a government official. One of them told me that he knows of cases where a persistent Muslim applicant has been told: 'You now have Pakistan, why don't you go there?'.

[...]

However, apart from the question of distribution of economic opportunities, it is useful to pursue the question of the attitude of the administration in general to the Muslim community, in view of the precarious majority–minority relationship in this country and the communal violence. As expressed picturesquely by an articulate lawyer in the town, the 'attitude of the government is reflected at the edges of administration'. What is important for our analysis is not the actual denial by the clerk in charge of a file, the loan or licence issuing authority, or the official at the municipal corporation, of some economic opportunity to a Muslim, but the burden of emotions which these people bring to the denial. For, the resentments which gather to burst into communal riots have their roots more in psychological deprivations rather than the relative economic deprivation. After all, the poverty of the mass of Muslims is as old as the hills. They were poor before and they are poor after the Hindu raj took over. In fact, as one Muslim handicraftsman pointed out to me, with the vastly enlarged market and a market which takes his craft into the orbit of international boundaries his economic condition is much better today than it could possibly have been in his father's generation—notwithstanding today's higher costs of living and higher prices of raw materials.

To understand the specific emotional burdens which intrude into the Hindu–Muslim relationship in X, we need to relate in brief the history of communal violence in the district.

Communal riots were rare in the Nizam's dominions as also in the rest of India in pre-British days. This, of course, is less due to the impartial benevolence of the ruler towards all communities than to the fact that one community being dominant in administration, the others usually submitted to the loss of privileges. Under the British, this situation changed; no one group being allowed to dominate another, each sought to assert its identity. In the Nizam's dominion, however, the Muslims continued to remain in a privileged position until 1947—although murmurs of Hindu discontent had already started decades earlier under the leadership of Arya Samaj workers.

However, in 1947, the *status quo* in the relationship between the two communities, which had lasted for centuries, broke down when the question of the accession of the Nizam's dominions to the Government of India was being negotiated. The Muslims, fearful of their fate in the Hindu-dominated India and reluctant to give up the privileges which they had enjoyed for centuries, organised themselves into the militant Ittehad-Ul-Musalmeen. The Ittehad-Ul-Musalmeen, under the leadership of Kasim Razvi, launched a movement which left some bitter memories. This was known as the Razakar movement. The Razakars (the 'volunteers') formed themselves into an armed militia with the object of keeping Hyderabad an independent state under continued Muslim domination. Armed with the theory that the sovereignty of the state does not reside with the Nizam but in the Muslims of the state, the Razakars denied the Nizam's government the right to negotiate the terms of integration with the Government of India. The tactic was to spread the terror of a communal holocaust and so to intimidate both the government and the Hindu population.

X is one of the districts which had suffered from the terrorist activities of the Razakars. However, if the violence perpetrated by the Razakars on the Hindu population was terrible, the police action taken by the Indian government let loose an orgy of exultation among the Hindu population resulting in equal violence towards the Muslim community in the district.

Memories Evoke Emotions

The memories of that year, of course, simmer in the minds of the people in the district, both Hindu and Muslim. However, my feeling was that these memories are, perhaps, more vivid in the minds of the administrators, the police officers, and the intelligentsia in the town such as teachers in the degree college—most of whom come from outside the district, and none of whom personally experienced the terrors of that year. There is a process at work which one might phrase as 'the intellectualisation of collective memories'. The memories evoke emotions which are expressed in prejudices and discriminatory practices and rationalised in terms of the memories. I would like to relate in detail the story of at least one ugly communal situation which took place in X.

In the official files kept on communal violence in the district, the incident is referred to as the 'the incident of the Madrasa'. The madrasa was built in the fifteenth century. The architecture is typically Persian. The madrasa was staffed at the time with most eminent philosophers, scientists and divines, and evidence still exists of a well-staffed library and a well-designed residential accommodation for students. The Muslims had used the madrasa throughout the centuries for imparting religious instruction to children. The mosque attached to the madrasa had also been used as a place of worship. Thus, by virtue of actual usage and emotional ties, the Muslim community could justifiably claim the monument to be their own.

However, the madrasa was a protected monument even during the Nizam's time. After police action, the monument was declared to be under central government protection. This was done through the Ancient Monuments and Archaeological Sites and Remains Act, 1851.

Immediately after the police action, some of the Muslims of the town left X and settled in Hyderabad. Many other Muslim families had also migrated to Pakistan. The prayer hall in the madrasa remained unused, as even the Muslims who remained in the town neglected use of it. The special officer of the Archaeological Survey of India locked the doors of the prayer hall, keeping some masonry materials inside.

In 1954, the Muslims who left X during the police action returned to their homes, and a few of them requested permission to use the hall for prayers as was their custom earlier. After some haggling over the matter, permission was given by the Deputy Commissioner.

The Pesa Imam and Kazi, who was looking after the maintenance of the prayer hall, went for Haj pilgrimage in 1964, entrusting the maintenance of the prayer hall to Ibrahim (fictitious name). The Kazi returned to X but he had become very old and did not take back charge of the prayer hall and left it to Ibrahim. Shortly thereafter, in 1964, the Kazi passed away.

Gradually, Ibrahim began to increase the activities in the madrasa. He started a religious school there in 1965. It started at first with 10–12 children, later increasing to 500. He occupied the first floor halls for this purpose, on the plea that the monument was an ancient university building for Islamic religion and culture. Next, he opened a sewing school and converted one of the rooms on the second floor to residential quarters for himself.

At this point, the officer of the archaeological department began to complain that he was not being given freedom to move around the building, and objected that the premises were being wrongly used for these various purposes. He put in a complaint to the police.

UGLY TURN

Thereafter, the situation took an ugly communal turn. Ibrahim was served with notice to vacate the premises immediately and to close down the school. The Muslim community became restive and threatened to be violent. But the District Collector (DC) and the Superintendent of Public took a firm stand, surrounded the monument with armed guards and forced the evacuation of the building.

The note in the official file on the incident goes to some length to allege that Ibrahim is an undesirable element, that he was in his early years recruited in the police service as a constable but was subsequently dismissed from service, that he was constantly quarrelling with his wife who left him, and so on and so forth. The note also objected to the use by him of one of the rooms in the building as residential quarters, since that involved the fixing of electric connection, cooking, furniture, and so on.

Now it seems to me that these specific complaints against the individual named Ibrahim ought not to have intruded in the stand taken by the administration. The situation could have been handled in a more civilised manner. For instance, alternative arrangements could have been made for the housing of the school, which was by then already 10 years old and catered to 500 children and many adults. Speaking of the incident, a lawyer (who is now the president of the municipal corporation) referred to the harsh and highhanded manner in which the DC treated the whole incident. Since this lawyer had represented the case on behalf of the Muslim community in the courts, I suggested to him that perhaps the government took the right stand since Ibrahim had put in fixtures, such as electric lights, in the building without any authorisation. The lawyer said that Ibrahim had written permission for putting up these fixtures and that he had shown these documents when he presented the case. When I referred to the reputation of Ibrahim as having an undesirable character, the lawyer agreed that the man had a bad record, but that he had turned over a new leaf, even though he was still eccentric in some ways. What is more important, the lawyer also mentioned the most unsympathetic attitude of the DC, with whom he had personally pleaded on behalf of the community, and he referred to the fact that the issue of alternative arrangements for a place where the children could continue to have their religious instruction was not raised.

Perhaps there is some element of exaggeration in the lawyer's version of the story, but the fact remains that the administration had not offered to do anything to house the school at a different location. When I met the DC himself, I asked informally as to what had happened to the school since it involved so many children:

did the government do anything about it? In reply, he merely shrugged his shoulders noncommittally, and I did not pursue the matter. As a matter of fact, the children's school continues to this day. Ibrahim is still running it in a different building. I would think that this testifies to the Muslim community's emotional investment in the whole incident.

The question which one might raise is: why was the incident defined as a conflict between the Hindu administration and the Muslim community? After all, the measures which were taken were in the interest of protecting a monument which is dear to the heart of the Muslim community in the whole region. Apparently it is the rhetoric and the idiom in which the whole issue was posed that put the minority community on the defensive.

Inwards Rather than Outwards

As is to be expected, the district officials' minds and hearts are turned inwards to the problem and the past of the district, rather than outwards towards the metropolitan centres and cosmopolitan problems. This, precisely, is considered the hallmark of the successful executive at the district level. When, moreover, the administrator is concerned with a district as rich in history and as well-endowed with splendid monuments as X is, the past becomes his cultural playground. The administrator may walk miles in the jungle (as I know one of them to do) to pick up a rare piece of sculpture, perhaps part of an old destroyed temple, he may look closely at an ancient Islamic monument and discover that it is built on a Hindu architectural foundation, and so on. And, of course, like all of us he evaluates the present in terms of the past. Consequently, if he is dealing with inter-community problems, insofar as the knowledge of the past is vivid in his memory, he carries a burden of emotion that tilts the balance of his judgment. This burden of emotion is almost a preconscious experience, so that it is difficult to label the acts which derive from it clearly as prejudiced or discriminatory.

Let me give an example. All the high school children in X have been receiving their education for more than five decades in the government school in the handsome building constructed in the heart of town. The medium of instruction was Urdu only. After the police action in 1950, the district schools almost immediately switched over to the language of the people, and this being a district with at least three language groups of considerable strength, the government high school became multimedia. The school offered courses in the Marathi, Kannada and Urdu mediums. The students continued to be housed in the same building having three different sections. The government girls' school also has these three sections and is housed in the adjoining building.

As the enrolment in the school began to increase, there was pressure on available space in the building. The administration decided to construct a new building for the girls, *so* that the twin buildings with common and spacious playgrounds could be used entirely for the boys. However, when the new building was completed, the staff and students of the girls' section were unhappy about moving because they would not be located as before in the centre of the old town—the new building was located at a distance of almost three miles from the old place. In addition, the administration of the boys' school was keen to separate the Hindu and Muslim staff and students, because of recurrent communal trouble after 1950. Since almost all the Muslim boys were studying in the Urdu medium, it was decided to shift the whole Urdu section to the new building. As a result, whereas during the Nizam's time there had been at least some measure of integration, albeit forced, today there is complete segregation of the school system along communal lines. If the students at least in the government high school had been physically located in the same building, with some common classes such as physical education, arts and crafts, English language, and so on, and if they had common playgrounds, there would have been opportunities for interaction between students of different communities. As it is, now the students and the staff from the different sections rarely meet together, even for common functions. The prejudices towards different communities, learned at the mother's knee are thus buttressed as he grows up, right from the primary school stage until he graduates from high school. By the time he attends the integrated college, it is too late; he has learnt only his own community's point of view. Apart from the government high school, during the last decade, several aided schools have been started, each of them catering to one or the other community.

Since the original high school was built by the Nizam, I have often wondered how the Muslim community felt about having to move into the new building which is some distance away. I visited the teachers there twice, but did not feel I could ask questions along those lines. There are probably good practical reasons why the Urdu section had to be moved out, just as there are in the government files good reasons given for summarily throwing the Muslims out of the madrasa. One cannot perhaps label these sections as discriminating against the Muslim community, but one might still raise the question whether a more imaginative handling of these issues was not possible in the long-run interests of communal harmony.

But then the question we have to ask is, is there a sincere concern on the part of the Hindu administration consciously to cultivate conditions for communal harmony? The attempt in the official files more often is to push the problem under the carpet.

The austere aloofness of the administration to the problems of this psychologically uprooted community is matched by the belligerence that it faces today in the political and civic processes. In the political field, the Jan Sangh has been steadily gaining ground. In fact, X is one of the first districts to send a Jan Sangh candidate to the state assembly.

As in many parts of India, the Jan Sangh wrested the seat from a Muslim candidate who had won the first two elections by a comfortable margin. I met this former Muslim MLA and Minister, Ayub (fictitious name) from X, and asked him whether he could comment on the fact that 20 years after Independence, the Jan Sangh is strengthening its hands in the district. After all, in spite of the post-Partition bitterness, the Hindus had voted him to the legislature for two terms. Ayub said that the work of organisations such as the Rashtriya Swayamsevak Sangh (RSS) and the

Arya Samaj have come to fruition only now. Children who have been indoctrinated in the discipline of the RSS in the 1940s are now in their 20s and 30s, ready to give returns to the organisation. As for being returned to the Assembly for two terms, Ayub modestly enough gave the entire credit to the Congress organisation. The Congress Party gave him the ticket; he underlined the fact that the Congress Party always appealed to community loyalties. Wherever there was a considerable proportion of Muslims, the Congress Party picked a Muslim candidate to represent it. ... Would the story have been different today if the Congress Party had not put up candidates not only in X but in many parts of India on the basis of communal appeal? Had some attention been paid in earlier years to the contribution of the candidates to the constituency, to their political career, and so on, we may have inherited a different tradition by now. The national parties did not, however, set the example in the early decades of parliamentary democracy when they could well have done it without too much risk. The result is the aggressive posture of the Jan Sangh and organisations like the RSS, and the retaliatory stand taken by the 'new' Muslim communal organisations (such as the Majlis-e-Mushawarat in Uttar Pradesh).

Secularism and the secular state would become living concepts in India only if an imaginative leadership and administration went about dealing with the communal problem in a self-conscious manner, and with the aid of some thoughtful long-range planning for decisions big and small which affect the minority community. My feeling is that, whereas the government bends over backwards to help and give prominent positions to a few qualified Muslims, there is in fact no consciously thought out policy for the masses of Muslims who continue to be socialised to a medieval world.

Note

1. These terms refer to holders of feudal land grants known as 'jagir' and 'inam'.

15

RELIGION AND POLITICS*

Role of Islam in Modern India

MOIN SHAKIR

I

The connection between religion and politics runs very deep. Religion, both in the West and in the East, influences political and non-political processes and affects the operation of the institutional framework of the state. Even in the developed countries where secularism has been accepted as an operative principle and where it is strengthened by the progress in the field of science and technology, religion continues to be more than a matter of personal and social significance. The reason seems to be, as pointed out by Grace Jones, that

> ...basic religious beliefs survive in disguised forms in moral assumptions and cultural norms and they continue to mould the attitudes of many people to such institutions as the family, marriage, and the education system. This influence is exerted in a concealed way, either at the individual subconscious level or through the medium of indirect pressure politics, and it is, therefore, impossible to assess with any precision. It is none the less real for that.[1]

Religion is more pervasive in India than in the West. Probably this prompted Whyte to conclude that India is a 'religious and not a political continent'.[2] Besides, till the advent of the British, the idea of secular civic society did not come into being in India and consequently religion, in one way or the other, dominated state and society. The advent of the British power constituted a break from the ancient traditions and became, to borrow the apt phase of Marx, 'the unconscious tool of history' in bringing about a fundamental revolution in the social state of the country.

Idealists as well Marxists agree that the rejection of religion as the opium of the people amounts not only to ignoring facts, but the historical process itself by which these facts have assumed attached values.[3] Gramsci's observation is quite pertinent: 'the three elements—religion (or 'active' conception of the world), State, Party—are

* *Economic and Political Weekly* 14 (7–8): 469–74 (24 February 1979).

indissoluble, and in the real process of historico-political development there is a necessary passage from one to the other'.[4] It cannot be disputed that religion has been a part and parcel of cultural and civilisational development of any community. It is a dominant theoretical pattern which filters into the major activities of the various religious communities.

Islam has been one of the most powerful religions of the world. Arising at the time of new class formations in Arab society, it consolidated the power of the state. The role of the Prophet as a ruler of the state distinguishes Islam from other religions like Christianity or Buddhism. The latter could turn hostile to the acquisition of greater power. In terms of doctrines, Islam is not much different, but the latter phase of the Prophet's life in Medina furnishes ample evidence of Islam's potentialities for managing a state. The subsequent Caliph's rule bears witness to many modifications, deviations and even contradictions in the political practices. These can be explained away by the fact that there is no definite political theory or practice which has the sanction of the Quran. It inevitably resulted in confusion. The benefit, of course, has been taken by the Ulema who by mystifying and obscuring the realities, justified the powers that be. By citing certain verses of the sacred book,[5] quite out of context, the Islamic fundamentalists all over the world argue that the concept of democracy and socialism are thoroughly un-Islamic. One fails to understand as to how Saudi Kingship or Pakistan's military dictatorship or Afghanistan's socialist government is Islamic. If the institution of kingship is Islamic, how is Ayatollah Khomeini's claim that the fight against Iranian autocracy is based on Islam justifiable? It is also significant that in professedly Islamic republics or in the Muslim majority countries, no mention is made of Islam's principle of social justice or equitable distribution of wealth, but[6] undue emphasis is placed on such petty points like cutting off of the hand for theft, prohibiting wine drinking, stoning to death for adultery, etc.[7]

Against this background, the role of Islam in Indian politics should be examined. Islam has always been the religion of a minority in this country. Although it has been the religion of the rulers, neither did it ensure equality nor emancipation from the feudal system. It remained fundamental to the system as it could call forth emotional allegiance of its adherents. The so-called custodians of religion wholeheartedly justified the institutions of monarchy, slavery and exploitation. The dissent, if any, was on the issues of fundamentalism or over socially irrelevant matters. Tolerance and broad mindedness, if any, was the result of pragmatism and expediency rather than religious (that is, Islamic) conviction.

Consequently, the Muslim government was founded not on Shariat (holy law), but on the laws and regulations of the king. What Allauddin Khilji told Qazi Mughisuddin seems to have been the policy of the Muslim rulers:

> Although I have not studied science or book, I am a Musalman of a Musalman stock. To prevent rebellion in which thousands perish I issue such orders as I conceive to be for the good of the State and benefits of the people. If men are heedless, disrespectful and disobey my commands, I am then compelled to be severe to bring them into obedience. I do not know whether this is lawful or unlawful. Whatever I think to be for the good of the State or suitable for the emergency that I decree.[8]

Under British rule, the position of the Muslim community underwent a change. The rulers were the bearers of a modern culture and civilisation superior to that of the native subjects. The first reaction was antagonism, which took a religious form. It was destined to collapse as it lacked ideological fervour and the support of the common masses, being merely a regional and emotional outburst rather than an all-India movement. It was, according to M. Mujeeb, 'a disintegrating rather than a unifying influence'.[9] When a section of the Muslim leadership decided to cooperate with the British and accept the modern system of education, it felt the necessity of change in socio-political and religious outlook, for other religious communities had already started thinking along those lines. The social reform movements in the Hindu community constituted a significant development as far as the religious outlook was concerned.

The case of the Muslim community was different. The nature and ethos of Islam is different from that of Hinduism. Hinduism has been flexible and tolerant, at least in the field of metaphysics. It has also been characterised by the absence of rigidity in matters of belief. In the process of interpretation and adaptation, Hinduism has been constantly reviewed and its base broadened. The basic tenets of Islam have, on the contrary, a rigidity which would not brook any such liberties of interpretation as Hinduism allowed. The Hindus could reject any scripture or doctrine which no Muslim could ever do because of the powerful orthodox divines. The Muslim intellectual also faced the difficulty of defining his attitude even to the Hadith literature. The Hindu intellectual had the freedom in matters of faith and belief which enabled him to launch movements for religious reforms and start various organisations for the purpose, while the efforts in the Muslim community centred on individuals who were careful while working on the secular plane not to disturb religious belief and there was no possibility also of creating organisations like the religio-social organisations of the Hindus. Syed Ahmed Khan's Aligarh Movement had little to do with religious reform. It was mainly an educational and political movement.

Mention of another point of difference will not be out of place here. Even after the decline of the Mughal empire, the religion-oriented leaders continued to believe and hope that Muslim power could be restored in India by the organised effort of Muslims, with the help of the Hindus, if necessary. When the Hindus were making efforts for educational advancement and social uplift, the Muslims thought that political power would solve all their problems. What is clear is that the Hindu elite was getting depoliticised while the Muslim elite's obsession with political power was complete. The defeat of the Mutiny in 1857 threw the Muslim community into a state of frustration. Syed Ahmed Khan and his movement failed to undertake the task of the modernisation of the religious and economic life of the Muslim community. The separatist political stance of the Aligarh movement provided an unhealthy bias to Muslim politics and thought in modern India.

It may appear strange, but it is true that the Hindu community practically remained indifferent and aloof towards the efforts of the Muslim revivalists. Similarly, the Muslim community was not stirred by the efforts made by the Hindu reformers. Thus, mutual apathy may be viewed as the perpetuation of the medieval legacy. People lived together for centuries but did not constitute a society. In the words of Louis Dumont, their 'co-existence was empirically accepted without being legitimised'.[10] In modern India, every leader stuck to his own community or caste even in initiating social reforms; Rammohan Roy neglected the need of religious and social reform in the Muslim community, just as Syed Ahmed Khan failed to take note of the problems of the Hindu community. In a similar way, when the extremists advocated Hinduism as the basis of nationalism, they never tried to anticipate the reactions of other communities. Similarly, when Mohammed Ali and other Muslim leaders expressed their support to pan-Islamism as a worthwhile goal, they likewise ignored its meaning for the Hindu community.

The British government released quite contradictory forces in Indian polity. The secular and liberal system of education, industrialisation, urbanisation, limited democratic experiment, new value pattern, growth of the spirit of rationalism, weakening of family ties, and understanding of politics in new perspectives did undermine the political potentialities of religion. But modernisation in a democratic framework never frees man from religion. Religion is not abolished, but its role changes. There is freedom of religion and not freedom from religion. The prevailing situation in India has not been conducive to the abolition of the institution of religion.

The British attitude provided a new lease of life to religion in politics. The British viewed the Indian people in terms of their religion. To them, horizontal divisions among the Indian people were not relevant; they deliberately emphasised vertical considerations. The vital realities of culture, language, religion and economic interests were thoroughly ignored. Conscious efforts were made to artificially divide the communities. Francis Robinson is quite right when he says that Syed Ahmed Khan was closer to Siva Prasad, his opponent, than to the Muslim weaver, as both belonged to what is called the Urdu-speaking elite group.[11] The fact was that the division between the elite culture and mass culture was complete. The British also introduced the politics of 'weightage' and 'counterpoise' which, directly and indirectly, compelled the religious communities to strengthen their communal identities. Religion was one of the strongest factors which could sustain and promote communal identity and differentiation. Religion reinforced political demands and furthered political ambitions. It supplied the wished for ideology necessary for backward classes as theoretical expression of their interests.[12] The introduction of separate electorates widened the gulf between the religious communities and permanently closed the possibility of a secular outlook on the problems of the community. The communities participated in politics as religious entities. The result was, as Harold Gould says, that

> Muslims came to regard their religious identity more and more as demarcator of the different life stages, power needs and economic interests which they felt set them apart from Hindus. The manoeuvres which followed the advent of separate Muslim electorates in 1916 symbolised the politicisation of the religiously demarcated ethnic identity.[13]

Communalisation of politics aggravated social tensions and perpetuated 'the struggle between those demanding a greater role for religion in the State and other demanding a secular polity'.[14] In such a situation, political organisations based on religion are bound to arise. Religiosity is used 'to create a system of instrumental means and secular objectives rather than theocratic ones'.[15]

Religion, in nineteenth and twentieth-century India, has been a motivating factor behind all major political developments. In the birth of the Indian National Congress, not only Theosophy but also Vedantic idealism were seen as the guiding principles. It was claimed that the revivalist movements were 'really so many threads in the strands of Indian nationalism'.[16] The manifestation and expression of Indian nationalism was 'predominantly in a Hindu idiom'; the prestige of Pandit and Pir was a force behind the national political bodies, and the revolutionary nationalist drew inspiration from Kali, Vedanta and Gita, which was decidedly religious in nature.[17] Tilak's view of Indian nationalism is quite significant:

> The common factor in Indian society is the feeling of Hindutva (Hinduness). I do not speak of Muslims and Christians as present because everywere the majority of our society consists of Hindus. We say that Hindus of the Punjab, Bengal, Maharashtra, Telengana (Andhra) and Dravid (Madras) are one, and the reason for this is only Hindu Dharma. There may be different doctrines in the Hindu Dharma but certain principles can be found in common, and because of this alone a sort of feeling that we belong to one religion has remained among people speaking different languages in such a vast country. And this feeling of being one is still alive...[18]

Tilak was for 'militancy, resurgent Hinduism, regional and communal sensitivity, caste-consciousness, and social conservatism'.[19] In the Swadeshi Movement and the Gandhi-dominated Congress, religious sentiments of the people were constantly exploited. Hindu symbols were used to mobilise the people. The Muslim community too adopted a similar strategy of using Islam for political purposes. Whether it was Syed Ahmed Khan's Aligarh Movement or Ameer Ali's Muslim Association, whether it was politics of the 'Old Party' or the 'New Party', or whether it was Mohammed Ali's Khilafat movement or the Moplah rebellion or the Pakistan movement, Islam has been a constant. It has been the unbroken thread of Muslim politics. The leaders wanted the members of the community believe that they were fighting for the cause of Islam. A lucid explanation of the relationship of religion and politics is found in the writings and speeches of the Muslim League leaders. The following is a classic statement of these attitudes:

> The Muslims cannot divorce their religion from their politics. In Islam, religious and political beliefs are not separated from each other. Religion and politics are inseparably associated in the minds and thoughts of all Muslims.... Their religion includes their politics and their politics are a part of their religion. The mosque not only constitutes a place of their worship but also the Assembly Hall.... They are born into a system. The system is not thrust on them. Religion and politics are the same to them. Hence Hindu-Muslim unity or nationalism, signifying homogeneity between them in all non-religions matters, is unimaginable. The Islamic polity in which religion and politics are inseparably united requires perfect isolation for its development. The idea

> of a common state with heterogeneous membership is alien to Islam and can never be fruitful.[20]

The implications of this approach are quite clear. It suited both the British rulers and the Indian elite. The former should have been satisfied with the growth of the separatist tendencies and the latter with the tremendous success in establishing a rapport with the illiterate masses. The British succeeded in trapping the Indian elite, which willingly played right into their hands.

It goes without saying that the British had a vested interest in communal polarisation. It came in the way of the unity of the poor of the different communities. Religious politics was the enemy of class politics. Religious politics, therefore, was neither genuine religion nor genuine politics. It ensured separate political existence to every religious community and made the consciousness of artificial identity a basic factor of political thinking. What M. Mujeeb said about the Muslim League of the United Provinces was true of the Muslim politician in general:

> I do not remember this belief (i e, of Islamic state as a guide and a corrective to political conduct) was shared by the prominent men and women of Uttar Pradesh in the Muslim League camp. They were just not the type of persons who would undertake the intellectual task of analysing the concept of an Islamic State. Their allegiance to it was rhetorical; they did not care to be intelligent or serious.[21]

II

After Independence, secularism has been accepted as one of the bases of Indian polity. The horrid experience of Partition riots convinced the Indian elite to minimise the role of religion in politics. But the great stumbling block in the way of such minimising has been the political heritage of the British era and the inability to deviate from the British approach to religion and politics. Except for the abolition of the separate electorates, the ruling elite in India has faithfully followed the British policy. Secularism is not viewed as separation of religion and politics, but as giving 'equal status' to all religions though in practice the new rulers consider Hinduism as the fundamental factor in the field of politics. The renaming of India as 'Bharat' in tune with old Hindu tradition, the urge to promote Hindi (of a Sanskritised kind) as the 'all-India' language, an emphasis on the adoption of such symbols like Dharma Chakra, popularisation of superstition-ridden festivals as Ramlila, broadcasting of Bhajans and devotional songs in the early morning programme of All India Radio, extension of the governmental patronage to the Sadhu Samaj,[22] etc., betray a strong Hindu bias in the approach of the new rulers. It is also argued that Hinduism not only provides ideological and cultural content to the Indian state, but also prepared the people to accept the social and political system.[23]

Islam is also destined to play an important role in the politics of the Muslim community. Even after the partition of the country, Indian Muslims remain the second largest segment of the total population. They are more prone to accept the authority of religion and the Ulema.[24] Notwithstanding the desire of a section of the Muslim elite for separating religion from politics, the stresses and strains of the situation underline the utility of uniting religious faith with political interests. After all, no community can be oblivious of its milieu and the larger setting of the community within the nation as a whole. In a competitive democratic polity, the principle of religious grouping as an instrument of pressure pays dividends; in the case of Muslims, it ultimately leads to Islamisation and political communalism. Engineered by the religious groups and exploited by the political elite, Islamisation separates 'Muslims from the cultural ties existing with Hinduism and increases identity consciousness and political mobilisation of the community'.[25] Even those Muslims who do not accept the autonomy of worldly life feel contended with the prevailing notion of secularism. In the emergence of new political culture,

> ...the contents of many religions are incorporated not because of their inherent spiritual authority, but because they are high parts of an existent national 'cultural' mosaic. Thus, orthodoxy withers, while a kind of religious revival blossoms... Indian device of cultural pluralism, conceived internally as an egoistic polity and probably secularising in its long term effects, nevertheless preserves for India a distinctly spiritual aura.[26]

The tendency to promote the religious grouping of a community for political purpose, in other words, the phenomenon of imposing religion on politics, is described as communalism. The Muslim elite has been using it for articulating grievances, in communicating with the masses, in framing political strategies and for maintaining a separate political status for the community. It has been a short cut to political power. It is strengthened by invoking the support from Islamic feelings, Muslim solidarity and Muslim culture which necessarily mean non-involvement in ideological and non-communal polarisation. The Muslim political organisations, like Jamaat-e-Islami, Muslim League and Majlis-e-Mushawarat, fall back on a romantic view of Islam implying that Islam alone is a perfect religion, while all other religions arc imperfect. The Muslims are acclaimed as champions of the Truth. The cause of their backwardness is seen as being due to the absence of training to draw upon the Quran in the solution of day-to-day political and social problems. The Muslims, according to this view, do not constitute a religious minority but an international community or a party to enforce the truth of Islam. Their mission is to reform mankind. The considerations of minority are alien to Islam. The political ideology of the Muslim political organisations is therefore opposed to the ideals of nationalism, secularism, democracy and socialism. Such concepts are viewed as the concomitants of modern culture, and not in consonance with the spirit of Islam. These principles, according to the Muslim leaders, provide for atheistic materialism, Hinduisatjon of the country and de-lslamisation of the Muslims.[27]

The effectiveness of the political ideology of the Muslim organisation should be judged in the context of the political behaviour of the Muslim community. Abid Hussain is not wrong when he says that it is not the religious feeling, but extraneous elements associated with religion and the name of the religion which are used by the elite for achieving certain political objectives.[28] The notion of identity consciousness or communalism owing to religion can also be questioned. It is not religion, but the plural character of society and the federal nature of the state that produces communalism. It is nurtured not by religion, but by the non-redressal of secular and genuine grievances of the Muslim community. It is not Islam, but a sense of discrimination which creates a sense of unity. It is the feeling of insecurity which provides the sheet anchor to the notion of solidarity. It is politics, not the ideal of Islam or pan-Islamism, which acts as the leveller of sectarian differences. Various studies of the political and voting behaviour of the Muslim community bear this fact out.[29] They also bring forth the concept and difference between the Muslim elite's perception of the political realities and that of the masses. The former always perceive the secular issues from the standpoint of Islam, while the masses do not. The Muslim support to the Congress can be instanced here, even though several leaders of Muslim opinion mounted determined and firm opposition to that party. In the 1971 elections, for instance, the consensus of the Muslim community, by and large, had been in favour of committed secular and democratic parties. The principle of en bloc voting on communal ground had been given up. The religion-oriented Muslim leaders who had asked the Muslim voters to boycott the elections proved to be ineffective. According to Gopal Krishna, the heavy penetration of the secular forces in and the political fragmentation of the Muslim electorate holds promise for those committed to secularisation of Indian politics and integration of the Muslims within the broad framework of a democratic secular political society.[30]

Nevertheless, one should not carry the impression that the goal of secularisation has been achieved. The obstacles are many. A comparative perspective regarding the growth of secularising tendencies in other groups of society and a meticulous analysis of socio-economic progress in the context of regions and communities is urgently called for. A probe into the existing gap between the common man and the elite is also necessary. Sufficient data about the class composition of the Muslim elite and the working of the Muslim organisations are not yet available. The present Muslim elite still carries the burden of the past on its shoulders. The reactionary heritage and fundamentalist legacy still haunts it. It still looks upon the issue of national integration as one of strengthening and uniting religious communities along sectarian lines and not as one of transcending and rejecting communal divisions. Its politics is of a compromise with the 'national' elite which is keen to accommodate it. This is how the facade of 'consensus' in the polity is being maintained. Both are interested in engineering the consent of the masses and legitimisation of elite rule. The simple law of asserting its (the Muslim elite's) hold in the community, as described by Marx in a different context, is to adopt a religious attitude to politics and political attitude to religion. Secularism in India, therefore, has amounted to no more than political rhetoric and a compromise with religion for political purposes.

The indifference on the part of the political parties to mobilising the Muslims on secular issues is another obstacle. The political and electoral processes encourage particularism and solidarity consciousness. The party setup and electoral system have not proved to be effective instruments of secularisation. They have failed to overcome the primordial allegiances of the electorate. Two trends in the Muslim political behaviour are quite significant in this context—political fragmentation, and social and religious solidarity. Political parties ought to recognise these two contrary trends in the Muslim community. The force of religious solidarity is being strengthened by the various cultural movements dominated by the authentic upholders of the fundamentalist legacy of Islam. Here lies the failure of the Muslim intellectuals who are wedded to a non-traditional approach. They are not only in India, but in the entire Muslim world, though isolated and few in number.[31] Their critical intellect and independent thought have, however, not shaken the inertia of the masses and of the administrative and governmental organisations.[32] Besides, they are keen to take into account the ideological postures of those in power and their directives while offering any new interpretation of socio-political principles of Islam. Consequently, the Muslim intellectuals in India have seldom been able to present a comprehensive analysis of the Muslim situation without myths and mystifications. The social and economic composition of the Muslim community is also not favourable to the growth of critical analysis. Consequently, the conservative succeed in asserting that Islam still continues to be 'the essence of the community' and not 'the essence of the difference'.[33]

NOTES AND REFERENCES

1. Jones, Grace. 1976. *The Political Structure*, second edition. London: Longman, 32. See also Stokes, Anson. 1950. *Church and State in the United States, vol. III.* New York: Harper and Brothers; and Pfeffer, Leo. 1953. *Church, State and Freedom.* Boston: Beacon Press.

2. Whyte, F. 1932. *The Future of East and West.* London: Sidgwick and Jackson, 37.

3. Mukherji, D. P. 1942. *Modern Indian Culture: A Sociological Study.* Bombay: Hind Kitab, 8.

4. Gramsei, Antonio. 1972. *Prison Notebooks.* New York: International Publishers, 266.

5. *al-Quran*, 12:40, 3:154, 6:50.

6. *al-Quran*, 57:25, 3:110.

7. For the 'fundamentalist' political viewpoint of Islam, see Ahmad, Khurshid, ed. 1977. *Essays in Islam: Its Meaning and Message.* New Delhi: The Islamic Foundation.

8. Habib, Mohammed, and Afsar Sultana. 1961. *The Political Theory of Delhi Sultanate.* Allahabad: Kitab Mahal, 8.

9. Mujeeb, M. 1970. 'The Partition of India in Retrospect', in *The Partition of India: Policies and Prospective*, 1935–1947, eds C. H. Philips, and Mary D. Wainwright. London: Allen & Unwin, 407.

10. Dumont, Louis. 1964. 'Nationalism and Communalism in India'. *Contribution to Indian Sociology* 8, March, 36.

11. Robinson, Francis. 1975. *Separatism among Indian Muslims.* New Delhi: Oxford University Press.

12. Krishna, K. B. 1939. *The Problem of Minorities or Communal Representation in India.* London: George Allen and Unwin, 187.

13. Gould, H. A. 1974. 'The Emergence of Modern Indian Polities (Part II)'. *Journal of Commonwealth and Comparative Politics* 12 (2), July, 181.

14. Almond, Gabriel A., and James S. Coleman. 1970. *The Politics of Developing Areas.* Princeton: Princeton University Press, 538.

15. Apter, David E. 1971. 'Political Religion in New Nations', in *Old Societies and New States*, ed. C. Geertz. New Delhi: Amerind Publishing, 89.

16. Beasant, Annie. 1917. *The Birth of New India*. Madras: Theosophical Pub. House, 358–59; Sitarammayya, P. 1946. *The History of Indian National Congress, vol. I*. Bombay: Padma Publications, 14. See also Hutchinson, L. 1937. *The Empire of the Nabobs*. London: Allen & Unwin, 184.

17. Srinivas, M. N. 1967. 'The Cohesive Role of Sanskritisation', in *India and Ceylon*, ed. Philip Mason. London: Oxford University Press, 81: Seal, Anil. 1974. *The Emergence of Indian Nationalism*. Cambridge: Cambridge University Press, 346; Underwood, A. C. 1930. *Contemporary Thought of India*. London: Williams & Norgate, 40–43; Farquhar, John Nicol. 1929. *Modern Religious Movements in India*. London: Macmillan & co., 358; Hutchinson. *The Empire of the Nabobs*, 192; Smith, W. R. 1938. *Nationalism and Reform in India*. New Haven: Yale University Press, 49.

18. Wolpert, Stanley A. 1962. *Tilak and Gokhale*. California: California University Press, 135–36.

19. Ibid., 325.

20. A Punjabi (pseudonym). 1932. *Confederacy of India*. Lahore: Nawab Sir Muhammad Shah Nawaz Khan, 88–89.

21. Mujeeb, M. 1970. 'The Partition of India in Retrospect', 408.

22. Desai, A. R. 1960. *Recent Trends in Indian Nationalism*. Bombay: The Popular Book Depot, 132–34.

23. Martindate, Don. 1967, in *India since 1947*, ed. A. Chakravarti. Calcutta: Allied Publishers, 44–45. See also Park, Richard. 1967. *India's Political System*. New Jersey: Prentice-Hall, 741.

24. Elder, Joseph. 1966. 'Fatalism in India'. *Anthropological Quarterly* 39 (3), July, 227–43.

25. Singh, Yogendra. 1973. *Modernisation of Indian Tradition*. New Delhi: Thompson Press, 76–77.

26. Marriott, McKin. 1971. 'Cultural Policy in the New States', in *Old Societies and New States*, ed. C. Geertz, 37.

27. See Shakir, Moin. 1972. *Muslims in Free India*. New Delhi: Kalamkar Prakashan, 46–78.

28. Husain, Abid. 1965. *The National Culture of India*. New Delhi: National Book Trust, 9.

29. For a more detailed discussion, see Shakir, Moin. 1977. 'Muslim Electoral Behaviour in India'. *Mainstream*, 12 February, 11–14.

30. Krishna, Gopal. 1972. 'Muslim Politics'. *Seminar* 153, May, 21.

31. Arkoun, Mohammed. 1977. 'Islamic Consciousness: A Cultural Profile'. *Cultures* IV (I), 89.

32. Merad, Ali. 1977. 'Reformism in Modern Islam'. *Cultures* IV (1), 120–21.

33. Marx, Karl. 1975. 'On the Jewish Question', in *Collected Works*, vol. 3. Moscow: Progress Publishers, 155.

16

Muslim Communalism*

Romesh Thapar

The clashes in Moradabad and the communal repercussions in various cities in the north have sent shock waves through the system. The stereotyped reactions of 'government circles' about conspiracies and the communal monster are I hope, only for public consumption. The story that is emerging is very much more complex and sinister, revealing a carefully coordinated attempt perhaps to use communalism as a weapon in the negotiations on foreigners in the north-east. That the clashes were engineered is quite clear to any independent observer.

What is disturbing are not the pigs which seem to have suddenly started encroaching on mosques, or the gun-toting Muslim worshippers who are on the ready to take it out on the police or the nearby Harijans, but the lazy bureaucratic and police system which is unable to take security measures. In so many places, following the Moradabad killings, posters hailing Pakistan were pasted on walls. No amount of warning seems to be adequate for those who are entrusted with public security.

I suppose one should not be so harsh with the civil servant and the policeman. Both have been bruised and battered since the days of the Emergency. If the Janata Party quite rightly tried to punish those members of the services who had violated procedure and misused their powers, a revanchist Congress (Indira) has launched vendettas against all those who tried to restore healthy administrative norms—Indira Gandhi's government is today served by a thoroughly demoralised police force and a near-paralysed civil administration. To expect vigilance from these services is apparently no longer possible—and the recent communal flare-up over a wide area is solid confirmation.

This is said not to divert attention from the new revivalist trends visible in the Muslim community and the charge that Arab funds are feeding a kind of communalism. The Ministries of Home and External Affairs are only too conscious of these aspects of the situation. Indeed, behind-the-scenes efforts have been made to insulate the Muslims of India from these disruptionist contacts, but to little effect.

* *Economic and Political Weekly* 15 (35): 1463 (30 August 1980).

The community, wherever it is concentrated in the north, is only too susceptible to the call of the Islamic activists who are now making their well-oiled presence felt.

When such facts are well-known and fast becoming part of normal political assessment, it is farcical for Muslim members of Parliament (MPs), largely of Congress(I) persuasion, to get together to issue statements which imply that every communal clash is organised by the Rashtriya Swayamsevak Sangh (RSS). This deliberate distortion of realities, designed largely to smear India as a communal cesspit before gullible Arabs and other foreigners, will one day be responsible for a terrible backlash, unless these elements begin a parallel effort to expose the various well-funded Muslim Jamaats now operating in India. Mistaken analysis can be forgiven, but not when doubts are cast about the secularity of so many Muslims who command positions of power because they were considered secular. A heavy responsibility now rests on Muslim leadership.

Hindu communalism cannot be fought unless there is simultaneous battle against Muslim communalism. Secularism in India cannot be turned into a weapon to be used exclusively against the Hindu, even though the Hindu must shed his big-brother chauvinism more demonstrably than others who are in a minority. Attitudes to the trends in the Muslim community are very important because of the size of the community (larger than the population of Pakistan!), and because these trends create reactions which influence the majority community's attitude to all minorities.

We have become such specialists in twisted logic and convenient rationalisation, at both official and non-official levels, that these truths seldom appear in print. And when they do, they are the subject of bitter controversy which seeks to muffle the truth. One would expect the Prime Minister (then Indira Gandhi) to be more guarded in her use of polemics against political opponents, particularly in the context of communalism, but caution is cast aside to score debating points. One would also expect the left to introduce a saner analysis, but these think-tanks are now more concerned with mobilising votes—yes, even in the shadowy areas of the polity. And, as for independent opinion, it is reduced to apathy or cynicism.

Whether it is the breakdown of the talks on Assam, or the flash of communal collisions in the north, it is about time that Indira Gandhi lifted herself out of her lazy notions about what is to be done and began to formulate a careful national response to these problems. Such a response can only crystallise at a conference of selected leaders drawn from all the major parties. The mechanics can be worked out in consultation with party chairmen. Indira Gandhi's reluctance to proceed along these lines, based largely on the hope that her various minions can pull off a settlement has already lost valuable time and damaged the credibility of the centre.

What use are pleas for national unity and reconciliation when the minimum initiatives are not attempted? Someone at the summit of power has to take courage in both hands and attempt a corrective. Indira Gandhi has to prove by word—and deed—that she is genuinely interested in a national response to key internal questions and the central issues of foreign policy. The two are closely connected, whatever the effort to treat them separately. The extraordinary doodling at the moment can only lead to disaster.

Seldom have I known the capital to be so full of rumours. They range from eye-witness accounts of clashes within the ruling family to reports of military deployments both internally and along the borders. Corruption is believed to be so rampant that a host of Congress(I) activists are named as brokers in massive government contracts, including the Defence Ministry, over which the Prime Minister presides. The old Sanjay slogan, of raising a crore of rupees a day to finance the cadres of the Congress(I), is repeatedly referred to, and no one anymore has any confidence of holding prices which have seen a dramatic rise during the past month.

The breakdown of a serious party system throughout the country, including the Congress(I) which is now shot through with factional suspicions and animosities, creates a profound impact on the crumbling political/economic system. A multi-cultural federal polity cannot drift in this fashion. It has to find a coherent structure of growth and consolidation. A political collective, either as a disciplined coalition or as a new formation, has to be forged. A deteriorating situation, whatever its expression, is a constant reminder about what needs doing.

17

Political Economy of Communalism in Contemporary India*

Imtiaz Ahmed

I

Communal tensions and riots have been a feature of Indian political life throughout this century. It is said that some communal riots had taken place during the reign of Aurangzeb, which means that they can be traced even further backwards. Nonetheless, the fact remains that they have been a recurrent phenomenon in Indian political life since the first decade of this century and have been particularly widespread in recent years.

Despite this recurrence, communal tensions and riots have not received from the social scientists the attention which they would seem to deserve. Usually, they have been seen as an extreme expression of the communal phenomenon without any serious attempt to discuss their distinctive local features as social events. Or, where they have been dealt with as local events, attention has usually been focused upon certain broad or universal causes without any attempt at analysing the dynamics of the local situation that can be said to cause or exacerbate them.

For instance, attempts at explanation of communal tensions and riots have usually concentrated on what may be called the civilisational or religious factors such as cow slaughter, playing of music before mosques or desecration of places of worship by pigs, etc. Even though these factors may be present in most of the communal riots, this does not necessarily mean that they can account for communal tensions by themselves. After all, cow slaughter, playing of music in front of mosques, or even desecration of religious places takes place in so many towns and cities and on countless occasions, but such occurrences cause ripples only in certain places or on selected occasions. Hence, it becomes necessary to understand those local factors that are crucial to spark off the deterioration of social relations that communal tensions and riots necessarily entail.

---

* *Economic and Political Weekly* 19 (22–23): 1196–97 (2–9 June 1984).

II

It is easy to understand the almost total lack of concern with the dynamics of local situations in discussion of communal tensions in India. For one thing, communal riots and tensions erupt suddenly and somewhat unexpectedly so that it is not possible for a social scientist to anticipate and be present at a place for research purposes when a communal riot is likely to break out. Second, studying communal riots is a risky and dangerous enterprise because of the violence and killing that accompanies them so that social scientists are reluctant to study them as events in process. Finally, an orientation has somehow been ascendant among social scientists that communal tensions owe themselves to the cultural and religious differences between the communities involved so that explanations of these occurrences must necessarily lie in macro causes centring around religious and cultural questions. Particularly where an understanding of communal tensions turn out to be a historical reconstruction of the events as reported by the people who themselves place a great deal of emphasis upon macro causes as the basis of tensions, attention easily gets deflected from local situation and factors.

Perhaps journalists are at an advantage in this respect as compared to the social scientists. As a rule, prompted by the demand of their profession to report events soon after they occur as they are occurring, they usually rush to the scene of a riot as soon as the first information of its outbreak is received. Even so, journalists operate under certain constraints which limit the range of what they are able to bring out into the open. First, they are limited by the code that requires them to refrain from reporting the gory goings on that are inevitably a part of communal riots. Second, since they are after the spectacular and the sensational which has greater news worthiness, they rarely have time enough to follow up the leads that their observations may initially suggest. Lastly, they go to the scene of a communal riot with few well thought out formulations which they might like to test or verify. Nor, indeed, do they have enough time to explore the many dimensions of the local situation which their first contact with the social reality of the venue of a riot might suggest to them as worth investigating. Even so, the journalistic writings contain much useful information which can be put to good use for social analysis.

Let me try in what follows to attempt a discussion of the local dimension of communal tensions and riots drawing partly upon the journalistic writings and partly upon my own understanding of trends in the communal phenomenon in general and communal relations in particular.

Given the paucity of detailed researches on this dimension, what we set out is perhaps by its very nature nothing more than a series of hypotheses whose validity can be tested only by more systematic research. Even so, where there is little definite knowledge, even good hypotheses should be a sound basis for administrative action.

III

If one takes a look at the accounts of communal riots during the last two decades, several distinctive features come out clearly. For one thing, communal riots have become fairly prolonged affairs recently. Earlier, they tended to be short-lived affairs, lasting a day or at best a few days. Once the tensions subsided, calm was restored and life returned to normal. One of the things that is shown by recent reports is that communal riots of the present times last longer. Even after calm returns, tensions keep simmering and contain the potential to erupt into a communal riot on the slightest provocation. This is confirmed by the events in Aligarh, Moradabad, Jamshedpur and Ahmedabad, which have all seen repeated recurrence of communal violence in recent years.

Second, communal riots over the last two decades have become considerably more gory affairs than used to be the case earlier and witness greater loss of life and property. Partly, this is a function of the easy availability of a more advanced arsenal to the public. Earlier, whenever communal riots took place, the weapons usually used tended to be either sticks or knives. Now, sophisticated guns and bombs tend to be used more frequently, resulting in greater loss of life and property.

Third, there is some evidence to suggest that communal riots these days are much more planned affairs than used to be the case earlier. Earlier, communal riots were usually confined to the streets and the loss to property resulting from a riot was largely accidental. It seems from the few accounts available that the targets of communal riots these days are specific properties and places and their destruction is ensured through the use of adequate arsenal.

Fourth, the ecology of communal riots during the last two decades has undergone a change. Earlier, and particularly before Independence, communal riots tended to occur more often than not in small townships usually called *qasbas*. This is no longer true today. Communal violence and tensions have, during the last two decades, become concentrated into what would generally be regarded as developing commercial and industrial centres. Even if they are not commercially or industrially developed, they at least have a tremendous potential for expansion of business and commerce as a result of the monopoly that they might enjoy in the production of specific local items with the potential of a large internal or international market. Jamshedpur, with its steel complex, and Ahmedabad and Bhiwandi, both of which are important centres of textile manufacturing, are examples of flourishing commercial and industrial centres. Aligarh, with its potential for lock-making; Moradabad, the home of brass wares; Varanasi, famous for carpet manufacturing and *zari* work; and Lucknow and Hyderabad, both feudal towns which have recently shot into commercial significance, are examples of traditional towns with potential for commercial growth.

IV

What is it about these townships or cities that makes them particularly prone to communal tensions and repeated recurrence of communal violence? Perhaps a detailed answer to this question must await a detailed and thorough-going analysis of the demographic, economic and social structures of these towns and the changes taking place in them during the last two decades or so. Even so, a few general observations can easily be hazarded on the basis of what is already known about them. For example, we can easily guess that one of the features that characterises them is a basic reorientation of communal relations arising out of the increased commercial and industrial potential of these cities and the keen economic competition that has come to characterise the relations between the communities over the last two decades.

Perhaps I would do well to elaborate this point. Each of the cities which have been prone to outbreaks of communal violence during the last two decades has a sizeable Muslim population, a large section of which comprised of what I would call artisans and craftsmen, menials and feudal retainers who led a parasitic dependence upon the landed aristocracy until the zamindari abolition, but found themselves dispossessed once the mainstay of their subsistence had been reduced. Given their misgivings and doubts about their prospects in independent India, often reinforced by the possibility of eventual migration to Pakistan or some other suitable location, these Muslims showed little enthusiasm for doing well economically. Either they engaged in their crafts as workers, supplying finished goods to middlemen and dealers who provided them with capital and material, or took to working as mechanics and technicians as most of these cities lacked a developed industrial base and could not absorb a large population that was dispossessed of its means of livelihood by the abolition of the zamindari system into the industrial sector.

This had resulted in the crystallisation of a structure of communal relations wherein economic stratification usually followed the lines of communal cleavage. Enterprising Hindus, mostly Punjabis and Banias, who enjoyed a virtual monopoly of capital resources and could see the commercial potential of the products that Muslim craftsmen could produce, tended more often to be middlemen and traders. The Muslims used to be workers and producers. Even if the relationship was exploitative and unequal, it was accepted by the Muslims as the uncertainty of their own future eroded their urge for doing better economically.

This situation changed drastically after the early 1960s. For reasons that do not concern us here,[1] the Muslims then realised that they had to swim or sink in this country and decided to swim. Growing economic opportunities as a result of economic development of the preceding decade and the expansion of the market for handicrafts goods abroad afforded opportunities for them to come up economically. Gradually, through generating savings out of increased wages flowing from the expanded quantum of work then available, at least a section of the Muslim artisans and craftsmen were able to work themselves into small entrepreneurs and began competing with Hindu traders and craftsmen. Over the years, some amongst them have been able to work themselves into businessmen of substance and are either running their own small manufacturing workshops where they employ Muslim craftsmen and workers, or engage as exporters of goods to foreign countries.

Export opportunities created by the sudden prosperity of oil-exporting countries have been a boon for some of these emerging Muslim entrepreneurs. For obvious reasons, they have found securing orders easy. A great deal was made at the time of the Moradabad riots about the foreign money which has flown into Muslim hands.

A great deal of this so-called foreign money that has come in is the result of the export orders that these emerging entrepreneurs have been able to obtain from the Gulf countries, one of the leading buyers of luxury goods. This has naturally added to the prosperity and economic visibility of Muslims in the cities that have been prone to communal tension in recent years.

Communal tensions have been exacerbated by the change which has come about as a result of the rise of the Muslim entrepreneurs and their greater economic visibility in the structure of communal relations. For one thing, the correspondence between the economic stratification system and the communal cleavage has broken down in that entrepreneurs are no longer necessarily Hindus nor are workers necessarily Muslims. Even though workers are still predominantly Muslim, the entrepreneurs today are also often Muslims though their size may not be large. Moreover, where an acute shortage of workers has come to prevail as the demand for the goods produced by them far exceeds the supply, the Muslim entrepreneurs are at an advantage over their Hindu counterparts. They seem to find it easier to get Muslim workers to work for them unless their Hindu counterparts agreed to pay better wages and offered better conditions of work. This makes the situation of Hindu entrepreneurs tighter and their competition with Muslim entrepreneurs tougher.

V

Emergence of Muslim entrepreneurs, however limited their size, and the filtering down of their newfound prosperity further down, however gradual, is producing other effects too in most of the cities that have been prone to communal tensions in recent years. Perhaps one is the outflow of Muslims to newer and less congested areas through extended investment in real estate. As is well-known, most cities in India have been characterised by clustering of communities in exclusive neighbourhoods. Usually, Muslims have been concentrated in the central parts of the cities and their neighbourhoods are usually dilapidated and congested besides containing comparatively small-sized houses as is equally true of old Hindu or other similar neighbourhoods. Moreover, there is little turnover of property so that anyone interested in investing in real estate has few investment opportunities there. If he wishes to invest in real estate he must do so outside. Enterprising Muslims who have been able to make good have found in real estate a good investment channel. And, as little scope exists for such investment in predominantly Muslim neighbourhoods, naturally they have been expanding into other areas. Almost all reports on Moradabad indicate that the newly rich Muslims in Moradabad have been buying up large chunks of commercial property along the main highway surrounding the city. It is also reported that large townships such as Wagidnagar, Mustafabad, Mahboobnagar and Islamnagar, which have come up during the last six or seven years around Moradabad, have been built by these Muslims. Even if these reports are exaggerated, proceeding on the assumption that whosoever in India has surplus money invests in real estate, there is reason to expect that considerable expansion of Muslims outside of their localities would be taking place in some of these cities.

Given this kind of a sudden and unplanned expansion of the city and enlargement of the real estate market, a second effect can also be easily anticipated. This is the sudden expansion of the demand for available land and the spiralling of price of lands available within the heart of the city. Where this happens, public funds or lands set aside for religious purposes are likely to become prized lands. Efforts are then likely to be made by vested interests to have these lands vacated for commercial purposes. Again, reports have it that repeated recurrence of communal violence in Aligarh owes itself to the fact that Muslim squatters occupy a patch of prized land in the heart of the city. It is alleged that vested interests are keen that this land should be vacated by the squatters so that commercial buildings may be raised there and engineer the riots to scare away the squatters. Even if we reject the conspiracy theory that underlies these allegations, the point is quite clear. Property values in these cities have gone up considerably as a result of the growing commercial and economic prosperity of these cities and this has naturally exacerbated tensions over lands which are susceptible to more profitable commercial exploitation.

Economic muscles, traditional or newfound, of any group or individual extend into the political arena. A third effect of the emergence of the Muslim entrepreneurs in some of the cities that are prone to communal violence has been their greater political assertiveness. Earlier, because of their relative economic weakness, they were unable to exert themselves politically and displayed comparative political dormancy, seeking the protection of the Congress umbrella. Few amongst them enjoyed positions of leadership which were an exclusive prerogative of either rich local Hindus or aristocratic Muslims. As they have prospered, they have also begun to stake claims to leadership positions and also tended to assert themselves in a manner that was not possible in a period of relative economic weakness. This too has sharpened the competition and disturbed the traditionally existing structure of communal relations. Of course, the rise to political significance of these Muslims is resented by the members of the old Muslim aristocracy, whose position they challenge equally, but the latter are having to concede to their political significance because of their greater economic strength and their growing ability to mobilise the support of the lower classes within the community who are often their beneficiaries.

Finally, the fourth effect of the newfound economic clout has been the greater cultural and social visibility of the Muslims. Earlier, they suffered from economic weakness which was reinforced by their residence in worn-out Muslim neighbourhoods, their absence at educational institutions, and the poor state of their religious and cultural institutions. Growing prosperity of Muslims, or some Muslims at least, in recent years has brought some of them out of Muslim neighbourhoods into newer parts of cities, where they are buying properties. This has enabled them to build schools, undertake the restoration and renovation of old and dilapidated mosques, and to engage in numerous community-betterment activities. All this has naturally made Muslims increasingly more socially and culturally visible than was the case earlier.

VI

At the outset of this chapter, we noted that analyses of communal tensions have usually concentrated on macro-level cultural and religious factors and tended to overlook the local dimension, which is highly significant. This discussion of some of the changes taking place in the towns and cities which have been particularly prone to communal tensions in recent years should serve to indicate the reasons for the macro-level cultural and religious factors to be commonly associated with communal tensions. As our discussion has shown, what is happening in these cities and towns is a natural process of economic and social development precipitated by bourgeoning trade and commercial opportunities. Even so, as perceptions of the people are greatly coloured by the stereotypes and prejudices which have crystallised as a result of recent political history, these purely 'secular' changes are seen through the coloured glass of prevalent stereotypes. Articulate Hindus see the newfound Muslim economic clout globally and entertain a number of latent fears which were frequently voiced at the time of the Moradabad riots. On their side, successful Muslims often project their recent economic prosperity as a triumph of the community. As such, these wholly 'secular' economic changes at once arouse communal fears and hopes and act as a powerful intervening variable to make a competitive local situation particularly explosive.

Politicians frequently make matters worse by using this situation of competitiveness to pursue narrow political ends by promoting communal mobilisation and playing up one community against the other. Perhaps it is worth observing in this context that in several of the community riots recently reported, trouble started as a result of clashes between Muslims and members of the scheduled castes. Perhaps a detailed study of the processes operating among the scheduled castes in these places and the pattern of their interaction with caste Hindus may throw useful light on this emerging dimension of communal tensions in recent years.

VII

Perhaps we may conclude this discussion by setting up a few propositions which are indicated by this analysis and need to be studied systematically. The first proposition that emerges from this analysis is that, while communalism has a long history in India, there is reason to argue that the character and nature of communalism has changed in recent years, particularly during the last two decades. This is suggested to some extent by the internal shifts in the nature, orientation and location of communal riots to which we referred earlier.

Second, this analysis suggests that communalism needs to be viewed in a different light than has been the case earlier. Communal tensions have traditionally been viewed in the past as an indicator of the breakdown of the system. This analysis suggests that communal tensions are actually a sign of its dynamism and the 'secular' changes that are taking place in it are a result of economic development and progress.

Communal tensions are usually seen at their roots as an illogical and irrational complex of actions and are usually responded to by people as such. So widespread in this tendency, indeed, that the word 'senseless' has become commonly associated with communal riots. Politicians and public figures too dismiss communal riots as irrational outbursts sparked off by an overriding attachment to a sense of community solidarity or religious fanaticism which have no basis in objective empirical reality. The third proposition that emerges from this discussion is that sociologically, communal rioting, like most social action, is a clearly directed, goal-oriented social action whose logic and rationality is clear to those who engage in it.

Finally, the fourth proposition indicated by this analysis is that communal tensions understood as tensions between Hindus and Muslims do not necessarily constitute a distinct category of tensions to be distinguished from the other forms of civil strife which too are known to occur widely in Indian society from time to time. Perhaps from the viewpoint of our emotional responses, the political weight of the Hindu–Muslim clashes in the context of the country's recent political history and the urge to move towards a secular social order, and the sheer magnitude of the problem, there may be a case for viewing them as a distinct phenomenon. However, there is nothing to warrant that they should not be seen as a part and parcel of the general civil strife that has been fairly frequent and widespread in recent decades. Perhaps a comparison of communal tensions understood narrowly with other forms of civil strife may serve to indicate the deeper social processes that are at work throughout Indian society and are producing an unusual exacerbation not only of communal tensions, but all varieties of social and civil conflicts and tensions.

NOTE

1. These reasons included closing down of the border by Pakistan through restrictions on immigration, growing confidence of the Muslims in the commitment of the government in secularism, their growing self-confidence that they could do well economically if they exerted themselves, and the expansion of trade and commerce arising out of the economic development of the previous decades. A detailed discussion of the reasons would be found in Ahmad, Imtiaz. 1972. 'Economic and Social Change', in *Muslims in India*, ed. Zafar Imam. Hyderabad: Orient BlackSwan; and Ahmad, Imtiaz. 1974. 'Pakistan and the Indian Muslims'. *New Quest* 93, 39–48.

18

Congress (I), Communist Parties and Communalism*

A. R. Desai

I

The recent developments in Assam, the Bhiwandi-Bombay complex in Maharashtra, Kashmir and Punjab and the astute use of religion by the Congress (Indira) in the mass media, including reshaping the content of the educational and other socialising processes, have revealed the limitations of the communist parties of India in analysing the use of religion made by the Congress Party to subserve the interest of the bourgeoisie in India. The brief note 'Congress (I) and Communalism' (A Correspondent 1984) has very rightly raised the crucial issue.

The communist parties of India have systematically avoided forthright analysis of the use of religion (particularly of Hinduism) made by the Indian National Congress headed by Jawaharlal Nehru and subsequently by Indira Gandhi to subserve the interest of the Indian bourgeoisie and to confuse and divide the exploited and oppressed masses. These parties have not made up till now a thorough class analysis of the reasons which prompted the Indian National Congress, headed by Mahatma Gandhi, Nehru and others, vociferous crusaders against communal vivisection of the country, to take a somersault and partition India on exactly the same religio-communal basis, and hurriedly forge a suitable state apparatus for the Indian Union appropriate for Indian capitalism. These parties have not even thought it necessary from the proletarian class point of view to assess how the Indian National Congress visualised the role, functions and uses of religion in the debates in the Constituent Assembly. Nor is there any appropriate evaluation of the justification given by the leadership for the subtle utilisation of religion by incorporating it in various sections of the Constitution as well as in various laws of the land, including personal laws founded on different religious faiths.

* *Economic and Political Weekly* 19 (30): 1196–97 (28 July 1984).

II

In fact, the Communist Party of India (CPI) and the Communist Party of India (Marxist) [CPI (M)], wedded to the two-stage theory of revolution and endeavouring to realise the first stage of revolution basically through the parliamentary path, have viewed till recently one section of the bourgeois—that represented by the Nehru and Indira-led Indian National Congress—as basically progressive, anti-imperialist, genuinely democratic, secular and anti-communal and as strategically pursuing the goal of the first stage of the revolution. They have also considered the rest of the bourgeoisie as compradore, closely tied to feudal, semi-feudal and other reactionary sections of the people, stooges and agents of the imperialist bourgeoisie and basically responsible for utilising communal, casteist, semi-feudal, religious, obscurantist ideas and practices obstructing the realisation of the national democratic or the people's democratic revolution. According to the communist parties, the compradore, semi-feudal, feudal and other sections of the reactionary classes are spearheaded by the Rashtriya Swayamsevak Sangh (RSS) and the main fire of the communist parties is directed at the RSS and the Bharatiya Janata Party (BJP).

III

The communist parties have articulated this position through various documents and publications and through a number of seminars conferences organised by the National Integration Committees officially launched by the Congress. Beginning with H. D. Malaviya, who wrote a full-length monograph entitled 'Danger of the Right Reaction' in 1965, a considerable mass of literature has been published by the communist parties or their front organisations on the dangerous role of RSS and its communalism. Only recently, against the background of growing communal and upper-caste violence in the country, the CPI published a pamphlet entitled 'National Integration for Democracy and Socialism', written by its senior leader S. G. Sardesai. It provides a clear insight into the party's analysis of the recent acceleration of communal, casteist and other forms of movements which, according to the party, 'have become the greatest danger to our national unity and hence to our democracy, integrity and national independence'. Sardesai writes: 'no progressive and patriotic Indian has any doubt about the forces behind this counter-revolutionary offensive. Everyone knows that it is the result of a conspiracy of most reactionary forces in the country backed by CIA. The Prime Minister Shrimati Indira Gandhi cannot be bracketed with these elements.' (Sardesai 1981) More recently, as pointed out in the *EPW* note referred to above, even E. M. S. Namboodiripad, Secretary-General of CPI (M), has absolved the Congress (I) of communalism.

The communist parties have further astutely shifted the analysis of the role of religion in Indian polity to what they call the role of 'communalism' in Indian polity. They thereby agree in fact with Nehru in distinguishing between what is called religion, in any real sense, and distortion of religion, that is, religion which is 'narrow and intolerant of other opinions and ideas, is self-centred and egoistic and which allows itself to be exploited by self-seekers and opportunities' (Goyal 1972).

Sardesai, the veteran CPI leader, defines communalism in the pamphlet mentioned above as 'the incitement of mass hatred between Hindus and Muslims, mass civilian violence between Hindus and Muslims ... done either for purpose of achieving or retaining political power'. According to him,

> [Q]ualitatively speaking, there is not a pin to choose between Hindu communalism and Muslim communalism. But Hindu communalism is far more dangerous in India. The reason is obvious. The great majority of Indians are Hindus. Hindu communalism has strength to achieve political power in the country which Muslim communalism obviously cannot do (Sardesai 1981).

According to Sardesai,

> We have to realise that while the RSS-BJP outfit is the spearhead of Hindu communalism, leaders like Morarji Desai, Charan Singh, etc, in other parties are profoundly communal and casteist, Hindu obscurantists. All sorts of Mahesh Yogis, Satya Sai Babas, Rajnishes, Anand Margis, Krishna Consciousnees people and so on, also bring grist to the same mill... so the danger of Hindu communalism is far broader than the influence of the RSS which no doubt is the arch villain of the piece (Sardesai 1981).

Sardesai highlights the 'reactionary' and 'counter-revolutionary' role of communalism spearheaded by the RSS in the following words:

> It has to be explained that Hindu and Muslim communalisms, with all their never-ending feud, meet in pro-imperialism, anti-communism and anti-Sovietism. Further, both of them are defenders of landlordism and free 'enterprise' in India. They never miss an opportunity to run down the public sector. There is an immense amount of material to expose Hindu communalism as the enemy, not only of secularism and national integration but also of democracy, socialism and India's national independence (Sardesai 1981).

IV

It can be seen from the above analysis that communist parties of India, wedded to the strategic alliance with the progressive, national, anti imperialist section of the bourgeoisie for realising the first stage of revolution and that too by parliamentary methods, have systematically conjured up and strengthened the myth that the Indian National Congress is secular and anti-communal. Only very recently, some questioning has started within these parties on this analysis. These parties have also tried to sedulously create an impression that the Congress does not basically use religion for befogging the masses and to divide and divert the attention of the exploited classes. These parties prevent the masses from locating the main enemy, that is, the Indian National Congress led by Nehru and Indira Gandhi, and to evolve their strategy and tactics of struggles for their liberation from that perspective. For evolving a proper strategy for the exploited and oppressed classes and strata of Indian society, whose conditions are worsening from day to day, and at an accelerated rate after the mid-1960s, it is urgently necessary that this myth, created by the communist parties, wherein the RSS is treated as the arch villain and the Indian National Congress as the saviour of secularism and national integration, is thoroughly exposed.

We will briefly indicate, for stimulating more discussion among revolutionaries, how the Congress led by Nehru and Indira Gandhi has, from the inception of Independence, utilised religion for the class needs of the Indian bourgeoisie as a whole.

The Nehru leadership defined secularism as respect for all religions and not religion as 'a personal affair of the individual'. This concept thus opens the ground for permitting all types of inequitous, unjust, superstitious, wasteful contradictory and conflicting beliefs and practices and their public observance. It also provides an avenue to be insensitive to the susceptibilities of atheists, agnostics, rationalists and materialists. This is evidenced by the fact that the subtlest purveyors and socialisers of the subjectivity of the citizens, namely the family and kin and caste life of the citizens, is left in the domain of operation of religion, through the personal laws of the land. These institutions deal with property, relations, sex relations, marriage, succession and inheritance, and are permeated through and through with religious ethos. They are preserved by the rulers and their most astute party led by Nehru and Indira Gandhi. The fundamental task of socialisation of the individual is thus left to institutions permeated by religion. The rulers have accepted as legal these religion-based relations connected with family, property, inheritance and succession, and a number of practices which vitally affect the life of the citizens from their childhood onwards are left in the hands of religion. The enactment of personal laws based on religion is not fortuitous.

The rulers have systematically pressed into service religious sectarian organisations like the Sadhu Samaj to spread moral and spiritual values among people. This practice exposes the major presumption accepted by the rulers—that materialist philosophy, based on the human being as the centre of values, is incapable of generating a humanist morality. They have also been utilising and creating associations specialising in singing devotional, non-secular, other-worldly and dependency and helplessness-generating songs ('bhajan mandalis') as special associations in villages, as a part of their cultural-associational network for development.

The state is actively trying through its various mass media to create a cultural ethos and climate wherein upper-caste Hinduism is basically glorified (with some veneering of similar trends in other religions) and the supposedly superior tolerant, spiritual values of Hinduism are being systematically boosted as the great national-cultural tradition of the people. A reverential other-worldly approach is being systematically and subtly inculcated among the people, which deadens the critical faculty of the masses and resurrects an atmosphere of awe and devotion towards higher-caste values. The systematic propagation of the spiritual ethos of holy places of pilgrimages in the Himalayas, the spread of awe and respect towards holy rivers, temples and festivals, *yagna*s and *hawan*s clearly indicate this use of religion by the state as an ideological weapon to subserve certain interests.

With the passage of time, as disillusionment deepens among the people about the pro-rich policies of the Congress, the rulers are systematically fostering elaborate rituals, festivals, religious *melas*, and ceremonial functions, even by actively associating with them, and thereby creating an uncritical, dependent ethos among the masses, and legitimising in the minds of people the authority and awe of godmen and priestly groups who constantly inculcate guilt-feelings among people. Dramatic worshipful gestures by Indira Gandhi and her entourage, her rushing to various temples to get the blessings of religious heads and patronising of some godmen—including permitting them to build ashrams, universities, research centres and even giving them licences to start factories and numerous mundane economic and other activities—have not been still understood in the light of their profound and dangerous implications. It is surprising to read in the above-mentioned pamphlet by Sardesai, only recently published, his view that boosting of godmen and religious heads is done only by the RSS.

The Congress government is very cleverly introducing an uncritical, religious content in the educational system, in the name of inculcating moral and spiritual values and what is called a spirit of national integration among teachers and students. This inculcation openly started with the Shri Prakash Committee Report published in the late 1950s and continues unabated till now, through a series of measures taken in that direction. The systematic endeavour to reshape the content of textbooks from primary to the highest level that is being carried on in a brazen manner to subserve this purpose is still not taken seriously by Marxist parties in terms of its dangerous ideological implications.

In the name of respect for different religions and also in the name; of not hurting the susceptibilities of various religious communities, the Congress government is very systematically suppressing critical movements which challenge the very basis of religions and the bizarre practices and beliefs prescribed by them. Further, the communist parties have not exposed how this approach basically harms and insults the susceptibilities of non-believers, humanists, atheists and materialists.

These few illustrations clearly show that the Nehru-Indira leadership of the Indian National Congress is very systematically utilising religion as a weapon to buttress its capitalist policies and programmes and is very subtly and astutely using it as one of the powerful ideological weapons to confuse the exploited and oppressed masses and to divert their anger into the wrong channels by provoking internecine conflicts. In fact, if properly comprehended, it is the use of religion by the Congress Party in the interest of the capitalist system that is the crucial precipitating factor for the rise of communal and castiest movements and atmosphere in the country. ... The RSS spearheads in a cruder, sometimes in a short-sighted manner, the forces and values generated by the Congress.

It is necessary for the revolutionary forces to systematically understand the subtle use of religion by the most astute ruling class party in the country, which is today the chief vehicle of the capitalist class. I wish a more systematic and basic discussion were launched to examine the assumption of the communist parties about communalism and their implications for the exploited and oppressed classes and masses unveiled. The issues raised in the *EPW* note referred to at the beginning deserve more extensive discussion.

REFERENCES

A Correspondent. 1984. 'Congress(I) and Communalism'. *Economic and Political Weekly* 19 (27), 7 July, 1010–11.

Goyal, D. R. 1972. 'Communalism vs Nationalism, The Nehru Approach', in *Indian National Consciousness*, ed. K. K. Gangadharan. New Delhi: Kalamkar Prakashan, 276–84.

Sardesai, S. G. 1981. 'National Integration for Democracy and Socialism'. CPI Pamphlet.

19

Cultural Context of Communalism in India*

Rajni Kothari

We need to come to grips with the growing crisis of confidence in the Indian state among various minorities, as well as among all but the privileged strata of the so-called 'majority' community known as the Hindus. Even the privileged strata—namely the 'twice-born' upper castes—seem to feel insecure in the face of what they feel to be the growing demands of the minorities and the already achieved upward mobility by some sections of the minorities. While all kinds of short-term explanations have been put forward (from the role of party politicians to foreign influences to the growth of 'fundamentalism') and while there is some relevance of each of these, there is need to go behind these and look at some longer-term tendencies. For, while it is clear that we are passing through a fairly serious phase of cultural conflict, a phase in which the assumption that we have had of preserving a pluralistic civilisation through a democratic political process is under shadow, it does raise a very large number of rather pertinent questions of both religio-cultural and socio-political kinds.

Before examining these questions, there is need to state some rather obvious points about India as a *cultural syndrome*, a cultural symbiosis of a kind. We need to remember that the essential identity of India is cultural; not political or economic. It is one civilisation that has withstood various vicissitudes and still endured, largely because of its basic identity being cultural. It never had a political centre except very recently. To that extent, it is very unlike countries like China and Japan.

India's fundamental integrative ethos and its self-identity have been drawn from a social reality that is composed of great diversity and plurality, running across which there were certain major cultural streams, and a cultural elite that shaped and interpreted these streams. In the old days, we used to call it a 'Brahmanic elite'. It has since widened, no doubt, but it is still quite a puzzle to outsiders how a society like this could survive and retain its identity without having a centralising mechanism that most societies have had in their development. It is, therefore, important to

* *Economic and Political Weekly* 24 (2): 81–85 (14 January 1989).

remember that until recently, up to the growth of the national movement and the founding of the Indian republic, what held us together was this basic identity of being a civilisation tied together by a set of values, by a set of cultural norms and by an interpreting elite, first within the broad stream of Hinduism which itself had an extremely plural framework and then through a multi-cultural, multi-ethnic and ultimately multi-national society which we are now.

Now, upon this sort of a pluralist unity has come, over the last 150 years, the cultural influence of the modern period essentially from the modern West, though much of it was also shaped by a particular elite that emerged here in response to the impacts of the West, so that ultimately, what came through was some kind of synthesis. Nonetheless, it is important to identify these influences because it seems to me that we need to sort out some real tensions that have emerged between an essential Indian identity and its cultural ethos and the identities generated by the modern period with which, I think, Indian society has not yet quite made its full equation. This is important because it is a society that has had its own modes of survival and perseverance and may indeed have some real contribution to make to the larger world which is itself in the throes of a serious crisis of survival.

IDEOLOGY OF NATION-STATE

First among the external influences is, of course, the whole ideology of a nation-state. It is the idea that societies round the world have to be organised around the notion of a state which would provide a centralised structure of power and authority, bolstered by a series of institutions. This is an idea that was not there in India. There have been periods when major empires have come up and they have tried to unify the country but by and large, in its full formation, it is really a modern conception. The idea that societies have to be organised around the authority of a centralised state, incorporated and legitimised by a set of institutions, is one to which India has tried to respond and is still trying to respond. There was a time when I would have said this was the most creative thing that had happened to India; but we now know that, while it has undoubtedly brought about a certain measure of power and a new sense of purpose, it has also meant that it has overridden and undermined the many diverse identities of which India was composed and that it has a highly centralising and homogenising ethos about it. ...

A second impact through which the country has passed is the whole notion of a modernising elite that undertakes 'development' with particular emphasis on economic development, but also on moving the whole society from tradition to modernity, rejecting the old and moving to the new, in its overall impact far more homogenising than respectful of diversities, straitjacketing rather than pluralising integrating into a world market of which India should become a part, seeking to 'deliver' the people from various traditional roots and making them available for modernising influences. ...

Third, there is the tremendous importance of technology, both as a mode of organising the material basis of life and as a mode of deciding the terms of conflict between opposing tendencies. It is important to remember that the two advantages that the West had in dealing with India were technological superiority and a particular superiority in armaments. So both technology in terms of shaping the material basis of life and technology in terms of militarisation have posed challenges to this society which was organised around a multiplicity of centres in a variety of ways where there was a lot of conflict no doubt, but there was no straitjacketing of a technological kind, not becoming part of a global military order. It is a technology which is more hard than soft and even where it is 'soft', it is more technocratic than humanistic. Techniques had always been there—all societies have had techniques—but the modern consideration of *technology* as an entire system of relationships is fundamentally one which replaces cultural and political perspectives by technocratic perspectives. It is not just technology in terms of importing some artefacts and machines and hardware, but also a mindset and a set of mental attitudes.

Fourth, there is the whole communication revolution in which again there are certain elites and there are certain centres that defuse communications packages and decide what will be communicated, and through which mass media. This has come to play an enormous role in which minds and social norms are sought to be influenced through all kinds of channels of which the latest, of course, is advertising and in which manipulation rather than spontaneous expression tends to be the norm.

Now, if we take all this together, the nation-state framework, the consequent stress on centralisation, the whole framework of development and modernisation and its stress on creating a homogeneous society rather than enabling various diversities to prosper, the impact of technology including arms technology and the impact of mass communications and an information technology, we can see that there is a fundamental dichotomy and dissonance between the old and the new, a dichotomy that India is trying very hard to overcome and synthesise.

[...]

We were told that when we became an independent nation-state, the main core of it was a steel-frame bureaucracy, but it was also true that an important core of it was the Indian National Congress. The Indian National Congress was indigenous, the steel-frame bureaucracy was alien. It is true that as we entered the money economy, a kind of class formation began to take place, here as in the West, but we also had, and we still have, a very strong social structure of caste. So there is caste as well as class. Or take the fields of business organisation and management. Again, there has been a traditional perspective on business and there is the modern management perspective. They are very different but they co-exist. Similarly, there is the humanistic learning which is very much part of the Indian core and there is the 'scientific' training which is part of what has been imported. Same with the ethnic reality—living with a great deal of ethnic plurality on the one hand and modern secularism which tends to organise things along one major stream of the authority of the state and these really have worked together for a long time and given rise to a new kind of Indian identity, a kind of Indian modernity with an Indian cultural ethos. However, in recent decades all this co-existence seems to be giving way to something that displays greater dualism and produces more confrontation than synthesis.

Synthesis and pluralism are being replaced by dichotomous understanding on the one hand and emphasis on choosing the modern, the latest, the scientific and the secular on the other. It is in that peculiar contour in which we are caught right now in this country. We would like very much to take our course as an Indian course while absorbing the best that comes to us and yet we are also caught in a global perspective as well as in a national perspective in which the more modern influences that I was stressing are beginning to overtake the Indian identity.

Meanwhile, accompanying these various influences we have also been experiencing another kind of cultural impact, through a set of ideas and a set of values. The core of the set of ideas and norms, it seems to me, is what can be called a competitive ethos—an ethos in which individuals, groups and nations are engaged in a competitive struggle. Even the concept of freedom in the Western worldview is sought to be thought in competitive and atomising terms. This is alien to Indian thinking. Even the conception of equality is based on this ethos. Equality is not the same thing as justice. There is a seeking for justice in all social orders but seeking it through the conception of equality has emphasised continually the competitive part of the modern worldview and this has influenced all thinking in the modern world and has obviously made its inroads into India. In the process, the idea of community has been undermined or is being undermined; the sense of community is being undermined. As against this, the sense of individual identity, the rights of the individual, the need for the individual to take recourse to anything in order to achieve what he wants, tends to be given much greater importance. This is central to the whole modernising ethos in which we have been caught. So we are caught in a kind of pincer, on the one hand the nation-state ideology and the stress on modern technology, on the other hand the competitive ethos based on the values of positivism, together undermining the basic sense of community and of plural identities which have informed Indian civilisation for so long.

It is precisely against this cultural backdrop and the contemporary growth of dualism and dichotomous orientations that the whole set of challenges that we have called 'communalism' need to be understood. We always had community conflicts arising out of trying to live with a vast series of groups and identities, all of them minorities (including groups within the so-called majority community) but we somehow managed to live with them for a very long time. What is new is a considerable escalation of not just strain and tension and violence but of a deep sense of alienation and distrust between communities and vis-à-vis the state.

This is new. And I think the real change that has taken place in this respect is in the relationship between the Hindus and the non-Hindus, between the Hindus and what are otherwise called the minorities. It is a relationship that was working relatively smoothly because of the overall Indian tradition of absorbing different cultures, different religions, different traditions and making them part of a plural ethos. What also helped a great deal in this respect was the whole democratic process given the nice fit between the democratic idea and the Indian tradition of living with differences, living with very great diversity.

Democracy was a very good instrument for continuation of this tradition in a world that was changing very fast. It was through the democratic process that the Hindu society came to terms with the modern world, while continuing to live with a number of other religions, linguistic regional and ethnic identities. On the whole, it was a matter of considerable pride for us—though of considerable surprise for outsiders—that a society as diverse as this could hang together and could move in a democratic way instead of falling apart.

And yet one must recognise that of late, for the last 15 years at least, there has been a set of problems which have today brought us on a point of crisis in respect of this very relationship between the Hindu 'majority' and the various minorities. By minorities I do not only mean Muslims, Sikhs and Christians, but also the great diversity of tribals and large parts of Hindu society itself, namely its various peripheries such as the dalits and various other socially depressed and 'backward' castes and communities. They are all minorities. In fact, one way to think about India is of a people and a land made up of a series of minorities, for Hindu society itself is internally highly structured, diverse and pluralistic. There are castes and subcastes and clans and all manner of groupings and sub-groupings. You go in any region and you will immediately be told that there is this caste and that caste, this grouping and that grouping, this ethnic identity and that ethnic identity—it is all really a set of minorities. It is thus wrong to think of Hindus as a 'majority' except that it is being thought like that of late and that is what is causing the problems.

Now it seems to me that, though I am a firm believer in the democratic process based on parties and elections, it seems to be that it is the narrowing of the calculus of politics by reducing it to electoral calculations that has produced the kinds of tensions in which we have of late moved. We have moved from considering politics as a coalition of diverse interests—the Muslims, the tribals, the other religious minorities, the dalits and certain poorer sections of the Hindus—producing a kind of 'winning coalition' because it gives to you a very populous basis to a perception that the key to winning an election is to mobilise the Hindu heartland in which a 'majority' of the people are located. To have identified the ruling party with the aspirations of this 'majority' which for some peculiar reason, while it is a majority, feels insecure with the democratic process was the height of political expediency and shortsightedness that will prove very costly in the long run (including, most of all, to the Congress). It is this that we are living through right now.

People have talked of a Hindu backlash, but what has taken place in the process is that this particular 'majority' has taken to thinking of itself at once in religious and political terms. It is felt—and this has been going on for quite some time—that here we are a very large majority and yet the state and the policy process have only benefited the minorities and all minorities at that—not only Sikhs and Christians and Muslims, but also the tribals and the dalits. They have everything—reservations, armaments, special economic deals—and can even flout the law of the land when it comes to regulating their personal lives. Only we have nothing. Precisely because we have been very tolerant that we have been taken for a ride and it is about time that we assert ourselves and we come out of this internal division that has plagued us, unify ourselves and meet the challenge of the minorities. This kind of jingoism has worked its way into the Hindu mind following the happenings in Punjab, Kashmir and the like, the caste riots in Gujarat and Bihar and, of course, the controversy over Ram Janmabhoomi and Babri Masjid in the north and that is what we are still in and I do not think we have recovered from it.

We have gone through this whole process of electoral manipulation which was used and exploited by the Congress Party. In the event of course, it greatly benefited because it could wipe out a number of opposition groups which had some kind of a communal leaning and it came out as a party with the most communal appeal, particularly in the Hindu heartland. But it can be no more than a short-term gain. Because when you think of the overall spread of the Congress Party, wherever there has been a good regional formation, wherever there has been a strong regional party, that is where the Congress has not made it. Everywhere, where there is a strong regional current with its own cultural identity, it has failed. And this is going to grow, not decline. It already includes the whole of the south, Punjab, Jammu and Kashmir, West Bengal and Tripura, large parts of the north-east and now Haryana where too a strong regionalist wave has been noticeable. Nor can the Congress survive in the Hindu belt any longer before the sweep of the Bharatiya Janata Party (BJP) on the one hand and the lower-class parties on the other. Yet the Congress is fast ceasing to be the centre party because, in its promotion of communalism and ethnic identities it has brought to an end its earlier coalitional and umbrella image.

Now the second aspect of this reduction of a plural society to a majority-minority calculus is that most of the minorities are unable to deal with this situation with any confidence, partly because they are small, partly because they are very defensive, partly because they have always tried to work with the Congress Party which has always been thought of as being the protector of their interests. But more than all this, there is also a fundamental philosophical problem. It is that their own dominant tradition, whether of Islam or of Christianity, has been one in which there *is* a centre, a well-defined core. It is very unlike the original Hindu framework although the modernisers of Hinduism want that Hinduism also should take on some of the characteristics of European Christianity or of Islam; that it should have a more unified ethos, a centralising church and an authoritative book, which was never there among the Hindus. Hinduism had no centre. They want to provide a centre. They want to copy more or less the same religions they want to fight against. I have deliberately used the word Western Christianity because I do not think eastern Christianity is anywhere like that nor is Indian Islam, which too is highly plural within and far less monolithic than in some other parts of the world.

What the Hindus are trying to do is to project certain ideal type images of these communities and then insist that the Hindus should become like them so that they have a much more centralised, unified, strong and hard core about themselves rather than the present very divided, weak and 'effeminate' way of doing things.

Hindus, the modernisers feel, are a very effeminate culture and they want to make it a macho culture. This is unfortunate but it is beginning to take place. It is a very great distortion of Hindu identity and of Hindu culture because central to the whole Hindu conception is a pluralist internal structure and so is its philosophical and metaphysical predisposition. My purpose in life and my relationship with the divine is my own but I have obligations and duties and rights which I have to respect just as I have to respect them in others. For it is not just me and my caste but there are other castes, other groups, other identities, other traditions which all have a right to survive and survive in dignity.

Such a broad, sensitive and eclectic position is now giving place to a wholly un-Hindu chauvinist reaction that is taking the form of a Hindu backlash. Underlying it or reinforcing it are two dominant themes both of which are fast overtaking the Hindu identity. One is that the nation is in danger; that national unity is in danger. The ruling groups have been successful in infusing this thinking and the anxiety that it in turn generates among nearly all sections of the people that something awful is happening to this country, that we are falling apart and we are falling apart essentially because of the politics of minorities on the one hand, and of course, the outside influences on the other hand, the much talked of 'foreign hand'.

Now it is not quite incidental that the 'foreign hand' that is thought of is often in a way associated with some group internally—Pakistan with Muslims, Western countries with the Christians, Sikhs being helped by both the Pakistanis and Westerners out to 'destabilise' the country. So that what we need to do is to develop a strong state, a state that will acquire a hegemonic position with its neighbours, which will emerge as among the most industrialised and powerful nations of the world. If you want to do that, you cannot go on in this very soft way towards all kinds of minorities and tribal and other groups. You have to build a hard core. Gradually, without always saying so, this becomes the notion of a strong Hindu state. It may not be completely like an Islamic state but it should still be one that is dominated by Hindus and in which the whole pluralist notion gives place to a more monistic perspective of a state.

This is of course a highly distorted notion of nationalism, not the creative nationalism of the movement led by the Indian National Congress. Rather it is a kind of nationalism that we find in a lot of other third world countries that have been taken over by authoritarian, militant or fundamentalist ideology. But it is a powerful ideology, an ideology that is slowly overtaking the middle classes, specially the upper middle class, in a big way, which then leads to and accentuates communal attitudes towards the minorities. Thus, we may be entering a very dangerous period, for once the Hindu gets the sense of becoming *macho*, and in the process legitimising violence in a big way, violence as a way of subjugating the minorities or of controlling them, there could be no return to a stable polity. There is a growing feeling that the Sikhs have always been very influential and have occupied positions of privilege, always making the Hindu neighbour feel inferior before him, so that the only way of dealing with them is to firmly and violently put them down; and the same is true of Muslims. Once that kind of thinking takes over, I do not think this society is equipped to deal with what will follow. It will involve a governing ethos in which the technology of violence and militarism become the main instruments of statecraft rather than the democratic political process based on bargaining, accommodations and coalition-making involving diverse interests which has been the essence of the Indian approach to politics and society.

The other side of this kind of thinking of building a strong nation-state at the cost of everything else is that the poor become its victims. You cannot build a strong and hard state of this conception and at the same time be generous to the poor. It is not possible. Given the resource situation, given the class character of the country, given the fact that the kind of development and modernisation and state-building that is involved in the conception of a hard state will necessarily divide the rich and the poor more and more, even the pretence of helping the poor will be given up. This is already beginning to take place. We are told that if you want 'progress' and modernisation, you have to pay the price for it and if in this process 30 or 40 per cent of the people become destitute and become more and more prone to various incapacities, that cannot be helped. Maybe when we become a very powerful and strong country and get enough of an economic base, maybe we will be able to take care of them, but if in the meanwhile they suffer and even die, that is too bad, it is *something one has to live with.*

Now this is a kind of mindset which was unthinkable even 10 or 15 years ago, but today it is beginning to take shape. It is not very unlike the thinking in some powerful circles in the West that yes, we must try to help this third world, these poor countries, but really they are increasingly becoming an embarrassment. If they were not there, how easy it would be to manage the world. Something similar is taking place within societies. In military science, there is a doctrine called 'triage' according to which, when you are on the battlefront, those who are more maimed or sick should be left behind. Those that can be put back on feet very fast should be taken along and of course, the other third, who are able to move, should move on. It is this idea of 1/3 (hence the term 'triage') that must suffer as a result of your wanting to move on. Similarly here, too, you have to move on and if you want to move on and if the sick and the poor and the weak are left behind, it is unfortunate but inevitable. This thinking is slowly emerging here too and it is not an accident that slogans like socialism, removal of poverty and so on are not even referred to any more even as a window dressing. We are moving into a hard-headed view of politics. Some call it a 'pragmatic' view of politics, according to which we will move into the twenty-first century with a pragmatic vision, not the soft ideologies like socialism and democracy and removal of poverty.

It is important to bear in mind that the two aspects that I have been discussing—the more cultural aspect governing the relationship between the minorities and the majority, and the more economic aspect governing the relationship between the rich and the poor—are related. Common to both is this whole drive of building a strong state, in which notions like state versus the people, strong versus weak, educated versus uneducated are emerging in which the poor, the backward and the illiterate become dispensable. If in the process you have to assert your might against the minorities, in order to get a certain clout, if you have to use violence, it is permissible. Therefore, the whole conception of Indian nationalism that is emerging (which, as I said, is contrary to Indian thinking and contrary to the norms that were laid out in the independence movement and in the Constitution) is one in which we will really become part of the modern world order dominated by the West and drawing into it some other powerful countries.

I have not, so far, dealt with another and very important aspect and that is the relationship between humans and nature. Because another price we are paying for this kind of progress is our natural environment. Central to Indian thinking through the centuries was a very close symbiosis between humans and nature in which the humans were seen as very much part of nature and that, I think, is something that we are beginning to give up; therefore, the tragedies of the kind that we have had in Bhopal and other places. But I am not referring simply to that tragedy, but something more basic and it is that when we have this view of the poor, this kind of a manipulative and egoistic view of other species, which again goes very much contrary to the original Hindu conception of its identity. What will be the cultural consequences of such a perspective?

First, of course, is the threat to the composite culture that India has always been, its community lifestyle, the whole Indian identity which was the basis of a very decentralised notion of living together, working together, having respect for each other's diversity, not having a sense of anything being alien. It is that which is under threat. Then I have already mentioned the threat to the natural environment, an environment that has sustained our diverse peoples. The reason I am bringing up the environment issue is that it is very central to the whole socio-economic problem. As we increasingly modernise, we are encroaching upon the resource base of the poor. We are cutting down our forests, we are denuding our soils, bringing down our water resources, in the process taking away the normal recourse to resources that the poor had, taking away their common lands, and reducing them to penury. We are forcing the tribals and others to migrate into the metropolitan areas where they settle in squatter settlements and slums from where too we then remove and send them off to resettlement colonies, all of which contributes to the kind of communal problems that we have. It is a very close relationship. A major study done by Earthscan recently shows that in many parts of the world, neglect of fundamental ecological issues and the growth of desertification and deforestation have led to migratory patterns which then produce communal and ethnic clashes. Among the countries and societies they have mentioned is India. The point is that all these factors are very related and unless one attends to the basics of Indian thinking—on the relationship between groups, between man and nature, between different occupations which may be poor or rich but always thought of together—unless one can keep all this in mind, it will be difficult to handle any of the problems that I have been trying to deal with in this chapter.

Finally, of course, there is the threat to the Indian personality. I think the Indian personality is a very fine balance between the aggressive component of human endeavour and the more feminine, soft and cultured conception which tends to integrate various dimensions rather than push along one dimension. That, I think, is again going to be very difficult, coming as it does under very difficult stresses as a result of the kind of nationalism that I laid out before you. There are two other forces with serious cultural implications. One is from below if you like and that is a very tremendous increase in crime, in criminalisation of politics, in criminalisation of the productive forces. The second is more from above and that is this whole conception that there is too much politics and what we need is to hand over our problems and the state apparatus to managers and technocrats. If we can simply do that we will solve problems very easily. We need to depoliticise, the people are told. All this tale of organising the poor and all that is no good. What we really need is to hand over things to people who are good managers, who can sort out our problems without becoming ideological or passionate about them. ... The politicians have messed it all up. Let's put an end to politics. ...

Now, some of these may not look to be cultural issues but they have very serious cultural consequences. The use of lumpen elements for fixing things, the use of paramilitary forces for fixing agitators and extremists and ultimately the army if it becomes necessary, on the one hand, and on the other hand this notion of handing over the state to people who may wear safari clothes but whose thinking also is hard-headed, pragmatic, no-nonsense all this has very serious cultural consequences.

Maybe I have painted too pessimistic a picture. Let me, therefore, move straight to what I consider to be important counter tendencies on which one will have to build. There is a very strong democratic spirit in this society. It is a spirit that is seen not so much in elections, party politics and so on, but at the grassroots. Whether you are working in tribal areas, or among the rural poor or among the agricultural labourers or among the dalits, and in a variety of settings among the women, there is a great deal of churning going on there, a great deal of organising going on there. Largely a result of the operation of the formal democratic process, there has been a great deal of awakening among the people, a great deal of sense that they can take their future in their hands and for that they need to organise, they need to politically organise themselves. Many of the atrocities on the scheduled castes and the landless generally are, one finds, a result of this awakening. It is because they are getting stirred up and because they are challenging the hegemony of the upper castes and upper classes that the latter are finding it necessary to hit back and to repress and to kill and to rape and to maim. But what is central is the democratic spirit that is taken very seriously by the ordinary people and by those who work with them.

Two processes are at work. One is the awakening of the ordinary people themselves and the other is the rise of the new breed of activists that are politically oriented, though not working through the parties. It is something like what began to happen during the national movement, when Gandhi asked the middle-class youth to go out there in the villages and do things. Today I think something like 50,000 such youth, perhaps many more, are active in this new genre of politics and they are all over the place. We will not see them in elections because they do not participate in elections but anybody visiting the districts and lower down and going in and seeing what is happening cannot miss them. They are imbibed by the democratic spirit. They range all the way from Gandhian, sarvodaya kind of people, to Marxist-Leninists, with a series of intermediate positioned people some of whom used to be at one time Naxalites, and believed in the violent way of killing landlords and so on, but who have now taken to this broader political process. Then there are the old socialists, the youth that was inspired by Jay Prakash Narayan, the Chhatra Yuva Sangharsha Vahini and various other such groups, a very large number of them.

Part of this grassroots process is also taking place in terms of organising the minorities and defending their rights. There are a large number of Christian groups that are active, a large number of Jesuits, operating from various institutions and cadre-based organisations. There are others too who have developed a sense of care and compassion as well as solidarity with the minorities and other deprived groups. In all this there is a great deal of spirit, of building an authentic, indigenous India, made a people with their own traditions, their technological know hows which are very rich and which we are trying to undermine and their powerful ethnic spirit. In all this, a large role is assigned to voluntarism that India has always had, of people looking after themselves, of organising things by themselves rather than looking to the state or looking to a capitalist.

Coming back to the grassroots, there is a great deal of effort underway and this is taking on new dimensions. I personally think that both the secular–communal problem and the poor–rich problem that I mentioned earlier which are two faces of the costs that we are paying for the kind of nationalism we are giving ourselves will be fought by these forces which believe in pluralism, which believe in the authenticity of ethnic identities, which believe in decentralisation, in regional autonomy, in federalism and so on.

Second, there is the productive process. No matter what happens, the peasant will keep going in this country. If he had not kept going, we would have been in a much greater soup and I do not think that the credit goes to new technologies or to the green revolution. There is something very basic in the Indian peasant and the Indian peasant will keep going and has always kept going no matter what struggles and conflicts he has to face. Empires have come up and gone down, but the Indian peasant with his resilience and hard work has survived.

What we have then is a struggle between two opposite tendencies or states of tendencies, a very serious struggle in which the macro tendencies that I have painted, of building a strong state by an elite that is appropriating nearly all resources of the country, or massive increase in poverty, destitution and disease on the one hand and, on the other hand the various counter tendencies that I have mentioned. So these are two sides of the Indian cultural syndrome and I for one am hopeful that in the long run, the democratic process and the grassroots movements will give rise to a different democratic process than the narrow electoral political process that we normally identified democracy with. But in the meanwhile, it is going to be a serious struggle and I am not very sanguine about the immediate future despite the tremendous change that has taken place on the electoral front.

The immediate future, I do not see, will solve the problem of Punjab. There may not be a Khalistan but I do not see how we can prevent that kind of thinking from growing in the immediate future, given the utter neglect of the issue by the powers that be. I do not see how we can handle the Kashmir problem. On the whole, I think, whether we like it or not, there is a tremendous alienation of that state from the centre. There is also a slowly growing alienation of south Indian states and the tremendous growth of regional identity, which of itself I am not against. In fact, the only antidote to the things that I have mentioned is the growth of regional identity and the role of various regional parties and, of course, the role of major non-party voluntary organisations working along with the regional formations. There is an emerging clash between centralising and decentralising tendencies, between democracy and authoritarian tendencies, between those keen on modernising along the Western style and building a strong state and those keen on keeping the voluntary ethos going, keeping the decentralising process going. These are the kinds of conflicts in which we have been placed. Indian culture and civilisation have enough of resources within them to come out of these conflicts, perhaps not unscathed, but still intact. But these will need to struggle for it as the tendencies that are pitched against them—both global and local—are too powerful to feel complacent about.

20

Muslims in A Multi-Religious Society*

Asghar Ali Engineer

The current controversy about Babri Masjid-Ramjanmabhoomi which has caused lot of bloodshed is proof, if any proof is needed, as to how relevant the past has become for the present conflict between these two principal communities. The past is glorified by both the communities and both try to establish supremacy over the other and come into sharp conflict with each other. History, in fact, has become a powerful weapon in the hands of communalists today. History's potential thus should not be underrated as far as conflict between Hindus and Muslims is concerned in India.

India is a multi-religious society and it has been so all through its known history. Pluralism, so to say, has been strength of Indian society rather than its weakness. It is also a fact that Hinduism has been a non-doctrinaire, non-formalistic, umbrella religion. Even protest movements which sprung from its fold like Jainism and Buddhism, remained part of the Hindu fold. These protestant religions were more doctrinaire than their mother religion, Hinduism.

However, with Islam it was different. First, Islam was a non-native religion which originated in Arabia. Second, as far as north India was concerned, it came along with the Muslim conquerors though the Sufi saints also accompanied them. So it was seen as a religion of aggressors. Third, and this is also important, Islam was highly doctrinaire in nature unlike Hinduism which was a non-congealed religion. In the south, it must also be noted, Islam did not enter as the conquerors' religion. It came through the Malabar coast as a religion of the traders and thus spread in that region quite peacefully.

Some light must be thrown on the conflict which developed between these two communities during the freedom struggle. Muslims, like any other community, were divided in their approach towards the British rulers. Sir Syed and other Muslim elites wanted to buy peace with the British rulers so that they could concentrate on education and thus consolidate their position in the elite British civil and other

---

* *Economic and Political Weekly* 25 (44): 2420–23 (3 November 1990).

services. The masses, led by the 'Ulama (theologians), were impatient with the British rulers and wanted to throw them out, if necessary, by joining hands with the Hindus. Thus when the Indian National Congress was formed, in 1885, Sir Syed urged upon the Muslims to keep away from it while the 'Ulama led by Maulana Rashid Ahmad Gangohi called upon them to join Indian National Congress and fight shoulder to shoulder with their Hindu brethren to drive out British from the country.

It is interesting to note that this remained the pattern almost throughout the freedom struggle. The 'Ulama formed an organisation called the Jami'at-al-Ulama and always stood by Indian National Congress and Indian nationalism, while the Muslim elite led by Jinnah and others developed a separatist trend in Indian politics which culminated in the formation of Pakistan. The Hindu and Muslim elite could not agree on division of power among themselves and thus decided to separate. The 'Ulama had rightly argued that the Partition is neither in the interests of Islam, nor of Muslims. It was not in the interest of Islam as Islam in the subcontinent will be weakened by division and not in the interest of Muslims as those Muslims who would remain behind would not only suffer, but remain weak. And this is precisely what happened. An outstanding Muslim leader Maulana Abul Kalam Azad had repeatedly warned Indian Muslims of the repercussions of Partition and he was proved right.

The 'Ulama also felt that there was nothing in Islam which went against composite nationalism. They cited the example of the holy Prophet who on migration to Madina, entered into an alliance with the Jews and pagans and formed a composite society. This *mu'ahidah* (agreement) was adhered to by the Prophet until the Jews betrayed it. Maulana Husain Ahmad Madani, a noted leader of the Jami' at al-Ulama, argued that *qaum* (nation) is a territorial concept and *millat* or *ummah* is a religious concept. The one should not be confused with the other. He also argued that Muslims could share territory with non-Muslims and hence nationality too and there was nothing un-Islamic about it. Maulana Husain Ahmad Madani also cited the Quranic verses to show that *kafirs* (unbelievers) and Muslims in the Quran belonged to the same territorial area.

These 'Ulama also argued that the Indian National Congress had assured Muslims that they would be free to practise Islam in free India and that no change would be made in any Islamic law unless the Muslims themselves consented to it. The Shari'ah law itself makes a distinction between the *harbi* (warmongering) *kafirs* and non-harbi kafirs. Muslims could fight only with the harbi kafirs but should live in peace with the non-harbi ones. Since the Indian National Congress had assured Muslims of non-interference in their religion, it was the duty of the Muslims to live in peace with it and those people whom it represented.

However, the real fight was not about religion, but about the share in power between the Hindu and Muslim elites and no satisfactory formula to either side could be found and ultimately India was divided, leaving its own bitter legacy behind. Jinnah was highly Westernised and was hardly bothered about theological positions. His only concern was the Muslim share in power in independent India.

The educated Muslim middle classes, who were also concerned with share in power, followed him and not Muslim theologians. The artisans, the weavers and other weaker sections among the Muslims were rather sceptical about the intentions of the Muslim League which had an upper-class, urban character.

Muslims constitute a significant section of Indian society. According to the Census of 1981, Muslims comprise 11.8 per cent of the population of India. In about 20 districts they constitute a majority including the state of Kashmir which itself is an arena of violent conflict today. The Indian National Congress adopted secularism as a sheet anchor of its political policy. The Muslims in India after Partition naturally accepted it in all good faith as it alone could guarantee their full participation in the political processes in independent India. For Jawaharlal Nehru, who headed the Government of India after Partition, secularism was a matter of creed. He was personally an agnostic and passionately committed to the concept of secular polity. Nehru, who deeply influenced the evolution of secular polity in India, was of the opinion that 'it was the prime responsibility of the Hindus to make the large number of Muslims in India feel at home and not see themselves as second-class citizens existing on sufferance'.[1] He also evolved a criterion for the success of secularism. The test of success, Nehru felt, was not what the majority community thinks, but how the minority community feels.[2] However, there were a great many problems in practising it. Nehru's personal commitment to secularism was not shared by all his party colleagues, much less by the administration and the law-enforcing agencies. Thus, we see that although Nehru stood firmly like a rock by secularism, a series of major communal riots look place in the early 1960s beginning with the major communal holocaust in Jabalpur in 1962.[3]

It is also interesting to throw some light on the concept of secularism in a backward and religiously pluralist society like that of India. There is of course a small section which takes it literally in the Western sense of the term which implies total indifference towards religion, at least in public matters. According to this concept, the state should have nothing to do with religion, neither of majority, nor of minority. However desirable it may be notionally, functionally for an Indian state, this is difficult to practise. Even during Nehru's time, the Indian state, could not strictly enforce this notion.

The Indian way of life is less individualistic and more communitarian. It is this communitarian way of life which creates serious problems for Indian secularism and religious pluralism. Every Indian citizen, though enjoying constitutional rights as an individual, behaves as a member of some caste or community socially and politically. No major social or political decision can be taken by individuals as individuals but only as members of some caste, community or collectivity. No wonder then that politicians aspiring for votes have to make appeals on the basis of these castes and communities. It is very difficult for any politician, however committed to the concept of secularism, to ignore this elementary fact of Indian life. Each political party has, therefore, to evolve its own strategy in this regard.

These political parties, and specially those which aspire to form the government either at the state or central level, have to appeal to the Muslims as a community in as much as they also have to appeal to certain Hindu castes, specially the scheduled castes and tribes, commonly known as Dalits. However, the Hindu communal parties that aspire to get the Hindu votes (which invariably means the upper-caste Hindus) denounce such appeals to Muslims as their *appeasement.* This is so as the parties aspiring for Muslim votes have to concede some religious demands of Muslims like non-interference in their personal law. According to the Muslim personal law as applicable in India, a Muslim man can take up to four wives and can divorce his wife at will without reference to any court of law. Muslims defend this as their Shari'ah law and resent any change in, or regulation of, it. Every ruling party extends assurances to Muslims that the Shari'ah law which is considered divine in origin will not be interfered with.

The Hindu communalists resent this non-interference in Muslim personal law and demand the scrapping of it and replacing it with a common civil code. They also denounce this non-interference in Shari'ah law as appeasement of Muslims. Muslims, on the other hand, argue that the Indian Constitution has guaranteed freedom of religion. The Indian Constitution lays down in its article 25(1), 'Subject to public order, morality and health and to the other provisions of this Part, all persons are equally entitled to freedom of conscience and the right freely to profess, practise and propagate religion'.

Muslims argue that Shari'ah law is part of their religion and religious identity and hence cannot be allowed to be tampered with. It should also be noted that it is not only the Hindu communalists who demand abolition of Muslim personal law, but also the secularists and rationalists. They too argue, though from a different point of view, that there should be no place for different personal laws in a secular and democratic India. Only a common civil law should govern all Indian citizens. Apart from the merit of this demand, what is of interest to us here is that Muslims refuse to agree to any change and would vote collectively against any government which interferes in, or tampers with, the Muslim personal law.

This can be best illustrated by the Shah Bano movement which began with the deliverance of a judgment by the Supreme Court in respect of maintenance of a Muslim divorcee. The Muslims considered this judgment as a gross interference in the Muslim personal law and began to agitate against it. It soon developed into a massive movement and lakhs of Muslims poured out on the streets to protest against the judgment. It soon became embarrassing for the government and it agreed to enact a law exempting the Muslims from application of Criminal Procedure Code section 125 under which a divorcee was entitled to get maintenance until she remarried or died. Thus, the Government of India enacted a law called 'The Muslim Women (Protection of Rights on Divorce) Bill, 1986'. With the enactment of this bill, the ferment among the Muslims died down.

However, the government now had to face the wrath of the Hindus. In a religiously pluralist society, concession given to one religious community evokes protest from the other religious community. Here, not only the Bharatiya Janata Party (BJP), but also the progressive and secular elements condemned the enactment of the above law. The government could not afford to alienate the majority community either. It quietly connived at opening of the doors of the Babri Masjid at Ayodhya in Uttar Pradesh, which the Hindus claimed to be the birthplace of Lord Rama and which they believed the Muslim king Babar converted into a mosque. With the opening of the doors of the Babri Masjid, a new fierce controversy started between the Hindus and Muslims.

The Vishva Hindu Parishad (VHP) on the one hand and the Muslim leaders, particularly the Shahi Imam and Syed Shahabuddin, on the other started an aggressive campaign on this question. The VHP demanded that they be allowed to construct a temple in commemoration of Lord Rama at the site of the Babri Masjid, thus avenging the 'insult' heaped on Hindus by a Muslim invader. The Muslim leaders on the other hand launched a movement to save the mosque. A huge rally was held jointly by the Muslims in Delhi in March 1987. This rally further inflamed the sentiments of the majority community and there prevailed in those days a high degree of communal tension in whole of north, western and central India. As a consequence of this, serious riots between Hindus and Muslims broke out in the Delhi–Meerut area in May 1987 in which more than 500 people perished.[4] Initially, Muslims were aggressive in Meerut but after a few hours, the Hindu mobs took over on 18 May 1987 under the protection of the Provincial Armed Constabulary (PAC).[5] The PAC fired at innocent civilians and carted away many Muslim youth from Hashimpura locality in a truck, killed them and threw their bodies into a nearby canal.

Amnesty International normally does not take up investigations of communal violence in India as it is thought to be a matter between two religious communities and not a matter of violation of rights of people at the hands of the state. But in case of the Meerut riots of May 1987, it, for the first time, took up the case of killing of innocent civilians at the hands of a state organ. It said in its report that 'there was strong evidence that north Indian provincial police had deliberately killed dozens of unarmed civilians and caused dozens more to "disappear" in the state of Uttar Pradesh earlier this year'. It further says:

> The PAC is alleged to have disposed of some of the bodies of those killed by throwing them into rivers and canals. Other bodies are said to have been burnt. At least 80 bodies have been recovered altogether. Amnesty International says it has the names of 29 victims known to have been killed and of another 32 listed as 'disappeared'. All were Muslims!

We have quoted from Amnesty International to show how serious the rioting was and how the state organs were involved in killing innocent civilians. Our interviews with those detained by the police in Meerut showed that the police had identified itself emotionally with the 'Hindu cause'. It kicked the detainees inside jail and said 'take your Babri Masjid'. The sentiments on both sides were running very high and relations between the two communities were at the lowest ebb.

This, in a way, has been the result of manipulations of religious communities in a religiously pluralist society by the political parties. It must be noted that the democratic polity is essentially a competitive polity and in a backward pluralist society, this competition takes place often on religious lines. With the deepening of the democratic processes, every religious community has become quite conscious of its voting power and its importance to the political system and tries to use it to the maximum advantage. Needless to say, both the communities compete with each other in asserting their importance, which naturally leads to competitive aggressiveness. This competitive aggressiveness is displayed through religious symbols like the Shah Bano issue or the Ramjanmabhoomi-Babri Masjid controversy. The symbols by themselves are not as important as the pent-up feelings on more secular issues behind them.

The Muslim aggressiveness on the Shah Bano issue was quite understandable. They had greatly suffered in many major communal riots which began with Moradabad in 1980 as if in a new phase of communal violence. A series of riots took place in Bihar Sharif (1981), Meerut and Baroda (1983), Neil[6] (1983), Bombay-Bhivandi[7] (1984), Ahmedabad (1985–86), Meerut (1987) and several other places. In these riots, it is Muslims who mainly suffered due to partial behaviour of the police. Also, due to aggressive propaganda by the Hindu communal elements, they felt their identity was threatened and that they must assert it equally aggressively to pressurise the government. Also, on the whole, their economic situation was far from enviable.

There is no denying, says Mushirul Hasan, that they [Muslims] have been at the lowest rung of the ladder in terms of the basic categories of socio-economic indicators of development.[8] Also, in modern industry and trade, except for isolated instances, they do not own large-scale industry or business and are generally found lacking in entrepreneurial traits. There is not a single Muslim house among the 50 industrial groups, while at the lower end of the scale, most Muslims are poor and backward.[9] And according to *Muslim India*, there are only four units owned by Muslim industrialists, in a group of 2,832 industrial houses owned by large corporate units, each with sales of Rs 50 million and above.[10]

Vir Singhvi points out that the benefits of various government schemes, aimed at improving the lot of the weaker sections, have not accrued to Muslims. Of the houses allotted by state governments to lower and middle-income groups, only 2.86 per cent went to them. Of the licences issued for Fair Price shops, only 6.9 per cent were awarded to Muslims. Finally, Muslims account for only 0.25 per cent of the tangible benefits extended to the artisans by the Khadi and Village Industries Commission.[11]

Of the loans advanced by financial institutions, only 3 per cent of those between Rs 50,000 to Rs 1 lakh went to Muslims. Of those between Rs 1 lakh to Rs 2 lakh, less than *2* per cent was received by Muslims. And of those between Rs 2 lakh to Rs 10 lakh, the figure was under 1 per cent.[12] As for the private sector, the situation is even worse. Muslim employment in the higher echelons is less than 2 per cent or nearly nil in some industries.[13]

At the lower rungs too, the situation is no better. In a survey conducted by the Institute of Islamic Studies, Bombay of 18 top private-sector industries, it was found that at the shop floor level, there were no more than 4 per cent Muslims although in Bombay, their population is nearly 15 per cent.

Thus, the economic situation of Muslims is quite dismal on the whole. Wherever they have made some progress locally on a small scale like in Benaras, Azamgarh, Meerut, Moradabad, Bhivandi, Malegaon, Hyderabad, etc., they face constant threat of communal violence. It has been observed by this writer that communal violence has been taking place where Muslims have been successful to some extent in competing either politically or economically and at the centres named above, Muslims have substantial presence to offer economic competition.[14]

Thus, Muslims have been feeling suffocated for a number of years and occasionally, their frustrations come out through some aggressive religious movements on issues like the Shah Bano movement or the Babri Masjid movement. These movements should therefore not be seen in isolation from the total Muslim situation in India.

However, it does not mean that religious assertion is solely due to the material situation of Muslims in the country. There are a number of other factors as well, Such as political assertion of Islam in Iran and the rise of Islamic movements in other parts of Islamic world and what is generally referred to as Islamic fundamentalism (although it is not very a precise term as far as Islam is concerned). A section of Muslim leadership in India has acquired vested interests in the aggressive assertion of Islam and Islamic identity. Also, Muslim society had been divided along caste lines (though there is no concept of untouchability among these castes and there is no rigidity like in the Hindu caste system and caste bonds among Indian Muslims are dissolving unlike in Hinduism, in which it is becoming more rigid) in the past and now lower castes like Ansaris and Qureshis are acquiring a measure of economic affluence in middle-sized cities and towns and they need in greater measure their Islamic identity and religious assertion for social legitimation vis-à-vis Muslims of traditionally high status.[15] Also, a large percentage of Muslim artisans are in urban areas. The artisan class as such is generally more formally religious than other classes. Also, their oppressive and exploitative conditions on one hand and their increasing anonymity in big growing cities on the other make them even more religiously oriented. This religiosity of the lower middle class Muslims is exploited by the political leadership.

It would be interesting to throw some light on the increasing religious militancy among the Hindus also. The upper-caste Hindus are in a much better economic position. The middle trading castes among them have used their traditional entrepreneurial skill to become big industrialists who virtually control the Indian economy today. The top castes (brahmins) control key government posts and dominate the cultural and educational scene. Thus, these upper-caste Hindus have taken maximum benefits of modernisation and economic change in the country. On the face of it, they should have been religiously more sober and socially and politically more confident. But what we witness, especially in the last decade, is an attempt on their part to use religious militancy to subdue other minorities, especially the Muslims and low-caste Hindus. Thus, a situation of outright confrontation between Hindus and Muslims has developed and often results in an outburst of communal violence.

Hindu militancy has found its expression in the Ramjanmabhoomi issue. Thus, a senior *Times of India* staffer says:

> The debate [on Ramjanmabhoomi] so far has been marked by an astounding level of hysteria. Rank communalists, trumped-up scholars and pure philistines have joined hands to prove that Hindus have every right to demolish the Babri Masjid which stands where a temple to Ram once stood in Ayodhya, his birthplace, and indeed that the laying of the foundation stone of the temple in the town on November 9 is not only an announcement by the Hindus that they will not tolerate discrimination but constitutes a revolutionary act which will rejuvenate the Indian nation.[16]

Further on he says:

> [T]he VHP campaign has drawn on the most...coarse elements of Hindu society, and represents the ugliest face of the semi-literate middle class Hindu in search of an identity. How else can one explain the preponderance of ash-covered sadhus in the decisions (going back to the Kumbh Mela this year)[17] pertaining to the Ram temple, in particular *shilanyas*? ...How is one to understand the large presence at the Ayodhya ceremony of Bajrang Dal volunteers, some of them dressed (if that is the word) like monkeys and unable to rise above the arboreal level of consciousness.[18]

No wonder then that this confrontational posture resulted in a series of communal riots in Uttar Pradesh, Bihar and other states in October–November 1989 when throughout north, central and western India, consecrated-brick processions were taken out by the VHP in collaboration with the BJP and the Rashtriya Swayamsevak Sangh (RSS). The worst violence broke out at Bhagalpur in which about 1,000 persons, among whom an overwhelming majority was of Muslims, perished. The communal violence at Bhagalpur was reminiscent of Partition riots in 1947. One wonders how low human beings can sink in religious bigotry and communal animosity.[19]

The BJP exploited this issue to the maximum and increased its strength in the Lok Sabha in the November 1989 elections from two to 85. In a pluralist society in a backward country, religious confrontation between the two communities can assume very dangerous proportions. Democratic competition in a socially and economically backward society can often degenerate, as the Indian case shows, to competitive communal militancy resulting in manslaughter. In Pakistan too, ethnic pluralism has resulted in a similar situation. Perhaps it is a degree worse.

In a religiously pluralist society, peace and harmony can be ensured only within the framework of democratic secularism. It is only within this framework that respect for pluralism is possible. D. E. Smith defines a secular state as 'a state which guarantees individual and corporate freedom of religion, deals with the individual as a citizen irrespective of his religion, is not constitutionally connected to a particular religion nor does it seek either to promote or interfere with religion'.[20] The Indian Constitution corresponds well to this definition of a secular state or perhaps Smith has defined secular state keeping the Indian Constitution in view. But what is unfortunate is that successive Indian governments have, in their eagerness to win or retain political power, tampered with this secular spirit of the Indian Constitution. Whatever the political compulsions, such tampering with secular values will weaken the unity of the people of India and the unity of the country. Secularism must be strengthened to preserve Indian pluralism and pluralism must be strengthened to consolidate secularism.

Notes and References

1. See Parthasarthy, G., and S. Gopal. 1987. 'Jawaharlal Nehru and India's Quest for Secular Identity'. Occasional Papers on History and Society XLII. Nehru Memorial Museum and Library, New Delhi, 18.

2. Ibid., 19.

3. For details of this riot, see Kolpe, S. B. 1984. 'Caste and Communal Violence and the Role of the Press', in *Communal Riots in Post-Independence India*, ed. Asghar Ali Engineer. New Delhi: Sangam Books, 313–25.

4. See Engineer, Asghar Ali, ed. 1988. *Delhi-Meerut Riots*. New Delhi: Ajanta Books.

5. The PAC has been notorious for its anti-Muslim bias and it displays this bias in every riot situation in Uttar Pradesh. Its counterpart in Bihar is the Bihar Military Police (BMP), which also displays a similar anti-Muslim bias.

6. See Engineer, Asghar Ali, ed. 1984. *Communal Violence in Post-Independence India* for details of these riots.

7. Engineer, Asghar Ali. 1984. *Bhiwandi Bombay Riots*. Bombay: Institute of Islamic Studies.

8. See Hasan, Mushirul. 1988. 'In Search of Integration and Identity: Indian Muslims since Independence'. Occasional Papers on History and Society LT1. Nehru Memorial Museum Library, New Delhi, March.

9. Singhvi, Vir. 1984. 'Coming to Terms with Hindu Backlash'. *Imprint*, July, 28.

10. *Muslim India*, February 1985, 82.

11. Singhvi, Vir. 1984. 'Coming to Terms with Hindu Backlash', 28; see also Hasan, Mushirul. 1988. 'In Search of Integration and Identity: Indian Muslims since Independence', 22.

12. See Saxena, N. C. 1983. 'Public Employment and Educational Backwardness among Muslims in India'. *Political Science Review* 23 (2–3), April–September, quoted in Hasan 1988, 23.

13. For industry-wise data, see *Muslim India,* January 1984, 17.

14. Engineer, Asghar Ali. 1984. *On Developing Theory of Communal Riots*. Bombay: Institute of Islamic Studies.

15. Engineer, Asghar Ali. 1985. *Indian Muslim—A Study in Minority Problems*. New Delhi: Ajanta Publications.

16. Bidwai, Praful. 1990. 'Appeasing Hindu Bigotry' in *The Babri Masjid Ramjanmabhoomi Controversy*, ed. Asghar Ali Engineer. South Asia Books, 139.

17. It refers to the year 1989.

18. Ibid., 141.

19. For a detailed account of the Bhagalpur Riots, see *Bhagalpur Riots*. New Delhi: People's Union for Democratic Rights, April 1990.

20. Smith, D. E. 1963. *India as a Secular State*. Princeton, New Jersey: Princeton University Press, 4.

21

THE WOMAN AS COMMUNAL SUBJECT*

Rashtrasevika Samiti and Ram Janmabhoomi Movement

TANIKA SARKAR

I

The Rashtrasevika Samiti, the little-known women's wing of the Rashtriya Swayamsevak Sangh (RSS), is not an isolable unit, complete within itself, but one tied into a whole nexus of interrelated communal institutions. The purpose of the present discussion is to see it in relation to the Ram Janmabhoomi upsurge—how and how much the '*samiti*' contributed to it, what new turns the movement imparts to the samiti and what possibilities the connection holds out for the present phase of Hindu communalism.

One of the most sinister features of the recent Hindutva movement has been the foregrounding of the militantly communal Hindu woman in a variety of unprecedented ways. Rural women at Bhagalpur in 1989 or upper middle-class Maruti-driving women at Ahmedabad last year have appropriated active roles on the centre stage of riot scenes where they would rarely put in an appearance before—an ironic inversion of the woman's traditional invisibility. According to Vishva Hindu Parishad (VHP) reckoning (which was conveyed to us at their Ramakrishnapuram office at New Delhi in February), 20,000 '*karsevikas*' courted arrest on 4 January 1991 alone and a total of 50,000 were involved in the entire December–January round of satyagrahas. The VHP fortnightly *Hindu Chetna* of 15 December displays a cover photograph of 'karsevikas' sporting the saffron headband. The caption says: *Matrishakti ka abhyuthhan* (the ascendance of maternal power [eds]). Its Ayodhya office is selling works by women poets, like the *Shraddha Suman Mala*, which celebrates sacrifices by mothers and wives of martyrs. An official VHP account of the October/November events, the *Amar Shaheed* pamphlet, accords particular importance to Vijayraje Scindia's arrest. If *Kalchakra*, a Hindi VCR news magazine, focuses long and pointedly on the victim figure of a lone woman resister being

* *Economic and Political Weekly* 26 (35): 2057–62 (30 August 1991).

dragged away by the police on 30 October, then the woman as a dynamic leader is highlighted by the *Newstrack* (covering the October events) where Scindia is striding purposefully between two senior and enormously respectful police officers towards a car from inside which she is shown again as leaving messages for the future conduct of the movement. VHP office-bearers in Delhi spent a long time explaining animatedly to us the precise differences in the quality of speech between Uma Bharati and *saddhvi* Rithambhara. And finally, and most obviously, if Advani and his 'rath' had been the visual emblems of Ram Janmabhoomi, then the voice and the words that fixed its message belonged to a woman.

[...]

Each of the karsevikas interviewed—VHP as well as non-affiliated ones—played a distinctive individual variation on the themes of Ram Janmabhoomi and Hindutva. For Vijay Dube, a would-be *sanyasini* from Ghaziabad, Hindutva implied a sweeping, millenarian vision of collectivity ('*samashtii*'). *Yah (Hindustan) samudra jaise gambhir hai, akash jaise vyapak hai...Hindu hi adi ant hai* (It is as deep as the ocean, as endless as the sky... the Hindu is the beginning and the end). Unlike other religions, it is not time-bound but eternal. It is not an individual, but a collective experience. It finds its centre of gravity in Ram

Janmabhoomi which then becomes; *Hamara sarvaswa hai, dharam ki bat nahin hai, sarvasarvaswa hai* (It is everything to us, it is not just a matter of religion; it is all, it is our everything). With the liberation of Ayodhya, *poora vishwa badal javega, ek naya shrishti ka nirman hoga* (The whole world will change, a new creation will come into being).

For Mithilesh Vashisht, a VHP worker from Modinagar, on the other hand, the value of the movement lay in the assertion of strength and self-respect against oppression: *Atyachar, anyay nahin sahenge, kisi chees ka seema hoti hai* (We will not tolerate oppression and wrongs; everything has limits). Another (unidentified) woman intervened with a more poetic-mythical version of the necessity: *Yah hamara ang hai, hamara abhushan hai... Krishna bhagawan ka chakra hai* (This is a limb [in our body], an ornament...it is the 'chakra' of Krishna 'bhagawan'). All karsevikas were bursting with speech—with arguments and descriptions, each had an accent very distinctively her own. Within an as yet limited social and geographical scope then, the Ram Janmaboomi movement seems to have enabled major breakthroughs in women's political self activisation, not available to earlier communal upsurges. The relevant parallel seems to be with phases within Gandhian mass movements or the final stage of revolutionary terrorism in Bengal when an intensely devotional form of patriotism admitted women as full-fledged activists.

In a curious way, the present movement inverts the usual pattern of symbolisation within national and earlier communal movements. So far, in both, the fetishised sacred or love object to be recuperated had been a feminine figure—the cow, the abducted Hindu woman, the motherland. When we had interviewed B. L. Sharma, secretary of the VHP Indraprastha unit last April, he had woven an entire anti-Muslim tirade around the figure of the endlessly raped or threatened Hindu woman. Sanatan Dharmi and Arya Samajist office-bearers extended the image into that of a perpetually exposed and endangered motherland. Here, however, the occupied 'janmabhoomi' belongs specifically to a male deity, and women are being pressed into action to liberate it and restore it to him, to bring back honour to Ram. Ram's army of monkeys and squirrels has now acquired a new combatant and Sita's sex[1] is coming to the rescue of Ram—an inversion of the epic narrative pattern where Ram and his army had to go and bring Sita back. The reversal of roles equips the communal woman with a new and empowering self-image. The woman has stepped out of a purely iconic status to take up active position as a militant.

[...]

A new shift has, therefore, occurred very recently, a shift that is pregnant with possibilities for Hindu communalism and with problems. Communal organisations have not allowed a demonstratively public or even a very active political role to women so far. The RSS is—and this is a very significant fact—an exclusively male organisation. When Lakshmibai Kelkar approached Hedgewar in 1936 with an appeal to admit women as members, she was refused and Hedgewar later helped her to set up a parallel but separate organisation with a small yet significant difference in name: the members of the RSS are Rashtriya Swayamsevaks while the members of the women's wing are Rashtrasevikas. There have been debates within the RSS about giving membership to women but so far the 'sangh' has remained uncompromisingly male. The Rashtrasevika Samiti has kept a remarkably low public profile through the six decades of its existence. Even though it is one of the oldest women's organisations in the country, its total membership is about a lakh now and is largely restricted to traditional RSS and Bharatiya Janata Party (BJP) bases—Maharashtra, Karnataka, Andhra Pradesh. The Delhi wing was formed in I960 and now includes about 2,000 samiti members. Sakhas are located almost entirely in middle-class areas: Karolbagh, Patel Nagar, Janakpuri, Naraina Vihar, R K Puram, Lajpat Nagar, Kamla Nagar. Volunteers come from enterprising trading families or from middle-ranking government service background. The VHP Mahila Mandal, which started operating in Delhi from the 1980s, has about 500 members. The two mass fronts of the VHP—the Bajrang Dal and the Durga Vahini—are strictly segregated. The growth in spatial, numerical end social terms has been quite low compared to the Delhi-based radical women's organisations which have come up much later, or to mass women's organisations under left political parties. ...

What does the apparent contrast between the austere reserve of the organisations and the recent flamboyant wave of a militant reclaiming of the public spaces by women denote? Is it a break, a total departure, or is it the culmination of a long drawn out strategy? Or, is it a consciously-planned extension that stretches out old boundaries?

II

It seems that we can usefully approach this problem through an extended reference to the very familiar cassette of saddhvi Rithambhara. One remembers that voice only too well: high-pitched, shrill, breathless, delivering a non-stop harangue with no modulation. The voice seems always almost about to crack under the sheer weight of passion, the overwhelming and constant impression is one of immediacy, urgency, passion, spontaneity. For over 60 minutes, extreme stress is continuously conveyed and speech seems to be improvised as if on the field of battle—an inspired voice speaking recklessly from the gut. The later ban would heighten the earlier impression of impending martyrdom while legends about the 'martyrs' of 30 October and 2 November would subsequently feed back into the effects of the cassette. The cassette, then, is not a finished product, but one that grows with events. New technology opens up unprecedented audio-visual possibilities for political messages and stretches boundaries of orality. The startling impact of the original maidan speech becomes simultaneously preserved and fixed and can duplicate its own efforts endlessly to ever-growing audiences at will in changed political conditions. By preserving and replaying the human voice and the spoken word, a different kind of impact is attained from the one resulting from rereading a written text. The latter also grows and acquires new meanings over time, but it remains an individual exercise, a private act. The spoken word addresses a whole congregation and proceeds through a continual interchange of passion between the speaker and the listeners. New technology is able to recapture that exchange *ad infinitum* for freshly or differently constituted congregations, and at the same time, allows the first message to fatten on new meanings and associations gathered from the movement unleashed by itself, growing from its own self-fulfilling prophecies. Rithambhara's words on martyrdom would have much enlarged and transformed meanings for people listening to them after 30 October.

The technology naturalises the intended effect to such an extent and covers its own traces so completely that we forget that what we are listening to is recorded speech and not a live recording of an actual speech either. That sustained high pitch and that non-stop delivery would be impossible to improvise without breaks or modulation. It is a studio composition, an artefact which, with meticulous deliberation and coordination, pieces together over long stretches, a carefully rehearsed address. The greatest success of technology lies neither in preservation nor in duplication, but in its naturalising abilities, in its self-effacement.

[...]

An intricate and delicately-balanced system of interlocking personnel, functions and interests is ultimately monitored by the apex parent organisation—the RSS. The sangh calls itself a family, not a political organisation. As proof of this, it claims that all its members are equal and uniform in dress, disposition and functions. This stems from a remarkably peculiar notion of what a family is, since there cannot be a family without women in it and there cannot be a family that is ever undifferentiated in functions and habits. Only by developing a women's wing, then, does the family metaphor partly realise itself. The Rashtrasevika Samiti was, after all, the first affiliate that the RSS helped to foster, although a good 11 years after its own foundation. The family model is not just a metaphor. All the samiti members that I talked to had male relatives in the RSS. In fact, the striking ease and self-confidence that animate the very vocal participation of even junior office-bearers in a discussion with their elders may partly be explained by the status of their male relatives within the sangh. This might carry greater importance than the order of ranking within the samiti itself. Within the Delhi VHP Mahila Mandal too, the three top figures are all married to VHP leaders.

The organisational principles of the sangh provide the pattern for the samiti. It does not have internal elections and the '*pramukh sanchalika*' nominates her successor. Office-bearers are selected by senior members. Samiti '*pracharikas*' are unmarried women, repeating the accent on celibacy that characterises RSS '*sarsanghchalaks*', all of whom so far have been bachelors. Much of RSS ritual is also replicated within the samiti. The strict and detailed code of regulations for setting up and disbanding the daily sakha, the physical and martial arts training (the samiti provides for lessons in yoga, sword and lathi play, judo and stengun fight), regular '*boudhik*' or ideological discussion and the discipline and protocol within sakha programmes are common to both. Whereas the RSS observes six annual festivals—five of which are connected with traditional religious events and the sixth, the Shivaji Utsav, is a Hindu nationalist celebration—the samiti observes five and omits the non-traditional festival. The major hymns are also more or less the same, and are recited individually and collectively in exactly the same order. At the same time, a fine tension exists between vociferous claims to complete autonomy and pride in sharing the RSS heritage. Viduhshi, a young office-bearer, told me rather defiantly that the two bodies are totally distinct as two railway lines are which run parallel, yet always separated. The analogy, however, comes straight from Golwalkar. In a different sense, too, as we shall see later, the samiti supplements certain kinds of sangh work, in a way thereby reiterating the conventional place of the Hindu '*dharampatni*' within the household—a related, yet subordinate sphere.

In the 'boudhik' sessions within the samiti, I came across the same finished structures of thought, the same basic themes on which variations are played by Rashtrasevikas, the BJP, the VHP, individual karsevaks and sevikas and loose fragments of which have come to constitute parts of popular common sense among non-affiliated informal support groups for '*Hindurashtra*'. Resonances of such views or values are heard even in the very different, far more rarefied academic atmosphere of sections of the radical right and the radical left. The RSS occasionally plugs into a whole range of otherwise radical issues—ecology, world peace, interrelated critiques of Western materialistic and monolithic notions of truth that lead to imperialist suppression of non-Western identities.

Here, I shall take up a single theme which I heard being expounded at a samiti training camp and about which I read up in samiti and RSS literature. This was the symbolism of the '*bhagwatdhwaj*' or the saffron flag which is ritually worshipped at the beginning and of each 'sakha'. The discourse starts with the unique philosophical concept of tolerance within Hinduism—*Sarva dharma sama bhava*—which celebrates pluralism and the many equally valid ways of reaching god. This very pluralism and tolerance, however, characterise a single national ethos which is essentially Hindu and to which all immigrant religions have adapted themselves. The notion of an essentially Hindu national ethos came under attack when 'fanatic' Muslim rulers ruled the land and tried to destroy it with 'brute strength'. The British, however, planned to subvert the Hindu mind itself. This was achieved through a seemingly superior and successful mode of Western knowledge which induced self-forgetting and which substituted alien categories of thought for self-knowledge. The perception of a single national ethos was broken up and Indian history was restructured to prove that the nation means simply a geographical space inhabited by different but equal communities, each with its separate ethos. This false and alien notion of secularism destroyed the single shared culture and fractured the sense of wholeness, led to communalism and violence, and eventually culminated in the Partition. The sangh aspires to recuperate that essential wholeness through its struggle for Hindurashtra. As an RSS pamphlet puts it, '*Vishal Hindu Bharatiya Samaj bhavi swayam sevak... sangh samaj me sangathan nahin, samaj ka sangathan hai*' (The sangh is not an organisation within society; it is organisation of society).

[...]

Somewhat like the sangh, but much more emphatically so, the samiti leaves alone charity or social welfare work and has no interest in union activities. Numerical expansion or extensive mobilisation has not, then, so far been the primary concern which explains their low growth rate. It is an intensive physical and ideological training centre out of which a small group of handpicked cadres is regularly selected and sent out to circulate among the affiliated organisations and movements.

That kind of intensive mobilisation works best during its first formative phase within a same-class situation where recruits and teachers do not constantly need to break down boundaries within their own disposition and habits to communicate and interact with one another. Mobilisation is then horizontal, unlike the vertical spread of radical women's organisations which reach out to less privileged sisters as soon as they form themselves. The breadth of the latter's concerns and connection is undoubtedly their greatest strength, yet the samiti does, perhaps, score over them in a greater initial ease in interaction among all its members. A VHP worker described the sangh–samiti combine as engaged in 'class work' rather than in mass work. Class here refers to a classroom situation where all participants usually share the same social milieu. The description is quite precise since the training is pedagogical in a very total sense. Not just the arguments, but an entire mode of arguing, a particular disposition is slowly nurtured within the person, leaving a distinct mark on the more engaged activists—a calm, quiet confidence, an unhurried, patient and seemingly reasonable exposition which proceeds by agreeing with the other person as much as possible and then gently suggesting and building up its own basic themes.

For the samiti, the daily sakha is not the sole or even the most major form of activity. The family concept is extended to cover the members' families in a number of ways. The samiti's guardianship role in the case of unmarried girls is carefully meshed in with an acknowledgement of the primary rights of the family. If the family obstructs the girl's desire for further studies, a particular profession, or a late marriage, the samiti at first tries persuasion. If this fails completely, the family's decision stands. The same policy is followed over problems of the girl's boyfriend or self-choice in marriage. Rekha Raje, a pracharika, hastened to assure me that the samiti tries to fill up their time with 'healthy' pursuits and such problems, therefore, rarely arise. If they do, the samiti first inspects the boyfriend. Once he is found to be suitable, it then tries to persuade the family. Again, it is the family which must ultimately decide and on no account should the girl be encouraged to disobey.

Prospects of persuasion are enhanced and problems of divided loyalties averted by regular visits to the girl's home and the systematic cultivation of warm personal connections. A young member told me that they make a point of visiting each other's homes and dropping in for tea whenever they happen to pass that way, so that the entire family is included within the circle of the samiti solidarity. *Adhyapika*s from the sakha go over regularly to discuss a member's behaviour and prospects with her relatives. The samiti is then carried right into the heart of the domestic space and ceases to be an institution within the public sphere. Even if the girl's own connections with her sakha snap for some reason, durable contacts had been made with the parental family and the zone of influence had been permanently expanded. For small towns where individual samiti workers find it difficult to keep a sakha going, the samiti sends instructions every three months, keeping the member posted on samiti developments, rituals to be observed within this period and on how to attain a base among women of her acquaintance on a non-formal basis. At Khurja in western Uttar Pradesh, Prabha Aggarwal, coming from a staunch RSS family, managed to set up a sakha which acquired 50 members. A scandal involving a local BJP pracharak, however, made parents withdraw their daughters from the sakha. Prabha now follows the 'correspondence course' of posted instructions, spreads samiti festivals and rituals on a home-based format. The local Saraswati Shishu Mandirs do the rest of the work, on school premises.

Solidarity and warm supportiveness are more actively expressed when samiti members take turns with cooking and nursing whenever there are major illnesses in a member's house. The sakhas have a strictly local character and these gestures find them strong roots in the entire neighbourhood. When a girl marries off into a non-RSS family and her new domestic situation prevents active sakha work, senior sakha members regularly visit her in-laws and strike up a close relationship with them. The married girl then acts as a pivot within a new domestic set up, a new neighbourhood. The samiti in fact encourages her to drop sakha work for the first few years after marriage, until her status in her new home is firmly established and her samiti friends are accepted by the entire family. If, however, the in-laws still discourage a connection with the old sakha, she is again not advised to assert her choice. Her old samiti members of the local branch keep in close touch with her and with her family. She is given a few easy exercises that may be done even within a fairly crowded home and she is told to teach them to women relatives in the new family. She is also advised to establish herself as an ideal counsellor and arbiter for women within the family. Once that position is attained, she can then informally discuss the ideas she had been trained in during her sakha days or which her samiti members have kept her attuned to. One can see how useful such a loose and informal network would have been to inculcate notions of 'Hindutva' and 'Hindurashtra' over a long period of time, and then, to swiftly link them up with a violent agitation which would find a ready support base without any direct and immediate organisational investment. Gradually, her reputation as a dependable adviser and friend in need will spread to the women in the neighbourhood and enlarge and stabilise a circle of dependents and listeners. For the women within the kinship network and the immediate neighbourhood, the presence of such a woman ensures an informal forum for the discussion of general topics. This way she fills up a crucial gap and appeases a very real hunger for serious intellectual discussion among women which traditionally only religious topics used to provide.

Women's religiosity is usually explained in terms of certain emotional, cultural or social needs. A very vital function of religion is hardly taken into account: that it alone gives her access to a world of meanings enclosed in epics, allegories or other forms of religious texts that she can interpret and dwell on, and thereby transcend her own immediate and closed world of limited experience. The samiti partly continues these themes and partly weaves them into a different and larger political fabric. A Haryana housewife activist told me that for her, the highest value of the samiti lay in exposing her to the world of thinking beyond household or personal matters. Golwalkar had seen a lot of possibilities in such household-cum-neighbourhood circles for women working for the sangh and these possibilities have been much extended since his times.

Informal training for unaffiliated wives of RSS activists is yet another important field for samiti work. At a samiti training camp, a whole session was reserved for them, followed by a joint lunch and a group discussion of their problems and possible activities. I found that the wives were as familiar with samiti activists and activities as any formal member. I met a school teacher wife of an RSS activist who has been married for five years, before which she had had no contact with that organisation. Now, even though she is not a member herself, she managed single-handedly to persuade her entire body of colleagues to join a day-long protest fast at Ajmal Khan Park after the 30 October deaths. Her account of the samiti and the sangh was as detailed and as confident as that of any activist's. Her work, she told me, was manifold. She has to coach her two tiny children thoroughly in the daily sangh mantra recitations and cultivate proper '*samskaras*' in them. She, along with other RSS wives, makes a point of bringing them over to samiti ceremonies as early as possible so that it becomes a second home to them. Another function was to help out with needy RSS families in her locality. Her husband, for instance, would tell her if one of them was getting a daughter married. In that case, all the more affluent wives would divide up parts of the dowry to be collected among themselves. They would also get together to help out if a distressed RSS member or someone in his family suddenly needed blood. RSS members are required to donate blood and keep their certificates precisely for this purpose—to have access to the blood bank in emergencies. Apart from being a far-sighted and practical form of support, this probably fosters the notion of a blood brotherhood. In her professional capacity, the wife is expected to gather influence and respect for her ideas and attitudes within her place of work. Much of the samiti's activity is then informal and directed at constructing an ideal, totalitarian RSS family. The concept of expansion is a family-by-family, mind-by-mind building up of the Hindu nation—an incredibly patient, long-term strategy. It is, to stretch a concept of Gramsci, a form of hegemony built up on a molecular model.

III

Is the samiti then merely filling up a space marked out for it by the sangh for its own purpose? And, if so, does not this conclusion contradict a statement that I had made earlier in the paper—that the strength of the movement lies in the exhilarating possibilities it creates for certain sections of deeply conservative women, in its being an expression partly of their own creativity?

I think that the original parameters worked out by sarsanghchalaks have proved to be flexible and accommodating. The major body of Golwalkar's instructions for women had carved out a sort of a '*Lakshman-rekha*' of faithful motherhood within which the properly instructed mother carefully guards her children from corrupting Western influences and instils in them the right sanskaras—filial piety, knowledge of patriotic heroes and of religious texts. Rashtrasevikas have travelled a long distance since then without overtly resisting the original instructions. The gap between the original impulse and the new self-definition may or may not open up fissures within the movement, depending upon the versatility and suppleness of the sangh ideology, both of which, I fear, are considerable.

Somewhat different pulls seem to be working within the samiti itself, though it would be crude and false to categorise them as potentially feminist versus overtly fundamentalist ones. Varieties of emphasis, nonetheless, remain interesting. In the first place, there are somewhat different versions of the origin myth of the organisation. Neither the authorised history of the samiti, nor the accounts of a senior office-bearer and a pracharika mentioned anywhere that Hedgewar was first approached to admit women into the sangh and that he refused and helped Kelkar to set up a parallel organisation. It is an RSS publication that dwells on this fact and claims that Hedgewar convinced Kelkar about the problems of a common organisation. Samiti accounts, then, seem to need to push away the fact of that refusal. Again, the official samiti history has a somewhat different explanation for the samiti's foundation. It says: '*Hindutva jagaran ka pramukh dhyeya lekar is swatantra sangathan ka shubharambha hua*' (with the primary aim of the awakening of Hindutva, this independent organisation began its auspicious start). Rekha Raje, a pracharika, however, narrated how Kelkar on a train journey had witnessed a young girl being raped by goondas (not Muslim ones, she replied to my question) in her husband's presence. She realised that since Hindu husbands cannot protect their wives, they have to strengthen themselves. Whereas the edge in this story is turned against the failures within Hindu society—Hindu male violent lust and Hindu male cowardice—the official text overlays that version by the broader and more general aim of Hindutva 'jagaran'.

In the self-explanations and self-definitions produced by the samiti, there is primary emphasis on physical courage and strength, on a trained, hardened, invincible female body. The sangh, too, defines this—cultivation of Hindu woman's physical strength—as the first principle and then goes on to list 'intellectual grasp of the values of Hindu culture and devotional attachment to the ideals of Hindu womanhood'. A samiti publication puts it in stronger terms: '*Swasangrakshankshham nari ki samaj me adhik pratishtha hoti hai*' (a woman who is able to defend herself gets a larger status in society). The specific deity which sums up their aspirations is the militant icon of '*ashthabhuja*' Durga who subsumes Saraswati, Lakshmi and Kali. Sevikas are meant to meditate on her weapons particularly. They see themselves as full-fledged soldiers in an impending apocalyptic war: their daily pre-meal mantra is translated as: 'Our limbs and bodies have been nurtured by our Motherland and we must give them back to her in her service alone'. Expounding on this theme, Asha Sharma, who is in charge of the Delhi organisation, explained that this binds up the notion of sacrifice with that of active fighting. When I asked if it was some kind of a civil war situation that she had in mind, she replied that it was a possibility. Certainly, then, the explicit purpose for which the empowered Hindu female body is trained is patriotic war against the Muslim combatant. The large place that the myth of Muslim lust occupies within the general mythology of Hindu communalism would also explain the need for self-strengthening.

Yet we must remember the oral version of the origin myth—Hindu goondas raping a girl in the presence of a Hindu husband—and also the reference to the larger status of the 'swasangrakshanksham nari' (a woman who is able to defend herself) within her own social milieu. Defence against and respect within her own environment is then the implicit subtext which might, in everyday calculations, become a more powerful motive force and a more real compulsion than the ultimate political intention of Hindutva jagaran. When we consider the context from within which the samiti mobilises and trains its women, the force of the immediate compulsion becomes clearer. Sevikas come from upwardly mobile, urban, solvent, trading or middle-ranking service sectors—a fertile breeding ground for dowry murders and the violence on wives that precedes them. Women's organisations that deal with huge numbers of divorce or maintenance suits arising out of this social level are very familiar with the violence and oppression that flourish here against women. In the big northern cities, if not in the rich small towns, so far, education and professional opportunities for women have come in late and recently but have come in a big way. Nor are families opposed to women's employment and professional training since it is regarded as a valuable source of extra income. Thrust into public and mixed spaces for the first time, women daily encounter yet new forms of overt or covert sexual discrimination and violence. It is no wonder that the physical training programmes of the sakhas prove extremely attractive to such women, with the promise of a powerful body and the attendant self-confidence. That body and that mental attitude that it generates would be a vital shield against gender oppression within domestic and public spaces.

We may then assume that despite the overarching aim of Hindu power, the woman needs also to utilise samiti facilities to empower herself against her own hostile environment. Problems of the newly mobile professional woman are often discussed in the *Jagriti*, the samiti journal. An article, for instance, describes how the author withstood the offensive behaviour of a police officer who partially undressed himself in her presence when she had gone in to report a street accident. Several others take up this theme: how to construct a responsible and fearless woman-citizen and teach her to exercise her civic rights and duties within a chauvinistic world.

Two very different readings of the precise location of the Hindu woman within her own society seem to be jostling each other within the samiti. The pramukh sanchalika's speech at the 1990 annual conference insisted that '*Bharat* (read Hindu for it) *ki nari sarvada se mukt hai*' (The women of India have always been free). An article in *Jagriti*, entitled 'Rashtra ka Adhar Nari' reiterates this conviction and traces a long history of her power within Hindu society from Manu to the current movement. Yet the same issue carries another article—Nari Jagaran—where the present women's movement in India (which is not equated with the specifically Hindu movement) is described as a result of and an antidote to the generalised oppression against women. Whereas the earlier trend is extremely critical of the global women's movement as a sign of Western corruption, the latter explains and legitimises it. Another article, 'Parivartit Parivesh me Bharatiya Nari' criticised Indian men for obstructing the larger entry of women into politics. It is interesting to see that while the more authoritative statements—Golwalkar, RSS strictures, the samiti's official accounts—applauds the new Hindu women for resisting Western modernism, women's own articles, when they deal with their everyday problems and perceptions, are little concerned about Westernised modernity. In fact, the new Hindu woman-citizen is cast in a mould which is very close to that of bourgeois feminism. *Nari ke sarvangin vikas ke liye uska arthik roop se swatantra hona paramavshyak hai, atah nari ki arthik swatantrata ke liye rozgar me sangrakshan hona chahiye tatha usse sambandhit sabhi mukadamon ke liye mahila nyayadhish chahiye* (In order to attain the comprehensive development of women it is extremely important for them to be economically independent. So, in order to ensure economic independence, they need reservation in employment and they need women judges to conduct all cases related to such issues). The new Hindu woman is, therefore, a person with professional and economic opportunities, secure property ownership, legal rights to ensure them and some amount of political power to enforce these rights.

How does this woman relate to Hindu tradition? I feel that Hindu tradition exists for her as a deeply cherished, yet somewhat remote, icon which requires ritual worship but is seldom brought out for daily use or inspection. There is very little interest in probing it and deciding on what it actually says about gender. In fact, very often the question of religious faith is interpreted as and completely displaced onto the realm of patriotic faith. The greatest triumph of the present communal moment has been to blend '*deshbhakti*' and '*Rambhakti*'—the two very potent sources of emotional involvement—into a homogenised whole so that adherents use them interchangeably. When our interviewer asked the karsevika Vijay Dube, a woman who plans to adopt sanyas, how Rambhakti has come to mean so much to her, she immediately traced back its source to her childhood experience of the China war and the passions it had aroused within her patriotic faith. In her case, this was the original impulse that stoked religious passion and she herself was not aware of any distinction between the two. The process of mutual collapsing works with equal felicity the other way round too. At Ayodhya, it was the banning of the usual 'parikrama' route that is a part of normal pilgrimage activity that turned pilgrims into karsevaks with great case.

On specific questions of gender within Hinduism, the verdict seems to be unequivocally modernistic. Sati was squarely denounced by all office-bearers. When I asked about voluntary sati, a young activist said with genuine revulsion: *Woh ho nahin sakta. Aurat jalegi kyoon?* (It is not possible. Why should a woman burn?). She then went on to explain that she might do it out of 'depression and frustration' that is, as a mark of weakness, not as a mark of strength—but neighbours and relatives must shore up her will to live. The samiti theoretically does not ban inter-caste or even inter-communal marriage, provided of course, the family agrees. The *Jagriti* cover page depicts two helpless women against a black background, crouching in a helpless mourning posture. And out of that dark frame, a young, rather grim-faced woman steps out on the radiant half of the cover with a fire step and uplifted head. There are no traditional Hindu marks on her body—no 'sindur', no veil, no 'bindi'. She wears chappals, her sari is draped tightly around her and her whole stance is free, even aggressive. Of course, she does wear the samiti uniform—the purple-bordered white sari. A surprising feature of this magazine is its uncompromisingly non-'feminine' nature. It makes no concessions to conventional women's topics. There are no hints on beauty aids, no cookery or embroidery section, no advice on child rearing. Stories are scrupulously bare of the romantic element. They deal with the romance of Hindu civilisation or that of modern patriotism instead.

Women's power is a theme that is discussed and celebrated, often in the most grotesque of circumstances. At the Ayodhya karseva, a crowd of women was chanting the beautiful feminist slogan: *Hum bharat ki nari hain. Phool nahin chingari hai* (We are the women of India. We are not flowers, we are embers). When our interviewer asked them why Sita was absent in the invocations to Ram, the men fell silent but women had their answers ready. One said that this was Ram's birthplace and not Sita's, which accounts for her absence. But Vijay Dube interrupted her to say that 'Shri' actually means Sita and hence in the chant Shri Ram, Sita is actually placed before Ram. The interviewer asked—'You mean Sita is contained in Ram?' 'No', said Dube, 'Sita comes before Ram'. Not only had thought gone into the location of Sita, there was also a recognition that Sita must come before Ram. In a VHP book for children, *Hanuman ki Kabaddi*, Hanuman declares himself to be neither Ram's '*bhakt*', nor Sita's bhakt, but the bhakt of Sitaram alone.

I do not at all want to convey the impression that a sort of women's liberation is going on happily within a somewhat unfortunate Hindutva framework. When I asked Asha Sharma where the samiti differs from other women's organisations, her reply was immediate: 'We do not believe that in marital disputes the husband is necessarily to blame. When we arbitrate, we do not take the woman's side, we are neutral. We tell the woman that she must do everything to preserve her home life. *Hum ghar torne-wali nahin hain* (We are not wreckers of home).' They offer no formal legal counselling to women, nor is divorce generally encouraged. Dowry is regarded as an evil, yet there obviously is no ban against its practice among sangh or samiti members. If a demand for full citizenship rights and affirmative action is made in *Jagriti* from time to time, there is no critical review of Hindu patriarchy. When karsevikas at Ayodhya were asked if their status would improve within

Hindurashtra, one of them said yes, because Muslims then would not be allowed to have four wives and that alone would ensure greater respect for women. She could not, on the spur of the moment, think of any other possibility within Hindutva for herself.

The same silence is maintained about caste. It is formally denounced and sakha members are not to submit their surnames when they enrol, so that their caste status does not become public knowledge. There is also community dining to ensure the absence of barriers. Yet the caste system is not a theme for discussion or criticism in boudhik study sessions. As with gender, class struggles are yet another field of resounding silence and non-involvement.

IV

Where do we feminists stand in relation to this manifestation of women's power? There is no denying that it does empower a specific and socially crucial group of middle-class women, if not in an absolute feminist direction then definitely in a relative sense. It helps hitherto homebound women to reclaim public spaces, to acquire a public identity, it confers upon them a political role and even leadership. It teaches the women not to regard themselves as merely feminine, but as full-fledged citizens. It gives her access to serious intellectual cogitation.

We know the costs too. The public identity is regimented, colourless, grim. Intellectual discussion and political involvement have reached their fulfilment in a violent campaign of blind hatred, and not in a critique of class, caste and patriarchy. It prepares the woman to be a citizen of an authoritarian Hindurashtra; to wreck secular, democratic politics.

This paradox of self-limiting and violent self-empowerment must not be appropriated within currently fashionable, flat and facile critiques of post-enlightenment modernity which read Hindutva as yet another problematic manifestation of a necessarily distorted Westernist discourse and seeks a resolution for it within a so-called unproblematic, accommodating, warm and generous Hindu tradition, in a shift from modernistic Hindutva to traditional Hinduism. Socialists and feminists can see no resolution for caste, class or gender issues within tradition, nor can they afford the luxury of ascribing all present distortions to an abstract, flat notion of colonial discourse. In any case, the specifically modernistic elements in the communalism of Hindu women are hardly ones that they can identify as sources of distortion or recommend their abolition. The samiti's verdict on sati would be an obvious example. The real problems lie in the realm of active politics, the resolution lies with more aware and sensitive forms of Left democratic and feminist movements alone.

NOTE

1. The author means persons of Sita's gender, that is, 'women activists'. [eds]

22

Gender and Communal Riots*

Bhavna Mehta and Trupti Shah

While it is true that both men and women living in riot-prone areas suffer during communal disturbances, rarely do evaluatory studies or reports examine the gender dimensions of adverse effects. In January 1991, the Women's Studies Research Centre of M. S. University of Baroda, in collaboration with Sahiyar Women's Organisation of Baroda, initiated a project to examine the effects of communal riots on women living in two areas of Baroda city which have been continually affected by communal disturbances since the early 1980s.

The interviews of women began in January 1991, four months after major riots had taken place in Baroda, sparked off during a Ganesh Visarjan procession in September 1990. During the period that followed, there was a constant tension for over 10 months in the selected areas, as an aftermath of L. K. Advani's *rathyatra.* There was an atmosphere of fear, feelings of insecurity, sporadic incidents of violence and anxiety that any minute another riot might break out. The interviews stretched over eight months mainly because of the difficulties in entering the area during those days and the team's concern for personal safety.

Two areas were chosen in the heart of Baroda city, Rajpura ni Pole and Navi Pole Ladwada. The reasons for selecting them being: (1) Sahiyar's earlier work among the Muslim women in the area, which had earned their confidence, making them willing to talk to the team about sensitive issues; (2) Rajpura ni Pole had been severely affected during the September 1990 riot, one narrow lane alone having been exposed to 80 rounds of police firing, and (3) Rajpura ni Pole is predominantly a Muslim area while Navi Pole and Ladwada are adjoining predominantly Hindu areas (This proximity is one factor contributing to riots). It was thus possible to interview women of both communities.

Detailed individual interviews were conducted with 40 women (22 Hindus and 18 Muslims). Six group interviews with about 16 Muslim women were carried out for the following reasons: the Muslim area is lower middle class, with houses arranged around an open quadrangle, where women sit and work during the day. An interview initiated with one woman would automatically result in others gathering

* *Economic and Political Weekly* 27 (47): 2522–24 (21 November 1992).

around. Further, because the area had been badly affected, any talk about riots would arouse interest and stimulate the neighbours to join the discussion.

In order to get the women to talk freely, the team also had to resort to various strategies to keep male family members away since otherwise they tended to dominate the conversation. If there were men around, one team member would engage them in conversation so that the women could be interviewed by the others without interruption. A few vegetable vendors and flower-sellers were also interviewed since their workplace is in the riot-affected areas, though they live elsewhere. While most of the Muslim women had small shops, they were self-employed or were home-workers.

During the interviews, we tried to gauge in precisely what ways communal riots affected women, what women perceived as reasons for riots, their attitudes towards the other community, what they thought was needed to be done to prevent riots, whether they perceive a role for themselves in preventing riots, and would they be willing to join a movement to promote communal harmony.

Summarised here are some illustrate responses (all names have been changed to protect the identities of the women):

Shantiben has been selling flowers near Nyaya Mandir (the district court) for 40 years, and has seen all the riots since Partition. She does not trust Muslims and feels insecure during riots. According to her, Babri Masjid is the reason for riots. She does not know more than that and even if she did, she would not speak out because 'they' will harass her. It is the government's responsibility to stop riots and prevent 'them' from indulging in violence.

Sakinabibi sells snack food for children at her home-based shop. Her son was severely beaten up and arrested and has been in jail for a year. She has sought help from the local (Muslim) leader to get him released but without success. She is in debt, has sold her goat and her jewellery trying to save her son. When the police came to arrest him, neighbours were too scared to help and just shut their doors. Her house was damaged and though a sum of Rs 2,500 was awarded as compensation, she got only Rs 250; the rest was swallowed up by officials. Her business collapsed during riots and she had to take a loan to pay her younger son's school fees. When the riot started, her pregnant daughter was present at home and later had to be sent back to her in-laws. She believes the riot was instigated by a leader of a communal political party. She says riots occur because the government fails to arrest anti-socials and the police remain passive.

Gaytriben is a Hindu living in a Muslim area. Her husband who is a factory worker was once beaten up by the police, for going out during curfew. She has no complaint of harassment by neighbours. She cannot sleep during riots. When there is a riot, they feel like leaving the place and going to live somewhere else, but when it is over they do not want to move.

Nadimabibis' husband sells footwear; her sons are employed. Once during the 1988 riot, she had gone to buy vegetables at Ghadialipol, accompanied by the young daughter of a neighbour. She was suddenly surrounded by a crowd, was frightened, and to protect the young girl, held her hand and ran home fast. She told no one in her 'mohalla' about the incident because if she had, they would have gone and fought with the boys in the crowd and the riots would only have gotten worse. Once when a building was on fire, her sons went to save people. She feels insecure all the time and when she goes out, she is constantly afraid that someone might come and attack her.

A group interview was conducted with young women who do 'badala' embroidery work. Their menfolk drive auto-rickshaws, During one riot, one man's auto was damaged. Income from both autos and embroidery falls during riot periods. When the husband is taking Hindu school children in the rickshaw, the wife feels insecure till he returns home. In another group interview, one of the women was a *papad*-maker, another gave tuitions. Once, some Hindu school children took shelter in her home when riots started and reached home safely the next day. During riots, children cannot come for tuitions and income falls.

Because women have the responsibility for keeping the household running, nearly all the women spoke of difficulties in getting milk and vegetables during riots, getting flour ground, of the high prices of food items, and the fear of going out to procure their daily needs. Those whose livelihood was affected, or whose menfolk could not earn during the riots, spoke of going hungry, taking loans and getting into debt. Those whose husbands or sons had government jobs (they were mostly Hindus) were less affected because government employees' salaries are not cut during riots. Some men could get curfew passes and continue to go to work. In such installers, the women were more concerned about interruptions in children's education, postponement of exams, etc. One problem in procuring articles of daily needs is having to go to far-off shops due to the compulsion to avoid the nearby shops belonging to the other community. Generally, women feel affected when husbands' or sons' jobs/earnings are affected, when menfolk are injured or arrested. They are anxious about men's safety when they are out at work.

Some women spoke of health upsets due to the outbreak of a riot—diarrhoea, high blood pressure, palpitations, sleeplessness, loss of appetite, shivering and vomiting. Intense fear and insecurity were frequently mentioned and the experience of being socially cut off because they could neither go out nor be visited by relatives. Women spoke of fear of going through nearby areas where the other community lived, even when there was no curfew.

Interestingly, those whose livelihood was affected were more worried about this than anything else. Like the vegetable vendor who plies her trade even when the situation is tense because she has a mentally disabled husband at home, and if she does not pay the rent, she will be evicted. She is more worried about her earnings than her life, works hard all day, does not know why riots occur, and has not the time to think about all these issues.[1] On the other hand, those who did not go out to work spoke of boredom at being confined to the house.

Some women were evasive when questioned, reflecting their feelings of insecurity. Shantiben, a widow working as a housemaid, stays in a predominantly Muslim area. She refused to give specific answers as she was being watched by a Muslim woman sitting in a nearby verandah, listening to the conversation.

Sayrabibi, who works in the family business of making and selling *samosas*, talks of acute financial crisis with the business collapsing during riots. When a male neighbour started interrupting, she became completely silent. After he went away, she was willing to talk but only in very general terms. She was not against people of the other community. The problem could be solved only if people unite, she felt.

Salma and Nagma clean garlic at home, they never go out, do not read newspapers or listen to the radio, and repeatedly stressed that they did not know anything because they live in purdah.

Movement outside the home gets severely curbed for women when the atmosphere of tension and danger persists after riots. One Hindu woman who used to go to a sewing class no longer does so because it is not 'safe'. Ayesha, a 17-year-old Muslim girl, longed to continue her studies but because of the unabating riot situation, her studies were stopped. She is most unhappy about it. Rakshaben, a professional singer, says they have to send their daughter away during riots because of eve-teasing and obscene gestures by 'them'.

Women talk of being able to usually anticipate probable riot dates. Those who can afford to, stock up the essential provisions. Those who cannot are badly affected. Getting milk and vegetables, however, remains a problem for all. Women admit that menfolk of their own families take part in the violence. They are aware of it but can do nothing to prevent it. They also acknowledge that they too help in stocking stones, etc., and in making acid bulbs for 'self-defence'. Swati, who lives in a Muslim area, says that neighbours tell her family to 'stay' when they are confident of being able to protect them. Sometimes they urge her to go somewhere else because 'if outsiders come we cannot protect you'. Mayaben has been staying in the area for the last 55 years. Once, her son was beaten up by the police. She is 'used' to riots; they no longer disturb her mentally.

Hindu women expressed strong anti-Muslim sentiments, while Muslim respondents seemed to be less vocal about anti-Hindu feelings. A possible reason could be that all the team members were Hindu and despite efforts, we were unable to include a Muslim investigator in our team. During one interview with a Muslim woman, a number of neighbours, male and female, joined in and became hostile when they learnt that the surname of one of the members of our team was similar to that of a local leader of a communal party. They associated her with this leader whom they regarded as responsible for the September 1990 riot and suspected that we were his agents. 'Why don't you go instead to the government and ask questions and tell them to reduce prices?', they retorted.

Among Hindu women, even those who saw a link between price rise, unemployment and riots and felt that politicians and goondas are responsible for them, blamed the police, still they expressed strong anti-Muslim feelings.

A few women did talk of members of the other community being kind and helpful. Shalini explains that her family has acquired a domestic flour mill, because getting flour ground during riots is difficult. Earlier, they used to go to a flour mill owned by a Muslim. 'He was a good and honest person but why should we take risk during riots?' She feels angry with youngsters of both sides who do rioting. She and her mother say that some Muslims are decent and cite example of Muslim friends who are 'good'. She adds that during Ganesh visarjan procession, Hindus shouted anti-Muslim slogans and Muslims reacted by breaking the head of the Ganesh idol. When Muslims start riots, the police do not prevent Hindu boys from retaliating. Instead, they urge them to answer back.

Sakinabibi says she has good relations with Hindu neighbours, and that during curfew, they help each other to get things; she adds that relationships do not get spoilt during riots. At the same time, she 'does not trust Hindus' and feels constantly insecure.

Hindu perceptions of why riots start are typical. Leaders are responsible. Muslims throw stones and dirty water on religious processions. Riots take place only during 'our' processions, not during 'theirs'. Riots occur because prices are high and people want to loot shops. Because Congress (Indira) supports Muslim politicians, smugglers, bootleggers and goondas, and anti-socials are responsible for riots. Youngsters start riots by using abusive language, throwing stones, petrol bombs, etc. Riots start from small events, personal fights among unemployed youth and ill-feeling between Hindus and Muslims. Riots happen when Muslims shout pro-Pakistan slogans during cricket matches.

Muslims perceptions of reasons for riots include: Local leaders of the communal party instigate riots; during religious processions Hindus shout anti-Muslim slogans; neither Hindus nor Muslims but 'outsiders' start riots and the police are responsible for allowing riots to continue by remaining passive spectators of arson and looting; people from nearby Hindu areas start the rioting and the government fails to do anything. Goondas start riot during religious processions to give Muslims a bad name; big leaders are responsible; riots occur because 'they' want to drive Muslims out of this country, etc. Muslims expressed much anger against the police for being passive or partisan. In one group interview, Muslim women said: 'When we stand in the queue for kerosene, Hindu and Muslim women wait together and nothing happens. Where does this hatred and violence suddenly come from? It is some outsiders who are responsible.'

What should be done to prevent riots? There was an overall feeling of resignation and helplessness among women of both communities. You cannot stop riots. It is like a game of cat and mouse. This time the Hindus will throw more stones, next time Muslims will throw more stones. It will continue like this. There will never be peace in this city. Riots will never stop. It will always be like this.

Both Hindu and Muslim women generally felt that in order to prevent riots, government must take action to stop price-rise and give jobs to all. It is for the government and the police to do something to prevent riots. A Hindu corollary to this was: 'government should drive Muslims from this country. If the Muslims are there, there will be riots. Send the Muslims to Pakistan. If they want to stay here they should stay peacefully.'

Do women have a role? Once again, the responses were of helplessness. 'We cannot prevent our own menfolk from indulging in violence. Who will listen to us?' There was also the argument that 'it is not *our* responsibility, we don't start riots'.

One Hindu woman suggested that women should try to stop youngsters from getting violent, and another Hindu woman suggested that children should be brought up in a secular way. In a broad sense, many agreed that there should be unity and communal harmony and all should strive for this (But at the same time, they also expressed communal sentiments). One Muslim woman said that the one thing women can do is to prevent the men from going out during riots (and thereby prevent violence from escalating). Among Muslim women, the feeling of helplessness and despair seemed stronger. 'Common people can do nothing. Only influential people can do something.' Nafisabanu, who irons clothes, says nobody can stop riots; women should understand that if we fight against price rise, then all will benefit. We should spread awareness of this and she is willing to join others to do so. Razia agrees women should strive for communal harmony and fight price rise but she herself has no time from papad-making and household work. Meenbai Menon says: 'How can we do anything? If we try to get together and do something there may be murder and the police will do nothing. Why should we risk our lives?'

Naseem, the 17-year-old whose studies were abruptly stopped, says: 'How can women do anything to stop riots? We want to do so many things but we are stopped by the males in our family. Someone is stopped by a husband, another by a father or a son.' Sharifabanu, the only graduate (Muslim) in our survey, says all Indians, both men and women, should try to stop riots. Women alone cannot do anything. Women should take jobs in the police. She herself cannot get involved in any movement because she is tied to the house, has a small daughter to look after and her husband will not give her permission to go out. She must be there when he comes home.

A broad conclusion from the above survey is that women certainly are affected by riots in specific ways because of their gender. However, some aspects of the impact are obviously common to both men and women. Though the project did not include interviews with men, it is not unreasonable to assume that feelings of insecurity and attitudes towards the other community need not be gender-related. It may not also be correct to say that women are affected in worse ways than men, for the nature of the impact is closely linked with class and community.

Interestingly, when we started the study, we assumed that women were unlikely to be directly involved in violence. We were partially proved wrong since women acknowledged that they helped in stocking stones, even though this was for 'self-defence'.

The question of involving women in a campaign for communal harmony is very complex, since identity with religious community was much sharper than gender. A campaign aimed at uniting women of both communities has to be linked to issues that both groups feel strongly about, and in this survey it was price-rise and unemployment which seemed to have this potential, along with anger against politicians and police. We cannot overlook the fact that even those women who cited the above issues as the underlying reasons for riots continued to have ill-feeling against the other community. This was particularly true of the Hindu women. Even though the latter cited religious processions as one provocation for riots, not one of them suggested a ban on processions as a measure to prevent riots. In fact, a suggestion to ban religious processions came from only one Muslim woman. One must also examine how, given women's feelings of utter helplessness to prevent their own menfolk from indulging in violence, they can be persuaded to join a movement for communal harmony without the active support of men.

NOTE

1. Earlier, during the Ahmedabad riots of 1985, the Self Employed Women's Association (SEWA) had noted that when the tools of self-employment of riot-affected women were restored, there was a marked change in their mood, and their dignity was partly restored (SEWA Annual Report, Ahmedabad, 1988).

23

INDIAN MUSLIMS SINCE PARTITION*

BALRAJ PURI

The title of this chapter may well have been 'Indian Muslims since Independence'. But the present title underlines the crucial impact, on Muslims, of the partition of the country. For in reality, it marked a division of the Indian Muslims, first in two and later in three nation-states; whereas the bulk of the Hindu community (and of other non-Muslim communities) was consolidated in what remained of India, retaining its historic and civilisational continuity.

PARTITION AND AFTER: EARLY YEARS

The idea of Pakistan, as is well known, had little support in the areas that now comprise that country. Its battle was fought essentially by those Muslims who lived in the Hindu majority areas, which remained a part of India. Iqbal, who is credited with the authorship of the idea, wanted to apply it to the Muslim majority areas of the subcontinent. In a letter to M. A. Jinnah dated 17 June 1937, he asked, 'Why should not the Muslims of NW India and Bengal be considered as nations entitled to self-determination?' But while suggesting establishment of Islamic states through the division of the country, he categorically advised Jinnah 'to ignore Muslim minority provinces'. He further urged him to concentrate on the Muslims of the north and west of India.[1] But the Muslim League leadership ignored this advice and found it easier to work upon the sense of fear and insecurity of Muslims in Hindu majority areas. It was able to persuade the Muslims that a separate Muslim state on either side of India would be a better guarantee of their rights.

Trauma

But soon after Partition, the entire Muslim League leadership, which alone had a popular base, left India along with most of the administrative, social, cultural and intellectual Muslim elite for the new, greener Islamic pastures, leaving Indian Muslims leaderless and impoverished.

* *Economic and Political Weekly* 28 (40): 2141–49 (2 October 1993).

Shaheed Subrawardy, who rose to the position of the prime minister of Pakistan, conceded: 'Pakistan has provided a home-land for the Muslims living in the majority areas but not for the Muslims in India. The Muslims in the Indian union have been left high and dry and must shape their own destiny.'[2]

The veteran Muslim League leader Khaliq-uz-Zaman went a step further and lamented that the Muslim community of the subcontinent had lost its collective weight due to the Partition. The two nations theory, according to him, 'proved positively injurious to the Muslims in India, and on a long view basis to Muslims everywhere'. Before the Partition, some observers used to refer to the Muslims as the largest community of India in view of the somewhat diffused and non-cohesive nature of the Hindu society. To this, Khaliq-uz-Zaman added: 'Pakistanis are not one-third as important as the pre-independence Muslim India was. Are the Indian Muslims one-third of their political forebears in their political weight? The Muslims of Bangladesh—well, you know, they do not count as much as even Pakistan.'[3]

For Indian Muslims, 15 August 1947 was the gloomiest day of their history. 'What the Muslim community got out of independence and partition was a sense of insecurity, frustration and uncertainty'.[4] A Pakistani scholar, I. H. Qureshi, predicted that 'in a hundred years, perhaps in a shorter time, the Muslim people may cease to exist in India'.[5]

The trauma of the Muslim community after Partition is often compared with what it suffered at the time of the collapse of the Mughal empire. But at that time, the community retained its self-esteem and the goodwill of its compatriots. This is borne out by the fact that a Muslim was accepted by the whole nation as a symbol and leader of the first war of independence in 1857. Moreover, the presence of British power ensured that the Muslims were not discriminated against.

But in 1947, the Muslims could not bank on a third power and lost much of the respect of the majority community for the role some of them had played in the disintegration of the country. In terms of their self-confidence, prestige and role, the Partition marked a break in the 800 years of Muslim history in India. In many respects, it was the birth of a new community.

The community received no guidance from its erstwhile leaders except a counsel of despair, resignation and withdrawal. Jamaat-e-Islami leader Maulana Maudoodi, who migrated to Pakistan, advised his followers in India 'to create a large-scale public opinion among the Muslims that they should, as a community, have nothing to do with the government and its administration'. While pleading for an Islamic state for Pakistan, he found nothing wrong in the formation of Hindu Raj in India.[6] The Indian branch of the Jamaat-e-Islami considered it 'terribly suicidal' for 'Muslims to strive for some communal rights'.[7]

The Muslim League leaders, while migrating to Pakistan, left just 'Khuda Hafiz' to tend their former followers in India. Those who remained behind became irrelevant.

Reversal of Communal Tide

It was Maulana Abul Kalam Azad, 'the lonely and tragic figure of Muslim politics',[8] who provided beacon light in this hour of darkness. In a touching and inspiring speech at the Delhi Muslim Convention on 4 November 1947, he called upon the Indian Muslims 'to take the pledge that this country is ours, that we belong to it and that fundamental decisions of its destiny will remain incomplete till we participate in them'. There is no place, he declared, 'for either cowardice or frenzy in a Muslim'.[9]

Maulana's status in the freedom movement and in the Government of India made him a source of hope and confidence for the Muslim community.

Two more factors had a decisive impact on the communal situation in the country. Accession of the Muslim majority state of Jammu and Kashmir to India on 26 October 1947 stemmed and reversed the anti-Muslim tide in north India. Gandhi's martyrdom on 30 January 1948 was another decisive blow to the communal hysteria. In addition, Jawaharlal Nehru's determined leadership consolidated the secular democratic basis of the Indian state.

The Partition did cast its shadow on the process of Constitution making. The traditional Muslim demands for reservation in jobs and legislatures, proportional representation, etc., were voluntarily withdrawn by the Muslim members of the Constituent Assembly. They ungrudgingly accepted Hindi as the official language of the country without pressing the claims of Urdu or Hindustani. The Partition also strengthened the case for a strong centre and against provisions for decentralisation and autonomy lest they should further threaten the unity of the country.

However, the founding fathers of the Indian Constitution provided for fundamental rights and minority rights which constitute the essentials of the principles of secularism and democracy. According to the noted constitutional authority D. D. Basu, 'the sum total of the constitutional provisions make our state more secular than even the US'.[10]

Achievements of India in the early years of Independence such as embarking on a planned development, laying foundations of democratic institutions, building an administrative edifice, ensuring internal stability and acquiring an international status owed a lot to its adherence to the basic principles of secular democracy and, in turn, strengthened the faith of its people in these principles.

India's goodwill in West Asia, symbolised by personal friendship of Nehru with Nasser, which isolated Pakistan in the Muslim world, was a more tangible dividend of secularism and a matter of pride for Indian Muslims.

Role of ideology in post-Independence India also undermined communal polarisation, for political parties in the 1950s were broadly formed on ideological bases, with the Congress on the left of the centre and the socialists as the main opposition. Other ideologies of the political spectrum included Marxism of the Communist Party, liberal capitalism of the Swatantra Party, and assertive nationalism of the Bhartiya Jan Sangh. There was no important party, except the Muslim League in Kerala and the Akali Dal of Punjab, which excluded members of the other communities from its membership.

Another factor that discouraged community-based identities in the period was the resurgence of regional identities, followed by linguistic reorganisation of the country in 1956.

Not that the Muslims did not have any problems in this period. But their expectations were low and fears high. The system offered more than they expected and was less hostile than they feared. Pakistan's comparatively poor performance in foreign affairs, functioning of democracy, and industrialisation, too, inspired better confidence in Indian Muslims in the system of their country.

These must have been the factors that encouraged eminent scholar of Islam, W. C. Smith, to predict in the mid-1950s that 'Islam in India would emerge as more progressive, dynamic, liberal and creative than Pakistani Islam'.[11]

How far did the promises of the 1950s, the decade of triumphant secularism, materialise? The later developments indicated that they were no less illusory than the prophecies of gloom in 1947.

Assertion of Self-identity

Gradually, the Muslim mood of withdrawal and resignation gave way to consciousness of rights, assertion of identity and protest against perceived injustices. A number of developments were responsible for this transformation.

During the 1950s, the Muslims lost three stalwarts among their leadership. Maulana Abul Kalam Azad and Rafi Ahmad Kidwai died, while Sheikh Abdullah was put under indefinite detention for allegedly conspiring to bring about Kashmiri secession from India. Azad's interpretation of the Quran and Islam had provided religious sanction to the concept of composite Indian nationalism and had reconciled its claims with urge for Muslim identity. Kidwai, as a fine specimen of the Ganga-Yamuna culture, could communicate with non-Muslims through a common idiom. Hafiz Ibrahim and M. C. Chagla who replaced Azad and Kidwai in the union cabinet could give neither religious, nor cultural expression to Muslim aspirations.

Abdullah had demonstrated the confidence of the Muslim community in the secular polity of India as also the tangible benefits of secularism to Indian nationalism. His arrest made many Muslims wonder why even Abdullah was not trusted in India. With his arrest, Kashmir, which had played a crucial role in reversing the communal tide in 1947, became, in later years, a factor in the revival of communalism in the country.

Azad, Kidwai and Abdullah not only inspired self-confidence in the Muslim community, but were also effective in building inter-community bridges. In their absence, the cause of inter-community understanding suffered.

Leadership Vacuum

At organisational level, the leadership of the Muslim community, after the Partition, was thrust upon the Jamiat-ul-Ulema Hind, an ally of the Congress Party. But it continued to suffer from the inadequacies on account of which it had lost the race for Muslim leadership the Muslim League before the Partition. Muslim political and cultural aspirations could not fully fit into its theological straitjacket. The Jamiat's concept of nationalism as a contract between Hindus and Muslims—along the lines of the Madina covenant that the Prophet of Islam had forged between Muslims and non-Muslims to form a common community at Madina—no longer impressed Hindus after the Muslim demand for a separate state had been conceded.

The Jamiat was all along an appendix of the ruling Congress Party, through which the latter sought to consolidate its vote bank. The Jamiat thereby acquired an image of a sarkari party and was as such incapable of representing anti-establishment sentiments which were bound to exist, in some degree, among the Muslims, as they did in any other community. But these sentiments could not get an adequate expression in the then prevailing one-party-dominant system in the country.

Conscious of its limitations, the Jamiat sought to broad-base its activities and took the initiative in convening an all-India Muslim convention in June 1961. It excluded what were called communal parties like the Muslim League and the Jamaat-e-Islami. But a group of the Jamiat-ul-Ulema, led by Mufti Atiqur Rahman, publicly favoured cooperation with the Jamaat. The convention was further split on a resolution of the communist leader Z. A. Ahmed aiming to ban communal parties.

All in all, the ground left vacant by the Muslim League, as a consequence of the Partition, and due to the absence of Azad, Kidwai and Abdullah could not be fully filled by the Jamiat or any coalition of Muslim parties or any secular party. Muslims, thus, lacked not only adequate articulation, but also a communication link with the Hindu majority.

Perhaps the first communal riot, which took place in Jabalpur in Madhya Pradesh in 1961, after a decade of communal peace, reflected this basic deficiency of the Indian polity at that stage rather than a mere aberration caused by a local event. The fact that a Hindu girl of a *bidi* manufacturer eloped with a Muslim boy of another bidi manufacturer could cause a sense of humiliation in the Hindu community and that the two communities had developed business rivalry due to competition of two bidi manufacturers merely indicated lack of trust between the two exclusive communal alignments.

Nehru was still the most effective inter-community bridge. He was shaken by the Jabalpur riot and renewed his offensive against communalism. He also set up the National Integration Council. However, the upsurge of patriotism among all communities following the Sino-India war of 1962 led the Asoka Mehta Committee, appointed by the council, to declare that its role had become redundant.

The euphoria over national integration was rudely shaken by the chain of communal riots in 1964 at Jamshedpur and Rourkela. But their epicentre significantly lay in the valley of Kashmir. Already agitated against a regime of corruption and repression imposed on them through rigged election, Kashmiri Muslims were enraged over the theft of a holy relic (sacred hair of the Prophet) from the Hazratbal shrine in early 1964. The reports of the suppression of the angry masses, including police firing on them, had a backlash in Dhaka, the capital of the then East Pakistan. A chain reaction of anti-Muslim riots within India followed thereafter.

Post-Nehru Era

The riots jolted the Muslims of India into a radical rethinking of their role. The riots were cited as the one main reason for convening what was called the Muslim Majlis-e-Mushawarat at Lucknow on 8–9 August 1964. It was convened by a veteran Congress leader, Syed Mahmud, at the initiative of a former socialist leader, A. J. Faridi, and was attended by about 80 Muslim leaders belonging to different schools of thought from all over India. In his address, as chairman of the reception committee, Faridi said: 'Since independence Muslims had almost retired from politics. But what happened in the two decades that followed showed that it was not a wise decision.'[12]

Though the Mushawarat was merely a coordinating body and not a political party, it was the most significant development in the Muslim politics of India after the death of Nehru and indicated decline of trust of the community in the post-Nehru leadership. It marked the first effective self-assertion by Muslims. In a way, the Nehru era had ended before his death in May 1964. After India's humiliating defeat by China in 1962, he had suffered a political, mental and physical setback from which he never recovered. The incidents in Kashmir and the reactions to them had taken place when he had been publicly declared to be ill.

Some more developments in the post-Nehru era adversely affected the Muslim mind. The new government at the centre took measures for the forced constitutional integration of Jammu and Kashmir with the union of India in the teeth of opposition of the Kashmiri Muslims. Change in the nomenclature of the head of the state and of the government, the change in the status of the former from being elected by the state assembly to being nominated by the president of India, extension of emergency provisions of the Indian Constitution to the state, and conversion of the regional National Conference to a branch of the Indian National Congress created an unprecedented wave of anger in Kashmir which tempted Pakistan to send armed infiltrators into Kashmir, leading to the Indo-Pak war of 1965.

Though Sheikh Abdullah had ceased to be a hero of Indian nationalism since 1953, the ideological umbilical cord between the Kashmiri nationalism and the Indian nationalism, led, respectively, by him and Nehru, was not cut during the Nehru era. But after the integrationist measures of 1964 and 1965, Kashmiri Muslim bitterness against India reached new heights; it eroded their ideological affinity as well.

The Indo-Pak war in 1965, following the developments in Kashmir, was another crucial impact on the Muslim situation. It was a war between two nation-states which established, as nothing had done before, the position of Indian Muslims as part of the Indian nation. Their participation in and contribution to the war effort, symbolised by Havaldar Abdul Hamid, who was posthumously honoured with the highest military award of Param Vir Chakra, added to their confidence in their Indian identity.

But the war also brought into sharp focus the perennial controversy over the Muslim attitude towards Pakistan. For, most Muslims could not match the intensity of hatred of an average Hindu towards the national enemy. This fact prepared the ground for a whisper campaign against Muslims in general and the Muslim dignitaries at the highest positions in particular, casting aspersion on their loyalty and patriotism.

Some people, of course, took a more sympathetic view of the Muslim mind on the subject. Commenting on this controversy, eminent journalist B. G. Verghese concluded: 'It was probably true that some or many Indian Muslims had a feeling of sympathy towards Pakistan and wished it well. But it hardly constitutes a charge of disloyalty.'[13] The veteran former communist leader B. P. L. Bedi asked in the same vein: 'Why should it be expected at all of any Indian Muslim to prove his loyalty to India through his enmity of Pakistan?' He asserted that 'there was nothing inconsistent in an Indian Muslim being at heart fully and totally loyal to India and a well-wisher of Pakistan'.[14]

But most of the Hindus would not take such a generous view. They rarely drew a distinction between transnational affinities and extra-territorial loyalty. Representing the other end of the political spectrum, the then Jana Sangh leader Atal Bihari Vajpayee asserted: 'It is a fact that many Muslims find Pakistan dearer than India and Al-Aqsa nearer than Jagan Nath'. Those who felt alienated, he said, 'are free to leave the country'.[15] Anti-Pakistanism almost became a litmus test of loyalty to India, in particular for Muslims who had not been forgiven for their alleged role in the vivisection of the country in 1947.

Shedding the Guilt

However, after 1965, the reaction of the Muslims to this view was no more apologetic. The post-Independence generation was not loaded with a sense of guilt for the creation of Pakistan and refused to be answerable for the sins the previous generation was supposed to have committed. In fact, some fresh evidence and theories were cited to prove that the Muslims alone could not be blamed for the Partition. Maulana Azad, for instance, in his book *India Wins Freedom*, especially the part that was released 30 years after his death, holds Congress leaders, including Nehru, equally responsible for it. In a more strident tone, the Jamaat-e-Islami's official organ *Radiance* editorially asserted: 'Post-independence Muslim is not prepared to listen to any non-sense with regard to his or his parents' role, if any, in the partition, for which, according to authentic history, Sardar Patel, Jawaharlal Nehru and Mahatma Gandhi were primarily responsible'.[16]

Thus started a new phase of assertion by the Indian Muslims of their Indianness and also of their Muslimhood. They no longer suffered from the schizophrenic pangs of the previous generation caused by claims of dual identity. They insisted on simultaneity of their Indian and Muslim identities. It was the awareness of the former that enabled them to shed all inhibitions in asserting their perception of Muslim identity and interests. They tended to believe that their right to assert themselves flowed from the fact that they were equal citizens of the country.

Many instances can be cited of the twin processes of indigenisation and assertiveness of the Indian Muslims in this period. Many Muslim communities started searching their indigenous roots. Some of them were able to trace their ancestry to the tribes of *Ramayan* and *Mahabbharat*, instead of the foreign Muslim countries as used to be the fashion so far. The growing popularity of the Bareilly school of Islamic learning as against the Deoband school indicated the same trend. For, the former permitted worship at tombs and 'ziarets' of local 'faqirs' and saints, which in a way is confirmation of attachment with the soil.

Symbols of Muslim Identity

So far as Muslim assertion is concerned, it was pronounced on three main issues which emerged as symbols of the Muslim identity, namely, Aligarh Muslim University (AMU), the Urdu language and Muslim Personal Law.

On 20 May 1965, the president of India promulgated the Aligarh Muslim University (Amendment) Ordinance which was enacted by Parliament in its autumn session. It reduced the court of the university to an advisory body, to be wholly nominated by the government. And it appointed a visitor with wide powers. The amendment was intended to bring the AMU at par with other central universities. An earlier attempt to drop Hindu and Muslim words from the names of the Benaras and Aligarh universities, respectively, in order to deemphasise their communal character, was abandoned due mainly to the opposition of the Muslim community. The new attempt to change the minority character of AMU alone met with greater opposition of the community.

The status of Urdu in Uttar Pradesh and Bihar also became a live issue. For, though Muslims reconciled to the displacement of Urdu from its preeminent position of pre-Independence days in view of the changed political situation, they aspired for at least a second language status for it.

The role of Urdu-speaking Muslims in the Muslim politics of India, before and after the Partition, needs no emphasis. The case of Urdu is often presented on the basis of secular arguments as it is claimed to symbolise a composite culture. But the fact is, observes Muhammad Qamaruddin, that 'a Muslim's love for Urdu is only second to the regard for his religion'.[17] Similarly, discussing the fate of Urdu in India, W. C. Smith opines: 'The Indian Muslim community is in danger of being deprived of its language, than which only religious faith is a deeper possession'.[18] Thus, though, there were many eminent Hindus among the 22 lakh signatories to the memorandum demanding rightful status for Urdu—the memorandum was submitted to the President of India, Rajendra Prasad—it reflected the innermost urge of the Muslim community.

The third symbol of the Muslim identity, namely, the Muslim Personal law, was soon to become the most explosive communal issue. As J. D. M. Derret had warned in 1968: 'If there is a frontal attack on the Personal Law in India, it will survive with a tenacity it has been unable to show in countries where the majority of the population are, and always have been, Muslims'.[19]

It is true that with the proliferation of educational institutions all over the country, increasingly a smaller percentage of Muslim students is dependent on the AMU for its educational needs. With the growth of regional languages and identities, fewer of Muslims need Urdu for self-expression. With the increasing awareness among women about their rights, and with the growth of the present socio-economic conditions, polygamy and some other provisions of the Muslim Personal Law have become obsolescent. But it is futile to argue against the utility of these symbols. For, a community adopts such symbols not out of a rational choice but under a certain combination of circumstances. In the case of Muslims, they emerged as a manifestation of their urge for identity.

The exclusivist trends in this urge were encouraged by the ambition of some leaders of the community to project it as the balancing force in a politics polarised between a weakened Congress and the united opposition in 1967. The Jamaat-e-Islami organ *Dawat* quoted S. W. Hussain to assert that there were not two (Congress and opposition) but three forces in the country; the third being the Muslims.[20] But the ambition of building a solid Muslim block balancing and dominating national politics was obviously too unrealistic to materialise and merely provoked the majority community to close its ranks at many places.

The assertive phase of Muslim politics witnessed communal tensions and riots. Starting from Jabalpur (1964), there were 3,646 riots in various parts of the country, in some cases for the first time, culminating in Gujarat, the state of Gandhi's birth, in his centenary year of 1969, taking a toll of 674 human lives, the worst till date since the Partition.[21]

Clash with Nationalism

In the 1970s, the Muslim community became further out of tune with the nationalist sentiments during the Bangladesh movement. Excepting the Bengali Muslims, the Muslim community felt culturally and emotionally closer to what was West Pakistan. The events in Bangladesh and the part that India played in the break-up of Pakistan in 1971 did not find favour, according to K. L. Gauba, among the Muslims in general.[22]

Articulating the general Muslim feelings on the subject, Maulana Abul Hasan Ali Nadvi regretted that 'in a country with Muslim majority, the idol of language prevailed... and national and racial zealotry smashed the brotherhood [sic] of Islam'. Its most shameful aspect, according to him, 'has been to arm the enemies of Islam with one more weapon against it'.[23]

Meanwhile, Indian nationalism, under the leadership of Indira Gandhi, hailed as an avatar of goddess Durga by Vajpayee, acquired a more strident and masculine character; it felt encouraged by the two victories against Pakistan (and its split), the annexation of Sikkim and a nuclear explosion.

While for M. K. Gandhi, Indian nationalism was a means for the attainment of a higher moral objective, and while Nehru formulated the demands of national interest in a moral idiom, Indira Gandhi's concept of nationalism was amoral and an end in itself. She aspired for a role for India on the basis of merely its physical strength, for which, she believed, solid support of the whole nation without dissent was necessary. Nationalism thus got differentiated from patriotism and political values like freedom and democracy became subordinate to it.

There were also some other political factors that contributed to the emergence of this situation, for example the imposition of the Emergency in the country in June 1975 against which Jayaprakash Narayan (JP) led a revolt. Muslims felt as suffocated during the Emergency regime as any other community and by and large supported the Janata Party in overthrowing it in the general elections of 1977.

For a while, Congress–Janata polarisation replaced the communal divide of the Indian politics. As co-sufferers of the Emergency and availing the opportunity for a dialogue in jails, the Rashtriya Swayamsevak Sangh (RSS) and Jamaat-e-Islami leaders developed mutual cordiality and exuded a fresh optimism about Hindu–Muslim relations. The basis of their dialogue was not made public. But in keeping with their known stand, the scope for evolving a community-based (instead of region-based) federal polity was perhaps explored. But it did not make much headway on account of the obvious impracticability of the idea.

Another hopeful pointer was the willingness of the RSS to consider JP's advice for allowing non-Hindus, including Muslims, into its fold. The erstwhile Jan Sangh, after its merger with the Janata Party, accepted all the secular formulations of the latter. Fresh initiative to improve Indo-Pak relations and the first fair election in the history of Kashmir, that went a long away in reviving the confidence of its people in Indian democracy and about their future therein, had a salutary effect on the communal climate in the whole country.

However, the Janata coalition, that JP had cobbled up together and had been cemented by anti-Congressism, collapsed under the weight of its own contradictions. JP regretted that the RSS did not implement his advice despite assurances to open its doors to Muslims.[24] The issue of the dual membership of RSS followers in the Janata Party led to its split and the return to power of Indira Gandhi, in the elections of 1980, with the slogan of a strong nation and a strong government. She is accused of playing the Hindu card in the election campaign.

Her frequent visits to Hindu shrines and religious personalities gave her a religious image. But what really endeared her to Hindu militants was her militant nationalism, which she first introduced in Indian politics in the early 1970s and which tended to fill in the ideological vacuum to which the Indira–JP confrontation had significantly contributed as none of the sides was ideologically based. Indira's no-nonsense attitude towards foreign powers and ethnic and religious minorities within the country reflected a militant nationalist mood.

Her refusal to condemn the entry of Soviet forces into Afghanistan, which aroused indignation of the Muslim world, the projection of Pakistan as a source of threat to India's security, and the reference to the possible role of the Gulf money in the conversion of the scheduled castes of Meenakshipuram to Islam in 1981 appealed to those Hindus who were scared by the resurgence of Islam outside and Muslim assertion within the country. The dismissal of the Akali-led government in Punjab in 1980, the army action at the Sikh Golden Temple at Amritsar in 1984, and the dismissal of the duly elected government of Farooq Abdullah in Kashmir in 1984 by engineering defection on the ground of his alleged anti-national role enabled Indira Gandhi to satisfy the militant nationalist sentiments of the Hindus.

The controversy over whether she became a staunch Hindu or remained a nationalist is irrelevant, for the dividing line between Hindu communalism and the extreme form of Indian nationalism is rather blurred. The majority everywhere tends to assume the right to define the parameters of nationalism. But in India's case, Hinduism is not merely another religion but a representative of the ancient and native heritage and may even be called a religionised version of Indian nationalism. The ancient national heroes being its gods, national epics being its scriptures, Indian mythology comprising the core of its theology, and Bharat Mata being its most sacred deity, Indian nationalism, ancient history and cultural heritage, and Indian mythology cannot be easily distinguished from the Hindu religion. The Hindu reaction to the Partition should be understood in the context. It was not treated merely as a separation of the Muslim majority parts of the subcontinent from its Hindu majority parts, which damaged Muslim interests more than the Hindu interests, but as a vivisection of the limbs of Mother India, the latter perception caused a spiritual and emotional shock to the Hindu consciousness and hence the Partition was seen as an unforgivable crime on the part of those who had demanded it.

It is on account of this conceptual ambiguity about Indian nationalism that it does not evoke the same degree of emotional response from all communities of India. How could Muslims, for instance, worship Bharat Mata, Ram and Krishna even though they might have reverence for them? For, 'Muslims particularly being non-idolatrous, are conscience-bound not to entertain any such loyalty that places them against God'.[25] Nor does an average Muslim share the degree of hatred for Pakistan that has become a second nature with many a Hindu nationalist.

Nationalism in India's case has never been a unifying force; not even when it was tempered with Gandhian compassion and Nehruvian sophistication. Jinnah's, after all, was a reaction to the Gandhi–Nehru brand of nationalism and not to that of Savarkar and Golwalkar who were non-entities at that time. But as Jinnah's remedy proved worse than the disease, Muslims in India had reconciled to that brand. But the crude and militant phase of Indian nationalism which prevailed in India in the 1980s after the second tenure of Indira Gandhi made fresh demands of conformity and uniformity which minorities, including Muslims and Sikhs, were unwilling to accept.

This phase of Indian nationalism coincided with what was called the Islamic wave, triggered off by the Khomeini revolution in Iran, in 1979–80. The ripples of this wave crossed over to the Indian borders which further encouraged the Muslim assertion that was rising due to autonomous indigenous factors already discussed.

[...]

NOTES AND REFERENCES

1. Sir Allama Muhammed Iqbal. 1977. *Rooh-i-Makateeb Iqbal.* Lahore: Iqbal Academy, 638.
2. Quoted in: uz-Zaman, Khaliq. 1961. *Pathways to Pakistan.* Lahore: Longman, 1961.
3. Letter to Khaliq-uz-Zaman dated 10 September 1947, ibid.
4. Shakir, Moin. N.d. *Muslims in Free India.* New Delhi: Kalamkar Prakashan.

5. Qureshi, I. H. 1954. 'Haya 'Alā-L-Falāh'. *Muslim World* 44 (1), 1 January, 1–11.

6. Quoted in the official organ of the Jamat-e-Islami Hind, the *Radiance*, New Delhi, 17 December 1960.

7. Ibid.

8. Krishna, Gopal. 1976 in *Muslim Communities of South Asia*, ed. T. N. Madan. New Delhi: Vikas, 154.

9. Quoted in: Karandikar, M. A. 1968. *Islam in Tradition to Modernity*. Hyderabad: Orient BlackSwan.

10. Quoted in: Bhamhri, C. P. 1992. *Financial Express*. 24 May.

11. Smith, W. C. 1957. *Islam in Modern History*. Princeton: Princeton University Press.

12. Gauba, K. L. 1973. *Passive Voices*. New Delhi: Sterling, 282.

13. *The Times of India*. 12 August 1965.

14. Bedi, B. P. L. 1965. *India, Indian Muslims and Pakistan*. New Delhi.

15. Quoted in *Radiance*, 18–24 February 1990.

16. Editorial in *Radiance*, 28 January–3 February 1990.

17. *The Times of India*. 28 April 1987.

18. Smith, W. C. 1957. *Islam in Modern History*, 266–67.

19. Derret, J. D. M. 1968. *Religion, Law and State in India*. New York: Free Press.

20. *Dawat*. Delhi, 7 November 1967.

21. Saxena, N. S. *The Times of India*. 4 January 1988.

22. Gauba, K. L. 1973. *Passive Voices*, 352.

23. Quoted in: Madan, T. N. 1976. *Muslim Communities in South Asia*. New Delhi: Vikas, 154.

24. Referring to the repeated but unimplemented assurance of the RSS leaders to include non-Hindus—Muslims, Christians, etc.—in it, JP lamented, 'It.. continuing like this for the last four years. After all there is a limit to everything'. *Dinman Weekly*. 8–14 April 1979.

25. Haq, Jalalul. 1992. *Nation and Nation Worship in India*. New Delhi: Genuine Publications, 89.

24

PUTTING GUJARAT IN PERSPECTIVE*

STEVEN I. WILKINSON

The exact course of events that began with the Godhra attack on 27 February 2002 remains unclear, as is almost always the case with 'communal' riots. What almost everyone agrees upon, however, is that by the beginning of April 2002, more than 800 people had been killed and many more injured in the communal riots in Gujarat even by the lowest estimates, primarily in the major cities of Ahmedabad, Surat and Vadodara but also in some smaller towns and a few villages. In many instances, the violence was targeted and highly organised, with rioters having apparently obtained detailed lists of Muslim-owned houses, flats and shops. Initial estimates of the economic damage in Gujarat have been put at around Rs 5,000 crore, or over a billion US dollars, and this figure does not factor in losses from the investments that will now not be made in the state.[1]

The response of Gujarat's Bharatiya Janata Party (BJP) government has, by common consent, been at best, weak and at worst, outright biased. Some riot victims have alleged that the police refused to come to their aid and others have alleged police complicity during the riots or partiality in their subsequent arrests and prosecutions.[2] Most notably, it came to light in late March that 60 Muslims involved in the initial Godhra violence had been arrested under the draconian Prevention of Terrorism Ordinance, but that the ordinance had been applied to none of the 800 Hindus picked up for participating in anti-Muslim violence.[3] Chief Minister Narendra Modi and several other politicians in Gujarat seemed to excuse the attacks by explaining that they were the outcome of 'public anger' over the Godhra attack, and that 'every action has an equal and opposite reaction'. The government stated several times that it was doing everything it could with the forces at its disposal, but it delayed calling in the Army, an action that everyone acknowledged could have prevented the riots from spreading.[4]

The Gujarat violence has been so truly awful that it is perhaps necessary to remind ourselves that seen in the context of the previous major riots in India, the recent events have not been exceptional. In all the largest communal riots since Independence—for example, in Mumbai in 1984 and 1992–93, Bhagalpur in

* *Economic and Political Weekly* 37 (17): 1579–83 (27 April 2002).

1989, Meerut in 1987, Jamshedpur in 1979, and in Ahmedabad in 1969—state governments from several various political parties have, as in Gujarat, delayed taking action to stop the violence for days or even weeks. In most of these riots, as in Gujarat in the past month, minorities suffered disproportionately. The Minorities Commission's figures on communal riots that took place from 1985–87, for example, found that 60 per cent of the 443 people killed were Muslims and that Muslims had suffered 73 per cent of the Rs 9 crore in reported property damage.[5] Commissions of inquiry prior to the 1980s found a similar pattern: in Bhiwandi in 1970, for example, the Madon Commission found that only 324 Hindus were arrested compared to 2,183 Muslims, that 'only Muslims died in police firings', and that half of the firings that took place were 'wholly unjustified'.[6]

This chapter will not revisit the events of the last month in Gujarat, or examine the sorry history of previous communal riots in India. Nor will I examine here the complex factors that determine why violence may be more or less likely to break out in one town or city rather than another in the first place.[7] Rather, my purpose in this essay is to ask why, given that state governments are responsible for law and order in India, some state governments prevent communal violence while others do not. I consider three possible explanations for differences in state performance: first, that decades of corruption, criminalisation, politicisation and a general lack of state capacity have left Indian state governments too weak to prevent riots; second, that Indian state governments are unwilling or unable to protect minorities because they systematically under-represent Muslims and other minorities within their governments, police forces and local administrations; and third, that the degree of party competition affects the value governments place on attracting Muslim swing voters, which in turn has an effect on whether governments will order their administrations to protect minorities. After providing some evidence that the first two explanations do not account for the pattern of state-level variation, I argue that the level of a state's party competition is the most important factor in determining the government's response to outbreaks of communal violence. My research suggests that the increase in political competition in India in recent years has made minorities a pivotal swing vote in many states, which in turn has forced state politicians to promise and provide greater security for minorities. Already, I argue, the actions of Indian state governments outside Gujarat in March 2002 should make us optimistic about ways in which greater political competition will reduce communal violence in the future.[8]

Are India's States Ethnically Biased?

After large-scale ethnic violence in India or in many other countries, there are often calls for state governments and police forces to be made more ethnically representative in order to prevent future riots. Proponents of proportionality or 'descriptive representation' argue that a larger number of minorities will increase minority confidence in the police, will serve as a check on biased officers within the force, and that greater exposure to officers from other communities will help to make officials more tolerant. After the 1969 Ahmedabad riots, for example, Khushwant Singh argued that the best way to stop communal violence was to ensure that most states' police forces contained 20–25 per cent minorities.[9] Arguments that increasing proportionality will reduce communal violence have also been put forward in recent decades by the 1983 Gopal Singh Committee on minorities, by Muslim leaders such as Syed Shahabuddin and even by a few Indian police officials.[10]

Unfortunately for proponents of this theory, the evidence that ethnic proportionality in a state's police force or administration always goes hand in hand with lower levels of communal violence is weak. In Table 24.1, I present a summary of some state-level data I have collected on minority proportionality in the police and state cabinets for 1975–95 for major Indian states, together with data on Hindu–Muslim violence in those states, drawn from a 1950–95 riot database I collected jointly with Ashutosh Varshney of the University of Michigan.[11] The two columns on the right hand side of the table display the percentage difference between the Muslim proportion in each state and the average percentage of Muslims in each state's cabinet and police force respectively. As we can see, while it is true that some states that under-represent Muslims in the police have had many riots (for example, Maharashtra and Gujarat where Muslims are underrepresented by 6 per cent and 3 per cent, respectively), other states with equally low levels of Muslim proportionality in their police forces or state cabinets (such as Rajasthan) also seem to have done quite well in controlling their levels of communal violence.

TABLE 24.1: Minority Representation and Communal Violence in States 1975–95

	State Muslim Per Cent	*Average Riots per Month*	*Average Killed per Month*	*Cabinet Under- or Over- Representation of Muslims Per Cent*	*Police Under- or Over- Representation of Muslims Per Cent*
West Bengal	23	0.09	0.42	–15	–16
Kerala	22	0.03	0.02	–10	–13
Bihar	14	0.19	2.86	–5	–12
Uttar Pradesh	17	0.49	4.28	–4	–10
Maharashtra	10	0.54	4.61	–4	–6
Gujarat	9	0.80	3.69	–4	–3
Rajasthan	8	0.07	0.29	–4	–3
Haryana	4	0.01	0.02	–1	–3
Karnataka	11	0.22	0.94	0	–3
Andhra Pradesh	9	0.15	1.27	–4	1
Himachal Pradesh	2	0.00	0.00	–2	–1
Madhya Pradesh	5	0.09	0.73	–1	0
Tamil Nadu	5	0.06	0.13	–1	0

Source: Muslim percentage in state population from Census of India 1991; Riot and death data from 1950–95 dataset collected jointly by the author and Ashutosh Varshney; Cabinet representation from a name analysis conducted by Wilkinson of state cabinets reported in the *Journal of Parliamentary Information* from 1975–95; Police representation from Table 11.17.2 *National Commission for Minorities Third Annual Report* (FY 1995–96), 143–46, and earlier reports.

The two states that on average under-represent Muslims the most in government and administration, West Bengal and Kerala, have levels of Hindu–Muslim violence that are considerably lower than states such as Andhra Pradesh and Madhya Pradesh where Muslims are much better represented in their cabinets and the state police forces. Kerala, for example, has fewer than half the number of Muslims in its police force that proportionality would require (10 per cent compared to a Muslim population of 23 per cent), and an even lower percentage of minority representation in other services.[12] As the table shows, however, Kerala has one of the lowest per capita levels of riots and deaths of any major Indian state. Some additional statistical tests I have carried out for a completed book manuscript (Wilkinson 2004) found that not only was police proportionality unrelated to a state's level of communal violence, but that factors such as the percentage of Muslims in a state's cabinet or full council of ministers also made absolutely no difference to a state's level of per capita communal violence.

I am certainly not trying to make the case here that ethnic proportionality is undesirable, simply that the evidence seems to show that proportionality is not a necessary condition for a force's ability to control communal violence. Additional support for this proposition comes, I would argue, from the fact that the central government forces that have the best reputations for impartiality and efficiency in stopping and preventing riots have exactly the same low proportion of Muslims as the state forces with the worst reputations. The central government's main anti-riot force, for example, the 1,50,000-strong Central Reserve Police Force (CRPF) was only 5.5 per cent Muslim in 1993, compared to the 12 per cent Muslim share of the general population.[13] Yet Muslim leaders frequently call on the CRPF to be stationed in towns because they do not trust forces such as the Uttar Pradesh Provincial Armed Constabulary or the Bihar Special Police, which have an identically low proportion of Muslims.[14]

Are India's States too Weak?

According to many students of Indian politics, a whole series of factors—the progressive politicisation of India's state police forces and bureaucracies, the deinstitutionalisation of the Congress Party after the 1960s, growing criminalisation, and Indian states' growing fiscal crises—has left state governments unable to prevent communal riots from taking place, or to quickly stop them once they do break out. Atul Kohli, in a fascinating study that examines amongst other things the effects of the politicisation of the bureaucracy and police since the 1960s, argues that, 'what started out as a strategy to enhance political control has unanticipated and unfortunate consequences: When leaders now need to call on the police arm of the state, that arm is relatively limp'.[15]

The problems Kohli and others identify are real: local officers are transferred in and out of positions too quickly; they are often reluctant to cross locally influential figures who might be able to have them transferred; some officials (though certainly not all) are unwilling to enforce the law without checking to see what the political fallout might be; and there is also growing corruption and factional politics within the police and bureaucracy that hampers their efficiency. All this does not mean, however, that India's state governments are incapable of preventing communal violence. For proof of this, consider that the state administrations that are generally regarded as being the country's weakest, such as Uttar Pradesh and Bihar, have proven quite effective, when given clear and unmistakable orders from their political masters, in preventing communal violence. Uttar Pradesh, for example, has had generally low levels of violence since 1993 though few would argue that the state has got stronger during this time. In 1995, most strikingly, the coalition BJP–BSP (Bahujan Samaj Party) government successfully prevented a repeat of the Ayodhya violence by restricting Vishva Hindu Parishad (VHP) plans to mobilise around another disputed religious site at Mathura.

Another reason for doubting a too-simple connection between state weakness and communal violence is that independent investigations into the very worst cases of violence have all identified the state government's lack of purpose and clear orders, rather than any lack of state strength, as the key factor prolonging the violence. After the September 1969 Ahmedabad riots, for example, the Reddy Commission found that the delay in imposing the curfew (a delay during which 250 properties were damaged, eight religious places attacked, five people murdered and four injured) took place because '...the Inspector General of Police before advising the commissioner was not prepared to act on his own and was trying to seek the prior approval of the government...'[16] Independent investigations uncovered the same pattern of politically inspired delay in other riots such as Ranchi (1967), Bhagalpur (1989) and Mumbai (1992–93).[17] And during the serious riots in Mumbai in January 1993, the police commissioner S. K. Bapat asked the government for permission to call in 40 army columns to control the rioting on the day violence broke out, 6 January 1993, but the government refused for four days before allowing 12 units into the city, and then only to perform limited duties.[18]

ELECTORAL COMPETITION

Why have some state governments been so much better than others at providing clear directions to their administrations to prevent riots and protecting minorities? Party ideology is often portrayed as the answer, as observers point approvingly to the record of the communist parties in Kerala and West Bengal, or to the performance of chief minister Digvijay Singh's Congress in Madhya Pradesh. Without wishing to undervalue the powerful secular credentials of these governments or their generally impressive record in preventing communal violence, I would argue that the degree of political competitiveness in a state has historically been an even more powerful factor. Focusing on political competitiveness can also help us explain, for example, why governments of all political persuasions in Kerala, not just the Left Democratic Front (LDF) governments, have acted firmly to prevent violence. And examining political competitiveness also helps us explain otherwise inexplicable anomalies such as the BJP–BSP coalition's firm action in deterring a mass VHP mobilisation around the Keshav Das Temple/Idgah complex in Mathura in mid-1995.[19]

Why should the competitiveness of state politics—the number of effective political parties competing in a state—be linked to government protection of minorities? The reason is that the greater the number of effective parties competing for power in a state, the more valuable minority voters become. This has long been true in southern India, for example. In the south, we find that the two major states with the lowest levels of Hindu–Muslim violence—Kerala and Tamil Nadu—are those in which middle and lower caste-based parties emerged earliest, strong party competition has existed since the early 1960s and changes of ruling party have been most frequent. These states have been so competitive, in large part, because the strength of pre-Independence political and social mobilisation by backward class movements allowed backward caste-dominated parties—the communists in Kerala and the Dravida Munnetra Kazhagam (DMK) in Tamil Nadu—to mobilise effective opposition parties to the Congress as early as the 1950s and 1960s. The continuing strength of middle and lower-caste mobilisation in the south and mobilisation around a Dravidian identity has prevented the Hindu–Muslim divide from becoming the central political cleavage there as it has been in the north.

Politics in the south has, since the early 1960s, been highly competitive, with Muslim voters and Muslim parties often the pivotal group that decides which party or coalition will gain power. Governments have in consequence been very active in preventing Hindu–Muslim violence. In Kerala, for example, the high degree of political competition between the LDF and United Democratic Front (UDF) means that the small Muslim political parties, which typically control 14–20 seats in a 140-seat state assembly, have been in a good position to forcefully demand security guarantees from the other parties as the price of their swing vote. In 1992, as the Ayodhya mosque agitation was reaching dangerous levels throughout India, the leader of the major Muslim party in Kerala pointedly invited the leaders of the main opposition party, the LDF, to dinner and threatened to bring Kerala's Congress-led coalition government down unless there was a speedy overhaul of the police and bureaucracy, and strong action against those who were trying to incite anti-Muslim riots.[20] Given the fact that Kerala governments typically have a majority of only a handful of seats, these Muslim security demands work. The state in Kerala massively deploys state forces to prevent riots, intervenes quickly and decisively when riots break out and punishes officials who fail to stop riots. After riots broke out in Kerala in 1971 for example, the police quickly cordoned off the town of Thalasseri and then rushed in armed reinforcements.[21] In the Kerala state capital, in 1985, the police opened fire to disperse large mobs that seemed to be on the brink of a communal riot.[22] In contrast to the pattern in states such as Bihar, Uttar Pradesh and Gujarat, press reports from the south suggest that almost all the deaths in riots in Kerala and Tamil Nadu over the past few decades have occurred due to police firing, rather than as a result of anti-Muslim pogroms.

My analysis of 1950–95 riot data I collected with Ashutosh Varshney shows that 79 per cent of all Hindu–Muslim riots in Kerala since Independence were stopped within a single day, 95 per cent within two days. In Tamil Nadu, a state that has also seen a healthily competitive state political system since the 1960s, the figure is even higher, at 91.67 per cent. By comparison, many of the worst riots in Uttar Pradesh in the 1960s and 1970s lasted for five or six days or even longer, and the data show that 45 per cent of all deaths in Hindu–Muslim violence since 1950 took place in the 17 per cent of riots that were allowed to drag on for three days or more. Independent inquiries into riots in Uttar Pradesh and similar states in which the level of political competition was low until the late 1980s found that the local police often illegally delayed action against rioters while they checked to see whether the state government wants them to intervene, and the state government takes its time deciding whether intervention to protect Muslims from Hindus was in its short-term and long-term electoral interest.

The good news for India is that, in part spurred by the growth of parties such as the Samajwadi Party and the BSP, political competition outside the south has increased in recent years, and that this increasing state-level competition, by making Muslim votes more valuable, is already having a moderating effect in many states. In a statistical analysis of party competition and levels of violence over several decades, I found that as the number of parties in a state goes up, the level of communal violence goes down, even when we control for factors such as a state's communal balance, income inequality or previous level of violence.[23] Since the late 1980s, Uttar Pradesh and Bihar have begun to change from one party-dominant systems (under Congress) to party systems in which two or three caste-based Hindu parties are competing for power, and none of these parties is strong enough to win power unaided. Political parties in both states have consequently become newly responsive to their Muslim minorities. In Uttar Pradesh, for example, the BSP forced its coalition partner to restrict a major Hindu nationalist mobilisation in 1995 around the Mathura Idgah complex, a mobilisation that was highly likely to lead to violence because it was attracting Hindu and Muslim militants from all over the state determined to carry out or stop a 'parikrama' at the site. The BSP forced the BJP to impose severe restrictions on the event because the BSP needed to appeal to Muslim voters if it was to have a real chance of victory in the elections to be held in the state in the following year.[24] In Bihar, we see the same link between coalition politics and state preventive actions. Chief Minister Laloo Prasad Yadav was elected with substantial support from Muslims, which he repaid by guaranteeing their security. Just to give one example, as soon as clashes broke out in the sensitive town of Biharsharif in July 1993, Yadav demonstrated his resolve by deploying two companies of central paramilitary forces and 32 fixed and six mobile police response teams to prevent further violence.[25]

In focusing on the agonies of Gujarat over the past two months, it is easy to overlook the important—and, I would argue, hopeful—events in other states. The increasing party competition in India's states and the pivotal power of minority voters has helped to prevent communal violence in 2002 from spreading nationwide as it did in 1992–93. In Andhra Pradesh, Karnataka, West Bengal and other states where Muslims are an important part of the support for the government, we have seen very strong and encouraging action by state governments to prevent Hindu–Muslim violence. In Table 24.2, I present some qualitative evidence that many states outside

TABLE 24.2: Good News: Some State Responses outside Gujarat during March and April 2002

State	*Polarising Events Likely to Lead to Large-scale Violence*	*State Response*	*Mass Violence*
West Bengal	VHP ceremony and processions: 10 March	WB Police firing at Taldi when karsevaks would not disperse: 1 killed; 29 injured; 100 arrests.	Prevented
	Mass Strikes called by VHP and BJP: 11 March	Massive Police Deployment	Prevented
Karnataka	Hindu–Muslim clashes in Mysore Rd area of Bangalore	Curfew and massive police deployment, 40 arrests and punitive transfer of officials. CM S. M. Krishna and former CM Veerappa Moily demonstrated for peace with Muslim politicians	Prevented
	Tensions in Bidar, Indi, Gulbarga, and Bijapur (burning of 'holy book'). 1 killed; 12 injured. Late March–Early April Holi clashes in several cities	Curfew and police raids in which petrol and weapons seized. Mass deployment of KSRP, mass arrests, tear gas fired. Police fired tear gas and carried out lathi charges. Mass deployment of KSRP.	Prevented
Bihar	Pre-Holi tensions. Statues damaged in Munger.	Massive police preparations and preventive measures before Holi; Heavy police deployment	
Rajasthan	VHP-sponsored strikes 1–2 March	Curfew and massive police response in Jaipur, Udaipur, Ajmer and elsewhere. Several killed in police firing in Gangapur and Simalwara as well as mass arrests	Prevented
	26 March: 300-strong Bajrang Dal mob blocking of Muharram procession route in Gangapur	Police ordered them to disperse and when they refused fired 30 rounds at mob, 2 killed and 15 injured	Prevented
Andhra Pradesh	Mid-March demonstrations to parallel Ayodhya movement	Government zero-tolerance policy while efforts to avoid mass deployment of police. Police firing against militants in Hyderabad.	Prevented
Madhya Pradesh	15 March demonstrations to coincide with Ayodhya temple-building ceremony	1,021 preventive arrests, curfews and prohibitory orders in 22 districts, state government considers banning VHP	Prevented

Sources: West Bengal—*Deccan Herald*, 11 March 2002; *The Times of India*, 11–12 March 2002; Karnataka—*Deccan Herald*, 15–16 March 2002, *The Times of India*, 15–16, 27 March, 1–3 April 2002; Bihar—*The Times of India*, 26 March 2002; Rajasthan—*Rajasthan Patrik*, 27 March 2002, Rediff.com 1–3 March 2002; Madhya Pradesh—*Hindustan Times*, 12 March 2002.

Gujarat where Muslims are important in the governing parties or coalitions took quick preventive action in February and March 2002 that prevented large-scale riots of the kind we have seen in Gujarat. The link between increasing party competition and greater government concern with protecting minorities is by no means specific to India. One of the most striking examples comes from the USA, where by the late 1940s and early 1950s, both the Democratic Party and the Republicans needed to win large northern swing states such as Illinois and Michigan in order to defeat the other in presidential elections.[26] To win these states, the Democrats in particular had to win heavily in the big cities, and by the 1940s, after several decades of Black migration from the south to the manufacturing heartland of the north, this meant that Democrats needed to win the support of an increasingly Black urban electorate, most of whom had relatives still living in the segregated south. By 1954, for example, the *Congressional Quarterly* calculated that there were 61 districts outside the south where the percentage of Blacks was greater than the winning candidate's margin of victory in the 1954 Congressional election.[27]

The increasing electoral importance of minorities in the north helped spur the US federal government to intervene to protect minorities in the south from racist local governments. The link between minority votes and protection for minorities is made explicit in a memo sent by the Democratic National Committee (DNC) in 1948 to Clark Clifford (who in turn passed it on to president Truman) that the Democrats had to win the support of 'working people, the veterans, and the Negroes' to win the election. To win Black support, the DNC suggested that president Truman,

> ...should speak out frankly and fully on his magnificent record as a fighter for Civil Rights—he should mention his votes in the Senate, his anti-poll tax and antilynching legislation, his support of the wartime FEPC, and his orders to end discrimination in the government and the armed services to prove that he acts as well as talks Civil Rights. The Negro votes in the crucial states will more than cancel out any votes he may lose in the south.[28]

India is, I suggest, now undergoing a similar transformation to the one that took place in post-World War II America, one in which greater political competition is already having a positive influence on state governments' efforts to prevent anti-minority violence.

Notes and References

1. Vora, Batuk. 'What's the Collateral Damage? Crores'. *The Times of India*, 31 March 2002.

2. See, for example, Syed Khalique Ahmed's account of the FIRs lodged in Vadodara, 'After Loot, "Fraud": Traders Say FIRs Fudged'. *The Indian Express* (web edition), 13 March 2002, and 'Opposition Sees Red in Gujarat's Saffron Bias'. *The Indian Express* (web edition), 21 March 2002.

3. Azmi, Shabana. 'POTO can Hurt our Secular Polity'. *The Times of India* (web edition), 23 March 2002.

4. 'What Modi Calls Public Anger the Home Minister Calls Plain Terror'. *The Indian Express* (web edition), 4 March 2002; 'Where Had All the Soldiers Gone?'. *The Telegraph* (Calcutta), 2 March 2002. *Deccan Herald* 10 March 2002.

5. *Minorities Commission Reports*, 1986–88. The 1985–87 Minorities Commission statistics on the ethnic balance of casualties are broadly consistent with the pattern found

for the 1960–80 period in Krishna, Gopal. 1985. 'Communal Violence in India: A Study of Communal Disturbance in Delhi'. *Economic and Political Weekly* XX (2), 12 January, 61–74.

6. D. P. Madon (Judge, High Court, Bombay). *Report of the Commission of Inquiry into the Communal Disturbances at Bhiwandi, Jalgaon and Mahad in May 1970*, Volume III, Part III (chapters 46–52), 9–14.

7. There is a huge literature on town-level factors that precipitate violence and a much smaller though hopeful literature on the town-level factors that can mitigate outbreaks of violence. See for a sample of the former, Pramod Kumar, ed. 1992. *Towards Understanding Communalism*. Chandigarh: CRRID; and for the latter, Ashutosh Varshney. 2002. *Ethnic Conflict and Civic Life: Hindus and Muslims in India*. New Haven: Yale University Press.

8. This article draws on my earlier analysis of all-India data on communal riots and their causes and on historical studies of the relationship between party competition and violence in Kerala, Tamil Nadu, Uttar Pradesh and Bihar. See, for example, Wilkinson, Steven. 'Weak States and Low Violence? Explaining State Variation in Hindu-Muslim Violence'. Paper presented at the August 2001 Meeting of the American Political Science Association (available at http://pro.harvard.edu/papers/012/012007WilkinsonS.pdf), and Wilkinson, Steven. 2000. 'Froids calculs et foules déchaînées: les émeutes intercommunitaires en Inde'. *Critique Internationale* 6, Spring, 125–42.

9. Singh, Khushwant. *Hindustan Times*, 15 October 1969, cited in Omar Khalidi. 1995. *Indian Muslims since Independence*. New Delhi: Vikas, 37.

10. *Muslim India* 261, June 1984; Shahabuddin's 'Note to the Home Ministry on Measures to Contain Communalism'. *Muslim India*, July 1989, 317–18, quoted in Omar Khalidi, *Indian Muslims since Independence*, 38. See also 'IUML: Memorandum of June 5, 1987 to the President of India', *Muslim India*, 55, July 1987, 296. For the views of one of the rare police officials in favour of proportionality to prevent riots, see V. N. Rai's interview in *Communalism Combat*, II, 6, February 1995.

11. Details of this dataset are provided in Varshney and Wilkinson. 1996. *Hindu-Muslim Riots: New Findings, Possible Remedies*, Rajiv Gandhi Foundation, Institute for Contemporary Studies, January 1996.

12. Muslims occupy only 2 per cent of the most senior Class I posts and 3–4 per cent of Class II posts in the state government service. U. Mohammed. 1995. 'Educational Problems of the Muslim Minority in Kerala' in *Kerala Muslims: A Historical Perspective*, ed. Ashgar Ali Engineer. New Delhi: Ajanta, 147–56, at p. 150.

13. *National Commission for Minorities Second Annual Report* (FY 1994–1995). 1997. New Delhi: Government of India, 111–12. The Rapid Action Force, specifically raised to deal with the problem of communal riots, had only slightly higher Muslim representation than the CRPF, at 6.9 per cent.

14. See the AMU Students' Union Statement of 21 December 1990 requesting the CRPF, Border Security Force (BSF) and Army to be posted in Aligarh instead of the PAC. *Muslim India* #98 February 1991, 78. See also the plea of the Muslim MP G. M. Banatwalla that the CRPF and BSF should be deployed in the town of Kalyan in preference to the Maharashtra armed police. *Lok Sabha Debates*, 25 April 1979, 297–98.

15. Kohli, Atul. 1990. *Democracy and Discontent: India's Growing Crisis of Governability*. Cambridge: Cambridge University Press, 217.

16. Justice P. Jagmohan Reddy (Judge, Supreme Court of India). 1971. *Report into the Communal Disturbances at Ahmedabad and Other Places in Gujarat on and after September 18, 1969*. Gandhinagar: Gujarat Government Press, 124–26.

17. See, for example, *Report of the Commission of Inquiry on Communal Disturbances, Ranchi-Hatia*, 22–29 August 1967 (1968), 108–09.

18. *Damning Verdict: Report of the Justice B N Srikrisna Commission Appointed for Inquiry into the Riots at Mumbai during December 1992–January 1993 and the March 12, 1993, Bomb Blasts*, Sabrang, Mumbai, nd, 221.

19. I explore how changing levels of political competition in Kerala, Uttar Pradesh, Bihar and Tamil Nadu have affected these states' attitude to protecting minorities in the articles cited in footnote 4 above, as well as in a forthcoming (Wilkinson 2004) book, *The Electoral Incentives for Ethnic Violence.*

20. *India Today*, 15 August 1992, 29–30; *Frontline*, 11 September 1992, 30–31.

21. *The Times of India*, 30 December 1971.

22. *The Times of India*, 23 December 1986.

23. Wilkinson, Steven. 'Weak States and Low Violence? Explaining State Variation in Hindu-Muslim Violence'. Paper presented at the August 2001 Meeting of the American Political Science Association (available at http://pro.harvard.edu/papers/012/012007WilkinsonS.pdf).

24. *Frontline*, 8 September 1995, 4–22, at p. 8.

25. *The Sunday Times of India*, 4 July 1993, at p. 13.

26. Carmines, Edward G., and James A. Stimson. 1989. *Race and the Transformation of American Politics*. Princeton: Princeton University Press, 33.

27. 'Negro Vote Could Swing House to GOP' *Congressional Quarterly*, April 30, 1956, pp. 225–27.

28. Italics added. Memorandum to Clark Clifford from William L. Batt, Junior Director, Research Division Democratic National Committee, entitled 'Notes on President's Campaign', 11 August 1948 [original in Truman Presidential Library, Clark M. Clifford Files]. Clifford sent Truman a virtually word-for-word version of this letter on 17 August 1948. Reprinted in Belknap, Michal R., ed. 1991. *Civil Rights, The White House and the Justice Department 1945–1968*. New York: Garland, Volume 1, 56–62.

REFERENCE

Wilkinson, Steven. 2004. *Votes and Violence: Electoral Competition and Ethnic Riots in India*. Cambridge: Cambridge University Press.

25

Communal Upheaval as Resurgence of Social Darwinism*

Jan Breman#

The recent pogrom against Muslims in Gujarat was not the first I have observed from close quarters. The wave of communal violence engulfing the state after the destruction of the Ayodhya temple coincided with a round of rural and urban research in which I was engaged during late 1992 and early 1993. I wrote on the shock and dismay in the village of my fieldwork when the news arrived of the urban carnage taking place in Mumbai, and on the state of disorder which still prevailed in Surat and Ahmedabad during my subsequent stays in these cities.[1]

In Spring 2002, the religious cleansing operation has been more severe, larger in scale and longer lasting than on earlier occasions, mainly because the state apparatus—both the leading political party and government agencies—condoned or even facilitated the pogrom, rather than stopped it, while it was taking place in late February and early March. The breakdown of civic society has been discussed from various angles, such as the unique history of Gujarat with deep-seated lines of fission between religious majority and minority, a progressive state of flux in the caste balance caused by upward mobility and the concomitant assertion of the middle class, or finally the character of the region as a cultural frontier.

I myself am inclined to give a lot of weight to the well-entrenched nature of the Hindutva movement and its predecessors in this part of the country, strongly opposed to communal harmony and to the design of society as a melting pot of diverse and open-ended social segments. The mobilisation of low and intermediate castes to participate in the activities of the Sangh parivar organisations in the last two decades has broadened the base of Hindu fundamentalism as a social-political force. The price these previously denigrated segments have to pay for their acceptance within the Hindutva fold is their willingness to express antagonism to Muslims as members of the religious minority and, in brutal acts of confrontation, to do

* *Economic and Political Weekly* 37 (16): 1485–88 (20 April 2002).

The author suggests that readers also consult the book sequel to this article: Breman, Jan. 2016. *Pauperism in Past and Present*. New Delhi: Oxford University Press.

the dirty work of cleansing on behalf of their high-caste brothers and sisters. The dynamics of inclusion and exclusion are intricately interwoven.

However, this explanation also has to be contextualised within the changing political economy of Gujarat. My following comments relate to Ahmedabad, the primary location of many of the horrors that have been reported. Since 1998, I have been carrying out research in localities in the city which used to be marked by the smoking chimneys of textile mills, many of which had a history of production for close to, or even more than, 100 years. To this branch of industry, Ahmedabad owed its fame as the Manchester of India. That proud record came to an end when, from the early 1980s onwards, these factories started to close their gates. Twenty years later, more than 50 mills have stopped production and, in this still ongoing crisis, at least one lakh workers have lost their jobs. While around the middle of the twentieth century half of the city's workforce used to earn its livelihood from employment in the composite textile enterprises dominating the industrial landscape, this percentage has now dwindled to a tiny fraction.

The dismissed workers were driven into the informal sector of the economy, to depend on casual rather than regular jobs, requiring no or only minimum skills, remunerated with very low wages and paid, moreover, not on time but on piece rate. Hired for hardly more than 15 to 20 days per month, most of them have been forced to strengthen the economy of their household by bringing former dependents, women and also young children, into the labouring process. Even all these efforts combined generally result in a life standard far below the poverty level. In the process of immiseratisation, the erstwhile mill workers have been made to surrender the regularity, stability and dignity they used to enjoy in the formal sector of the economy.[2]

Pauperisation is not only contained within the sphere of these households, but has become publicly visible in the run-down quality of the industrial localities in and around the old city centre. In contrast to the new prosperity displayed so glamorously in the middle-class neighbourhoods on the right bank of the Sabarmati river, the low-income districts on the left bank, inhabited by a huge labour reserve army of underemployed own-account producers, home workers and casualised wage earners, have been thoroughly deprived of their former economic dominance and vitality.

The closure of the textile mills has resulted in more than just massive loss of earnings and employment. Hardly less dramatic is the collapse of the social infrastructure that has accompanied it. It is certainly not a coincidence that the orgy of violence that has taken place in Ahmedabad since the end of February seems to have reached a climax in ex-mill localities populated by social segments from which a major part of this industrial workforce used to be recruited: subaltern Hindus (mainly dalits, OBCs and intermediate castes, especially patels) and Muslims.

Whenever communal tensions have flared up and erupted in street riots in the past, these clashes could be defused by appealing to working class solidarity, which transcended the boundaries of primordial loyalties. The social consciousness produced by factorised employment did not arise spontaneously but had been built up during the social struggle in which the Majoor Mahajan Sangh (MMS) played a pivotal role. Over a period of many decades, this famous trade union, established in 1920 as the outcome of a strike led by Mahatma Gandhi, successfully galvanised the collective interest of workers in the textile industry. Preaching an ideology of class harmony instead of class conflict and with unconditional acceptance of the composite character of its membership, the Gandhian leaders of this social movement aroused the need for concerted action and tried to scale down more parochial interests along the lines of caste and religion.

No doubt, there were communal disturbances also then. When riots broke out in 1969, the police agreed to set up a control room at the headquarters of the trade union and on the basis of messages received by phone from its cadre in the mill localities, the leadership kept the authorities informed of the latest incidents. The factories had stopped production but on the third day of the riots, the call came for members of the MMS to report back to duty. Workers of the same shift but with different caste and religious identities were told to go to the mills and back home in mixed batches in order to safeguard each other's wellbeing. Nowadays there is hardly any space left for that sort of inter-communal sharing and mutual protection. The union which at that time with more than 150,000 members was one of the largest and best organised in the country is a spent force, reduced to less than one-tenth of its former strength and depleted of all economic and political power. In mid-March 2002, with parts of the city still under curfew, I met the secretary general in his office, a big building once vibrant with activity but which now stands desolate in the heart of the old city. This veteran, at the age of 88 years and in failing health, told me with anguish how a fortnight ago he had endeavoured for many hours to reach the police commissioner and prominent politicians. When he received no response to his incessant calls on 28 February, he realised that the state machinery deliberately refused to give shelter to the victims and to protect life and property when the rampage of killing and looting was at its worst. In the relentless drive towards a regime of informality as the dominant mode of employment, labour appears to have forfeited not just its economic value, bargaining power and dignity. In vain, this Gandhian stalwart had tried to persuade his office staff, cut down from its former impressive size to a few helpers, to come along with him on a tour of the industrial localities in order to pacify the incited mob. In addition to their blunt refusal to go out into the streets, they also warned him against risking his life on such a hopeless mission.

The trade union movement which used to be the main platform for collective action has withered away. Neither have other kinds of social movements been able to stem the rising tide of communalism. Apart from a few exceptions, the wide variety of non-governmental organisations in Ahmedabad, which claim to represent civic society, remained by and large lethargic under the communal onslaught. In the words of one commentator:

> The space, which allows, mediates and keeps alive the possibility of dialogues, seems to have disappeared from our social, cultural, political and even our educational life [my note: in Gujarat]. Public life has become so implicated and impoverished that in the

face of crisis there is no one individual or collective which can exercise moral authority and rescue the dialogic space.[3]

AT SABARMATI

This state of paralysis could not have been better illustrated than by the decision of the board of the Sabarmati ashram to close its gates when the violence spread through the city on 28 February. Where the founding father of this institution would not have hesitated to rush to the scene of the 'hoollad', the lame excuse of the ashram's trustees was that they had to protect Gandhi's heritage. The way they did this betrayed the very ideals the Mahatma stood for all his life and which in the end also became the cause of his death.

The MMS did not merely negotiate better labour standards with the captains of the textile industry in the city. Throughout much of the twentieth century, a large outreach staff worked together with social workers assigned by municipal agencies to dignify the circumstances of the working class by promoting a wide range of welfare practices—such as sport clubs, reading rooms, classes for adult education, family care and counselling courses, day nurseries, primary health centres—in the mill localities. All these activities naturally became meeting points, which facilitated interaction between people of different identities. The 'Other' was not at a distance, but highly visible and touchable as a workmate, a neighbour or a friend with whom close contact was maintained both within and outside the mill. This mesh of social cohesion that transcended the separate niches of caste and religion broke down once the MMS started to fade away and municipal welfare agencies, due to lack of funding, had to cease or drastically curtail their activities.

The trend towards spatial segregation which already began several decades ago should be understood as both cause and effect of the erosion of inter-communal networks. The formation of ghettos has taken place within and beyond the neighbourhood. In the first round, segregation came about at the level of the locality itself, as people moved to blocks inhabited by members of the same community or faith. Living together creates the illusion of having found adequate shelter and a feigned ability to resist in case of attack. In this restructured setting, streets become zones of demarcation. In times of unrest, crossing from one side to the other means putting your life at risk. Nevertheless, bridges are kept intact by peace-makers on both sides who discreetly exchange information on what to do or not to do, even at the height of the upheaval. They try to keep their own youngsters, who are eager to make mischief, in check and agree on rules of engagement or disengagement. Passing from one zone to the next during the latest round of mayhem, one cannot but be impressed by the quality of the grassroots leadership and the goodwill that continues to exist between people now separated but who still remember the years when they used to work and live together. One Muslim in Gomtipur, a former jobber in a textile mill, narrated his nightmarish experiences but added that he refused to see Hindus as his enemy. He was sure that the large majority of them, on his count four out of five, did not wish him harm. As a matter of fact, a few hours before the signal for the hunt on Muslims spread like wildfire, a Hindu friend had phoned with the urgent warning to stay at home and see to the safety of his family. With trusted friends like this one, he was accustomed to sharing food, participating in their rituals and celebrating festivities in the house.

In the second round of ghettoisation, members of the minority are driven out of localities in which they themselves have lived all their lives, and often generations before them. I witnessed and described such instances of collective deportation during my stay in Ahmedabad in early 1993.[4] Also, this time, there are reports of large-scale treks of members of the minority fleeing to marginal sites on the outskirts of the city. Juhapura, on the right bank of the river, has emerged as a huge Muslim enclave. It is an overcrowded district which has been inundated with many tens of thousands of refugees in a short period of time. The area is known popularly as 'mini Pakistan' and most of the people living there seem to have slid into a state of utter deprivation. In the mind of the Hindu outsider, they constitute an anonymous mass. It is with reference to such alien landscapes at remote distances from more 'civilised' parts of the city that the Other is constructed as having neither name nor face and becomes demonised as an anti-social, criminal underclass which cannot be accepted as part and parcel of mainstream society.

No End in Sight

The end of the Hindutva politics of exclusion is not yet in sight. Before my departure from Ahmedabad, I acquired a pamphlet urging the Hindu majority to avoid all economic transactions with Muslims. The call for a total boycott—do not buy from their shops or engage in business with them, do not employ or be employed by Muslims—is not a new one and the same message of systematic discrimination already circulated in previous rounds of communal rioting. There is also the appeal in the text to Hindu men to keep their daughters and sisters under close scrutiny lest they fall prey to the lust of the bestial Other. The hatred radiating from these sentences is as ignominious for the targeted males as it is for the females belonging to the majority, who are portrayed as lacking the will and the capability to be in charge of their own virtue. One could, of course, argue that the separate niches occupied by Hindus and Muslims in the labour market militate against exclusion from economic life of a newly created segment of untouchables. I am not so sure that such a plan of action, contingent upon a more comprehensive blueprint and backed up by the kind of intimidation we have already witnessed, would prove to be abortive in the end.

The design does not seem to be so dissimilar from what happened during the initial phase of the Nazi regime in Germany. Prior to the actual elimination of Jewish people from mainstream society by the state, their property was identified and either destroyed or confiscated. In the latest orgy of violence in Ahmedabad, which combined a killing spree with the selective and ruthless destruction of Muslim shops, garages and other business establishments, I see a notable resemblance to the Kristallnacht[5] in the early 1930s when the policy of German Nazification began in earnest. Seen from that perspective, it is quite alarming to observe the complete absence of feelings of shame and remorse among those who propagated or participated in the Ahmedabad onslaught after the worst of the pogrom was over. The dominant mood was rather one of glee and satisfaction, or even a sense of fulfilment, expressed in statements such as 'they had it coming' or 'they got what they deserved'. The chairman of the Vishva Hindu Parishad (VHP) in Ahmedabad went on record as proudly claiming that 'it had to be done'.[6] What sort of future does the Sangh parivar leadership have in store for the religious minority in the country? As second-class citizens, as the apex body of the Rashtriya Swayamsevak Sangh (RSS) made clear at a recent Bangalore meeting: 'Let the Muslims understand that their real safety lies in the goodwill of the majority'. Such phrases come dangerously close to labelling them as Untermenschen.[7]

Both first-hand reporters and more analytical commentators have squarely laid the blame for the communal upheaval in Ahmedabad on the proponents of the Hindutva movement, helped by the power of the state—which, in Gujarat, happens to be under control of the Bharatiya Janata Party (BJP). Although I have no qualms about accepting that verdict, my argument is that the viciousness of Hindu fundamentalism still needs a follow-up explanation which takes into consideration the globalised nature of the political economy that has emerged. The welfare capitalism that was both cause and outcome of the emancipation of labour in the Atlantic part of the world from the end of the nineteenth century onwards arose out of a specific mode of production, distribution and consumption which, in retrospect, proved to be time-bound and did not spread to the colonised economies. During the struggle for national freedom in the first half of the twentieth century, the Indian leaders made promises to the working class for a better deal. The new society to be shaped after the end of foreign rule would be just and fair to all. Although repeated again and again, this pledge has fallen into abeyance in the post-colonial era. The brand of lumpen capitalism that came to dominate in the so-called development decades is based on an ideology of social-Darwinism, and could not care less about the urgent need to raise labour standards and shows precious little interest in increasing the dignity of the working poor.

In a recent essay on how the regime of neo-liberalism has worsened the plight of labour at the bottom of Ahmedabad's urban economy, I concluded that: Gujarat could be understood as an experiment for trying out what will happen to state and society under a policy regime which does not attempt to harness the most brutal consequences of a market-led mode of capitalist production. The total eclipse of the kind of Gandhian values which, for the better part of the last century were so important in the promotion of a public image both within and outside the country, has also led to the shrinking of social space needed for humanising economic growth. The disappearance of a climate leaning towards social democracy and tolerance has been accompanied by an increase in communal hate politics.[8]

EFFECT ON LABOUR

Public order had not yet been restored when I left the city close to the end of March. The curfew was lifted in some parts of the city one day, only to be re-imposed the next day in the same or other localities because new incidents had occurred. There has been hardly any discussion of what all this has meant for the large number of working class households who fully depend for their daily subsistence on the erratic and meagre yield of their labour power. Even under so-called normal circumstances, steady employment is difficult to come by, but for more than three weeks at a stretch now these people have not been able to move around in their cumbersome search for gainful work. For many of them, the regular state of deprivation in which they live has further deteriorated into destitution. Without any food reserves left and bereft of all creditworthiness, they have to survive on whatever private charities are willing to dole out to them. It comes as no surprise that the front organisations of the Sangh parivar were able to mobilise mercenaries from this lumpenised milieu of subaltern castes to assist in the operation of killing, burning and looting.

One should, however, be careful when implying that underprivileged segments in the underbelly of urban (or for that matter rural) society can easily be incited to engage in indiscriminate and sustained combat against each other. Indicative is the recent change in meaning of the term communal. The riots which broke out in the early 1980s were a reaction by the high and intermediate castes against the reservation policy introduced by the Congress government to favour their clientele from the lower social classes. The first anti-reservation agitation targeted the dalits, while the second round of the same backlash which erupted in 1985 included the other backward classes, which stood to gain from the proposed expansion in the system of reservation. While the notion of communal until then tended to refer to frictions between top and bottom of the caste hierarchy, the social forces pushing the Hindutva agenda gave a different slant to the term by propagating the unity (although most certainly not on par) of Hindus high and low. In their guidelines for societal reconstruction, inferiority and subjugation were coined as the exclusive stigma of Muslims. It remains to be seen whether, as part of a long-term strategy—if not dictated then at least inspired by the interests of classes higher up in society—the fragmented segments of the labouring poor can be trusted to go on waging war against each other. Particularly in the localities inhabited by dalits, it is not only possible to detect remnants of a previous class-based solidarity, but there is the realistic awareness that in a next round of violence they might again be at the receiving end of the discriminatory policies that have been practised by the powers that be from generation to generation. Of undiminished and even striking relevance here is the observation with which Gooptu ends her study of the urban poor in India at the beginning of the twentieth century:

> [I]n the case of the untouchable or the Muslim poor, their caste status and religious affiliation further reinforced their stigmatisation and social exclusion by the urban upper and middle classes, who were predominantly higher-caste Hindu, and included orthodox commercial groups as employers of labour and as zealous promoters of Hindu revitalisation movements. All sections of the poor in varying degrees found themselves culturally and socially distanced, at times even physically segregated as the middle classes retreated into the safe havens of new urban residential areas.[9]

We need historical reports not only for the sake of writing the chronicles of today's events, but also to get an idea of things to come. Accounts with a focus on *la longue duree* might give us a handle on the kind of future we are heading for, or drifting towards.

NOTES

1. See 'Rural Impressions of the Urban Carnage'. *The Times of India*, January 1993; Breman, Jan. 1993. 'An Anti-Muslim Pogrom in Surat'. *Economic and Political Weekly* 28 (16), 737–41; Breman, Jan. 1999. 'Ghettoisation and Communal Politics: Inclusion and Exclusion in the Hindutva Landscape' in *Institutions and Inequalities: Essays in Honour of Andre Beteille*, eds R. Guha, and J. Parry. New Delhi: Oxford University Press, 259–83.

2. Breman, Jan. 2001. 'A Turn for the Worse: The Closure of the Ahmedabad Textile Mills and the Retrenchment of the Workforce'. Wertheim Annual Lecture 12. Centre for Asian Studies, Amsterdam School of Social Science Research, University of Amsterdam.

3. Suhrud, T. 2002. 'No Room for Dialogue'. *Economic and Political Weekly* 37 (11), 1011–12.

4. See Breman, Jan. 1999. 'Ghettoisation and Communal Politics'.

5. Kristalnacht (literally 'crystal/glass night', translated as 'Night of Broken Glass') refers to the Nazi state-sponsored pogrom against Jews on 9–10 November 1938. Police watched passively as stormtroopers and civilians attacked Jewish businesses, homes and synagogues. Hundreds are supposed to have been killed and around 30,000 arrested and deported to concentration camps. The name derives from the broken glass that littered the streets after the pogrom. [eds]

6. Bhatt, S. 2002. 'VHP's Startling Revelation'. *Mainstream* 40 (13), 16 March.

7. Plural form of 'untermensch', literally 'under or inferior man', a term used by the Nazis to refer to Jews, Gypsies, Slavs and others that they considered sub-human species worthy of elimination. [eds]

8. See the S. Chakravarty Memorial Lecture which I delivered on 16 November 2001 at the Delhi School of Economic Growth. The text of the lecture is part of a larger essay: Breman, Jan. 2001. 'An Informalised Labour System; End of Labour Market Dualism'. *Economic and Political Weekly* 35 (52), 4804–21.

9. Gooptu, N. 2001. *The Politics of the Urban Poor in Early Twentieth-Century, India*. Cambridge: Cambridge University Press, 420.

26

MEMORIES, SAFFRONISING STATUES AND CONSTRUCTING COMMUNAL POLITICS*

BADRI NARAYAN#

Managing the memories of different communities and reinterpreting them at the local level to suit the logic of a particular political group is an oft-observed phenomenon in the ongoing political processes of the country. This entails digging out lesser known historical events associated with particular communities and converting them into popular memory, after making additions and deletions that suit the political agenda of the concerned political forces. Sometimes, historical events are placed in confrontation with each other, and communities are mobilised by creating warring memories and warring identities against other communities. In this process, a space is forged in the collective memory of the communities concerned.

Political forces that follow this strategy succeed in their efforts by using arresting and powerful memory-kindling devices like constructing memorials, organising festivals, staging theatres and circulating their stories in the form of popular literature for popularising their own version of a historical event. Popular memory is created by selectively remembering and conveniently forgetting. The Rashtriya Swayamsevak Sangh (RSS) or the Association of National Volunteers, and its political wing, the Bharatiya Janata Party (BJP) are the main players of this game and they have been following this strategy ever since the BJP joined the political bandwagon. Even after the 2004 general elections held in which the party lost to the Congress and Communist Party of India (Marxist) combine, it reiterated its objective of following and implementing its Hindutva ideology by creating warring memories among various communities, especially dalit castes (Laxman 1994).

* *Economic and Political Weekly* 41 (45): 4695–701 (11 November 2006).

The material presented in this article is based on the fieldwork conducted during the data collection of the project, 'Myth, Memory and Politics: A Study of the Language of Political Mobilisation of Grassroot Dalits', funded by the ICSSR, New Delhi. I am thankful to ICSSR for providing me financial support for the project. I would like to thank the members of my research team Mousumi Majumder (MM) and S. P. Upadhayay for their help with the survey and data preparation.

The method adopted to mobilise these castes was by searching for lower-caste heroes who suited the Hindu way of thinking. Local histories were explored, popular dalit heroes were dug out, and their stories were circulated back among the people from whom they were originally taken. The present article tries to show that these stories are not always produced by the people themselves and should not be treated as original, primary and sacrosanct cultural and narrative constructions. They are constructed through complex processes by outside socio-political forces and diffused among the common people through various means of transmission. Often, these local myths are integrated into the grand history of the community as a whole that is being created as a part of the ideology of the party. This phenomenon can be commonly observed in the political scenario of Uttar Pradesh in which the BJP is trying to mould and reinterpret the local histories of various regions according to their own political agenda and create a metanarrative of all the communities in their political fold.

This chapter studies one such attempt of the RSS and BJP to search for space among the dalits of Uttar Pradesh by searching for heroes of their communities and relocating them in their broader project of construction of communal memories among Hindus as a whole. In the study that is based in Bahraich and an adjoining village Jittora, we will document the local history behind myths, and the politics of communalisation around these myths. Bahraich is approximately 160 kilometres from Lucknow, the capital of Uttar Pradesh. In the north, it touches the Nepal border. A famous *dargah* (mosque containing a tomb) of a warrior called Salar Masood Ghazi, who is popularly called Ghazi Mian, is located here. This dargah is visited by thousands of devotees each day and an annual fair is held in May. Lakhs of devotees (jayren), the maximum being Hindus, attend the fair to pray for the fulfilment of their wishes. In Jittora, on the other hand, there is a temple built in the memory of Suhaldev, a pasi (dalit) king who supposedly killed Ghazi Mian and himself died in the battle. The BJP, which is one of the many parties active in the region, also organises a festival in May each year around the same time as the one held in the dargah, to commemorate the memory of Suhaldev and to emphasise among the dalits and Hindus together, that Suhaldev was a Hindu warrior who sacrificed his life to safeguard the original residents from Ghazi Mian. Thereby, it is trying to create a warring heroic identity of Suhaldev and positing it against a so-called Muslim invader. This hero is then being used for asserting the identities of the Hindus and dalits of that region, which the party hopes will ultimately lead to the political mobilisation of these communities in their favour.

[...]

CONTESTING HISTORIES, WARRING IDENTITIES AND MAKING OF POPULAR DOMAIN

... This project was launched on 2 May 2004, when a Maharaja Suhaldev Sewa Samiti, Uttar Pradesh was formed in Bahraich, which organised a five-day celebration in memory of Suhaldev. The organisers of the programme were Mahiraj Dhwaj Singh, the 'pracharak' of RSS and Sureshwar Singh, also of the RSS. The other members of the organising committee were members of the BJP. The headquarters of the organising committee was mentioned as Keshav Bhawan, Model House, Lucknow, which is also the head office of the RSS in Uttar Pradesh. Shri Yogi Adityanathji Maharaj, a BJP member of Parliament from Gorakhpur, inaugurated the function. The other names mentioned in the invitation letter were mostly of local leaders of the BJP, Hindu Parishad and the RSS. According to the letter, it was being held to commemorate the memory of maharaja Suhaldev, the great warrior who defended the Hindu religion and religious people from the foreign invader Masood who despoiled Indian cultural traditions, ravaged women and killed children and men without facing obstruction from anyone. They proclaimed that it was essential to sing the glory of such great sons of the nation, otherwise the defender will be erased from the pages of history while the cruel invader will be glorified.[1] Many programmes were organised as a part of the function, including a 'kalash yatra', 'yajna', sports competitions, a huge (virat) wrestling match and a 'Ram katha' (discourse on Ram).

On 6 May 2004, another fair began in Bahraich at the dargah of Salar Masood, who was claimed by the RSS to be the foreign invader who had caused ruin and desolation among the people. Surprisingly, he seems to be revered more by Hindus than by Muslims since they attend the fair in large numbers each year.[2] According to a news report published in the Hindi newspaper *Amar Ujala* on that day, the fair symbolises communal harmony in the region. The report said that the 'baraat' (marriage ceremony) of Ghazi Mian will be held on 9 May, which will be attended by almost five lakh people, of which the maximum will be from the majority community of Hindus (*Amar Ujala* 2004). On the same day, another report was published in the same newspaper saying that Kunwar Manvendra Singh, the president of the legislative assembly and council, and a leader of the BJP, who had come to inaugurate the Ram katha on the last day of the five-day fair of maharaja Suhaldev mentioned above, termed the worship of Salar Masood Ghazi as unfortunate. He said it was tragic that maharaja Suhaldev had been resurrected so late, but everyone should attend the victory celebrations of such a great person. Proclaiming maharaja Suhaldev as a great martyr, he said that earlier governments had not understood his greatness. He appealed to the people to follow his footsteps and emulate his ideals (Ibid.).

From these two reports, it is obvious that two parallel, but contesting and warring histories are being celebrated in the same region which the two communities inhabit. The BJP–RSS is trying to create a warring history of Suhaldev by projecting him as the defender and saviour of the Hindu religion who had laid down his life to save the people from the hands of the foreign invader who was ruining and destroying the existing culture. The managing committee of the dargah of Ghazi Mian, which organises the fair every year, on the other hand, projects him as a symbol of communal harmony between Hindus and Muslims. The committee is a non-political one comprising members affiliated to all political parties.[3]

The story about Suhaldev and Ghazi Mian that is popular in the region is that Suhaldev was the king of the *bhar kaum* (community) living there. He was also the leader of 17 small kings in the region but was very cruel and oppressive. At that time, that place was a jungle. Ghazi Mian, whose actual name was Salar Masood, and who was the nephew of Mahmood Ghaznavi and also his son-in-law, had come to the jungles to hunt. He set up his tent inside the jungles and was supposed to leave after hunting. The Muslims of the region, who had all been converted from Hinduism, went to him and requested him to protect them. Ghazi Mian agreed. Suhaldev, suspecting that Ghazi Mian was trying to overthrow him, attacked him and after a fierce battle, killed him and his entire army. He himself died in the battle.[4]

Another myth in circulation is that Salar Masood was in love with a girl named Zohra, who lived in a nearby village called Rudauli. Unfortunately, he died before his marriage. The girl then built a tomb for him and also built her own tomb. She died soon after that on a Sunday, which was also Salar Masood's death day. That is why a baraat or marriage procession of Ghazi Mian is taken out from the dargah each year on a Sunday as a part of the annual fair held there, and a symbolic marriage ritual is performed in their memory. Even today, people from the Rudauli village pose as members of the bride's family and lay a 'chadar' (bed spread) on her tomb.[5]

The reason why Ghazi Mian is so popular among the Hindus of that region is that when Ghazi Mian's tomb was built, it was believed to have acquired magical powers. The local people narrate that both Hindus and Muslims are blessed after praying there. According to the popular history of that region, the first person to have experienced his miracle was a yadav woman. She had no offspring but after praying there, a son was born. Since then, many miracles have occurred. Lepers who come to pray at the shrine during the annual fair get cured and people in whom ghosts enter are exorcised there. More than 75 per cent of the visitors to the annual fair are Hindus and all the political leaders standing for elections visit the tomb to get Masood's blessings both before filing the nomination and after winning the elections.

INVENTION, INCARNATION AND INTERPRETATIONS

[...]

The myth of Suhaldev is developed around the story of the battle between him and Salar Masood. According to the *Gazetteer*,[6] Masood was a nephew of Mahmood of Ghaznavi. He was born in Ajmer in 1015. At the age of 16, he started on his invasion of Hindustan. After travelling through Multan, he reached Delhi and from there he went to Meerut, Kannauj and Satrikh in Barabanki. Before arriving at Bahraich, he sent two 'kotwals' (lieutenants) of his army, Saiyad Saif-ud-din and Mian Rajab, there. A confederation of the nobles of Bahraich threatened them and tried to push back the army. Masood then himself marched to Bahraich reaching there in 1033 CE. The chieftains of the region were at first daunted by the young warrior but gradually took heart to fight against him. But Masood defeated them repeatedly, until the arrival of Suhaldev turned the tide of victory. He was overthrown and slain in 1034 CE and buried by his servants in Bahraich, where his dargah was built in 1035.

Suhaldev was the eldest son of the king of Sravasti, called Mordhwaj. According to the stories circulated popularly, he had many names like Suhaldev, Sakardev, Suhirdadhwaj, Rai Suhriddev, Suhridil, Susaj, Shahardev, Sahardev, Suhaaldev, Suhildev and Suheldev. But in contemporary print culture, he is referred to as raja Suhaldev.[7] It is popularly believed that he was the king of the bhar community, from which emerged the pasi community, a dalit caste of the region. Some people of the forward castes of Bahraich project him as a vais kshatriya (suryavanshi kshatriya) (Shukla 2003), but there are no historical records to substantiate this. In 'Mirate Masudi', he is mentioned as bhar tharu. Boys, a British historian, mentions him as bhar rajput.[8] Cunningham mentions him as tharu (*Gazetteer* 1903). Some writers claim that he was pandav vanshi tomar; some say that he was a bharshiv and some pasi.[9] Gonda *Gazetteer* mentions him as rajputvanshi jain. Gewail, in the Bahraich *Gazetteer*, calls him tharu kalhans. The paragana book of Bahraich mentions him as nagvanshiya kshatriya and the Kaifiyat Paragana Ikauna writes of him as visen kshatriya. Kanth Charitra and Shankar Vijay texts refer to him as suryavanshi kshatriya (*Gazetteer* 1903).

Gradually, with the flow of time, the pasis became convinced that Suhaldev belonged to their caste and started glorifying him as their caste hero. Just before the 2004 elections, Guddi Rajpasi, a pasi candidate standing from Barabanki Lok Sabha region, a neighbouring region of Bahraich, as a member of the Bharat Kranti Rakshak Party (BKRP), appealed to the pasis in her election leaflet to vote for her in the name of Rashtra Bhakt Maharaja Suhaldev and other heroes of the pasi caste such as Maharaja Satandev, Bijli Pasi, Virangana Udadevi, Ganga Baks and other dalit heroes like Jhalkaribai, Mahatma Buddh, Mahatma Gandhi, Baba Saheb Bhimrao Ambedkar, Sardar Patel and Amar Shaheed Abdul Hameed.[10]

As the second largest dalit community in Uttar Pradesh, the pasis are the targets of various political parties who would like to marshal them as vote banks. Understanding this, the RSS launched a campaign to search for heroes that suit their Hindu political agenda. They found such a hero in Suhaldev and started organising festivals in Jittora to evoke his memory among the common people. Suhaldev is projected as a 'rashtra rakshak shiromani' who defended Hindu society, culture and the country from Muslim intruders by forming a confederation of local kings. In the narratives, Suhaldev is depicted as an ideal Hindu king who protected cows ('go rakshak'), protected Indian culture, provided a respectful position to saints ('sant rakshak') and worked for the uplift of Hindu culture ('dharma rakshak').[11]

Cow as a symbol is used for glorifying both Suhaldev and Salar Masood. In another version of Salar Masood's story narrated by the dafalis, a low-caste Muslim community whose profession is to sing songs praising Ghazi Mian at his dargah, it is said that when Salar Masood was sitting at his marriage 'mandap' (tent) just before his marriage, a woman ran up to Salar Masood saying that some people had unchained her cows. Hearing this, Ghazi Mian rushed to rescue them, but lost his life. He was thus unable to marry his lover and died before consummating his marriage.[12]

The narrative glorifying Suhaldev says that Salar Masood, realising the significance of cow in the Hindu psyche, placed a herd of cows in front of his army as a shield. As a counter strategy, Suhaldev unchained the cows on the eve of the battle both to save the cows and so that Salar Masood would be forced to fight man-to-man.[13] Thus, one narrative glorifies Ghazi Mian as a cow protector while in the other narrated by the RSS glorifying Suhaldev, Ghazi Mian is depicted as being insensitive towards dumb animals, and who used the sacred cow against Hindus. Through this narrative, Suhaldev emerges as a saviour of the cows that were being needlessly killed during the battle.

Through the print media also, the BJP–RSS tried to carve the image of Suhaldev as a pasi hero who was a pride to Hindus. In the booklet 'Hindu Samaj ke Gaurav, Pasi Veer Maharaja Suhaldev ki Shaurya Gatha', written by Triloki Nath Kol, a local RSS activist and BJP leader of Bahraich (Kol 1997), he tried to influence the pasi community in favour of Hindutva agenda. He also attempted to create a narrative instigating hatred against Muslims within the pasis by exaggerating and fantasising the attitude of the community towards them by showing how the Muslim rule in the medieval period was very oppressive towards pasis. The pasis were the earlier rulers of that region and had been dethroned and dispossessed by the Muslims. According to the narrative, Muslims consider pasis to be their greatest enemy. It is commonly believed that when the pasis lost to the Muslims, they were forced to do jobs like filling water from tanks. This gave them the title Bharpasi. At that time, the pasis welcomed this name since filling water is a respectable Hindu work. They did not realise that this name would later turn into a curse for them. Tremendous efforts were made to divide and weaken the pasis. The Muslims married pasi girls and forced them to change their religion. Under these circumstances, the pasis started eating pork that is hated by Muslims and marrying off their children at young ages. Kol lamented that it was unfortunate that due to lack of historical information, these events are not given much importance (Ibid.: 10–11).

[...]

MYTH MAKING AND POPULAR NARRATIVE

It is interesting to note that the story circulated by the RSS and its various wings is contradicted by the popular narrative of the mostly Hindus devotees who worship Ghazi Mian. Ghazi Mian is not perceived as an intruder, but as a hunter who wanted to settle down here because of the beautiful environs. Suhaldev was the king of a local sun-worshipping tribe called bhar. He was a great tyrant and an oppressor of the Muslims and lower castes. When Ghazi Mian arrived, all the people requested him to save them from the oppressions of Suhaldev. Very reluctantly he agreed, and a fierce battle ensued in which both Suhaldev and Ghazi Mian were killed.[14] Thus, Suhaldev is looked upon as a villain while Ghazi Mian is a hero. Even today, when a strong wind blows, it is believed to be the evil spirit of Suhaldev and an iron chain that is full of magical powers is tied at the front gate of the dargah to prevent the spirit from entering. No one is allowed to enter or leave the dargah at that time.

The month-long annual fair at the dargah of Ghazi Mian held in May is organised by the Dargah Committee and Sunni Central Board, Bahraich that was formed in 1902 (Shukla 2003). On the first Sunday of the month, all the people living in the neighbourhood gather there to dip in the water tank called Suryakund (lake dedicated to Sun god) near the dargah. The RSS claims that earlier, an idol of the Sun god stood there. Thousands of years ago, before Salar Masood's advent, big fairs used to be held there during solar and lunar eclipses. Later, the Muslims changed its name to 'Hoz Shamshi', which is the Persian translation of the word 'Suryakund'.[15] Sunday being the day of the Sun, Hindus observe a fast and pray to the Sun god. This is the reason why Hindus go there with flags and 'trishuls' (tridents) to pray. It is commonly believed that when lepers bathe in the water of the Suryakund, they get cured.[16] The RSS, however, propagates that the lake actually belonged to Balarkmuni and it was sanctified by 'rishis' and 'munis' over the ages, which gave it miraculous properties. This is how lepers get cured after bathing in this lake.

Statue, Image and Myth Making

The logical, intellectual and narrative resources which the RSS uses are heavily drawn from the narratives created and circulated by the Arya Samaj, Ram Rajya Parishad and the Hindu Mahasabha Sangathan that tried to spread ideas of Hindu nationalism derived from socio-religious movements initiated by high-caste Hindus (Jaffrelot 1996: 11). The basis of the image of Suhaldev was invented and constructed by a schoolteacher and poet of Bahraich, named Guru Sahay Dikshit Dwijdeen, who, influenced by the Arya Samaj, composed a long poem in 1940 based on the character of Suhaldev called 'Sri Suhal Bavani'. The poem composed in 'veer ras' (emotion portraying bravery) projected him as the saviour of Hindu pride against the foreign intruder Salar Masood. Bitter words were used against Islam and Salar Masood, in particular. The poet himself recited the poem in local poetry conferences in a grandiloquent manner with a sword in his hand and a headband around his head. This manner of recitation brought Suhaldev to life in his chivalrous glory to the audience. A local resident of Bahraich who had attended one such recitation, narrates that this created an arresting image of Suhaldev in the minds of the audience.[17] The oral rendition and the printed version, which appeared in 1950, helped to build up and diffuse a heroic image of Suhaldev in that region. It is interesting to note that in the poem, Suhaldev was not labelled as a pasi king, but was said to be a Jain king who was a passionate anti-Muslim and a staunch Hindu loyalist. Inspired by the poem, the local intellectuals like lawyers and schoolteachers started writing articles in newspapers glorifying this image of Suhaldev.[18]

The Partition of India and the ensuing communalism played an important role in the reconstruction and transmission of the myth of Suhaldev as an anti-Muslim, Hindu hero. After Independence, an incident took place in the region which reinforced the memory of Suhaldev in the minds of the local people. The Arya

Samaj, Ram Rajya Parishad and the Hindu Mahasabha Sangathan had launched a movement demanding the installation of a memorial to Suhaldev.

[...]

In the beginning, although the RSS was involved in the movement, the leadership was in the hands of the Arya Samaj, Hindu Mahasabha and the Ram Rajya Parishad. Later, due to the agenda of involving dalits under their fold and the fear of conversion of lower castes into Islam in the Indo-Nepal border after the opening of a number of madrasas in the region, the RSS intensified the move of projecting Hindu warring icons to perpetuate the anti-Muslim hatred and started creating memories of Suhaldev as a Hindu hero against Muslim invaders not only in Jittora, but also in the adjoining regions. The movement had dampened for a few years; it picked up momentum in 2001 when the Maharaja Suhaldev Sewa Samiti was formed under the banner of the RSS. As mentioned earlier, this association aggressively revived the memories and celebrations around Suhaldev by creating new festivals, publishing pamphlets, leaflets and booklets and organising various popular activities so that the narrative of Suhaldev may transmit to the grassroots level. Interestingly, the Raj family, that earlier patronised the Sri Suhaldev Smarak Samiti led by Ram Rajya Parishad and the Arya Samaj and the Hindu Mahasabha, shifted their allegiance to the Sri Suhaldev Sewa Samiti under the RSS. In the stationery used by the Sewa Samiti to circulate information about their various activities, the names of pasi leaders associated with the organisation like Poonam Verma and Padma Sen Chowdhry were mentioned prominently. In the 2004 elections, they appealed to the voters to vote for the party which had elevated the glory of persons who had laid down their lives in the defence of their motherland, whether it was Suhaldev or the martyrs of the Kargil war.[19] Murli Manohar Joshi too, in his address to the pasi community, transformed the myth of Suhaldev into an electoral resource by specifically mentioning that Suhaldev had stopped the conversion of many Hindus to Islam.

As a part of the transmission of Suhaldev in the popular memory of people of Uttar Pradesh, various statues of Suhaldev were installed in different parts of the state. The statue installed in Lucknow by the RSS reflects their urge to propagate an aggressive image of Suhaldev. It is markedly different from the statue in Bahraich installed in the 1950s based on the painting by the Nag brothers. In the Lucknow statue, he is shown in as a valiant, militant stance similar to the image of Maharana Pratap. He is wearing iron armour, iron headgear and iron breeches, and is holding a spear while a sword is tucked in his waist. On the other hand, the statue in Bahraich depicts him more as a medieval folk hero wearing a crown and holding a bow and arrow. Maharana Pratap is another myth propagated by the RSS and the attempt to carve Suhaldev in his image might be a reflection of the desire to homogenise the militant Hindu heroes and their iconography. The residents of Bahraich, however, believe that the statue of Suhaldev in Bahraich is a true depiction.

Before 2002, the festival was restricted to performing Ramkathas, 'kalashyatras' and 'havan' and taking out processions. In 2002, at a meeting in Saraswati Shishu Mandir, a branch of a school run by the RSS all over India to culturally condition young children, it was decided that depicting the life of Suhaldev through theatre would be a more effective medium of transmitting the message of the RSS to the masses. The Berunapur theatre company was commissioned to prepare a drama based on the life of Suhaldev. The script of the drama was prepared by Mahiraj Dhwaj Singh, a Sangh pracharak with the help of literature and writer Gopal Shukla.[20] The drama, when it was performed for the first time during the Suhaldev fair organised at the premises of the Suhaldev temple, evoked a thunderous applause, especially in the scene when Suhaldev chopped off Ghazi Mian's head. Seeing the response of the audience, the organisers decided to make the drama a regular feature and make that particular scene even more gruesome and aggressive. This version of drama is used by various other drama companies of the region, which they perform on various occasions. Thus, the drama prepared for the celebration of the memory of Suhaldev is now emerging as a popular culture of theatrical performance of the region and is helping in creation of popular memory in one religious community against the other.

[...]

Notes

1. *Panchjanya*, 6 April 2003 and 23 January 2004, New Delhi; and various other interpretations of BJP and RSS leaders published in other issues of *Panchjanya* and other publications.

2. Invitation letter-cum-pamphlet distributed by Maharaja Suhaldev Sewa Samiti to propagate Suhaldev Memorial celebration, May 2004.

3. Ishar, Muhammed. Field diary, MM, time: 3.00 pm, place: Dargah of Ghazi Mian.

4. Yadav, Sakharam. Field diary MM, 23 April 2004, time: 5.00 pm, place: Bahraich.

5. Ishar, Muhammad. Field diary MM, 23 April 2004, time: 4.00 pm, place: Bahraich.

6. *Bahraich: A Gazetteer*, vol. XLV of the District Gazetteers of United Provinces of Agra and Oudh, Government of British India, 1903.

7. Kol 1997 and Pasi 2005.

8. *Bahraich: A Gazetteer*, vol. XLV of the District Gazetteers of United Provinces of Agra and Oudh: 1903.

9. Kol 1997, 2; see also: Fisher, F. H., and J. P. Hewett, eds. 1884. *Statiscal, Discriptive and Historical Account of the NWP of India*, vol. VIII part 2, comp. C. D. Steel. Allahabad: Government of British India, 49.

10. Leaflet published during the parliamentary election, 2004 by the Bharat Kranti Rakshak Party (BKRP) at 207, Lekhraj Gold Munshi Pulia, Indira Nagar, Lucknow.

11. 'Rashtra Rakshak Veer Shiromani Maharaja Suhaldev': pamphlet published by Maharaja Suhaldev Sewa Samiti, Bahraich, 2003.

12. Ali, Gulle Abbas. Field diary MM, 21 February 2003, time: 4.30 pm, place: Shahabpur.

13. Projection of the image of Suhaldev as a cow protector is a method that had earlier also been used by the RSS to mobilise dalits and backward communities. Rai, Vibhuti Narain. 1998. *Combating Communal Conflicts: Perception of Police Neutrality during Hindu-Muslim Riots in India*. Allahabad: Anamika Prakashan, 49.

14. Ishar, Muhammed. Field diary, MM, time: 3.00 pm, place: Dargah of Ghazi Mian.

15. S. P. Singh, a local pracharak, Chowk Bazaar, Bahraich of RSS; interview recorded on 25 April at 1.30 pm, 2004.

16. Ramsnehi, Hospital Road, Bahraich; interview recorded on 26 April, at 4.00 pm, 2004.

17. O. P. Agrawal, age 70 years, a local resident of Bahraich; interview recorded on 24 April 2004, at 3.00 pm.

18. Shri Shyam Lal Shrivastava, a lawyer and Shri Devi Charan Shrivastava, the principal of a local college, were two such writers.

19. 'Path Sanket', the pamphlet published by the RSS, 8 April 2004, Lucknow.

20. Interview of Gopal Shukla.

REFERENCES

Amar Ujala. Lucknow, 6 May 2004.

Jaffrelot, C. 1996. *The Hindu Nationalist Movement and Indian Politics 1920s to the 1990s*. New York: Columbia University Press.

Kol, Triloki Nath. 1997. *Hindu Samaj Ka Gaurav: Pasi Veer Maharaja Suhaldev Ki Shaurya Gatha*. Allahabad: Samajik Samrasta Abhyan Samiti.

Laxman, B. 1994. 'Samajik Manthan ki Aavashyakta'. *Panchjanya*, 23 January, New Delhi, 14.

Pasi, Raj Kumar. 2005. *Ek Barabanki ka Vishmrit Ithihas*. Lucknow: Pasi Shodh Evom Sanskriti Sansthan, 71.

Shukla, Gopal. 2003. *Aitihasik Kal Khand ke Prishth*. Unpublished manuscript, Bahraich, 108.

27

Judicial Inquiries into Communal Violence*

Relevance of Vishnu Sahai Commission

Rajeshwari

The immediate reaction of any state government following a communal riot is to constitute a judicial inquiry commission. It was not a surprise, therefore, when the Akhilesh Yadav government constituted a one-member judicial commission led by Justice Vishnu Sahai to inquire into the Muzaffarnagar riots. What is the message that a government wants to convey in appointing a judicial inquiry commission? The paramount concern of any government after a communal riot should be to restore the confidence of the victim community after the acts of violence and judicial commissions are primarily set up for this purpose. The rationale is that an independent inquiry would help bring forward credible information related to the riot, as often it has been observed that there are different versions emerging and there is an attempt to define or attach meaning to incidents of communal violence. The government orders a probe to demonstrate its neutrality, particularly when there are questions raised on the actions/inactions by different agencies of the state during the riots. The commissions are expected to compile a report on their findings and name the groups or persons responsible for the communal riot and also recommend adequate compensation for the victims.

Since the main purpose of appointing judicial commissions is to bestow an aura of neutrality and fairness, it would be useful to analyse whether judicial commissions in the past have been successful in fulfilling this purpose. Can we come up with a singular and universal conclusion on judicial inquiry commissions inquiring into communal riots? What are the parameters under which the Sahai Commission and others like it should be judged? What lessons can there be for the Sahai Commission from the past experiences of judicial inquiry into communal riots?

* *Economic and Political Weekly* 48 (40): 13–15 (5 October 2013).

JUDGING JUDICIAL COMMISSIONS

In India, there have been a number of reports and critiques of how commissions do not meet the purpose because of inherent delays and the long time taken to come out with findings. This criticism is not completely unwarranted. According to government records since Independence, among the numerous incidents of communal riots, commissions of inquiry have been appointed on 40 occasions. These commissions were appointed to inquire into some of the major riots where two groups belonging to different castes or religions were involved. Among the 40 commissions appointed, action taken reports (ATR) by the government are available for only 11 commissions of inquiry. Only 14 commissions have submitted the report within a span of one year and the rest have taken between two to eight years to finish the inquiry and submit a report. Most of the perceptions of inquiry commissions are, therefore, based purely on these data, which are important, but do not bring forward the complete picture. Any comprehensive understanding of these commissions can emerge only if we look at the substantial issues that come before them.

In taking up the task of inquiring into a sensitive matter like a communal riot, the Sahai Commission would have to deal with all the issues faced by the others inquiring into the incidents of communal rioting. These issues relate to credibility, vagueness in terms of reference, lack of cooperation from the state government concerned and most importantly, collecting credible evidence. The past experiences of judicial commissions on communal riots suggest that the manner in which a commission tackles these issues becomes important in deciding its efficiency and success. Some examples can be given to illustrate this point. The inquiry commission on the Bhagalpur riots resulted in further controversy with two different reports coming from the same commission. It could not play the mediatory role between the people and the government and restore the confidence of the victim community.

The mandate of a commission or its terms of reference have a relevant role to play in determining its fair and neutral character. Whether commissions strictly stick to the mandate before them or whether they manoeuvre the terms for the benefit of the issue under inquiry has an important bearing on the character of the commission. The Srikrishna Commission interpreted the mandate for the larger benefit of the issue under inquiry and was, therefore, one of the popular commissions.

The procedure a commission follows while inquiring into matters of public importance is another important parameter for assessing them. For example, a commission that makes an in-camera inquiry like the Ranganath Mishra Commission which probed the anti-Sikh riots would certainly be viewed with suspicion as against a commission which conducts an open inquiry. How a commission goes about the process of collecting evidences is another important aspect. The process of collecting evidences is not only tedious, but has several constraints and challenges.

Sometimes, as was pointed out by the Venkatagiri Commission, it is not just public apathy that stops witnesses from coming forward and giving evidence. There are other aspects like fear and lack of protection that make it difficult for genuine witnesses to file their statements before an inquiry commission. The Aligarh Riots

Commission headed by Justice Shashi Kant Varma appointed on 20 October 1978 was wound up on 31 July 1980. The commission was expected to examine 200 witnesses but from January to April 1980, it was able to examine just eight witnesses and the Uttar Pradesh state government suggested that it wind up the inquiry. Some commissions believe in a passive role wherein they wait for the evidence to emerge before them. Others take a more active role by going in search of evidence and create the space for new evidences to emerge before them. The Sahai Commission has both the options available before it and has to make a choice based on how it wants to be viewed.

Scoring Political Points

The next significant issue is the relationship between the government and the commission. The government's power to appoint and dismiss commissions and the arbitrary use of this power has time and again undermined their relevance. Sometimes, commissions have been appointed for political gains. For example, the Tamil Nadu government appointed the Sivasubramanian Commission of Inquiry on 14 August 1992 to probe charges against the Dravida Munnetra Kazhagam (DMK) leader, M. Karunanidhi, but did not give convincing explanations for its appointment. Since the chair of a commission enjoys the same perks and salary as that of a judge of the Supreme Court and there is a lot of public money involved in the inquiry process, governments are expected to be careful in appointing judicial commissions. It is difficult for any judicial commission to enjoy the confidence of the people if the reasons for their appointment are not rooted in the letter and spirit of the Commission of Inquiry Act and such an inquiry, even if it does exemplary work, would be viewed with suspicion and its fairness and neutrality would always remain a question mark.

Also, who is appointed as the chair of a commission acquires importance. The ideal situation is when the government's appointment is met with agreement all around. While this ideal is difficult to achieve, it is important that a broad consensus emerges. The integrity of the judge presiding as the chair of a commission comes into question especially when s/he is rewarded with appointments and coveted positions, transfers and post-retirement benefits. The appointment of Justice K. Venkataswami, who was chairing the Tehelka Inquiry Commission, as the chair of another statutory body even before he submitted his report is a case in example. The performance of the commission and the final recommendations along with proceedings are given shape by the chair of a commission. Therefore, functioning in a neutral manner is essential for producing a balanced report which safeguards the rights and provides justice for the citizens of a country. In the context of the Sahai Commission again, it would be interesting to see how the victims perceive the commission. Some views expressed by the Deoband do not reflect in favour of the commission.

Another problem that commissions often face is with regard to the relevance of their report. It is argued that commission reports have little relevance since they are not implemented by the governments concerned. However, it is important to remember that whenever commission reports have not been implemented, these issues have come back to haunt the respective governments and become serious subjects of debate within the legislative assemblies and Parliament. The resurfacing of issues and their 'longevity' along with the mechanism of going back to the recommendations of the commission perhaps make them a relevant public institution in a democracy.

However, if these are the parameters on the basis of which commissions should be adjudged, then can we bracket all of them together? The effectiveness of public institutions like judicial commissions needs to be located outside 'black' and 'white' categorisation. Some commissions succeed largely in restoring the lost trust of people and re-establishing the legitimacy of the state, while others are not able to achieve this. The difference between commissions appearing to function/not function in a fair and neutral manner is rooted, to a large extent, in both the procedural and substantial aspects of their functioning. At a more substantial level, commissions that do not appear meek or overawed by the governments in their working, and show an ability to grasp the larger political context of their appointment while taking decisions accordingly have been viewed as fair and neutral. It would be unfair to suggest that all commissions are unable to name the perpetrators or implicate authorities in their reports. There have been cases like the Madon and Srikrishna Commissions which have recognised and identified those who were responsible for the riots that they were looking into respectively. Others have given indications of probable involvement of politicians, important ministers (Nanavati Commission) and dereliction of duty by individual police officials. The differences among commissions and their ability to apportion responsibility for riots is based on the nature of evidence, how a commission interprets such evidence, the different competing explanations which emerge for the same incidents of riots and how a commission deals with these different versions.

LEGACY OF COMMISSIONS

While it would be easy to dismiss the work done by judicial commissions as irrelevant and view them as public institutions of little value, it is significant to understand the legacy left by these commissions. The detailed accounts of riots, proceedings and reasons for following a certain type of inquiry, evidences for and against a certain contentious issue, the key findings and recommendations—all these are not just information on the events which the commissions inquire into but also an account of how inquiries into communal riots are conducted. It would be interesting to wait and watch the progress that the Vishnu Sahai Commission makes, particularly with regard to the pressures that it would face given that its recommendations and findings can be used by different political groups for electoral gains.

28

Communal Riots in Uttar Pradesh*

Badri Narayan

India's democracy exerts constant pressure on political parties to mobilise people for electoral purposes. Electoral mobilisation is often based on evoking emotive issues such as religion, language, caste and parochialism. Development and other rational issues also get transformed into emotional issues because of the unequal distribution of resources and opportunities, and the growing expectations of the people.

A study of the history of electoral mobilisation in India would show that religion and caste have always been the most effective issues for mobilising people. Indian political parties have often used the issue of caste to stop religious mobilisation, and the issue of religion to stop caste mobilisation. In the 1990s, both the politics of communal hatred, which emerged around the demolition of the Babri masjid, and caste politics, which emerged after the implementation of the Mandal Commission report, were strengthened. Since then, communal politics has been used to neutralise caste politics, and religious politics to defuse caste politics. Caste feelings often remain active even after being submerged in the cauldron of religion, and the rise of middle-and-dalit caste identities work against communal politics. These two are not always opposed to each other, and work together to take a complex form for electoral mobilisation. Thus, both caste consciousness (*jati bhav*) and communal consciousness (*sampradayik* bhav) are necessary for political parties, depending on their electoral compulsions. Often, caste and communal consciousness join with politics to become aggressive—in its outer and inner forms, in its form and content, and in its process and consequence.

The politics of emotive issues and identity politics introduced by the Bharatiya Janata Party (BJP) and Sangh parivar in the 2014 parliamentary elections was born of a mixture of the 'desire for development and communal consciousness' which shattered the dichotomy between communal and caste identity in Indian politics and society. The BJP understood that communal politics by itself would not succeed, and it had to be linked with the desire for development in the minds of the common people. It successfully combined these two elements while devising a

* *Economic and Political Weekly* 49 (37): 29–32 (13 September 2014).

strategy for mobilising people of all castes and communities, including Muslims. If the promised development does not happen, disillusionment will set in quickly. This would limit the degree to which the BJP can succeed in communal polarisation in the future, just as it did in Muzaffarnagar and Moradabad.

PHENOMENON OF SMALL RIOTS

Communal riots do not occur; they are engineered, and the people engineering them have motives that usually have to do with political mobilisation and elections (*Amar Ujala* 2013). If one studies the history of the forms of communal riots in the post-Independence period, one finds several changes in them over time and space. Putting aside the riots that reflected communal moments at the time of Partition, historians and social scientists have always considered communal riots as an urban phenomenon. However, in post-liberalisation India, communal riots have been spreading to villages as well.

The second change is that there used to earlier be big communal riots at large intervals, but now under a new strategy for reaping electoral gain, different religious groups are mobilised by creating communal moments through small communal conflicts and riots over a long period of time. Through this, communal consciousness is made a continuous presence, not a momentary one. In this strategy, the making of a communal consciousness requires a string of communal moments that produce and reproduce communal polarisation directly and indirectly. Political parties try to exploit these small riots or communal moments, and arouse and sustain a communal consciousness through them. Through these small riots, they also want fear to grow in their target oppressed group or opposed group. This accumulation of fear takes an aggressive and vicious form at the time of elections in the name of saving a community's honour or avenging its humiliation.

Bigger riots need long-term preparation for the making of a communal moment. This includes collecting arms and ammunitions, and making pyramids of multiple tensions between communities. Given the pyramid of tensions, even playing loud music or throwing stones may erupt into big violence. However, for small riots, one does not need long-term preparations, and waiting for or engineering a pyramid of tensions (Rai 1998: 61). They may erupt because of an immediate small issue, which is fuelled by political forces who politicise it. In the visual media and newspapers, their mobilisational impact multiplies and influences both the quarrelling communities, sometimes across a region and state. This is further aggravated by an alert and active communal consciousness among the people. Thus, the impact of small riots is no less than that of big riots, but the political parties inciting them are not subject to as much criticism.

The phenomenon of small riots needs the eruption of a series of low-key communal conflicts, and through them a constant reproduction of communal consciousness. This is more suitable for political forces to harness communally mobilised votes. A cadre of a communal organisation asked me during an interview, 'Agar kam mehnat, loss and investment me jyada fayada ho raha ho to kyon bara risk le?' (If there is more profit with less effort, loss and investment, why should we take a bigger risk?). This does not mean that small riots may not turn into big communal riots, but that in the absence of long-term preparation, it is difficult to transform them into big communal riots. In the past, communal moments used to lose their effect after a few days. But the small riots stretch communal moments over a long duration.

According to an investigation by the *Indian Express*, police records show that more than 600 'communal incidents' or small religious conflicts took place in Uttar Pradesh after the Lok Sabha elections, between 16 May and 25 July 2014. The largest number of riots, 259, took place in western Uttar Pradesh. In the Terai region, 29 clashes took place; in the Awadh region, 53; in Bundelkhand, six; and in eastern Uttar Pradesh, 16 (Express Investigation Part I 2014). A further analysis of the statistics shows that the regions where most of the communal riots took place are the constituencies where assembly by-polls will be held very soon. For example, in western Uttar Pradesh, polls are due in five seats; in the Terai region, in two seats; in the Awadh region, in one seat; in Bundelkhand, in two seats; and in eastern Uttar Pradesh, in two seats. The roles of political classes and parties are clearly evident in these riots.

Political Economy

In western Uttar Pradesh, where polls are due in five seats, 259 riots took place, while fewer riots took place in the regions where polls are due in fewer seats. However, the proportion of riots is much higher in western Uttar Pradesh than in other regions. This implies that the socio-economic and political ground of the region is conducive for communal riots to occur.

Western Uttar Pradesh is the most developed region of the state. It reaped the maximum benefits of the green revolution and came to be known as Harit (green) Pradesh. However, the benefits of the green revolution were not spread evenly, and were confined to a few castes. The region is steeped in feudalism, and prosperity widened the gap between various castes and communities. Jealousies and anxieties spawned by uneven development further increased existing feudal pride. The gap between Hindu jats and the Muslim (Mulla) jats significantly increased after the green revolution. The percentage of Muslims in this region is the highest in the state. There is no parliamentary constituency where they are less than 20–25 per cent, and in some constituencies, they are more than 40 per cent. Muslims here are not a passive community, but highly active and aspiring. They are trying hard to increase their space and visibility in the region.

If we analyse the nature of the small riots that took place in western Uttar Pradesh, we find that most of them were conflicts for dominant visibility, that is, to establish domination over other communities.

Several of them were over trivial issues such as the volume of loudspeakers. As many as 120 of the 600-odd communal incidents were triggered by clashes over the use of loudspeakers (Express Investigation Part II 2014). Although loudspeakers and religious festivals do not have any direct connection, all religions use them to assert their identity and 'dominance of visibility'. The Calcutta High Court banned them many years ago, but this ban has not yet been implemented. Far from being an assertion of freedom, the use of loudspeakers shows a greater tendency to spread anarchy and hurt the feelings of other communities. Other trivial reasons for the communal incidents were arguments over who should be served first in a local eatery; the use of a public latrine by one community; the grazing of cattle; the cutting of a neem tree; collisions between children riding cycles; and minor motorcycle accidents (Express Investigation Part IV 2014).

POLITICAL PARTIES

... The spread of trade and commerce has played an important role in the expansion of different branches of the Rashtriya Swayamsevak Sangh (RSS), which is trying to promote the cultural dominance of Hindutva. Immediately after Independence, the Arya Samaj was active in west Uttar Pradesh and it played a very progressive role. But when this declined, the Hindutva mindset took over. The dalit community in Uttar Pradesh was particularly influenced by the Arya Samaj, which later became the cause for bonding with Hindutva.

... The BJP has recently been working on the politics of linking the desire for development with a desire to create a 'Maha Hindu identity' through communal mobilisation, and has reaped great profit from it.

For the Samajwadi Party (SP), the Bahujan Samaj Party (BSP) and the Congress, communal riots are now a no-profit game because Hindu polarisation has cut their Hindu base and marginalised them. All the three have to obtain a share of the remaining, mainly Muslim, votes. They are thus compelled to play the politics of communal mobilisation. To reply to the BJP, the SP mobilised Muslims in Uttar Pradesh, and the Congress also took advantage of it when there was the possibility of linking the caste vote bank with the Muslim vote bank. In the new political scenario, when the yadav base of the SP, the dalit base of the BSP, and the urban and upper-caste votes of the Congress have moved towards the BJP, the communal game is a losing one for them. At the local level, it is possible that these three political parties may gain some advantage, but that will happen only if their Hindu vote banks remain intact and Muslims vote for them. Since all three parties are struggling for a share of the same set of Muslim votes, they participate in riots because of a compulsive fear that they may lose the remaining Muslim votes as well. Thus, there is anxiety about their political base, which is under threat.

Like in the fable of the snake and the mongoose, the BSP is neither able to swallow the situation nor ignore it because the communal mobilisation of the Sangh parivar is creating dalit–Muslim tensions. A ninth of all communal incidents since 16 May 2014 were dalit–Muslim confrontations (Express Investigation Part III 2014). One such incident took place in Katauli Kala in Azamgarh district on 4 August 2014. A minor argument over widening a village road led to a violent clash, leaving eight people injured, even though there was no history of tension between the two communities (Express Investigation Part III 2014). The dalit vote of the BSP, which was strong in western Uttar Pradesh, is being lost. The party's politics of forging a link between dalits and Muslims is now in crisis. If it tries to bring Muslims under its umbrella, dalits might go their own way, and if it sides with dalits, Muslims might break away. That is why Mayawati is unable to take any action.

The ... Sangh parivar ... vision of Indian villages is one where upper-caste Hindus govern, while the dalit castes are imbued with brahminical values. They should willingly function as soldiers of the upper castes and fight battles on their behalf. For this, the growing chasm between the upper and lower castes should be reduced, and social harmony has to be restored (Narayan 2009: 42).

The small riots will continue to take place before the 2017 assembly elections in Uttar Pradesh. There will also be a marked effort to spread them to places such as eastern Uttar Pradesh and Bundelkhand. If the SP is unable to reduce the growing communal space in Uttar Pradesh society and politics through its state agencies, the BJP will have an advantage, while the others will have none.

References

Amar Ujala. '18 Sthalon par Sadbhav Bigarhne ki Ashanka'; 'Kaushambi ke 20 Netaon ke Pratinidhion par hai ATS ki Nigah', Allahabad, Pratapgarh, 24 September 2013.

Express Investigation Part I. 'Over 600 "Communal Incidents" in UP since LS Results'. *The Indian Express*, 5 August 2014.

Express Investigation Part II. 'My Loudspeaker versus Loudspeaker'. *The Indian Express*, 6 August 2014.

Express Investigation Part III. 'Dalit-Muslim Divide Deepens, Goes Rural'. *The Indian Express*, 7 August 2014.

Express Investigation Part IV. 'Fighting Kids to Dhaba Bill: Takes Little to Keep Communal Pot Simmering'. *The Indian Express*, 8 August 2014.

Narayan, B. 2009. *Fascinating Hindutva: Saffron Politics and Dalit Mobilisation*. New Delhi: Sage.

Rai, V. N. 1998. *Combating Communal Conflicts*. Allahabad: Anamika Prakashan.

Section IV

Accounts and Analyses of Specific Riots

Introduction to Section IV

Articles in this section deal with individual cases of sectarian violence. Given the ubiquity of the phenomenon and the periodicity of the *EPW* as a weekly, there were naturally a very large number of articles to choose from and the choice was not easy. In selecting the articles, we were neither guided by the scale or gruesomeness of the incidents, nor by the endemic nature of the violence at some sites. We were looking for variety in the approaches to riots, attempts to consciously set aside predictable explanations and bring in fresh perspectives. Since the political economy approach, or, what can be more broadly called a search for objective material factors precipitating violence, dominates the coverage by *EPW*'s 'Correspondents', we have tended to select articles which deviate from this standard narrative.

The essays in this section cover roughly two decades from the late 1960s to the late 1980s. In terms of the calendar of riots, the opening piece is Ghanshyam Shah's analysis of the 1969–70 riots in Ahmedabad (published 1974), while the most recent commentary is on the aftermath of the 1987 Meerut riots, including the Hashimpura killings, by Iqbal Ansari (published 2004). We have also included two pairs of pieces on the same riot just to illustrate the similarities and differences produced by a different viewpoint on the same events. Thus, Sudhir Chandra and Ghanshyam Shah write on the Surat riots of 1993; incidentally, both were residents of Surat at that time. By contrast, the Bijnor riots of 1990 are the subject of two articles by researchers based abroad. However, Patricia and Roger Jeffrey (based in the United Kingdom) have been doing intermittent fieldwork in Bijnor district for over a decade, while Amrita Basu (based in the United States of America) spent two months making repeated visits to Bijnor town for her fieldwork. No researcher can ever hope to be an 'insider' to the social processes that produce riots, but different kinds of relationships to the 'field' would presumably yield different insights.

When riots take place anywhere, our social scientific instinct looks for causes, discriminates between the underlying conditions and the 'trigger', the demographic profile of the locality where the violence was acute, migration pattern, the local economy and its vicissitudes, the history of disputed sites, and the electoral politics. A few of the articles included in this section follow the trail of riots and try to identify their origins in the complex weave of actions and conditions. Such analysis can be illuminating but its utility in preventing future outbreaks is limited. If riots are 'staged conflicts', or 'routines' belonging to the political repertoire, as we saw in the chapter by Paul Brass (in Section II), then what we have really is not a sudden outbreak over an emotionally potent issue, nor animosities going back across decades and centuries, but an elaborate system of riot production.

One way in which objectivist accounts can be complemented is by exploring mutual perceptions of the members of the two communities, men and women who have some degree of identification with the respective communities. Some of the chapters included here (for example, the second part of Gopal Krishna's essay) do it by presenting results of post-riot surveys, or giving us accounts of conversations with persons from both the communities. By talking to a cross-section of people in the affected areas, they try to find out what the Hindus and Muslims think of each other, what their self-images are, and whom they blame for the violence. The timing of these surveys and interviews is significant. The immediacy of the riot lends urgency to the reflections by the respondents, it makes them think and introspect, but the same closeness of extraordinary events might also influence the responses in ways not easy to gauge. Therefore, to see in them probable causes of the riot retrospectively may not be justifiable. The authors are alive to the problematic nature of the testimonies and of the complexity of the interaction between the investigator and the traumatised people. This comes up in Gyanendra Pandey's chapter in Section II as well. But what perhaps needs to be reiterated is that the relationship between what is said and what is done is not simply that of beliefs and emotions causally producing actions. In narrating, mourning or bitterly complaining to the investigator, the respondents are doing something. The verbal responses are actions by themselves—at once revealing and ambiguous—and not just causal clues to the past and future actions.

There is another kind of ambiguity discernible in some of the cases, this time ambiguity of actions and not of verbal responses. Reading Shail Mayaram's chapter, one can see that a local politician or a member of a right wing outfit is perfectly capable of protecting or leaving unharmed his neighbour belonging to the 'other' community and also at the same time, actively participating in rioting elsewhere. People are guided by multiple codes and they switch from one to the other in a manner that is hard to understand and harder to predict. Incidentally (and here we are moving away from Mayaram's overall argument), this also shows that the bulwark of local age old ties between Hindu and Muslim neighbours are perhaps less resistant to the macro ideologies and the pull of electoral calculations than we would like to believe. So, to modify slightly the title of one of the essays, local riots are not always local.

29

Communal Riots in Gujarat*

Report of a Preliminary Investigation

Ghanshyam Shah

[...]

The Riots of September

We shall now try to reconstruct the sequence of events that produced the holocaust in Gujarat. We report the events in some detail, both because the details have not yet been presented in a proper form anywhere and also in order to bring out the general point that the casual sequence in collective violence is not so much determined by the 'first cause' as by certain intervening factors which transform a low-tension situation into a high-tension one.

Jagannath Temple Incident

On 18 September 1969, while Congress leaders from all over Gujarat were busy discussing the 'unity resolution' of the Congress Party at a meeting held in Ahmedabad, some sadhus and Muslims were reported to have clashed a little distance away. This was, of course, a pure coincidence. The venue of the clash was the Jagannath temple, situated at the end of Jamalpur area, thickly populated by Muslims. In 1946 too, when the last major communal riots took place in Ahmedabad, the cause was the same, namely a *rathayatra* (chariot procession [eds]) of Jagannath.

As part of a festival held every year, about 1,000 Muslims, including women and children, had assembled for Urs near the Jagannath temple along a narrow road about 30 feet wide. Also, as happened every day, at about 3 pm, a herd of cows was returning to the temple, led by two sadhus who were quite familiar with the Muslims of the area. ... In this atmosphere of tension and commotion, a scuffle developed between the Muslim young men and the sadhus. The sadhus used their sticks, while the Muslims used stones. The two sadhus, being fewer in number,

* *Economic and Political Weekly* 5 (3–5): 187–200 (17 January 1970).

rushed into the temple. As they went inside the temple, the crowd threw stones at the temple. The two sadhus came back with a few others to retaliate. But they were still too few against the crowd. About 13 sadhus were injured by stones. There was also some damage to the temple, such as breakage of glasses of photo-frames covering the picture of a deity. Meanwhile, police came and brought an end to the fighting. On the whole, it was an ordinary incident sparked off by a minor accident.

Organised Protest

A few hours after this episode, at 8 pm, a meeting of the trustees of the temple was held. The meeting issued a press statement expressing distress, appealing to the government to appoint a commission of inquiry and punish the criminals and asking the people of Ahmedabad to offer a prayer to Lord Jagadish and maintain peace.

On the same night, several sadhus of the temple, including Sevadas-ji, the head priest, went on fast to protest against the attack and to demand justice. Similarly, the Hindu Dharma Raksha Samiti called a public meeting on 19 September at 7 pm outside the Raipur gate for condemning the attack on the temple.

Although there were these loud expressions of protest, the rest of the city life went on quite normally. Several rumours, of course, went around the town. Also, as a measure of retaliation, on the night of 18 September and early morning of the 19th, three shops belonging to Muslims at three different places were set on fire.[1] But, barring this, the city passed the evening and the night quietly.

19 September

The next morning, 19 September, brought news of the attack on the temple to newspaper readers. Different newspapers gave different descriptions of the episode. We shall examine the role of newspapers later in this article. Suffice it to note here that the news media only succeeded in spreading confusion in the minds of the people. People also read the statement of the trustees of the temple and the call of the Hindu Dharma Raksha Samiti. From all this, they concluded two things: the attack on the temple by the Muslims was a serious one and had been pre-planned; and the government and the press were not giving a correct picture of the casualties. Though newspaper reports were short, it was mentioned that the attackers used acid bulbs and arms.

However, despite this general impression and expression of concern about it, there was as yet no sign of an outburst of communal feeling. The burning of the three Muslim shops had not been reported in the newspapers. The morning of the 19th in Ahmedabad appeared to be pretty near normal. Workers went to the factories, students attended their classes and businessmen carried on their work as usual. The overriding topic of discussion in the town was, of course, the Jagannath temple. And the nature of the discussions revealed deep-seated prejudices.

Atmosphere of Suspense

As the day passed, however, these prejudices were to be actively nursed and incited. During the day, unsigned handbills were circulated which gave exaggerated accounts of the Jagannath temple incident from the point of the view of the Hindus. The reports contained in these handbills were taken at their face value, and most people were furious against the Muslims. Second, about noon, organised groups of people began moving around various areas, asking people to close their shops. By 2 pm, most of the markets were closed. Schools were closed a little later. Evening shows of cinemas were cancelled. By the afternoon itself, a grim atmosphere of suspense had overtaken the city.

Meanwhile, several delegations met the Chief Minister to press for appointment of an inquiry committee on the Jagannath temple episode. The government had declared the appointment of such a committee. Leaders of all communities issued appeals, condemning the attack on the temple and urging the citizens to maintain peace. Muslim leaders were not found lagging behind in these attempts. Fifteen Muslim leaders belonging to different parties condemned the attack on the Jagannath temple, demanded an immediate inquiry, and asked for severe punishment to the offenders. They appealed to Hindus and Muslims to maintain peace. But the news of all these appeals, and the government's decision to appoint a committee of inquiry, were published only the next day in the newspapers. Long before that, mob fury had taken hold of the situation. And there was no sign yet of any firm action on the part of the government.

Already between noon and the evening, several scattered instances of arson and fire had taken place in different places within the walled area of the town. At 7 pm, the scheduled meeting of the Hindu Dharma Raksha Samiti was held outside the Raipur gate despite section 144 of the Cr.PC having been promulgated. It was a big congregation. The leaders of the Samiti came to the venue of the meeting in a procession. Anti-Muslim slogans were shouted. The speakers condemned the attack on the temple in very strong words and asked for an inquiry committee, failing which, according to a swami of the Gita Mandir, all sadhus of the Mandir would observe fast from the next day and would not hesitate to sacrifice their lives on the issue. Another very popular religio-political leader said that he would violate section 144 of the Cr.PC, no matter what sacrifice was involved. Most of the speeches at the meeting were delivered in a firm and decisive tone.

Mob Fury

Although the meeting was dissolved in 20 minutes, while it was in session, a section of the meeting attacked a radio shop of the area and set fire to it. The fire brigade soon came but was met with stones from the crowd and was forced to return. Later on, the police controlled this particular situation. But mob fury had been sparked off and there was no stopping the looting and large-scale rioting in various parts of the city. However, the government imposed curfew in Khadiya, Jamalpur and Kalupur wards from 10 pm to 7 am.

The direction of mob action was determined by this partial action on the part of the government. The rest of the city was left at the mercy of the rioters. They first turned to Gita Mandir Road, adjoining the Raipur gate. Gita Mandir temple is located in this area and the sadhus of the temple were active in the protest organised by the Hindu Dharma Raksha Samiti. The inhabitants of the area also had a special grievance which had turned them against Muslims. A political bully of the area, whom the Congress leaders were alleged to have protected so far, happened to be a Muslim. Residents had felt helpless and were critical of the government. Now, in the general excitement against the Muslims, they found an opportunity to retaliate against the hooligan and his community. They became active in the riot. Close to Gita Mandir road was the Beharampura area where the *Ramayana* incident had taken place only a week ago. There was also the slummy Shah Alam Taka, reportedly the abode of many a hooligan. This combination of circumstances provided fertile ground for the spread of the mood of retaliation and revenge that started with the Raipur meeting and its aftermath.

Evidence of Planning

By 11 pm, the mob had taken complete control over the area. There was not a little planning in their actions. In order to prevent police vans from entering the area, they dug ditches at the three ends, some volunteers occupying seats near the ditches and watching. Meanwhile, Muslim shops were broken open, goods were looted or set on fire. Even in this, the mob showed a calculated sense of discrimination. Muslim shops in Hindu-owned buildings were plundered but not set on fire; similar shops in Muslim-owned buildings were set on fire; shops owned by a Hindu and Muslim in partnership remained undisturbed. It was reported to me that riot organisers in this and other areas moved with voters' lists to identify Muslim houses. On the whole, though they tried to resist the attackers in the beginning, the Muslim population found itself overwhelmed in number and utterly demoralised in the face of such a massive attack.

The momentum came with the burning of two big 'kabadi' markets dealing in second-hand tubes and tires, colour and cloth printing for which Ahmedabad is famous and oil which provided the rioters with ready fuel. No fire brigades came to the help of the Muslim shopkeepers, most of whom were themselves not on site. The flames spread wide. Even the roads were hot. Yet throngs of Hindu householders, including women, were out as participants, as observers or simply to enjoy the fun. Some of them joined in shouts of 'Jai Jagannath', while others distributed *prasad* to the onlookers.

[...]

By the afternoon of Saturday, 20 September, the flame of Gita Mandir and Raipur had spread through the whole town—labour and upper-class areas. The mob violence that was let loose did not spare even the Sabarmati Ashram. On Saturday evening, a relatively small crowd of about 50 people went to the Ashram with axes, stones, lathis and iron bars to attack Imam Manzil, the house of 70-year-old Gulam Rasool Kureshi, an Ashram inmate since 1921. For him, it should be noted, this was not the first attack by communalists. In 1939, he had been assaulted by Muslim Leaguers. But this time, as the ashramites stood together against the crowd, no serious damage was done to Imam Manzil. However, the houses of Kureshi's two sons, one of whom had married a Hindu woman and had allowed her to follow the Hindu religion, were set aflame. In the process, both the *Quran* and the *Ramayana* were burnt by the mob.

[...]

No One Spared

In the same way, the crowd attacked the house of Ramjan Lakhani, whose brother Rajab had sacrificed his life[2] to prevent Hindu–Muslim riots in 1946. Similarly, high government officers who lived in the government colony were not spared. Officials could not protect their Muslim colleagues who happened to be their neighbours. In this inventory, mention should also be made of Kamal Hostel of Vadaj, a Muslim hostel for university students in which there were also 30 Hindu students as boarders. The hostel provided a possible platform for expressing solidarity among the two communities. Instead, it was completely destroyed; pillars and slabs of the huge building were physically removed, suggesting that skilled engineers were employed in the destruction.

The worst affected areas were the labour areas Khokhara-Mehmadavad, Amaraivadi, Raipur, Rakhiyal, Bapunagar, Chamanpura and New Mental Hospital Colony. Villages nearby Sabarmati and Ranip were also affected. Chawls consisting of rows of huts had been destroyed, their woodwork burnt and mud and brick walls demolished. Even such property of Muslim labourers as earthen pots, a pair of clothes, bed and a broken chair were burnt or destroyed. Old cycles, the only vehicles of mill labourers, were broken into bits. Atrocities multiplied by the evening of the 20th, when several poor labourers were either burnt alive or murdered. ... In this mad orgy, animal instincts of the worst kind seem to have got hold of the people of Ahmedabad.

Orgy of Violence

The riots had spread from Ahmedabad into various parts of the state.[3] Trains were not spared. On the night of the 20th, when several Muslims were escaping from Ahmedabad, four trains were stopped, Muslim passengers pulled out, looted and killed. Four days later, two trains were again stopped and 17 passengers were killed. On 23 September, as the government lifted the curfew for three hours, 40 persons lost their lives.

This orgy of violence—massacre, arson and looting—continued unstopped for three days. By Tuesday (23 September) afternoon, Ahmedabad was under the control of the army. The coming of the army brought about a radical change in the situation, but scattered instances of stabbing continued to take place for more than a month. More than 1,000 people, a large majority of them Muslim, lost their lives. Several hundreds ran away to their native villages. About 15,000 took shelter in relief camps. 3,969 dwellings and shops suffered destruction by fire, and 2,317 more were physically destroyed. About 6,000 families lost their belongings and shelter.[4] The value of property destroyed ran into crores of rupees. Just the city being under curfew for 10 days caused loss in income of at least Rs 33.70 crores.

THE QUESTION OF RESPONSIBILITY

A major issue in all chain occurrence of collective violence is how stray incidents get transformed into conflagrations. Who were the organising agents and what were the positive and negative contributory factors?

Looking to the nature of destruction in Ahmedabad, one is led to believe that there was some sort of planning in organising the riots. Soon after the Jagannath temple clash, a group of people seems to have systematically started spreading rumours. Who these people were and what the mechanics of spreading rumours were need a separate inquiry. However, it is well known that by noon of 19 September, hundreds of handbills were distributed in Ahmedabad regarding the Jagannath incident. In the handbills, it was said that a cow had been killed and the Mahant seriously injured, that the Muslims had entered the temple and that the idol of the god had been damaged. There was no truth in any of this. (In Baroda too, rumours were spread about the burning of the Swaminarayan temple.) As the riots continued, handbills were published which gave false, exaggerated and provocative news.

Masks Used

Besides the handbills, the Raipur Gate meeting in Ahmedabad (as the Wadi meeting in Baroda) provided evidence of advance planning. Moreover, it is clear that local neighbours had not done any harm to each other, most of the damage was done by crowds who came from outside. In certain mixed localities, every house and shop belonging to Muslims had been gutted. Voters' lists were used to locate Muslim houses. Muslims living in Hindu houses and Muslim houses in which Hindus were residing were separately marked. Kerosene and petrol were freely available at the trouble spots. Transportation facilities were provided to take a belligerent crowd from one area to another. I was also told that some persons in the crowd covered their faces with masks in order to conceal their identity.

By and large, all sections of the Hindu community participated in the riots in one way or other. Some were actual participants, some were observers providing facilities for the rioters if needed, and some were sympathisers and morale boosters.

However, one can say that businessmen, irrespective of caste, creed or region, did not take a direct part in the riots. Even Punjabi and Sindhi businessmen who had deep-rooted grievances against the Muslims remained aloof from the riots. They could not afford disturbances and, moreover, their business with Muslim merchants would be affected. Nevertheless, I came across a few businessmen, engaged in building construction and owning small factories, who supported rioters with money and materials. They gave them their vehicles and even participated in making riot 'plans'.

Workers Main Participants

The most active participants came from textile workers, manual labourers and scavengers. In Ahmedabad, 31.08 per cent of the population consist of workers. It should be noted that devotion to Jagannath is marked among workers. Sevadas-ji, the chief priest of the temple, is held in high regard by them. When they heard of the attack on the temple and the sadhus, they were very angry. Later, when the rumour spread that the chief priest had been killed, they were ready to take revenge.

Several textile mills had been closed down during the last few months, rendering 6,000–7,000 workers jobless. On the other hand, a large number of Muslim workers were permanent employees in textile mills. Some of the unemployed Hindu workers might have thought that Muslim workers stood between them and new jobs.

A sizeable number of labourers in Ahmedabad are non-Gujaratis. They are from Uttar Pradesh, Rajasthan, Maharashtra and other parts of the country. Classification of the migrants is given in Table 29.1. One can see from the table that a large number of them, particularly from Uttar Pradesh and Rajasthan, stay in Ahmedabad without their families. Workers from these regions are religious and have deep-rooted animosity towards the Muslims. Moreover, as they live alone, they have no roots in the cultural life of the city. And as they greatly value the *Ramayana*, the insult to it caused by a Muslim police inspector in the incident in which 'Bhaiyas' from Uttar Pradesh were involved, had already inflamed them. Most of all, it is difficult for a man who lives with his family to risk his life in riots, but these immigrants were free from immediate family bonds. They were thus available for mob action.[5]

TABLE 29.1: Non-Gujarati Migrants Classified by Sex, Religion and Place of Birth

Place of Birth	*Hindu*		*Muslim*		*Others*	
	M	*F*	*M*	*F*	*M*	*F*
Maharashtra	14,379	11,944	2,398	2,164	1,428	1,594
Rajasthan	29,940	15,858	5,136	3,683	1,987	1,146
Uttar Pradesh	23,149	7,423	11,784	4,504	324	165
Other States	12,633	8,194	4,649	2,782	1,750	1,361
Outside India	9,906	7,990	947	432	770	609

Source: Census of Gujarat, 1961.

It should also be added that the pattern of recruitment in textile mills and the functioning of the Majoor Mahajan, the dominant trade union of Ahmedabad, have come in the way of developing a sense of belonging to the working class among the labourers. Several departments are under the almost exclusive control of one or another caste or community. For instance, spinners are mostly Harijans, whereas winders and weavers are mostly Muslims. Labourers live with their kin in particular localities and 'would decline to leave them in order to be nearer a particular mill',[6] thus reinforcing community patterns. The Majoor Mahajan also works on the basis of departmental unions, which often correspond to caste and communal groups. All this has perpetuated social barriers and strong communal identifications among labourers, who have continued to be Harijans, Rajputs or Muslims, and have failed to be identified as members of an urban working class.

Among the Gujaratis themselves, Vagharis, Harijans, Bhois and Kolis were in the forefront in looting and killing. Many of these castes belonged to tribes classified by the colonial government as 'criminal tribes' [eds] till as recently as two decades ago. But Patidars and Rajputs also actively participated in killing Muslims. The former in many cases encouraged and financed people from the lower castes.

Even a few days before the carnage, the government of Gujarat believed that the state was 'traditionally free from communal trouble'. It did not, therefore, accept a suggestion of the National Integration Council for setting up state-level committees comprising representatives of various sections to help in the maintenance of communal harmony. For the same reason, the state government did not heed to the warning of the central government that communal tensions were building up in the state. Again, the trustees of the Jagannath temple had repeatedly requested the government to locate a police station near the temple, as quarrels between sadhus of the temple and local Muslims were not new in the Jamalpur area. However, the request had not been taken seriously.

[...]

Always Too Late

Decisive action came in slow and patchy measures. On 19 September, the government imposed curfew only at some places; curfew was later extended to other parts of the city. Then, as the situation went out of control on the 19th, the State Reserve Police (SRP) and the Central Reserve Police (CRP) forces were called in by the morning of the 20th. As these failed in controlling the situation, the army was called in on Sunday, the 21st. Troops were first posted in the suburbs. Later, they were given complete control of the city. 'Shoot at sight' orders were given to the soldiers on Sunday. More than 5,000 persons were arrested for participating in riots during the 10 days of the curfew. Because of the vigilance of the army, the situation came under control.

However, the authorities were almost always late in taking decisions. It took two days to call the army and, according to reliable information, only after one of the cabinet ministers had insisted on this and threatened to resign. Even after this, a whole day passed in discussions whether the entire city should be handed over to the army. ...

Reluctance to Use Force

Apart from the delay in taking decisions, the state government was half-hearted in using force. ... Besides this reluctance to use force, the curfew was not strictly imposed in Ahmedabad till the army took control. A large number of organisations and individuals were authorised to issue curfew passes. I was told that Congress House alone had distributed about 5,000 passes. Consequently, there was virtually no curfew in practice. I have come across some persons who participated in the riots with curfew passes in their pockets.

Instead of taking firm action to curb the riots, Gujarat politicians were in search of scapegoats. In the beginning, they discovered that the riots were instigated by 'Pakistani agents'. Later, they suspected communists of creating disorder. ...

The police in Ahmedabad had utterly failed in its duty of maintaining law and order impartially. At several places, killing and looting took place in the presence of policemen. They often ran away from the place and allowed a free hand to the rioters. Often, SRP and CRP cadets told Hindus that Muslims needed 'such treatment'. (I was told that in Baroda, policemen had encouraged onlookers to be courageous and take part in looting.)[7]

The indifferent, and in some cases partial, attitude of the police can be attributed to two reasons. First, it is an open secret in Gujarat that police and anti-social elements have close ties. More often than not, illicit liquor, gambling and smuggling which are rampant in the towns and villages of Gujarat run under police protection. For this, policemen get a regular amount every month which is often many times their salaries. Such association between bootleggers and policemen has paralysed the functioning of the police (prohibition's contribution to public life!). For the same reasons, the police were reluctant to arrest known goondas. If a few were arrested, they were released on bail immediately. In the course of my investigations, I have come across a case in which a police officer informed a hooligan in advance that a warrant was to be issued against him.

The second reason concerns the state of demoralisation of the police in Gujarat. In order to appease mischief mongers, the Gujarat government had time and again disowned responsibility for police actions, making the police itself responsible for them. During recent years, in three cases, the government did not defend police action but, on the contrary, asked the police to apologise to mischief makers.[8] The attitude was revealed when a senior Congressman close to the ruling circles told me that 'the police might have failed in controlling the riots but not the Government'. Obviously, such treatment had demoralised the police and made them indifferent and reluctant to take risks. They did not know when the government would ask them to apologise for firing on communal fanatics!

Press also Responsible

The press seems to have contributed its own bit to the worsening of the situation. It appears that most of the reporters did not move about in the riot-affected areas. The editors had instructed them not to take any risks. Consequently, the reports that were published were based either on hearsay and rumours, or on official versions released by the government. Because of this manner of reporting, inaccurate and false reports were published, which aggravated the situation. For instance, *Sevak*, an afternoon edition of the leading daily *Sandesh*, reported on 20 September that several women—obviously Hindu from the description—had been stripped and raped in public in Lal Millni Chal. It appears that the reporter had not visited the place but got the news from someone he knew who had come from that area. On the next day, the report was officially contradicted by the paper, but the damage was done. By the afternoon of the 20th, killing of men and women, molestation and raping, had already begun.

Biased Reports

An objective analysis would clearly indicate that the reporters, being Hindu, were partial in reproducing the news. Whenever a temple was attacked, the news was 'a temple was attacked', whereas when a mosque was attacked, it was 'a religious place was attacked'. The whole policy of spacing and display was biased. Newspapers gave headlines to rumoured reports of attack on Hindu temples. For instance, a newspaper told its readers in headlines that the Gita Mandir temple had been attacked on the 20th. The report was entirely false. In fact, by the 20th, Hindus were in complete control of this area. Similarly, reporting on the Jagannath temple was confusing to readers, and not a little provocative. On the same page, at three places, three different figures would be given regarding injured sadhus. The report would be embellished by descriptions of the attack as 'pre-planned' and 'cruel' and the revelation that acid bulbs and weapons had been used against the temple. The damage to the temple was, in most cases, exaggerated.

Newspapers generally suppressed news and letters which criticised the riots. Muslims did not get a place to express their reactions and views. This was true even in regard to clarification of facts, as when some Muslim—or a secular-minded Hindu—wanted to give a 'true picture' of some incident or the other that had taken place during the riots with a view to clarifying prevailing false impressions or bias.

As we have seen in Ahmedabad, rumours about the riots played an important role in worsening the situation. But no attempts were made by the government or the radio to counter the rumours. The radio simply repeated the 'do not believe in rumours' advice and broadcast various appeals of political leaders. But no authoritative news was given to actually counter the rumours.

Political Parties

No Gujarat Congressman had come out to stop the frenzy. Congress House distributed curfew passes in numbers, but did not refute any rumour or provide any information to workers. Office bearers of the Congress were inactive in preventing and controlling the riots. The only exceptions were some old Gandhian Congressmen who were really disturbed by the carnage, but they were too old to do anything or had no moral courage to come out in the midst of looting and killing. They, therefore, simply offered prayers.

In the words of a DCC President, most of the Congressmen were communal in their outlook. This was apparent during the post-riot period. Thus, the District Congress Committee of Baroda did not criticise the riots. On the contrary, it blamed the Muslims for such riots. It said in the resolution that the pro-Pakistan attitude of some Muslims had caused the tension in the state. The same attitude was in evidence at meetings of Congress workers. Responsible Congressmen criticised Muslims for their communal attitude and suggested that they should go to Pakistan. ...

Jan Sangh and Swatantra workers were also subject to the same communal prejudices, although the Jan Sanghis were more active than the Swatantrites. ... The only secular political force on the scene was the leftist parties—Praja Socialist Party, Samyukta Socialist Party and, above all, the communists—who tried their best to prevent the riots. More than anyone else, communist workers even at the cell level functioned as secular citizens. Three prominent Muslim communists lost their lives in their attempts to prevent the riots. There were other elements too, more isolated but effective, such as the radical humanists of Ahmedabad and their labour union. I have come across several cases in which a Hindu communist or radical humanist had saved Muslim neighbours and vice versa. A labour area between Hathi Khai and Kamdar Medan is an illustration of this. This area is known for frequent riots. In 1960, during the labour movement, a police officer was killed by local residents. But this time, it was an undisturbed area. In some of its chawls, there were 60 per cent Muslims and 40 per cent Hindus; in others, 70 per cent Hindus and 30 per cent Muslims. But both communities worked hard to maintain complete harmony. In thickly populated Muslim localities in this area, shops of Hindus remained not only undisturbed, but were protected by Muslims. Both Hindu and Muslim communist leaders of this area worked day and night to avert any conflict.

Some Final Remarks

The Gujarat riots may now be a matter of the past, though not necessarily so. In any event, neither the government, nor the social and intellectual elite can afford to underrate the causes and consequences of the communal holocaust. And some of the lessons of Gujarat have relevance for the country as a whole.

[...]

The concrete lesson of Gujarat is the most elemental requirement of civil society, namely that government should maintain law and order. In fact, the Gujarat experience shows that unless violence of this type is suppressed as soon as it occurs, and the government's will to suppress it is widely recognised, things soon get out of hand, and a democratic society degenerates to a level where the worst animal instincts that can be imagined dominate. The government has also to create confidence among citizens, irrespective of community or religion, that there exists an authority that will provide security against any anti-social elements, no matter where they come from. And in doing this, the government ought not to hesitate to use force with firmness. The growing attitude of waiting for the army to come and restore peace is, in this context, disquieting.

[...]

Notes

1. One of these was an oil shop outside the Sarangpur gate, the second was a laundry at Raipur Chakala, and the third was a laundry on Relief Road.

2. The role of Rajab has now become—or at least had been until the 1969 riots—a legend of Gujarat. During the 1946 communal riots, Vasant Hegiste, a Hindu, and Rajab

Lakhani, a Muslim, both members of the Congress Seva Dal, sacrificed their life. The legend has been immortalised through a memorial, the 'Vasant Rajab Shahid Smarak'.

3. Our investigation has also covered several other riot-affected areas of Gujarat. However, limitations of space do not permit us to include them in this report, which is mainly confined to Ahmedabad. In order to highlight a few points, however, there are a few references to other areas.

4. Ramesh Bhatt and others. 1969. 'A Study of Rehabilitation Problems of Riot Affected Areas in Ahmedabad'. Ahmedabad: Mangal Prabat's Sarsapur Arts and Commerce College; mimeographed.

5. Some newspapers had highlighted the role of non-Gujaratis in the riots. This immediately made Gujarati Hindus defend the non-Gujaratis. They argued that this was an attempt to divide the Hindu community into Gujaratis and non-Gujaratis. Some said that had there not been non-Gujaratis, they would have been crushed by the Muslims. They were, in fact, grateful to the outsiders.

6. Gillion, Kenneth L. 1968. *Ahmedabad.* Berkeley: University of California Press.

7. I have come to know from reliable sources that sometimes even the police diary was filled in with false or twisted information. The police diary of Baroda notes that Muslims first attacked the Swaminarayan temple and that thereafter, Hindus attacked the mosque Miya Mahamad ni Masjid. The true fact is that the mosque was attacked at 3 pm, whereas the temple was attacked after 6 pm.

8. The instances of *Quran* and *Ramayana* have been discussed earlier. The third one was of student riots in Baroda in July 1969. In order to control a violent mob of students, the police had used force. But later, the police commissioner was forced to tender an apology for this.

30

COMMUNAL VIOLENCE IN INDIA*

A Study of Communal Disturbance in Delhi: The Riot of 5 May 1974

GOPAL KRISHNA

POST-RIOT SURVEY

The May 1974 riot was the worst that Delhi had experienced after Independence. Because of the gravity of the riot, the Centre for the Study of Developing Societies decided to undertake an in-depth study of some of the larger questions of inter-community relations in the riot-affected area and in the wider city with a view to arriving at some understanding of how people were directly affected, what those living at a distance thought about the riot and what implications that, in turn, had for national integration. Our objective in this study was not to test hypotheses bearing on inter-community relations, but to explore the mentalities of the relevant sections of the citizens.

The study entailed preparation of a suitable questionnaire, drawing up of a sample of male and female cross-section and elite respondents both from among the Hindus and the Muslims in the riot-affected area and elsewhere in the city. It was decided to interview a larger number of Muslims than Hindus partly because the Muslim minority is concentrated in the riot-affected area and because the Muslim orientations are crucial for understanding the larger consequences of communal conflict. The overall distribution of the sample was determined in the ratio of 2 Muslims to 1 Hindu respondent.

The questionnaire was prepared soon after the May riot and trial interviews were carried out during the course of June. The cross-section sample was drawn from the electoral rolls for the riot-affected areas. The elite sample was drawn up in consultation with informants of the area and was designed to ensure that certain types of notables were interviewed for the study.

The survey covered 10 localities in the Sadar Bazar area. These were: Kishan Ganj, Bara Hindu Rao, Qasab Pura, Deputy Ganj, Sarai Khalil, Azad Market,

* *Economic and Political Weekly* 20 (3): 117–31 (12 January 1985).

Beriwala Bagh, Nabi Karim, Motia Khan and Sadar-Thana Road. In these localities, a total of 153 interviews were conducted between 1 July and 17 September 1974. They consisted of 133 cross-sections (49 Hindu—34 men and 15 women, and 84 Muslim—59 men and 25 women) and 20 elite (8 Hindus and 12 Muslims) respondents.

Outside the Sadar area, a further 56 interviews were conducted, consisting of 19 Hindus [18 cross-section (13 men, five women) and one elite, and 37 Muslims [26 cross-section (all men) and 11 elite (three men and eight women)]. They were drawn from 12 areas of the city: Ballimaran, Kucha Pandit/Lal Kuan, Naya Bans, Chandni Chowk, Ajmeri Gate, Turkman Gate, Chawri Bazar, Bazar Sitaram, Jama Masjid, Darya Ganj, Nizamuddin and Jamia Nagar.

The total sample consisted of 209 persons: 177 cross-section and 32 elite respondents. The Muslim interviews were carried out by three trained Muslim investigators, and the Hindu interviews by a Hindu investigator. Women's interviews were done by a female investigator. All the interviews were conducted in the respondent's own language. The elite respondent categories covered for this study are: journalists, civil servants, teachers, businessmen, political leaders, writers, doctors, lawyers, artists and moulvis.

In the following paragraphs, we provide some relevant characteristics of the sample. Table 30.1 gives the age break-up, separately for Hindus and Muslims, for the cross-section and elite samples.

TABLE 30.1: Age Break-up of Population

Age	*Cross-Section*			*Elite*			*Grand Total*
	Hindus	*Muslims*	*Total*	*Hindus*	*Muslims*	*Total*	
Less than 20 years	3	–	3	–	–	–	3
20–29 years	26	34	60	–	5	5	65
30–39 years	17	34	51	1	2	3	54
40–49 years	9	19	28	3	11	14	42
50 years and over	9	23	32	5	5	10	42
NA	3	–	3	–	–	–	3
Total	67	110	177	9	23	32	209

Source: Author.

The dominant age group in our sample, accounting for 77 per cent of the respondents, was between 20 and 49 years. This is the active element in the population. But in public affairs, age carries very considerable weight, on account of experience and understanding associated with it, and this was provided for in our sample by persons of 50 and above who represented just over 20 per cent of the respondents.

There is a rather marked overrepresentation of the educated in the sample: 65 per cent of our cross-section respondents and 87.5 of the elite respondents have had some education. The preponderance of the educated among the Hindu respondents was greater than among the Muslim respondents. This is no great disadvantage in an enquiry of this kind, provided those without education are adequately represented. The educational profile of the sample is presented in Table 30.2.

TABLE 30.2: Education Profile of Population

Education	*Cross-Section*			*Elite*			*Grand Total*
	Hindus	*Muslims*	*Total*	*Hindus*	*Muslims*	*Total*	
No education	8	53	61	–	3	3	64
Primary	10	15	25	–	1	1	26
Secondary (High School)	20	22	42	3	9	12	54
College and above	25	17	42	5	9	14	56
Technical	3	3	6	–	1	1	7
NA	1	–	1	1	–	1	2
Total	67	110	177	9	23	32	209

Source: Author.

The next relevant variable is the length of residence in the area. Most of our respondents have been long resident in the areas in which they were living at the time of the survey, and thus well able to answer our questions with adequate knowledge of the conditions of the area, the state of inter-community relations and offer reflections on the causes of communal conflict.

Table 30.3 provides the distribution of respondents by length of residence in the area. Table 30.4 shows the occupational distribution of the respondents.

TABLE 30.3: Length of Residence in the Area

Length of Residence	*Cross-Section*			*Elite*			*Grand Total*
	Hindus	*Muslims*	*Total*	*Hindus*	*Muslims*	*Total*	
Always	32	51	83	2	13	15	98
Less than 5 years	4	9	13	–	1	1	14
5–10 years	4	10	14	–	2	2	16
11–19 years	12	12	24	–	1	1	25
20 years and more	7	12	19	7	4	11	30
NA	8	16	24	–	2	2	26
Total	67	110	177	9	23	32	209

Source: Author.

All the major elements in the composition of the population are well represented in our sample. A four-fold classification of all the respondents would produce the following distribution: I. Manual + artisans + service (low) = 59 (28.36 per cent); 2. Service (middle) + service (high) + professional section and political work = 57 (27.40 per cent); 3. Business (petty) + business (substantial) = 44 (21.53 per cent);

TABLE 30.4: Occupation

Occupation	*Cross-Section*			*Elite*			*Grand Total*
	Hindus	*Muslims*	*Total*	*Hindus*	*Muslims*	*Total*	
Manual	4	19	23	–	–	–	23
Service (low)	8	9	17	–	1	1	18
Service (middle)	19	14	33	1	1	2	35
Service (high)	2	1	3	2	4	6	9
Professional	4	4	8	2	1	3	11
Artisan	–	17	17	–	1	1	18
Business (petty)	11	14	25	2	1	3	28
Business (substantial)	1	6	7	–	9	9	16
Household duty	14	24	38	–	4	4	42
Student/Retired	3	2	5	1	–	1	6
Social and Political worker	–	–	–	1	1	2	2
NA	1	–	1	–	–	–	1
Total	67	110	177	9	23	32	209

Source: Author.

4. Household duty + student/retired = 48 (23 per cent). Here too, one should not look for representativeness of the sample, but adequacy of representation of the different segments of the population divided into broad classes. This is well provided in our sample.

Lastly, we come to the political orientations of the respondents. These are considered crucially important, for communal conflict always has strong political overtones. It is, therefore, necessary to ensure that all the major political tendencies are adequately represented in the sample. Since the sample is weighted in favour of Muslims there is, relative to its electoral support, over-representation of the Congress supporters among the respondents, and relative under-representation of the Jan Sangh supporters. Since party membership is acknowledged by only about 35 per cent of the respondents, we have used the alternative measure of closeness to a particular party to determine their political affiliation. The distribution is presented in Table 30.5.

In the following pages, we present the qualitative and quantitative results of the survey. The primary focus of the survey was on inter-community relations, and it is to the questions relating to these that we turn first. It is increasingly recognised in literature on communal conflict in India that it does not originate wholly, or even primarily, in the religious concerns of the Hindus and the Muslims. Members of both the communities are intensely religious in their orientation and consider religiousness as a good, indeed noble, quality. In our survey on Muslim communities, we had asked a simple question: 'It is said that for the good of the country, Hindus should cease to be Hindus and Muslims should cease to be Muslims or Hindus

TABLE 30.5: Party Preferences

Party Preference	*Cross-Section*			*Elite*			*Grand Total*
	Hindus	*Muslims*	*Total*	*Hindus*	*Muslims*	*Total*	
Congress	22	30	52	4	9	13	65
Jan Sangh	14	3	17	–	–	–	17
CPI/CPM	2	2	4	1	3	4	8
Others	1	23	24	–	3	3	27
No party	25	16	41	3	6	9	50
NA	3	36	39	1	2	3	42
Total	67	110	177	9	23	32	209

Source: Author.

should become better Hindus and Muslims should become better Muslims, what do you think?' The responses we got showed that there was an overwhelming preference for the latter position: 96.6 per cent of the cross-section and 98.1 per cent of the elite Muslim respondents preferred that for the good of the country, Hindus should become better Hindus and Muslims should become better Muslims. Among the Hindus, 88.1 per cent of the elite and 84.1 per cent of the cross-section expressed the same view. In the present survey, a very large majority of respondents indicated that they practise religion. This was particularly evident from responses to question number 11, which asked whether the respondent offered prayer, and how often, or if s/he performed *puja* and how often. The results are presented in Table 30.6.

TABLE 30.6: Performance of *Puja*/Offer of Prayer

	Every day		*Once a Week*		*On Special Occasions*		*Never*		*Total*	
	No.	*Per Cent*	*No.*	*Per Cent*	*No.*	*Per Cent*	*No.*	*Per Cent*	*No.*	*Per Cent*
Hindus	49	64.47	–	–	19	25.00	8	10.53	76	100.00
Muslims	74	55.64	42	31.58	12	9.02	5	3.76	133	100.00

Source: Author.

Given this disposition towards religion, neither Muslims nor Hindus would view it as a possible source of communal conflict, which they do consider to be utterly evil. It is also relevant to note that in the twentieth century, the dominant Indian political ideology has emphasised the idea of the 'fundamental unity of all religions', and secularism in our society has not been presented as antithetical to religion but as supportive of freedom of religion on the premise that, religion is basically a good thing.

Despite this, inter-community relations have been characterised by tension, ill-will and increasing violence. Our respondents have tended to see the source of this in politics. For Hindus and Muslims alike, politics has been a dominant concern at least for the last 100 years, if not longer. Politics is about power, and in an agglomerative society, concern with power is paramount because it determines the access to economic and cultural resources and thus determines the relative ranking and the future of the constituent elements of the society.

There is a general, and justified, presumption that when people appraise each other negatively, they develop antipathy towards each other, and this then becomes a source of hostility/tension, leading to violence. What leads people to make negative appraisals of others is a different question. Nor should one attach much weight to the contents of such appraisals, for their truth value is extremely small. In the literature on inter-community relations, a great deal of attention is paid to prejudice, with the expectation that prejudice is likely to be replaced by enlightenment once it is identified as such. This appears to me an unwarranted expectation because prejudice is not merely ignorant opinion, but has an important function in the struggle for dominance that is such an overwhelming feature of inter-community relations in India, as elsewhere. And yet, it is important to discover what people think about each other for it is on that basis that they order their own strategies, responses, expectations, etc. It is also important to discover what people think of themselves and the consequent dissonance this must produce between the two sets of appraisals. So we asked our Hindu and Muslim respondents what deficiencies they saw in their own and in the other community. Since the question was open-ended and responses qualitative in character, I reproduce below a representative sample of the responses in an abbreviated form.

Hindu View of Muslims

Bring religion into everything; without thinking quarrel in the name of religion; lack sentiment of nationalism; look up to Pakistan; are poor, backward in education; there are no deficiencies in them; a Muslim defends another Muslim even if he be in the wrong; do not see the man but look to his religion; are frightened; accord low status to women; fanatical in religious matters; forgetting their religion and those who forget religion are lost; ignorant; cast evil eye on other people's women; religious and communal minded; think of themselves as superior; we have nothing to do with them and do not know anything about them; because of excessive religious feeling they cannot live in harmony here; do not bother about cleanliness; get excited in the name of community when in India they are not lacking in anything; weak, engaged in increasing their population; narrow-minded; think of themselves as separate; do not regard the country as their own; their religion and traditions are against us; so long as they do not practise family planning their condition will not improve; too many children means lack of education for them; also makes for over-crowding and there is always the danger of quarrels; consider Hindus Kafirs; untrustworthy; quarrelsome and harsh; marry several times; we do not like their ways; eat meat.

Muslim View of Muslims

Muslims quarrel among themselves, persecute others, lack capacity for caring, womanise, waste time on bird games; have moved away from religion, shave beard, listen to music on radio; run away from prayer; do not learn from experience; jealousy; waste money on self-indulgence; lack of education, which is the source of all the problems; they are ignorant and speak plainly, which is a sort of deficiency in this age; lack of unity, poverty, cowardly; live in dirty environment; gamble; do not work hard; do not get together on a common political platform; do not know how to do business; no leadership; ignorant of the times and the scheming ways of the world; deceive; are untrustworthy; loss of character; have moved away from religion; lack of foresight; the worst thing is that they are Muslims, and even worse is that they live in India; have become victims of inferiority feeling; have forgotten their own principles and are following in the footsteps of others; dislike of secularism; there is nothing wrong with Muslims—it is all made up by the Hindus that they are anti-nation; they lack a leader who will show them the right way and build unity among them; no movement, no leadership; gundaism; not enough religious education; lack of faith; produce too many children; no motivation to progress; do not practise family planning and are therefore poor; circumstances have compelled them to think of themselves as slaves; their so-called leaders injure them for their own selfish interests; blind belief; lack political awareness; limited opportunities of progress; spend-thrift; wrong kind of religious fanaticism; the ulema have neglected their duty; do not help each other; unreliable; do not take advantage of the facilities provided by the government.

Hindu View of Hindus

There is nothing wrong with the Hindus; there is no unity among the Hindus; get misled; poverty, lack of education; selfish, superstitious; run away from light, backward in religion, engaged in pulling each other down; religious fanaticism; consider India only their own country; want of cooperation; blinded by religion; casteism; communal-minded, quarrelsome; are democratic; do not help Muslims and take advantage of their weakness; lack political consciousness; not farsighted; rich-poor sentiment; have forgotten their own religion; divided between many castes; victims of blind faith; enmities over money; decline in religious faith.

Muslim View of Hindus

Hindus hate Muslims, whom they consider to be dirty, which is not true; Hindus do not have business dealings with Muslims; untouchability; dislike of Muslims; dislike of Kashmiris; there is nothing wrong with the Hindus—practise a little discrimination; do not consider Harijans human; are afraid of meat; seek to dominate with the help of the government; drink alcohol, gamble, womanise; there is a lot that is wrong with the Hindus, but wealth hides it; do not respect religion, run after wealth, worship money; refugees have created a mentality of discrimination against Muslims; suspect everyone; are wicked; do not have much dealing with Hindus; very cowardly; commerce and trade is their special occupation, and doing everything proper and improper they consider good; every Hindu practises discrimination; do not trust Muslims, look upon them as Pakistani agents and remove them from offices; do not respect other communities in the country; greedy; communal minded; not only Muslims, but no other community in the world has been able to understand Hindus; they are duplicitous; one thing inside, another outside, do not try to understand Muslims; do not live in friendship, do not consider Muslims to be Indians; are engaged in finding ways to weaken Muslims materially; weak-minded; do not help in need; quarrel over trivial matters; hoarding habit; do not buy goods from Muslims; narrow-minded; unreliable; cannot bear to see Muslims happy; there is nothing wrong with the Hindus, except that they are hostile to Muslims; put barriers in the path of progress of other communities; want to expel Muslims from India, take interest; enmity towards Muslims in trade; consider people of other religions inferior; the greatest deficiency in them is that they are not willing/able to accept Muslims; lack progressive outlook; saturated with communal feeling—even for a doctor they want a Hindu; nothing wrong with them—they are sharp and making progress; victims of inferiority complex; moving away from their own religion; decline of character; the ordinary Hindu is not so communal-minded, although during a riot a few communal-minded came to the forefront; on the whole Hindus are good—Muslims by their own ignorance (*jahalat*) make them hostile (towards Muslims).

Although our question may be said to be biased towards eliciting negative responses, which it was intended to do, it is important to notice the contents of the responses themselves. On the whole, the Muslim responses are more expressive than those of the Hindus. It is clear that the Muslims think that the Hindus are suspicious of them and practise discrimination, while Hindus, on the whole, confirm the suspicion and see Muslims as 'excessively religious'. Other identified deficiencies seem to me to lack the force of this particular characterisation, especially in its implication for inter-community relations and national integration.

The next question I want to consider is the one relating to the perception of the state of inter-community relations in the Sadar Bazar area during the preceding five years. Our question was: 'How have been Hindu–Muslim relations in this area during the past five years? Good, bad, or indifferent?' Since this was a closed question, the answers of our respondents are presentable in a tabulated form (Table 30.7).

TABLE 30.7: Hindu–Muslim Relations Five Years Ago

Respondents	*Good*		*Bad*		*Indifferent*		*Total*	
	No.	*Per Cent*	*No.*	*Per Cent*	*No.*	*Per Cent*	*No.*	*Per Cent*
Hindu CS	31	46.26	10	14.92	26	38.82	67	100
Hindu Elite	5	55.56	2	22.22	2	22.22	9	100
Muslim CS	17	15.46	23	20.91	70	63.63	110	100
Muslim Elite	13	56.52	1	4.34	9	39.14	23	100
Total	66	31.58	36	17.23	107	51.19	209	100

Note: CS = Cross-section.

Source: Author.

Of the whole sample, half thought that the relations between Hindus and Muslims in the preceding five years were 'indifferent'. Both Hindu and Muslim elites thought they were 'good', but it is the Muslim cross-section who thought that they were in the main 'indifferent'; very few of them thought that they were 'good'.

We could probe this a little further by reference to age and self-assigned class status. If we divide the respondents in three age classes and tabulate the responses to the question, we got the following results, given in Table 30.8. The table brings out the fact that more of those below age 40 in 1974 thought that Hindu–Muslim relations were either bad or indifferent than those of 41 and above. It is a cause for concern that 68.41 per cent of the respondents believed that Hindu–Muslim relations were not good in the areas in which they lived.

Table 30.8: Hindu–Muslim Relations Five Years Ago—By Age Groups

Respondents	*Code Categories*							
Age	*Good*		*Bad*		*Indifferent*		*Total*	
	No.	*Per Cent*	*No.*	*Per Cent*	*No.*	*Per Cent*	*No.*	*Per Cent*
Less than 25 years	12	26.66	9	20.00	24	53.34	45	100
26–40 years	26	29.54	14	15.91	48	54.55	88	100
41 and above	28	36.84	13	17.10	35	46.06	76	100
Total	66	31.58	36	17.23	107	51.19	209	100

Source: Author.

Table 30.9 gives responses by self-assigned class status, stratified in three categories—high, middle, low. (The numbers of respondents falling in each of these categories were: High—Hindus 1, Muslims 3; Middle—Hindus 58, Muslims 62; Low—Hindus 8, Muslims 25.)

Table 30.9: Hindu–Muslim Relations Five Years Ago

Respondents	*Code Categories*							
Self-assigned Class/Status	*Good*		*Bad*		*Indifferent*		*Total*	
	No.	*Per Cent*	*No.*	*Per Cent*	*No.*	*Per Cent*	*No.*	*Per Cent*
Less than 25 years	5	16.66	4	13.34	21	70.00	30	100
26–40 years	50	34.96	25	17.48	68	47.56	143	100
41 and above	11	30.54	7	19.44	18	50.00	36	100
Total	66	31.58	36	17.23	107	51.19	209	100

Source: Author.

A related question was whether, in their view, Hindus and Muslims entertained sentiments of hostility towards each other, and the extent of it—a great deal, somewhat, very little, or not at all. It has been my experience that direct questions of this sort not only do not put off the respondents, but introduce the necessary candour in a discussion of what is an extremely serious concern for the respondents and their community. The replies we got are summarised in Table 30.10.

TABLE 30.10: Extent of Mutual Hostility between Hindus and Muslims

Respondents	*Code Categories*								*Total*
	A Great Deal		*Some*		*Very Little*		*None*		
	No.	*Per Cent*	*No.*	*Per Cent*	*No.*	*Per Cent*	*No.*	*Per Cent*	
Hindus (A) (i)	28	36.85	14	18.42	31	40.79	3	3.94	76
(A) (ii)	44	57.89	8	10.52	22	28.94	2	2.65	
Muslims (B) (i)	16	12.02	56	42.11	45	33.87	16	12.02	133
(B) (ii)	43	32.34	34	25.56	41	30.83	15	11.27	

Notes: (A) (i) Hindus are hostile towards Muslims. (ii) Muslims are hostile towards Hindus.
(B) (i) Muslims are hostile towards Hindus. (ii) Hindus are hostile towards Muslims.

Source: Author.

There is an interesting and marked discrepancy when Hindu respondents express themselves on Hindu hostility towards Muslims, and their appraisal of the Muslims' hostility towards the Hindus. The same phenomenon obtains when we consider Muslim appraisal of Muslim hostility towards the Hindus and their appraisal of Hindu hostility towards Muslims. Thus, 57.89 per cent of the Hindus think that Muslims entertain 'a great deal' of hostility towards Hindus, while 36.84 per cent of them think that Hindus harbour 'a great deal' of hostility towards Muslims. A much smaller proportion of our Muslim respondents (12.03 per cent) think that Muslims harbour 'a great deal' of hostility towards Hindus, but many more (32.33 per cent) believe that Hindus do so towards them. Some measure of hostility towards each other is acknowledged by most of the respondents, though quite clearly each views the other as being more hostile.

Given this picture, we should consider the normal range of interaction between Hindus and Muslims. This was done through a question which asked respondents to tell us on what occasions they met with members of the other community. The results are presented in Table 30.11.

TABLE 30.11: When Do Hindus and Muslims Meet?

Respond-ents	*Code Categories: Occasions*											
	Social		*Political*		*Business*		*Every day*		*Do not Meet*		*Total*	
	No	*Per Cent*	*No*	*Per Cent*	*No*	*Per Cent*	*No*	*Per Cent*	*No*	*Per Cent*	*No*	*Per Cent*
Hindus	11	14.47	4	5.26	22	28.94	16	21.05	23	30.28	76	100
Muslims	31	23.31	5	3.76	55	41.35	20	15.04	22	16.54	133	100

Source: Author.

We are now in a position to consider questions relating to the Sadar riot itself. In one of our questions, we asked our respondents to give us their explanation of the riot—why did it take place? It was an open-ended question and the responses are summarised in the following pages.

Muslim Explanations of the Sadar Riot

A shopkeeper (barber), age 30: In this area Muslims had some good business; Hindus had been trying to destroy them for quite some time, and when they could not defeat them in competition, they organised the riot.

A labourer, age 48: Because of Pakistan, meaning that 99 per cent of the population of Kishanganj is Muslim, and Hindus call it 'little Pakistan'.

A Moazzin, age 55: It gives a setback to Muslim business; to destroy Muslims in Sadar Bazar; to frighten them so that they leave this area.

A Shia shopkeeper, age 34; The primary reason for this riot is the uplift of the Harijans; Harijans consider Muslims to be their enemies, and in a riot they kill Muslims.

A railway employee, age 34: This was the result of religious intolerance; Hindus do not trust Muslims and Muslims do not trust Hindus; the first thing they want to see is whether a person is a Hindu or a Muslim, not what sort of a person he is, however good he might be.

A small wire manufacturer, age 38: The main reason is poverty, and non-availability of essentials; when people get exasperated, they become quarrelsome; when they are happy, they do not quarrel; second, Hindu–Muslim enmity; Hindus cannot tolerate so many mosques—that is why the Kishanganj mosque was made a target of attack.

A small shopkeeper, age 32: I do not know. A mob came to my shop shouting 'burn the shop'. I took shelter in a Hindu friend's place, and saw that my shop was looted and burnt.

A small shopkeeper, age 38: This is an old enmity which surfaces on different occasions and excites emotions on both sides.

A BA student, age 23: This riot was started by the gundas, and spread to Hindu and Muslim population; the police acted in a partisan manner and got Muslim property damaged.

An artisan, age 23: It was the work of the Hindus; there was a plan to expel Muslims from this area.

A tailor, age 30: The real reason is the non-wearing of the veil by Hindu girls, Hindu boys teased a Hindu girl, and Muslims saved her, but they were the ones who were attacked—that is how things are.

A welder, age 25: It is an old habit of Hindus; they are always thinking of how to get rid of Muslims from India; they also say that when there is Pakistan for Muslims, why should they be here? This riot is a part of that same chain.

A salesman, age 25: This is a mentality which is now flourishing; the reason is that hearts are not clean; now Hindus must understand that Muslims are inhabitants of this place, and Muslims must understand that they are living in the country of Hindus, where they are in the majority.

A tailor, age 45: The real source of the riot lies elsewhere, namely in the making of Pakistan and its acceptance by our Congressmen; second, the Jan Sangh mentality, which is increasing among the Hindus. The trouble started at the cinema where deliberately a girl was teased; she then went to a typing shop and complained that she was teased; the man who runs the shop is a troublemaker and he spread the story. Then there was trouble in the shop that sells sugarcane pieces. The gamblers who were gambling thereabout got into the fray when they heard that a riot had started; they got involved in this way because they saw the police coming, who were shouting 'hit the Muslims', and so they joined in because they thought otherwise they would be arrested for gambling; every Sunday all these people gamble, and Hindus and Muslims both participate.

A binder, age 26: The government and the Congress caused the riot jointly.

A tea-stall owner, age 30: This was a small affair which was turned into a communal riot; there was a conspiracy to destroy the Muslims, but it did not succeed.

A dyer, age 46: Outside elements caused the riot—local people are not like that.

A tire-tube merchant, age 32: The trouble started at the cinema, the RSS [Rashtriya Swayamsevak Sangh] people gave it a communal turn.

A shopkeeper, age 45: The riot was part of a scheme, and if we had not defended ourselves there would have been a 'Hiroshima' and 'Nagasaki' here; in truth it is the Congress people who instigate riots. They all have the RSS mentality, but the difference is that these people keep it hidden while the RSS people talk openly; it is true that the riot was the work of the Jan Sangh, but the Congress leaders gave full support.

A shopkeeper, age 45: Hindus do not like to see Muslims in one place. This was a well-thought-out scheme and these people will do it again; the result will be that Muslims will become guerrillas.

A political worker, age 59: The riot was the result of police incompetence.

HINDU EXPLANATIONS OF THE SADAR RIOT

Our Hindu interviews, by comparison, are far less interesting, and produce standard responses, asserting that the riot was the work of the gundas, or that it was a consequence of earlier troubles, or that they did not know the cause of the riot. There were strong references to trouble over girl-teasing, the role of the political parties, pre-planning by Muslims, work of communal elements; that it was a diversionary act, due to election politics; a conspiracy of the capitalists, and interference by political parties; some quarrel among shopkeepers which assumed the shape of a communal riot; selfish pursuit behind the shield of religion.

The analysis of the responses shows that the Hindus had not been much affected by the Sadar riot and despite the killing of nine Hindus in the firing (assumed to be by Muslims) had made no effort to formulate any understanding of the causes of the riot. The Muslim responses, on the other hand, reflect both a great concern and an attempt to construct some *rationale* for the riot. The rationale assumes that Hindus are hostile to Muslims, that they will do anything to hurt Muslims materially, and that the authorities are collaborators with the Hindus in this type of activity.

A communal riot is an event that envelopes the entire community—not only in the directly affected areas, but over a much broader region—and is thus an occasion for the expression of community solidarity. This takes the form of statements of concern for the people affected, demands on the authority that protection be given to them, denunciation of the perpetrators of violence, and collection of funds and articles for relief. In the affected areas, the immediate manifestation of solidarity takes the form of anxious consultation, especially among the leading elements of each community. They are an index of *communitas*. We tried to identify the extent of it by asking our respondents whether people consulted among themselves when a riot occurred. Among the Muslims, 53.48 per cent of the area respondents told us that no consultations were held by Muslims, while 34.88 per cent said that consultations did take place; 11.62 per cent did not know if they did or did not. Among the Hindus, over 60 per cent of the respondents reported that consultations did take place, while 15.87 per cent that they did not, and 23.80 per cent did not know. From these data, it is obvious that consultations do take place, but not all are aware of it, and this applies especially to women. One inference from our data would seem to be that there is perhaps a relatively greater degree of *communitas* among the Hindus of Sadar Bazar than among the Muslims.

Impact and Effect of Riot

What do people actually do in the event of a riot? That was the question we asked our Hindu and Muslim respondents. Their answers tabulated in six categories are presented in Table 30.12.

Table 30.12: What Do Hindus/Muslims Do in the Event of a Riot?

Respondents	*Code Categories*													
	Discuss		*Pray*		*Seek Government/ Police Help*		*Plan Self Protection*		*Seek the Help of Influential People*		*Other*		*Total*	
	No.	*Per Ccnt*	*No.*	*Per Cont*	*No.*	*Per Cont*	*No.*	*Per Cent*	*No.*	*Per Cent*	*No.*	*Per Cent*	*No.*	*Per Cent*
Hindus	20	26.31	8	10.52	13	17.11	27	35.53	2	2.64	6	7.89	76	100
Muslims	18	13.54	69	51.88	13	9.78	6	4.51	8	6.01	19	14.28	133	100

Source: Author.

This table reveals remarkable passivity on the part of Muslims, despite known acts of violence in the May riot. One obvious consequence of the riot was to enhance suspicion between the Hindus and the Muslims; the other was to increase alienation between the Hindus and the administration; the third was the disruption of the economic life of the area, and the impoverishment of a large number of families. We asked our respondents to tell us what impact the riot had more generally and more specifically on Hindus and Muslims. The Muslim appraisal of the consequences of riots reflected strong emotion, anxiety and resentment. Their responses are summarised below.

MUSLIM APPRAISAL

Muslims have received a setback in the economic field for a few years; whatever contacts had been established between Hindus and Muslims have been destroyed, and they now look upon each other with suspicion; the Hindus knew well when and where the riot was going to take place; and therefore, they had made full preparations to protect themselves; they did suffer some loss of life, as did the Muslims; but Hindus did not suffer material losses, which only Muslims did. Muslims used to feel insecure—now they do even more so because until now, the administration has only frightened the Muslims.

Hindus are pleased because Muslims suffered losses. Muslims became frightened and have started thinking of self-defence.

The police got bribes. Some parties have appropriated relief funds. Prices have risen. Muslims lost businesses. They are frightened, but have begun to think that they must become united and take steps (to protect themselves); relations among Muslims have improved to some extent, Hindus have begun to think that Muslims are also strong.

The Hindus are very agitated over the resistance offered by the Muslims, and are therefore preparing for a big riot; Muslims have become united, fearless.

There is a tension in the area; all, whether they are Hindus or Muslims, are bothered.

Very adverse effect on Muslim businesses; Hindus get the sleep of ease; Muslims have been destroyed—many factories and houses have been burnt.

Riot makes Muslims communal-minded.

People have become more religious now; along with earning a living, people have started thinking of defence, especially the Muslims.

Those who were arrested have been ruined. There has been no loss to the Hindus. Many Muslims started thinking of leaving India.

Impact on business: Those Muslims who did not suffer in the riot found that afterwards, they could not do business with the Hindus.

I only know that my business has been reduced to half. My dealings were mainly with the Hindus. On account of the riot, they no longer come here and do not place orders (with us). No one knows how many such cases must be.

Danger of further conflict: Now both Hindus and Muslims have started keeping some weapons in their houses. Because more Hindus were killed in this riot, they are thinking of taking revenge. Muslims have lost confidence in the government.

Everyone had become afraid for his life, and has become suspicious of others. What impact can a riot have on the Hindus? Even if they suffer, their people make up the loss. Muslims have become anxious for life and property, and have begun to think of leaving (the area).

The poor suffered hunger; there was no milk even for children; businessmen suffered heavy losses; the business of the butchers was completely closed for 10–15 days. The police discriminated against Muslims during the curfew.

My work stopped; had to go hungry for three days. Many good Hindus and Muslims have suffered distress. It is the poor Hindus and poor Muslims who have suffered on account of the riot.

The riot showed to the Muslims that even now, we are not safe in this country. Hindus suffered no loss, but it is said that the people they brought over from Meerut to fight here are dissatisfied with the local Hindus because they did not get adequate compensation and are now thinking of taking revenge. Muslims have been strengthened in their faith, and are firm in the belief that only Allah can protect them.

Both Hindus and Muslims suffered loss of trade; thousands of men lost work, and labourers had to go hungry. The main thing is that the plan of the Hindus did not succeed, and even now in Kishanganj and Sadar Bazar areas, Muslims have survived well and are pursuing their trades and businesses.

The government was exposed; our police never wants to act in time.

Mutual dislike between Hindus and Muslims has greatly increased. It has had a great impact on the Hindus—they now know that Muslims are not a weak community; all their plans have failed. They had made full preparations, and the police was with them but we fought them even without weapons, and showed no weakness after the riot; this has made a great impression on the hearts of the Hindus. The Congress-Muslims have also started criticising the Congress leaders. Muslims have lost confidence in the police and the administration.

Hearts got poisoned. They were not clean earlier either, but this riot has worsened the condition. There was some secular atmosphere in Delhi, but that has been destroyed by all this.

Feeling of enmity between Hindus and Muslims: There is propaganda among Hindus that Muslims used firearms against Hindus and that this was improper. The truth is that these people wanted to destroy all the Muslim businesses in the area. After this riot, Muslims are depressed. They say they had to resort to firing in order to save their lives and property. Despite this, the right to self defence has been taken away from them.

Hindu Response

The Hindu responses have been qualitatively poor. They mentioned 'loss of life and property' as the general consequence of the May riot. Some also spoke of social consequences, for example, 'relations have stopped coming into the area, and people have started thinking of changing houses' (that is moving out of the area). Some also spoke of increase in tension, that 'the real mentality came to the forefront' and also 'the old relationships broke up'.

The last series of questions to be considered for this report relates to our respondents' views on what ought to be done to prevent communal violence. In one question, we asked what should be done to prevent communal riots generally and in another question, we asked what should be done to the same end in the Sadar Bazar area. Responses to both these sets of questions are merged in what follows because our respondents often did so themselves.

MUSLIMS RESPONDENTS' IDEAS ON WHAT OUGHT TO BE DONE TO PREVENT COMMUNAL RIOTS

In my view, Muslims feel that they are always under a threat, and that Hindus do not consider them Indians. If government provided employment to Muslims in the administration, this feeling will diminish and communal conflicts will also decline. Muslims should try to enter all the political parties; this way they will get into those parties which instigate riots, and they will not then be able to do so. Jan Sangh-Hindus will never want to see the end to communal riots. Other Hindus should establish good contacts with Muslims; they should consider Muslims as their fellow-countrymen.

All Muslims must support the Jamaat-e-Islami. Hindus should befriend Muslims. There should be good police arrangements.

Hindus and Muslims must live together; remove jealousy; do their own work in peace. Muslims should join the Jan Sangh; must not be misled by the secularists; Hindus should be instructed in Mahatma Gandhi's politics. The government must assume responsibility for the protection of Muslims. Muslims must strengthen the Islamic sentiment.

The government must treat the Muslims well; India must not be viewed as a Hindu country, Muslims should live together, break off relations with the Hindus. Muslims should be recruited into the police.

People must become secular, separate politics and religion; Muslims ought to keep away from communal parties.

Muslims should get united; Muslims should be recruited into the police and the army so that they are able to defend themselves. Hindus must stop charging Muslims with disloyalty.

Muslims must boycott the Muslim League. There should be a ban on communal organisations. Hindus should subscribe to secular ideology.

If Muslims follow Islam, they will automatically become good, and then Hindus will not have the courage to lift their eyes towards Muslims. Muslims should turn a blind eye to Hindu narrow mindedness. Hindus should look upon Muslims as equal.

What can the Muslims do? They are backward in every sphere. The government should strengthen the CID [Crime Investigation Department].

Muslims should not look up to Pakistan and other Muslim countries, instead they should think of Muslims of their own country; government must protect Muslims.

It is not easy to stop riots. Muslims must build their character. It is the government's responsibility to protect them. Hindus should help in removing communalism; at least in business dealings, there should be no communalism.

Hindus and Muslims should be settled in separate areas; if there is less contact, friendship might develop; Muslims should defend themselves.

The difference between rich and poor should be abolished, and everyone should be given work.

Hindus and Muslims must develop a common mentality; they should have equal rights according to the Constitution; unless there is a common law, quarrels like this will continue.

People from congested areas should be dispersed; riots occur mainly in congested areas. Narrow mindedness should be eliminated; people should live in friendship with other communities, but in the event of a confrontation, Muslims must not retreat from self defence. In the police and the army, Hindus and Muslims should be recruited in equal proportions; punish the guilty.

Improve education; increase interaction (between Hindus and Muslims).

Muslims should leave Hindu areas where there is always danger to life; they must discharge their own duty. There should be more police in the area.

Muslims should progress by working with other communities; they should live in other, far-away areas; cultivate friendship with Hindus.

Muslims should pray five times.

Where Hindus and Muslims live together, there should be more CID to keep a close watch on the situation; small incidents should be amicably resolved; in the police, there should be Hindu officers over Muslim police and Muslim officers over Hindu police.

Government should find a solution. Such a powerful government that can fight Pakistan and China cannot control the masses of this country! Muslims should separate themselves from politics and attend to the improvement of their own conditions; they should acquire capacity to bear up, avoid quarrels.

Muslims do not want to make trouble because these are the times when 'one who has the stick claims the buffalo'; they should cooperate with the administration.

Muslims should not be viewed as a minority, but the second majority; they must get their constitutional rights. But the government is involved in these riots and it wants the Muslims to remain depressed, and support the Congress out of necessity.

There should be no communalism in textbooks. Both Hindus and Muslims should avoid hurting each other's sentiments.

Muslims should unite on a common platform, acquire political awareness, be political in dealing with the Hindus; Muslims should get representation in the police, the military and the administration in proportion to their share in the population.

Jan Sangh, Muslim League, RSS must go. The government should stop its interference. Congress must be defeated. Muslims should give their votes to the Communist Party. As long as conditions are bad, there will be no riots; when conditions improve there will be riots.

Muslims must protect themselves from a communal propaganda; they should work as a pressure group in every political party, and take active part in national matters; Hindus should take upon themselves the responsibility of protecting the Muslims and create confidence in them.

It is necessary that there should be 25 per cent Muslims in the police and the army; there should also be a Muslim women's police force so that veiled women are not outraged. Lists of persons living in the midst of the majority should be made and the majority charged with the responsibility of protecting them; should they suffer, they should be compensated by imposing a fine on the majority. There is a section among the Hindus which is angry with the Muslims because they made Pakistan, dividing the country into two, and those who stayed behind have not joined the national mainstream, so much so that some Jan Sanghis insist that Muslims should adopt wholly Hindu customs and manners, and if they do not do so, they should be forcibly expelled from India and settled in some other country.

In areas where Muslims are in small numbers, there should be Muslim police officers. History must be presented in a right manner. Muslims cannot do anything. Instead of thinking in terms of Hindus and Muslims, it should be considered that if a 15 per cent section of the population, that is, Muslims, were to be made backward, that would be a great economic loss to the country because neither can such a large population be killed, nor can it be sent to Pakistan; if they have to live here then why not live in friendship so that the country may progress?

HINDU RESPONDENTS' IDEAS ON WHAT OUGHT TO BE DONE TO PREVENT RIOTS

People are distracted by unemployment, high prices, etc.; military rule is the only remedy. Hindus and Muslims should live together peacefully; all should obey the law.

Strict measures by the administration are necessary; there is frustration; necessities are not satisfied; there is no housing; there must be a law of family planning.

Muslims must cultivate national feeling.

Improve education; provide employment.

There should be no discrimination; people should learn to live together.

Muslim isolation in an area should be broken; then there will be friendship between Hindus and Muslims and the problem will disappear.

Instruction in secularism should be provided.

Eliminate gundaism; provide education and work—that will end gundaism. Participate in each other's festivals.

Impart education that would create national awareness.

Politicians start these troubles for their own ends; people cannot make sense of them.

Punish the gundas; make proper use of education; misunderstanding caused in the name of truth, not religion, should be removed.

Military rule.

Since my ideas do not agree with them (government), I cannot make suggestions; Muslims should prevent the entry of political parties in these matters; Hindus should keep away from political parties.

Firmness is necessary; when there is fear there will be no riots.

Muslims should go to Pakistan.

Religion-based ideas should be abolished; end casteism and impart instruction in nationalism. Muslims should reform themselves.

Muslims should not go along with communal elements, and should not bring religion into everything.

The troubles are caused by gundaism; ordinary people have no time to spare from their toil. Muslims must understand that this is their own country; not get excited by the gundas.

Muslims should be Indianised.

Congestion is the cause of the trouble. If there was a more open atmosphere, more spacious houses, quarrels will disappear. Muslims should cultivate the spirit of nationalism and eliminate religious differences.

In place of the present government there should be a government of the poor. Only the poor class can eliminate communal feeling. Muslims should support the Communist parties instead of the Congress.

Muslims should feel that no party is against them; government should be impartial and alert; Muslims should acquire nationalist feeling, should regard India as their country.

DIR [Defence of India Rules] should be applied.

Build a secular society.

End the capitalism system.

People should be made to understand that all men are one and that differences of religion, caste, etc., are created by a few like Tata, Birla, etc. for their own advantage; communal organisations like Jan Sangh, Jamaat-e-Islami, Hindu Maha Sabha, Muslim League should be destroyed. Muslim should regard this country and other people in it as their own; give up the idea of high and low.

Muslims should pay attention to their own economic progress.

Hindus should accept Muslims as their brothers.

Government should stop discrimination.

Expel the Muslims, reply brick with stone.

Hindus should not have much to do with Muslims.

All parties of Muslims give encouragement to gundas; Muslims should look upon Hindus as their brothers; Hindus should forget what has happened.

Muslims should not eat meat and respect the Hindus; government must protect both the communities; remove Muslims from this locality (Kishanganj/Sadar Bazar).

General Inferences

If one were to draw some general inferences from these extraordinary statements, one would say that Muslim responses to our questions on what should be done to prevent riots reflect despair, while Hindu responses express a strong feeling that Muslims are lacking in national sentiment. There are several points of views represented here, among the Muslims there is the extreme political position formulated by the Muslim League respondent that Muslims should be treated as the 'second majority'; among the Hindus its counterpart, voiced by a housewife, that Muslims be expelled. But these extremes are few and far between. The vast majority of respondents seek accommodation and mutual goodwill. Among the Muslims, self-reliance in community's defence is far outweighed by resignation and the demand that government should protect them. There have been resentful responses, accusations that government instigates the riots, and Hindus enjoy the misfortunes of Muslims, but these are few. There are a few practical suggestions, regarding reducing over-crowding, education, etc., but not many, and not specific enough. Different party men, above all those of the communist parties, have articulated their party's line that communal violence cannot be ended except by putting an end to the capitalist order.

As part of this discussion, it might be useful to see the status accorded to secularists among Hindus and Muslims, for they are the people most actively engaged in preventing communal conflict though they are not without their critics. We asked a simple question to our respondents: What did they think of the secularists; whether they thought them to be 'useful', 'dangerous', or 'useless'? The results are presented in the following Table 30.13, collapsing the two categories 'dangerous' and 'useless' into one 'use less'.

TABLE 30.13: What Do You Think of the Secularists?

	Useful				*Useless*			
	Hindus		*Muslims*		*Hindus*		*Muslims*	
	No.	*Per Cent*	*No.*	*Per Cent*	*No.*	*Per Cent*	*No.*	*Per Cent*
Secularists among Muslims	59	77.63	55	41.35	17	22.36	78	58.64
Secularists among Hindus	59	77.63	81	60.90	17	22.36	52	39.09

Source: Author.

Secularists enjoy a somewhat wider acceptance among the Hindus than they do among the Muslims, though they view Hindu secularists more favourably than the Muslim ones.

CONCLUSION

Since the completion of our survey of the communal disturbances in Delhi and their aftermath, the communal situation in India has continued to be a cause for anxious concern to the nation. There has been a second, gruesome riot in Bhiwandi this year, 15 years after the first one in 1969. There have been riots in Jamshedpur,

Meerut, Moradabad, Baroda and elsewhere; in Hyderabad there has been a more or less continuous series of communal incidents over the past two or three years. In the south, the issue of conversion holds a dangerous potential for communal conflict.

[...]

Even though the capacity of the contemporary Indian state to control communal violence is wholly adequate, the signs of alienation are growing, and this should cause concern. In our survey, we made use of two questions to measure (a) alienation of Hindus and Muslims from the machinery of the state, and (b) anxiety and desperation felt by the Muslims. In one set of questions, we asked our respondents to tell us whether they had any dealings, on any count, with the administration and whether they found the encounter satisfactory. More than 65 per cent of our Hindu respondents and 54 per cent of our Muslim respondents found their encounters with the administration unsatisfactory. And when it came to the protection of Muslims, twice as many Muslim respondents thought that they and their own organisations will have to protect them as did those who looked up to the central government.

To measure the sense of anxiety expressed by Muslims, we had asked a straightforward question about the expectations they held for their future: 70 per cent of the Muslim respondents were despondent about it, holding that the conditions of the Muslims will either remain as they are (bad) or they will deteriorate further; those who thought that they will deteriorate outnumbered those who thought that they will remain as they are. The concern Muslims felt for themselves and their families, and the alienation they obviously felt from the nation, or even from the Muslim community as a collectivity, was strikingly brought out in responses to a question we asked on the rank-ordering of their own responsibilities towards their own family, community, the state and the nation. 82.70 per cent of our Muslim respondents considered their own family to be their primary responsibility (against 38.15 per cent of the Hindu respondents), while 4.51 per cent chose their community (against 0 per cent by Hindu respondents); when it came to the state and the nation, only 3 per cent of the Muslim respondents gave primacy to the state and 9.77 per cent to the nation; of the Hindu responses, 5.26 per cent accorded primacy to the state, and 56.57 per cent to the nation.

Neither 'Indianisation' of Muslims, dear to Hindu communalists, nor religious corporatism, the chosen remedy of the Muslim communalists to the problem of religious diversity, can serve the ends of the nation. The process of integration in India has to be organic, and the degree of unification we should expect to achieve in a vast and diverse population cannot be more than modest by standards of relatively more homogenous societies.

[...]

31

UNDERSTANDING COMMUNAL VIOLENCE*

Nizamuddin Riots

PRADIP DATTA, BISWAMOY PATI, SUMIT SARKAR,
TANIKA SARKAR AND SAMBUDDHA SEN

On 17 March this year [1990], a riot in the heart of south Delhi left two Bangladeshi Muslim refugees dead in police firing and about 50 other Muslims injured. The clash occurred in Nizamuddin, when a large gathering of Hindus began building a boundary wall without police sanction (but nevertheless with careful police protection) on a piece of land that is disputed between the Wakf board and the municipal corporation of Delhi. An Urdu weekly, *Akbar-e-Nau*, later carried a photograph of wall-building going on in a relaxed manner within a police ring, while smoke billows from refugee jhuggis and a clash is obviously going on in the background. Municipal water tankers provided water to mix mortar for the wall, but not to put the fires out. The disputed land lies between an old Muslim burial ground and a relatively new and expanding Arya Samaj *shamshan-bhoomi* (cremation ground [eds]) that requires additional land for a very large car park. An Arya Samaji leader compared the wall building with the proposed 'shilanyas' ceremony in Ayodhya, but he also called it 'kar seva'—a term that suggests how Hindu organisations in Delhi are increasingly inviting the participation of Sikhs in a united front against Muslims.

By today's standards, the 17 March event was almost a non-riot. Only two Muslims were killed, and the settled inhabitants of Nizamuddin were not directly involved. Paradoxically, this gave us the reason to investigate it. Since violence was negligible, it would not overwhelm our attention, and it would leave us free to investigate larger social processes, like the organisation of communal identities and the problems of localities caught up in uneven urban development.

The Nizamuddin we investigated comprises three habitational zones. At the centre is the *basti* (which means here an old settlement and not slum), that is, the traditional pilgrimage centre, clustered around the shrine of Nizamuddin Chisti. To its west, occupying a minuscule corner, is the densely populated refugee jhuggi.

* *Economic and Political Weekly* 25 (45): 2487–95 (10 November 1990).

On the east, in very sharp contrast, lies the posh residential 'colony' of modern Nizamuddin, with an overwhelmingly Hindu population. On the left, between the basti and the jhuggi, is the disputed land. The whole area is located on one of the most important arteries of Delhi, which, with three flyovers, offers the speediest connection between the most booming part of south Delhi, and both Connaught Place and Old Delhi.

The Nizamuddin event seemed to occupy a middle ground between a riot and an invasion. It had not taken place in a shared space: an organised Hindu crowd coming from other parts of the city, ably supported by the police, had invaded an overwhelmingly Muslim settlement. We discovered during the course of our investigation that this was contributing to a marked asymmetry in our own research. The section on Muslims tends to see them in terms of an aggregate of different individuals, dispersed, though not separated in their relationship with their identity as Muslims, and united by physical proximity. Our search for those who organised the Hindus, in contrast, led us to visit offices and residences in several different parts of the city and put us in touch with only the politicised Hindu—who shared a common, fairly organised, groundwork of beliefs and objectives. Matters were further complicated by our lack of expertise in dealing with the religious beliefs of the Muslims (which itself reflects the biases of liberal academics in our country). Nevertheless, we have retained these asymmetries in our report, not only because we do not know any better, but more crucially, because we feel that these reveal a new critical structuration of communal relations in our country, when a single aggressive communal ideology is poised against a community that at present lacks the resources to produce an equally unifying ideology.

The history of the land dispute that sparked off the riot is an index of the growing and aggressive demarcation of communal boundaries. This land—sandwiched between the Nizamuddin basti and the gleaming opulence of Lodi Hotel—is triangular in shape. It has three segments, two of which are occupied by the *kabristan* (graveyard [eds]) and the shamshan-bhoomi respectively, and the third, which lies adjacent to the refugee jhuggi, is disputed. It belonged to the government: Settlement Reports from 1927–28 onwards indicate that it had been leased out for cultivation on a temporary basis from time to time. The burial ground is obviously pretty ancient, while the cremation area came into existence in the 1950s, no doubt with the southward expansion of the city. For years, the burial and cremation grounds co-existed without friction. The situation started altering in the 1970s. The Wakf board (in charge of customary burial grounds) had entered into litigation with the municipal corporation regarding part of the disputed land, and in 1976 they were awarded 18 bighas. It was also from the late 1970s, an observer recalls, that the shamshan-bhoomi, managed by the Arya Samaj, started building more permanent structures. The 1970s, it must be recalled, was a decade of immense urban development, when a large number of residential colonies dominated by affluent Hindu gentry came up in south Delhi, and the Nizamuddin flyover was constructed. The shamshan-bhoomi grew in importance, as it was very conveniently located for south Delhi (the other major cremation ground being more than 10 kilometres away). The situation was further unsettled by the expansion of a brand new *prachin* (ancient [eds]) Shiv Shakti temple, located on disputed land right next to the old Muslim basti. Starting as a little wayside shrine, it quickly acquired a big brick-and-concrete structure, and was inaugurated by H. K. L. Bhagat in 1982. Meanwhile, the Wakf board was somehow prevented from building a boundary wall around the area awarded to it in 1976.

Not the least communally significant element in the land dispute was that a reference point was the kabristan. Though the graveyard is directly under attack, it provides visible legitimacy to the authority of the Wakf board. The emotive significance of the graveyard is enhanced by its proximity to Nizamuddin basti; it is seen socially as its extension.

Graveyards are integral to the identity of Nizamuddin, built, as it is, around the grave of a great Sufi saint, Nizamuddin Aulia. For the Sufis, the grave of saint signifies not so much death as the constantly renewable connection with his grace and spiritual presence. This does not, of course, extend to the graves of ordinary folk, but the layout of the graveyards around the dargah (which includes that of Mirza Ghalib) suggests a sense of community among the dead, a community that is linked to the living through a shared desire for *barkat* (grace) from the saint.

The dargah of Nizamuddin has a sacred and monumental history of 700 years. To retain this institutionally has been the task of the Nizami family which claims direct descent from the saint and claims most of the land. Their superior patriarchal presence has helped to maintain the identity of this place, 95 per cent of whose inhabitants are Muslims, the rest consisting of Hindus and Christians. This fairly stable religious composition of Nizamuddin is remarkable, considering the vicissitudes of Partition, which saw the emigration of a major component (Ghosi converts, who had tended cattle). Their place has been taken by Muslims who came from Bihar, Rajasthan and Uttar Pradesh.

Much has altered, however, despite the sway of the Nizami family. The occupational profile changed with the departure of the Ghosis: now the dominant professions are linked to the urban offices. Yahya Nizami, a member of the family, is a retired accountant. Besides there are new centres of prestige such as the principal of the Ghalib Academy to whom Nizami was fairly deferential. Foreign money has also begun to make a distinct impact. There is an organisation called the Tabligh-i-Jamait, which engages in purification campaigns and is funded, according to some sources, by French and Dutch money.

The big buildings in which the Ghalib Academy and the Tabligh are housed look exceptional. The rest of the Nizamuddin basti wears an unchanged 'mofussil' appearance. Small *pucca* houses sit next to each other and are woven together by small narrow winding gullies. In contrast to its plush south Delhi neighbours, the Nizamuddin settlement has a concentrated and confined look: it covers barely 2–3 square kilometres.

While not looking depressed, there are few signs of economic activity here. All of it is limited to the approach to the dargah, which is speckled with shops selling pan, flowers, incense, mementoes and food. There are no signs of mechanical workshops, petty offices, xerox shops that are normally visible on the central lanes of similar south Delhi settlements. The reason is that Nizamuddin is not '*laldora* land', a status that enables a Delhi 'village' to claim subsidised electricity for manufacturing and commercial centres. Here, Nizamuddin is characteristic of Delhi's town planning which has failed to develop Muslim habitats except for the authoritarian attempt at evacuating Turkman Gate during the Emergency. Clearly, Nizamuddin's stability is not simply self-generating; it is enforced by an implicit communal bias in urban planning.

[...]

On 17 March, the refugee jhuggi lying adjacent to the basti on disputed land had been the principal target of Hindu onslaught, mounted at 6.30 am by a huge crowd (some say as many as 10,000 participants) mobilised from many parts of the city to build the boundary wall by collective labour. The crowd had been led by B. L. Sharma, secretary of the Indraprastha unit of the Vishva Hindu Parishad (VHP). Top ranking Bharatiya Janata Party (BJP) leaders like M. L. Khurana and V. K. Malhotra had also been present. Police action backing up the Hindu onslaught, however, quickly swept beyond the jhuggi into the basti. There was random firing at basti houses, and a bullet hole can still be seen on the window panes of the state-sponsored Ghalib Academy, where a seminar was on when the bullet was fired.

The events of that day created a common predicament of vulnerability and fear for two otherwise very different settlements—the basti with its 700-year-old history, and the very recent refugee jhuggi, started only a few years ago, and sustained economically by the *kabari* (rag picking) trade. The wall threatened to enclose much of the open space where the refugees kept their kabari dumps, from which waste is recycled. The jhuggi-dwellers therefore had protested, and, on police advice, we were told, the Hindu volunteers started burning the dumps. This led to stone throwing from jhuggi, and the alleged beating up of two policemen. Firing promptly killed a young man and a boy from the jhuggi.

Life in the jhuggi is brittle and unsettled—a small precarious existence at the foot of a swank flyover, in a part of the city that has no comparable settlement. Covering approximately an area of 1 square mile, it is densely packed with miniature hutments covered by wooden sheets. More than one family may inhabit a single room. Najma, the pregnant widow of one of the firing victims—a very young girl of about 13—stays with her sister's family along with other dependents. The people who live here are recent migrants, mainly from Bangladesh, and some from West Bengal and Bihar. To protect themselves from eviction, they claim that they are not Bengalis, but 'Darbhangis'.

The loss of identity, however, has been compensated for by a livelihood acquired through the kabari trade. Its importance was latent in the words of an inhabitant who stated, just a few days after the riot: 'We live in great peace here. My children get enough to eat!' The kabari trade forms the heart of the jhuggi: it is the livelihood of the jhuggi-dwellers and is also what organises their community. There is a hierarchical structure in the trade with the lowest rung consisting of those who move around actually collecting refuse, and whose earnings vary between Rs 6–8 to

Rs 30–60 a day. The waste, which consists mainly of plastic and paper, is carefully arranged into bundles which are then neatly stacked in the courtyard (referred to as *gola* in the local parlance) of the kabari intermediaries. There are 18 golas in the locality. At the top of the hierarchy are the prosperous intermediaries of kabari, one of whom, Imamuddin, had his substantial stocks burned in the 17 March disturbances. But the goods threatened or destroyed also included those of other, lesser jhuggi-dwellers—the attack hence mobilised the entire jhuggi.

[...]

There is, of course, a larger binding force in their being Muslims. It does give them a source of sustenance, for it cannot be a coincidence that they have chosen to settle in the immediate periphery of a historic Muslim settlement. The relationship between the refugees and the inhabitants of the basti is, however, we shall later see, problematic.

The assumption of implicit continuity between the basti and the jhuggi is read as such by their more prosperous Hindu neighbours. This was evident in the mobilisation which preceded the wall-building of 17 March. Throughout some of the surrounding colonies (many of which had witnessed major anti-Sikh riots in 1984), there was a drive by different Hindu organisations to raise funds for the bricks which would go into the building of the wall. One colony which contributed in a big way was Nizamuddin West.

Besides the name, Nizamuddin West shares another common feature with its poorer neighbourhood—like it, Nizamuddin West is inhabited by migrants. But for the rest, it supports a life that is the exact opposite of what we saw in the basti and the jhuggi. The overwhelming number of Punjabi migrants here live in modern bungalows, often double-storied, which overlook roads wide enough to allow speeding cars to pass each other. The growing communalisation of Delhi has dovetailed with some cases of petty theft by some residents of the jhuggi to develop into a larger resentment against the two Muslim settlements. The problem has been exacerbated by recent migrations of some very wealthy Muslims from Old Delhi; inside West Nizamuddin Muslims have been discouraged from actively participating in residents' committees. Clearly, the aggressiveness of the Hindu communalists and the violence of the police could only occur on the basis of such powerful grounds of sympathy.

All around the Nizamuddin complex are solidly prosperous Hindu and Sikh traders' settlements—Jungpura, Bhogal, Lajpat Nagar. Such areas are today dotted with Sanatan Dharam temples, Arya Samaj mandirs, VHP offices, and Rashtriya Swayamsevak Sangh (RSS) *shakhas*.[1] ...

From the killing of women and children in police firing within an enclosed mosque at Id prayers in Moradabad in August 1980, through the Central Reserve Police Force atrocities in Meerut and Malliana in 1986, down to Bhagalpur, Gujarat and Nizamuddin in recent months, the overwhelming majority of those killed in communal violence have been Muslims. The offensive almost invariably has come from Hindus, and police and paramilitary forces have been blatantly partial. In Nizamuddin, Hindu volunteers disregarded police requests and built a wall on disputed territory and burnt Muslim habitations. Yet only Muslims were killed or injured in the police firing, once more confirming the general pattern.

Islamic fundamentalism certainly exists, but for the moment it seems to have turned inwards, resulting in a defensive conservatism; backlashes against community members who rebel against orthodox norms and occasional de-syncretising efforts. A Jungpura Hindu leaflet complains that a Muslim has been forcibly installed at a dargah with a syncretist tradition, which had so far been looked after by a Hindu. There is a great deal of anger still against Muslims who had opposed the Muslim Women's Bill; a general consensus is that they had colluded with anti-Islamic forces. 'Islam has been stripped naked', said Saheed Siddiqi, a Nizamuddin journalist. A Janwadi Mahila Samiti school started some years ago in the Nizamuddin basti had to close down in the face of conservative opposition. There is a closure to self-criticism and opposition to reformism within Islam even among Muslims completely non-traditional in their own ways of life.

[...]

Intra-community social divisions breed much tension. ... The subtly-graded subcontracting system in the jhuggis, from master kabaris, through various intermediaries down to the rag pickers, produced very different voices about the meaning of the crisis. Each voice also changed its inflection according to changes in the situation. ...

If the widely assumed concept of a coherent, unified, organised Muslim community remained widely unrealised even in a crisis, we did come across at least some latent tendencies that could point in that direction. ...

Overriding all divisions and differences looms a shared memory of terrible wrongs which still go unrectified, even unheard. Ever since 1987, the Jama Masjid has kept its main entrance draped in black banners with 'Tears of blood' written on them in three languages. They demand punishment for those guilty of the 1987 killings. The poignancy of the banners lies in the fact that these demands have not only remained unfulfilled, but also gone largely unheard, in contrast to the demands for justice for the anti-Sikh genocide of 1984 which have now come to form a part of the secular consciousness in the city. A poster at the Nizamuddin basti pays homage to the shaheeds of 17 March, thus expressing kinship with the Bangladeshis. ... Delhi Muslims share too, a strong sense of growing marginalisation in the social life of a rapidly expanding metropolis, which in turn breeds in them an acute sense of spatial constriction. It is difficult for Muslims of any income group to rent houses from non Muslims, and Muslims wanting to settle down in Nizamuddin have to pay artificially inflated rents and sale prices. The West Nizamuddin Residents' Association tends to exclude Muslims even though Muslims comprise 15 per cent of the population there. Areas with large Muslim populations—Jama Masjid, Turkman Gate, Nizamuddin basti—have remained untouched by urban development, retaining the congested look of old medieval lanes. They stand in shocking contrast to the vast open boulevards, gardens, parks and planned colonies of the 'modern' city.

[...]

The pattern of recent urban development has dispersed the bases of inter-community cultural interaction in mixed local communities. Opposite the Pusa Road Springdales School stands an old dargah which some years ago was at the centre of a bustling village. Development of the ridge area and the construction of a shopping centre on the Pusa Road broke up the village. The dargah now stands isolated, obsolete, without any recognised social or cultural role, an oddity. ... It is very remarkable that the few remaining dargahs that still draw mixed batches of devotees nowadays are generally isolated from the main thoroughfares and often exist under the shadow of giant, empty ruins. ... The contrast with the public ostentatiousness of the Prachin Shiv Shakti Mandirs, with their shining marble, gaudy decorations, flourishing bazaars and blaring loudspeaker music, could not be sharper. ... Another instance of the eviction of Muslims from a shared culture is the ghettoisation of the preeminent Urdu culture of Delhi which in total defiance of history has been branded a 'Muslim' language. A curious feature about the present state of Urdu is that this very act of separation has also created a new, though entirely sectoralised, vitality. There has been a recent leap in newspaper readership and in many Muslim homes, girls are being given an exclusively Urdu-based education.

[...]

Desperate survival strategies in a BJP-dominated Delhi probably make Muslims represent themselves as a peace-loving, mild, tolerant people, to counter the usual stereotype of aggressive, proselytising militant Islam. The Nizamuddin basti people try to conflate local associations of communal harmony—a shared musical culture, a charity-oriented Sufi dargah that offers its generosity to all creeds—with the image of Islam as a whole. In any case, an alternative self-image, rooted in peace and charity rather than in militancy, is probably needed to legitimise this period of rather unsuccessful negotiations with far more powerful adversaries. At the same time, one must not underestimate the potential for resistance in desperate situations. Siddiqi was clearly impatient with the fears and compromises of local bosses and Ahmed Bukhari, son of Imam Bukhari had, a few years ago, formed an Adam Sena as an abortive challenge to the Bajrang Dal. The *Akbar-e-Nau* report on the riot stated that the Muslims began to stone the police as soon as they had trained their guns on the Muslims: that is, the report made it a point to claim that Muslim stoning had preceded the actual firing. A subtext, affirming courage and militancy, informs the report. Peaceability should not be confused with cowardice and endless submission.

Since colonial times, secular and progressive forces have used fairly well-established explanations for communal violence. At the operative, organisational level, communal conflict has been seen as the handiwork of criminals aided and abetted by excesses of the Hindus, police and the paramilitary forces. At a more generalised level, communalisation is seen as distorted class struggle, the distortion being introduced, on the one hand, by manipulating the religious 'passions' of the masses, and, on the other, by alien policies, notably 'divide and rule', which skilfully taps these energies. The net effect of these approaches is to detach communal violence from any understanding of the beliefs that go into its making, and the organisations that shape their production. Consequently, the masses and the elite are saved from complicity, and communalism is always located as an exterior force.

At a first localised glance, Nizamuddin seems tailor-made for these explanations. First, it has a history that has not witnessed communal violence. Second, the violence on 17 March was engineered from outside and was not located in a common space. Finally, the deaths occurred among the non-local Bangladeshi population and were solely due to police firing.

The picture, however, became quite different once we extended the geographical scope of our investigations. In order to understand the motivations of those who participated in the attack, we decided to investigate the surrounding localities from where they had come. These included relatively affluent south Delhi residential colonies like Nizamuddin West, Lajpat Nagar, Jungpura and the less affluent Bhogal. What we found was a network of mass organisations which in turn led us to head offices that were located in places quite distant from Nizamuddin.

[...]

As we went looking for offices of organisations, we discovered intimate interconnections. At the Arya Samaj mandir in Jungpura, we were directed to the Sanatan Dharam mandir which lay a furlong away. There, the pujaris told us that they shared an office with the VHP at Lajpat Nagar. At the Namdev Temple Samiti office on Lodi Road, we saw mobilisation going on for a VHP march against the US Supreme Court on behalf of the ISKCON. On Ram Navami day, we saw the same trucks carrying signboards of the VHP and the Arya Samaj. VHP leaflets mentioned the fraternal involvement of several Sikh and Buddhist organisations in the Ram Navami celebrations. In this connection, it is interesting that one of the sponsors for the burial ground shilanyas was the Sikh Singh Sabha.

Despite the fact that none of the organisations had surrendered their individual nomenclatures, the overwhelming impression was of deliberate orchestration. 'We are all Hindus, we are all the same!', all the different organisational spokesmen told us at the beginning of their expositions; all reduced any difference in beliefs or practices among themselves to personal eccentricities. All the representatives we talked to emphasised the oneness of Hinduism which, by consensus, was seen to spring from its unique location on Indian soil. The word 'Hindu' applied to all home-grown religions, while caste, rituals, deities were seen as matters of personal and local differences. What was striking was the exchange of icons between organisations. The local Arya Samaj president we visited sported a picture of Bajrangbali in his house. Ram, Sita and Hanuman were the main deities in the Prachin Shiv Shakti temple at Nizamuddin. None claimed an exclusive monopoly over a fundamental truth of Hinduism or, in fact claimed any truth beside the word 'Hindu' as fundamental; no one even sought to propagandise their individual excellence or superiority. Hinduism, unlike its nineteenth century incarnations, had no dogmatic basis here. On the contrary, it was being realised as a pluralism of beliefs—the whole packaged in the word Hindu. Given this picture, an interpretation of present day Hinduism as 'fundamentalist' is clearly a misnomer.

This particular notion of Hinduism has its roots in the discourses of Hindu revivalism in the 1920s, most notably perhaps the writings of V. D. Savarkar. (See, for instance, his 1923 publication, *Hindutva/Who is a Hindu?*, which defined the Hindu not by doctrine or ritual, but as 'a person who regards the land of Bharatvarsha as his father land, as well as his holy land, that is the cradle land of his religion'.) What was surprising was that it had become a basic assumption amongst all the Hindu participants of the 17 March incident. Clearly, this revealed a high and prior degree of institutional exchange. ...

The master text of all these festivities is of course the Ramjanmabhoomi issue. It is this which has contributed most to the professed pluralism of Hindu revival. The shilanyas programme which, till now, has been the main feature of this issue, has successfully combined the contours of a ritual with that of a cultural and political movement. As such, this combination has been prefigured earlier, such as in Tilak's Ganpati experiment. Where it has marked new frontiers, is firstly in its all-India scope, combining both rural and urban areas at a moment when all the anxieties of this country seem to hinge on the fear of disintegration. Second, this ritual movement has the character of a specific, time-bound project which sharpens its mobilising edge. And finally, of course, it has a single external enemy, which, as current talks by communalists of killing 50,000 Muslims to save Kashmir suggests, is physically expendable. ...

Above all, the pluralist Hindu revival is defined by what it excludes. These are specifically listed in the VHP leaflets as Christians, Muslims and communists. Paradoxically, communists in VHP literature are seen not so much as foreign agents as misguided intellectuals who are victims of alien Western rationalist categories, the evidence of which is to be found in their criticism of Hinduism. ... VHP fears about communist and Christian conversions seem to sum up older Hindu nationalist strategies of classifying any criticism of 'Hinduism' as 'alien' a device through which all criticism was sought to be closed.

Sooner or later, however, anti-Islamism crops up to provide the central polemic and guiding emotion. Interestingly, discourses on Muslims have different moments of passion and raised varied associations with fear. We went to meet B. L. Sharma, who was identified by many as the man who had personally directed the 17 March action. The Indraprastha VHP office was adjacent to one of the main temples in Delhi. In his robust manner, Sharma declared that riots were inevitable and desirable, given Muslim duplicity and treachery; he easily admitted that Hindus may have burned the Nizamuddin jhuggis. He showed little awareness of the land dispute. The organising principle of his theme was Muslim lust and violence. Recalling the 1947 riots in Punjab, he depicted them as a series of abductions by Muslims of Hindu women, who were for him mothers and sisters, that is, embodiments of chastity. For him, that history carries on. Muslims are constituted by lust: '*Unke aankhon mein lust hai*' ('There is lust in their eyes' [eds]), though they seek to cover it up with politeness and charm.

[...]

In the written VHP discourse, however, the lust factor is relatively absent. Lust here gets translated into Muslim virility and self-multiplication, and the penetration of Muslim money from outside; the last two being permanent themes. For the Sanatan Dharam representative, the main concern was with Muslim attacks on temples and their multiplying numbers. The Muslims interpret family planning as:

'*Hum panch, hamara pacchis.*' The force of numbers operates through their takeover of temples and other kinds of land. His paranoia was so confident that he claimed that the images in the Shiva Shakti temple in Nizamuddin had been defaced, which was patently untrue. The Wakf board, he said, can put up notices claiming any piece of stray land, and if that is not disputed within a year, the land is taken over by them. Moreover, Muslims can establish dargahs and shrines simply by putting a few bricks on an open field and then claiming that it is a pir's grave. For Khosla, president of the Arya Samaj, Lodi Road, the Muslim raised fears about permanently open and exposed Indian boundaries. Though a much travelled man, he insisted that it was not necessary to possess visas to enter India. Consequently, India was open to hordes of Muslim refugees and invaders. This led to a specifically Arya Samaji notion of crisis. An Arya Samaj leaflet that was circulating in Nizamuddin some days before the riot alleged that the Muslim burial ground there encroached upon the burial grounds of Hindu and Sikh infants. It made the further point that whereas lakhs of Hindus could be cremated in the same spot, each time a Muslim died and was buried, the land was lost forever. Thus, for Muslims, even death was a device for expansion on land. The Muslim, in fact, does not have to be overtly hostile. By the mere process of birth, breeding and dying, that is, by going through the natural biological cycle, he poses a threat.

Numbers—with which these Hindu politicians associate Muslims—gained a peculiar importance during early nationalism, particularly after the census operations commenced. The nationalist hymn *Bande Mataram,* for instance, shows an obsessive concern with the exact number of arms, hands and mouths of the children of the mother. But what was a source of strength in nationalist discourse became a sign of weakness among Hindus in Bengal with the onset of electoral politics and the corresponding anxiety about the minority position of Hindus within Bengal's population. The latter rhetoric of numerical weakness seems to be now taken over and woven into an overwhelming majoritarian Hindu discourse. The Hindu majority can cite its very numerical strength as a threat of impending loss because of its overwhelming historical associations, just as the older nationalist self-image of a threatened, weak and subjected country is fully retained in present-day self-projections of what is actually a fully independent nation-state with a big military-industrial complex.

Very little space in VHP leaflets is given to doctrinal dialogue or debate; only one leaflet lists Koranic strictures against idolatry. The Muslim is almost exclusively seen as a simple racial stereotype, whose true political loyalties become visible from time to time when they cheer for the wrong side during Indo-Pak cricket matches. These instances then get conflated into rumours that they fly Pakistani flags during days of national mourning. Such political suspicions, vastly accelerated now because of the Kashmir issue, have become part of the living common sense, especially in the media. The chief minister of Himachal Pradesh recently described Pak designs on Kashmir as the disrobing of Draupadi, conjuring up instantaneously, an identical scene made familiar by the TV Mahabharata representation across the entire country. A wide range of discourses—media, mythology, official speech and exhortations by communal organisations—thus come together weaving in sexual anxiety, physical fears and political problems in shared, popular audio-visual representation.

In a fundamental way, Muslims provide Hindus with history. After touching on the epic beginnings of Hinduism, the historiography of VHP Hinduism quickly jumps to the advent of Muslims, passing over the entire 'Hindu period' very lightly. It is at this moment that Hindu history becomes alive. Muslim invasion firstly summons up a spectacle of pride. According to B. L. Sharma, Islam managed to evict all religions wherever it went. But in India, brahmanical Hinduism did manage to survive, albeit in a debilitated and defensive form through puja, shastric study and, later, in the rather feminine forms of *krandan* (lament [eds]) and *artanad* (outcry [eds]) of the Bhakti tradition. He, therefore, ascribes a rather negative (because of its feminine character) definition to Bhakti traditions, which are popularly associated with syncretism. Hindu history matures with the coming of the British. It was then that Vivekananda introduced to it the idea of the motherland. He was followed by Savarkar, whom Sharma designated as 'the greatest man in history': he made Hindus self-aware, a nation not just in itself but for itself. Hedgewar succeeded him with the idea of organisation, through which Savarkar's notion of the self-arming Hindu could be actualised. This was the real period of creation, for it was then that the RSS, 'the mother of us all', was born. The RSS remains the dearest and most divine entity: '*gun jo hai, sab uske hai, dosh hoga to hamara hoga*' ('whatever is good in us, we owe it to the RSS; the flaws are because of us' [eds]). The RSS is the true centre, it is 'cadre based', while the VHP and other organisations are its 'mass fronts'. Incidentally, Sharma did not really dilate on the role of the BJP. This silence probably allows greater flexibility to BJP manoeuvrings, though the latter has consistently participated in VHP programmes. The Sanatan Dharmi official, after some hesitation, also stated that the real Hindu community began in 1925 with the inception of the RSS. Like the VHP spokesman and the Arya Samaji, he, too, considered the present state of Hinduism as a moment of *jagarukta* or 'about to be awakened'.

All of them acknowledged the positive contribution of the media, especially of the televised Ramayan, for this awakening. The success of the serial, it may be noted, is evident not only in the bare fact of its pan-Indian viewership, but also in the way it marks a new development in Hinduism. For the first time, all Hindus across the country saw and at the same time listened to the same thing: the serial, in fact has introduced a congregational imperative into Hinduism. ...

The combined effect of the serialised Ramayan with the Ramjanmabhoomi/Babri Masjid issue has been the most ambitious attempt to popularise the VHP idea of the Indian state. For them, the Hindu is one for whom India is the sacred land. As such, it seems a 'secular' depiction of Hinduism. In fact, this definition seeks to remove the distinction between secular and communal, just as it takes over, even more easily, the authority and ideology of the nation-state. But then, it proceeds to Hinduise the land completely, by appropriating and sacralising its geographical, historical and even zoological features. ... Yet, the moment this 'secular' religion is made co-extensive with the country alone, the land itself is reinvested with Hindu marks.

In doing this, the VHP draws on some very central, profound longstanding and evocative traditions of Indian nationalism. Communalism or, rather, this variant of nationalism, predates the Gandhian and Nehruvian moments of Indian nationalism, and may prove to be ultimately stronger. Right now, it seems to have become part of the common sense regarding the assumptions of the Indian state. It remains to be seen, whether it can, as the VHP seeks to do, alter the premises of the Indian Constitution.

To achieve such aims, contemporary Hindu revivalism needs to establish the unity of Hindus vis-à-vis the predominantly Muslim other as absolute, unconditional and 'natural'. Faced in real life with tensions of gender, class and caste, however, its ideological response can recognise and even claim to celebrate difference, but only within given hierarchical and conservative limits. ... And the real limits of this supposedly 'unifying' 'pluralistic' discourse have been revealed in [a] flash by the high-caste backlash on the reservations issue. ... Hence, for all Hindu communalists and their intellectual fellow travellers, the 'renewed importance of Ayodhya'.

Note

1. An RSS shakha is both a unit and a daily meeting of the members of the unit at an open place. [eds]

32

KHURJA RIOTS 1990–91*

Understanding the Conjuncture

UMA CHAKRAVARTI, PREM CHOWDHURY, PRADIP DATTA,
ZOYA HASAN, KUMKUM SANGARI AND TANIKA SARKAR

[...]

I

On our first visit to Khurja, we were struck by the fact that the pottery industry cropped up in most connections and we spent some time looking for direct connections between the pottery industry and the riots. In our present understanding, pottery is at the heart of the political economy of the city and is implicated in the riots to the extent that communal differentiation and riots are themselves embedded in the conjuncture of political and other social processes.

With its brisk export inside and outside India, pottery accounts for the prosperity of Khurja, while much of the economy and politics of the city centre around it. This industry is not only at the nodal conjuncture of a whole network of social relations—of labour and capital, intra-class conflicts and alliances, communities and communalism—it also condenses a whole social relation of petty bourgeois, small-town urbanisation.

The pottery trade-manufacture seems to be the main agent of change, economic expansion and social mobility in Khurja; with coal, clay and some of the capital and labour[1] of this industry coming from outside the city, the life of the town must have altered considerably in the last two decades. One of the new elements is related to the black market in coal which is not only the particular form in which criminalisation is said to have entered Khurja, but the surpluses generated by it seem to have played a significant role in the riots.

Pottery production, the principal industry,[2] now said to be the main source of livelihood for nearly half the town's population, received a boost after the establishment of the Pottery Development Centre in 1962, the setting up of

* *Economic and Political Weekly* 27 (18): 951–65 (2 May 1992).

training centres and financial assistance for new units. The ensuing boom, generated by the transition from cottage industry to factory production, led to a dramatic expansion in pottery manufacture in the mid-1970s, with the really large factories and big capital entering the scene. At this time, the quality and design of pottery also improved vastly. Till then, it had been a small capital enterprise, with people setting up little units on their own land at a cost of Rs 30,000–40,000. Most of this expansion was concentrated in the private sector and there is only one government controlled pottery unit.

The Khurja pottery industry is, in relative terms, a low-capital and low-technology industry considering that this was the period of industrialisation in Uttar Pradesh, and establishment of several centrally sponsored industries with priority being given to small-scale and medium-sized industries in the Sixth Five Year Plan. There are about 500 units, about 50 'large' ones and the rest small-scale. Any unit with a capital of Rs 7.5 lakh, excluding land and buildings, is deemed as small-scale. There are over a 100 such small-scale units which are called dependent units since they rely on the common kiln and other facilities provided by the Uttar Pradesh Small Industries Corporation. In 1989, there were 396 private units registered as independent. These units are considered 'large' because they are self-sufficient. Altogether, only about 250 units are said to be effective producers which work and produce pottery throughout the year.

The logistics and mechanics of 'ineffective' production seem to be tied to the black market. From Jaiprakash's (a Bharatiya Janata Party (BJP) pottery owner) account, it seems that the limited and erratic supply of coal from the government has by now acquired a structuring role in pottery manufacture which integrates it into a parallel black-marketing economy and functions to guarantee under-production and corollary high prices. Too much coal leads to overproduction, lack of demand and a drop in prices. According to the Sub-divisional Magistrate (SDM), coal is bought from the government at Rs 1,250 a ton and sold at Rs 2,000 in black and the black turnover is around three crores. Paradoxically, shortage of coal appears to be a favourable condition for the prosperity of the Khurja pottery industry, because when there is an abundant supply of coal, the market suffers a decline! Regulation of coal supply enables manufacturers to control production so as to inflate product prices.

The coal factor also seems to be one of the determinants of the daily wage labour system and the preference of some manufacturers for farming out work to home-based units. Most of the units officially employ barely 10–20 workers and another 10–12 on contract. This is in order to avoid providing employees state insurance facilities, which no owner wants to do. A pottery owner told us that an owner will 'declare' only 9–10 workers. The most skilled workers—most of the moulders and all the glazers—are Muslims and their artisanal skills are still indispensable, especially since there is a shortage of skilled craftsmen. Workers are mostly contracted on a daily wage basis except in the glazing departments, which require the longest supervision of products, where they are given monthly contracts. Not surprisingly, the workers are not well organised and Khurja pottery has a sparse history of trade union activity. There is only one recent Centre of Indian Trade Union's union and that is located in the government-owned pottery works. This too helps the manufacturers in keeping wages to a minimum and maintaining abysmal work conditions. The majority of units do not have roofed sheds, carry out work in the open air and work very little in the rains.

Production is also carried on in home-based units. Muslims predominate in the home-based units, which also have a small number of Bihari migrants. Government training and bank loan facilities and mechanisms for new small-scale industries seem to have left home-based potteries in Muslim hands and worked in favour of factory-based production which is mostly owned by Hindus. Many manufacturers prefer to get their work done in home-based units rather than in factories. This may be convenient in a situation where many factories do not produce at all, many erratically, and only some regularly, relying as they do on black market profits.

In fact, the high black market value of coal may well be part of the attraction of the pottery industry for investors. Excepting the strong component of Punjabi refugees, most of the manufacturers are locally based. Some of the capital comes from as far as Bihar and Calcutta, but anyone who has money in Khurja, made from retail trades in the *mandi* (market [eds]), farming or fruit orchards, considers it a good investment, and since the pottery boom, some of the old landowning aristocracy and some of the rural rich are also investing in it. We were told that of the Hindu labourers who had come from Bihar, around 50 have become pottery owners with the help of bank loans. According to Sarwar Husain, some 'sainis' ('kumhars') have also become pottery owners and support the BJP now. He said, at one time, all pottery units were owned by Muslims, their monopoly was broken by the new manufacturers, most of whom were Hindus. Even now, Muslims own about 150 of the approximately 500 private units, but gradually, Hindus have come to own the largest number of pottery units. The reason offered by him was that there was better education among Hindus and he cited the example of an uneducated Muslim owner whose Hindu manager and contact-man had now become an owner in his own right, taking over all the lucrative government contracts in the process. Though there are some Muslims in the wholesale pottery trade, it seems Hindus largely control the distribution while Punjabis control about 35 per cent of the pottery retail trade.

Though much of the production is carried on in private units and households, the manufacturers depend on the government for obtaining coal which is the crucial component in pottery production. This is then siphoned and sold for domestic consumption, fetching a high price in the black market in Khurja and the Ghaziabad industrial area. The proximity of Khurja to the industrial belt of Ghaziabad, Noida and Okhla industrial estate may also be an added incentive. Permits are required to take coal out and bribes are required for these; it is said that Rs 250 is collected as bribes for each truck and the money so collected amounts to around Rs 2 lakh every month. It was alleged by one pottery owner that the Station House Officer gets Rs 50,000 and another Rs 50,000 has to go towards bribes to the administrative and police network in the area. A coal mafia involving hired goondas is involved in this operation.

Accounts of the number of non-productive units and the amount of coal sold in the black market varied from 50 to 95 per cent! Prakash Chandra Goel, a shop owner and Communist Party of India (Marxist) supporter, said nearly 95 per cent of the coal was sold on the black market; according to the ex-SDM, 425 of the 500 units do not work and are registered for the purpose of procuring coal; a manager in the government pottery said 50 per cent of the coal-based units do not function at all. The Muslim reporter and other Muslims engaged in retailing pottery claimed that 75 per cent of the pottery units are engaged in black marketing coal, and that the Pottery Manufacturers Association is directly involved in the black marketing business. According to one owner, a common technique for black marketing in coal was the establishing of 'farzi' [fake] glass units and coal briquette units by pottery owners, a few years ago, in the names of their wives and sons for the sole purpose of procuring coal licences.[3] The huge amounts of coal coming to them end up in the black market.[4]

Pottery owners have resisted newer technology. According to a manager in the government factory, they refused to switch over to an efficient, low-cost Japanese innovation introduced in 1984 which uses diesel and stops the use of coal!

Given their stake, the pottery owners, in contrast to the workers, are extremely well-organised under the aegis of the Pottery Manufacturers Association (PMA), which includes the 396 owners of independent units but excludes home-based units. The PMA acts as a pressure group in obtaining licences for coal and maintains close relations with political parties in power. Control of the PMA is vital in cornering licences and eliminating rivals and competitors, and for control over the parallel economy. In 1986, the Khurja Ceramic Association merged with the Khurja Pottery Manufacturers Association, intensifying the struggle and the number of people involved. Past, present and would-be office-bearers include prominent Punjabis and Muslims. According to ex-SDM Sharma, pottery owners seek to exploit politicians and to dominate the administration and police. There is said to be another trade association, the 'vyapar mandal', but the PMA is said to dominate that as well. Thus, the mandi itself seems to be connected to pottery manufacture both through the association and as a field of investment.

II

The pottery owners then subsist within a quadrangular relation comprising criminals, politicians, municipal politics and the mandi.

It was alleged that important local personalities, both Hindu and Muslim, are engaged in the coal black market while prominent leaders of the coal mafia—one Hindu and one Muslim—wished to enter municipal politics, with the former aspiring to be chairman of the municipal board in Khurja. Members of the Legislative Assembly and members of Parliament (MPs) from the district, both

Hindu and Muslim, seem to be involved and it is alleged that they have been getting a fixed share of the profits, at least in the past few years. D. P. Yadav, ... a leader from Bulandshahr who has a dozen cases against him, is also said to be associated with these activities and these politicians. A recent struggle for power by this group seems to have been over control of the PMA. Elections for office-bearers are held each year and have become the scene of intense manoeuvring and manipulation since the stakes are the siphoning of black market profits. The bitter infighting and most rivalries seem to have been largely on intra-community and not on communal lines.

The corruption itself and the allegations of corruption recognised no communal boundaries! It was, however, a contradictory situation. While the intra-class and intra-community rivalries have a 'secular' character, the corruption itself produces a social space ripe for communalisation in the present conjuncture, and communalisation is occurring. One curious and longstanding feature of Khurja potteries is the display of the 'communal' identity of capital—'chand sitaras' or three-pronged 'trishuls' adorn the tops of most factory chimneys. A small Muslim factory owner insisted that such separation was necessary. An Imam told us that the old Muslim-owned kilns carried chand sitaras and the trishuls put up five to seven years ago could be a self-assertive response to them—'*apne ko zahir karne ke liye*'—and added that new Muslim factories do not carry any insignia. One BJP owner relegated them as mere lightning conductors.

However, in some cases, economic and political rivalry seems to be getting contoured by 'Hindu' ideology. The Muslim reporter told us that the factionalism in the PMA was responsible for the riots, and that a coal agent and black marketeer, part of the politician-led mafia, was involved in the riots. A member of the mafia is alleged to have given money out of the coal black market for starting the riots to Mathrawali. The relative of a resident Muslim MP, who belonged to the Congress as well as to the opposite faction in the PMA, held that his rival was directly responsible for instigating both Muslims and Hindus, thereby strengthening his power over both. This explanation seemed to follow the contours of an established interpretation of the origins of communalism as lying in the 'divide and rule' policy of the British, except that the figure of a single MP replacing the overwhelming presence of a colonial power could well represent an exaggeration in the MP's role. One Muslim feared that riots were intended to close down Muslim potteries by keeping out Hindu labour. There was indirect evidence of this in the baseless, but vicious rumour picked up by the media, denied by the SDM, that Hindu labourers had been shoved into the kiln of a Muslim-owned pottery.

At some level, the operation of political parties and the coal mafia obviously dovetail, and it was a common perception that profits from the black market and the coal mafia were directly involved in the riots. The transferred SDM even suggested that the coal mafia was communalised and had links with some BJP doctors and teachers who started the riots. Neither the tangible grounds, nor the precise relation between the coal mafia and the riots could of course be determined from these testimonies, since most were also using the riots to smear opponents.

There was greater local unanimity amongst administrators, pottery owners and others about the diversion and reinvestment of the black market profits last year into the satta on riots which in turn may have created a vested interest in their occurrence. Apparently, people staked different sums of money ranging from Rs 1–10 on the occurrence of a riot and a receipt was issued by the organisers of the satta (whom nobody was willing to name) and huge sums were collected. Dates were indicated by which rioting must occur. If it did not occur, then a lot of money would change hands. The sum staked is said to have gone up to Rs 15–90 lakhs at the end of January before the second round of rioting.

This bizarre phenomenon seems to be new. Asghar Ali Engineer mentions the unprecedented entree of the satta bazaar into speculation on the riots in Agra in 1990.[5] The entree of a speculative activity which exists at the periphery of most commercial centres may speak of the extent to which riots have been, or are sought to be, naturalised as a recurring urban phenomenon in Uttar Pradesh and also of the extent to which a cynical common understanding exists about how little it can take to spark off violence once communal tensions have been built up.

The mandi, at present replete with signs of allegiance to Hindu communal organisations, may be another factor dragging the PMA into communal friction. Though, according to a pottery owner, there were only about 10 per cent banias in the pottery business, the bania preponderance in trade has long historical roots[6] and even now, banias dominate the 'anaj mandi' and control the grain trade along with some 'sonars' who are also very visible in other retail trade. Muslims are mostly in meat (for which there is an export factory), vegetable and fruit trade and some iron hardware sales and in the transport business. They also seem to form a minority in other commercial activities such as shoe shops. Today, as in the past, the ghee and anaj mandi links Khurja to the surrounding rural areas; additional links are the cold storage and political networks. According to a local CPI(M) source, active communalisation in surrounding rural areas is restricted to the two or three brahmin-bania dominated villages.

Our own understanding, that the parallel economy cushions the big pottery owners who do not seem to have suffered very much in riots, despite their statements to the contrary, was shared by at least one person in Khurja, the Muslim reporter. It seems that the economic elite of the town is in a position to contain the losses of production caused by the riots, even if their units shut down, since the parallel economy in coal continues to bring in steady profits. Their link-up with a politics in which riot-hardened boundaries and identities assist electoral mobilisation both in a spatial and in an ideological sense, may mean that the dislocation of trade and manufacture caused by riots in the short run may be offset by the possibility of long-term gains. The effects of the riots, according to Jaiprakash, have been a labour shortage due to the departure of migrants and communalisation of workers, tension on communal lines within the PMA, and damage to about 15–20 factories However, the real losers are those who have no such cushioning. Frightened workers had not returned until April because there was no one to guarantee their security.

While Sobha Ram, a pottery owner, is said to have sponsored the kar sevaks from Khurja, ironically, according to the ex-SDM, there is a peace committee in town which is filled with pottery owners. The owners seem to be playing a game of brinkmanship or to be living out a contradiction, characteristic of our ruling elites,[7] between a desire for stable co-existence and an endorsement of communal differentiation even through violence! Though the Rashtriya Swayamsevak Sangh (RSS) may be offering them a Utopia beyond the corrupt political present, this section has an enormous stake in that corruption in terms of its own immediate survival. The offered 'pure' space can be read as a socio-economic imperative: the creation of a petty producer-speculator culture which has benefited from this process of corruption but needs the (re)introduction of institutional checks to 'stabilise' competition.

III

In all our discussions with the owners, administration, etc., criminalisation was always objectified upon an 'other', deflected outside one's self and usually outside one's social and political class. For a current political leader, the poor and lower classes, whether Hindu or Muslim, were because of lumpenisation and frustration, out in search of a better deal, as either criminals or mercenaries; where intra-class conflicts were at work then established power wielders and new 'wheeler dealers' accused each other. The discourse of criminalisation (which often clusters around riots) explicitly links politics and economics, even though the notion of the criminal itself circulates differently. For the Hindu communalists, of course, Muslims are criminal; their targeting of upper and lower strata is to some extent a reflection of the profile of Muslims in Khurja composed primarily of labourers, artisans and an upper strata.

The Muslims in Khurja, as in western Uttar Pradesh as a whole, are more prosperous than their counterparts in central and eastern Uttar Pradesh. There is an air of confidence among them and they seem to be well integrated into the politics of mainstream parties. The formation of the Muslim aristocracy seems to have been part of a long process.[8] There are several well established 'feudal' Muslim families with extensive kinship networks who have now moved into politics and the pottery business and who constitute a thin but important upper layer of landed, orchard-owning town politicians.

However, despite the political profile and economic clout of some sections, the Muslims have not been able to make a sizeable transition into professions unlike their counterparts from the majority community. Their presence in the liberal professions such as law is small and there are few teachers outside purely Islamic educational institutions. They seem to lack a formal non-traditional intelligentsia. Though present in trade and transport, the majority are labourers. There was a tendency among some Hindus to represent the Muslims in the city as a minority in every sense and among some Muslims to represent themselves as a minority but in a position of strength—'*aadhe se kucch kam*' (a little less than half).

While on the whole Muslims have a lower class and educational profile than Hindus, it is important to note that Muslims are a sizeable urban group which has the potential for becoming a 'natural' target for, or coming into conflict with, similar rising Hindu petit bourgeoisie. Even in 1931, the majority of Muslims were urban residents. In the 1951 Census, the highest proportion of Muslims lived in central and western Uttar Pradesh districts. Their relative dependence on non-agricultural occupations is reflected in the fact that nearly 30 per cent of them were located in urban areas and that they constituted 31.3 per cent of the urban population of the state.[9] After Partition, the urban concentration continued partly due to a migration of Muslims from rural to urban areas between 1946 and 1950 for reasons of insecurity.[10] According to the 1981 Census, the total urban population of Muslims in relation to the total population of Uttar Pradesh was 28.5 per cent.[11]

Ironically, the early integration of Muslims into mainstream politics in Khurja, historically assisted by the fact that Khurja (along with Roorki, Meerut and Muzaf farnagar) was one of the first centres of the Deoband school in 1877–78,[12] has exacerbated internal divisions and political rivalries. In recent years, with Hindu communalist organisations making a practice of vilifying Muslims in positions of public visibility, the Muslims of the upper strata now occupy a position of double vulnerability.[13] Corruption had already been dramatised as a national issue by the Bofors scandal. The continuing unregenerate decay of institutions, which can be seen so palpably in a place like Khurja, produces the need to look for other political ideologies and programmes which uphold the value of honesty, while simultaneously resurrecting an old, readily accessible target of attack in the Muslims. The whole issue of corruption and its displacement on Muslims assists Hindu communal organisations in legitimising their struggle for wresting political control of the state from those 'corrupt' persons currently in power. This constellation can be seen in the municipal elections which opened a new theatre of conflict and competition in Khurja.

The revival of municipal elections from 1988, after a gap of 17 years, coincided significantly with the Ramjanmabhoomi campaign, which probably lent a greater urgency to them. Gaining command of municipal administration with the aim of controlling essential services, sources of patronage and creating a political machine has been a tried and tested gambit of political parties in Uttar Pradesh. The Jan Sangh tried, without notable success, to develop an urban base through running candidates for municipal elections in the 1960s.[14] Now, the BJP has stepped into the fray. The BJP, which had been marginal to the politics of Khurja earlier, gained a fair degree of influence in these elections, though they did not win the post of the chairman of the municipal board; at the same time, all Muslim candidates were said to have won on very high polling while the total number of seats they won were said to have been equal to the number won by Hindus. An ex-president of the BJP who teaches in a local college, Bhardwaj, interpreted this as a sign of a cohesive Muslim group politics, since the Hindu vote was split between the Congress and the BJP, all of whom had fielded Hindu candidates. He claimed that while the Congress and BJP candidates were businessmen, teachers and traders, Muslims included rickshaw-pullers, butchers and barbers. This representation sought to evoke a communal spectre of a violent plebeian mob ruling town politics. There was a persistent effort by Bhardwaj to castigate the upstart character of Muslim pottery owners, one of whom has allegedly managed to make good with government loans and does not come from a 'good moneyed background'. So a fear and envy of Muslim landed wealth and status, upward mobility and plebeian power is sought to be built.

[...]

NOTES

1. Migration into Bulandshahr district is low, only 11 per cent of the district's population are born outside the district. The workforce in Khurja was said to largely consist of local people; along with some from neighbouring rural areas and migrants from eastern Uttar Pradesh, Bihar, West Bengal and Orissa, who work on daily wages and come without families. While the migrants seem to man most of the production process, the locals work in transportation, painting and packaging. According to P. K. Dasgupta of the Central Industrial Security Force, the migrant Bengali and Bihar labourers are extremely underpaid, live in overcrowded rooms and survive on two chapatis a day.

2. There are some small-scale industries like nut and bolt, and surgical cotton, while electrical insulators made of clay are also produced by pottery units. The origin of Khurja pottery is traced to the manufacturing town of Bahadurgarh in Meerut district. The craft of pottery making is at least a century old. Manufacture of glazed potteries started in the 1920s. Glazed flower pots and 'chilams' in dark blue and dark red were marketed in the neighbouring towns. Before 1942, red parched clay was used; this was replaced by blue pottery in the mid-1940s.

3. The coal briquettes are meant to make the small balls of coal used in domestic consumption.

4. This is a phenomenon which is not confined to Khurja pottery. Another documented instance is the bogus units common in the Firozabad glass bangle and glassware industry in Agra district, with 70 per cent of the registered units being non-working. Owners of bogus units can earn as much as Rs 10 lakh a year without lifting a finger through black marketing coal. They have even shifted from employing permanent labour to a daily wage labour system. See Burra, Neera. 1986. 'Glass Factories of Firozabad'. *Economic and Political Weekly* 21 (46), 15 November, 1983.

5. Engineer, Asghar Ali. 1991. 'The Bloody Trail'. *Economic and Political Weekly* 26 (4), 26 January, 158–59.

6. Khurja stands on the Grand Trunk Road, from where two principal roads lead to the central main bazaar and to the 'ganj'. By the early nineteenth century, the flourishing commercial agriculture in northwest India had already given rise to a new merchant class in towns such as Khurja, Deoband, Saharanpur and Pilibhit, and these in turn were important centres of sugar and wheat trading (Bayly, C. A. 1983. *Rulers, Townsmen and Bazzars*. New York: Cambridge University Press, 205). At the turn of the century, there was large-scale financial activity, as far out as Punjab, by 'seths' in banks and grain trading. At this time, traders were mostly agarwals, there were a few khatris, and the rest were barasainis, maheshwaris and rastogies (Government of Lucknow. 1980. *UP District Gazetteer, Bulandshahr*).

7. See Rai, Alok. 1989. 'Addled only in Parts: Strange Case of Indian Secularism'. *Economic and Political Weekly* 24 (50), 16 December, 2771.

8. The Muslim quarter of Khurja is typical of north Indian *qasbas* (small towns [eds]); the dominant families are pathans, sheikhs, sayyads, whose influence has persisted because of the strong base of landed property they have maintained through endogamy. The pathans, the earliest Muslim settlers in the district, came from clans of Ghori, Yusufzais, Afridis and Lodis. Another important clan, Khesgi, migrated from Punjab and settled in this area during the reign of Firoze Shah.

9. Graham, Bruce. 1990. *Hindu Nationalism and Indian Politics: The Origin and Development of the Bharatiya Jana Sangh*. New York: Cambridge University Press, 156.

10. Aslam, M. 1990. 'The UP Muslims—1947, 1967, 1987', in *India: Creating a Modern Nation,* ed. Jim Masselos. New Delhi: Stirling.

11. Economic and Statistic Division. 1986. Statistical Diary, Uttar Pradesh, State Planning Institute. According to this source, Muslims comprise 19.3 per cent of the total population of Bulandshahr district.

12. Khurja is located near Deoband, the important centre of religion and reform which trains men in professional careers. (The wife of a present day Deobandi imam referred to her husband's work as 'service' and not as a vocation.) The Deobandi ulema were champions of a composite nationalism, though deeply traditional and revivalist otherwise, and had a base among the Muslim peasantry. They were opposed to the Partition and actively participated in khilafat, non-cooperation, boycott of famine commission, civil disobedience and other nationalist campaigns. Interestingly, Khurja was also linked in the same period to the obverse revivalist tendency. Dayanand was preaching heavily in the area in the 1870s (*UP District Gazetteer, Bulandhshahr,* 1980) and several Arya Samaji religious centres were opened in Bulandshahr district between 1870 and 1875.

13. A Muslim pottery owner, educated in Aligarh and active in the Congress, said it was impossible for Muslim administrators to function effectively to protect Muslims because of communal targeting; the ex-DM of Bulandshahr was such a target about two years ago.

14. Graham. *Hindu Nationalism and Indian Politics*, 242.

33

Communal Violence in Jaipur*#

Shail Mayaram

Rajasthan, which has hardly had a history of communal violence, has now joined the list of communally sensitive states with the events of 1989 and 1990. This paper is an effort to understand the violence that occurred in Jaipur in terms of the penetration of the ideology of religious nationalism. The political economy of collective violence emphasises large-scale structural processes, in particular urbanisation and industrialisation.[1] The causal relation between violence and levels of modernisation is undeniable, but not absolute in the case of Jaipur. For instance, Rajasthan is low on the list of industrialised states. On the other hand, ideological factors are of primary significance with respect to communal violence. Hindu religious nationalism through a highly effective institutional base has spread deep and wide in the body politic.[2] This ideology can be seen as a master narrative comprised of distinct segments. Here [in the unabridged version of the article] we examine three narratives relating to the communal violence of 1990 in Jaipur which left over 50 persons dead. These relate to:

(1) The ideology and organisation of the dominant party, the Bharatiya Janata Party (BJP), in Rajasthan and its supporting organisations.
(2) The orientation of the state apparatus, specifically the police administration.
(3) The regional print media.

The three narratives are analysed here in terms of the attempt to reorganise space and time: indeed, they demonstrate a symbolic convergence. It is also possible to identify other narratives such as the rumours, the politics of relief, and so on. Quite clearly, these threaten to constitute a master narrative that frames individual consciousness and action and threatens to become hegemonic. The master narrative constructs the Muslim as the masculine other who is a foreigner, invader and aggressor. Its contrast is the effeminate, weak Hindu community, in which 'dharma' is perceived as requiring 'raksha' (protection) from the enemy within. Apart from

---

* *Economic and Political Weekly* 28 (46–47): 2524–41 (13 November 1993).

The paper is based on three months of fieldwork in the affected areas, but the names of persons interviewed have been suppressed or changed for reasons of their security.

explicit violence which expresses itself in direct attacks, there is also a need to develop a notion of implicit violence. This was manifest particularly in the speech of persons belonging to the middle class that gave legitimacy to the violence in comments such as, '*Thik hua Musalmanon sabak sikhana hi tha. Ye to har dange mae nihattae Hindu ko marte hae*' (It was right. The Muslims needed to learn a lesson. In every riot they attack unarmed Hindus). '*Dekho Musalmanon ki kitni jansankhya badh rahi hae*' (Look at the way the Muslims are multiplying and the numbers of Hindus are being reduced). 'Ye to appeasement ka natija hae' (This is an outcome of the policy of appeasing Muslims). This certainly contributed to creating what Feldman has called an 'oral culture' of violence.[3]

An assessment of the penetration of this ideology, however, is not possible without an examination of resistance to this ideology at the ground level. Accounts of such resistance can be obtained only by treating individual behaviour as a text, that is, from people's testimony about their action in a crisis situation where violence is occurring. It is argued that instances of individuals intervening at considerable risk to their own life, family and property to protect persons belonging to the other community are indices of resistance to communal ideologies. They counter boundaries constructed by hegemonic ideological frameworks grounded in the self–other distinction. The category of the 'survivor' has been developed by Lifton with respect to the victims of the nuclear holocaust at Hiroshima.[4] Its intellectual ramifications have meant a sociological focus on the subject who experiences violence.[5] Here, I attempt a theoretical shift in the category by arguing that the category of 'survivor' be expanded to include not only those who are victims of violence, but also those who are able to survive because they experience protection from members of the other community. This theoretical expansion thus enables us not only to look at victimhood in terms of pain and suffering, but also at the therapeutic processes of care and healing. Temporally speaking, this approach is focused not only on the moment of violence, but on the context which gives meaning to people's action and on the aftermath of violence.

A large number of studies on communal violence take their epistemological departure from a position where the juxtaposition of two groups is taken for granted. In the Indian subcontinental context, the mutual antagonism between groups is sometimes presumed to be part of their natural state: this is the view from without. The enquiry from within the starting point of which is the survivor shows both the penetration of the ontology of communal ideology and how, if at all, it is contested at the level of the subject. Rishi Ghalav Nagar, a colony to the north of Jaipur city, where communal violence was most intense during the rioting of 1990, can be seen as a microcosmic universe of the conjuncture of national, regional and local politics. The case study of this colony in this paper analyses the problematic nature of 'community' formation among Hindus and Muslims. Rishi Ghalav Nagar shows the brutal onslaught of neighbours, of acquaintances and friends, who descended in murderous suddenness on unprepared people as a result of the sustained creation of frenzy. In Jaipur, Rishi Ghalav Nagar became representative of the violence of sections of Hindus on Muslims. The focus on survivors, however, also suggests that the large numbers of Muslims survived only because of the intervention of a cross-section of Hindus and Sikhs. The theoretical shift in the category of the survivor also makes possible an understanding of the impact of violence and how victims renegotiate their life-worlds. The exploration of the role of the protector enables a retrieval of the role of human agency in contesting hegemonic ideologies. It sears open the contradictions within seemingly homogeneous, unified communities demonstrating how violence ruptures the self, the family and the community created by totalising systems. Perkin's contention that victims totalise their categories, hence, needs to be phenomenologically reconsidered.[6]

[...]

SOURCES OF RESISTANCE

The issue of the sources of resistance to communal ideology is central to an estimation of its penetration. The question also needs to be asked whether the term 'communal riot' expresses what 24–25 October were all about. But a closer reading of the violence suggests that the riot becomes an omnibus for all variety of conflict, not all of it communal. In fact, the evidence suggests that communalism becomes a rubric that covers all kinds of motives. In Jaipur, it was used to settle personal scores and acquire quick material gain through looting.[7] Rioting also provided an occasion to eject tenants.[8] To categorise these conflicts as 'communal' suggests that there is an inexorable divide among people, and that primordial religious identities are the source of conflict. In the case of the Jaipur riots, sectarian conflict was not given: its primacy was politically established. Barely three weeks before the *rathyatra* (chariot procession [eds]), using the same pattern of political mobilisation which precipitated the riots, the upper castes sought to divide the Hindus to protect their sources of employment against the affirmative action of the state in favour of backward castes. Only with the stay order on the Mandal issue, the time became opportune for the Hindu 'ekta' or unity of all castes.

The media privileges violence in its reports on death and arson, and aggressive assertion of ethnic barriers. The police draws a similarly polarised picture concerned as they are with law and order. In their concern to justify firing and police action, an essentially endemic and inevitable conflict is portrayed. Similarly, the accounts of communal organisations completely obscure the mutuality between persons who helped, reassured, protected each other, and shared the moment of immense fear and tension. In *mohalla* (suburb [eds]) after mohalla, one gets a record of people risking their life and property for others. At Koliyon ki kothi, the women reported how their Muslim neighbours prevented intruders telling them, '*Bich mae ham hae, kuch nahin hoga*' ('we won't let you proceed' [eds]); near the park a Muslim boy extricated an old woman who would have died otherwise; in the Ramganj area, three orphaned children came to Shamin—a Harijan family had taken care of them till such time as it was safe to move out;[9] Shanti, whose brother had been killed (it is presumed by a Muslim), found it safest to stay with Baba Mohammed sahab for 45 days. Similarly in 1992, 11 mali labourers who managed to survive the mob from Idgah were protected by the local Muslim rangrez family.

All the survivors of Rishi Ghalav Nagar who were the victims of violence also experienced help and protection in some form or other from members of other religious groups. Hammu, whose wife and brother-in-law were killed, took shelter in the house of a Sikh. His small children were brought safely to a relative's house by Raju Pandit.[10] Darbar Ali's daughter, Tahira, was similarly saved even as his wife and son were killed and he himself lay brutally assaulted.[11] Shabuddin's aunt was killed and he would have been killed too had it not been for two *khatiks* (butchers [eds]) who helped them hide and then misdirected the rioters. At Hakim's house, Hakim himself and several persons belonging to a pinnara family lay dead. Abdul Hakim's children were taken in by the Harijan woman although her son was on the rampage with the rioters.[12] She recounts:

> I worked at Hakim's house. He was a very good man. They should not have killed him. Only we women were inside when it happened. The children were crying, 'my abba ammi have been killed'. We took them in and closed the door. The young child kept crying. I told my daughter-in-law to suckle him. They stayed here the entire night. We sent a message to their *nani* (grandmother [eds]) who stays at Loharon ka khurra. She came to take them.

Communal constructions are directly contested here both in speech and action. There were also more complex cases at Rishi Ghalav Nagar. For instance, Gupta, the local BJP leader, said to have tacitly supported the violence, locked in his Muslim neighbour, Ali Sher Khan and his family to prevent the rioters getting to them.[13] Ali Sher's mind is badly affected by the experience and this is manifested in a fragmented account in which there is a continuous loss of memory:

> Although we did not agree on the masjid issue, Guptaji helped me. This was at two in the day. He said, '*Chacha*, you sit here quietly upstairs. Nothing will happen to you.' At 11 in the morning, when the corpses had fallen in front of my house, he helped me. If he'd wanted, he could have got me killed. Downstairs, things were broken and set on fire. There were around 11,500 people. This started at 11.30 in the morning. Within half an hour, 45 persons were dead. Hammu's sadhu was killed and Darbar's child, and two–three more persons in the side lane whom I did not see as I'd taken the children in...I made my children read the *kalma*. But Gupta and Dhan Singh (a Sikh) did not allow them (the crowd) to use the (gas) cylinder. See I was the leader of the masjid, I was in charge. I was responsible for looking after it, so I was a target. But they said, 'This is a Hindu colony. It is wrong for Muslims to live here.' But there was *mahobbat* (affection) between us, the only problem was due to the masjid. When I was tailoring, I used to supervise the construction of his house. I would stand there all day. Gupta and Dhan Singh were my good friends. Two years before the riot I got his house made...But the Lord saves one. They came again at 9 in the night... When the police came, I left with my children at 3.30 in the night.

Another local Harijan leader similarly locked up a large number of his Muslim neighbours and their families, then joined the mob for the prospects of loot. Indeed, his case and that of Ali Sher suggest that the penetration of communal ideology is so uneven it even ruptures the self and the family, leading to apparently contradictory behaviour.

Perkin uses the category of totalisation to suggest that victims totalise their categories. But the evidence is uneven in this respect. Ali Sher's badly affected family was rehabilitated only with the assistance of Deepak Purohit, gemstone dealer and previous employer of his son, Gulsher. Ali Sher says, '*Ye hamari zindagi mae madat dene vale farishte the. Hamko dedh lakh diye*' (He was an angel who brought help to us; gave us a sum of Rs 1.5 lakh). His son's statement, '*Vo hamari madat nahin karte to ham bagi ban jate*' (If he had not helped us, we would have turned rebellious), is a crucial pointer to the possibilities of a healing process. Those who remain untouched by it are ready sources for mobilisation into future mobs.

Adjacent to the zone of rioting at Rishi Ghalav Nagar is the extension colony where rioters were not even permitted to enter the area. According to Yousuf Ali, a khatik called Ram Narain told a crowd of 200, '*Chale jao sab makan hamare hain. Koi kuch nahin karega*' (Go away. All houses are ours; no one will do anything). Ram Narain, he adds, is a 'history sheeter', a man with a criminal record. He runs a taxi, lives in a hut near their house and would often come to take water. Along with Lal Chand, a khatik meat seller, and the Punjabi Harishji, he refused to allow rioting in their area. Razia Sultan's family living in four houses collected together in fear after they saw the smoke rising over the city. This is her account:

> The boys started banging our door with sticks, yelling '*Musalmanon bahar ao*' (Muslims come out). A crowd of about hundred collected with swords, cycle chains and *sariya*s (iron rods). We went to the roof and four of us women jumped over to the Kajods' roof. We hid among the goats but they had seen our shadows and started shouting. We went down to the Kajods' house, all of us crying. They made me wear 'ghagra-lugdi' and said, that you are with us. Nothing will happen. '*Anch nahin ane denge*' (We shall not let the fire touch you). Then Kajod went and talked to them and told them, 'Leave them they are good people otherwise you will have to deal with us'. Then the police jeep came and the rioters ran away. This was at about 8.30 at night. Later Kajod told us, 'Our house is now unsafe'. He took us to Jai Singh's, next door. But the men had seen us and we jumped onto the Sindhi's roof. He locked us inside for the night. They came again at 9.30. All night, we heard cries and saw people with *mashal*s (flames), burning houses. In our colony people sat at the 'nukkad' (crossing) all night so that nothing would happen. No one came that night. At 5.30 in the morning, we left for Pahadganj where my *devar* (brother-in-law [eds]) lives. Jai Singhji and the Sindhi had come to leave us. At the crossing, five persons with sticks stopped us. They said, '*Bolo Jai Siya Ram*'. All of us said, 'Jai Siya Ram'. Then they let us go. We were again stopped at the mandi and said 'Jai Siya Ram'. A little ahead, we told them, 'Now we are in the Muslim area. Go back now!' We stayed two months at Pahadganj, then went to Sanganer, then Tonk for three months. People from our colony were very good. They still come to see us (at Van Vihar) on festivals, our children tie rakhis on them.[14]

Razia's account allows one not merely to relive the fear and the trauma that the family lived through, but also their survival made possible through their community ties with their Hindu neighbours. Kajod and his wife, Badaam are khatiks. According to Kajod, it was a 'dharma ki bhavna' that made him save Razia's family. 'Brothers come in later', he said, 'it is neighbours who can help each other in the first instance'. The khatiks follow Bhairuji, said Kajod, whom he described as a pir. 'I gave her my ghagra and lugdi', said Badaam, 'and put a *tiki* on her forehead so nobody would recognise her although he (Kajod) kept watch outside all night. I am not educated, I don't know history. But where we live, we live like brothers!'

Possibly the families of the Rishi Ghalav Nagar extension colony had been living together for a longer period as they had been shifted from a slum following the floods of 1981. The presence of a lone Muslim tenant in a neighbouring house was reported to Pappu, the young son of Chatar Singh. 'We dragged Jamilbhai to safety', Pappu said. For two days he was kept in their neighbour, the vegetable vendor, Babu Lal's house. His daughter-in-law had just delivered a baby and he was shaven clean and passed off as the girl's uncle who had come from Bihar. Pappu's mother, Prem devi, said that when he left, 'I put a *tilak* on his forehead, tied *kalaya* (sacred thread) on his hand so no one would think he was a Muslim'.

Two conversations with Prem devi and Ganga devi, the wife of Babu Lal 'bijwala', are transcribed here as they indicate ways in which people express resistance to communal ideology, and the sources of resistance.

> I follow all Hindu *devtas* (gods [eds]) and I also believe in Muslim gods. I believe in Ajmer's Khwaja saheb and Saiyyad baba. You find his *sthans* (sites [eds]) everywhere. He fulfils all desires and brings peace of mind. I even follow the *isai* devtas (Christian gods), Isamasi and Guru Nanak. The gods tell us to do one's karma. They were men but great men and we must fold our hands. All people who do good work must be worshipped. There are fanatics in all communities, whether Hindu or Muslim. Compassion is within all... The best thing for Ayodhya is if both the mandir and the masjid remain. They are god's homes, not made to be destroyed. The janmabhumi is a fight for the chair, between politicians, and the poor public dies.

Prem devi's account indicates the rootedness of a humanism in religious belief. Ganga devi described her family's close relations with the Muslim Manihar family:

> For 20 years, we lived together in the *basti* (settlement [eds]) below in huts. They had a *jhaunpdi* (hut [eds]) and so did we. Then they were allotted a plot. We had very good relations with them, no sense of being Hindu or Muslim. We came here in 1973 and lived together after that. There was '*boli ka prem*' (language of affection) between us. When I faced a problem like when my child had an accident on Moharrum, Munna (the eldest son of the Manihar family) rushed with her to the big hospital. She had come under a truck when she was going with her grandfather to see the tazia. She was saved but her foot was cut. She has an artificial foot. And so we shared each other's '*dukh-sukh*' (joy and sorrow). (On whether Hindus go to see the tazia) Always. This is the first time I've heard of such a thing (referring to the riot). But nothing happened in our basti.
>
> When we learnt of Jamil (a Muslim trapped in the Manihar house), we jumped across and fetched him. We were so scared, thought someone might kill us. My mind was already failing. My elder son had gone to Ayodhya for kar seva—he ran away because of his friends, I had the responsibility of my daughters-in-law and grandchildren. I don't go anywhere, to any temple. My temple is in my home where I worship all gods. For Ram and Rahim I light agarbattis, for Sayyad baba I light an agarbatti. I said to Jamil, 'see *beta* you are just like this beta here'. Then I gave him tea and dinner. If anyone asked I said, 'He is our guest, my *bahu*'s [daughter-in-law]

chacha from Delhi'. The next day my nephew came, to sell some newspapers. I told him to leave Jamil at Galta Gate. So we sent him on the truck to Galta. After 8–10 days, his relatives, his mother came to thank me. Possibly it is that *dua* [blessing] due to which my son returned from Ayodhya where so many had died. His mother had said, 'You have saved my son, your son will also come back safely'. He's not in the BJP but went because of his friends. He was only 20 years old. The police came to leave him in a car. He said, 'I was put in jail'. I said 'Good, even better if they'd broken your hands and legs. Here you come back in 22 days, and you know your wife has had a baby'. My granddaughter, elder son's child died. She had loose motions. I was going mad. Some strangers would pass by our house spreading rumours saying, 'They are coming. Coming in a bus, in a truck.' I said, 'Let them come. I was so sick of the rumours'. We were all together, the people of this colony. We'd been together for 20 years. But who listens to poor people? Our daughter was killed for dowry. It is now one-and-a-half year. The police doesn't listen. She was hanged. Who bothers... Our Muslim neighbours left the colony even though we did not want them to. But when our daughter was killed by her in-laws they all came to share our sorrow.

Ganga devi's account, like Ali Sher's, brings out the centrality of everyday interaction in sustaining resistance to totalising ideologies. Ganga devi describes it as the sharing of dukh-sukh. This also emerges from Tahira's account. Her family frequently bought milk and vegetables from the brahmin vegetable seller in the area. It was the latter's son who came to her rescue when her house and its occupants were set on fire. Raju recalls:

I work at Phutakhurra, Pataudi House, above the maniharan. I learnt gemstone work from Hanif bhai for six months and from Khemraj Pataudia for two-and-a-half years. In the evening at 6–6.30, my mother sent me to see if my sister Bhanwari devi was alright. The gate to their house was closed. The house next door was of a Muslim family. People were breaking things inside. Near the crossing of Hammu bhai's house, I saw Rais' *khala*'s daughter, Tahira, and two other children. Tahira called me, 'Raju bhaijan'. I asked her, 'What are you doing here?' She said something about her mother and father having been killed. I took them to Rais' house and left them there. I did it because she was my good friend's sister. I know Rais since childhood. He is still my special friend although he lives in Idgah, Van Vihar and works in the university. We have grown up eating and living together. He is uneducated but like my brother. I was not bothered about my life and neither did I have the time to think about it then. She was my friend's sister and I had to save them.

Raju's interaction with Muslims was at many levels. At the workplace, he had learnt his craft from a Muslim; his best friend was a Muslim and he and his family lived in proximity to Muslims. His mother said, 'all the *mia*'s *chora-chori* (the Muslim neighbour's children [eds]) call me "*mataji*". They come here for their vegetables.'

Interviews with a group of kolis suggest the complexity of social relationships that the ideology of religious nationalism has still not been able to homogenise.[15] A koli began with, '*Bahut mare sahab* (they killed many people). Eight to 10 corpses were found: all after curfew. They had been so badly burnt by Muslims, they were unidentifiable.'[16]

Nathuram, a more elderly koli, gently corrected him, 'No two were killed'. Keshav Lal said, 'We learnt that koli houses had been burnt. My son and his friend went to the park to see what had happened. He saw thousands of Muslims. As he was running away, another group of Muslims surrounded him. He was stabbed. Another was hit by an iron rod.' But the women of koli households gave a differing account. One said, 'Of the two who had gone to investigate and were injured, one was a Hindu, the other a Muslim!' Hemlata remembered that the crowd had come shouting 'Jai Siya Ram'. 'The Muslim who lives in the house across, Rais, who does "nagina" work, protected us!' Toshibai, her mother confirmed, 'Then the Muslims who had come [to attack], did nothing. They did not burn my house, break anything. During curfew Rais and Jumma came to our home, sat with us, and helped us!' Keshav Lal, whose son had been stabbed, was treated by Seraj, the Muslim doctor, at what is called the Mahavaton ki dispensary.[17]

At several koli homes, the machine for 'bindai' is in evidence, suggesting their shift from unskilled labour ('*beldari*'), which fetches Rs 30–40 a day, to the gemstone business. They get their work from Muslim manufacturers in the area. Dalchand refers to his patrons as 'Rajak bhai' and 'Babu bhai'. 'Are they Hindus?' I ask him. 'No, they are Muslims'. The Muslims, he feels, are '*milansar*' (sociable); at least the '*purane admi*' (older folks) are. 'If we don't go to their weddings and festivals then they send us food'. 'What about the practice of "*jat pat*" (discrimination) against scheduled castes?', I ask him. 'No, we do not do that, it's the Brahmins and banias who practise untouchability against us', he replies. 'Now see what a struggle it is to get a "piao" [drinking water fountain] at Manak Chowk. But the banias of Jauhari bazzar, the "seth-log", refuse to permit the release of the order [to set up a piao];' The question of upper and lower caste relations remains problematic.

The future of the ideology of religious nationalism is contingent upon the sustaining monolithic, homogenised structures of community consciousness. The interviews with both kolis and Muslims suggest how fragile and tenuous Hindu and Muslim identities are. The attempted distribution of the spoils of Rishi Ghalav Nagar's mosque plots between self-seeking, self-styled 'Hindu' and 'Muslim' leaders is symptomatic of what goes on in the name of communalism. Kolis, raigars and some other lower castes in Jaipur bemoan of how they have been duped by the BJP 'dharm ke nam par' (in the name of religion). What emerges instead is their far better relations with the Muslims of their area. In fact, the lower castes such as the raigars and kolis have shown a complete lack of enthusiasm for the 'paduka pujan' campaigns launched by Ashok Singhal of the Vishva Hindu Parishad in Jaipur in 1992. There are scattered reports of conversion to Islam of the low caste jatavs following caste rioting in Bharatpur. Although the urban middle class is a strong source of support to the BJP, the question of its spread in rural Rajasthan is dependent on the extent to which it can control the middle and lower castes.

NOTES

1. See Tilly, Charles, Louise Tilly, and Richard Tilly. 1975. *The Rebellious Century 1830–1930*. USA: J. M. Dent and Sons. They examine the association between collective action and structural factors in England and France.

2. In Jaipur, I have been repeatedly questioned about 'minority communalism'. In this context, it is important to state that Muslim fundamentalism as an ideological formation is as yet underdeveloped in the city. At the judicial hearings inquiring into the rioting, police officials discounted the presence of Muslim organisations such as the Jamaat-i-Islami and the Muslim League. In terms of the organisation of Muslims, kinship and neighbourhood organisation play a far more significant role.

3. Feldman, Allen. 1991. *Formations of Violence: The Narrative of the Body and Political Terror in Northern Ireland*. Chicago: University of Chicago Press.

4. Lifton, Michael Jay. 1968. *Death in Life: Survivors of Hiroshima*. New York: Random House.

5. See, for instance, Das, Veena. 1990. 'Introduction: Communal Riots, and Survivors'; 'Our Work to Cry: Your Work to Listen'; and Srinivasan, Amrit. 1990. 'The Survivor in the Study of Violence'; and Kanapathipillai, Valli. 1990. 'July 1983: The Survivor's Experience', in *Mirrors of Violence*, ed. V. Das. Oxford: Oxford University Press, 1–36, 345–98, 305–20, 321–44. Also see Chakravarty, Uma, and Nandita Haksar. 1987. *The Delhi Riots: Three Days in the Life of a Nation*. New Delhi: Lancer International.

6. Perkin, David. 1986. 'Violence and Will', in *Anthropology of Violence*, ed. David Riches. Oxford: Basil Blackwell.

7. Our fieldwork brought out frank confessions from rioters that they joined in the rioting because of the prospects of looting.

8. In Jauhari bazaar, this happened with a large number of Muslim tailor shops whose landlords were Hindu. In many cases, the belongings were thrown outside the shop before being set on fire so that the building would remain intact.

9. Interview of Shamin by Mamta Jaitly, October 1990.

10. FIR 480/90 of Shabuddin, 24 October 1990; interview with Raju. This section is based on separate interviews of both survivor and protector.

11. Interview, 6 September 1992.

12. I am grateful to Mamta Jaitly's assistance in tracing this case.

13. Interview with Ali Sher Khan at Pahadganj, 16 July 1992.

14. Razia Sultan on 30 April 1992. Her account was followed by in-depth interviews of Jai Singh, Kajod and Jai Singh.

15. Koliyon ki kothi, 7 May 1992.

16. Kesar Lal's affidavit is very similar. According to him, the Muslims set fire to koli homes so that several were burnt alive. Exhibit B-1, Tibrewal Commission.

17. Dalchand acknowledged his good work among the poor as he charges only Rs 3 per person irrespective of religion.

34

Of Communal Consciousness and Communal Violence*

Impressions from Post-Riot Surat

Sudhir Chandra

I

Following the demolition of Babri Masjid on 6 December 1992, Surat witnessed some of the most gruesome manifestations of communal violence. Recurring a month later, in January, this violence was marked by a ferocity and traits that even areas traditionally prone to communal disturbance could scarcely match. This happened in a city that had, for decades, taken pride in the peaceful coexistence of its religious communities. More and more cities and towns in Gujarat had, since the country's partition and independence, fallen prey to communal violence which, at least since 1980, seemed to find its preferred habitat in Ahmedabad and Baroda, the state's prime cities. All this while, Surat, the chief city of south Gujarat, remained an oasis of communal peace.

The oasis was then abruptly transformed into a microcosm of communal India. For the first time in its history since 1927–28, the city experienced communal rioting. Arson, loot, physical assault and killing, rape, destruction or desecration of places of religious worship, nothing from the repertoire of communal violence was missing in this orgy. ...

The death toll was estimated by government agencies to be in the vicinity of 200; and they do tend to underestimate. More than 19,000 women, children and men—almost all of them Muslims—sought shelter in 43 relief camps. Such for them has been the trauma of the December terror that many of them have not to date returned to their homes in localities where unprecedented brutality was let loose upon them (Neither government officials nor voluntary organisations active during relief operations have much idea of the number of such people and of the places where they have gone after the relief camps were wound up).

* *Economic and Political Weekly* 28 (36): 1883–87 (3 April 1993).

In December, as if driven to make up for the time lost owing to its long peaceableness, Surat took to communal violence with a vengeance. In the process, it sharpened the distinction that marks ordinary criminal violence from communal violence (which does not, on that count, cease to be criminal). The latter, unlike the former, is often converted into a spectacle. Depending on the degree of communalisation within the society, it is valorised by larger or smaller sections of the concerned communities.

[...]

Events in Surat, thus, reflect a disturbing approximation between the manifestation of communal violence and the enunciations of the relatively less rabid ideologues of Hinduism. Hindu communal violence in Surat seems to have made another alarming contribution to the escalation of communalism. It broke a crucial psychological barrier that had hitherto divided the physical perpetrators of communal violence from those who verbally justified or even abetted it.

Following this division, once communal violence broke out, the Hindu middle classes' reaction would be one of reluctant approbation. Usually prefaced with regret about the incidence of violence, it would proceed to justify violence as a necessary lesson that, having been harassed and harried in their own land, the Hindus felt compelled to teach the 'others'. Over the last couple of years, the proportion of regret decreased dramatically; what has replaced it is unalloyed approbation, *a la* Chinmayananda. The actual work of administering the 'lesson', during all these long years, was the prerogative of the underclasses of the community.

In Surat, a new low was registered in the Hindu middle-class association with communal violence, as well-off men and women joined in the looting of Muslim shops. While the riots were on, stories began to circulate of middle-class men and women in their Maruti cars defying the curfew and returning home with the choicest booty. Women, the stories said, ransacked Muslim shops to pick up saris that matched their blouses and blouse-pieces that matched their saris. They helped themselves to the finest jewellery, including rings that fitted their fingers. 'Respectable' people drove to Muslim shoe shops to try and take away shoes and chappals of their choice.

That these stories may be exaggerated is their least important part. What is worrying is that the exaggeration rests on actual cases of middle-class participation in an aspect of communal violence from which they had hitherto kept aloof. However limited the participation, it can hardly be dismissed as an ugly aberration; one that, even if not repeated in Surat, would also not infect middle-class behaviour elsewhere in the country.

At the level of actual physical participation, one fears, future eruptions of communal violence may involve larger segments of the community across class and gender divisions. Put differently, the breaking of the psychological barrier implies a qualitative lowering of the middle-class Hindus' threshold of resistance to communal violence.

The savagery of December and January in Surat, then, means more than the transformation of an oasis of communal peace into a microcosm of communal India. It threatens to be the portent of a fall into further depths.

No one familiar with the history of Surat would argue that it has been free from communal consciousness. But the city had evolved a social anastomosis that enabled strong communitarian identities, with their separate interests and socio-religious peculiarities, to exist within a subtly changing social equilibrium without needing to resort to violence against one another. Recent rioting and, even more, its extraordinary ferocity and ritualism brought about the collapse of the defences which had earlier prevented the resolution of the city's communal tensions by means of violence.

[...]

II

No one suspected till the very last that Surat would be seized by such violent frenzy. Over the decades, even as they would apprehend communal riots at the slightest pretext in different parts of Gujarat, people got progressively convinced that, whatever happened elsewhere, Surat would remain peaceful. From its history of communal harmony to its demographic composition and the nature of its communally inter-textured business nexus, a whole variety of reasons would be advanced by lay citizens and experts alike for the city's immunity to communal violence. Even the stereotyped image of the average inhabitant of Surat—the happy-go-lucky 'Surati lala'—was perceived as an insurance against the outbreak of communal violence. In fact, in popular memory, the city was remembered as having forever been free from any kind of group violence. Let alone the disturbances of 1669 and 1795, even the riots of 1927–28 did not figure in the Suratis' collective cognitive map.

The worst then happened in this bastion of peace. Overnight, literally, what needed to be explained was not the city's immunity but its vulnerability to communal violence.

There is an aspect of these explanations which helps us place in some kind of a perspective the savagery of December and January. The stress in the preceding narrative on the representative and portentous character of the Surat violence needs to be balanced by an account of developments that seems to offer a modicum of hope for the overall situation is quite complex and people's attitudes betray a measure of unresolved tensions and ambiguities. This is best revealed in the Suratis' determined refusal during the first phase of rioting to implicate themselves. They argued, and seemed desperate to believe, that the violence was organised and committed by 'outsiders'. These outsiders were not all non-Gujaratis. Besides the migrant industrial workers from Orissa, Bihar and Uttar Pradesh, the perpetrators of violence included a large chunk of Saurashtrian migrants. As for the middle-class involvement in looting, the accusing finger was, again, pointed towards outsiders, particularly Punjabis. These migrants had damaged the general atmosphere in the city. But the Surati had valiantly stood by his/her tradition.

Another explanation that served a similar function found a scapegoat in the city's police commissioner, P. K. Datta. Within less than two months that he had been in charge of the city, Datta had come down heavily on the bootleggers who, in collusion with the police, had been carrying on a lucrative business. So complete had been Datta's drive that women engaged in bootlegging were, with unmistakable exaggeration, said to have been forced into prostitution for a living. The drive created two disgruntled elements: the unemployed bootleggers and the police deprived of their regular commission from the illicit trade. The demolition of Babri Masjid came as a godsend to the bootleggers who, given their penchant for criminal activities, organised anti-Muslim riots; and the police force refused to obey the orders of a chief who had deprived them of a rich source of income. The two conspired to create a situation in which their *bête noire* would be transferred from Surat.

Widely believed in Surat, this explanation was invested with further credibility following its publication in *India Today* (Gujarati edition, 6–20 January 1993, 42–44). The need to believe it, and get rid of guilt, was so deep that people completely ignored that, given the state's venal political leadership, vested interests did not need to cause diabolic disturbances to bring about an honest officer's transfer. They also ignored the question as to how the underworld dons could ensure the frenzied participation of so many people in the communal orgy.

This guilt was neither squarely faced, nor consciously exorcised. And, however deviously suppressed and indirectly felt, guilt was not the only feeling entertained with regard to the riots. It was related to a complex structure of feeling produced by the events in Ayodhya. There was a widely shared sense of shock and disbelief when the news first came of the demolition of Babri Masjid. But, for a variety of reasons, including the sympathy that by its inept handling the Government of India restored for the Hindutva combine, the realisation that something ugly was happening in their city was accompanied by a resurgence of enthusiasm for Hindutva. The latter may not have completely overpowered the former. But it permitted a different look at the local barbarity.

A very persuasive factor was found for the different look. The riots were seen as a reaction to the aggressiveness of the local Muslims in the wake of the demolition in Ayodhya.

[...]

The whole question of backlash is related to a particular view of the historical relationship between phenomena that are, significantly, described as Muslim communalism and Hindu/Indian nationalism. According to this view, the Muslim has always been the aggressor and the Hindu has always felt driven to react, maybe of late with a ferocity missing earlier. At a deeper, and more universal, level, the question is related to the psychology that a besieged minority almost invariably develops.

That apart, I should like to draw attention to the wide hold exercised by such historical stereotypes. For one, the Surat riots are perceived as a Hindu reaction to Muslim action even by scholars who are not Hindu communalists—one of them is a Christian priest. This view, further, exists in spite of the assertion that these riots were pre-planned. If they were pre-planned, how did it matter whether the Muslim reaction to the Ayodhya vandalism was restrained or exaggerated? The chronology of Hindu violence, in fact, belies the theory of Hindu reaction to Muslim action. Lancy Lobo and Paul D'Souza provide evidence that Hindus in the city struck without waiting for the Muslims to react—or overreact—when they attacked four Muslim families on 6 December and set their houses ablaze ('Images of Violence', *Economic and Political Weekly* 28 (5), 30 January, 152–54).

If serious scholars, and those who by their religious affiliation are unlikely to be tainted by Hindu communalism, fail to see through the stereotypes about Hindu behaviour, one can imagine the great comfort it must be offering to the generality of Hindus. It enables them, in the face of their undisputed implication in savage violence, to feel varying degrees of guilt and yet transfer it on to the ever-obliging Muslim aggressor.

I may offer here a few illustrations of Hindu ambiguity during the tragic days of December and January. Speaking about the riots to the correspondent of *India Today,* Bhagwati Kumar Sharma, an illustrious Gujarati litterateur and winner of the prestigious Sahitya Akademi award, expressed his anguish in a pithy question. 'How can human beings', he asked, 'go to such an extent?' (The Gujarati edition cited above.) Sharma also looks after the leading Gujarati daily of Surat, *Gujarat Mitra.* Under his stewardship, the paper all along supported Hindutva and attacked the Muslims.

The other example comes from a very different social segment. A bearer in Surat's solitary health food restaurant was in the midst of an animated conversation with some of his colleagues as I reached there to buy some bread. The snatch that I heard related to how politicians were making fools of both Hindus and Muslims who were senselessly killing one another. Impressed by the outburst, I asked him: 'Then how does it happen that the very people you live with don't understand this and kill their Muslim neighbours?' With equal conviction, and realising no contradiction in the two statements, he explained: 'You don't know, saheb. These Muslims are by nature very cruel and violent.'

A young doctor at the local government hospital who had worked zealously to attend upon riot victims, most of whom were Muslims, remarked that Muslims were prone to be violent as they ate non-vegetarian food and practised professions such as the butcher's. Similarly, at a meeting organised at the local university, a young entrepreneur suggested the spread of vegetarianism as a cure for communal violence.

Rooted deep in people's consciousness, this ambiguity is manifested in many ways. A sad manifestation of it was visible in the thinking of some professionals who were among the first to join the Communal Unity Committee which was formed to help relief operations and peace efforts. With obvious enthusiasm, which may in some cases have been informed by an all too human desire for publicity, they devoted their time and energies for days on end. Not a few among them believed that the Muslims really needed to be taught a lesson. In private conversation, they expressed their admiration for the Bharatiya Janata Party (BJP) and Hindutva.

To the same category belong many of those who braved obvious risks to help their beleaguered Muslim neighbours. For, if there were some who wrote a melancholy chapter in the annals of communal violence by turning against their neighbours, there were others whose behaviour conformed to tradition. They either offered the protection of their own homes to their Muslim friends and neighbours or helped them escape to safety. However, even such people do not necessarily take a secular stance. They even betray an anti-Muslim bias. They reconcile the two positions by positing a distinction between the Muslims they care for and Muslims as a people/community about whom they share a stereotype that seems to have entrenched itself since the nineteenth century. The Muslim they know may be the very picture of human virtue; but for these Hindus, such a Muslim can never be more than an exceptional figure.

III

[...]

Compared to Bombay, where the post-Ayodhya communal violence was inextricably enmeshed in the economy of real estate with its attendant mafia rivalries, Surat saw a violence that was but marginally affected by entrenched material interests. This was particularly so in December, for the recrudescence of rioting in January was taken advantage of by a speculator to clear one slum area. It is too early to assign a critical significance to this shift between December and January. But there are suggestions that, looking for new pastures after the near saturation of the slum-clearing business in Bombay, top mafia lords like Arun Gauli and Dawood Ibrahim have trained their eyes on Surat. Should this be so, and should they succeed in skewing business relations in the city, the outbreak of communal violence in the wake of Ayodhya will certainly have initiated a new and ugly phase of communal relations in Surat; and the phase would only gain in strength from the growing saffronisation of its sprawling slums.

There are, however, also indications that eruption of communal violence may not easily recur in the city again, which means that the collapse of the city's traditional defences against the spilling out of its communal antipathy into violence may well have been temporary. Ground for this hope is provided by the way calm has been maintained during the last five months in spite of the proliferation of causes that would ordinarily have precipitated a communal confrontation. Ever since the January round of rioting ended, there have been numerous incidents of stray stabbing and assault. These did not produce any Hindu 'reaction'. Even the disfiguring of an idol in a Hanuman temple provoked a controlled reaction which, clearly on design, did not make Muslims its target. A protest march was organised in the city. The same day, before the march could begin, a bomb explosion injured about 40 persons at the local railway station. And while the march was meandering through downtown, an irate Muslim youth with a criminal record killed one Hindu processionist. Neither of these incidents caused any reprisal.

It may be tempting to see the absence of Hindu retaliation in the context of the Bombay bomb blasts and argue that what happened in Surat is not exceptional. But then, these stray incidents occurred fairly regularly before the Bombay explosions. If calm was still maintained, it cannot be ascribed to the deterrence supposedly produced by the Bombay bomb blasts.

It seems reasonable to assume, instead, that business interests in the city have recovered from the immediate euphoria and shock of the riots, and realised the overriding need for peace and order. Hindu businessmen soon got over their euphoria to grasp the meaning of an exodus from the city of its predominantly migrant labour population; an exodus that caused 85,000 tickets to be sold in a single day at the Surat railway station. Nor did Muslim businessmen take much longer to get over their shock and humiliation. Both combined to contribute to the restoration of peace. And both need to maintain it.

Hindu businessmen may have suffered, as indeed they did, immense material losses as a result of the riots. But that has not alienated them from the BJP and Hindutva. Material and ideal interests are not always easy to weigh in relation to each other. The ideal interests served by Ayodhya seem to have more than compensated for the material loss caused thereby. The BJP is not, in consequence of this loss, seen as an expensive liability. In its own turn, the party's local leadership has shown great concern for the city's business interests. Kashi Ram Rana, Surat's BJP Member of Parliament, took a delegation to Orissa in order to persuade the runaway Oriya workers to return to their city of promise, assuring them perfect safety and all facilities. Some of these workers had participated in the violence against the Muslims, and fled as they feared administrative action. Assurances by a BJP leader were all the more likely to create a favourable impression upon a workforce that had demonstrated its communal propensities.

The Surat riots, it seems, deepened sympathy for Hindutva among large sections of the city's Hindu population. The return of peace only strengthened the trend. The BJP, consequently, hardly needs further communal violence in the city. The existing level of communal consciousness among its Hindu inhabitants will serve its purpose. Also the personality of Kashi Ram Rana, whom the party has recently made its chief for the Gujarat state, is bound to win it more friends and sympathisers. In a society where arrogance and venality are synonymous with political power, this man has not changed his ways since he was an ordinary political worker.

There has been increasing intra-party tussle within the BJP. Still, its leadership compares favourably with what most other political parties have to offer. There was reason for the BJP during the last parliamentary elections to woo the voter with the slogan: 'You tried others. Try us now.' The slogan was aimed to make use of mounting despair among the Indian people. In such a situation, the qualitative difference that someone like Kashi Ram Rana offers the electorate in terms of human material may prove decisive. When a sworn enemy of the BJP like Ashok Mitra is forced to concede to its leadership difference of quality in comparison to other parties, the ordinary voter may find it hard not to be beguiled by the difference.

The BJP's gains from the riots and the peace thereafter have been earned at the cost of deepening the Hindu–Muslim divide. If ever the party really meant to create a toehold among the Muslims, the design would appear to have suffered a setback. But considering its much higher other stakes in the political gamble, it cannot possibly rue whatever it has lost on the Muslim front. In fact, the loss has been more than compensated by the completion of the Muslims' disenchantment with the Indian National Congress.

The BJP does not, however, seem content with this compensatory gain alone. It has, with singular cynicism, renewed its efforts to build its bridges with the Muslims. It may not say so, but it seems to believe that the fear and despair produced among them by Ayodhya and its aftermath will incline the Muslims more than ever to consider accepting its overtures. The maintenance of peace in Surat despite an unending series of stray provocations may be seen as a move in that direction. For, consolidation of its gains among the Hindus apart, so far as Muslims are concerned, peace gives the BJP's punish-and-woo policy a semblance of chance. After all, it was after Ayodhya that the party decided to field 100 Muslim candidates in the recent West Bengal panchayat elections; of them 28 won.

While these efforts cannot be written off—their value as gestures remains in any case—they are unlikely to mitigate appreciably the general Muslim hostility against the BJP. However, an occasional Muslim does trifle with the idea of buying safety through the BJP. Meanwhile, the hurt and anger felt against the Congress will take long to heal; if they heal at all. But if despair can produce the wild thought of going to the BJP, it will prompt some Muslims to stick to the Congress as the lesser evil.

Facile speculations apart, it must be admitted that for a non-Muslim Indian, a Hindu particularly, it is difficult these days to establish rapport with the Muslims. As one of them put it, they have had their noses rubbed into the ground. They would rather be left alone and lick their wounds. However, from whatever one can gather from Muslim friends who still retain some capacity for trust, their dominant mental state seems to combine deep humiliation and utter uncertainty. Contradictory feelings keep coming, as if on a pendulum, in this state of uncertainty. Which ones of these feelings will stay and what ensembles they will form is hard to predict.

In this turmoil, one question assails the Muslims constantly: 'What is our place in this country?' The question recurs in many forms: 'Don't we belong here?' 'What have we done to deserve this?' 'What can we do to persuade them that we belong here?' That these questions really admit of no answer was brought home to me with a blinding clarity by an exceptionally articulate Muslim who had organised relief for riot-affected people from an area in Surat where the worst kind of ritualised violence was enacted. He reeled off various variations of the root question, and came to: 'What can we do to persuade them that we belong here?' At this point, he described the rape and killing of a young Muslim school teacher. The chilling narrative ended, he added: 'Why did they kill her? She was not a Mussalman. She was in every way a Hindu.' She dressed, he clarified, like a Hindu woman, even putting on a bindi on her forehead, and observed perfect vegetarianism. Yet she was killed.

To understand the disturbing implications of this particular account, we need to recall the fate of those Jews in Hitler's Germany who, out of genuine conviction, behaved like Germans in every possible way. They fared no better than their coreligionists who, while believing that they were German, retained their distinguishing Jewish marks.

One thought that frequently occurs to Muslims in this state of impotence and confusion is that of terrorism. In 1990, when a rash of Muslim-bashing erupted in the wake of the so-called massacre of '*kar sevaks*' (volunteers) in Ayodhya, one ran into a Muslim youth now and again who would talk of the possibility of Muslim terrorism as an answer to Hindu militancy. This time one is struck by the spread of such sentiments. Someone may talk of the possibility of Muslim terrorism, while someone else may talk pointedly of the bomb blasts and the killing of the Shiv Sena and BJP legislators in Bombay. A third may even lay stress on the lessons to be learnt from the absence of retaliation from the Hindus this time.

But, and this is significant, these outbursts end in speculations about the possible choices the Muslims, as Muslims, can make at the next elections. For, on the outcome of the elections, they still believe, will depend the fate of the question that plagues them most: the question of their place and their future in India.

But this is not a question that concerns only the Muslims of the country. On the answer that the Indian polity finds to this question will hang its very fate. At this level the problem that ought to engage us relates not merely to the BJP's place in the Indian political system. At stake in the present turmoil is the very conception of the Indian nation-state. A federal, plural and secular polity is sought to be converted into a regimented Hindu monolith.

In this turmoil, the threat posed by the BJP is, in one sense, the most serious and brazen, for it proposes a counter-ideology and seeks to realise it. There is also a less brazen but no less sinister threat to the polity. It operates subterraneously, eroding cherished values, political practices and institutional arrangements. So much so that today, if communalisation of politics is taken as a critical variable, very little would seem to divide most Indian political parties from the BJP. Even the United Left Front, after its long spell in power in West Bengal, is beginning to feel worried about the communalisation of its rank and file (Some observers feel that even sections of the intermediate Left Front leadership are communally tainted).

Let us not forget that until the very last, P. V. Narasimha Rao was dangerously close to effecting an understanding with Hindutva. In Gujarat, to cite a similar example, Chiman Patel was obliged to do some political tightrope walking before he decided to join the Congress as the best way of ensuring his chief ministership. With a slightly different political arithmetic in Delhi, he could well have joined the BJP. With such fluidity marking political alignments—bringing into currency a telling term like Hindutva Congress—can we possibly afford to worry only about the position of the BJP in the Indian political system?

35

IDENTITY, COMMUNAL CONSCIOUSNESS AND POLITICS*

GHANSHYAM SHAH

Inquiries into the nature and intensity of communal riots in Surat and elsewhere reveal that though agents provocateurs and participants in acts of violence were few, a large number of onlookers occasionally joined the crowd and extended subtle support to the rioters. On the eve as well as during the riots in the city, the atmosphere was surcharged with emotions reinforcing communal categories and idioms. To what extent do the cross-sections of a society share the communal ideology which provides legitimacy to such riots? In order to understand this, we need to explore perceptions and opinions of the people on the subject of communal division and related issues. As a preliminary exercise to understand the complexities of 'mind-sets' of people, let us examine the nature of individual identity and communal consciousness and also how they get manifested in the political arena. The present study is confined to Surat city which witnessed communal riots in December 1992, soon after demolition of Babri masjid. The study is based on survey research, interviewing 723 persons in May–June 1993 from various parts of the city.[1]

IDENTITY

[...]

In order to ascertain as to what was uppermost in respondents' minds about their identity, we asked open-ended questions:

> Different people introduce themselves differently. Given the fact that some introduce themselves by their occupations such as businessman, worker, teacher, etc., some by region such as Gujarati, Tamilian, Bihari and the like, some by 'jati' and some by their 'dharma', how would you introduce yourself to a stranger asking for your introduction?

The question was somewhat repeated to know the second identity. Of course, one's introduction to a stranger does not necessarily capture complexities of identity. This is only one tentative clue to unfolding one's identity. A caveat needs to be entered

* *Economic and Political Weekly* 29 (19): 1133–40 (7 May 1994).

about the context that people were interviewed in May–June 1993, soon after the second phase of riots. And respondents were told that our study was regarding the recent communal disturbances in the city.

The responses are reported in Table 35.1. It is a cross-table giving first and second identity. Since 9 per cent of the respondents did not answer the first question, the second question was not applicable to them. One-fifth of the respondents did not give their second identity. For them there was no difference between their first and second identity.

TABLE 35.1: Self-Introduction to a Stranger (Percentages)

Second Introduction in	*First Introduction in*						
	Religion	*Caste*	*Region*	*Occupation*	*Indian*	*Indian Name*	*Total*
Religion	24	23	59	–	33	5	31
Caste	44	61	18	5	24	31	40
Region	3	5	10	16	6	3	6
Occupation	2	2	1	68	–	11	4
Indian	19	5	10	–	29	5	11
Indian name	9	4	2	11	8	45	8
Total	22	36	24	3	8	7	100

Source: Author.

One-fifth of the population identified themselves as belonging to specific religious groups. All of them, however, did not introduce themselves as Hindus or Muslims. A few expressed their identity by sect. 'I am none but a Swaminarayani and all those who follow the Swaminarayan sect are my brothers and sisters', a businessman dealing in the diamond trade told us. He had a 'tilak' placed on his forehead, which is a distinct mark of the sect. Similar instances were also found among the Muslims. For example, a Sunni Vohra businessman preferred to be called a Sunni Vohra rather than a Muslim. One-fourth of those giving religion as their first identity also repeated it to be their second identity. In this case, they gave the name of their sect. That is, the first identity is Hindu and the second is Vaishnava or vice versa.

A majority who placed religious identity over other identities are workers in white-collar jobs and students. Religious identity was expressed in larger proportion by the minority groups. Their number is larger among the Jains, Christians and Buddhists than the Muslims. Among the adivasis, expressing religious identity was preferred only by a handful of persons. The highest proportion of those who preferred to be introduced by their religions is found in middle and upper-caste groups.

Self identity expressed through caste is pronounced among a sizeable section of both Hindus and Muslims. Those giving caste as their first identity constitute the single largest group. Even in terms of expressions related to the second identity, caste remains predominant. Many reiterated their caste status and identification by placing themselves within specific sub-castes as the second identity. In other words, while the first time one identifying himself as a kshatriya called himself koli at the second level of identity. Thus, it appears that for the majority, the caste identity is either the first which precedes religious or regional identity, or the second, next to regional identity. While many who preferred to express caste as their first identity are distributed broadly in similar proportion across all occupational groups, they are, however, slightly more among casual labourers. A large number of them belong to the other backward classes (OBCs) and only a small proportion belongs to the scheduled castes (SCs). In Surat, OBCs have emerged as a political force only recently and are an upwardly mobile group.

One-fifth of the respondents expressed their first identity by the place of their origin cither by region or city. Significantly, a majority of those inclined to be introduced in this manner are local Suratis. Twenty-three per cent of the Suratis as against 17 per cent of the immigrants preferred to place their regional identity over identities like caste or religion. However, for many of them the second identity was expressed through their religion. Thus, to them, regional and religious identities go together, as it is the case of caste and religion.

Only a few (9 per cent) liked to be identified by their names that I am so and so. Many among them also repeated that as the second introduction. A majority among this group are white and blue-collar workers and belong to OBCs, SCs and scheduled tribes (STs). Seven per cent of the respondents preferred to be introduced as Indians first and a majority among them chose to express their second identity through religion or caste. This does not seem surprising in a situation where religion and nation are seen as co-terminus with one another. Only a few expressed their first identity through their occupation. They are mainly factory owners, businessmen and white-collar employees, belonging generally to upper and artisan caste groups.

The nature of economic growth in India in general and Surat in particular with a significant portion of its labour force placed in its informal sector has had little impact in the formation of the secular identity. Electoral politics has helped in reinforcing primordial identities. In such a milieu, it is not surprising for an overwhelming section of the population to pronounce caste as their first identity irrespective of their sex, age, educational status and occupation. The campaign of the Sangh parivar and Islamic fundamentalists has not succeeded even in weakening caste and/or sectarian differences. It is, however, noteworthy that a relatively large section among the artisan caste groups, SCs and STs have preferred to introduce themselves first by their names, occupations or as Indian rather than by castes. This is because a secular identity becomes more advantageous.

Communal Consciousness

'Qaum' (in Gujarati it is pronounced as 'kom') or 'jat', that is commune or community, is more often than not understood and referred to in day-to-day parlance as caste or cluster of castes in India. While inferring in this manner, one imagines having an immediate or a distant social relationship, sharing common heritage and 'sanskar' (culture) and fraternity with members of the 'qaum'. Such a notion of 'qaum' is not only prevalent among the caste Hindus, but also among various Muslim social groups. We have already seen that in the midst of religion-based communal polarisations, many caste Hindus and Muslims prefer to identify their 'qaum' as 'jati' or 'jamat'. Even while the Muslims as a minority are forced to join hands as Muslims on religious grounds for their security and survival, a number of them (28 per cent) continue to identify themselves as maleks, memons, vohras, khojas, more salams Garesiyas and so on.

This does not mean that religious 'qaum' as Hindus or Muslims do not exist at their collective consciousness. The above data show that after caste, most of them identified with the religious 'qaum'. This is because of a variety of reasons. It is partly because of their real or imaginary historical heritage, linked with other social groups within the larger caste structure in the Hindu framework. Certain commonality among members of the 'same' religion through sharing of festivals, chanting name/s of the same god/s, performance of certain rituals, considering certain texts and scriptures as holy, etc., contribute to developing a common religious identity. State, religious leaders and intellectuals codify people as Hindus or Muslims for at least the last two centuries and see them as 'juxtaposed' in relation to one another. Significantly, social and religious reformers and political leaders who mobilised various 'jatis' and 'jamats' at various regional levels amongst Hindus and Muslims since the mid-nineteenth century also helped in strengthening such boundaries.

Both meanings of the term 'qaum', 'jati' or 'jamat' and Hindu or Muslim seem to exist almost simultaneously at a cognitive level. Within a milieu of communal riots, both the meanings interfuse and overlap when one speaks to respondents on issues related to 'qaum' without specifying any religious community. It hence becomes difficult to conclude as to what exactly the term 'qaum' encompasses.

Consciousness of one's 'qaum' or the communal consciousness in this context is not just a question of belonging to his/her community, but also the intensity of one's identification with it. In a 'communalised' situation, intensity of communal consciousness is related with one's perception about 'others' who are considered rivals. We have examined five dimensions of this complex state of mind. They are (i) identification with one's 'qaum'; (ii) commonality of interests of the members of the 'qaum' and hence the need of their protection; (iii) perceptions about 'others'; (iv) economic relations with others; and (v) political power for the 'qaum'.

[...]

An overwhelming number of persons irrespective of occupation, sex, income or political affiliation expressed ... 'I am proud of my "qaum"!' Since we did not specify the term 'qaum' as a religious community or a caste, it is difficult to say to which 'qaum' they referred. For some, the 'qaum' meant caste and for others their religious identity. However, all those who clearly professed being proud of their 'qaum' do not subscribe to the Sangh parivar's or the non-Hindu fundamentalists' ideology of superiority of their 'qaum' over others. Thirty one per cent refused to take such a position and said that each community has good and bad aspects.

While trying to ascertain the extent of agreement with statements regarding common interests of the 'qaum' and need for unity to protect such interests, except for a small minority (3 per cent), all subscribed to the view of having common

TABLE 35.2: Communal Consciousness (*Percentages*)

	Item	*Fully Agree*	*Somewhat Agree*	*Fully Disagree*	*Somewhat Disagree*	*DK NA*
1	I am proud of my 'qaum'	89	5	1	3	2
2	My 'qaum' is superior to the others in all respects	40	26	5	26	3
3	Social, economic and political interests of all members of my 'qaum' are the same and for the protection of these interests all members of the 'qaum' should work together.	78	15	1	2	4
4	Unity and organisation of the 'qaum' are necessary for the protection of its interests	88	7	1	2	2
5	If it is necessary to acquire political power in the interests of 'qaum', it should be done.	41	36	2	16	5
6	Interests of the Hindus and Muslims are mutually opposite, if one gets advantage, the other gets disadvantage	26	24	4	37	9
7	Problems and difficulties faced by Hindus/Muslims, people belonging to Muslims/Hindus are largely responsible	17	25	9	41	8
8	We should not transact with shopkeeper/factory owner/vendor belonging to other 'qaum'	14	20	6	55	5
9	We should not rent or sell a house to members of the other community in our locality/housing complex	16	19	6	53	6

Source: Author.

Don't Know (DK); No Answer (NA) excluded. N = 575.

socio-economic interests among all the members of a 'qaum'. It is true that the idea of 'qaum' and its interests are not understood similarly by all. While the respondents were not asked to clarify their concept of 'qaum', some explained as to what they understood by the term. For a majority, it was a caste-based community. But at the same time, a few also identified its meaning with a religious community. A similar pattern emerged while examining the aspect of common interests of a 'qaum'.

All castes and religious organisations propagate that their members have common interests and that they should work together for the protection of their interests. During the last assembly and parliament elections, the Vishva Hindu Parishad (VHP), many of the sadhus and saints, and several front organisations of the Bharatiya Janata Party (BJP) issued statements and distributed posters asking people to vote for the party which would protect the interests of Hindus. A question arises as to whether all members of a 'qaum' have common social, economic and political interests. Here, the understanding of common interests varies from individual to individual and no neat answer emerges. At a normative level, they wish to have and perceive common interests of the members. They believe in belonging to the same social group and thereby inherit a common culture—the culture of caste or the culture of religion. Political interests for them are either political dominance or protection, while economic interests mean economic uplift of all members in the 'qaum'. This means job opportunities, business prospects, better living conditions, etc. They do not consider, at least while thinking in terms of common interests of the 'qaum', that the factory owners and the labourers or the landlords and the tenants belonging to the same 'qaum' have conflicting interests.

To a question as to what they consider as common interests of the members of the 'qaum', a postgraduate student wrote:

> I am proud to be a Hindu because 'Bharatiya sanskriti' (culture) is very old and the Hindu religion is considered to be 'mahan' (great) in the entire world. Geeta, our religious book, provides inspiration to us, to the country, to human society, to all individuals, and to the whole world. I greatly adore and respect the Geeta. Bharat is a Hindu nation and it is Hindustan. We should work in the direction of improving the social and economic condition of our Hindu brethren and for that we should get ourselves organised and united so that others cannot harm our interests.

Another respondent who also understood the term 'qaum' in terms of a Hindu identity, while elaborating what he meant by common interests, extended repetitive and fuzzy answers. He said that, 'dominance of the other "qaum" should not be upon us'; and that 'our interests may be endangered by the other "qaum"' or that we are one and therefore our interests are the same.

A Muslim said that the 'socio-economic and political interests of people in my community are equal and none in our community should be higher or lower. They all should work for the protection of the interests of all. But in reality this is not seen to be practised.'

Another Hindu belonging to a SC group said:

> According to the Constitution of India, interests of the members of our 'qaum' are not opposite to each other. They are equal. However, there is inequality as far as economic interests are concerned and that ought not to be so. Therefore I believe that we all should work together for the protection of our interests.

A member of a Scheduled Caste, who read 'qaum' as caste said that his 'qaum' was socially, economically and politically backward than the others and they should try to get equality with others. Another respondent from an OBC said, 'In my village, members of certain castes own lands and are educated and powerful whereas members of our "qaum" are poor and illiterate'.

The communality of economic, cultural and political interests of the members of a 'qaum' as perceived by the respondents in this context seemingly indicates two things. First, most of them are vague and talk about 'common interests' without specifying what they mean by it. They very nearly repeat what politicians say in public meetings—more of rhetoric than facts. It is *vox et praeterea nihil.* Second, many visualise and consider 'common interests' only at a normative level for which they feel that members of their 'qaum' should work together. Third, those who interpret 'qaum' as caste, perceive their 'qaum' as 'social class' having social ties, uniform lifestyle and similar economic status among its members.

[...]

Those believing in commonality of interests among members of a 'qaum' do not, however, necessarily subscribe to a view that there is a need to capture political power. As much as 18 per cent of the respondents did not agree with the view that it was necessary to obtain political power for protecting their interests. On the other hand, more than three-fourths did express a need to have political power for the interests of the 'qaum'. However, we do not know as to what they actually meant by 'capturing power' and wonder whether it meant voting in elections for a member of their 'qaum' or forming a political party or it was a pure and simple empty expression.

Communalists often invoke among members of their 'qaum' feelings against other 'qaum', tribals against non-tribals, kshatriyas against patidars, upper castes against backward castes, and so on. Hindus are told that they face various problems for which Muslims are responsible. To a set of two questions aimed at ascertaining the views of respondents about the extent to which they thought their interests (we specified in the question as Hindus or Muslims) conflicted with the interests of the other 'qaum', while some did not reply, there were others who felt that it was difficult for them to say anything categorically. However, 50 per cent of the respondents expressed a view that the interests of the two 'qaums' were antagonistic. Some among them shifted their position by not blaming the other 'qaum' for their problems with 42 per cent holding the other 'qaum' (Muslim/Hindu) responsible for the problems being faced by their 'qaum'.

During the riots, the Sangh parivar, the BJP, and some other local organisations and individuals appealed to people through public meetings, street-corner gatherings and by distributing leaflets to boycott goods manufactured or sold by Muslims. Hindus were asked to boycott Muslim autoricksha-walas. In one case, a professor apparently looking like a Hindu woman stopped an autorickshaw for going to the railway station. The driver asked, 'Madam! I am a Muslim, would you mind hiring my rickshaw?' The professor, who did not subscribe to communal segregation, was emotionally moved by the question. A few reported cases suggest that Muslims were asked or forced to vacate their houses located in predominantly Hindu localities. Even before riots, other things being equal, there has been a general tendency to prefer neighbours of similar social background. Living clusters of Jains, Vanias, Marwadis, Punjabis, low castes, etc., within the same colony is a testimony to this. Nonetheless, except among a few having aversion to non-vegetarian food habits, tendency of segregation on the basis of caste and community in newly constructed apartments and colonies did not seem to exist. This situation has, however, changed for the Muslims, particularly after the riots. Communalists from both groups now talk openly that the 'others' should not be allowed to acquire a house in their localities. Let us attempt to ascertain to what extent the people of Surat subscribe to such views.

A majority of the people (nearly 60 per cent) do not support the idea of economic boycott. Though soon after the first phase of riots, Hindus avoided Muslim shopkeepers or vendors, an act determined partly by emotional anti-Muslim feelings and rumours about poison being mixed in food and the like; it did not continue for long. Even those believing in boycott did not necessarily put that into practice owing to the intricate economic relationships. Similarly, a majority (69 per cent) did not support the idea of segregating houses on communal lines.

To get a clearer picture about the overall communal consciousness, an index based on nine variables was prepared. The 92 cases not responding to any of the questions have been dropped from the index. Each of the items has a four-point scale. Anyone strongly agreeing to all the propositions is given 36 points, and the one strongly disagreeing is given 9 points. Based on such scores, respondents have been divided into three categories. Those getting 22 or less points have been considered to have a lower degree of communal consciousness as against those getting 29 or more points and treated as highly communally conscious persons. Even while this is an arbitrary decision, according to the score, 51 per cent have moderate communal consciousness and 26 per cent high communal consciousness.

Intensity of communal consciousness was found to be more or less uniform among males and females. The pattern is also the same among all age groups. There is, however, some variation when we examine their education; 25 per cent of the illiterates as against 32 per cent of college educated persons were found to have a high degree of communal consciousness (Table 35.3).

Table 35.3: Socio-Demographic Characteristics of High Communal Consciousness (*Percentages*)

Sex		*Occupation*	
Male	26	Factory owners	24
Female	27	Professionals	43
Age		Traders	24
15–25 years	25	White-collar workers	27
26–35 years	27	Factory workers	28
36–46 years	28	Vendors	29
47–55 years	24	Casual labourers	22
Above 55 years	28	Others	29
Education		*Caste/Community*	
Illiterate	25	Upper castes	28
Primary	29	Middle castes	22
Secondary	22	Artisan castes	25
College	32	Low castes	33
		Scheduled castes	32
		Scheduled tribes	31
		Other Hindus	16
		Muslims	29
		Christians/Jains/Buddhists	37

Source: Author.

Intense communal consciousness was found more or less in the same proportion among various religious groups, though it was found to be more pronounced among the Christians, Jains and Buddhists compared to the Muslims and the Hindus. They are 37, 29 and 26 per cent respectively. Among Hindus, the proportion is higher among the dalits, adivasis and other backward castes compared to the upper and middle castes (Table 35.3). Among the dalits and adivasis, the phenomenon seems perplexing, for as seen earlier, the tendency among them to opt for secular individual identity is generally high. The data suggest that collectivity, be it through religion or caste, is felt by them as necessary for their mobility or protection of interests. It seems to be a dilemma for many dalits or adivasis, for at one level they tend to shun their caste identity but at the same time need to inculcate communal consciousness while aspiring for political power and economic benefits.

Seemingly, communal consciousness is widespread in different degrees among all occupational groups. Twenty four per cent of the factory owners or big businessmen and petty shopkeepers, and 27 per cent of white-collar as well as blue-collar factory workers have intense communal consciousness. The case of self-employed professionals like doctors and lawyers suggests a different pattern with 43 per cent among them falling in the category of intensely communal individual. However, their number in the sample being too small, it might be hasty to draw conclusions.

The trend is more or less similar among the economically well off and contented and those having difficulty even in making both ends meet (Table 35.4). The proportion of intensely communal persons is slightly higher (33 per cent) among those who are worse off than those who are contented (27 per cent).

TABLE 35.4: Perception of Family's Economic Condition and Communal Consciousness (*Percentages*)

Perception of Economic Condition	*Level of Consciousness*				
	Low	*Moderate*	*High*	*Total*	*N*
Very bad	14	53	33	100	55
Bad	23	52	25	100	397
Not bad	24	49	27	100	176

Source: Author.

The highest proportion of intensely communal persons was found among those who preferred to identify themselves by regions. But as mentioned earlier, regional and religious identities are not mutually exclusive, for a majority who gave regional identity as their initial introduction stated religion to be their second identity. Thus, if we take the first and second identities together, the pattern emerges as expected. Table 35.5 shows that intensely communal persons are strikingly low among those who preferred to identify themselves by their name or as being Indian. And it is significantly lower among those who identify themselves in terms of their occupation.

Table 35.5: Individual Identity of Intense Communal Consciousness (*Percentages*)

Identity	*Proportion of Intense Communal Consciousness*	
	First	*Second*
Religion	23	37
Caste	24	30
Region	40	5
Occupation	5	1
Indian	15	8
Indian name	22	4

Source: Author.

Religiosity and Communal Consciousness

Some scholars consider that religion breeds communal consciousness. For them, religion and secularism cannot exist together. For some others, communalism is a political construct and is not related to an individual's faith in a religion. In order to probe into these propositions, five questions were asked about participation in various religious activities. Table 35.6 shows that one-third of the respondents visit religious places regularly. Most of them did not, however, participate in other religious activities like attending 'katha' or discourses regularly. A majority did not read the sacred books and only 2 per cent had gone regularly on pilgrimage, that is, 'jatra' or 'haj'. A low proportion of only 4 per cent regularly donated for various religious activities.

Table 35.6: Participation in Religious Activities (*Percentages*) ($N = 723$)

	Hardly	*Occasionally*	*Sometimes*	*Regularly*
1 Visiting mandir/masjid/church	8	26	29	35
2 Attending bhajans/discourses	24	35	28	12
3 Reading sacred books	33	21	28	18
4 Providing financial support	21	42	30	4
5 Had gone on pilgrimage	48	28	20	2

Source: Author.

In order to get an overall picture of their participation in religious activities, an index of five activities was prepared. Those receiving 16 or more points have been considered to be relatively more active in religious activities. (They may be called persons having high religiosity.) Only 11 per cent of the respondents have shown such high level of religiosity and 40 per cent have low level of participation in various religious activities. Table 35.7 shows that it is hazardous to say that religiosity and communal consciousness go together, that is, religious persons are not necessarily communal and vice versa. Proportionately smaller number of persons (19 per cent) having low communal consciousness are found among those who are active in religious activities. Nevertheless, it seems that if other things are constant, religiously active persons tend to become communal. This may be because the meaning of religion has undergone change in which identity of being 'we' against 'they' is getting sharper and composite folk religion is getting weaker. Moreover, religious platforms have been used in invoking communal politics during the recent times.

TABLE 35.7: Religiosity and Communal Consciousness (*Percentages*) ($N = 723$)

Communal Consciousness	*Religiosity*		
	Low	*Moderate*	*High*
Low	28	18	19
Moderate	49	53	53
High	23	29	28
Total	100	100	100
N=	230	317	62

Source: Author.

POLITICS AND COMMUNAL CONSCIOUSNESS

Political leaders and social scientists often assert that communalism is a political issue. It may mean two things: one, political leaders appropriate communal issues in order to obtain larger support in mobilising people of one or the other community in electoral politics and two, that intensely communal persons are also politically active. We shall examine the second aspect of the problem, that is, the relationship between communal consciousness and political participation.

Three indicators have been used to measure political participation, these being (i) interest in politics; (ii) participation in meetings/processions; and (iii) working for a party in election campaigns. Though one-fourth of the respondents reported taking interest in politics, only 4 per cent had a great deal of interest in such matters. All those interested in politics do not necessarily participate in various political activities. Twelve per cent of the respondents participated in public meetings and/or processions, and a smaller number worked for any party in election campaigns. Taking these activities together, only 11 per cent may be identified as politically active. Table 35.8 shows that there is no relationship between political participation and communal consciousness. A vast majority of politically active persons do not have intense communal consciousness and vice versa. What is striking, however, is that the proportion of intensely communal persons is more among those who are politically inactive. The question naturally arises here what can one infer from the above evidence: is there de-politicisation in electoral politics of the intensely communal individuals? Or would it mean that political participation in electoral politics tends to soften communal consciousness? These important questions with wider theoretical relevance need further examination.

Table 35.8: Political Participation and Communal Consciousness (*Percentages*) (*N* = 723)

Communal Consciousness	*Political Participation*	
	Low	*High*
Low	22	25
Moderate	51	53
Intense	27	22
Total	100	100

Source: Author.

It is now widely accepted that there is hardly any difference between the Congress and thc BJP as far as communal politics is concerned. The Congress distributes party tickets in elections and positions on caste and community lines, shares platforms with religious and caste leaders who speak in a communal idiom. Their support is often sought to mobilise voters. The Congress has not made any effort to develop secular politics in the country, except for chanting populist slogans of secularism or Hindu–Muslim unity. As mentioned earlier, several Congress leaders hold similar views about the Muslims, believe in the dominance of the majority community and 'over-protection' to minorities. BJP politics in this matter is open. In such a situation, how far are BJP and Congress supporters different in their communal consciousness? In order to identify Congress and BJP supporters, a question was asked, 'Whom would you vote for in the next elections?' Fifty per cent respondents reported that they would vote for the BJP. An overwhelming number (88 per cent) of them were committed voters who voted for the same party in the 1991 election too. Thus, the BJP has gained 10 per cent more supporters. The Congress has more or less retained 26 per cent supporters, which was the case during the last election.

Table 35.9 shows that both the Congress and the BJP have almost equal proportion of supporters who have intense communal consciousness and their size is not insignificant. Together, they add up to 30 per cent of the respondents. The number of such persons is significantly low among the supporters of Janata Dal, the Communist Party and other parties. Even among the undecided or non-voter

Table 35.9: For Whom Would You Vote in Forthcoming Elections? (*Percentages*) (*N* = 723)

Communal Consciousness	*Religiosity*				
	Congress	*BJP*	*Others*	*Undecided*	*DK/Would Not Vote*
Low	24	17	32	41	41
Moderate	46	53	56	60	44
Intense	30	30	12	19	15
Total	(100)	(100)	(100)	(100)	(100)
N=	162	316	25	67	61

Source: Author.

individuals, the proportion of intensely communal conscious persons is significantly lower than among the BJP and the Congress supporters. Does it suggest that they find no difference between the Congress and the BJP on the communal issue or they are fed up of these parties?

Construction of Mandir and Communal Consciousness

Another political dimension of communalisation is reflected in people's views on the construction of the Ram mandir or Babri masjid at Ayodhya. Communal riots in Surat are closely related with the BJP and Sangh parivar campaign for construction of the Ram mandir. The campaign had been built up brick by brick for the last five years. And the riots followed soon after the demolition of the Babri masjid. Though in its campaign, the BJP raised other economic and political issues, it essentially banked upon the issue of temple construction. This intensified communal division in society. We tried to ascertain as to how a certain person viewed the priority of the temple. In order to probe into this question, respondents were asked to prioritise five problems according to the importance that they gave to each of them. The problems were: (1) construction of the Ram mandir/mosque at Ayodhya; (2) price rise; (3) unemployment; (4) corruption in public life; and (5) the rising population.

About 5 per cent of the respondents did not reply to this question. Some responded that they did not understand as to what was more important and there were others for whom the day-to-day problems were more pressing than bothering about questions which fall in the domain of political leaders.

Among those prioritising the five issues (Table 35.10), only a small proportion of 13 per cent considered construction of the Ram mandir or mosque at Ayodhya as the most important issue to be solved, whereas as high as 68 per cent gave it the last priority. Many among those giving first priority to the construction of the temple did so because it was a question of faith and dignity for them. One of them said:

> I know that the BJP is not going to solve the problems of our community and is in no way different from the Congress. It aspires for power. But who is really bothered about solving problems? ... at least the BJP would unfurl the saffron flag on the Lal Killa. This is more important.

TABLE 35.10: Prioritisation of Issues according to their Importance

	Priority					
	First	*Second*	*Third*	*Fourth*	*Fifth*	*Total*
Construction of Ram mandir/ mosque at Ayodhya	13	9	3	7	68	100
Price rise	40	20	18	16	6	100
Unemployment	9	31	30	23	7	100
Corruption	9	18	24	39	10	100
Population rise	29	21	25	17	8	100
N=	200	150	169	114	55	688

Source: Author.

Another respondent said that the Babri masjid was a symbol of slavery and a beginning of Muslim rule. Babar built the mosque by destroying the temple. Construction of the Ram mandir would be a new era for Hindutva and it would bring prosperity. Therefore, we should not talk about poverty or unemployment. Once the temple is constructed, other problems would be solved. The Muslims giving priority to the construction of the mosque felt that by the demolition of the Babri masjid, 'we were badly insulted. This was a direct assault on our very existence, and on our dignity.' Another Muslim respondent said that the reconstruction of the mosque on the same site was necessary for secularism and that the minority community was protected by the Indian state. However, a handful of respondents gave priority to the construction of the temple just to end the communal problem once and for all. A medical doctor said that once the temple was constructed, the series of communal riots of the last few years would come to an end and the country would be able to concentrate more on the other pressing issues.

Supporters of the construction of the temple/mosque over other priorities are found in small proportion among both males and females, various age groups and also among educated and illiterate (Table 35.11). They belong to all varieties of occupational and social groups. Contrary to general belief, their number, however, is small among white-collar workers and upper-caste individuals. It is also significant to note that none among the respondents from STs gave priority to the construction of the temple.

Table 35.11: Socio-Demographic Characteristics of those who Gave First Priority to Construction of Ram Mandir/Masjid

Social Groups	*Percentage*
Sex	
Male	12
Female	12
Age	
15–25 years	13
26–35 years	12
36–46 years	10
47–55 years	16
Above 55 years	15
Education	
Illiterate	10
Primary	12
High School	8
College	9
Social groups	
Upper castes	9

(Contd)

Table 35.11 (Contd)

Social Groups	*Percentage*
Middle castes	12
Artisan castes	15
Low castes	20
Scheduled castes	19
Scheduled tribes	–
Other Hindus	16
Muslims	14
Christian/Jains/Parsi, etc.	2
Occupation	
Factory owners	14
Professionals	14
Shopkeepers	15
White-collar employees	8
Factory workers	15
Vendors	11
Casual labourers	19

Source: Author.

As is apparent from Table 35.12, those who give first priority to construction of temple/mosque are in equal proportion among those who have moderate or high communal consciousness, but are expectedly in smaller proportion among those who have low communal consciousness. Similar pattern is found among people with different rates of participation in religious activities. They are fewer among those who rarely participate in religious activities than the ones who participate in such events more actively. Construction of the mandir or masjid has become a political issue. However, a large proportion (23 per cent) of politically active individuals gave priority to the construction of temple/mosque. This means that for them, the Ram mandir is a political issue. This is further substantiated by the fact that despite equal proportion of highly communal persons in both the parties, a larger number of BJP than Congress supporters gave priority to the construction of the temple. This is not surprising, for the BJP has made it a political issue.

OVERVIEW

Caste identity is uppermost in the minds of most people even in an urban area like Surat. It is more so among the OBCs than dalits and members of the upper castes. The OBCs in Surat have recently improved their condition and are upwardly mobile through caste idioms, organisation and solidarity in economic and political spheres. There is a tendency among the dalits to underplay their caste identity and opt for secular identity through occupation. This is more common among those who have

TABLE 35.12: Political and Religious Participation, Party Affiliation and Communal Consciousness of those who Gave First Priority to Construction of Temple/Mosque

Occupation	*Percentage*
Level of Political Participation	
High	23
Low	10
Supporters	
Congress	10
BJP	15
Other parties	
Communal Consciousness	
Low	6
Moderate	15
High	15
Religiosity	
Low	6
Moderate	17
High	14

Source: Author.

higher education and are engaged in white-collar jobs or as entrepreneurs, for they feel that they have very little to be proud of their caste. It is important to note that despite a call and programmes for a Hindu or a Muslim unity, sectarian and caste identities continue to dominate. Caste and religious identity, however, is not opposite or contradictory at a personal level. For many, religious identity is but a continuation of the caste identity. Both co-exist though their emphasis changes with varying contexts.

Individual identity based on caste and religion reinforces communal consciousness—the consciousness of being member of one's 'qaum' . The connotation of the term includes both caste and religious community. But for many, a notion of caste-based community is closer and more identifiable than religious community. It is a 'social class' whose members not only share an identity, a particular lifestyle and a definite value system but also have more or less similar socio-economic position as rich, business community, service class, labourers, poor, backward, etc. While doing so, economic differentiations within a caste, if they exist, are noticed but do not seem antagonistic. But it is not so in the case of religion-based community consciousness. Economic and cultural differences between caste Hindus are so sharp and antagonistic that 'community of interests' as Hindus or Muslims is vague and rhetorical.

Caste or religious communal consciousness is widespread in Surat among people in all walks of life irrespective of their sex, age, education and place of belonging (local or immigrants). All of them, however, do not share communal consciousness to a similar extent. Most do not ascribe superiority to one's own community over others or economic polarisation between the communities. Nearly one-fourth of the population (of course not insignificant, especially with potential of being fanatic) were found to have high communal consciousness which may tend to be fanatical. They are found in all social and occupational groups with only slight variation in their proportion. High communal consciousness is neither particular caste or class, local or immigrant, literate or illiterate group phenomena. Significantly, neither religiosity nor political participation is related to intense communal consciousness. This makes the problem more complex than is generally recognised and requires multipronged strategies to deal with it.

Despite predominance of caste and religious individual identity and communal consciousness, when it comes to choice on issues, people do not give preference to religious issues over the economic ones. Even soon after the riots when communal passions were high, an overwhelming number of them did not give preference to construction of the Ram mandir or masjid over price rise or unemployment. Thus, though communal consciousness is widespread and people are susceptible to communal slogans and symbols and may indulge in rioting for the time being, they do not continuously get swept away by communal categories and issues. They see that as the game of politicians.

NOTE

1. Surat has 36 municipal wards. The biggest ward has 49 polling booths and the smallest ward has just three polling booths. We have selected minimum one or 10 per cent of the polling booths from a ward. Fifty-three polling booths were selected. From each polling booth, 25 voters were selected with the help of random table for interview. The total number of respondents was 1,325. From them, we could interview 723. A number of them were either wrongly listed or shifted their residence. Some were not available at the time of interview, they either left the area or were out of station or not available after two visits. A few avoided us.

36

When Riots are not Merely Local*

Bringing the State Back in, Bijnor 1988–92

Amrita Basu

In October 1990, the town of Bijnor, in western Uttar Pradesh, experienced a major Hindu–Muslim riot. Official sources estimate that 87 people were killed; unofficial estimates range from 198 to 300.[1] This was among the most serious of the many riots that took place in the wake of the Bharatiya Janata Party's (BJP) campaign to build a temple at the supposed birthplace of Lord Ram in Ayodhya. Other violent events took place in the cities of Ahmedabad and Baroda in Gujarat, and in Shamili and Gorakhpur in Uttar Pradesh; tensions were also reported in Allahabad, Faizabad and Bareilly.

I first visited Bijnor five months after the riot had taken place and returned there several times over the next two months. The question of why a majority community should engage in extreme brutality against members of an impoverished and relatively powerless minority haunted me. But my questions centred not only upon why the riot had occurred, but more broadly on how scholars and activists might go about studying Hindu violence against Muslims.

[...]

Over the course of several visits to Bijnor, I asked caste Hindus and Muslims from a range of social backgrounds for an account of the riot of October–November 1990. Although their accounts differed in many important respects, the people with whom I spoke sharply demarcated the year before 1988 in which communal violence had been absent, from the succeeding years. However they considered the riots of 30 October–3 November a continuation and culmination of a series of other events. The four incidents that they repeatedly mentioned were: the municipal council elections in November 1988; a conflict over a plot of land in town on 23 August 1990; the banning of the so-called *ram jyotis* (devotees of Ram) from Bijnor on 4 October; and a rally organised by the chief minister on 9 October. ...

* *Economic and Political Weekly* 29 (40): 2605–21 (1 October 1994).

THE RIOT

The BJP–Vishva Hindu Parishad (VHP) combine had arranged for thousands of so-called *kar sevaks* (voluntary workers) to converge on Ayodhya from all over the country on 30 October. Acting on instructions from the chief minister, the administration arrested 637 of these young men from various points surrounding Bijnor, at Balwali, Hardwar and the barrage near the Ganges.[2] Since there was no room for them in the local jail, it detained them in a girls' intermediate college in Bijnor. The next day, 26 October, the kar sevaks launched a protest against 'prison conditions', demanding better food, sanitation and other amenities. That evening they attempted to escape. The police intervened and opened fire. Although K. L. Joshi, a *Dainik Jagran* reporter, visited the jail and found that the police had only killed one person, it was rumoured that the police were gunning down kar sevaks by the dozens. On 27–28 October, shopkeepers closed down their shops with allegations that the government had treated the kar sevaks inhumanely. The following day, several hundred people marched from the Arya Samaj mandir to the collector's office where it engaged in a 'jail *bharo andolan*' ('fill the jails campaign' of voluntarily courting arrest). Hindu women from Bijnor were at the forefront of this protest.

Many observers denied that kar sevaks had been mistreated while in confinement. Ashok Varma reported that he had inspected the girls' intermediary college and found that the kar sevaks were better housed, fed and clothed than the large majority of prisoners. Furthermore, the term 'imprisonment' was highly misleading, for security at the girls' college was minimal; the kar sevaks would usually spend the evenings in town fermenting disturbances and return to their lodgings at night.

By 30 October, the day when the kar sevaks reached Ayodhya, tensions dramatically escalated. The VHP had organised a large group of women to assemble outside the Arya Samaj mandir to do '*kirtan*' that morning. They were joined by the hundreds of kar sevaks who had been detained en route to Ayodhya. The atmosphere was extremely tense. Around 11 am, a police officer who had been listening to the radio rushed to the mandir with news he claimed he had heard over the BBC: the kar sevaks had reached Ayodhya, placed their flag on the mosque and started to demolish it. Within an hour, a victory procession of several hundred people marched through Bijnor shouting slogans about their determination to build a temple in Ayodhya. The procession marched towards '*ghanta ghar*', a clock tower in the centre of town where the road forked, dividing the Muslim and Hindu quarters. The group disagreed over which way to proceed. The more militant members prevailed and the procession marched through the Muslim section.

Muslim families had congregated on their roof tops, from which they watched the procession with horror and fear. The Hindu demonstrators shouted ugly, provocative slogans like: '*Musalmaan keh dohistaan*, Pakistan *aur kabristan*' (There are two places where Muslims belong: Pakistan and the graveyard); and '*Tel lagake Dabar ka, masjid girao babar ka*', (by applying Dabar [a brand name] kerosene, eradicate Babar's mosque); '*Hindu bachcha ram ka, Musalman haram kah*' (caste

Hindus are the children of God; Muslims are bastards). At some point along the way, Muslims began to pelt stones at the processionists, who responded in kind.

Then one of the most tragic and inflammatory incidents of that day took place. Mushir Ahmed, a Muslim doctor who had a clinic in the centre of town, saw that Hindu women who were at the forefront of the procession were getting caught in the crossfire and provided them shelter. The account that follows was provided by Fazlul Hyder, a Muslim veterinarian:

> Ahmed was the most humane and secular-minded person. He had kept his clinic open that day because he felt that people should resist chauvinistic attempts to divide the two communities. That was also why he took those women into his clinic. But a rumour spread that Ahmed had abducted Hindu women; some angry Hindu men broke into the clinic and murdered him.
>
> When Muslims carried Ahmed's body back to *mohalla* [locality] Charshiri, where he had lived, people went out of their minds with grief and rage. A group of Muslims marched to Barwan (the neighbouring Hindu mohalla) and attacked the caste Hindus there. Once the violence started, some other Muslims joined in because they wanted to settle scores with a Hindu from Barwan who had been having a love affair with a Muslim's wife. Several hours later, the Muslims had killed 12 people in Bartaan. By the evening, the administration had declared a curfew and all the Muslims went home. ...

Significantly, Muslim violence in Bartaan was directed at the other backwards classes (OBCs), a relatively vulnerable, subordinate group among caste Hindus. Upper-caste Hindus later capitalised on this by plying jhuggis with both relief and BJP propaganda. Riots in Bijnor, as in other parts of the country, galvanised caste Hindus to overcome caste divisions and confront their common enemy.

The period of Muslim violence against caste Hindus was short lived. Sharma from the *Dainik Jagran* reported that whereas Muslims observed the curfew, for they were afraid that they would be pulverised if they stepped out, caste Hindus roamed freely through the town, looting Muslim shops. What the administration termed a curfew in fact trapped Muslims within their walled quarters, while giving caste Hindus free reign.

From 31 October to 3 November, violence took on a wholly different character: it was no longer perpetrated by one community against the other, but rather by the state against Muslims. During this phase, as elaborated in greater detail below, district administrators, the police and above all, the Provincial Armed Constabulary (PAC), accompanied by local Hindu residents, tracked down Muslim shops which they looted and destroyed. They searched out Muslim men and women, tortured them and shot them at point-blank range.

It would do great injustice to the riot victims to shift too quickly to questions of causality without first providing a fuller account of the violence itself. As Gyan Pandey aptly notes, the liberal media often assumes that even if one community has suffered disproportionately more, objectivity necessitates equal time to both communities.[3] To rectify the distortions associated with such attempts at even handedness, the account below mainly relies upon Muslims' testimony. I visited the mohallas which had experienced the most severe violence, and spoke to informants I met there who then put me in touch with others. All of the people I describe below are ordinary men and women; none of them were political leaders or activists.

The first Muslim mohalla I visited was Charshiri, a site of some of the most severe violence. I met Abdul Shamim sitting on the stoop of his house and asked him to describe the violence that he had personally witnessed. He recounted:

> The PAC arrived here on 31 October around 2.30 pm. Some boys from the Bajrang Dal and Shiv Sena were identifying houses. One of the PAC members was holding a gatore [an instrument used to spray pesticides in the fields] which was filled with petrol. They systematically went from one house to the next, spraying each house with petrol and setting it on fire.
>
> There is a masjid across the street (he points it out to me) where about nine Muslims had taken shelter. I saw the PAC march in, drag people onto the streets, and beat them severely. None of these people tried to escape. But the sub divisional magistrate [SDM] ordered the PAC to open fire and shoot seven people. Two men who had been beaten severely still lay there. The PAC poured kerosene over them and burned them. The PAC did not want to shoot them because their bodies were covered with bruises so instead the officers burned them to death.

Shamim took me to visit his friend Abdul Sarkar, who lived a few homes away from him to introduce me to some of the people who had personally experienced the violence. We found the old man sitting in his bed which, I was told, he rarely left. Tears streamed down his face as he spoke:

> They killed both of my sons, my two only sons. I am a widower and now I have no one in this world... they killed both of my sons... The SDM and sub-inspector of police came to my house and searched for arms. We have no arms but I had collected Rs 40,000 for my older boy's wedding; he was to be married on 5 June. That was all the money I had. They took the money, then they hauled my sons out of the house and shot them.
>
> When the sub-inspector who had been searching my house leaned over, his identification card fell out of his pocket. I kept it and made copies of it. Then I wrote to the prime minister and enclosed a photocopy of the ID. I said, 'This officer has killed my son. I saw him shoot my son with my own eyes. What sort of a government do you run?' The government then awarded me Rs 1,00,000 rupees in compensation.

Shamim gave me a copy of the ID card bearing a picture of a clean-cut young man who must have been about the same age as his own son. For several weeks, I carried it around with me and often stared at the photograph as if it would give me some explanation for these senseless murders. When I would imagine to myself that I had surely heard the worst because I could not bear to hear more, there were always more people, often with strikingly similar stories to tell. Within the same mohalla lived a widower named Habib Afshar.

> When we heard that the PAC was invading Muslim homes and killing innocent people, we wanted to run away. But where could we go? A curfew was in force and the police had been given shoot on sight orders—which meant that any Muslim roaming the streets would be at great risk. So we could not run away. We were trapped in our houses like prisoners.

> On the 31st afternoon, the PAC accompanied by Rampal and Jaspal, two local (Hindu) boys, broke into my house. They looted my house and took all my savings. Then they dragged my son out of the house and tied his feet to a '*bhel gari*'[4] (ox-drawn cart) and took off. Once we could safely leave the house, we searched everywhere amidst the stench of decaying corpses. I could not give up hope until I found his body near the railway crossing. He was my only son. He lived with me. He supported me. He was my reason to live.

I visited Qasaban, a small, isolated, extremely poor Muslim mohalla, accompanied this time by a few Muslims whom I had met in other mohallas. Since I wanted to meet some Muslim women, they had brought me to the home of a widow who had suffered greatly. In order to reach her house, we had to pass through a long, narrow cobblestone path lined on either side by high walls. We went to a small house where I met a woman who must have been in her late 30s and her five-year old daughter. The child sat by my side looking haunted and sometimes terrified. Her mother spoke:

> It happened on the 31st afternoon. Four PAC men entered my house and said they had learned we were storing arms so they had come to search my house. Then they made all of us leave the house except for my fourteen-year-old girl. They spent the whole night in the house violating my daughter. (She breaks into uncontrollable sobs.) I was outside, banging on the door, throwing my whole body against the door, trying to get in. The next day they brought her out to the courtyard and locked me inside. They doused her with kerosene and burned her to hide all proof of rape and murder.
>
> My home has become like a prison now. I wanted to run away but I had no place to go and for days I lay awake all night afraid that they would come back and attack us.

The Bijnor Times reported that four mosques (but no temples) had been destroyed. I spoke with the imam of norrani masjid, near B24 mohalla Charshiri, a frail and saintly man, whose home adjoined the mosque. He reported:

> On the 31st afternoon the PAC barged into my house. My daughters Tasleen, Nusrat and Rani were with me. They stripped Rani and took her to the other room. Then the SP [Superintendent of police] and SDM entered the house. I thought that they would stop the PAC but instead the SP was shouting orders: 'shoot, shoot, shoot!!' They seemed to have lost control of their senses. The SDM shouted at us 'we have destroyed your chairman Zafar Khan and now we will destroy all your imams' [religious leaders]! After they had left my house I watched them from my courtyard. Twenty-one Muslims were killed in this mohalla and five are missing; I saw the PAC kill three of them with my own eyes. And I saw that the SDM was goading them on.

Most of the violence was confined to urban Bijnor, but there were reports of some violence in the surrounding villages, above all in Rampur Bakli, which was about a mile east of Bijnor. Although judged by the extent of construction, Bakli bore greater resemblance to an urban area than a village, most of its residents depended on agriculture for a livelihood. Patterns of agricultural production were quite typical of western Uttar Pradesh as a whole. Bakli contained 256 houses of which 106 are Muslim and 150 Hindu. According to one account by Sharma from the *Dainik Jagran*, the damage done included: 17 people killed, 15 missing and 620 injured;

21 houses were burned and 66 looted; 223 people were arrested. Sharma reported that although he did not have precise figures of the damage incurred by each community, Muslims had suffered much more than caste Hindus.

My first interview was with a Muslim family who owned about six acres of land and a spacious pucca house surrounded by a large courtyard. According to a woman in her late 30s:

> There is no history of communal violence here—not at all. When we heard news of the tensions in Bijnor we wanted to leave but our Hindu neighbours persuaded us to stay on. They said, 'whatever happens in Bijnor, you know you are safe here'. At the time we believed them but now we feel that they deceived us.
>
> On the first night, hordes of people descended on the village. Most of them had come from the town. With them were some members of the PAC. They went to the Hindu homes and asked for help. Our neighbour Rakesh was helping them.
>
> When the Muslims saw this, most of them ran away. Some went to Bakshwala (a neighbouring village); some hid in the fields. We left at that time too. Those who remained here were killed. After about four days, the police came and found us and escorted us back to our houses. What a sight we found when we returned.

The woman walked with me through her compound. The granary had been set on fire and all the stored grain had been burned; the walls and roof of the granary were charred black. She then led me to the field where the tube well had been damaged and the plough dismantled. Inside her house was a small store room which had been ransacked and all the household valuables—money, jewellery and equipment—had been looted. The most lasting damage was to their agricultural equipment. Since they could not afford to repair it, work on the land had virtually come to a standstill. The theft of the money they had been accumulating meant postponing their son's marriage. I asked this woman how she explained what had happened. She responded:

> It all began on 9 October with Mulayam Singh's rally. We did not attend; in fact we were opposed to it but it made people very angry. Then there has been this whole Ram Janmabhoomi issue. Frankly we don't care whether a mosque or a temple stood there. What does it matter to us? And it didn't matter much to our neighbours either until recently. But now they have changed. Now we no longer trust them and we never can trust them again. Because when the mobs came here, Hindus became caste Hindus.

Her comment suggests how the identities of even those Muslims who were indifferent to the Ayodhya dispute were redefined by it. Once caste Hindus had assumed the role of aggressors, Muslims inevitably became defined as victims.

[...]

POSTSCRIPT

I returned to Bijnor briefly in January 1993, less than a month after the destruction of the mosque in Ayodhya. I was curious to learn how it was that Bijnor, like most of western Uttar Pradesh, had remained peaceful, when major riots had occurred throughout the country. The fact that a riot did not occur in this region is especially striking since western Uttar Pradesh was in the eye of the storm: the state in which

Ayodhya is located, where a BJP government had occupied office and then been dismissed by the central government, and all of this amidst growing Hindu–Muslim polarisation. Why then had violence not erupted?

My first observation is drawn from conversations with the Hindu men and women who I had interviewed two years earlier. Although most of them continued to be as militantly anti-Muslim and as chauvinistically Hindu as they had been in the past, they no longer depicted themselves as victims. Once I became aware of this subtle but significant shift in their self perceptions, its underlying logic quickly became evident. The 1990 riot had helped restore these caste Hindus' sense of agency. Perhaps the complicity of the district administration in aiding Hindu groups had dispelled their assumption that the state discriminated against them in favour of Muslims.

The destruction of the mosque at Ayodhya represented a further symbolic victory for caste Hindus—and blow to Muslims—particularly in light of the central government's weak and ineffective response. Ashok Varma commented that the BJP combine had proved that its promises of a temple in Ayodhya had not simply been empty rhetoric; thus, it was no longer necessary for militant Hindu organisations to signal to the BJP leadership their readiness to engage in violence. M. N. Tyagi, a BJP activist who I had interviewed extensively in previous visits, commented: 'There was no riot here this time because we put Muslims in their place. We have found that after a riot, Muslims remain silent for the next eight years.'

What did contribute to some sense of Hindu victimisation was the central government's ban on the Rashtriya Swayamsevak Sangh (RSS) and VHP. However, the sense of victimisation that the ban caused was partially compensated for by the merriment that surrounded discussions of its ineffectiveness. Hindu leaders went underground just after the mosque was destroyed but resurfaced shortly thereafter. Local RSS, VHP and Bajrang Dal leaders had removed sign posts from above their front entrances but otherwise went about their business as usual. 'All a ban means is that we stay inside more', Tyagi commented. 'When someone knocks at the door, I send my son to answer so he can say I am out. That all this ban has meant!'

Another mark of the 'success' of the 1990 riot was that it effectively removed Muslims from Bijnor's political landscape. In August 1991, within six weeks of coming to office, the BJP government took up charges that Arya and Saxena had made months earlier concerning Zafar Khan's alleged misconduct as chair of the nagar palika. Once Aftab was dismissed, he relinquished all political ambitions and maintained a low profile; the same was true of other Muslim leaders.[5]

In electoral terms too, the riot had worked. The BJP candidate won with overwhelming support in the parliamentary elections from the Bijnor constituency in 1991.[6] Mangal Ram Premi won the parliamentary elections in Bijnor with 53 per cent of the popular vote or 2,47,000 votes, a significant increase from the 1,73,977 votes he had received in the 1989 elections. Asha Chaudhury of the Congress (Indira) polled 39,738 votes compared to the 1,10,690 votes she had polled in 1989.

Similarly, all seven BJP candidates from Bijnor won the legislative assembly elections in 1991; the BJP won 47 per cent of the popular votes while the remainder was shared among all the opposition parties. One significant development in 1991 was the shift in political loyalties on the part of Hindu jats towards the BJP, most likely because they resented having been excluded from the list of OBCs who were deemed eligible for reservations in the Mandal recommendations. The Chandpur constituency for the legislative assembly, for example, which had traditionally been strongly identified with Ajit Singh, elected a BJP candidate by a wide margin.

Tidal support for the BJP had also decimated the Bahujan Samaj Party (BSP), and the fledgling alliance it had been constructing between Muslims and scheduled castes. While caste Hindus had voted on communal lines, the Muslim vote had been divided between the Congress and the BSP in part because Zafar Khan and a coterie of his Muslim supporters had left the BSP. Aftab denied the rumour that he had left because the BSP had prevented him from contesting the elections and alleged that the BSP had not been sufficiently active in assisting Muslims after the riot. However the BSP's actions might be judged, an additional deterrent to Muslims' voting for the BSP might well have been that at best the BSP's influence was limited to the state level, while the dangers Muslims were experiencing were national in scope. Moreover, several observers commented that while the riot prompted a large Hindu turnout, to achieving domination through electoral means, it had the opposite effect on Muslims, who stayed away from the polls out of fear.

However, some positive lessons might also be derived from the absence of a riot in 1992. The local press reported on events in Ayodhya in 1992 in a much more responsible fashion than it had in 1990. Of even greater significance was the role of the district administration in taking effective preventative action. The district magistrate who was posted in Bijnor was a south Indian and the additional district magistrate a Muslim; they had learned from what the district magistrate characterised as the administration's appalling conduct during the 1990 riot. Thus, he undertook numerous measures that helped prevent the build-up of tensions. With the exception of some conflict in the Nagina locality, these measures were largely successful: upon learning of the destruction of the mosque in Ayodhya, he immediately called in the army; Muslims were undoubtedly relieved to see the Central Reserve Police Force rather than the hated PAC posted in their mohallas. He also declared a curfew in selected parts of the town, made some preventive arrests, and required that all arms be deposited in his office. Efforts were also made to closely involve both the Hindu and Muslim communities in peace-keeping efforts by organising meetings in various mohallas, posting Hindu and Muslim citizens alongside the armed forces on picket lines, and meeting with Muslims to reassure them that this time, they could trust the administration. Certain small, symbolic measures appeared to be quite effective. For example, a mosque in the town was damaged, presumably by some Hindu groups. The administration asked caste Hindus to pay to have it repaired and ensured that a builder would be on hand throughout the day and night to repair other damaged mosques or temples before they generated tension. Officials roamed the towns in cars with loud speakers that issued reports reassuring people that the administration was closely monitoring the situation.

It is not necessary to accord the state exclusive responsibility for the 1990 riot in Bijnor by acknowledging that if it had taken such simple-measures earlier, it might have prevented a major riot from taking place in Bijnor. Nor should the nature of state intervention distract us from the forces at work within civil society that have heralded the growth of an increasingly violent, polarised, communal society. Indeed, the very recognition that riots can be willed serves as a reminder of how purposefully violence is used by particular groups to attain particular objectives: not primordial, but rational; not mainly economic, but more often political; and yet not born simply of the desire to dominate, but also by feelings of powerlessness and victimisation.

Notes

1. Estimates of casualties vary widely. Official estimates, according to Raj Kumar, the current district magistrate, are: 87 persons killed, 127 injured (of which 42 were identified as serious injuries and 85 as simple injuries) and 1,038 cases of arson and looting. Kumar noted that the previous district magistrate had reported only 36 people killed; after he had been replaced, many more people had come forward and filed reports. The district magistrate had no record of how these figures broke down by religious community. However, all unofficial estimates, including those of militant Hindu nationalists, report much higher casualties, mostly among Muslims. Nandaji, the *pracharak* (propagandist [eds]) of the RSS in Bijnor, estimates that 14 Hindus and 184 Muslims were killed. According to J. B. L. Sharma, a reporter for the *Dainik Jagran* who toured Bijnor right after the riots, 75 Hindus and 225 Muslims were killed and 400–500 people were injured.

2. *The Bijnor Times*, 21 October 1990, 4.

3. Another example of the way in which scholarly biases against Muslims are manifest is found in the tendency for works which proport to address the problem of communalism in India to confine their attention to Muslim communalism as if Hindu communalism was non-existent.

4. An alternative spelling is *bail-gadi.* [eds]

5. Arya and Aftab are pseudonyms for local politicians in Bijnor and were rivals in the municipal council politics. Zafar Khan was the Chairman in the local municipal council and Abhay Saxena was the local VHP president.

6. In the Bijnor parliamentary elections, the BJP won with 47 per cent of the vote; the remaining votes were divided between the BSP, Congress (I), and the Communist Party of India (Marxist). In the Bijnor legislative assembly elections, the BJP won with 53 per cent of the vote, while the BSP followed with 41 per cent of the vote.

37

THE BIJNOR RIOTS, OCTOBER 1990*

Collapse of a Mythical Special Relationship?

ROGER JEFFERY AND PATRICIA M. JEFFERY

[...]

In this chapter, we set out our understanding of the sequence of events in August–November, 1990, and how the violence was perceived locally. A secondary aim is to begin to explore some possible longer-term implications, both locally and nationally.

[...]

LOCAL EXPLANATIONS FOR THE TROUBLES

Outside Trouble-makers

One common set of explanations was that the violence was caused by outsiders—Hindu 'communalists' or 'secularists', later unspecified outsiders. Immediately before the August incidents, there had been a Bajrang Dal convention in Bijnor, with their bunting spread over the main roads, and they were accused of inciting the attempt to build a temple in Bijnor town in such a provocative place. The most obvious whipping boy for the events in October was Mulayam Singh. After his rally on 9 October, a *Bijnor Times* editorial asserted that there were riots wherever such meetings had been held. Other outsiders were also implicated. In the reports of the worst rioting (30 Octobcr—2 November), a *Bijnor Times* headline on 3 November said that 'most of those arrested were from outside', people from Moradabad and as far away as Bihar, claiming they had relatives in Bijnor but unable to give their names or addresses. The new senior superintendent of police told the press that the trouble had been caused by outsiders, some of whom 'spoiled the minds of local people' (*Bijnor Times*, 5 November 1990). The local administration also acted on this theory, cutting access to the town from outside during thc riots, and refusing permission for politicians (including the local member of Parliament) to tour the riot-affected areas in the immediate aftermath.

---

* *Economic and Political Weekly* 29 (10): 551–58 (5 March 1994).

State Negligence or Active Encouragement of Violence

Local Muslim accounts usually blame the local police for conniving at the holding of the provocative march on 30 October. The superintendent of police is said to have ignored the district magistrate's ban on demonstrations; if so, he must have known that a riot was the almost inevitable outcome. When the fighting was underway, outside paramilitary police—especially the Provisional Armed Constabulary (PAC)—joined in with the worst attacks on Muslims. Others—including some Hindus—agreed that the major troubles coincided with the arrival of the PAC on the evening of 30 October. Many shops were burnt and looted; to begin with, those owned by Hindus in the centre of town, but as the PAC gained more control, shops owned by Muslims in other areas were targeted. When it was announced that five more people had died on 4 November, we were told that the PAC were trying to terrorise the population so that there would be no trouble when they lifted the curfew. Or as a prominent politician's son put it, 'the ordinary police loot for 363 days in the year and the PAC try to make the best of the two or three days they are given'.

Local Hindus made equivalent charges against the local administration's role until the outside police were called in. At that time, the district magistrate in Bijnor and the divisional commissioner (based in Moradabad) were both yadavs and regarded as tools of Mulayam Singh's policies; and Javed Aftab (with no force at his disposal, but considerable influence) was regarded as in the same camp. The *Bijnor Times* reports a series of complaints about the inefficiency of the administration in dealing with the arson and looting after Mulayam Singh's rally. But throughout October, the Bharatiya Janata Party (BJP), the Vishva Hindu Parishad (VHP), Bajrang Dal, Shiv Sena and the Rashtriya Swayamsevak Sangh (RSS) leaders and members (all, of course, Hindus) were being arrested, claiming injured innocence, and then being released on conditional bail.

As with the 'outsiders' argument, 'blaming the state' allows both sides to claim that they have no serious differences with locals from the other community. The 'basic' disputes are seen as 'political' (in the pejorative sense) and externally motivated (the BJP led conflict with the local administration and then the paramilitary police Muslim conflict) rather than resulting from endogenous cultural or economic differences.[1]

'Aggressive Muslims' versus 'Provocative Hindus'

One alternative discourse does locate the blame on local people. It is not entirely coherent, but it has a series of elements which collectively make sense to local people. To begin with, ethnic stereotypes abound, and are long and deeply held. Day-to-day relationships between members of different groups have distinct limits. We were continually surprised at how little our Muslim friends knew about common features of daily life amongst Hindus, and vice-versa. One example: in 1982, Patricia hosted a hilarious session at which Muslim and Hindu women discussed the relative advantages and disadvantages of 'dhoti-kurta' (worn by Hindu women) and 'shalwar-kamiz' (worn by Muslim women) for discrete defecation in the jungle and for avoiding sexual advances. She realised that the Hindu women did not know that there are latrines in the Muslim village. Amicable economic relationships—as employees, clients, trading partners—are restricted to these activities; very few men or women move easily across caste and communal boundaries into friendship, let alone kinship. The major taboo area is sexuality; elopements which are intra-caste can be handled relatively easily, affecting only the honour of the girl's family; cross-caste or cross-religious liaisons are potential dynamite.[2]

People in the north Indian countryside use a variety of different markers as symbols of the basic and essential difference between different groups—castes and religions. As outsiders, we were continually asked questions which seemed designed to find out if we were more 'like' one group or the other. These range from clothing (saris versus shalwar-kamiz) and colour preferences (saffron versus green) through eating styles (separate *thalis* versus sharing a common plate; respecting vegetarianism versus preferring meat; avoiding beef versus avoiding pork); attitudes to alcohol; marriage patterns (clan- and village-exogamy among Hindus versus a tolerance of 'close-kin' marriage and village endogamy among Muslims, seen by Hindus as marrying one's 'sisters') to kinds of religion (polytheism and idolatry versus a religion of the Book) and funeral practice (cremation versus burial). These can be manifested in apparently trivial ways: one abiding memory is from 1982, when we were infested with bed-bugs. The differing slanderous explanations we were given all hinged on which of our varied guests had low standards of hygiene and were thus most likely to have brought the bed-bugs with them.[3]

These ethnic markers of course co-exist with many similarities in diet and clothing, with shared class-based practices and even with the presence of members of one religion in the religious rituals and sacred sites of the other. We do not wish to give priority to signs and symbols of difference over those of similarity; but to point out that sets of cultural codes are available if people want to foreground difference rather than similarity. When people explain or justify inter-communal hostility, they give general differences more forceful interpretations. Each side can produce a closed or circular account which creates a hostile, frightening 'Other' to justify pre-emptive strikes or violence in response.

We were given one chilling example one day soon after the curfew was lifted in November 1990, when we returned to a jat-dominated village where we were carrying out research. Seated in the brahmin doctor's clinic, we were given a powerful account of the 'Hindu' argument by supporters of the BJP (hardly surprising, given their use of *Dainik Jagran* as their daily newspaper).[4] Hindus, we were told, are soft-hearted, whereas all Muslims are hard-hearted—as witness, their willingness to sacrifice animals at Eid. Muslims would even cut off women's breasts; Hindus would never do that. In this view, Muslim toughness explains why there is only trouble where there are a lot of Muslims, and why only Muslims have fire-arms; why Muslim kings knocked down temples, but Hindu kings never knocked down mosques. For these supporters of the BJP, Muslims have lost their rights to protest: they had no right to attack the procession on 30 October (no matter what may have been chanted) because there was no trouble when the Muslims took out a procession for the Prophet's birthday on 3 October. Muslims have forfeited their right to protection under Indian law because they raise slogans in favour of a second Pakistan in India (as well as supporting the Pakistani cricket and hockey teams against the Indian one); and because they forced changes in the law (on maintenance for divorced wives, after the Shah Bano case) rather than obey it. The violence was organised by Javed, and when he was arrested, the police found a bomb factory, stengun and rocket-launcher.[5] The only Muslim houses burned were those between two Hindu houses being burned by Muslims. Only Hindus would protect isolated or vulnerable Muslims (from whom?); in similar circumstances, they said, Muslims would kill Hindus. Muslims are symbols of the 'alien' invaders whose coming led to 700 years of subordination for Hindus. Even the man who had been the Congress Party organiser in the village suggested that the PAC should be let loose to produce a 'final' solution: all Muslims should leave for Pakistan, be killed, or convert to Hinduism if they want to stay in India. These men seemed convinced of the BJP arguments that Muslims either started the trouble, or deserved what they got.

Muslim accounts stressed how Hindus, backed up by the might of the police, taunted Muslims through slogans and hostile marches. Muslims portrayed themselves as valiant in the face of overwhelming odds, or as victims. Muslims were not responsible for the riots, but whether or not they stood up against provocation by people like the Shiv Sena, the police (and especially the PAC) connived in violence in order to be able to attack Muslims, their homes and their property. Muslims claimed that the Hindu marchers on the morning of 30 October were not only allowed to take a provocative procession through Muslim areas, but after they were attacked and ran away, they were persuaded by members of the PAC to go back again, in order to create more serious trouble.[6] Muslims provided their own tales of isolated Hindus protected in numerically dominant Muslim areas; and of Hindu atrocities to match Muslim ones. Some of the accounts from Muslims, however, were willing to differentiate Hindus by caste and economic interest: at a crude level, urban brahmin and banias were regarded as 'soft', unlike rural jats and rajputs. But for most Muslims, independent India is really a Hindu-raj (it is, after all, as often called Hindustan as it is Bharat), which systematically excludes Muslims from the benefits to which they are entitled; and in Uttar Pradesh, Hindus use their control over the PAC to enforce their will, whoever is in power in Lucknow.

Organised by Muslims

The idea that the troubles were 'organised' also appeared in the *Bijnor Times* on several occasions; unravelling the code in which newspaper reports are written, we think it meant that the riots were organised by Muslims, and we spoke to many ordinary Hindus who accepted this version of events. Originally, the *Bijnor Times* argued that 'no-one thought that the minority community would get involved' (31 October 1990), but the next day it argued that the bombs, arms and stones had all been collected in advance and that the attack on the procession singing 'holy songs' was pre-planned. Blame was allocated through a series of questions. Why did the police first have to fire at the upper storey of Irshad's house? Why else were the first shops set light those of Hindus in a Muslim mohalla, and why were people first attacked with swords and set alight there?

> These things must have all been prepared in advance, they could not have come suddenly. All of these were done in mohallas where the minority community lives and where there are elements stirring up partiality between Hindus and Muslims (*Bijnor Times*, 1 November 1990).

'Elements stirring up partiality' may be code for 'those close to Javed'; the *Bijnor Times* also reported that Muslims made their most concerted attack on the police immediately after Javed was arrested, in an attempt to get him released.

A Jat Plot

We also have more nuanced accounts from those standing on the side. In particular, they suggest that people were acting not only as Hindus, but also as members of specific caste groups. Dhimars told us that there was only trouble in large jat-dominated villages. In their view, jats were using the Ayodhya dispute in an attempt to reassert their traditional authority in the face of 'uppity' lower Hindu castes, Harijans and Muslims. Some self-proclaimed neo-Buddhist chamars gave us a similar account: that the mandir–masjid dispute was not their argument, since they would not pray in either. As chamars, they were not treated with respect by Hindus and indeed were still excluded from one of the local temples.[7] In this perspective, jats were leaping on the Ayodhya bandwagon as a way to pull chamars into a Hindu pogrom on Muslims, one which would do nothing beneficial for the chamars.

EXPLANATIONS OF TROUBLES: OUTSIDER PERSPECTIVES

Like Gyan Pandey (1991), we would suggest that all these accounts may have something of the truth in them, but separately they are too simple. To say that 'Bijnor City was famous for peace and brotherhood but today, suddenly, riots started on a large-scale' (*Bijnor Times*, 31 October 1990); to blame outsiders; or to pass the riots off as momentary madness, are clearly too conveniently aimed at removing responsibility from the shoulders of all locals and encouraging a return to 'normal' life which does not look too closely at local causes. Using anti-Muslim stereotypes seemingly exonerates the Hindus, but makes little sense of the numbers of Hindus reported (even by the *Bijnor Times*) to have been injured while making bombs, or the attacks on the mosques.

Blaming the jats makes them out to be more significant in the towns than they really are. Despite the evidence of preparations made by 'organised groups', clearly far more local people were involved than just the hard-line supporters of Javed or the members of the Sangh parivar. It seems likely that the escalating violence grew out of pre-existing negative stereotypes, which were fertile soil on which mutual fear and distrust could grow (Spencer 1990). The stereotypes and rumours justify retaliation, leading to further incidents cited as confirmation of the original rumours and stereotypes.

Certainly the arrival of the *kar sevaks* gave an amazing fillip to longer-term attempts by the Sangh parivar to encourage its base, particularly among the urban, upper-caste, Hindu middle classes into becoming more active. One element in the Bijnor riots was the ending of Bijnor's semi-isolation from the mainstream of national affairs. Some of this was a unique feature of the events of 1990, for which Bijnor was suddenly strategically placed. With its important Ganges rail and road bridges (the latter only 10 km from Bijnor town), and its northern border (the Shivaliks) it was one of many convenient points for the administration to try to stop people getting to Ayodhya. The success of the BJP strategy—drawing activists from all over north India into the attempt to reach Ayodhya—and the aggressive response of the Uttar Pradesh government combined to create a highly volatile situation in Bijnor. The events of 20 August, 9 October, and then the firing, attacks on kar sevaks, demonstrations and protest marches on 28–29 October 'disrupted everyday order', making it possible for rumour and fear 'to dominate people's perceptions of the world' (Spencer 1990: 615–16).

Many supporters of the VHP and BJP expressed a strong sense of injustice, which drew 'upright citizens' into unprecedented activity. One example is the frequency with which, as we have seen, women were prominent in the demonstrations of 28–30 October. Similarly, the tacit or active support of Mulayam Singh may have encouraged Muslim leaders to more provocative acts. But it is not clear whether these were the same people as those who threw bombs, set fire to houses, or led the PAC to areas of Muslim residence.[8]

We should note two forms of economic and cultural explanation which we have not yet fully considered. As Pandey (1991: 565) points out, much writing about riots by those on the 'left' looks for economic interests as the 'real causes' lying behind the incidents which apparently spark communal violence. We do not know enough about the economic niches of the different groups in Bijnor town to comment on the extent to which there is cooperation and competition in the various markets for labour and trade. Such knowledge as we have is insufficient to say whether or not particular economic categories were targeted by mobs. It may be that in the course of the riots, Hindu moneylenders or rapacious traders were targeted by Muslims, and rising Muslim merchants saw their investments destroyed by people working as agents for established Hindus. But we have no reports from Bijnor which suggest a targeting of violence other than on the basis of a simple religious identification.

The major cultural concept, used by locals and by some observers to explain the violence of the emotions involved, is '*izzat*' (honour, respect) and people's conceptions of themselves as worthy and respected. Collective taunting is a way of enhancing one's own izzat at the cost of the other; and one obvious effect is to exaggerate and increase the unity of those being taunted. Humiliations of one kind or another are often cited among the antecedents of rioting and the form of some of the violence that results often seems bent on humiliating the 'Other', not merely on killing, burning or looting (Spencer 1990). The tussle over Ayodhya is, in large part, seen locally as a matter of izzat; if the temple is built, Hindus across north India will feel a sense of pride, a previous wrong will have been redressed and their izzat will be enhanced; while the mosque stands, Muslims can feel they still have some izzat left. Such an argument may account for the cultural terms in which hostility and competition are expressed, or the importance of violence against women; but concern for izzat does not necessarily mean that the other must be disgraced. In one of our research villages, for example, there was much criticism of the jat who attacked a Muslim visitor, on the grounds that the izzat of the village required that a guest should be treated properly. More generally, people who offered their protection to those in a minority in a particular village may say that they are acting to maintain their izzat. Explaining only the riots in terms of izzat, then, is inadequate.

LONGER-TERM PROSPECTS

Of these local and outsider perspectives, none seems totally satisfactory, though all may have a part to play in explaining what happened in the short term (August–November 1990). Possibly, the short term is all that matters, and these events are only of passing significance. Maybe, for chance reasons of location, a particular conjunction of external influences impinged on Bijnor, a town 'waiting for riots to happen'. A state chief minister attempted to weld together a political alliance of 'backward castes' and Muslims, feeding into and enhancing a period of militancy among some Hindus over the Ayodhya disputed site. Bijnor was one among many places where these factors interacted in mutually reinforcing ways, and may be unlikely to recur.

Clearly, however, the short term must be extended at least up to the 1991 national and state elections. In Bijnor, as in most of the rest of western Uttar Pradesh, the Congress and the Janata Dal collapsed. In the Bijnor Lok Sabha election, there was no alliance against the BJP; the Bahujan Samaj Party, the Communist Party of India (Marxist) and the Congress (I) divided 48 per cent of the vote between them, so the BJP won with 47 per cent of the total. In the Vidhan Sabha election for the Bijnor seat, a tacit anti-BJP strategy gave the BSP 41 per cent of the vote, but the BJP won by a clear margin with 53 per cent. The BJP's core of urban middle-class Hindus, especially shop-keepers, lawyers and teachers, was able to attract rich and middle peasant jats, gujjars and rajputs—for whom the history of the past 20 years has been one of steady reduction in prestige and in their rights over their social inferiors. The growing urban middle class is in part being recruited from these same jats and rajputs, so these are not entirely separate groups.[9]

Some have argued that the success of the BJP is purely temporary and that it will succumb to the same problems of factional infighting and an inability to be all things to all people, as with all the other Indian political parties (Misra 1992). Clearly, keeping jat farmers and bania jewellers (for instance) in the same camp will not be an easy task. In Bijnor, the key to future electoral success lies with the jatavs (chamars) and other scheduled castes; with 20 per cent of the district population, they were being wooed from both sides. As one jat ex-Congress election agent put it, the trouble with the jatavs was that they did not know which way to vote, like the proverbial dhobi's dog (*'dhobi ka kutta, na ghar ka na ghat ka'*). The BJP's 1991 victory in Bijnor may indeed be short-lived.

Nonetheless, this political shift could be a sign of the decay of an old order and its replacement by a new one. The Bijnor riots may be a *crise revelatrice* of a moment of transition, of the collapse of one system of regulated violence in Bijnor and the absence, as yet, of its replacement (Bastian 1990: 289). ...

The revitalisation of militant Hinduism seems to be the key to the BJP's chances of keeping a simple identification of all Hindus as the 'us' referred to above. Until recently, there were no mass-based national organisations of Hindus. Hinduism might have been defined by outsiders as a cohesive religion; to its adherents, it was a set of household beliefs which varied by caste and region (Thapar 1989). Temples have little day-to-day significance in the lives of most people in rural Bijnor; the temple priesthood is unimportant and regarded cynically by most. Now, across much of north India, a more unified sense of Hinduism has emerged, fostered by phenomenally popular TV screenings of the Ramayana and the Mahabharata. The VHP has sponsored this so-called semitisation of Hinduism, and has used a variety of symbols—Kashmir, Punjab, Ram Janmabhoomi—to harness these forces in political mobilisation using practical actions (such as the transmission of the Ram Jyoti flames, 'shilanyas' bricks, and 'asthi kalash', as well as kar seva itself). Religious leaders have created modern bureaucratic structures (local groups, newsletters, books) to encourage allegiance to a set of behavioural ideals. But the appeal of the 'religion as belief' elements in this transformation is quite narrowly restricted. Most supporters of both the political and confessional forms of Hinduism are urban, high-caste, and well-educated. Western Uttar Pradesh Hindus (especially jats and rajputs) are notorious for their low level of interest in organised religion; but that does not weaken their commitment to 'religion as identity'. All the complex issues which inform national politics (Shah Bano, Ayodhya, Mandal) were interpreted by the jats we knew in anti-Muslim or anti-chamar terms. Ayodhya provided an opportunity to threaten and beat Muslims, to lower their izzat and demand their subservience.[10]

In town and countryside alike, Muslims are losing the battles for education and jobs. Organised industry is still weak in Bijnor, but the town's role as an administrative, legal and educational centre is bringing in more educated Hindus from the surrounding rural areas and from elsewhere in the state. Figures for the communal distribution of the district urban population for 1991 are not yet published, but they will probably show the continuation of a trend of a rising Muslim percentage, up from 61 per cent in 1951 to 66 per cent in 1981. Muslims have, until recently, been unable to translate their numbers into the ability to influence school and college admissions or appointments to local jobs—in the sugar mills, local government, nationalised industries, schools and colleges. Javed and his supporters claim that the municipality would be suspended or packed with opponents if he systematically tried to do this. Muslims increasingly see their numbers as their only resource, and this only gives them control over the town council. But playing the 'numbers game' gives the BJP a further stick for beating Muslims, claiming this is evidence of both a Muslim plot to take over the country by out-breeding Hindus, and a lack of commitment to the national progress that could follow if population growth were brought under control.

Our sense is that Muslims see themselves as standing up for themselves in almost the only way available to them—by stressing their Islamic identities. We witnessed missionary activities by supporters of the Tablighi-Jamaat as they exhorted Muslims to cleanse their lives of Hindu-like practices. Islamic education is flourishing as never before, and on the outskirts of Bijnor is a Muslim Fund Bank building. Like all new, visible, Muslim endeavours, it is rumoured to have been funded by Saudis, or at least from money sent back by migrant workers in the Gulf. Young Muslims in particular are increasingly denying the old style of accommodation to a dominant non-Muslim political order. They are trading in the 'weapons of the weak' and replacing them with a rhetoric of demands for rights and entitlements in the face of manifest discrimination and exclusion.

It is not just Muslim youth who are discontented; there are also growing numbers of disillusioned young Hindu and Jatav men, educated and articulate but with nowhere to go. These young men are said to be running out of control and turning to violence or other forms of immorality (crime, drunkenness) which threaten public order. This is often expressed through reference to the deteriorating 'mahol' (atmosphere). Women are seen as increasingly vulnerable. Attacks on women were often reported during the riots. Even before that, Muslim girls, who have to pass the boys' intermediate college on their way to the girls' degree college, were being taunted to say '*Jai Shri Ram*' in place of the Islamic greeting, '*A-salaam-alaikum*' or the more neutral '*namaste*' or '*namaskar*'. In April 1991, as Eid approached and the election campaign began to hot up, we were told that the district magistrate had announced that he would not consider himself responsible for anything which might happen to any woman out on the streets, until several days after Eid was over. The 'atmosphere' now inhibits parents from allowing their girls to go beyond the village or town for schooling or for medical care, and makes people worried about sending new brides off to their in-laws in their wedding jewellery. At the very least, it is hard to see how more rigid communal divisions can benefit women; they are much more likely to suffer from everyday symbolic attacks and experience greater seclusion (under the guise of protection) and possibly earlier marriage in response.

Our prognosis for the future of communal relations in Bijnor is thus not a good one. Bijnor seems likely to experience the 'criminalisation of politics' which is characteristic of the larger Uttar Pradesh towns. Within the nascent form of democracy, 'ethnic politics and collective violence (are) an integral component' (Tambiah 1990: 758). Despite the fact of close interrelationships on a daily basis, people are increasingly seeing themselves and others in 'communal' terms. The violence of 1990 has reinforced this process. Neither side really allows the other the legitimacy required for more substantial accommodation, and there are fewer and fewer institutions which bridge the communal divide. In our view, Muslims will continue to suffer most from this 'crisis of governability'—from those entrusted with the governing as well as from those who benefit most from the status quo.[11]

NOTES

1. For accounts of the extent to which the PAC in Uttar Pradesh has treated Muslims in the neighbouring district towns of Moradabad in 1980 and Meerut in 1987, see Akbar 1988; *The Business and Political Observer*, 26 December 1990, 3; and Saberwal and Hasan 1991.

2. We have cases from our own field notes where intra-caste liaisons hardly raise more than gossip; intra-religious ones which were handled with censure on the girl's parents for not maintaining better control and possibly with the removal of the young man for a while; and inter-religious ones which required full panchayats and extended negotiations to keep the peace.

3. Of course, religious caricatures are not the only ones which circulate: caste-based stereotypes are also legion. In almost any dispute, the opposing party may be said to manifest characteristics of his or her particular sub-caste, village or urban residence, education or class position, and (or instead of) their religious identification. Further, as Barth (1969) theorised, and many others have noted, the content of the differences between such categories may appear trivial to an outsider.

4. Pandey (1991: 566–67) reproduces a list of points made in a leaflet which was circulating in Bhagalpur in 1989–90 which makes all these points, and some more we regularly heard in Bijnor (such as the relative population growth rates). As he argues, Muslim men are often identified with 'aggression, conversions, and unbounded sexuality' (566). Kakar (1990) argues these are 'disavowed aspects' of Hindu identity. We have no similar accounts in the academic literature of whether (and if so, how) Muslims displace onto Hindus 'disavowed aspects' of their identities.

5. Among the many rumours about Javed's involvement was that the police found 15 abducted Hindu women in his house when he was arrested.

6. This account is strikingly similar to Brass's account of the political interpretation of communal riots by Muslim leaders in the mid-1960s (Brass 1974: 218).

7. The riots in Delhi on 15 November 1990 were said to be provoked by a 'peace march' which brought together Muslims, Sikhs and dalits and raised anti-Hindu slogans (*Frontline*, 8–21 December 1990: 111–15; Engineer 1991a: 157). Some reports of the rioting in Patna, Bihar also stressed a realignment of 'backward castes' (notably, yadavs) who protected Muslims from attack (*India Today*, 15 December 1990: 44–46. See also *India Today*, 31 December 1990: 88–94).

8. We can get a hint of which kinds of people were involved in the violence from the reports of households where bomb-making equipment was found (usually as a result of a bomb going off accidentally). In mid-October, the *Bijnor Times* gave some details of two houses—one with a Shiv Sena member, the other the house of a market trader. In one of our research villages, bombs were found in the house of a very substantial jat farmer (owing 35 acres) who also rents out buildings used as a country alcohol shop, tea stall, etc., on the main road. One of his sons also attacked a Muslim visiting someone in the village.

9. The jats of one of our research villages defected from Congress well before the election. More than a dozen young jat men had been arrested on 22 October as members of the Shiv Sena; and 18 of them went into the local town to court arrest on 29 October. Of these youths (10 aged under 20, only two aged more than 24) who went to court arrest, most (16) were middle or small peasants, expecting to inherit four acres or less; only two were from wealthier families. Three were married; the rest single. All but two had completed high school (eighth class). Elsewhere, as far as we could ascertain, brahmins, jats and at least as far 'down' the caste hierarchy as the sahnis voted for the BJP; and even some jatavs had put their names down as members of the Shiv Sena.

10. Banerjee (1991) captures much of the spirit of the appeal of the BJP and its allies for many urban and rural middle- or upper-caste Hindus in Bijnor; Engineer (1991b) presents a view of how Muslims respond to these attacks.

11. Das (1990: 24) notes that according to official figures, in the 1950s, 86 per cent of those killed in riots were Muslims; that during the more recent riots of the 1980s, more people are killed in police violence than in communal clashes; and the number of Muslims killed by the police is larger than the number of Hindus.

REFERENCES

Akbar, M. A. 1988. *Riot after Riot: Reports on Caste and Communal Violence in India.* New Delhi: Penguin Books.

Banerjee, S. 1991. 'Hindutva—Ideology and Social Psychology'. *Economic and Political Weekly* 26 (3), 97–101.

Barth, F., ed. 1969. *Ethnic Groups and Boundaries.* Boston: Little, Brown and Company.

Bastian, S. 1990. 'Political Economy of Ethnic Violence in Sri Lanka: The July 1983 Riots', in *Mirrors of Violence*, ed. V. Das. New Delhi: Oxford University Press, 286–304.

Brass, P. R. 1974. *Language, Religion and Politics in North India.* London: Cambridge University Press.

Das, V. 1990. 'Introduction: Communities, Riots and Survivors', in *Mirrors of Violence*, ed. V. Das. New Delhi: Oxford University Press, 1–36.

Engineer, A. A. 1991a. 'The Bloody Trail: Ramjanmabhoomi and Communal Violence in UP'. *Economic and Political Weekly* 26 (4), 155–59.

____. 1991b. 'Remaking Indian Muslim Identity'. *Economic and Political Weekly* 26 (20), 1036–38.

Kakar, S. 1990. 'Some Unconscious Aspects of Ethnic Violence in India', in *Mirrors of Violence*, ed. V. Das. New Delhi: Oxford University Press, 135–45.

Misra, A. 1992. 'Uttar Pradesh: BJP Gains by Default'. *Economic and Political Weekly* 27 (8), 393–94.

Pandey, G. 1991. 'In Defence of the Fragment: Writing about Hindu-Muslim Riots in India Today'. *Economic and Political Weekly* 26 (11–12), 559–72.

Saberwal, Satish, and Mushirul Hasan. 1991. 'Moradabad Riots 1980: Causes and Meanings', in *Communal Riots in Post-Independence India*, ed. Asghar Ali Engineer. Hyderabad: Sangam Books, 209–27.

Spencer, J. 1990. 'Collective Violence and Everyday Practice in Sri Lanka'. *Modern Asian Studies* 24 (3), 603–23.

Tambiah, S. J. 1990. 'Reflections on Communal Violence in South Asia'. *Journal of Asian Studies* 49 (4), 741–60.

Thapar, R. 1989. 'Imagined Religious Communities? Ancient History and the Modern Search for a Hindu Identity'. *Modern Asian Studies* 23 (2), 209–31.

38

HASHIMPURA KILLINGS*

Is there any Hope of Justice?

IQBAL ANSARI

Is there any hope that those found guilty of the violence and killings in Hashimpura in 1987 will ever be brought to justice? The sequence of legal proceedings to date does not inspire much confidence in the justice system.[1]

The chief judicial magistrate, Ghaziabad continued issuing bailable and then non-bailable warrants against the 19 Provincial Armed Constabulary (PAC) men who faced charges of murdering 40 Muslims of Hashimpura (Meerut) in 1987, 23 times between January 1997 and April 2000. They were never arrested and produced before the court, though all along this period they were in active service with known postings and residential addresses. At the end of May and early June 2000, 16 of the accused surrendered and got bail. The trial court fixed dates in September, October and December 2000 for framing of charges, for which the government counsel was not prepared. On 13 December, the Crime Branch-Criminal Investigation Department (CBCID) submitted that it wanted time for appointing a Special Public Prosecutor. The case has been adjourned for 25 January 2001.

This sequence of legal proceedings can hardly inspire confidence in the aggrieved parties and the public that justice will be done in the case.

On 22 May 1987, during curfew in Meerut in Uttar Pradesh, the PAC picked up several hundred innocent Muslims, mostly youth, from their homes and took them away in trucks, while there was no rioting in that area of the city. A few days later, about 40 dead bodies of some of those arrested were found floating in the upper Ganga Canal in Murad Nagar, district Ghaziabad. Inquiry reports by reputed journalists like Nikhil Chakravarty and Kuldip Nayar, and organisations like the People's Union for Civil Liberties (PUCL) and the People's Union for Democratic Rights (PUDR) revealed that it was a case of barbaric cold-blooded murder by the PAC personnel. Nikhil Chakravarty compared the event with 'Nazi Pogrom against the Jews, to strike terror and nothing but terror in a whole minority community'.

* *Economic and Political Weekly* 35 (52): 4601–02 (30 December 2000).

The Amnesty International's inquiry report observed that 'there is evidence to suggest that members of the PAC have been responsible for dozens of extra judicial killings and disappearances' (AJ Index: ASA 20/06/87). In a joint statement, eminent persons including I. K. Gujral, Rajindar Sachar, Kuldip Nayar, Subhadra Joshi and Badr-Ud-Din Tyabji demanded that 'the government must prosecute all those who have disgraced their uniforms. Their misdeeds must be treated at par with treason and tried by special courts.' The government of Uttar Pradesh ordered an inquiry into the ghastly incident by the CBCID. A thorough inquiry report was submitted by the CBCID in February 1994 in which 66 PAC-Police personnel of all ranks were indicted.

A writ petition (no. 1379 of 1995 MIB) was filed by Jamaluddin and others of Meerut on 15 February 1995 before the Lucknow Bench of the Allahabad High Court for making the report public, prosecuting all those indicted and payment of adequate compensation to victims. The government of Uttar Pradesh filed cases against only 19 PAC men of lower rank in the court of Chief Judicial Magistrate (CJM) Ghaziabad on 20 May 1996 under sections 374/307/302/201 of the IPC (case no. 1267/96). In the counter-affidavit filed on 13 March 1997 in the High Court, the CBCID admitted that 'the remaining detenues were taken in the PAC truck URU 1493 to the Hindon Canal (Village Makanpur) and the Platoon Commander and PAC men shot them dead'. Para 10 of the affidavit states that 'it is submitted that the incident and human rights violations not denied'.

In spite of this background of admission of guilt, the following is the sequence of proceedings in the law courts at Ghaziabad from May 1996 till October 2000. The accused were never arrested and produced before the court, although they were all along serving members of the PAC whose posting and home addresses were known even after issuance of bailable warrants six times between 31 January 1997 and 16 February 1998 and of non-bailable warrants 17 times between 20 April 1998 and 29 April 2000 by the CJM Ghaziabad. On 16 February 1999, the CJM had also ordered for proceedings to be taken against the accused under sections 82/83 CrPC for declaring them absconders and for confiscation of their properties. During those five years of the pendency of the case, the lack of will on the part of the successive governments of Uttar Pradesh is matched by equal lack of interest by the Muslim organisations, the Human Rights groups and the media. Things, however, started moving after this writer personally visited Meerut and Ghaziabad in May 1999 to collect papers related to the case. Subsequently in a meeting convened by the Minorities Council on 7 July 1999, a decision was taken that the council in cooperation with other organisations willing to lend support, including PUCL, would pursue the cases in the Lucknow High Court and Ghaziabad CJM's Court. I also published an article under the title 'Forgotten Massacre or Hashimpura case from 1987 till August 1999' in the Autumn 1999 issue of the Quarterly IOS Bulletin *Human Rights Today* that I edit, which made some impact and led to Siddharth Varadarajan of *The Times of India* taking interest in the case, who published a front-page story in *The Times of India* on 17 May 2000 on the bizarre proceedings in the CJM Ghaziabad Court.

That was the time when on our representation, the National Commission for Minorities (NCM) impressed upon the union home minister and the government of Uttar Pradesh to take early measures for payment of adequate compensation and speedy trial. This pressure from the Minorities Council, the NCM and *The Times of India* seems to have forced the state government to realise that it could no longer shield the guilty PAC men. As a consequence of this pressure, 16 of the 19 accused PAC men surrendered in groups in the last week of May 2000 and early June 2000. One accused is absconding and another is reportedly dead. They were refused bail by CJM, Ghaziabad. However they were allowed bail by the district judge R. P. Mishra on the ground that there was no direct evidence against them and that being members of the PAC, there was no chance of their absconding.

Apparently their practically being absconders from January 1997 to May 2000 did not weigh with the learned court while easily allowing bail to all 16 in groups on 2 June 2000 (Bail Application no. 1353/2000), 5 June 2000 (no. 1412/2000), 27 June 2000 (no. 1564/2000) and 4 July 2000 (no. 1620/2000).

None of the 16 PAC men have been suspended from service. On 11 July 2000, the case against these 16 accused PAC men was committed to district judge for trial, who transferred the case to the additional district sessions judge (IV) (Room no. 204) as case no. ST 1362/2000. The case has been adjourned three times for framing of charges against the accused. Charges, however, have not yet been framed. The following order was passed by the learned court, '30.10.2000: Called out. Accused are present. State Counsel is not in a position to open his case for charge. As a last chance fixed December 13, 2000 for charge sd/ Additional session judge.' On 13 December 2000, on the plea of the CBCID, the case has been adjourned for 25 January 2001.

The entire sequence of legal proceedings since the submission of CBCID report in February 1994 till date has been rightly summed up by Siddharth Varadarajan of *The Times of India* in the following words: 'Even by the lethargic and Kafkaesque standards of the Indian judicial system, the Hashimpura case is in a class of its own' (*TOI*, 17 May 2000). Such is the apathy in the Human Rights movement, the press and legislators that except for the PUCL president Ravi Kiran Jain's filling of PIL in the Allahabad High Court in May 2000, no one made it a serious public issue even after the publication of the story in *The Times of India*. The surrendering of 16 accused PAC men and their easily getting bail and the government counsel not being in a position to get charges framed in September–October and the additional district sessions judge (IV) strangely passing order that 13 December 2000 is being fixed as last chance for framing charges, did not become news in national, regional or local newspapers. *The Times of India*, however, after our briefing again published a detailed story on 11 December 2000.

Maulvi Mohd Yameen and others of Meerut had approached the NCM through their representation of 2 April 1997 on which no action was taken. Subsequently, after the Minorities Council's representation of 8 March 1999 and persistent reminders impressing upon the chairman the gravity and uniqueness of the case, the deputy secretary NCM addressed a letter to the chief secretary, government of

Uttar Pradesh on 12 October 1999, which was not further pursued. The present chairman, however, promptly advised the government of Uttar Pradesh, for speedy trial in May 2000, but did not monitor the progress as had been requested by the Minorities Council.

It needs to be noted that at my instance the NCM has requisitioned an official copy of the CBCID report on Hashimpura killings. In its latest letter of 27 November to the chairman, NCM, the Minorities Council has urged the chairman to intervene effectively in the case. Being a case of custodial killings, the Minorities Council sent a representation to the National Human Rights Commission on 2 August 2000, which has remained unacknowledged till date.

Is there any hope that members of state forces guilty of crimes against humanity shall be brought to justice and the next of kin of those killed will get adequate compensation? The government of Uttar Pradesh maintains that the amount of Rs 40,000 it paid for each of those killed is enough. It needs to be kept in mind that Hashimpura is a case of custodial killings by the PAC, not that of killings during riots because of failure of governance as in 1984 in Delhi for which the Delhi High Court awarded compensation of Rs 2 lakh.

NOTE

1. On 31 October 2018, 16 former PAC men were convicted by the Delhi High Court for their role in the massacre. [eds]

Notes on the Authors

Imtiaz Ahmed retired as Professor of Sociology from the Jawaharlal Nehru University, New Delhi.

Iqbal Ansari was Professor of English at the Aligarh Muslim University and a prominent human rights activist.

Amrita Basu is Paino Professor of Political Science and Sexuality, Women's and Gender Studies at Amherst College, Massachusetts, USA.

Ward Berenschot is a researcher at the Royal Netherlands Institute of Southeast Asian and Caribbean Studies (KITLV), Leiden, Netherlands.

Paul R. Brass is Professor Emeritus at the University of Washington, Seattle, USA.

Jan Breman is Emeritus Professor at the University of Amsterdam and Honorary Fellow at the International Institute of Social History, Amsterdam, Netherlands.

Uma Chakravarti taught History at the Miranda House College for Women in Delhi University.

Sudhir Chandra retired as Senior Fellow at the Centre for Social Studies, Surat.

Prem Chowdhury is an independent researcher.

Pradip Datta is Professor, Centre for Political Theory and Comparative Politics, Jawaharlal Nehru University, New Delhi.

A. R. Desai was Professor of Sociology at the University of Mumbai.

Ratna Dutta (later Ratna Naidu) retired as Professor of Sociology at the University of Hyderabad.

Asghar Ali Engineer was a well-known social activist and headed the Centre for the Study of Society and Secularism, Mumbai.

Zoya Hasan is Professor Emeritus,Centre for Political Studies at Jawaharlal Nehru University, New Delhi.

Sasheej Hegde is Professor, Department of Sociology at the University of Hyderabad, Hyderabad.

Patricia M. Jeffery is Professor Emerita in Sociology, Chair of British Association for South Asian Studies, UK.

Roger Jeffery is Professor of Sociology of South Asia at the University of Edinburgh, Edinburgh, UK.

Rajni Kothari was a Senior Fellow at the Centre for the Study of Developing Societies, New Delhi.

Dharma Kumar was a Professor of Economics at the Delhi School of Economics, Delhi University.

Gopal Krishna, formerly a member of the faculty at the Centre for the Study of Developing Societies, Delhi.

Shail Mayaram is Professor at the Centre for the Study of Developing Societies, Delhi.

Bhavna Mehta is Professor of Social Work, Faculty of Social Work at the Maharaja Sayajirao University of Baroda, Vadodara.

Badri Narayan is Professor and Director at the G. B. Pant Social Science Institute, Allahabad.

Gyanendra Pandey is the Arts and Sciences Distinguished Professor of History at the Emory College of Arts and Sciences, Atlanta, Georgia, USA.

Biswamoy Pati was a historian who taught for many years at Sri Venkateshwara College in Delhi and at the Delhi University.

Balraj Puri was a journalist and peace activist with a long-term involvement with Kashmir.

Arvind Rajagopal is Professor, Department of Media, Culture and Communication at New York University, New York.

Rajeshwari is an independent researcher.

Rowena Robinson is Professor of Sociology, Department of Humanities and Social Sciences at the Indian Institute of Technology, Bombay.

Kumkum Sangari is William F. Vilas Professor of English and the Humanities at the University of Wisconsin-Milwaukee, USA.

Sumit Sarkar retired as Professor of History at Delhi University.

Tanika Sarkar retired as Professor of modern history at Jawaharlal Nehru University, New Delhi.

Sambuddha Sen is Professor, Department of English at Shiv Nadar University, Greater Noida.

Ghanshyam Shah is an independent researcher and has worked at the Centre for Social Studies, Surat, and Jawaharlal Nehru University, New Delhi.

Trupti Shah was a well-known human rights and environmental activist and the founder of *Sahiyar*, a women's organisation in Vadodara, Gujarat.

Moin Shakir was Professor of Political Science at Dr. Ambedkar Marathwada University and author of many books on Muslims in India.

Pritam Singh is Professor of Economics at Oxford Brookes University, Oxford.

Romesh Thapar was a well-known journalist and founding editor of the journal *Seminar*.

Surya Prakash Upadhyay is Assistant Professor, School of Humanities and Social Sciences at the Indian Institute of Technology, Mandi.

Ashutosh Varshney is Director, Center for Contemporary South Asia, Sol Goldman Professor of International Studies and the Social Sciences; and Professor of Political Science, Watson Institute for International and Public Affairs, Brown University.

Steven I. Wilkinson is Chair, Department of Political Science, Professor of India and South Asian Studies at Yale University, New Haven, USA.